Social-Ecological Resilience and Sustainability

EDITORIAL ADVISORS

ASPEN COURSEBOOK SERIES

Social-Ecological Resilience and Sustainability

Shelley Ross Saxer
Laure Sudreau Endowed Chair
Pepperdine School of Law

and

Jonathan Rosenbloom
Dwight D. Opperman Distinguished Professor of Law
Drake University Law School

Wolters Kluwer
Attn: Order Department
PO Box 990
Frederick, MD 21705

Printed in the United States of America.

1 2 3 4 5 6 7 8 9 0

ISBN 978-1-4548-7224-5

Library of Congress Cataloging-in-Publication Data

Names: Saxer, Shelley Ross, author. | Rosenbloom, Jonathan D., author.
Title: Social-ecological resilience and sustainability / Shelley Ross Saxer,
   Laure Sudreau Endowed Chair, Pepperdine
   School of Law and Jonathan Rosenbloom, Dwight D. Opperman Distinguished
   Professor of Law, Drake University Law School .
Description: New York : Wolters Kluwer, 2018. | Series: Aspen coursebook
   series
Identifiers: LCCN 2018000450 | ISBN 9781454872245
Subjects: LCSH: Environmental law--United States. | Sustainable
   development--Law and legislation--United States. | Environmental
   law--Social aspects. | Sustainable development — Law and
   legislation — Social aspects.
Classification: LCC KF3775 .S29 2018 | DDC 344.7304/6 — dc23
LC record available at https://lccn.loc.gov/2018000450

About Wolters Kluwer Legal & Regulatory U.S.

Wolters Kluwer Legal & Regulatory U.S. delivers expert content and solutions in the areas of law, corporate compliance, health compliance, reimbursement, and legal education. Its practical solutions help customers successfully navigate the demands of a changing environment to drive their daily activities, enhance decision quality and inspire confident outcomes.

Serving customers worldwide, its legal and regulatory portfolio includes products under the Aspen Publishers, CCH Incorporated, Kluwer Law International, ftwilliam.com and MediRegs names. They are regarded as exceptional and trusted resources for general legal and practice-specific knowledge, compliance and risk management, dynamic workflow solutions, and expert commentary.

To Gary, Jennifer, Robyn, Randi, and Jonalyn
Shelley Ross Saxer

To E and Cheetah, Bunny, Dolphin, and Blankie—correte libere
Jonathan Rosenbloom

Summary of Contents

Contents

Chapter 2: Challenges and Root Causes   63

Part II: Resilience and Sustainability in Context 115

Chapter 3: Water 119

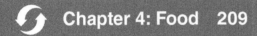

Chapter 4: Food   209

Chapter 5: Shelter and Land Use   269

Chapter 6: Energy Production and Consumption   357

Chapter 7: Natural Resources   453

Chapter 8: Pollution 509

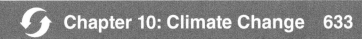

Chapter 9: Disasters   589

Chapter 10: Climate Change   633

Preface

Resilience and sustainability (R&S) provide analytical frameworks to help understand and, ultimately, address new, changing, and complex economic, environmental, and social challenges. These challenges threaten critical social-ecological systems, the health and safety of communities, and fundamental necessities, such as water, food, and shelter. R&S offer two different, overlapping, and, at times, conflicting paradigms to help understand and address these challenges. R&S do so in new and innovative ways that help explain complex systems and in turn help rethink traditional notions of law and policy.

Importantly, this book aims to help students learn about R&S and utilize resilience theories and sustainable principles. It does so by illustrating how we use these concepts in various contexts, such as water systems and climate change. The book does not aim to teach all of the law and policy of the various contexts (for example, all water law doctrine). Rather, the book focuses on where R&S play a role in the contexts presented. Nonetheless, the authors intend the book to provide enough information about these various contexts to serve as a survey course for those schools who do not have the teaching resources, or the student demand, to offer separate courses for each area of the law and policy we address.

This book has two primary parts. Part I, encompassing Chapters 1 and 2, introduces resilience and sustainability as analytical frameworks and their relevance to law and policy. These chapters review the various definitions and parts of R&S. By the end of Part I, students should have a good conceptual foundation to explore the interdisciplinary nature of R&S and the meanings of, complexities embedded in, and the overlap and differences between R&S.

Part II builds off Part I by viewing R&S in eight law and policy contexts—with one chapter corresponding to one context. Part II is focused on operationalizing the theory described in Part I. Part II explores how to understand R&S in context, assess R&S, and translate R&S into policy. Part II explores R&S in eight contexts where they can influence law and policy, including: water, food, shelter and land use, energy, natural resources, pollution, disaster law, and climate change.

Strategically placed throughout Part II, we describe eight useful tools to help utilize R&S as analytical frameworks. We refer to these tools as "Strategies to Facilitate Implementation" and they are:

1. Understanding Collective Action Challenges (Water Systems, Chapter 3)
2. Precautionary Principle (Water Systems, Chapter 3)
3. Ecosystem Services Management (Water Systems, Chapter 3)
4. Systems Thinking (Energy Systems, Chapter 6)
5. Baselines and Metrics (Energy Systems, Chapter 6)
6. Adaptive Governance (Natural Resources, Chapter 7)
7. Life Cycle Sustainability Assessment (Pollution, Chapter 8)
8. Risk Analysis (Pollution, Chapter 8)

Many of the case studies used throughout this book consist of human decisions that led to unsustainable and non-resilient systems and societies. At times, those decisions were based on a lack of information and at other times, decisions were based on policies notwithstanding the availability of relevant and accurate data. The Strategies to Facilitate Implementation are designed to help address sustainability and resilience challenges, both by providing mechanisms to obtain pertinent information and by establishing policy approaches that utilize that information. While we cannot cover all the tools that help provide data and policy approaches relevant to R&S, the eight described in Part II provide a foundation to explore questions necessary to obtain data relevant to R&S and help decision makers transform data into policy. By the end of this book, students should have a solid understanding of several approaches to help obtain data and transform it into policy in a way that considers systems' resilience and sustainability.

The genesis of this book was a panel discussion co-sponsored by the Section on Environmental Law and Section on Natural Resources at an American Association of Law Schools conference in New Orleans in 2010. The panel, titled "Climate Change and Legal Education: It's Getting Hot in Here," discussed how law schools are teaching various new courses centered around climate change. One theme that emerged from these discussions and questions from the program attendees was the problem of "too many important courses to teach and too little time." We thus concluded that a survey course and accompanying textbook would be helpful to schools with limited resources and to students who wish to learn more about the area without taking multiple courses. Because this textbook is ambitious in its goal to cover many complex areas of the law, which are generally taught as separate courses, the authors used the overarching themes of social-ecological sustainability, resilience, and global relevance to select the appropriate materials to incorporate.

The authors give special thanks to Craig "Tony" Arnold, Dan Tarlock, and Hari Osofsky, who helped guide the book through its beginning conception and proposed publication. Rick Mixter at Wolters Kluwers provided invaluable guidance, enthusiasm, and support for this project, which has taken eight long years to come to fruition. The whale has been mostly eaten.

Acknowledgments

"America's Income Gap Is Really an Education Gap." Copyright © 2011 by the Tax Foundation. Reproduced with permission. All rights reserved.

Anacostia River Watershed. Courtesy of the Metropolitan Washington Council of Governments/U.S. Army Corps of Engineers.

Area of Virgin Forest, 1620, 1850, and 1926. Courtesy of William B. Greeley/U.S. Forest Service.

"As Oceans Absorb CO_2, They Become More Acidic." Courtesy of the U.S. Global Change Research Program.

Atlantic cod. Courtesy of Saipal/Flickr.

Atmospheric CO_2 measured at Mauna Loa, HI. Courtesy of Narayanese/Sémhur/National Oceanic and Atmospheric Administration/Wikimedia Commons.

Bluehead wrasse. Courtesy of James St. John/Wikimedia Commons.

"Bottom Dissolved Oxygen Contours." Courtesy of the National Oceanic and Atmospheric Administration.

"Building Resilience Against Climate Effects (BRACE)." Courtesy of the Centers for Disease Control and Prevention.

Bycatch. Courtesy of Joan Dwinkwin/U.S. Fish and Wildlife Service.

"Carbon Dioxide, Shell building, and Ocean Acidification." Courtesy of Bvelevski/Wikimedia Commons.

Carbon price. Courtesy of the Sightline Institute.

Climate Change 2014: Synthesis Report. Contribution of Working Groups I, II and III to the Fifth Assessment Report of the Intergovernmental Panel on Climate Change [Core Writing Team, Pachauri, R.K. and Meyer, L. (eds.)], Figures 1.6 and 1.12. Courtesy of the Intergovernmental Panel on Climate Change, Geneva, Switzerland.

"Climate Feedbacks Can Be Positive and Negative." Courtesy of the Met Office.

"Collapse of Atlantic Cod Stocks (East Coast of Newfoundland), 1992." Courtesy of Lamiot/Wikimedia Commons.

Coltan mine near Rubaya, North Kivu. Courtesy of Sylvain Liechti/ United Nations Organization Stabilization Mission in the Democratic Republic of the Congo.

Confined animal feeding operation (CAFO). Courtesy of the Wisconsin Department of Natural Resources.

Cycle of adaptive change. Copyright © 2010 by Noah Raford. Reproduced with permission. All rights reserved.

Dadaab Refugee Camp, Kenya. Courtesy of Bjørn Heidenstrøm/Flickr.

Dakota Access pipeline protest. Courtesy of Fibonacci Blue/Flickr.

Devil's Tower National Monument. Courtesy of Guido da Rozze/Flickr.

"The Disaster Cycle" from Farber, Daniel A. "Legal Scholarship, the Disaster Cycle, and the Fukushima Accident." *Duke Envtl. L. & Pol'y F.* 23 (2012): 1. Copyright © 2012 by Daniel A. Farber. Reproduced with permission. All rights reserved.

Dogfish caught during a trawl survey. Courtesy of John Wallace/ National Oceanic and Atmospheric Administration.

Earth crust cutaway. Courtesy of Surachit/Wikimedia Commons.

Earthquake-triggered tsunamis in northern Japan. Copyright © 2011 by Kyodo News/AP Images. Reproduced with permission. All rights reserved.

Electronic waste near Accra, Ghana. Courtesy of Marelene Napoli/ Wikimedia Commons.

"Energy Consumption in the United States (1776-2016)." Courtesy of the U.S. Energy Information Administration.

Erosion from loss of riparian vegetation near Los Altos, CA. Courtesy of Schmiebel/Wikimedia Commons.

"Estimates of GHG Net Emissions in Brazil in 2015." Courtesy of the World Resources Institute.

"Farm Bill: 'It's like a Swiss Army knife.'" Courtesy of the U.S. Department of Agriculture.

"Federal Tax Rate by Income Group." Courtesy of Booga Louie/ Wikimedia Commons.

Food Not Bombs logo. Courtesy of Keith McHenry/Food Not Bombs.

Fukushima Daiichi Nuclear Power Station. Courtesy of Greg Webb/ International Atomic Energy Agency.

"Gapminder World 2012." Courtesy of the Gapminder Foundation.

"Geoengineering Methods." Courtesy of Climate Central.

"Geothermal Power Generation." Courtesy of Billy Roberts/National Renewable Energy Laboratory.

"Global Land-Ocean Temperature Index." Courtesy of the Goddard Institute for Space Studies, National Aeronautics and Space Administration.

Global wind power cumulative capacity. Courtesy of Delphi234/ Wikimedia Commons.

Grand Coulee Dam. Courtesy of the U.S. Bureau of Reclamation.

"The Greenhouse Effect" from *Climate Change Indicators in the United States*, 2nd Edition (2012). Courtesy of the U.S. Environmental Protection Agency.

Grenfell Tower fire. Courtesy of Natalie Oxford/Wikimedia Commons.

"Gross Domestic Product Per Capita 1500-1950." Courtesy of Kanguole/Wikimedia Commons.

Hanging gardens of One Central Park, Sydney, Australia. Courtesy of Rob Deutscher/Flickr.

Holling's panarchical connections from *Panarchy* by Lance Gunderson and C.S. Holling. Copyright © 2002 by Island Press. Reproduced by permission of Island Press, Washington DC.

Homeless camp. Courtesy of Natalie HG/Flickr.

Honey bee. Courtesy of Bob Peterson/Wikimedia Commons.

Hot water hydrothermal system. Courtesy of Goran Tek-En/Wikimedia Commons.

Hurricane Harvey; soldiers conduct rescue operations in Houston, TX. Courtesy of the National Guard.

Hurricane Irma; damage to buildings in Nanny Cay on the British Virgin Island of Tortola. Courtesy of the U.K. Department for International Development.

Hurricane Maria; homes damaged in Puerto Rico. Courtesy of the U.S. Air Force.

Hurricane Sandy; damaged homes along New Jersey shore. Courtesy of Greg Thompson/U.S. Fish and Wildlife Service Northeast.

"Impact of Climate Change on Human Health." Courtesy of the Centers for Disease Control and Prevention.

"Internet Users (Per 100 People)." Copyright © 2015 by GlobalPost/Public Radio International. Reproduced by permission. All rights reserved.

Johns Hopkins Glacier, Alaska. Courtesy of Alan Wu/Wikimedia Commons.

Marine mammal sightings submitted to TMSS from *Thames Marine Mammal Sightings Survey Ten Year Report (2004-2014)*. Courtesy of the Zoological Society of London.

Maslow's "Hierarchy of Needs." Courtesy of J. Finkelstein/Wikimedia Commons.

"Meat Consumption Per Capita in Industrialized Countries." Courtesy of Heinrich Boell Foundation/Friends of the Earth Europe.

Miami, FL skyline. Courtesy of Tom Schaefer/Miamitom/Wikimedia Commons.

Mississippi River Watershed. Courtesy of the National Park Service.

Moai at Rano Raraku, Easter Island. Courtesy of Aurbina/Wikimedia Commons.

"Most U.S. Farms Are Small Family Farms", from *Family Farm Report* (2014). Courtesy of the U.S. Department of Agriculture.

"Number of Oil Spills from Tankers Worldwide, 1970-2016." Courtesy of Max Roser/Our World in Data.

"Obesity Rates Have Increased Substantially Over the Past 20 Years and Are Highest in the U.S." Copyright © 2013 by NewsHour Productions. Reproduced by permission. All rights reserved.

Ocean trash. Courtesy of Jason Karn/Wikimedia Commons.

"One Metric Ton Carbon Dioxide." Courtesy of Real World Visuals.

Pacific Ring of Fire. Courtesy of Gringer/Wikimedia Commons.

"Percentage of Wetlands Acreage Lost, 1780s-1980s." Courtesy U.S. Fish and Wildlife Service.

pH scale. Courtesy of the U.S. Environmental Protection Agency.

"Planetary Boundaries." Copyright © 2015 by Félix Pharand-Deschênes, Globaïa. Reproduced with permission. All rights reserved.

Ploughing with a yoke of horned cattle in Ancient Egypt. Courtesy of the Yorck Project/Wikimedia Commons.

Polynomials under Newton's method. Courtesy of Georg-Johann Lay/ Wikimedia Commons.

"Predominant Renewable Fuel for Utility-Scale Electricity Generation, 2011." Courtesy of the Energy Information Administration.

R6 Quality Housing Regulations. Reproduced with permission of the New York City Department of City Planning. All rights reserved.

"Recent Sea Level Rise." Courtesy of Robert A. Rohde/Global Warming Art/Wikimedia Commons.

The Rhine. Courtesy of Daniel Ullrich/Wikimedia Commons.

Sediment in the Gulf of Mexico. Courtesy of Jeff Schmaltz/National Aeronautics and Space Administration Earth Observatory.

Shell buttons from Coker, Robert E. (1921), *Fresh-water Mussels and Mussel Industries of the United States, Bulletin of the United States Bureau of Fisheries*, vol. 36, 1917-1918, Washington, DC: Government Printing Office.

Solar panels and wind turbine. Courtesy of Gerry Machen/Flickr.

"Splitting Backbones and Final Inspection." Courtesy of the Library of Congress.

Squash, corn, and green beans. Courtesy of Chris Feser/Flickr.

Sugarbeet harvester. Courtesy of Rasbak/Wikimedia Commons.

Sumatran village in ruin after tsunami. Courtesy of the U.S. Navy.

Thermohaline circulation. Courtesy of the National Aeronautics and Space Administration.

Three Spheres of Sustainability. Courtesy Johann Dréo/Wikimedia Commons.

Total amount of energy produced in the United States since 1949. Courtesy of the U.S. Energy Information Administration.

"Total Greenhouse Gas Emissions by Economic Sector." Courtesy of the U.S. Environmental Protection Agency.

Transfer of Development Rights (TDR). Reproduced with permission of the New York City Department of City Planning. All rights reserved.

Volcanic ash and pollution. Courtesy of the U.S. Geological Survey.

"The Water Cycle." Courtesy of Ehud Tal/Wikimedia Commons.

"Water Stress by Country." Courtesy of World Resources Institute.

"What Do We Do When We Lose Power?" Courtesy of the Public Library of Science.

"Where Is Global Warming Going?" Courtesy of Skeptical Science/Wikimedia Commons.

"World Energy Consumption by Fuel" from *International Energy Outlook 2013*. Courtesy of the U.S. Energy Information Administration.

World population. Copyright © 2017 by the United Nations. Reproduced with permission. All rights reserved.

Social-Ecological Resilience and Sustainability

Part I
Building a Foundation

Part I of this book, encompassing Chapters 1 and 2, starts the important task of understanding resilience and sustainability (R&S) as analytical frameworks and their relevance to law and policy. The objective of this part is to build a conceptual foundation by focusing on the knowledge and skills helpful to identify, evaluate, and apply R&S. Chapter 1 introduces and defines the terms "resilience" and "sustainability." This chapter explores the interdisciplinary nature of R&S and the meanings of, complexities embedded in, and the overlap and differences between R&S.

Chapter 2 explores the evolution of R&S by describing the economic, social, and environmental challenges and systems relevant to R&S. Many of these challenges and their root causes are interconnected, multi-disciplined, and multi-scalar—making them extraordinarily complex and dynamic. Helping to understand this complexity and dynamism serves as one of the primary benefits of turning to R&S, as these concepts help us assess complex multi-faceted systems.

Defining Resilience and Sustainability

1

At their core, resilience and sustainability (R&S) represent new and innovative ways to help understand our role in creating, exacerbating, or remedying challenges arising in economic, social, and ecological systems. R&S help assess the properties of systems (see adjacent note describing "system") to inform how those systems are functioning under certain conditions. But what do the terms "resilience" and "sustainability" mean? This chapter explores this question by first considering what they are not.

Importantly, one thing they are not is identical. They are distinct analytical frameworks. Although we group them together, we do so only where relevant and applicable. Where R&S diverge, we discuss resilience separately from sustainability and vice versa.

Throughout this book, we use the terms "system" and "social-ecological system." A "system" is a group of interconnected parts that interact or act independently to form a more complex whole. We typically organize various parts of the system around a common purpose or function. Systems may be natural, such as ecosystems, or human-made, such as a stormwater management or monetary system. Particularly relevant to R&S are "social-ecological systems." Social-ecological systems are the joining of natural systems (for example, coral reefs) with social systems (for example, fishing in the coral reefs). Fikret Berkes and Carl Folke "started to use the term 'social-ecological' system to emphasize the integrated concept of humans in nature and to stress that the delineation between social and ecological systems is artificial and arbitrary." Carl Folke et al., *Adaptive Governance of Social-Ecological Systems*, 30 ANNUAL REV. ENVIRON. RES. 441, 443 (2005). Put another way, social-ecological systems are the linkage of "the 'human system' (e.g., communities, society, economy) and the 'natural system' (e.g., ecosystems) in a two-way feedback relationship." Fikret Berkes et al., *Guidelines for Analysis of Social-Ecological Systems* (2014), at 2, *available at* http://www.community-conservation.net/wp-content/uploads/2016/01/FINAL_CCRN-Guidelines-for-Analysis-of-Social-Ecological-Systems-September-2014.pdf.

I. CASE STUDY: *EASTER ISLAND AND WHAT IS NOT A RESILIENT NOR SUSTAINABLE SOCIETY*

Today, Easter Island is a well-known tourist destination because of the over 800 gigantic head and torso stone carvings measuring over thirty feet

tall. Notwithstanding its marvelous sculptures, the island's history is a remarkable tragedy.

Best-selling author Jared Diamond pieces together the rise and fall of the people and society on Easter Island, located in the Pacific Ocean over 2,000 miles from Chile and 4,000 miles from New Zealand. In describing Easter Island, Diamond paints a compelling picture of the possible disastrous results stemming from practices and behaviors that resulted in a community that was neither resilient nor sustainable. While there have been several critiques of Diamond's writings on Easter Island, it is uncontested that he has widely highlighted the notion that societies bring about their ruin when they fail to grow in resilient and/or sustainable ways.

According to Diamond, contact with Western culture began in 1722, when a Dutch explorer, Admiral Jacob Roggeveen, came upon the island inhabited by approximately 2,000 people. When Roggeveen arrived, there were few, if any, natural resources left on the mostly barren island. There were no trees over ten feet high, and no wildlife larger than insects, although the inhabitants had domesticated chickens. Without large trees the inhabitants did not have access to large pieces of lumber, and thus, the boats Roggeveen saw were no more than flimsy canoes, suited only for patrolling the shallow waters and not deep sea fishing or traveling.

Notwithstanding Roggeveen's account of the island, Diamond notes that modern scientific analysis reveals the island was once host to a thriving ecosystem and a robust human population. It is believed that seafaring Polynesian people settled the island sometime between 400 and 700 A.D. At that time and for at least 30,000 years before, there was a rich forest with some of the largest palm trees on Earth. The trees helped support an abundantly diverse ecosystem, including multiple species of large sea birds, land birds, and seals. Pollen analysis indicates that the island had bushes and shrubs, as well as ferns, herbs, nut trees, and grasses — all of which were gone before Roggeveen arrived.

Diamond and others estimate that the Easter Island human population reached approximately 7,000, three to four times the population Roggeveen found. Paleontologists discovered evidence that early inhabitants hunted dolphins in the deep sea. To do so, fishers would have had to design and build boats significantly larger and sturdier than those Roggeveen found in 1722. In addition, constructing the large stone monuments required far more sophisticated tools to sculpt and transport the monuments than the ones discovered by Roggeveen. The advancements of the pre-Roggeveen Easter Island society led one author to state: "The result was the creation of the most advanced of all the Polynesian societies and one of the most complex in the world for its limited resource base."[1]

What could have happened to the deep sea fishing society and robust ecosystem on Easter Island? How did Easter Island, its inhabitants, and its society go from a fertile island rich with natural resources to the wasteland Roggeveen found? Diamond theorizes that the *inhabitants used the natural resources faster than they were regenerating*, leading to a depletion of the resources and associated unforeseen consequences. The lush forest succumbed to *overpopulation* and *increased consumption* as settlers used the trees to build canoes and shelter and used palm hearts for food. Others have suggested that settlers introduced an *invasive species*, Polynesian rats. The rats, which had no natural predator on the island, most likely ate palm nuts. These nuts are the palm trees' seeds and without them, they cannot naturally reseed, reducing the number of trees further.

Massive deforestation would have left inhabitants without their primary material for building houses and boats, leaving them with the primitive huts, caves, and flimsy canoes Roggeveen found. Loss of the trees would have degraded soil quality for purposes of harvesting crops. The forests were also habitats and without them, there was no habitat for insects to re-pollinate and for animals to reproduce and feed. All birds went into extinction. As resources became scarce, internal fighting escalated. There is even evidence that human relations devolved to the point of cannibalism.

Questions and Note

1. In the next section, we begin the task of defining R&S. Based on your own experience, what might cause someone to define the Easter Island society Roggeveen found as not resilient or sustainable? Is it foreseeable that these characteristics could be replicated elsewhere?

---

[1] Clive Ponting, A GREEN HISTORY OF THE WORLD: THE ENVIRONMENT AND THE COLLAPSE OF GREAT CIVILIZATIONS 4 (2011).

2. The Easter Island example raises the question of, "why?" Why would a society do this? Or as Diamond asks in one of his articles: "Why didn't they look around, realize what they were doing, and stop before it was too late?"[2] Did the inhabitants have the information necessary to estimate the consequences of their actions? Were the changes too incremental for the people to notice? Was it too difficult to stop someone from having unintended consequences when jobs, food, or shelter were at stake?

3. The following concepts are highlighted in the Easter Island story: inhabitants used the natural resources faster than they were regenerating, overpopulation, increased consumption, and invasive species. These are concepts we will return to throughout the book. Can you identify why those concepts are important to the Easter Island story and the demise of the Easter Island society? How might they be applicable to other scenarios, such as climate change?

4. Former president of the Environmental Law Institute, William Futrell, notes that it may be easier to identify "unsustainable conduct," than it is to identify sustainable conduct because information pertaining to behaviors or impacts that conclude with our or another's ultimate destruction is more readily available than information indicating sustainable conditions, which requires complex projections.[3] Can you use the Easter Island story to help explain Futrell's point?

5. Keep the Easter Island example in mind as a cautionary tale. It may be difficult to convince someone that current global conditions are such that we are going to suffer the same fate as the society on Easter Island. We can use the example to illustrate the connection between decisions and behaviors and long-term negative consequences. The challenge is identifying, assessing, and altering those decisions and behaviors before it is too late.

II. DEFINING "RESILIENCE" AND "SUSTAINABILITY"

The Easter Island story illustrates a society that collapsed due to a number of decisions that led to an unsustainable and vulnerable community. Who makes those decisions and what information they have are critical to assessing R&S. Throughout this book we often point out who or what public or private entity makes a particular decision. It is important to remember who that body is, whom they represent, and how they came to be authorized to make that decision. These factors may change the

---

[2] Jared Diamond, Easter's End, DISCOVER (Aug. 1 , 1995) http://discovermagazine.com/1995/aug/eastersend543.

[3] J. William Futrell, *Defining Sustainable Development Law*, 19 NAT. RES. & ENV'T 9 (2004).

decision makers' perspective and alter the assessment of R&S. Similarly, what information a body has to make its assessment may also alter the determination as to whether a system is resilient or sustainable.

Let us continue to enhance our understanding of R&S by looking at what properties are resilient or sustainable. The following situations seem to conjure notions of resilience and/or sustainability relative to particular systems or conditions:

- a soap company extracting discarded plastic waste out of the ocean and reusing it
- a building producing more renewable energy than it needs and capturing more water than is uses
- a solar company providing solar electricity to thousands of underserved households
- a city maximizing the natural purification of water by preserving a watershed

How are these examples the same, how are they different, and how can we understand the links between them and the thousands of similar actions or events? In other words, how would you define resilience or sustainability?

Some definitions are quite straightforward. *Oxford Dictionary*, for example, defines sustainability as something, "[a]ble to be maintained at a certain rate or level,"[4] and resilience as, "[t]he capacity to recover quickly from difficulties; toughness."[5] Thus, the Earth's rotation around the sun might be sustainable and Chicago Cub fans might be resilient.

Notwithstanding these relatively straightforward definitions, R&S embody an enormous interdisciplinary complexity. Because R&S are applicable to many diverse subjects simultaneously, there is not an agreed upon single definition for either. Professor and author Gregory Unruh highlights concepts relative to sustainability:

> It doesn't take much to discover that sustainability means different things to different people. Try engaging on the topic with external stakeholders. Labor advocates see it differently than Greenpeace. Community leaders see it differently than regulators. Who you're talking to affects what they hear.[6]

In other words, *R&S are contextual.* There is no general or overall sustainability or resilience. Rather, R&S are relative to something, such as a

---

[4] Sustainability, OXFORD DICTIONARY, https://en.oxforddictionaries.com/definition/sustainability (last visited Dec. 22, 2017).
[5] Resilience, OXFORD DICTIONARY, https://en.oxforddictionaries.com/definition/resilience (last visited Dec. 22, 2017).
[6] Gregory Unruh, *Sustainability Dialects*, MIT SLOAN MGMT. REV. (June 10, 2014), http://sloanreview.mit.edu/article/sustainability-dialects/.

system or condition. For example, agriculture and the harvesting of food are critical for the survival of humans. That fact could result in both resilient and sustainable systems and vulnerable and unsustainable systems. Increased land use and water use for agricultural purposes could help support sustainable human development, but it could also lead to unsustainable ecosystems, destroying habitats and depleting water resources. The *trade-offs* between and among systems that result from law and policies are concepts we return to frequently.

While R&S are contextual, there are commonly used definitions and characteristics to help understand R&S. Some of the most common definitions characterize R&S as properties of a system. Law informs that system by altering behaviors and R&S can help determine the law's impact on a system. In this section, we begin by dissecting the various parts that make up resilience and then sustainability. From international, national, and subnational discussions and research, numerous widely accepted definitions have emerged. Keep these definitions in mind as you work through the rest of this book. Try to identify which definition is used in the given context and whether it meets certain goals. Finally, as we move through the definitions, keep in mind that each definition requires *scientific and sociological information* to assess the resilience and sustainability of a system. R&S are complex terms, and information is necessary to assess them properly.

A. Resilience

Before diving into tools to help assess the resilience of a specific system or condition, let us explore some of the definitions and parts of "resilience." To be sure, the term "resilience" has multiple meanings depending on the context and has no single definition.[7] In psychology, for example, resilience is a personal trait or the process of adapting to trauma. The context most relevant to our inquiry is how we use the term relative to social-ecological systems. In that context, we begin by distinguishing between "engineering resilience" and "ecological resilience." In the excerpt below, C.S. Holling sets forth some of the key distinctions between engineering resilience and ecological resilience. Following the excerpt, we explore in more depth the various parts of ecological resilience.

---

[7] *See also* Janine S. Hiller & Jordan M. Blanke, *Smart Cities, Big Data, and the Resilience of Privacy*, 68 HASTINGS L.J. 309, 313 (2017); Robin Kundis Craig, *Putting Resilience Theory into Practice: The Example of Fisheries Management*, 31 NAT. RESOURCES & ENV'T 1, 1 (2017); Dan Sage & Chris Zebrowski, *Resilience and Critical Infrastructure: Origins, Theories and Critiques*, INTERNATIONAL SECURITY HANDBOOK 1-2 (R. Dover & M. Goodman eds., Palgrave MacMillan 2016); Thomas P. Seager et al., *Redesigning Resilient Infrastructure Research* 4 (Igor Linkov & Jose Palma Oliveira eds., 2017) (noting "the necessity of a pluralistic understanding of resilience").

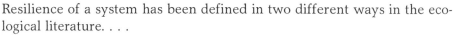

C.S. Holling, *Engineering Resilience versus Ecological Resilience*

AT 31-44 *IN* P. SCHULZE ED., ENGINEERING WITHIN ECOLOGICAL CONSTRAINTS
(NATIONAL ACADEMY, WASHINGTON, D.C., 1996)

Resilience of a system has been defined in two different ways in the ecological literature. . . .

The first definition, and the more traditional, concentrates on stability near an equilibrium steady state, where resistance to disturbance and speed of return to the equilibrium are used to measure the property. . . . That view provides one of the foundations for economic theory as well and may be termed *engineering resilience*.

The second definition emphasizes conditions far from any equilibrium steady state. . . . In this case the measurement of resilience is the magnitude of disturbance ["disturbance" is described in more detail below] that can be absorbed before the system changes its structure by changing the variables and processes that control behavior. We shall call this view *ecological resilience*. . . .

The two contrasting aspects of stability — essentially one that focuses on maintaining *efficiency* of function (engineering resilience) and one that focuses on maintaining *existence* of function (ecological resilience) — are so fundamental that they can become alternative paradigms. . . .

Those who emphasize the near-equilibrium definition of engineering resilience, for example, draw predominantly from traditions of deductive mathematical theory . . . where simplified, untouched ecological systems are imagined, or from traditions of engineering, where the motive is to design systems with a single operating objective. . . . There is an implicit assumption of global stability, that is, that only one equilibrium steady state exists, or, if other operating states exist, they should be avoided . . . by applying safeguards. . . .

There are many examples of managed ecosystems that share this same feature of gradual loss of functional diversity with an attendant loss of resilience followed by a shift into an irreversible state, such as occurs in agriculture and in forest, fish, and grasslands management. . . . [In these examples,] the ecosystem evolves to become more spatially uniform, less functionally diverse, and more sensitive to disturbances. . . . That is, ecological resilience decreases even though engineering resilience might be great. Short-term success in stabilizing production leads to long-term surprise. . . .

In the examples of resource management that I have explored in depth, not only do ecosystems become less resilient when they are managed with the goal of achieving constancy of production, but the management agencies, in their [drive] for efficiency, also become more myopic, the relevant industries become more dependent and static, and the public loses trust. . . . This seems to define an ultimate pathology that typically can lead to a crisis triggered by unexpected external events, sometimes followed by a reformation of policy. . . .

[T]he initial diagnoses of the pathology as I saw it in the early 1970s were as follows:

- Successful suppression of spruce budworm populations during the 1950s and 1960s in eastern Canada, using insecticide, certainly preserved the pulp and paper industry in the short-term by significantly reducing defoliation by the insect so that tree mortality was delayed. This encouraged expansion of pulp mills but left the forest, and hence the economy, more vulnerable to an outbreak that would cause more intense and more extensive tree mortality than had ever been experienced before. That is, the short-term success of spraying led to moderate levels of infestation and partially protected foliage that became more homogeneous over larger areas, demanding ever more vigilance and control.
- Effective protection and enhancement of salmon spawning through use of fish hatcheries on the west coast of North America quickly led to more predictable and larger catches by both sport and commercial fishermen. That triggered increased fishing pressure and investment in both sectors, pressure that caused more and more of the less productive natural stocks to become locally extinct. . . .

There is a puzzle in these examples and this analysis. It implies that efficient control and management of renewable resources in an engineering sense leads initially to success in managing a target variable for sustained production of food or fiber but ultimately to a pathology of less resilient and more vulnerable ecosystems, more rigid and unresponsive management agencies, and more dependent societies. . . .

The above conclusion is based on two critical points. One is that reducing the variability of critical variables within ecosystems inevitably leads to reduced resilience and increased vulnerability. The second is that there is, in principle, no different way for agencies and people to manage and benefit from resource development. . . .

Holling's excerpt above describes some of the key differences between engineering and ecological resilience and points out how these concepts can be contrary to one another. Engineering resilience focuses on stability at a near-equilibrium state. We measure the resilience of a system by the speed of a system's return to equilibrium after a disturbance. Holling also notes that engineering resilience's focus on "near-equilibrium" requires "an implicit assumption of global stability" and that "only one equilibrium

steady state exists, or, if other operating states exist, they should be avoided
. . . by applying safeguards."[8] Professor Robin Kundis Craig echoes this
point, stating engineering resilience assumes "there is an equilibrium balance of nature to which natural systems will return after a shock or disturbance."[9] Craig continues by noting that engineering resilience presumes
nature is "knowable, predictable, and largely controllable. . . . This assumption is perhaps most obvious in the reigning legal presumption that . . . we
can keep important systems from changing in the first place and that we
can restore any system that we've already changed to its previous state."[10]

Rather than focus on a steady state, ecological resilience predominantly focuses on "maintaining existence of function" and accommo-
dates changes in variables and processes.[11] It focuses on the disturbance
that can be absorbed before the system shifts from one state to another.
Importantly, it does not depend on whether the system is at or near an
equilibrium state. In other words, an ecological resilient system can be in
chaos, but an engineering resilient system cannot.

Ecological resilience recognizes and embraces uncertainty, change,
and the ability of ecosystems to adapt and thrive in more than one stable
state. Craig describes ecological resilience as "acknowled[ging] that change
and coping with change are a continual reality within natural systems."[12]
Ecological resilience recognizes the regularity of changes in ecosystems by
accounting for their adaptability and transformability.[13] Importantly, the
failure to account for change and uncertainty can increase system vulnerabilities. Ecologist Brian Walker and author David Salt state:

> At the heart of resilience thinking is a very simple notion — things change — and
> to ignore or resist this change is to increase our vulnerability and forego emerg-
> ing opportunities. . . . Sometimes changes are slow . . . sometimes they are
> fast. . . . Humans are usually good at noticing and responding to rapid change.
> Unfortunately, we are not so good at responding to things that change slowly.[14]

As Walker and Salt recognize not only do systems change, but also failure
to acknowledge this change can result in increased vulnerabilities and
lost opportunities. With the correct information, policymakers can make

---

[8] C.S. Holling, *Engineering Resilience Versus Ecological Resilience, in* The National Academy of
Sciences, Engineering Within Ecological Constraints 33-34 (Peter Schulze ed., 1996).
[9] Craig, *supra* note 7, at 1.
[10] *Id.*
[11] Holling, *supra* note 8, at 33 (alteration in original); *see also* Hiller & Blanke, *supra* note 7, at 342.
[12] Robin Kundis Craig, *Learning to Live with the Trickster: Narrating Climate Change and the Value of
Resilience Thinking*, 33 Pace Envtl. L. Rev. 351, 388 (2016).
[13] Carl Folke et al., *Resilience Thinking: Integrating Resilience, Adaptability and Transformability*, 15
Ecology & Soc'y 1, 3 (2010) (Transformability is "[t]he capacity [of people] to create a fundamentally new [social-ecological] system when ecological, economic, or social structures make the
existing system untenable.").
[14] Brian Walker & David Salt, Resilience Thinking: Sustaining Ecosystems and People in a Changing
World 9-10 (2006).

decisions that can address vulnerabilities, help prepare for future changes, and leverage new insight to ensure the continued functioning of those systems.

In the rest of this section, we focus almost exclusively on ecological resilience. To give a bit of background and general description of ecological resilience, we turn to a piece by Professor Tracy-Lynn Humby. Following Humby's piece, we break down five key terms relevant to resilience (disturbances, thresholds, adaptive cycles, panarchy, and boundaries) and provide brief examples for each term to help better understand ecological "resilience."

1. BACKGROUND AND INTRODUCTION

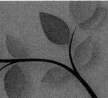

Tracy-Lynn Humby, *Law and Resilience: Mapping the Literature*

4 SEATTLE J. ENVTL. L. 85, 89-95, 104-106 (2014)

The theory of resilience has its roots in the discipline of ecology. The origins of the "resilience perspective" lie in studies on predation [the research of animals preying on others] conducted by C.S Holling during the 1960s and early 1970s. . . . Contrary to the conventional belief that ecosystems oscillated around a single equilibrium . . . Holling discovered that ecosystems could "flip" between more than one stable state; they were both complex and adaptive and thus, characterized by surprise and inherent unpredictability. . . . Holling's use of the term serves as the basis for the most popular definition of resilience: *"the capacity of a system to absorb disturbance and still retain its basic structure and function."* [Emphasis added.]

The complex and adaptive nature of ecosystems places limits on the predictability of how the system will behave. . . . [T]he behavior of the system cannot be predicted by understanding the individual mechanics of its component parts or any pair of interactions but must take into account the feedbacks between the elements of the system and how those feedbacks in turn transform the component parts. . . .

[E]cosystems are affected by many variables. . . . Along each of these key variables are *thresholds* [explored in more detail in subsection II.A.2.b] [emphasis added] and if the system moves beyond them, it will start behaving in a different way. . . . Once a threshold has been crossed it is usually difficult—and in some cases, impossible—to cross back. . . .

A system's resilience can be measured in terms of distance from the thresholds of key variables. The closer a system lies to any one threshold the less it takes to be pushed into a new regime. . . .

[Critical to resilience are] social-ecological systems (SES) . . . the idea of the synergy and "fundamental interdependency" of the human and environmental subsystems in determining the condition, function, and response of either subsystem (and of the system as a whole) to a disturbance, perturbation, or hazard.

Ecological systems refer to biological and biophysical processes, while social systems are made up of rules and institutions that mediate human use of resources. . . .

One of the key insights of resilience theory is that . . . [r]esource management strategies that attempt to optimize only particular elements of an ecosystem . . . frequently weaken the entire system. Such interventions are blind to the fact that while resource management practices keep one component of an ecosystem constant, the other elements continue to change at other spatial and temporal scales. This tends to tip the social-ecological system more precariously toward a regime shift. . . .

While much work has gone into understanding how social-ecological systems absorb disturbance so as to retain essentially the same structure, function and feedbacks, emphasis is now also being increasingly placed on the capacity of systems to reorganize while undergoing change. . . .

[A]s a concept, resilience not only connotes persistence, but also adaptive capacity or adaptability; the capacity for both the human and ecological components of a system to respond to, learn from, create, and shape variability and change in the state of the system and influence resilience. [Emphasis added.] Assessment of the resilience of social-ecological systems can therefore proceed along three inter-dependent dimensions: (1) the degree to which the system can absorb disturbance and still remain within the same state or domain of attraction; (2) the degree to which the system can self-organize and the quality of that self-organization; and (3) the degree to which the system can build and increase the capacity for learning and adaptation.

Questions and Notes

1. As the piece above illustrates, ecological resilience has been refined a number of times and is now a complex term with several facets. While it may have begun as an exploration into the ability of a system to absorb a disturbance, today it includes the ability of the system to also adapt and transform. Carl Folke et al. state it this way:

   Resilience thinking addresses the dynamics and development of complex social–ecological systems (SES). Three aspects are central: **resilience, adaptability and transformability.** *These aspects interrelate across multiple scales.* **Resilience** *in this context is the capacity of a SES to continually change and adapt yet remain within critical thresholds.* **Adaptability** *is* *part of resilience. It represents the capacity to adjust responses to changing external drivers and internal processes and thereby allow for development along the current trajectory (stability domain).* **Transformability** *is the capacity to cross thresholds into new development trajectories.*[15]

2. As mentioned above, *trade-offs* are a reality of law and policy. Often trade-offs impact systems' resilience inversely. For example, C.S. Holling describes efforts to create a resilient salmon industry from an economic perspective, which simultaneously negatively impacted the resilience of natural salmon runs.

3. Based on Humby's and Folke et al.'s description of resilience, what makes the Easter Island society resilient or not? What changes did the society experience? Was the society able to absorb, adapt, or transform to the changes?

4. How a system naturally builds ecological resilience or how humans help artificially build engineering resilience is not dictated by resilience thinking. Rather, resilience is a framework to help understand a given system's ability to maintain a state of equilibrium (engineering resilience) or the ability of the system to i) "bounce-back," ii) withstand, iii) adapt, or iv) modify after shock from changes (ecological resilience), regardless of how the system accomplishes these. In other words, resilience is a system's property, not normative guidance for law and policy, although it is instructive.

2. EXPLORING THE SUBPARTS OF ECOLOGICAL RESILIENCE

Many words and concepts embedded in Humby's and Folke et al.'s writings above are not part of everyday parlance, but are critical to understanding resilience. Below we describe in more detail the following key subparts to enhance our understanding of resilience: disturbances, thresholds, adaptive cycle, panarchy, and boundaries. After a description of each subpart's relevance to resilience, we provide a summary of an article discussing the term. The summaries, written by The Resilience Alliance, www.resalliance. org, illustrate how the subparts are important to understanding resilience.

a. Disturbances

Disturbances are external influences that disrupt a system's core characteristics and impact the system's resilience. Outside influences can alter disturbances by changing their intensity, prevalence, and extent. Such

---

[15] Folke et al., *supra* note 13 (emphasis added).

influences are often extensions of law, policy, and behaviors. A system's ability to bounce-back, resist, adapt, or transform following or in response to a disturbance is a measure of the system's resilience to that disturbance.

Identify the various disturbances affecting the resilience of salmon populations (the system) in the example below and how humans can alter the disturbances and impact the system's resilience.

> **Example.** Salmon, during the river-bound part of their life, are adapted to live in dynamic habitats. Short term perturbations of habitats occur during landslides, floods or low flow periods. The frequency, magnitude, duration, and predictability of these events describe the system's disturbance regimes. Humans change these attributes of the disturbance regimes directly and indirectly. When these altered disturbance regimes assume characteristics outside the evolutionary history and the range of random fluctuations previously experienced, the resilience of salmon populations could be compromised.
>
> Anthropogenic activities can either reduce or increase the frequency of disturbances. Dams and water storage in reservoirs typically suppress peak flows and augment low flows, thereby dampening flow variation throughout the year. Large floods create new channels and recruit wood from the floodplain. Flood mitigation or large reductions in frequency of this key habitat-forming process reduces the complexity of salmon rearing habitats. Timber harvest, urbanization and agricultural land uses often increase the frequency and/or magnitude of floods and landslides. Each of these impacts reduces habitat variation in the river landscape, which narrows the diversity of salmon that survive.
>
> Disturbance regimes are a critical feature of salmon landscapes. Human activity has disrupted the disturbance regimes resulting in a limitation in habitat diversity, exaggerated the frequency and/or magnitude of disturbances that result in high mortality events, and broken down connectivity between habitats.[16]

---

[16] *See* Robin S. Waples et al., *Evolutionary History, Habitat Disturbance Regimes, and Anthropogenic Changes: What Do These Mean for Resilience of Pacific Salmon Populations?*, 14 ECOLOGY & SOC'Y 1 (2009).

Many social-ecological systems, including those relevant to salmon, involve rivers in Oregon. The following two provisions from the Oregon Revised Statutes are relevant to some of the flow issues raised in the example above. They illustrate how the law can influence a system's resilience by affecting disturbances.

537.332 Definitions for ORS 537.332 to 537.360. . . .

(1) "In-stream" means within the natural stream channel or lake bed or place where water naturally flows or occurs.

(2) "In-stream flow" means the minimum quantity of water necessary to support the public use requested by an agency.

(3) "In-stream water right" means a water right held in trust by the Water Resources Department for the benefit of the people of the State of Oregon to maintain water in-stream for public use. An in-stream water right does not require a diversion or any other means of physical control over the water.

(4) "Public benefit" means a benefit that accrues to the public at large rather than to a person, a small group of persons or to a private enterprise.

(5) "Public use" includes but is not limited to:
   (a) Recreation;
   (b) Conservation, maintenance and enhancement of aquatic and fish life, wildlife, fish and wildlife habitat and any other ecological values;
   (c) Pollution abatement; or
   (d) Navigation.

537.336. . . .

(1) The State Department of Fish and Wildlife may request the Water Resources Commission to issue water right certificates for in-stream water rights on the waters of this state in which there are public uses relating to the conservation, maintenance and enhancement of aquatic and fish life, wildlife and fish and wildlife habitat. The request shall be for the quantity of water necessary to support those public uses. . . .

(2) The Department of Environmental Quality may request the Water Resources Commission to issue water right certificates for in-stream water rights on the waters of this state to protect and maintain water quality standards established by the Environmental Quality Commission. . . . The request shall be for the quantity of water necessary for pollution abatement. . . .

(3) The State Parks and Recreation Department may request the Water Resources Commission to issue water right certificates for in-stream water rights on the waters of this state in which there are public uses relating to recreation and scenic attraction. The request shall be for the quantity of water necessary to support those public uses. . . .

b. Thresholds

A *threshold* represents the "tipping point" of a given system that serves as the maximum measure of that system's resilience relative to a disturbance. Thresholds are baselines of important and often slowly changing characteristics of a system. If a disturbance pushes a system across a threshold, the system enters a new state and trajectory, beginning a "regime shift."

The closer a system is to a threshold the less resilient the system is to a disturbance affecting that threshold. For example, a water source that can absorb more pollution and not pass through a threshold, altering the core characteristics of the water source, is more resilient to the pollution-based disturbance than one that cannot. Thresholds can be constantly in flux and can be influenced by time and other changes in the system. Thus, one way to assess a system's resilience is whether it is close to or whether it has surpassed a threshold.

The following example sets forth some of the key considerations relevant to identifying thresholds and the importance of crossing a threshold. In the example, identify the disturbances that have been introduced to the ecological system and how those disturbances are pushing the system through thresholds, leading to irreparable changes.

Example. Phosphorus (P) is a common element that is necessary for plant growth and is often added to agricultural fields as fertilizer to increase crop yields. Some of the P is carried in runoff to surrounding areas. Over time, with continuous inputs, the P accumulates in mud (sediments) at the bottom of lakes and supports increased growth of phytoplankton that can result in algal blooms.

The amount of P in lake sediments is a key factor determining whether the lake tends to be clear with green plants (one state), or murky with algae blooms (alternate state). As with other cases where resilience is diminished, the threshold associated with lakes that suffer from large and persistent algal blooms, is linked to system components that change slowly and thus may give the appearance of being stable.

A century ago, in many regions human sewage was typically funneled into lakes, eventually resulting in state changes of the lake system. Even after decades of water treatment to remove phosphorus from sewage, many lakes have not returned to their original clear-water state. In many systems, once thresholds have been crossed, it is difficult (if not impossible) to return to the previous state. Although 'natural' recovery is possible if stressors such as farm runoff are removed, it can take a period of time equivalent to multiple human generations before recovery may occur. During this time, society must cope with the undesirable outcomes of state changes that, in the case of freshwater lakes, may include lower provision of ecosystem services related to water quality, fisheries and recreation.[17]

---

[17] *See* Marten Scheffer & Stephen R. Carpenter, *Catastrophic Regime Shifts in Ecosystems: Linking Theory to Observation*, 18 TRENDS ECOLOGY & EVOLUTION 648 (2003).

PHOSPHORUS, FERTILIZER, AND STATE PREEMPTION

Knowing that a system is or is not resilient can help direct policy decisions, however, it does not have to do so. For example, in many states where algal blooms strain water resources, states prohibit local communities from regulating the use of phosphorus in fertilizers. In these states, state legislatures have expressly preempted local governments from regulating phosphorus. Ohio (Toledo, Ohio experienced an algal bloom in 2014 that left hundreds of thousands without potable water) provides a typical example:

No political subdivision may enact, adopt, or continue in effect local legislation relating to the registration, packaging, labeling, sale, storage, distribution, use, or application of fertilizers. See Ohio Revised Code s. 905.503.

Thus, even if Toledo, Ohio wanted to regulate fertilizer to protect its citizens from phosphorus runoff, it could not do so. Although states prohibit local governments from regulating phosphorus, many state governments fail to establish phosphorous use regulations statewide. The EPA found that Ohio and 27 other states failed to establish numeric nutrient criteria for phosphorus and nitrogen (nutrients found in fertilizer).

E.P.A., *State Progress Toward Developing Numeric Nutrient Water Quality Criteria for Nitrogen and Phosphorus*, https://www.epa.gov/nutrient-policy-data/state-progress-toward-developing-numeric-nutrient-water-quality-criteria.

c. Adaptive Cycle

Adaptive cycle depicts four phases social-ecological systems may experience.[18] The phases help categorize a system's level of resilience to a disturbance or disturbances. They contemplate changes in systems and reorganizations as part of ecological resilience. The four phases are:

- an initial stage of *development showing rapid growth* (shown as the "r" stage in Figure 1-1), where the system is highly resilient, leading to the second stage;
- a *rigid or conservation* phase (shown as the "K" stage in Figure 1-1), where the system is less flexible and resilient, ultimately resulting in the third stage;
- a *collapse or release* phase (shown as the "Ω" or omega stage in Figure 1-1), where the system's resilience is strained, leading to the fourth stage;
- *reorganization* (shown as the "α" or alpha stage in Figure 1-1), where the system restructures and closes the cycle.

---

[18]Eric Desjardins et al., *Promoting Resilience*, 90 Q. Rev. Biology 147, 149 (2015) (describing the four stages as growth, conservation, release, and reorganization).

In each phase, we can understand the system as resilient, not resilient, trending toward resilience, or trending away from resilience. In Figure 1-1, the outer edges of the r-K loop (first two phases) reflect a more stable and predictable system, while the outer edges of the Ω-α loop (last two phases) represent a rapidly changing system. A disturbance may facilitate movement from one phase to the next.[19]

The example below illustrates the adaptive cycle relevant to the lumber industry in and around the Tongass National Forest in Alaska. As you read the example, look for the four phases and think about how they help indicate the system's level of resilience to the disturbances affecting the system.

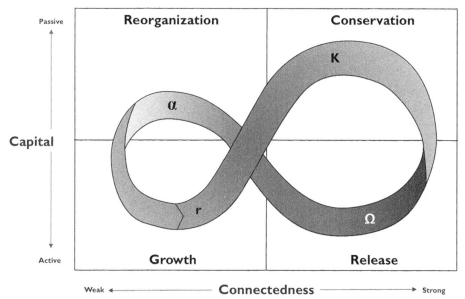

Figure 1-1

Example. A boom-bust cycle of industrial forest management that occurred on the Tongass National Forest in Alaska demonstrates a remarkable fit with the adaptive cycle.

During the early 1900s, efforts to establish this system in the remote and rugged landscape of southeastern Alaska were hindered by a number of economic and logistical factors. This period, the organization phase [α phase to r phase], was when the foundational elements of the Tongass resource system first emerged. Eventually, demand for lumber supplies during World War II created the opportunity to initiate the Tongass forestry system. With legislation

[19] Adapted from C.S. Holling, *Understanding the Complexity of Economic, Ecological, and Social Systems*, 4 ECOSYSTEMS 390 (2001).

providing the political authority and economic subsidies to harvest large tracts of primary old-growth forest, the Tongass system was established upon long-term leases that provided guaranteed low-cost timber. These new factors allowed the Tongass system to change rapidly and initiate a period of vigorous growth that lasted over two decades (1948-1970) [r phase].

During the latter years of this growth phase, reforms in environmental policy began to erode the authority of the Tongass to harvest timber, leading to a period when the system sought stability in the face of change — the conservation phase [r phase to K phase]. Changes occurring during this time were mostly external to Alaska, but affected the Tongass in many ways, including globalization of timber markets, stronger environmental protection policies, and institutional reforms at the U.S. Forest Service [K phase].

In 1990, when the U.S. Congress reformed the establishing policies and removed timber subsidies, during a market downturn for Alaskan forest products, the long-term leases were terminated and the Tongass system entered the collapse phase [Ω phase]. Collapse of the Tongass system led to dramatic declines in employment and major changes in local and regional economic conditions. Another legacy of system collapse has been a degraded forest ecosystem in several areas and a highly contentious atmosphere of mistrust among managers, stakeholders, and policy makers.

As of 2010, the Tongass remains trapped in the collapse phase [Ω phase], unable to reorganize and begin a new adaptive cycle [α phase]. A primary reason this occurred is because the system rigidly resisted change, instead of being adaptive to change. Another lesson from this case study was that change only occurred in the Tongass system — i.e., a shift from one phase to the next — when two of its subsystems (economic and social) moved to that next phase at the same time. In other words, the larger system did not experience dramatic change until several smaller-scale factors pushed it in the same direction.[20]

---

[20] *See* Colin M. Beier et al., *Growth and Collapse of a Resource System: An Adaptive Cycle of Change in Public Lands Governance and Forest Management in Alaska*, 14 ECOLOGY & SOC'Y 1 (2009).

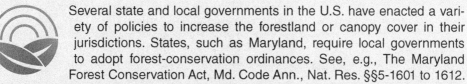

Several state and local governments in the U.S. have enacted a variety of policies to increase the forestland or canopy cover in their jurisdictions. States, such as Maryland, require local governments to adopt forest-conservation ordinances. See, e.g., The Maryland Forest Conservation Act, Md. Code Ann., Nat. Res. §§5-1601 to 1612. These laws require local governments to establish plans and in some cases minimum conservation standards. For an example of such a plan drafted pursuant to Maryland's law, see Forest Conservation Ordinance, Washington County, Maryland: Department of Planning and Zoning, http://www2.washco-md. net/planning/forest.shtm.

Cities have taken the lead to increase their urban canopy cover. In 2007 New York City, for example, started an initiative to plant and care for one million trees. Through contributions from the public and private sector, the initiative, MillionTreesNYC, accomplished its goal in 2015. "This landmark program . . . has led to a host of valuable research regarding the urban forest and has transformed acres of parkland and streets into ecologically healthy forests that provide benefits to all New Yorkers."[21]

d. Panarchy

Panarchy is the interaction among related adaptive cycles that together form larger systems. The concept of panarchy helps capture the complexity of systems and their interconnectedness. Each system may have numerous social and ecological subsystems, existing at various scales and connected to one another. Each subsystem and its adaptive cycle can influence the other subsystems and adaptive cycles and thus, the overall resilience of the larger system. Panarchy reflects this interdependency and connections among adaptive cycles.

Revolt, indicated in Figure 1-2, shows a disturbance that leads to collapse in one adaptive cycle (Ω phase in the bottom adaptive cycle) can cascade up to additional and vulnerable systems, initiating additional collapses (indicated in the middle adaptive cycle by the arrow showing Ω to K to Ω—rigidity leading to collapse). *Remember* illustrates the renewal capacities of one adaptive cycle (in its rigid K phase) to reach back and to help another cycle remember its prior incarnation.[22] *Revolt and Remember* help explain how a larger system's resilience is dependent upon multiple adaptive cycles.

The example below describes the panarchy that helps shape the reindeer husbandry and forestry systems in Sweden and their resilience to a variety of disturbances. Be sure to identify the disturbances and the interconnectedness of the systems.

---

[21] *MillionTreesNYC*, New York City Parks, https://www.nycgovparks.org/trees/milliontreesnyc (last visited Sept. 24, 2017).
[22] Carl Folke, *Resilience: The Emergence of a Perspective for Social-Ecological Systems Analyses*, 16 Global Envtl. Change 253 (2006).

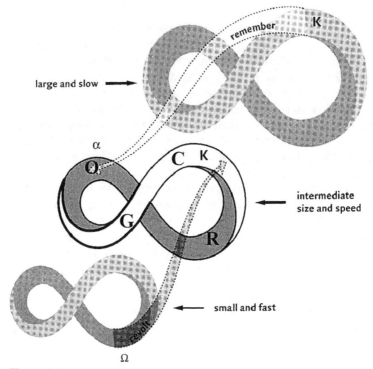

Figure 1-2

Example. Reindeer husbandry and forestry are two landscape-use sectors in the boreal forests of Sweden. Each of these sectors has a complexity of political, economical, and ecological dynamics changing and shaping their development. The shared natural resources and geographical space ensures that forestry and reindeer husbandry interact and influence each other.

Reindeer husbandry is a central livelihood for the Sami people, the indigenous people of northern Scandinavia. At first they raised small herds. Then, increased enforcement of national boarders cut off winter and summer grazing grounds. This resulted in a migration southwards and a transition to large herds used mostly for meat production.

At the end of the 19th century new economic opportunities opened the forestry sector in Sweden. After initial clear cutting, sustainability mandates were imposed by the government for several decades until 1979 when clear cutting, coupled with regeneration criteria became law. An increased focus on optimization and intensified silviculture [the cultivation of trees] has changed the ecological makeup of forests and spawned a network of forestry related industries. The sector can now be described as industrial forestry. From the local to the international level forestry has its own panarchy of adaptive cycles interacting at different scales.

These sectors share a landscape. The actions taken within one sector influence the other. With the backing of economical strength, forestry dominates most conflict discussion. Reindeer husbandry is dependent on the forest for winter and summer grazing areas. The increase and optimization of the forestry industry has decreased the herding landscape and increased fragmentation. Management of the two sectors takes place on different scales, but they influence one another immensely. In this way, this system represents interlocking panarchies. There are complexities within each sector and then there are complex dynamics operating at different scales of the whole system. Understanding the internal dynamics within each sector, as well as the interactions between them [i.e., panarchy] is necessary for assessing the sustainability [and resilience] of the system as a whole.[23]

e. Boundaries

Boundaries are the borders in which a system or subsystem resides. Drawing the boundary for a given social-ecological system is difficult, similar to other aspects of evaluating a system's resilience. It is also critical because it dictates what additional social and ecological subsystems and adaptive cycles may influence the base system that we are assessing.

Drawing boundaries is particularly difficult because it often involves overlapping systems that conflate out in potentially unrelated manners and directions. For example, if we intend to assess the resilience of Lake Michigan's watershed, do we measure only those systems within the ordinary high water mark around the Lake? Do we include the surrounding terrestrial areas? River banks? The dozens of tributaries feeding into the Lake? What about the flora and fauna along the shoreline? What about those systems embedded in the soil, which may serve as food for a number of other systems, which may then serve as food for larger amphibians or mammals, and so on? Thus, determining the system's boundaries heavily impacts what is analyzed for purposes of assessing resilience, thereby also affecting the results.

---

[23] *See* Jon Moen & E. Carina H. Keskitalo, *Interlocking Panarchies in Multi-Use Boreal Forests in Sweden*, 15 ECOLOGY & SOC'Y 1, 9 (2010).

The Gouritz River in Africa illustrates the challenges and importance involved with drawing the appropriate boundaries. The River's watershed is affected by numerous subsystems, including subnational governments, diverse flora and fauna (including an estuary), and varying land uses and topographies. As you read the example below, consider where you would draw the boundary to examine the resilience of the Gouritz River watershed. In essence, which subsystems are necessary to evaluate in order to gain reliable information on the watershed and its resilience to a variety of disturbances?

Example. The Gouritz area is the central part of South Africa's Cape Floristic Region; spanning a coastal plain, two east-west parallel mountain ranges, and the Little Karoo Basin between them. The coastal area is used for resort development, recreation, pasture-raised livestock farming, and indigenous vegetation harvesting. The foothills of the mountainous region are used for agriculture, while the higher elevations are mostly state owned and preserved for nature conservation and water production.

The conservation strategy proposed for this dynamic landscape is the implementation of conservation corridors. Conservation corridors act as linkages between crucial wildlife habitats.

The boundaries of this case evolved by using the established nature conservation areas and then broadening out using topographic maps and aquatic processes to establish a wider region that incased entire water catchments. Expert workshops with conservation managers, aquatic biologists, botanists, entomologists, ornithologists, zoologists, archaeologists, and land use planners ensured the proposed project boundaries represented the biodiversity [discussed in more detail in Chapter 2, Section II.B.3] and land use diversity that defines the system.[24]

3. CRITIQUING ECOLOGICAL RESILIENCE

People have criticized the concept of resilience on a number of fronts. Below we set forth four of those critiques. As you work through each critique, ask whether you agree with it. Why or why not? Can you think of other challenges facing attempts to assess a system's resilience?

---

[24] Amanda T. Lombard et al., *Designing Conservation Corridors in Production Landscapes: Assessment Methods, Implementation Issues, and Lessons Learned*, 15 ECOLOGY & SOC'Y 1 (2010).

The first critique expresses concern that analysis of a system's resilience applies equally to social and ecological systems. In *Why Resilience Is Unappealing to Social Science: Theoretical and Empirical Investigations of the Scientific Use of Resilience*, Lennart Olsson et al. argue that resilience thinking fails to recognize important differences between human-made social systems and ecological systems, thus, skewing the analysis and results.

One key difference Lennart Olsson et al. note is that social systems are products of human thought and reason, while ecological systems are not. This difference, the authors claim, makes understanding social systems and their adaptive systems fundamentally different from ecological systems:

> [C]ore concepts and theories in social science — such as agency, conflict, knowledge, and power — are absent from resilience theory. . . . Given its . . . lack of attention to agency, conflict, knowledge, and power, resilience can become a powerful depoliticizing or naturalizing scientific concept and metaphor when used by political actors. . . . Resilience is a unifying concept within ecology and environmental studies but not in the social sciences. . . . The unifying ambition in resilience theory and thinking to go beyond natural science is counterproductive to successful interdisciplinary and integrated research.[25]

A second critique of resilience thinking questions whether we should base policy on assessing resilience. As discussed above, assessing a system's resilience requires an understanding of disturbances. Critics claim that this focus on disturbances too narrowly views systems and their place in the world. Why, for example, should we measure human behavior and decisions against a disturbance and/or the ability of something to withstand or adapt to a disturbance or allow such disturbance or adaptation to dictate human response? What about the benefits, economic or otherwise? And development? Should they yield when a system's resilience is stressed? If so, why?

A third criticism of resilience thinking is that the adaptive cycle, its four phases, and panarchy are too rigid to cover the many variations found in both social and ecological systems. The adaptive cycle and panarchy do not account for, for example, deviations from the four phases. Critics claim this rigidity fails to acknowledge realities. Some systems, they allege, do not follow the order of the four phases, raising questions about the usefulness of the adaptive cycle and panarchy.

Finally, resilience thinking simultaneously considers transformation as a positive measure of a system's resilience and regime change as a negative measure. Critics claim transformation and regime change are often the same thing and thus, cannot simultaneously express negative and positive

---

[25] Lennart Olsson et al., *Why Resilience is Unappealing to Social Science: Theoretical and Empirical Investigations of the Scientific Use of Resilience*, 14 Sci. Advances 1, 9 (2015).

qualities concerning resilience. You recall that modern definitions of resilience include a system's ability to transform following a disturbance. However, a system is not "resilient" when it shifts regimes. Is it possible for a system to transform (and thus, exhibit resilience) and not change regimes (showing vulnerabilities)? If so, how? Relatedly, is it possible to change regimes (and thus, breach a threshold beyond a system's resilience capacity) and not transform? If so, how?

4. SUMMARIZING RESILIENCE AS A CONCEPT

In the sections above, we covered some of the fundamental characteristics of ecological resilience. Let us now summarize the core materials. This summary will give us a jumping off point for Part II where we explore resilience in context and tools to assist in doing so.

- There are many ways to view "resilience." Two types are *engineering resilience* and *ecological resilience*. Some differences between the two include how they view stability and functionality. In this book, we focus predominantly on ecological resilience.
    - Ecosystems may become less resilient from an ecological resilience standpoint when we manage them with the goal of achieving "constancy of production" (engineering resilience).
    - Ecological resilience is an attempt to assess the functioning of, relationship among, and the limits of social-ecological systems.
    - Evaluating a system's resilience can help more completely comprehend the impacts and consequences associated with human behaviors and decisions relevant to social-ecological systems.
- Resilience analysis necessitates a drawing of *boundaries* to determine which systems we will analyze.
- *Disturbances* impacting those systems are identified and explored to ascertain whether and under which circumstances they can pierce a system's *thresholds* such that the disturbance irreparably changes the system (i.e., regime-shift).
- The system's ability to *resist, adapt,* or *transform* following a disturbance is the measure of the system's resilience.
- The *adaptive cycle* characterizes a system's life in four potentially repeating phases and identifies where in those phases a system is most resilient.
- The *adaptive cycle* and *panarchy* also help depict the relationship among systems. This relationship includes how changes in one system follow the crossing of a threshold and may alter related systems.

B. Sustainability

In addition to resilience, scholars, scientists, policy makers, and others have implemented a variety of approaches to help understand and assess many social-ecological challenges as "sustainable." Professor John Dernbach notes that sustainability "is best understood as a framework (or a perspective, lens, or approach) for the integration or balancing of environmental protection, economic development, and social justice."[26] Similarly, Professor Klaus Bosselmann has stated that sustainability "provides crucial guidance for the interpretation of legal norms and sets the benchmark for the understanding of justice, human rights and state sovereignty. In doing so, sustainability represents the foundational concept of emerging 'sustainability law' based on ecological justice, human rights and institutions."[27]

Over the last 40 years, international, national, and subnational bodies have spent an enormous amount of time and resources debating the definition of "sustainability" and drafting policies that coalesce around sustainability. From these discussions and intense negotiations, at least two widely accepted definitions for the term have emerged—one tied to "intergenerational equity" and the other tied to the "triple bottom line."

Before we explore intergenerational equity and the triple bottom line, we first set forth some of the history relative to defining sustainability. Most of the events and documents covered below originated through discussions at the international level, which in many ways became the most influential force in defining sustainability around intergenerational equity and the triple bottom line. What follows is not an all-encompassing chronology of the origins of these two definitions, as their development was much more organic with inputs happening simultaneously from many different disciplines at many different levels. Rather, what follows highlights some of the key legal documents helping to form the modern definition of sustainability.

1. MODERN ORIGINS OF SUSTAINABILITY

We can trace the origins of intergenerational equity and the triple bottom line back to major international conventions, beginning with the 1972 U.N. Conference on the Human Environment in Stockholm, Sweden. The Stockholm Conference was a key moment for forming sustainability as a concept. It solidified the connection between environmental harms, human behaviors, and the economy. It was the first official international

---

[26] John C. Dernbach, *Sustainable Development and the United States*, in Agenda for a Sustainable America 9 (John C. Dernbach ed., 2009).

[27] Klaus Bosselmann, The Principle of Sustainability: Transforming Law and Governance 41 (2d ed. 2009).

action to acknowledge that humans could do *irreversible damage* to the environment — i.e., act unsustainably.

In addition to establishing a new institution, called the United Nations Environment Programme (UNEP), and designating it as the primary international body concerning international environmental issues, the Convention produced the Stockholm Declaration containing seven proclamations and 26 principles concerning the environment and a desire to protect it from human deterioration.

INTERNATIONAL LAW

International law is decentralized. For the most part, individual sovereign nations make the laws. The United Nations (U.N.) has very limited authority to make binding laws. In addition, the U.N. has no compulsory jurisdiction over sovereign nations. This means no central authority can compel jurisdiction of one entity over another.

However, compulsory jurisdiction and binding law can occur through treaties or customary international law. Article 38(1)(d) of the Statutes of the International Court of Justice sets forth four types of laws that are binding in international law:

1. Treaties often called conventions: "international conventions, whether general or particular, establishing rules expressly recognized by the contesting states";
2. Customary international law: "international custom, as evidence of a general practice accepted as law";
3. General principles of law: "the general principles of law recognized by civilized nations"; and
4. Judicial decisions, excluding decisions of the International Court of Justice pursuant to Article 59.

The materials in this chapter focus primarily on treaties. For an overview of international law sources see Malcolm N. Shaw, INTERNATIONAL LAW 49-91 (7th ed. 2014); Sean D. Murphy, PRINCIPLES OF INTERNATIONAL LAW 77-124 (2d ed. 2012). For additional information on customary international law see Daniel Bodansky, *Customary (and Not So Customary) International Environmental Law*, 3 IND. J. GLOBAL LEGAL STUD. 105 (1995).

The following Stockholm Declaration principles were influential in forming sustainability as a concept:

Principle 1
Man has the fundamental right to freedom, equality and adequate conditions of life, in an environment of a quality that permits a life of dignity and well-being, and he bears a solemn responsibility to protect and improve the environment for present and future generations. . . .

Principle 2

The natural resources of the earth, including the air, water, land, flora and fauna and especially representative samples of natural ecosystems, must be safeguarded for the benefit of present and future generations through careful planning or management, as appropriate.

Principle 3

The capacity of the earth to produce vital renewable resources must be maintained and, wherever practicable, restored or improved. . . .

Principle 5

The non-renewable resources of the earth must be employed in such a way as to guard against the danger of their future exhaustion and to ensure that benefits from such employment are shared by all mankind.

Principles 1 and 2 declare that the current generation has a responsibility to future generations. We call this "intergenerational equity" and explore what responsibility the current generation has to future generations in more detail in the next section. Principles 3 and 5 are concerned with the renewable capacities of the Earth and resource exhaustion. We explore this concept in more depth in Chapter 2 in a text box on "Planetary Boundaries."

Prior to the 1972 Stockholm Convention, numerous relevant events were happening around the world. For example, beginning in the early and mid-twentieth century many of the first modern ecologists, such as Charles Sutherland Elton, George Evelyn Hutchinson, and H.T. Odum helped expose the interconnectedness between the environment and human actions. They also helped formulate the concepts of ecosystem ecology and systems thinking.

In addition, dramatic environmental catastrophes were widely reported, including the igniting of the Cuyahoga River in Ohio on several occasions due to pollution. Such reporting highlighted the connection between economic growth and the environment. Rachel Carson, author of *Silent Spring* in 1962, helped popularize the idea that human behaviors and economic growth can have profound impacts on human and animal health.

In response to these and other events, the U.S. Congress passed a series of federal statutes aimed at managing a variety of environmental impacts. These statutes include the Clean Air Act in 1963 (and major amendments several times after including in 1970, 1977, and 1990), the Air Quality Act of 1967, the National Environmental Policy Act in 1969, which set the standard for national environmental impact statements, the Clean Water Act in 1972, and the Endangered Species Act of 1973. Many of these statutes are covered in Part II of this book.

Around the same time, Congress enacted a number of other statutes to manage natural resources based on a "sustainable yield" standard, including the Multiple-Use

Sustained-Yield Act of 1960 and the Forest and Rangeland Renewable Resources Planning Act of 1974. In part, those statutes state:

43 U.S.C.A. §1701. Congressional declaration of policy

(a) The Congress declares that it is the policy of the United States that . . .
(7) goals and objectives be established by law as guidelines for public land use planning, and that management be on the basis of multiple use and sustained yield unless otherwise specified by law. . . .

16 U.S.C.A. §1852. Regional Fishery Management Councils

. . . (g)(1)(B) Each scientific and statistical committee shall provide its Council ongoing scientific advice for fishery management decisions, including recommendations for acceptable biological catch, preventing overfishing, maximum sustainable yield, and achieving rebuilding targets, and reports on stock status and health, bycatch, habitat status, social and economic impacts of management measures, and sustainability of fishing practices.

16 U.S.C.A. §1853. Contents of fishery management plans

(a) . . . Any fishery management plan which is prepared by any Council, or by the Secretary, with respect to any fishery, shall. . . .

(a)(3) assess and specify the present and probable future condition of, and the maximum sustainable yield and optimum yield from, the fishery, and include a summary of the information utilized in making such specification. . . .

16 U.S.C.A. §1802. Definitions

. . . (34) The terms "overfishing" and "overfished" mean a rate or level of fishing mortality that jeopardizes the capacity of a fishery to produce the maximum sustainable yield on a continuing basis.

For a critique of these statutes and others, see Robin Craig, *"Stationarity is Dead"— Long Live Transformation: Five Principles for Climate Change Adaptation Law*, 34 HARV. ENVTL. L. REV. 9 (2010).

About ten years after the Stockholm Convention, the U.N. General Assembly by a vote of 111 for, 18 abstentions, and 1 against (the U.S.) adopted the *World Charter for Nature*, which more fully integrated human impacts on the environment, stating:

> *The General Assembly [acknowledges that]: . . .*
>
> *(a) Mankind is a part of nature and life depends on the uninterrupted functioning of natural systems. . . .*
>
> *[The General Assembly is c]onvinced that: . . .*
>
> *(b) Man can alter nature and exhaust natural resources by his action or its consequences and, therefore, must fully recognize the urgency of maintaining the stability and quality of nature and of conserving natural resources. . . .*

At approximately the same time, the UNEP's Governing Council adopted the Nairobi Declaration, which, among other things, urged "Governments and peoples of the world to discharge their historical responsibility to ensure that our planet is passed over to *future generations in a condition that guarantees a life in human dignity for all*[.]"[28]

From 1983-1987, the World Commission on Environment and Development (WCED) convened and ultimately produced the pivotal document, *Our Common Future* (also known as the "Brundtland Report," named after Gro Harlem Brundtland, former Prime Minister of Norway and chair of WCED). The Brundtland Report has turned into one of the most influential documents on defining sustainability. The Brundtland Report defined "sustainable development" — as opposed to "sustainability" (sustainability and sustainable development are contrasted below in subsection II.B.4) — as *"development that meets the needs of the present without compromising the ability of future generations to meet their own needs."* (Emphasis added.) Although we used this definition to define sustainable development, it has been frequently, and some have argued incorrectly, used to help define sustainability. The Brundtland Report went on to state, "Even the narrow notion of physical sustainability implies a concern for *social equity between generations,* a concern that must logically be extended to *equity within each generation."* (Emphasis added.) Thus, the Brundtland Report not only raised the relevance of social equity in sustainability, but also highlighted the need for intragenerational equity.

We developed other documents that served as an early basis for helping frame the initial contours of sustainability at the 1992 Rio de Janeiro U.N. Conference on Environment and Development (also known as "Rio Earth Summit"). These documents include Agenda 21 (a detailed framework for achieving sustainable development making connections between "a high quality environment and a healthy economy for all") and the Rio Declaration on Environment and Development, which stated, in part:

Principle 3
The right to development must be fulfilled so as to equitably meet developmental and environmental needs of present and future generations.

Principle 4
In order to achieve sustainable development, environmental protection shall constitute an integral part of the development process [chain] and cannot be considered in isolation from it.

Principle 5
All States and all people shall co-operate in the essential task of eradicating poverty as an indispensable requirement for sustainable development. . . .

---

[28] G.A. Res. 37/219, ¶ 4 (Dec. 20, 1982) (emphasis added).

Principle 6
. . . International actions in the field of environment and development should also address the interests and needs of all countries.

Twenty years later in 2012, world leaders met again in Rio to create a framework for sustainable development. In doing so, the parties emphasized seven core areas relevant to sustainability: jobs, energy, sustainable cities, sustainable agriculture, water, oceans, and disaster preparedness. The first paragraph of the primary report from 2012, entitled *Report of the United Nations Conference on Sustainable Development*, described the principal focus as:

1. We, the Heads of State and Government and high-level representatives . . . with the full participation of civil society, renew our commitment to sustainable development and to ensuring the promotion of an economically, socially and environmentally sustainable future for our planet and for present and future generations.

In this statement, the Report simultaneously noted the importance of achieving economic, social, and environmental sustainability and protecting the planet for future generations.

Questions and Notes

1. When considered together the conventions and documents above provide some of the most influential and foundational pieces for forming the modern definition of sustainability. In the quoted portions above, the following key phrases are italicized. Do you see trends or consistencies among the phrases?
    *   for present and future generations
    *   for the benefit of present and future generations
    *   capacity of the earth
    *   guard against the danger of their future exhaustion
    *   shared by all mankind
    *   life depends on the uninterrupted functioning of natural systems
    *   Man can alter nature and exhaust natural resources
    *   maintaining the stability and quality of nature and of conserving natural resources
    *   passed over to future generations
    *   guarantees a life of human dignity for all
    *   development that meets the needs of the present without compromising the ability of future generations to meet their own needs

- social equity between generations
- equity within each generation
- equitably meet developmental and environmental needs of present and future generations
- environmental protection shall constitute an integral part of the development
- eradicating poverty as an indispensable requirement for sustainable development
- interests and needs of all countries
- promotion of an economically, socially and environmentally sustainable future for our planet and for present and future generations

2. In addition to the provisions mentioned above, the Stockholm Declaration, Principle 21 provides:

> *States have, in accordance with the Charter of the United Nations and the principles of international law, the sovereign right to exploit their own resources pursuant to their own environmental policies, and the responsibility to ensure that activities within their jurisdiction or control do not cause damage to the environment of other States or of areas beyond the limits of national jurisdiction.*

What do you think about Principle 21? What are the key components of Principle 21? Do they help assess or achieve sustainability in, say, a watershed that crosses national borders?

3. As the term sustainability developed, two views of it emerged. The first, called "weak sustainability," allows current generations to substitute built capital, such as dams and bridges, for natural capital, such as trees, in what passes to the next generation. The second, "strong sustainability," requires that the next generation receive the same amount or level of natural capital.

2. TWO FUNDAMENTAL UNDERSTANDINGS OF SUSTAINABILITY

In understanding sustainability, two consistent themes are "intergenerational equity" and the "triple bottom line." In the next two subsections, we summarize these two common and widely accepted definitions. We also point out some of the assumptions embedded in understanding sustainability as intergenerational equity or based on a triple bottom line. Keep these definitions and their corresponding assumptions in mind throughout the book and try to identify how, if at all, specific policy decisions support each definition.

a. Intergenerational Equity

Stockholm Principle 1 and 2, the Brundtland Report, the 1992 Rio Declaration Principle 3, and other provisions raise intergenerational equity as a core sustainability concept. Pursuant to intergenerational equity, the current generation should not destroy or exhaust the things, known and unknown, that may be necessary or desirable to future generations. Present generations have an obligation to ensure that future generations have the capacity to flourish. In this regard, present generations must, among other tasks, manage natural resources and ecosystems in a way that allows future generations to access those resources and systems.

Professor Edith Brown Weiss' piece on intergenerational equity excerpted below remains one of the most influential pieces on intergenerational equity and details the core components.

In addition to those set forth above the following international agreements have incorporated intergenerational equity into policy:

- *Rio Declaration on Environment and Development*, Principle 3: "The right to development must be fulfilled so as to equitably meet developmental and environmental needs of present and future generations."
- *Non-Binding Authoritative Statement of Principles for a Global Consensus on the Management, Conservation and Sustainable Development of all Types of Forests*, Principle 2(b): "Forest resources and forest lands should be sustainably managed to meet the social, economic, ecological, cultural and spiritual [human] needs of present and future generations[.]"
- *U.N. Convention on Biological Diversity*, Preamble: "conserve and sustainably use biological diversity for the benefit of present and future generations."
- *U.N. Framework Convention on Climate Change*, Article 3(1): "The Parties should protect the climate system for the benefit of present and future generations of humankind, on the basis of equity and in accordance with their common but differentiated responsibilities and respective capabilities."

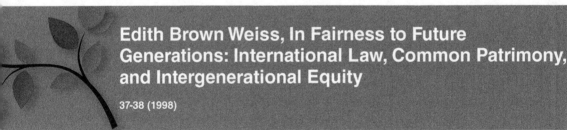

Edith Brown Weiss, In Fairness to Future Generations: International Law, Common Patrimony, and Intergenerational Equity

37-38 (1998)

The theory of intergenerational justice says that each generation has an obligation to future generations to pass on the natural and cultural resources of the planet in no worse condition than received and to provide reasonable access to the legacy for the present generation. What then are the principles of intergenerational equity that will fulfill these purposes?

Four criteria should guide the development of principles of intergenerational equity. First, the principles should encourage equality among generations, neither authorizing the present generation to exploit resources to the exclusion of future generations, nor imposing unreasonable burdens on the present generation to meet indeterminate future needs. Second, they should not require one generation to predict the values of future generations. They must give future generations flexibility to achieve their goals according to their own values. Third, they should be reasonably clear in application to foreseeable situations. Fourth, they must be generally shared by different cultural traditions and generally acceptable to different economic and political systems.

We propose three basic principles of intergenerational equity. First, each generation should be required to conserve the diversity of the natural and cultural resource base, so that it does not unduly restrict the options available to future generations in solving their problems and satisfying their own values, and should be entitled to diversity comparable to that of previous generations. This principle may be called "conservation of options." Second, each generation should be required to maintain the quality of the planet so that it is passed on in no worse condition than the present generation received it, and should be entitled to a quality of the planet comparable to the one enjoyed by previous generations. This is the principle of "conservation of quality." Third, each generation should provide its members with equitable rights of access to the legacy from past generations and should conserve this access for future generations. This is the principle of "conservation of access."

Questions and Notes

1. *Conservation of options.* Weiss' first basic principle is that each generation should be required to "conserve the *diversity* of the natural and cultural resource base." (Emphasis added.) The current generation has to do so in a way that "does not unduly restrict the options" future generations have. Future generations should be entitled to diversity comparable to that of previous generations. How would you translate this into a specific obligation that each generation has and can you see embedding that obligation into the law?

2. The first criteria (as opposed to principle) notes that the present generation should not be "impos[ed with] unreasonable burdens." How should the current generation balance conserving a resource (part of the first basic principle) to allow future generations to utilize it while allowing the current generation to not be unreasonably burdened by use restrictions?

3. Conservation of *quality.* Weiss' second basic principle is that "each generation should be required to maintain the *quality of the planet* so that it is passed on in no worse a condition than the present generation received it." (Emphasis added.) What could "quality of the planet" mean in this context and how would you measure that? Weiss also notes that the "quality of the planet" passed on should be comparable to the one inherited—a concept now often discussed as having a "net positive" impact in which the current generation would pass on a planet in better quality to the one it inherited.

4. Conservation of *access.* Weiss' third and final basic principle is that "each generation should provide its members with *equitable rights of access* to the legacy from past generations and should conserve this access for future generations." (Emphasis added.) This incorporates an additional *temporal component* to sustainability. It connects contemporary actions with future impacts and opportunities and past legacies. Should it mean that each generation should allow each individual access, rights, opportunities, etc. to natural resources in a similar fashion to prior generations in terms of quality? Quantity? Opportunity?

5. A challenge involved with intergenerational equity is trying to determine the relevant body of people that qualifies as the current or future generation. Relatedly, there are challenges in determining what amounts to an equitable result among those people. Weiss raises this point in her second criteria, noting that one generation should not predict the values of another generation. How would you define your generation? Who is part of that generation? Who is part of your preceding or succeeding generation?

6. What are some of the intergenerational issues of our time? Pick an issue; how does it impact future generations? Why should we consider intergenerational equity in determining law or policy as it relates to that issue? How could we balance the needs of the present generation with those of the future?

---

i. Case Study: Catching Water in a Net, the Population Collapse of the Atlantic Cod

 In exploring the concept of intergenerational equity and its relevance to understanding sustainability, consider the role of intergenerational equity in the following story about the Atlantic cod. To assess the sustainability of any given system, we must understand complex scientific and social information and recognize how disruptions

in the system can result in pervasive and potentially irreversible consequences, destroying the system for future generations. Of course, having the information does not mean that we will alter law and policy to
enhance a system's sustainability. The ecological and social systems that
collapsed around the depleted Atlantic cod provide an illustration.

A bottom-dwelling fish, the Atlantic cod represented the lifeblood of
fishing in the Northwest Atlantic Ocean for many centuries. Gradually
fishing turned into overfishing, and in the early 1990s, cod numbers
crashed, leaving future generations without a vital economic, cultural, and
ecological resource.

 How law and policy can move forward in the face of a lack of information or changing information are topics we discuss in more detail with
the Precautionary Principle in Chapter 3 and Adaptive Governance in
Chapter 7.

Reports dating back to the fifteenth century, when fishing consisted
of small boats and fishing lines with single-baited hooks, indicate that
the Atlantic cod was an important part of some societies' subsistence and
economic life. In 1497, Italian explorer, "John Cabot" (Giovanni Caboto),
marveled at the abundant population of the Atlantic cod. One early writer
even speculated that no human effort could deplete the stock.

Over time, the plethora of cod led individuals to settle in Newfoundland,
an island off the coast of what was later Canada. For early settlers, the cod
served as a means of personal consumption and a form of trading with
local buyers. For the next several centuries, the abundant cod and its associated social and ecological systems supported families and port towns on
Newfoundland and the surrounding areas.

Beginning in the nineteenth century, subsistence around the Atlantic
cod expanded to entrepreneurship. The cod-seine, "[a] large net, up to
600 feet (182.8 m) in length, set around a school of cod, the 'foots' drawn
together to form a bag,"[29] which had been the predominant method of fishing, was replaced by the cod trap. The cod trap was developed in the late
1860s/early 1870s. The cod trap funneled cod into an underwater room
with walls, floors, and one door all made of netting.

Codfish enter the trap through a doorway in the front wall, guided by a . . . long
wall of netting that extends from the doorway. The traps are set in areas where
fish swim along the shore or rock shoals, whereby they encounter the [long wall
of netting and] are diverted . . . into the trap.[30]

---

[29] DICTIONARY OF NEWFOUNDLAND ENGLISH 106, (G.M. Story et al. eds., 2d ed. 1990).
[30] *The Invention of the Cod Trap*, WHITELEY MUSEUM, http://www.whiteleymuseum.com/codtrap.
asp?id = 3 (last visited Sept. 24, 2017).

The cod trap quickly became the industry standard because it was efficient at catching cod and lowered costs. Where the cod-seine required a crew of at least six people and several boats to set and haul, the cod trap reduced the necessary crew size and no longer required constant monitoring.

New technologies continued to facilitate the catching of cod — this time in the form of the steam engine. Boats powered by steam engines allowed international fishing fleets from across the Atlantic Ocean to reach Atlantic cod stocks. French steamboats began dragging or trawling nets across the ocean floor in the early 1900s. During this time, harvesting increased, but was limited because of the rapid rate cod perishes when pulled out of the sea. Each boat's catch was limited to the time necessary to return to shore to salt the fish immediately for preservation.

In the 1950s, technology changed again. This time the appearance of the factory-freezer trawler, which was essentially a floating ice box/processing facility, allowed fleets to stay at sea and increase their fishing capacities.[28] Further advances in radar and navigation systems facilitated even larger catches. By the 1970s, the Atlantic cod was supporting crews from New England, Canada, Europe, the Soviet Union, and elsewhere, all with sophisticated methods of catching the cod.

In Chapter 2, we explore the role of technology in sustainable systems. In the Atlantic cod example, technology played a dual role: expediting the exploitation of the Atlantic cod, while also helping to provide information to ascertain whether the social-ecological systems relevant to the cod are sustainable.

As catch numbers increased, some began to question whether the industry was sustainable. In 1914, the U.S. Commissioner of Fisheries wrote, "unregulated fishery eventually may result in injury." Similarly, in 1930, scientists warned that continued high rates of trawling could cause substantial damage to the cod population and to the sea bed. Nonetheless, generally permissive regulations and subsidized fishing operations continued to increase yields.

"But then, you know, that changed when, when the fish started declin[ing] and we, and we all could see what was happenin'. I mean they were fishin', right and then their fish would get smaller

---

[31] George A. Rose, Cod: The Ecological History of the North Atlantic Fisheries 388 (2006).

and smaller and smaller and smaller. . . ."[32] In response to declining cod catches and sizes, in 1976, the Canadian government prohibited foreign trawlers (except U.S. trawlers) from fishing the Atlantic cod within its Economic Enterprise Zone, as defined under the U.N. Convention on the Law of the Sea (see adjacent box).

The U.N. Third Convention on the Law of the Sea (UNCLOS) divides the Ocean into four basic zones: 1) territorial zone, extending 12 nautical miles from the coastline; 2) contiguous zone, extending 12-24 nautical miles from the coastline; 3) exclusive economic zone (EEZ), extending 200 nautical miles from the coastline; and 4) high seas, extending out after the EEZ.

The EEZs set the rules to abate clashes over fishing and oil rights. Within its EEZ, a nation:

- has sole exploitation or conservation rights over all natural resources, Art. 56;
- may build and has sole operation of artificial islands and installations, Art. 60;
- is responsible for determining the allowable catch, Art. 61, with the idea that the nation "shall promote the objective optimum utilization of the living resources" and "shall ensure through proper conservation and management measures that the maintenance of the living resources in the exclusive economic zone is not endangered by over-exploitation"; and
- shall "promote the objective of optimum utilization of living resources," Art. 62(1).

For an example concerning national dispute over EEZ, see *Bangladesh v. Myanmar*, International Tribunal for the Law of the Sea, Judgment 14 March 2012, No. 16, https://www.itlos.org/fileadmin/itlos/documents/cases/case_no_16/published/C16_Judgment.pdf.

As shown in Figure 1-3, cod fish landings first decreased dramatically, and then slowly increased, shortly after the 1976 laws went into effect. The increase, known as "the glory years," saw Canadian and U.S. fishing fleets take advantage of their monopoly over the cod in Canada's Economic Enterprise Zone and increase their harvests. "Canadian catches reached new highs in the late 1970s and early 1980s, then stayed above historical levels until the late 1980s. . . . When some dragger skippers noticed that cod were becoming smaller and harder to find in the mid-80s, they adapted by illegally lining their nets with smaller-size mesh . . . effectively targeting juvenile fish."[33] Not surprisingly, the species did not have a chance to rebound following the 1976 law and the cod population in the Northwest Atlantic fell to approximately 1% of its original size.

---

[32] Lawrence C. Hamilton et al., *Above and Below the Water: Social/Ecological Transformation in Northwest Newfoundland,* 25 POPULATION & ENV'T 195 (2004).
[33] *Id.* at 13.

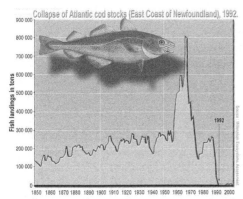

Figure 1-3

In 1992, the Canadian government instituted a full moratorium on fishing the Atlantic cod within its EEZ. This decision enraged tens of thousands of workers who lost jobs up and down the supply chain related to the cod, although it is debatable whether they would have had jobs as the cod stock was already drastically reduced. Government efforts addressing impacts from the loss of cod included buyouts of fishing boats and unemployment payments for the crews and other industry workers. The Canadian government spent approximately $8 billion to mitigate the damage to the coastal economy, half of which consisted of unemployment benefits.[34]

SUBSIDIES, POLICY, AND SUSTAINABILITY

Consider the following facts describing some of the subsidies involving the Atlantic cod. Who benefits from these subsidies? Who pays the costs associated with them? Which subsidies tend to support sustainable systems? What about unsustainable conditions?

- During the 1960s, 70s, and 80s, Canada funded new and upgraded Canadian fleets to compete with foreign fishers' fleets. Such subsidies amounted to 35% of fishing costs.
- From 1972 to 1991, the Canadian federal government spent about $4 billion on the Atlantic fishing industry.
- When the moratorium was announced in 1992, the federal government also agreed to pay fishers and plant workers.
- From 1994 to 1999, Canada paid an additional $1.9 billion in income payments and fishing license buybacks.[35]

The effects of aggressive cod fishing rendered the cod population so crippled that it has yet to recover, more than 25 years after the 1992 moratorium. Social-ecological systems, developed around the cod for hundreds of years, were shattered. The entire ecosystem of the Northwest Atlantic and the cod population in particular, has undergone fundamental changes that we cannot reverse simply by ceasing to harvest the cod. Many of the changes have made it more difficult and less hospitable for young cod to grow. For example, trawling nets demolished the reefs along the ocean floor where young cod used to hide from predators; herring, which fed

[34]Elizabeth Brubaker, *Unnatural Disaster: How Politics Destroyed Canada's Atlantic Groundfisheries*, in POLITICAL ENVIRONMENTALISM: GOING BEHIND THE GREEN CURTAIN (Terry L. Anderson, ed., 2000).
[35]Suzanne Iudicello et al., FISH, MARKETS AND FISHERMEN: THE ECONOMICS OF OVERFISHING 53-69 (2d ed. 1999).

on cod eggs, have greatly increased in population; and grey seals, which once competed with cod for food, have become more numerous, making it difficult for cod to reach mature size.

Fishing crews, which have been prohibited from landing cod since 2003, began "fishing down food webs," meaning they have turned to harvesting lobster, shrimp, and capelin, some of the cod's natural prey — illustrating panarchy and how the resilience of one system to a disturbance can impact the resilience of other related systems. Harvesting these species reduces the cod's basic diet, providing fewer opportunities for cod to survive and reducing their likelihood of reaching spawning age. This phenomenon, called *trophic cascade*, is where the absence of one species causes fundamental changes throughout a food chain.

Other social and economic systems relative to the cod also continue to suffer. An entire generation of former cod fishers had to find alternative employment and lost their cultural and historical identities. When the cod population crashed, the U.S. and Canada instituted programs to help individuals and local economies. Notwithstanding these efforts, for the first time in decades, there was a decrease in local populations along former cod fishing villages. Further, government assistance remains significantly above the Canadian national average in these areas, increasing to "nearly 40% of all income."[36]

The Atlantic cod provides a cautionary tale of how using a natural resource beyond its renewable capacities and failing to more completely understand social-ecological systems can result in economic, environmental, and social disasters that limit future generations' options, quality, and access as defined by Edith Brown Weiss in the excerpt above. The once-thriving cod industry that provided substantial quantities of fish to eat and jobs for thousands of people has folded, and there is no apparent remedy.

Questions and Notes

1. What do you think about the fishers in this story? Did they breach some kind of obligation to future generations? If so, what is that obligation? Do others have similar obligations? What obligation should the present generation have to live out the ideals of intergenerational equity?

2. Edith Brown Weiss' piece notes that each generation must ensure access to a variety of resources and options for future generations, including rights of access to past generations' legacy. What does that mean in the context of the Atlantic cod? What makes up the legacy of a generation?

---

[36] Hamilton et al., *supra* note 32.

Do these principles require that each individual have identical access to resources? Or is it sufficient to secure access to opportunities that may be comparable, but different?

3. The Atlantic cod story raises a fundamental issue we will struggle with throughout this book, namely, how to rectify economic interests with social and environmental ones. Policy decisions often require *trade-offs*. For example, Newfoundland and Labrador, where many of the Atlantic cod fishers lived, had some of the highest levels of Canadian national government monetary assistance to live and fish in the area for decades before the moratorium. How can we understand or justify the national assistance if it helped sustain individuals' livelihood, but also encouraged an unsustainable cod industry? Here is an example of a trade-off, where sustaining individuals' financial well-being led to or encouraged behavior that depleted the Atlantic cod.

4. Edith Brown Weiss's second criteria for intergenerational equity does not require that one generation predict the values for future generations. This means future generations must have the flexibility to achieve their own goals based on their own values — not what the present generation values. Note the difficulty with this. The current generation has an obligation to preserve the future generation's options (the first guiding principle), but they cannot confine future generations to a certain set of values (the second criteria). Is it possible to ascertain and protect options or opportunities without setting values?

In 1993, the Supreme Court of the Philippines held that a group of citizens for themselves and on behalf of future generations could use the court system to direct the government to stop the continued harvesting of rainforest timber. The Philippines is a nation of over 7,100 islands, which, in 1973, was 53% covered in rainforests. By 1987, rainforest cover was reduced to 4%, and in the early 90s that number had fallen to 2.8%. This severe deforestation resulted in serious impacts, including water shortages, drastic erosion, increased endangered species, disruption of indigenous cultures, silted rivers, destruction of coral deposits, increased wind velocity in typhoons, lowland flooding, and loss of carbon sequestration. By the time the plaintiffs sued, the government had issued permits sufficient to authorize the razing of the rest of the forest several times over.

The Supreme Court of the Philippines did not issue a moratorium on deforestation, but the ruling is historic. It incorporates principles of intergenerational equity into the law from the highest national judicial authority. The court emphasized the "intergenerational responsibility insofar as the right to a balanced and healthful ecology is concerned." The court also prioritized the conservation of access, saying that nature must "be equitably accessible to the present as well as future generations." How can the present generation, which inherits a legacy of 2.8% rainforest cover, provide for itself and utilize its right of access without impairing access in the future? Did we breach the duty we owed to them? If so, what could and should be the remedy? This raises the related question of to what extent should the current generation deprive themselves to preserve opportunities for the future.

b. Triple Bottom Line

[Sustainability] means that the choice of goods and technologies must be oriented to the requirements of ecosystem integrity and species diversity as well as to social goals. Elements of all three perspectives—economic, ecological, and social—are essential to an understanding of the requirements for sustainability.[37]

The most widely understood and accepted definition of sustainability describes a framework in which we simultaneously assess the environment, economy, and society. Accounting for the environment, economy, and society is commonly known as the "three-legged stool," 3Es (environment, economy, equity), 3Ps (planet, profit, people), or the triple bottom line (TBL), which we use in this section.

The modern origin of the TBL is rooted in the 1972 U.N. Conference on the Human Environment, covered above. One of the primary objectives of the Conference was to harmonize economic activity with environmental conservation. In doing so, the Conference parties sought to better integrate the development of economic systems with ecological systems.

Following major societal events, such as racial segregation in South Africa and its use of financial tools to maintain segregation, the international community added social systems as a third component, as seen in the Brundtland Report quoted above. The social component requires a consideration of equity needs such as, education, health, equality, human happiness, democracy, and justice. As Professors Richard E. Stren and Mario Polèse state, the social equity component consists of "policies and institutions that have the overall effect of integrating diverse groups and cultural practices in a just and equitable fashion."[38] (Emphasis omitted.)

These three parts — economy, environment, and society — are reflected in a number of international agreements throughout the 1980s and 90s. *Our Common Future* and Rio Earth Summit, for example, draw directly from the connections between a strong environment, economy, and society. These international documents serve as the backbone for framing sustainability as the TBL.

---

[37]Jonathan M. Harris, *Sustainability and Sustainable Development*, INT'L SOC'Y FOR ECOLOGICAL ECON. INTERNET ENCYCLOPAEDIA ECOLOGICAL ECON. 1, 2 (2003).
[38]Richard E. Stren & Mario Polèse, *Understanding the New Sociocultural Dynamics of Cities: Comparative Urban Policy in a Global Context, in* THE SOCIAL SUSTAINABILITY OF CITIES: DIVERSITY AND THE MANAGEMENT OF CHANGE 3 (2000).

States around the U.S. have incorporated the TBL into a variety of regulatory actions. Oregon Revised Statute §468.153, which incentivizes good behavior as well as establishes minimum standards, provides such an example:

(3) The Legislative Assembly finds and declares that it is the policy of this state to *promote sustainability* and provide incentives for the voluntary prevention, elimination, reduction or control of air pollution, water pollution, solid waste and hazardous waste through the voluntary application of innovative solutions to achieve the environmental goals of this state. [Emphasis added.]

(4) *The Legislative Assembly declares it to be the policy of this state to promote social, economic and environmental principles of sustainability by providing incentives to individuals and businesses that support social, economic and environmental sustainability goals.* [Emphasis added.]

It was not until 1994 that John Elkington coined the actual term "triple bottom line." In his 1997 book, *Cannibals with Forks: Triple Bottom Line of 21st Century Business*, Elkington described the TBL in more detail:

> *Sustainable development involves the simultaneous pursuit of economic prosperity, environmental quality, and social equity. Companies aiming for sustainability need to perform not against a single, financial bottom line but against the triple bottom line.*[39]

In the adjacent quote from *Cannibals with Forks* note how Elkington seems to equate sustainability and sustainable development, using "sustainable development" in one sentence and "sustainability" in the other—both referring to the triple bottom line. We return to the sustainable development versus sustainability debate in the next section.

Elkington continues by describing the TBL as "an inevitable expansion of the environmental agenda" that "focuses corporations not just on the economic value that they add, but also on the environmental and social value that they add—or destroy."

Elkington's principal concern was to motivate the use of TBL in the private sector. One of the most influential guidelines to help private sector entities track TBL sustainability is the *Reporting Principles and Standard Disclosures* by the Global Reporting Initiative, which states:

---

[39]John Elkington, CANNIBALS WITH FORKS: THE TRIPLE BOTTOM LINE OF 21ST CENTURY BUSINESS 397 (1997).

An ever-increasing number of companies and other organizations want to make their operations sustainable. Moreover, expectations that long-term profitability should go hand-in-hand with social justice and protecting the environment are gaining ground. . . . A sustainability report conveys disclosures on an organization's impacts—be they positive or negative—on the environment, society and the economy.[40]

The Venn diagram (Figure 1-4) is a common portrayal of the TBL. It illustrates how TBL represents sustainability. It also helps acknowledge unintended consequences that each leg of sustainability can have on the other legs.

Assessing sustainability based on the TBL requires that social and environmental concerns and their associated capitals (for example, natural capital, which is explored as having value in Chapter 3 under Ecosystem Services Management) be integrated into decision making and are considered equal components for purposes of decision making.

The case study below illustrates how we can integrate TBL into policy and use it to help us assess the sustainability of a city in relation to a number of factors. The case study describes a city's plan to become more sustainable, while using sustainability as a framework to measure improvement.

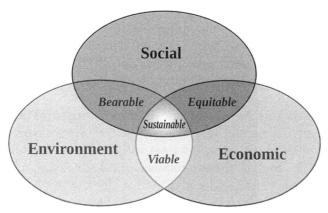

Figure 1-4[41]

i. Case Study: pLAn(ing) for the Future by Incorporating the TBL

The City of Los Angeles has adopted an aggressive sustainability plan, called "pLAn," that will be implemented over the next 20 years. The pLAn

---

[40] *Reporting Principles and Standard Disclosures*, GLOBAL REPORTING INITIATIVE 3 (2013), https://www.globalreporting.org/resourcelibrary/GRIG4-Part1-Reporting-Principles-and-Standard-Disclosures.pdf.
[41] *What Is Sustainability?*, VANDERBILT UNIV., https://www.vanderbilt.edu/sustainvu/who-we-are/what-is-sustainability/ (last visited Sept. 24, 2017).

consists of a complex set of baselines, metrics, and action steps designed to integrate sustainability into municipal workings. Although there are many pieces to the pLAn, the overarching theme is to achieve sustainable systems in 14 areas by identifying, quantifying, and calculating environmental, economic, and social impacts.

In setting its goal to become more sustainable, the pLAn adopts a TBL understanding of sustainability. In the Preface, Mayor Eric Garcetti states it this way:

> *The Sustainable City pLAn is a roadmap for a Los Angeles that is environmentally healthy, economically prosperous, and equitable in opportunity for all—now and over the next 20 years. . . . LA's first-ever Sustainable City pLAn connects the dots for Los Angeles by building on the three legs of the stool needed for any thriving city: environment, economy, and equity.*[42]

In developing its goals around the TBL, Los Angeles identified 13 topic areas framed within the three pillars of sustainability. A fourteenth topic area is to "lead by example," by fully integrating our assessment of the city's sustainability into every part of municipal governance. For each topic, the pLAn provides:

1. an explanation as to why this topic is one of the critical 13;
2. a vision;
3. near- and long-term outcomes, setting forth objectives for 2017, 2025, 2035;
4. a description of what the City has done to date; and
5. strategies and priority initiatives for each topic.

The pLAn begins by addressing the **environmental** leg of sustainability. The environmental topics focus on five areas: local water, local solar, energy-efficient buildings, carbon and climate leadership, and waste and landfills. For each of these topics the pLAn states the information for the five points above. The City's vision for "local water," for example, is to "lead the nation in water conservation and source the majority of our water locally." It plans to do this by reducing its per capita water use by 20% by 2017, reducing its purchase of imported water by 50% by 2025, and sourcing 50% of water locally by 2035.

For the **economic** leg of sustainability, the pLAn identifies four key topic areas: housing and development, mobility and transit, prosperity and green jobs, and preparedness and resiliency. The pLAn seeks economic prosperity through projects that improve equity and strengthen the

---

[42] *pLAn: Transforming Los Angeles*, THE CITY OF LOS ANGELES 8, https://d3n8a8pro7vhmx.cloudfront.net/mayorofla/pages/17002/attachments/original/1428470093/pLAn.pdf?1428470093.

environment. For example, by 2017, Los Angeles has a strategy to add more "green jobs" through water and energy efficiency than any other city in the U.S. The pLAn notes that this may also address environmental issues (presumably by reducing GHGs by improving technologies) and social issues (by creating jobs).

The pLAn's final section, **equity**, explores four key topic areas: air quality, environmental justice, urban ecosystem, and livable neighborhoods. These topics again illustrate how the three legs of sustainability can work together. Air quality, for example, is clearly an environmental issue, but the pLAn lists it as an equity topic, pertaining to poor air quality in economically depressed areas. Pursuant to the pLAn, Los Angeles will improve air quality by adding more mass transit infrastructure by 2025 and will provide more access to urban rivers than any city in the U.S. by 2035.

The pLAn is helping guide the City's work to improve the environment, social conditions, and economic opportunities simultaneously. For example, it aims to clean the most polluted and underserved neighborhoods, while providing better and safe transit (such as creating more bike lanes) and more opportunities for engagement and the formation of a strong community. By focusing efforts to revitalize urban social-ecological systems, Los Angeles prioritizes sustainability as part of its future. It also enhances environmental, economic, and societal conditions without sacrificing one of the three. As the Mayor notes: "To ensure our bright future, we must protect what makes our city great: our incredible natural environment, our diverse economy, and the people that make our city thrive."[43] Along these lines, the City recognizes:

> that sustainability is not a narrowcast endeavor, the efforts of the [sustainability office] . . . permeate everything we do as a city. . . . [W]e are incorporating sustainability — and now, this pLAn — into each of our 35 departments and bureaus, from airports to police to water and power and everything in between. . . . This pLAn sets the course for a cleaner environment and a stronger economy, with a commitment to equity as its foundation.[44]

Questions and Note

1. In his opening letter in pLAn, the Los Angeles Mayor, Eric Garcetti stated:

> We expect at least 500,000 more people to call Los Angeles home by 2035. So the question before us, like it was to those Angelenos of the past, is how

---

[43]*Id.* at 6.
[44]*Id.* at 5.

can we improve our city today, and ensure future generations enjoy a place that is environmentally healthy, economically prosperous, and equitable in opportunity for all?

Note the interplay between population, TBL, and intergenerational equity. Are they all necessary to address in order to achieve a sustainable city in Los Angeles?

2. The U.S. Environmental Protection Agency defines sustainability as being "based on a simple principle. . . . Sustainability creates and maintains the conditions under which humans and nature can exist in productive harmony, that permit fulfilling the social, economic and other requirements of present and future generations." This definition, like Mayor Garcetti's quote above, brings together intergenerational equity and the triple bottom line. How would you describe the overlap between these two important concepts?

3. While the pLAn focuses on the TBL, the pLAn does not go into depth on how any one of the three pillars impacts the other two pillars. For example, how will reducing waste that goes to landfills (a pLAn environmental goal) impact the social and economic systems? Or how will more access to urban rivers (a pLAn equity goal) impact the environmental and economic systems? Or how will enhancing "mobility and transit" (a pLAn economic goal) impact the environmental and social systems? Each of the three pillars is constantly in flux. Assessing each and their impact on the entire system help assess the sustainability of the system.

4. Should we consider one of the three pillars more important than the others? For example, what if water-use changes impact species diversity, cost more than current practices, and burden individuals with lower incomes? Which pillar should take precedence? This question raises the issue of *trade-offs*. It also highlights how assessing sustainability requires social and scientific information.

3. SUSTAINABILITY AND SUSTAINABLE DEVELOPMENT: RELATED, BUT SEPARATE, CONCEPTS

The concept of sustainability has garnered a lot of attention around development. As mentioned above, economic development was at the forefront of international negotiations throughout the latter half of the twentieth century when the modern concept of sustainability originated. These negotiations often featured two broad categories of nations with competing economic development priorities. Many "developed" nations believed that environmental protections would serve a vital role in preserving ecosystems and would foster human well-being in the wake of recent discoveries concerning widespread industrial pollution.

Many "developing" nations largely blamed developed nations for caus-ing the environmental challenges and pollution and asserted their right to develop in similar ways. Developing nations saw an injustice in requiring them to mitigate environmental impacts as it would impede their prog-ress — a burden that developed nations did not have during their growth periods. Further, developing nations claimed that individuals were entitled to establish minimum standards of living notwithstanding environmental impacts — something developed nations had already been able to do.

The 1987 Brundtland Report attempted to strike a balance between the developed and developing nations' perspectives. In bringing the countries together, the Brundtland Report defined *sustainable development* as "develop-ment that meets the needs of the present without compromising the ability of future generations to meet their own needs."[45] The Brundtland Report's definition presents a vision of sustainable development that attempts to reconcile both developed and developing nations' concerns. Those nations who sought to prioritize environmental protections negotiated with those who sought to develop notwithstanding environmental challenges.

Some have conflated the Brundtland Report's definition for *sustainable development* with the definition for *sustainability*. Many scholars, policy makers, scientists, commentators, and others use the terms interchange-ably. As Professors Robin Craig and Melinda Harm Benson stated, "out-side of 'pure' natural resources management, sustainability has become almost inextricably enmeshed in sustainable development."[46]

The International Society for Ecological Economics in *Internet Encyclopaedia of Ecological Economics* provides another example. It begins by noting it is setting forth a definition of sustainable development and ends by stating it just defined core parts of sustainability:

> [T]here has been a growing recognition of three essential aspects of sustainable development:
>
> * Economic. . . .
>
> * Environmental. . . .
>
> * Social. . . .
>
> These three elements of sustainability introduce many potential complications to the original, simple definition of economic development.[47]

Some scholars note that while conflation of sustainable development and sustainability is inadvertent,[48] others note that it is also a product of

---

[45] THE WORLD COMMISSION ON ENVIRONMENT AND DEVELOPMENT, OUR COMMON FUTURE 43 (1987).

[46] Robin Kundis Craig & Melinda Harm Benson, *Replacing Sustainability*, 46 AKRON L. REV. 841, 849 (2013).

[47] Harris, *supra* note 37, at 1.

[48] *See, e.g.,* Myria W. Allen et al., *Sustainability Discourse Within a Supply Chain Relationship: Mapping Convergence and Divergence*, 49 INT'L J. BUS. COMM. 210 (2012).

political realities. "[I]t is politically important for many people to avoid making a distinction"[49] between sustainability and sustainable development because "sustainable development [i]s a term that ultimately g[ives] priority to development, while the idea of sustainability [i]s primarily [believed to be] about the environment."[50]

In 2015, the United Nations adopted The Sustainable Development Goals (known as *Transforming our world: The 2030 Agenda for Sustainable Development*). The Goals, amending the Millennium Development Goals (2000), are 17 goals that join with 169 targets/indicators. The Goals materialized through negotiations among 193 member states. They apply to developed and developing countries equally and are due for completion by 2030.
The Goals are:

1. End poverty;
2. End hunger, improve nutrition, and promote sustainable agriculture;
3. Ensure healthy lives;
4. Ensure quality education for all;
5. Ensure gender equality;
6. Provide access to water and sanitation;
7. Ensure access to affordable, reliable, and sustainable energy;
8. Promote employment;
9. Build resilient infrastructure;
10. Reduce inequality within and among countries;
11. Make cities inclusive, safe, resilient, and sustainable;
12. Ensure sustainable consumption;
13. Combat climate change;
14. Sustainably use the oceans, seas, and marine resources;
15. Sustainably manage forests and stop biodiversity loss;
16. Promote just, peaceful, and inclusive societies; and
17. Promote global partnership for sustainable development.

Note how some of the goals incorporate "sustainable," "sustainably," and "resilient." Some, such as Goal 11, concerning cities, include both "resilient and sustainable" to describe the goal.
What does sustainability mean in this context? For example, what does sustainable agriculture mean? We probably all have examples of what sustainable agriculture could look like, such as cover crops or buffer strips. If we look at it from the lens of our two definitions—triple bottom line and intergenerational equity—we might say:

Sustainable agriculture is the production of food, fiber, or other plant or animal products using farming techniques that protect the environment (including animal welfare), society (such as public health), and the agriculture community without compromising the ability of future generations to meet their own needs.

---

[49]Simon Dresner, The Principles of Sustainability 71 (2d ed. 2008).
[50]*Id.*

Also important, each goal has a number of targets or indicators. For example, Goal 13 (Quality of the Planet) has the following targets:

1. Strengthen resilience and adaptive capacity to climate-related hazards and natural disasters in all countries;
2. Integrate climate change measures into national policies, strategies, and planning;
3. Improve education, awareness-raising, and human and institutional capacity on climate change mitigation, adaptation, impact reduction, and early warning;
4. Implement the commitment undertaken by developed-country parties to the United Nations Framework Convention on Climate Change to a goal of mobilizing jointly $100 billion annually by 2020 from all sources to address the needs of developing countries in the context of meaningful mitigation actions and transparency on implementation and fully operationalize the Green Climate Fund through its capitalization as soon as possible; and
5. Promote mechanisms for raising capacity for effective climate change-related planning and management in least developed countries and small island developing states, including focusing on women, youth, and local and marginalized communities.

United Nations, Sustainable Development Goals, *Goal 13: Take Urgent Action to Combat Climate Change and its Impacts,* http://www.un.org/sustainabledevelopment/climate-change-2/.

A few data sets and statistical indicators are surfacing to help measure efforts relative to the sustainable development indicators above. Some of those efforts include:

• Sustainable Development Solutions Network, Bertelsmann Stiftung, *SDG Index and Dashboards – Global Report,* http://sdgindex.org/download/#dashboards (July 2016)
• Green Growth Knowledge Platform, *Measuring Inclusive Green Growth at the Country Level,* http://www.carlocarraro.org/wp/wp-content/uploads/2016/07/Measuring_Inclusive_Green_Growth_at_the_Country_Level.pdf (Feb. 2016)
• Fondazione Eni Enrico Mattei, *APPS Project,* http://www.feemsdgs.org/ (providing assessment of 27 of 169 sustainable development indicators).

Others argue that conflation of the terms can be problematic because it assumes sustainability is integrated into and a part of development. Sustainability, they argue, is morphed into existing economic development paradigms rooted in neoclassical economics and the Industrial Revolution (discussed in more detail in Chapter 2). As one scholar noted "sustainable development has come to signify 'sustained economic growth,' thus jeopardizing environmental protection [and] . . . thus fails to question the assumption that continuous economic growth will eventually lead to the destruction of the planet."[51] In other words, sustainable development

---

[51] Annie Rochette, *Stop the Rape of the World: An Ecofeminist Critique of Sustainable Development,* 51 U.N.B. L.J. 145, 162 (2002).

could continue a track of economic growth that results in *unsustainable* environmental or social conditions — again, highlighting the importance of *trade-offs.*

Some prefer to separate the terms, asserting that sustainable development is part of a process to achieve a sustainable system. In this regard, sustainability describes the system or the analytical framework based on environmental, economic, and societal benefits. Sustainable development is part of that system or framework relevant to those portions described as "development."

Similarly, others argue that the terms are potentially inconsistent. Development, they argue, is not an inherent characteristic of or necessary for achieving a *sustainable system.* However, development is an integral part of *sustainable development.* When we conflate the terms, any assessment of a system's sustainability is from the perspective of development. In this light, the two are inconsistent in that one could seek to sustain a level of open space that may require no additional construction or development, sustainable or not.

Another way to think about the differences between the two is that sustainable development is a normative statement expressing a value or objective of what development should be. Whereas, sustainability does not prescribe a normative goal, rather it sets forth an analytical approach (evaluation of environmental, economic, and social concerns) or characterization without casting judgment.[52]

In practice, it is difficult to differentiate between the two. There is also a question as to whether there is value in differentiating between them. That said we try to avoid using them interchangeably in this book, discussing "sustainability" almost exclusively.

4. SUMMARY OF SUSTAINABILITY PRINCIPLES

In the sections above, we covered some of the fundamental characteristics of sustainability. Let us now summarize the core materials. This summary will give us a jumping off point for Part II where we explore sustainability in context and tools to assist in doing so.

- *Law and policy have an essential connection to sustainability.* That connection involves the influence law and policy have on behaviors, which implicate systems' sustainability.
- Sustainability is a *framework* to analyze conditions and/or systems.
- Two ways to view sustainability as a framework include *intergenerational equity* and/or *triple bottom line.*

---

[52]*See* Harris, *supra* note 37, at 2.

- Intergenerational Equity is the idea that the present generation has an obligation to ensure that future generations have the capacity to flourish and that our use of natural resources will allow for later usage by those generations.
  - Edith Brown Weiss' piece set forth four criteria to consider when viewing intergenerational equity.
  - She also set forth three basic principles:
    - *Conservation of options.* Each generation is required to conserve the diversity of the natural and cultural resource base. However, we should not burden unreasonably the present generation by use restrictions.
    - *Conservation of quality.* Each generation is required to maintain the quality of the planet so that we pass it on in no worse a condition than the present generation received it.
    - *Conservation of access.* Each generation is required to provide its members with equitable rights of access to the legacy from past generations and should conserve this access for future generations.
- Triple Bottom Line bases an assessment on the balancing of environmental, economic, and social factors when analyzing a system, condition, or effects of a policy.
- Distinguishing between sustainability and sustainable development is helpful.
  - Sustainable Development Goals (2015)
- Other key factors that influence a sustainability analysis include:
  - *Trade-offs*, which play an important role in assessing sustainability. Policy decisions often require making determinations to benefit one system or group of individuals over another system or group of individuals.
  - *Institutional arrangements* and which body or bodies are making decisions relating to sustainability. Is that body public? Private? Inclusive? Exclusive? International? National? Or Local?
  - *Context*, which can alter how to measure sustainability and what sustainability may mean in a given area.
  - *Technology* (something we discuss in more depth in Chapter 2), which can help obtain critical information necessary to analyze sustainability. It can also provide enhanced access to exploit natural resources, which can implicate sustainability both positively and negatively.
  - *Population and Consumption* (something we discuss in more depth in Chapter 2) and how they can implicate the sustainability of a system or condition.

III. OVERLAP AND DIVERGENCE BETWEEN RESILIENCE AND SUSTAINABILITY

While R&S have different origins and analytical approaches, they both represent new and innovative ways to assess multi-disciplined and diverse systems and challenges. While their analytical approaches may vary, there is overlap between R&S. In this section, we set forth some of that overlap, interaction, and divergence.

A. Core Commonalities and Characteristics: Interdisciplinary Nature, Geographic Variation, and Institutional Arrangements

R&S both help us better understand human interaction and interplay with planetary ecological systems. In doing so, they can inform new policies to address challenges facing many disciplines. In this way, assessing a system's resilience or sustainability may implicate many different and complementary fields and can incorporate many systems at many different points in time. Changes in one system that alter the system's resilience or sustainability may alter another system that may be predominantly located in another discipline. For example, whether a system is resilient or sustainable in the context of land use planning (discussed in more detail in Chapter 5) may be different from the context of agriculture (discussed in more detail in Chapter 4), even though the two (land use and agriculture) may overlap.

The Atlantic cod example illustrates this point. The Atlantic cod story implicated many complex economic systems (covering large geographic areas and diverse contexts), environmental systems (trophically cascading through the food web), and social systems (impacting legal and cultural aspects of society). Combined, these subsystems and their associated adaptive cycles comprised the Atlantic cod system. When the subsystems began to fail or become less resilient or sustainable, pervasive and potentially irreversible consequences followed. The system began to crumble, impacting the resilience or sustainability of many subsystems.

Further complicating attempts to define R&S is that their meaning may change not only by discipline, but also by *geographical location*. Because local communities understand local conditions, norms relative to R&S often change based on location. For example, the data and questions necessary to assess and ask for purposes of R&S relative to stormwater management systems in California are fundamentally different from what is necessary for purposes of stormwater management in parts of Eastern India, where some of the highest levels of precipitation in the world are experienced. A further complicating factor is that R&S are applicable at a variety of *institutional arrangements*, such as those in the private sector and at all levels in the public sector from international to national to regional to local to neighborhood.

> ### INSTITUTIONAL ARRANGEMENTS
>
> Political scientist Oran Young describes institutions as "collections of rights, rules, and decision-making procedures that give rise to social practices, assign roles to the participants in these practices, and guide interactions among the participants."[53] The United Nations Development Programme adopts a similar definition: "Institutional arrangements are the policies, systems, and processes that organizations use to legislate, plan and manage their activities efficiently and to effectively coordinate with others in order to fulfill their mandate."[54]

B. Areas of Further Interaction

In this subsection, we look more closely at how resilience and sustainability play off each other. To begin, *a social-ecological system that is not resilient is unlikely to be sustainable* (below we discuss whether an unsustainable system can be resilient). Any system or characteristic of that system lying close to one or more thresholds such that a minor disturbance would irreversibly alter the system is more likely to experience change. When in this state of vulnerability, the system is susceptible to change, and thus, is likely to be unsustainable as it may eventually be in a state of flux and change its core features — one definition of "unsustainable."

"Sustainability is also about knowing if and where thresholds exist and having the capacity to manage the system in relation to these thresholds."[55] In this way, resilience is "an element of the broader discourse of sustainability"[56] or "a boundary concept to integrate the social and natural dimensions of sustainability."[57] We can assess both resilience and sustainability in relation to the *distance core characteristics are from thresholds*. Passing through a threshold not only alters the regime for purposes of measuring resilience, but also implicates a system's sustainability.

---

[53] Oran R. Young, *Sugaring off: Enduring Insights from Long-Term Research on Environmental Governance*, 13 Int'l Envtl. Agreements: Politics, L. & Econ. 87 (2013).
[54] United Nations Economic and Social Council, *Trends in National Institutional Arrangements in Geospatial Information Management* (Jun. 25, 2014), http://ggim.un.org/docs/meetings/GGIM4/E-C20-2014-5%20Trends%20in%20Institutional%20Arrangements%20Report_cleared.pdf.
[55] Walker & Salt, *supra* note 14, at 63.
[56] Tracy-Lynn Humby, *Law and Resilience: Mapping the Literature*, 4 Seattle J. Envtl. L. 85, 86 (2014).
[57] Olsson et al., *supra* note 25.

Another area where R&S interact is where we determine *what we desire to sustain*. C.S. Holling and Lance Gunderson stated that one form of resilience "focuses on persistence, adaptiveness, variability, and unpredictability — all attributes embraced and celebrated by those with an evolutionary or developmental perspective. The latter attributes are at the heart of understanding and designing for sustainability."[58] Integrating sustainability into a system (in a way that achieves the triple bottom line or intergenerational equity) is also likely to require the system to be resilient.

While a system that is not resilient is unlikely to be sustainable, *a system that is unsustainable may still be resilient, although it is likely to be strained*. If a social or ecological system is unsustainable it may affect the resilience of the system, but the system may be sufficiently resilient to withstand collapse or alteration. For example, a system may achieve economic objectives, but not social or environmental objectives or it may utilize natural resources in a way that leaves fewer or no options for future generations; and thus, is not sustainable. However, that same system may be resilient. It is entirely possible that toxic, destructive, and unsustainable systems could be extremely resistant to change, even in the face of major disruptions. For example, the idea that economic development or growth is inherently beneficial may not be sustainable, as it has led to social inequalities and environmental degradation. However, the idea has shown to be immensely resilient at almost all levels of government and in the private sector.

Professor Tracy-Lynn Humbly adopts a similar view on the relationship between R&S, stating:

> *Since resilience is a property of a system, an evaluation of how well the various parts cohere notwithstanding external shocks and the emergent characteristics that arise from the system's own internal dynamics, it is correct to apply the term even to social-ecological systems that are not sustainable, at least over the short to medium term. Such unsustainable systems may be propped up by a host of social practices (pumping of underground water, the application of fertilizer, use of fossil fuels, subsidies, insurance, property rights; etc) that are very difficult to change and thus exhibit a form of resilience. Over the long term, however, the capacity of these various elements to hold together will be eroded.*[59]

As Professor Humbly notes the longer a system remains unsustainable, the more strain the system experiences, tending to lower its resilience. Additional examples of unsustainable systems "propped up by a host of social practices" may include deforestation, filling and loss of wetlands,

---

[58]C.S. Holling & Lance H. Gunderson, *Resilience and Adaptive Cycles, in* PANARCHY: UNDERSTANDING TRANSFORMATIONS IN HUMAN AND NATURAL SYSTEMS 27 (2002).
[59]Humby, *supra* note 56, at 104 n.106.

ocean acidification, and soil degradation. In many of these, the economic system driving human choices has shown resilience in the face of unsustainable environmental systems. Forests are destroyed for timber faster than they can regenerate, losing the resource for future generations, disrupting ecosystems and habitats, and negating health benefits associated with trees, including water filtration, soil retention, and carbon capture. The longer the behaviors that result in an unsustainable system continue, the higher the risks that the system will cross a threshold.

Policies that support a resilient system may also support a sustainable system. The U.S. Environmental Protection Agency adopts a similar perspective:

> *Understanding resilience is important for assuring the sustainability of economic, social, and environmental systems. . . . Resilience Analysis is still in its infancy as a formal sustainability assessment tool, and the form of analysis used can vary depending on the type of system examined and the definition of resilience employed. Since resilience analysis is a means of assessing a system's vulnerability based on properties of the system itself, it can help assess the effectiveness of policies meant to reduce risk even in instances where full knowledge of specific risks is absent.*[60]

There is a lack of uniformity in the scholarship as to whether assessing resilience or sustainability is *normative*. Some argue that neither term requires a normative approach, others argue that both are normative, and still others argue that one but not the other is normative (see the next subsection). On the one hand, R&S do not dictate whether we should have a sustainable or resilient system. Rather, they focus on analytical frameworks, which help us to understand humans' impact on their surroundings. On the other hand, others argue that both are normative and seek to achieve a "good" result or a desirable state.[61] We want, for example, a resilient and sustainable community or city because it will bring equality in education, wealth, and enhanced natural resources. It is important to recognize that even when not normative per se and instead addressed in strictly analytical frameworks, R&S require a number of value judgments. They may require us, for example, to decide what we should assess to determine a system's resilience or sustainability and what we will use to measure such assessment.

---

[60] *Sustainability*, U.S. EPA, http://www.epa.gov/sustainability/analytics/resilience.htm (last visited Oct. 10, 2015).
[61] *See* Per Olsson et al., *Sustainability Transformations: A Resilience Perspective,* 19 ECOLOGY & SOC'Y 1 (2014).

C. Areas of Divergence

Some argue *sustainability connotes a value judgment, while resilience does not.* Understanding sustainability as something we can achieve, such as inter-generational equity, implies, if not compels, that healthy long-term results are good and desirable. Pursuant to this perspective, sustainability seeks "specific, sustainable outcomes for the system and possible pathways to achieve these conditions"[62] while resilience "focuses on building a system's adaptive capacity to favorably respond to shocks and stresses without predetermining the specific outcome of the actions."[63] Similarly, while resilience assesses a system's state and its ability to retain its essential characteristics moving forward, resilience does not assess whether those characteristics are positive or negative, or sustainable or unsustainable.

Another area of potential divergence between R&S is that *resilience relies on adaptation and change and sustainability constitutes "stationarity."*[64] Those scholars advocating this view note that sustainability requires an acknowledgment of the status quo and requires the capacity to maintain a level of "stationarity." In other words, sustainability, they claim, requires keeping the system operating within an unchanging envelope of variability. In contrast to sustainability's requirement of stationarity, resilience accounts for continual change and explores adaptive capacities. As part of their argument, these scholars point to innumerable changes stemming from climate-changing conditions. With the excess of changes, sustainability is not a proper framework, they argue, because it cannot cope with change.

Professor Melinda Harm Benson describes it this way:

> [T]he pursuit of sustainability inherently assumes that we: (a) know what can be sustained; and (b) have the capacity to hold onto some type of stationarity and/or equilibrium. These assumptions are no longer appropriate given the dynamics of [social-ecological systems (SES)].
>
> In contrast, resilience thinking is grounded in an acknowledgement of uncertainty and disequilibrium within SESs, with a ground-level acknowledgement that change is not only always possible but also to be expected. Resilience, as employed here, is defined as "the capacity of a system to absorb a spectrum disturbance and reorganize so as to retain essentially the same function, structure, and feedbacks—to have the same identity." The focus is therefore on change *as well as the system's capacity to meaningfully respond to change. In*

---

[62] Charles L. Redman, *Should Sustainability and Resilience be Combined or Remain Distinct Pursuits?*, 19 Ecology & Soc'y 1 (2014).
[63] *Id.*
[64] *See, e.g.,* Robin Kundis Craig & Melinda Harm Benson, *Replacing Sustainability*, 46 Akron L. Rev. 841 (2013) (also differentiating resilience by the need to identify baselines and metrics and an acknowledgement of human harm to the environment for sustainability).

contrast to the sustainability narrative, the emphasis in resilience thinking is on understanding the dynamics and complexities of the SESs, not on determining and then maintaining a fixed system state. The emphasis is building adaptive capacity rather than maintaining stationarity.[65]

Importantly, scholars with this view define sustainability as an attempt to maintain *contemporary* levels of natural resources — a possible, but not certain goal of sustainability. Intergenerational equity and TBL do not inherently require the establishment of a baseline founded in current conditions. They can also project into the future and account for temporal changes through intergenerational equity or the establishment of a framework for analysis without establishing baselines. Further, "stationarity" as it relates to a resource is only one metric that we use to assess sustainability. We could also look to measuring the ability to sustain quality of life, happiness, health, or even continual change — all things that could be measured within a sustainability context that are not subject to the same criticism of stationarity as they require movement or flexibility in the use of resources to be sustained.

Questions and Notes

1. In Chapter 10, we discuss the 2015 Paris Agreement. The Agreement is an international treaty that addresses climate change. The three following provisions from the Agreement mention both resilience and sustainability. Explain the role of resilience and sustainability in each of these three provisions and how R&S relate to each other.

   a. *Article 2(1)*: "This Agreement . . . aims to strengthen the global response to the threat of climate change, in the context of *sustainable development* and efforts to eradicate poverty, including by . . . (b) Increasing the ability *to adapt to the adverse impacts of climate change and foster climate resilience.* . . ." (Emphasis added.)

   b. *Article 7:* "(1) *Parties hereby establish the global goal on adaptation of enhancing adaptive capacity, strengthening resilience and reducing vulnerability to climate change, with a view to contributing to sustainable development* and ensuring an adequate adaptation response in the context of the temperature goal. . . ." (Emphasis added.)

   c. *Article 7:* "(9) Each Party shall . . . engage in adaptation planning processes and the implementation of actions, including . . .

---

[65]Melinda Harm Benson, *Reconceptualizing Environmental Challenges — Is Resilience the New Narrative?*, 21 J. ENVTL. & SUSTAINABILITY L. 99, 115-116 (2015).

(e) *Building the resilience of socioeconomic and ecological systems,* including through economic diversification and *sustainable management of natural resources."* (Emphasis added.)

2. *Reintroduction of wolves to Yellowstone National Park.* Throughout the nineteenth century wolves, a top predator, were hunted in Yellowstone National Park (the Park was designated the first national park in 1872). By the late 1970s, no one had seen a wolf pack in the Park in 50 years and lone wolves were rarely seen if at all. In 1995 and 1996, several wolves, captured in Canada, were reintroduced to Yellowstone.

While there are many aspects and disputing science concerning the reintroduction, several studies indicate a "trophic cascade," in which reintroducing the wolves at one end of the food chain impacted the entire chain, and related flora and fauna previously at-risk have returned. Studies have shown a decrease in browsing (animal feeding on vegetation), an increase in new growth of plant species, such as willows, aspens, and cottonwoods, helping to foster bird and beaver populations. Further, these studies have tied the effects to the wolves preying on elk, and the elk decreasing in population (or grazing areas) and eating less of the vegetation. Further cascading has tied forest stabilization to reduced soil erosion and stabilizing riverbanks.[66]

Throughout Part II of this book, we describe several methods to help assess or understand R&S. Based on the definitions of R&S in this chapter, analyze which systems or subsystems became more resilient or sustainable with the reintroduction of wolves. How, if at all, does your analysis differ whether you assess the system's resilience or sustainability? Can you identify a system or subsystem that is resilient, but not sustainable and vice versa? Does it matter if you are in favor of the reintroduction or opposed to it? Who should make the decision as to which definition is best suited for this circumstance or any circumstance?

3. Above we discuss how some systems can be resilient, but not sustainable and vice versa. Can you make an argument that the exhaustion of oil deposits for fossil fuels is resilient, but not sustainable and vice versa? Where do you see the difference between R&S in this example?

4. The pLAn, described above as an applied example of TBL, incorporates resilience as one of its topic areas on economic development, stating:

We must prepare Los Angeles for future earthquakes and increasing climate disruptions . . . including bigger wildfires, longer and hotter heatwaves, and

---

[66]For a brief video summary of some impacts related to the trophic cascade stemming from the wolves, see Sustainable Human, *How Wolves Change Rivers* (Feb. 13, 2014), https://sustainablehuman.tv/remix/how-wolves-change-rivers.

rising sea levels. . . . [I]t is immediately necessary to have proactive solutions to prepare the city [including]. . . .

Improve our preparedness and resiliency so the city and commercial activity can "return to normal" after a disaster as quickly as possible

· Develop measurable targets for post-disaster service restoration in the areas of water, electricity, communications, and surface transportation

· Develop measurable targets for post-disaster service. . . .

What does the pLAn use for a definition of resilience and how does it overlap with its goals to become more sustainable?

REVISITING EASTER ISLAND

In 1971, American philosopher John Rawls wrote *A Theory of Justice* in which he partially wrestled with defining the contours of "justice" and "equality." Instead of placing a definitive definition on the terms (and how they relate to one another), he developed a theory on the proper perspective or process to arrive at something one could characterize as "justice" or "equality." Part of the process Rawls developed involved a thought experiment called the "original position." In the experiment, he asked each member of a theoretical society to create the institutional structure in which he or she would want to live. All members know that they live in a diverse society (for example, diversity of gender or social status). However, they are cloaked behind a "veil of ignorance" in which they do not know to which diverse group they belong. Rawls designed the experiment to produce a reasoned, equitable, and impartial form of "justice."

Assume we asked you to participate in a Rawlsian exercise to define a society based on R&S. What would it look like? Who would participate? Would there be "winners," "losers"?

IV. BUILDING ON DEFINITIONS

In this chapter, we explored commonly used definitions of R&S and where the terms overlap, interact, and differ. As we explore the terms throughout this book, you will see that R&S are applicable to an extraordinary number of contexts. We can best understand R&S through illustrations. For this reason, Part II of this book (Chapters 3 through 10) focuses on common questions and inquiries one could or should make to help assess and understand R&S regardless of the context. Those contexts include water, food, shelter and land use, energy, natural resources, pollution, disaster, and climate change. Incorporated into Part II are eight tools, "Strategies to Facilitate Implementation," to help identify, assess, and implement R&S. You can find them at:

1. Understanding Collective Action Challenges (Water Systems, Chapter 3)
2. Precautionary Principle (Water Systems, Chapter 3)
3. Ecosystem Services Management (Water Systems, Chapter 3)
4. Baselines and Metrics (Energy Systems, Chapter 6)
5. Systems Thinking (Energy Systems, Chapter 6)
6. Adaptive Governance (Natural Resources, Chapter 7)
7. Life Cycle Sustainability Assessment (Pollution, Chapter 8)
8. Risk Analysis (Pollution, Chapter 8)

The next chapter helps contextualize R&S by describing some of the *challenges* that test the resilience and sustainability of many systems and disciplines.

Challenges and Root Causes

2

The challenges facing the world today are complex, interrelated, and interdisciplinary. Much of the complexity associated with those challenges stems from their connection to complicated social-ecological systems. R&S help us understand not only the challenges, but also characteristics of the underlying social-ecological systems and the potential for irreversible and catastrophic ramifications when failing to adopt policies that result in sustainable and/or resilient systems.

This chapter describes some of the challenges facing critical social-ecological systems and their root causes. The information set forth below does not capture all of the challenges stressing all critical systems or their root causes. Rather, the information provides context to understand R&S and to illustrate the interconnectedness and multidisciplinary nature of the challenges R&S help illuminate.

As an introduction to the challenges, we begin with a series of benign mollusks in the center of the United States. As you read about the mollusks consider the challenges each party and system face. Also, consider whether the individuals or institutions in power made decisions that strained various systems' resilience or sustainability based on what we covered in Chapter 1.

I. CASE STUDY: *THE PEARL CITY*

In this case study, we highlight a number of key terms and phrases that we will return to at the end of the case study. Consider how these terms and phrases help explain why the parties may have made decisions that resulted in vulnerable or unsustainable conditions. What motivated the parties to make those decisions? Did they have the right information? Were they driven by competition or economic gain?

Muscatine, Iowa, a town of about 23,000 residents, lies on the Mississippi River 250 miles upstream from St. Louis, Missouri. Today, the town holds few remnants of its illustrious past as the world epicenter of a

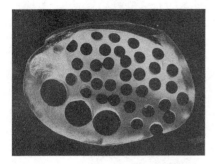

booming pearl button industry. What follows is the story of Muscatine and the pearl buttons, mussels, ecosystems, and economics that built, consumed, and helped deteriorate the city — in short, it is a story about R&S.

When John Boepple arrived in Muscatine sometime between 1884 and 1891, he found abundant and diverse beds of mussels: ebonyshell, washboard, threeridge, elephantear, fat pocketbook, winged maple leaf, and Higgins' eye mussels. Boepple, a German immigrant, who manufactured buttons in his homeland, began making buttons from the pearls and mussel shells pulled from the Mississippi River. Not long after, others — *many of whom were reeling from the demise of the local timber industry* — began to follow Boepple's lead, sparking the "gold rush of the Mississippi."

Boepple and others did not have to wait long for the pearl button market to rapidly expand and they received help in this expansion from unexpected places. *Changing laws and policies* helped drive demand for the Muscatine pearl buttons. The federal Tariff Act of 1890,[1] commonly known as the "McKinley Tariff," raised import duties (taxes on goods brought into the country) significantly taxing imported buttons and raw materials used to make buttons (see adjacent box). The import duties made non-domestic buttons prohibitively expensive and domestic buttons, such as the pearl buttons made in Muscatine, more affordable and desirable.

The McKinley Tariff Act of 1890, named after then-U.S. Representative William McKinley and, later, the 25th President of the United States, increased tariffs for many imported goods. The Act increased a variety of products' duties (essentially, a tax imposed by the U.S. on goods imported) between 38% and 50%. The Act added duties to some goods that were once duty-free, such as wool and hides, while others, such as sugar and coffee, remained duty-free. The new duties helped protect and make national industries more competitive by increasing the price of similar imported goods. The Act also required that:

> all articles of foreign manufacture, such as are usually or ordinarily marked and all packages containing such or other imported articles, shall, respectively, be plainly marked, stamped, branded, or labeled in legible English words, so as to indicate the country of their origin; and unless so marked, stamped, branded, or labeled they shall not be admitted to entry.

Tariff Act of 1890, ch. 1244. §6, 26 Stat. 567, 613 (1891) (the Wilson-Gorman Tariff Act of 1894 lowered tariff rates).

---

[1] The U.S. Federal Tariff Act, ch. 1244, 26 Stat. 612 (1890).

Simultaneously, *changes in cultural norms* relevant to fashion helped expand the pearl button market. New clothing styles with more buttons per garment became popular. The combination of new laws and changing styles gave domestic buttons, like those manufactured in Muscatine, a captive and growing market. It was not long before Mississippi mussels were in high demand.

The process to manufacture pearl buttons initially involved multiple *laborers*. Making pearl buttons began with clammers "polly wogging," wading into the Mississippi River and feeling for mussels with their feet. The clammers then pulled the mussels out by hand.[2] Newly caught mussels were put into large vats of boiling water often right at the river's edge. The mussels were then opened, cleaned, soaked, the shells cut, and the buttons polished, finished, and sold.

As demand increased, *technological developments* helped factories produce buttons more quickly. Clammers replaced polly wogging with "brailing" to extract more of the mussels faster. Invented in 1897, brailing consisted of attaching 30 or more lines with crowfoot hooks to a cross bar on a boat. The clammers dragged the lines across the river bottom where mussels clamped down on the hooks. Brailing allowed clammers to greatly expedite and expand their catch. Simultaneously, factories in and around Muscatine developed automated machinery that required less time and fewer laborers per button. As these harvesting and production techniques improved, making buttons required fewer people and less effort to extract more mussels.

The industry grew rapidly.[3] "Clammers harvested less than 100 tons of shell in 1894. By 1897, the amount had grown to 3,500 tons — a 3400% increase in 3 years. Two years later in 1899, clammers took nearly 24,000 tons" — another 586% increase in two years.[4] Similarly, in 1894, when the harvest was less than 100 tons, the total mussel harvest gross in terms of dollars was about $2,000. Total mussel harvest in dollars skyrocketed to about $100,000 in 1899 — a growth of 4900% in five years.[5]

During the expansive growth of the pearl button industry Muscatine grew rapidly. The city grew to accommodate 28 button factories, employing hundreds of people and leading to an almost 100% increase in population from 1880 to 1910.[6] By comparison, the State of Iowa's population increased from 1,624,515 to 2,224,771, approximately a 37% increase during that same time.

---

[2] Melanie K. Alexander, MUSCATINE'S PEARL BUTTON INDUSTRY 233 (2007).
[3] Lisa Knopp, WHAT THE RIVER CARRIES: ENCOUNTERS WITH THE MISSISSIPPI, MISSOURI, AND THE PLATTE 36 (2012).
[4] Alexander, *supra* note 2, at 7.
[5] *Report of the Bureau of Fisheries*, U.S. DEP'T COM. & LABOR 714 (1904).
[6] *Id.* at 715.

Year	Muscatine Population	Year Percentage Increase
1880	8,295	23.5%
1890	11,454	38.1%
1900	14,073	22.9%
1910	16,178	15.0%
1920	16,068	−0.7%

Ripple Effects

As button factories and mussel harvesters clamored to build their businesses, the freshwater mussel, the lynchpin of the pearl button industry, *quickly dwindled in numbers.* Harvests began yielding smaller loads and fewer mature specimens.

As is often the case, individuals closest to the industry began noticing the declining resource. In 1898 — *before some of the highest annual yields* — Dr. Hugh M. Smith, who would later become the Director of the U.S. Bureau of Fisheries ("Bureau"), *published an investigation* of the mussel fishery and the pearl button industry. In his report, Smith called for conservation measures, expressing concern at the rapid removal rates.[7] Similarly, in 1902 a U.S. Bureau of Fisheries Report stated that "[t]he mussel beds in the vicinity of Muscatine have become very much thinned out by continual fishing during the past few years, and the scarcity there has necessitated bringing the shells from a greater distance every year."[8]

Just as the birth of the industry was a function of *several factors,* its demise resulted from a confluence of several factors. As clammers picked the local beds clean, many of the factories tried to stay open and the clammers sought new beds to exploit, *harvesting from farther and farther away.* Further, the easing of federal tariffs opened foreign markets, making nondomestic buttons less expensive and reintroducing foreign competition. While private industries continued harvesting at rapid rates, the declining numbers of the mussel drew the attention of the federal government. The Bureau made *concerted efforts to recreate the mussel ecosystem and promote the species,* but those efforts were not enough to remedy or replenish the mussel. The Bureau built and operated a research station, intended to develop methods of propagating mussels back into the habitat. This turned out to be no easy task.

Although being a relatively simple creature (for example, they have an unsophisticated nervous system and no brain), the life cycle of and the

---

[7] *A Historical Analysis of Mussel Propagation and Culture: Research Performed at the Fairport Biological Station,* U.S. ARMY CORPS OF ENGINEERS (2001), http://www.fws.gov/midwest/mussel/documents/an_historical_analysis_of_mussel_propagation_and_culture.pdf.
[8] U.S. DEP'T COM. & LABOR, *supra* note 5, at 715.

ecosystem surrounding the mussel were difficult to recreate. Almost all freshwater mussel species have an obligatory phase as a parasite, where microscopic larvae, known as glochidia, latch on to the fins or gill filaments of a fish. The glochidia undergo an important development phase before they fall away as juvenile mussels. Those glochidia, which do not find a host fish, never mature and die. Efforts to replicate glochidia and mussel development in the lab experienced only minimal success, as researchers struggled to discover the proper compatibility between fish and mussels.

One of the difficulties researchers encountered was that the mass exploitation of the mussels altered the mussels' *original habitat*. Depleted mussel beds had been replaced by plant growth or sand bars. In addition, pollution and dredging made reestablishing the mussels even more difficult as the riverbeds were no longer an ideal habitat for mussels.[9] Because efforts to re-establish the once-thriving mussel beds of the Mississippi River never produced the desired results, we exhausted federal funding for repopulation in 1934 and other propagation efforts ceased in 1942.[10]

Employers and employees, who struggled to survive as mussel populations plummeted, did little to conserve the resource, and adopted few, if any, measures to ensure species and ecosystem survival. Those companies that did survive adapted to new realities and transitioned to making plastic buttons. Today, only a fraction of the number of people employed during the pearl button heyday are employed making buttons in Muscatine, Iowa. Further, only three Muscatine button companies remain open and they all focus predominantly on making plastic buttons.

Coda

Human interaction with the Mississippi River mussels impacted global markets, created a boom and bust economy, led to development, exhausted an ecosystem, and affected a number of other social, economic, and environmental systems. Freshwater bivalves, like the mussels, are not likely something that most people think about on a daily basis. Yet, decisions relative to them impacted thousands of lives and numerous generations.

Similar to these decisions, millions of other decisions each day concerning critical systems and fundamental aspects of society have serious known and unknown implications for the future. John Boepple probably had no idea how his introduction of pearl buttons made from Mississippi River mussels would blossom into a phenomenon, how new fashions or federal tariffs would disrupt the delicate market balance of the industry, or how difficult it would be to repopulate the barren mussel bed once the resource was exhausted.

---

[9] U.S. ARMY CORPS OF ENGINEERS, *supra* note 7, at 36.
[10] *Id.* at 6.

Questions and Notes

1. The story of *The Pearl City* is a good place to begin our exploration of the challenges stressing the R&S of many systems because it raises a number of external influences that can alter systems' resilience or sustainability. Several factors relevant to those challenges are italicized in the story and include:

   - shifting from one resource to another after exhaustion of the first (timber industry to mussels);
   - changing laws and policies;
   - changing cultural norms;
   - promoting economic development and jobs;
   - development of technological advancements;
   - increasing rates of resource extraction;
   - obtaining the proper information to make decisions;
   - complexity of ecosystems;
   - repopulation attempts; and
   - habitats.

   a. How would you describe the role each factor played in altering *The Pearl City* saga?

   b. Would those alterations tend to stress or support the resilience or sustainability of the mussels? Could some actions both stress and support? How might they impact the Muscatine society or community?

   c. Can you think of an example in which one of the factors listed above challenges a social-ecological system not associated with mussels?

2. While humans are often responsible for leading a species to extinction, humans also make Herculean attempts to preserve species, usually with mixed results—a subject matter we return to throughout the book. When the Mississippi River mussel crossed a threshold and was no longer resilient or sustainable, humans attempted to intervene and bring the species back to life. In *Helping a Species Go Extinct: The Sumatran Rhino in Borneo*, Alan Rabinowitz detailed the unsuccessful efforts to save the Sumatran Rhino. Rabinowitz noted the numerous impacts humans have had on rhinoceroses, including hunting and destroying their habitat. Based on the declining numbers, some individuals created a special group and program in the 1980s to capture rhinos thought to be in danger.

   Forty Sumatran Rhinos, representing a sizable percentage of those left in the wild, were captured from 1984-1996 with the intent to breed them in captivity. Of those, 20 died before 1996. Following more deaths and a Surra disease outbreak in 2003, all but three survived and were transported to zoos in Los Angeles, New York City (Bronx), and Cincinnati, where the first successful rhino calf from this program was born in captivity. Today, less than 100 Sumatran Rhinos exist in the wild and that number may be as low as 80. The program designed to save Sumatran Rhinos resulted in 37 dead rhinos and 2-5 newborns bred through an intensive and invasive process.

The story of the Sumatran Rhino exhibits the complexity and fragility of natural systems. The Sumatran Rhinos had flourished without human assistance for millions of years. Do you think humans can and should engage in recreating ecosystems? Does it matter if humans were responsible for their demise? Resilience and sustainability provide frameworks to analyze systems and decisions in the face of dwindling species.

3. The Mississippi River mussels and Sumatran Rhino stories also raise the question of whether we need "wild" mussels or rhinos at all. What about other flora or fauna? Is recreating an ecosystem necessary? Keith Hirokawa partially examines this question and a provocative 1973 article by Martin Krieger entitled *What's Wrong with Plastic Trees?*:

> *Some time ago, when questioning the feasibility of preserving environmentally sensitive areas, urban-design professor Martin Krieger considered this point:*
>
>> *What's wrong with plastic trees? My guess is that there is very little wrong with them. Much more can be done with plastic trees and the like to give most people the feeling that they are experiencing nature. We will have to realize that the way in which we experience nature is conditioned by our society — which more and more is seen to be receptive to responsible interventions.*
>
> *Krieger's point is merely a constructive one: What we value about nature is influenced by our social practices and norms and generally arises as a construct of our collective imagination. If what we value is the opportunity to engage in a "natural" experience, the degree to which we achieve this goal depends on the context in which we seek the experience (or further, that we will first need to be told what constitutes such an experience).*[11]

---

[11] Keith H. Hirokawa, *Sustainability and the Urban Forest: An Ecosystem Services Perspective*, 51 Nat. Resources J. 233, 247-248 (2011) (quoting Martin H. Krieger, *What's Wrong with Plastic Trees?*, 179 Sci. 446, 453 (1973)).

II. CHALLENGES FACING THIS GENERATION

The story of the Mississippi River mussels and the once-thriving pearl button industry of Muscatine is a good place to start exploring the challenges facing the world today. The story raises critical issues relevant to R&S and foreshadows many challenges riddled throughout this book. In Chapter 1, we explored the modern origins and definitions of R&S. It is helpful to reflect on the challenges facing the world in order to better understand these definitions. R&S are means to understand these challenges. We can base law and policy on a more informed understanding of the systems they are regulating. Like R&S, the challenges are interconnected, multifaceted, and multi-scalar, making them extraordinarily complex.

Importantly, our starting point is to understand the challenges and how they strain a system's R&S—it is not our ending point. This book is about exploring how to reverse unsustainable and vulnerable trends through law and policy. It is about proposing innovative legal and policy solutions. In order to do so, we must first gain an introduction to the enormity of the grim social-ecological challenges facing the world today.

A. A Product of Our Past

Many of the environmental, economic, and societal problems we face today are direct extensions of practices and behaviors developed during and rooted in the Industrial Revolution. While those practices and behaviors may have resulted in enhanced material benefits, they also resulted in ecological consequences and inequities that continue today. In this subsection, we briefly review only those key developments in the Industrial Revolution most relevant to challenges that strain the resilience or sustainability of social-ecological systems. We end this subsection with two contemporary critiques of the Industrial Revolution that reflect important aspects of resilience thinking and principles of sustainability. We explore how these critiques are relevant today and whether the critics' fears came to fruition.

1. THE INDUSTRIAL REVOLUTION

There are hundreds of books detailing various economic and social aspects of the Industrial Revolution (approximately early eighteenth to the late nineteenth century, commonly thought to begin when Thomas Newcomen invented the earliest usable steam engine to pump water out of coal mines in 1712). Rather than focus on a detailed account of the Industrial Revolution, we focus on economic growth as a primary driver and three themes or narratives that helped achieve economic growth:

1) assertion of human moral and physical domination over nature; 2) connection between economic growth and human happiness; and 3) classic economic theory.

The three themes center on a concentrated belief that economic development and progress benefits all members of society. As can be seen in Figure 2-1, prior to the Industrial Revolution the Gross Domestic Product (GDP) per capita was relatively stable with modest increases. GDP per capita exploded in many areas around the world during the Industrial Revolution. However, many did not equally experience this GDP per capita explosion and there were significant inequalities in wealth and income. In addition, the environment suffered greatly, with mass pollution, often experienced by the least wealthy segments of society. The three themes and their promotion of economic development often occurred at the expense of social and environmental impacts and helped give rise to R&S as frameworks to better understand the challenges facing social-ecological systems.

The first of three themes is an *assertion of human moral and physical domination over nature*. This theme was an outgrowth of the Enlightenment (late seventeenth and early eighteenth century), which viewed humans as supreme over nature. Nature was not only subordinate to humans, but also at humans' disposal. Science, technology, and reason served only as tools to help humans overcome any natural barriers to exploitation.

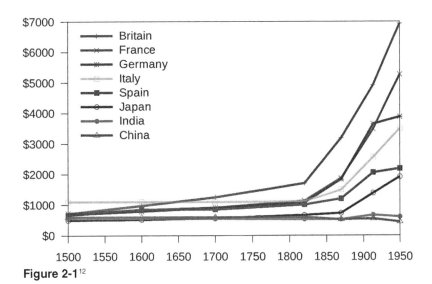

Figure 2-1[12]

---

[12] Donald Devine, *Romney Right on Culture*, U.S. Action News (Aug. 29, 2012), http://usaction news.com/2012/08/romney-right-on-culture/.

Many believed that science and reason could break through any obstacles or limits presented by nature, thereby allowing humans to tame and manipulate the environment to optimize its use. As author Kirkpatrick Sale noted, "[t]he Industrial Revolution was the first spectacular triumph of the human species over the patterned, ancient limitations of the natural world." After thousands of years, humans were no longer asking how to protect themselves from nature, but rather how to extend their dominance over nature to ensure economic progress.

The second theme, also built off the Enlightenment, *connects economic growth to human happiness*. Industrialization and economic growth helped achieve a new level of material benefits that inherently equated with improved lives. The best way to enhance the standard of living among the poor was to promote economic growth. A primary view held by many supporters of economic growth during the Industrial Revolution was that enhancing economic growth was a desirable end goal as more growth meant improved standards of living. Relatedly, a principal belief among supporters of economic growth was to connect moral progress with economic progress. In other words, growth, in and of itself, was considered a laudable and praiseworthy goal as it was believed to lead to better lives and more happiness. When combined with the first theme, humans accepted the moral and physical approval to exploit nature to ensure economic growth, which would lead to happiness.

As many of the industrialized nations migrated from feudal systems to economic systems based around capitalism, *classic economic theory* — the third theme — helped facilitate further economic development. Most people trace classic economic theory to Adam Smith's 1776 seminal piece, *An Inquiry into the Nature and Causes of the Wealth of Nations*. In *The Wealth of Nations,* Smith wrestled with formulating an economy around self-interested individuals. While this may sound like a good description of many contemporary economies today, it was a novel description of the economy emerging from the Industrial Revolution. Prior to the eighteenth century (as well as after) many societies had a much more protectionist or common good approach in which free trade was restricted.

While the precise contours of Smith's work relative to classic economic theory has been debated, one of the more salient points that helped form the classic economic theory is the idea that *free markets driven by self-interested individuals can regulate themselves* (often called a "laissez faire" approach to market regulation). Smith and others, such as Jean-Baptiste Say and David Ricardo argued that we should determine a nation's wealth by trade and the value purchasers place on the trade. Governments, they argued, should let the purchasers and sellers freely exchange and compete, which will determine the proper market regulations — something Smith called the "invisible hand" — so long as they are free from coercion.

Combined, these three themes — human dominance over nature, the connection between economic growth and happiness, and the classic economic theory and a free market regulatory approach — formed an overall narrative, which gave rise to a consumption-based society in which humans and nature were often in conflict. Although each theme went in and out of favor for brief periods, the themes were driving forces throughout the Industrial Revolution.

The themes also established an order of priority in which economic development was superior to the environment and equality. This order had and continues to have significant consequences. For example, while GDP clearly increased, less clear is whether social and environmental standards were proportionately, if at all, improved.

Conflicts and trade-offs between and among economic growth, social equity, and/or the environment are visible in many decisions made during the Industrial Revolution. The following two subsections look more closely at these conflicts. Although each subsection sets forth a contemporary critique of the Industrial Revolution, each subsection also describes a critical issue facing the R&S of systems today. The critiques zero in on the role of *technology*, *economic development*, and *population*.

2. ENVIRONMENT AND SOCIETY VERSUS ECONOMIC GROWTH AND THE ROLE OF TECHNOLOGY

What is or should be the role of technology in making decisions that impact social-ecological systems? On one hand, technology helps provide access to information previously unavailable. We can then use this information to assess a system's sustainability. On the other hand, during the Industrial Revolution, technology was a tool to help humans control the environment and to maximize natural resources to promote economic growth.

What is the best use of technology? To answer this question, we must ask:

- whether and how we can use technology to access resources (for example, deep water drilling for oil);
- whether technology can substitute for natural resources (for example, repopulate Mississippi mussels or Sumatran Rhinos or install plastic trees);
- whether that substitution sufficiently addresses public needs; and
- whether we should use natural resources just because technology makes them available.

In other words, if technology continues to advance, can we simply consume natural resources without limit?

CAPITAL

"Capital" refers to a "set of assets capable of generating future benefits for at least some individuals. The set of individuals involved may be relatively small, such as a family or a work team, or quite large, such as the participants in an economy or a political system. The flow of benefits generated by capital may all be positive or a smaller group may be benefited while a larger group is harmed." Elinor Ostrom & T.K. Ahn, FOUNDATIONS OF SOCIAL CAPITAL, INTRODUCTION (2003). Examples of varying capitals are physical capital, such as roads and hospitals, natural capital, such as forests and wetlands, and human capital, such as skills and knowledge.

In his 1627 novel, *The New Atlantis*, Francis Bacon provided some of the theoretical underpinnings for society's fateful move toward science-based domination over nature. A particularly telling passage begins "I am come in very truth leading to you Nature with all her children to bind her to your service and make her your slave." Bacon and others believed that man was superior to nature and should dominate nature. This idea became an accepted thought among philosophers and theorists called "Rationalists" including Rene Descartes (1596-1650), who believed only humans possessed rationality. Such a statement allowed Descartes and others to remove moral obstacles to dominate nature. It also justified technological advances to expedite this domination.

French physicist and philosopher Blaise Pascal challenged and disagreed with Rationalists' justification for human dominance over nature based on science. Pascal wrote, "we colour [the natural world] with our qualities and stamp our own composite being on all the simple things we contemplate," believing that humans do not have the capacity to understand and explain the natural world. Pascal did note, however, that humans have the capacity for thought, which allows and/or obligates us to maintain moral standards:

> For after all what is man in nature? A nothing in relation to infinity, all in relation to nothing, a central point between nothing and all and infinitely far from understanding either. The ends of things and their beginnings are impregnably concealed from him in an impenetrable secret. He is equally incapable of seeing the nothingness out of which he was drawn and the infinite in which he is engulfed.

Blaise Pascal, *Pensées* No. 72.

> The human being is only a reed, the most feeble in nature; but this is a thinking reed. It isn't necessary for the entire universe to arm itself in order to crush him; a whiff of vapor, a taste of water, suffices to kill him. But when the universe crushes him, the human being becomes

still more noble than that which kills him, because he knows that he is dying, and the advantage that the universe has over him. The universe, it does not have a clue.

All our dignity consists, then, in thought. This is the basis on which we must raise ourselves, and not space and time, which we would not know how to fill. Let us make it our task, then, to think well: here is the principle of morality.

Blaise Pascal, *Pensées* No. 200.

The idea that reason, often exhibited in technological advances, allowed human dominance over nature and would lead to enhanced happiness did (and does) have its critics. Jean-Jacques Rousseau (1712-1778) and other Romantics, believed that humans would only achieve true happiness by returning to be a part of nature. Technology, the Romantics believed, can overreach and disconnect humans and nature, obstructing true happiness. The Romantics thought science was best when it worked in tandem with nature and not in an effort to subdue it.

Simultaneously, several writers and scholars recognized that nature has value other than promoting economic development. Ralph Waldo Emerson, Henry David Thoreau, George Perkins Marsh, and John Muir (founder of the Sierra Club) all challenged the idea that nature's primary, if not sole, use was to promote modern luxuries. Thoreau challenged humans to recognize the larger ecological systems around them and humans' place within those systems, stating, "[w]hat we call wildness is a civilization other than our own."[13] Similarly, Perkins Marsh believed that humans have an ethical responsibility to conserve the environment; and that the responsibility is equal to or more important than the ability to extract economic value from the environment.

ETHICS, RELIGION, AND THE DOMINANCE OF NATURE

In addition to providing a rallying call for environmental preservation through legal action, the[] writings [of Aldo Leopold, John Muir, Rachel Carson,] and others provided the foundation for environmental ethics as a new discipline. Professor Eric T. Freyfogle . . . quoted the leading Leopold scholar, J. Baird Callicott, who described this diverse field as "includ[ing] articles by and in criticism of animal liberationists, biocentrists, deep ecologists, strong anthropocentrists, weak anthropocentrists, nonanthropocentric holists, neo-pragmatists, ecofeminists, process philosophers and theologians, Taoists, Zen Buddhists, Christian apologists, Muslim apologists, . . . [and] Jews."

Environmental ethics as a discipline seeks to define and incorporate ethical values into the human response to environmental issues. Aldo Leopold's land ethic, as expressed in his essays in *A Sand County Almanac*, is probably the most famous and most referenced view of an environmental ethic. According to Leopold, a land ethic "reflects the existence of an

---

[13] THE QUOTABLE THOREAU 365 (Jeffrey S. Cramer ed., 2011).

ecological conscience, and this in turn reflects a conviction of individual responsibility for the health of the land." "In short, [Leopold's] land ethic changes the role of Homo sapiens from conqueror of the land-community to plain member and citizen of it. It implies respect for his fellow-members, and also respect for the community as such." As Professor Freyfogle noted, "Leopold spoke to the reader as an individual and challenged the reader to develop an ethical attitude toward the land." Developing such a change of heart requires that we look beyond science or economics to the individual minds and souls of people. Leopold was not a preacher, but instead recognized the evolutionary nature of this spiritual path and attempted to shepherd his readers to find their own ways to an ethical relationship with nature.

Daryl Fisher-Ogden & Shelley Ross Saxer, *World Religions and Clean Water Laws*, 17 DUKE ENVTL. L. & POL'Y F. 63 (2006).

The Romantics and other individuals and groups expressed concern that technology is also eroding social systems. They claimed that we would need fewer jobs as technology improved efficiency. As individuals lost their jobs, they lost their income, and they experienced poorer — rather than better — living standards.

FRANKENSTEIN AND THE ROMANTICS

Early in the Industrial Revolution, the Romantics, such as Rousseau, took note of the separation of humans from nature. Mary Shelley, a Romantic and the author of *Frankenstein*, was an early forecaster of potential disasters that could result from the unchecked use of technology to manipulate nature. In *Frankenstein*, she describes Dr. Frankenstein's quest to avert nature: "With unrelaxed and breathless eagerness, I [Dr. Frankenstein] pursued nature to her hiding places . . . a resistless, and almost frantic impulse urged me forward; I seemed to have lost all soul or sensation but for this one pursuit."

Before the end of Emerson's, Thoreau's, Marsh's, and Muir's life, however, it was clear that Bacon, Descartes, and others had won the day as manufacturing activity facilitated by technological advances exploded. Human dominance over nature escalated to previously unseen levels as new and more natural resources became available. As you read Section II.B, which describes some of the challenges facing the world today, consider the role of technology and whether it is helping to create a better, more sustainable, or more resilient world.

Questions and Notes

1. What is the role of technology in assessing resilience or sustainability? On one hand, technology provides critical data to help assess a system's resilience or sustainability. On the other hand, technology

can lead to the straining of a system by using that system beyond its capabilities. For example, if technology makes a resource available, say a rare metal on the continental slope, should we extract and use the resource? Should there be any limitations? If so, what are the limitations? What information would you want to know before extracting the metal? These questions may help establish laws and policies for extraction that result in more resilient or sustainable systems associated with the use of the metal.

2. Today, there are many examples of human attempts to rectify the destruction of the environment through technology. Often called "geo-engineering," this is the process of remedying environmental harms through further manipulation of the environment. For example, to combat climate change (discussed in more detail in Chapter 10), some have proposed reducing carbon dioxide by "vacuuming" it out of the atmosphere, capturing and burying CO_2, or injecting sulfate particles or other aerosols into the stratosphere to reflect sunlight and cool the planet. Can you think of other examples in which we relied on technology to correct the results of human behavior that had destroyed a natural resource? Is this a good idea? What do you think about technology as a post-damage remedy? Which is easier and less expensive: to correct behavior or to use technology to remedy damage? Do either of these approaches tend to promote sustainability and intergenerational equity around the resource?

3. ENVIRONMENT AND SOCIETY VERSUS ECONOMIC GROWTH AND THE ROLE OF POPULATION

In addition to technology, the Industrial Revolution raised concerns about population, consumption, and whether natural environments can sustain constant or endless economic growth. Thomas Robert Malthus (1766-1834), a supporter of equal and economic rights, believed that population growth was correlated to economic growth. Further, Malthus stated that population growth would always increase faster than the food supply and thus, more economic development would lead to more people without the proper nutrition. In essence, population growth (increasing exponentially or geometrically, that is at a consistent *rate*) would increase faster than resource availability (increasing arithmetically, that is at a consistent *quantity*), ultimately leading to the collapse of social systems and reduced living standards. In *An Essay on the Principle of Population*, Malthus concluded that misery and not happiness for large portions of the population was the inevitable result of unchecked economic growth.

Indirectly, Malthus raised the issue of ecological limits—a theory many have tapped into since. William Jevons (1835-1882), an economist and author of *The Coal Question*, estimated that by the twentieth century it would be too expensive for Britain to extract coal, as the resource would be scarce due to depletion. In doing so, Jevons connected Britain's economic and population growth directly to the availability of natural resources. Further, he raised the question of whether natural resources can sustain unchecked growth.

PLANETARY BOUNDARIES

In 2009, Johan Rockström, director of the Stockholm Resilience Centre and professor at Stockholm University, Will Steffen, emeritus professor at Australian National University, and others identified nine "planetary boundaries." The boundaries help locate a "safe operating space for humanity," and how much more some systems can absorb before risking "irreversible and abrupt environmental change." The researchers identify not only the boundaries, but also how far we are from crossing seven of the boundaries. The nine boundaries are:

1. Climate change
2. Change in biosphere integrity (biodiversity loss and species extinction)
3. Stratospheric ozone depletion
4. Ocean acidification
5. Biogeochemical flows (phosphorus and nitrogen cycles)
6. Land-system change (for example deforestation)
7. Freshwater use
8. Atmospheric aerosol loading (microscopic particles in the atmosphere that affect climate and living organisms)
9. Introduction of novel entities (e.g., organic pollutants, radioactive materials, nanomaterials, and micro-plastics)

In 2015, the scientists updated the planetary boundaries and found that human activity has caused four of nine planetary boundaries to be crossed. Those four are climate change, loss of biosphere integrity, land-system change, and altered biogeochemical cycles (phosphorus and nitrogen). Further, the scientists found that two of these four are "core boundaries" that if significantly altered would "drive the Earth System into a new state." *Planetary Boundaries — An Update*, Stockholm Resilience Centre http://www.stockholmresilience.org/research/research-news/2015-01-15-planetary-boundaries---an-update.html.

Describing the planetary boundaries, the 2015 update states:

The planetary boundaries (PB) approach aims to define a safe operating space for human societies to develop and thrive, based on our evolving understanding of the functioning and resilience of the Earth System. . . .

A planetary boundary as originally defined is not equivalent to a global threshold or tipping point. . . . [E]ven when a global- or continental/ocean basin-level threshold in an Earth System process is likely to exist, the proposed planetary boundary is not placed at the

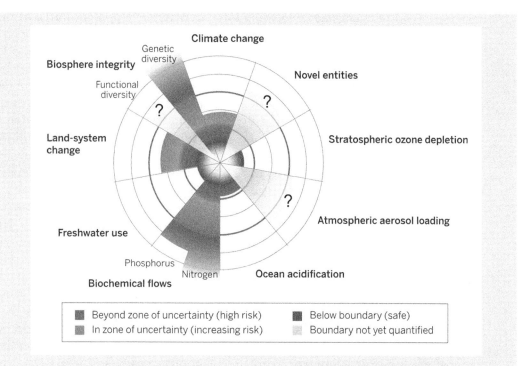

position of the biophysical threshold but rather upstream of it, i.e., well before reaching the threshold. This buffer between the boundary . . . and the threshold accounts not only for uncertainty in the precise position of the threshold with respect to the control variable, but also allows society time to react to early warning signs that it may be approaching a threshold and consequent abrupt or risky change.

Will Steffen et al., *Planetary boundaries: Guiding Human Development on a Changing Planet*, SCIENCE (Jan. 15, 2015).

Malthus had his critics that helped define the role of population and consumption in economic development. For example, William Godwin (1756-1836), father of author Mary Shelley, believed, among other things, that economic development would equate with better lives as living standards would correspondingly continue to improve even as populations increased. Years after Malthus' death, Karl Marx (1818-1883) and Friedrich Engels (1820-1895) argued that scientific and technological progress would keep pace with population growth and would equally distribute wealth and resources as development occurred. Thus, they argued that science and technology are means to achieve growth and improve living standards, notwithstanding population increases. Godwin, Marx, and Engels paid little attention to the limits of nature. Rather, there was an implicit, if not explicit, acknowledgment that if technology had no limits, population growth had no limits.

While Engels was advocating for economic development (often at the expense of ecological systems), he also had great sympathy for workers and advocated for social equality. When sent to Manchester, England to work at his father's manufacturing plant, Engels wrote a detailed report on the destructive conditions facing workers, entitled *The Condition of the Working Class in England* (1844). In the report, Engels described the difficult lives workers faced under the Industrial Revolution, including living in dilapidated housing, having no sanitary facilities and toilets, and little access to potable water. He also noted that laborers performed physically rigorous work for long hours, were often children, and received little payment — none of which improved "happiness."

Engels was struggling with conflicts that arose as part of trade-offs among economic development, the environment, and society. He expressed concern for the health of workers as connected to the environment. He was one of the first writers to do so, acknowledging the awful water and air pollution laborers experienced. He challenged the idea that uncontrolled economic development provided benefits to all segments of society, recognizing that the Industrial Revolution had a cost and that cost was pollution (as it pertained to a social cost to laborers) and poverty. In essence, Engels simultaneously recognized the potential of economic development to enhance laborers' wealth and its potential to enhance economic inequities. He recognized that economic development required the use of natural capital and that the poor often experienced the negative ramifications of using that capital. These conflicts and trade-offs and many others repeated throughout the Industrial Revolution and continue today. R&S help elucidate these trade-offs by analyzing systems, their functioning, and disturbances.

Questions and Notes

1. It is clear that world population continues to increase, as shown in Figure 2-2. As population increases, so too does consumption (although advocates of technology might suggest that consumption could decrease in the face of population increase if the correct technology was in place to help lower per capita consumption). Figure 2-2 indicates the correlation between population increases and energy and grain consumption increases. How might population and consumption levels impact the resilience or sustainability of the food system?

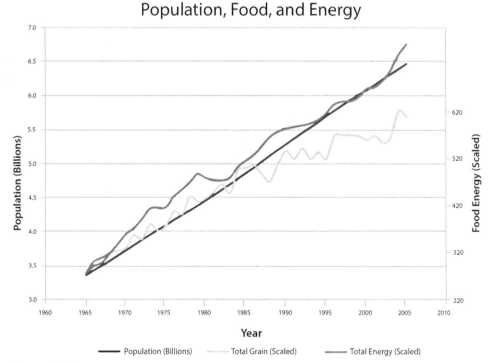

Population, Food, and Energy

Population (Billions) ——— Total Grain (Scaled) ········· Total Energy (Scaled) ———

Figure 2-2[14]

2. *A sustainable society must ultimately imply a stable level of population. Thus population policy must become a central element of economic development. [Sara J. Scherr] suggests that maintaining environmental integrity depends on slowing rates of population growth in the developing world, and that policies to do so require a focus on social equity and women's rights.*[15]

Do you agree with this quote connecting sustainability to population? Are populations stressing natural resources or societal equity? If so, how? Do you think governments and societies around the world should address population increases? Should they do so through law and policy? If so, how? If not, how do we ensure that future generations have the resources they require?

3. In light of the three subsections above on economic growth, technology, and population, what do you think about the following passage, and what is or should be technology's role in addressing population increases and associated demands on social-ecological systems:

"*Two of the fundamental axioms of ecological and evolutionary biology are that organisms are exuberantly over-productive, and that limits set by time,*

---

[14] Paul Chefurka, *What Drives Population—Food or Energy?* (2007), http://www.paulchefurka.ca/PopulationFoodEnergy.html.

[15] Jonathan M. Harris, *Sustainability and Sustainable Development*, Int'l Soc'y for Ecological Econ. 7, http://isecoeco.org/pdf/susdev.pdf.

space, and energy are inevitably encountered." . . . In an ecological perspective sustainability must involve limits on population and consumption levels. These limits apply to all biological systems. While humans may appear to evade them for a time, they must ultimately accept the boundaries of a finite planet.[16]

4. SUMMARY OF FORCES AFFECTING THE CHALLENGES

In this Section A, we reviewed a number of challenges that can impact diverse systems' resilience or sustainability. Those challenges include:

- three Industrial Revolution narratives:
  - ○ assertion of human moral and physical dominance over nature,
  - ○ connection between economic growth and human happiness, and
  - ○ classic economic theory;
- one of the more salient points that helped form the classic economic theory — the idea that *free markets driven by self-interested individuals can regulate themselves* (often called a "laissez faire" approach to market regulation);
- the complex role of technology in the context of R&S;
- the role of population and consumption; and
- planetary boundaries.

B. PICTURE OF THE PRESENT

Many concepts and changes born during the Industrial Revolution, including the themes of human dominance over nature, correlation between economic growth and happiness, a free market regulatory approach, technological advances, and increased population, persist today. Particularly relevant to the R&S of many social-ecological systems today is the persistence of classic economic theory — which is remarkably resilient.

During and after the Great Depression (beginning in 1929 and going through the 1930s and in some countries through World War II), classic economic theory began to lose favor as unregulated business was partially blamed for deteriorating social conditions. In *The General Theory of Employment, Interest and Money*, economist John Maynard Keynes developed an alternative to classical economics that supported government or other types of intervention to stimulate the economy, as private markets were unable or unwilling to do so, ultimately called "Keynesian" economics.

---

[16] Jonathan M. Harris, *Basic Principles of Sustainable Development*, *in* 1 DIMENSIONS OF SUSTAINABLE ENVIRONMENT 29 (Kamaljit S. Bawa & Reinmar Seidler eds., 2009).

When social conditions deteriorated again with both high unemployment and inflation in the 1970s, we began to replace Keynesian economics with neoclassical economics. Neoclassical economists advocate for, among other things, a return to free markets and a reliance on individuals to self-regulate and promote the highest possible level of economic growth. Neoclassical economists believe, as classic economists believed, that this economic growth leads to improved lives across income and wealth brackets.

As the images and text in the next three subsections indicate, while some things have improved since the Industrial Revolution, others have deteriorated, including many social-ecological systems. Toxic industrial sites, polluted waters, greenhouse gas emissions, soil pollution and erosion, species decimation, and many others—all by-products or indirectly related to economic growth—have greatly increased since the beginning of the Industrial Revolution and a pursuit of economic progress.

Rather than detail the many economic, social, and environmental challenges, we provide a snapshot of the diverse challenges straining systems' R&S. The information below does not encompass all challenges we face or all challenges straining R&S. Rather, the information below provides a sense of some key data points and illustrates the diversity of the challenges and systems relevant to R&S.

We group the topics below into three areas: economic, social, and environmental. As you view the images and read the text below, consider how the topics overlap. We may categorize one issue as "economic," but we may just as easily have categorized it under "social" or "environmental." The topics touched upon are:

Economic Indicators	Poverty levels	Income inequality	Accumulated wealth inequalities	General levels of consumption	Energy consumption levels	Food consumption levels
Social Indicators	Life expectancy	Education inequality	Obesity levels	Malnourishment	Computer and Internet access	
Environmental Indicators	Deforestation	Wetland loss	Biodiversity	Coral reef loss	Freshwater depletion	Climate change and air pollution

1. ECONOMIC INDICATORS

A quick glimpse at several key economic indicators shows a growing disparity between wealthy and poor individuals as well as between wealthy and poor countries. The excerpt below discusses how income and wealth continue to accumulate in a small group of individuals at rapid rates, leaving vast swaths of society in poverty. This excerpt gives a broad overview of wealth and income in the United States based on a comprehensive review of capital income (such as dividends, interest, rents, and business profits) from federal income tax returns since 1913. As you read the piece below, consider whether promises of economic growth and equality stemming from the Industrial Revolution are coming to fruition.

Emmanuel Saez & Gabriel Zucman, *Wealth Inequality in the United States Since 1913: Evidence from Capitalized Income Tax Data*

AT 22-26 (OCT. 2014), HTTP://GABRIEL-ZUCMAN.EU/FILES/SAEZZUCMAN2014.PDF

The average net wealth per family is close to $350,000, but this average masks a great deal of heterogeneity. For the bottom 90%, average wealth is $84,000, which corresponds to a share of total wealth of 22.8%. The next 9% (top 10% minus top 1%), families with net worth between $660,000 and $4 million, hold 35.4% of total wealth. The top 1% — 1.6 million families with net assets above $4 million — owns close to 42% of total wealth and the top 0.1% — 160,700 families with net assets above $20 million — owns 22% of total wealth, about as much as the bottom 90%. . . .

Top wealth shares have followed a marked U-shaped evolution since the early twentieth century. . . . [T]he top 10% wealth share peaked at 84% in the late 1920s, then dropped down to 63% in the mid-1980s, and has been gradually rising ever since then, to 77.2% in 2012. . . . While the top 10% wealth share has increased by 13.6 percentage points since its low point in 1986, the top 1% share has risen even more (+16.7 points from 1986 to 2012). . . .

Over the 1978-2012 period, the top 1% income share has gained 13.5 points, the top 1% wealth share 19 points, and the top 1% taxable capital income share 29 points. Wealth inequality has grown less than taxable capital income inequality because the concentration of housing and pension wealth — which do not generate taxable income — has increased less than that of directly held equities and fixed income claims.

Wealth concentration has increased particularly strongly during the Great Recession of 2008-2009 and in its aftermath. The bottom 90% share fell between mid-2007 (28.4%) and mid-2008 (25.4%) because of the crash in housing price. The recovery was then uneven: over 2009-2012, real wealth per family declined 0.6% per year for the bottom 90%, while it increased at an annual rate of 5.9% for the top 1% and 7.9% for the top 0.1%. . . .

At the very top end of the distribution, wealth is now as unequally distributed as in the 1920s. In 2012, the top 0.01% wealth share (fortunes of more than $110 million dollars belonging to the richest 16,000 families) is 11.2%, as much as in 1916 and more than in 1929. . . .

The losses experienced by the wealthiest families from the late 1920s to the late 1970s were so large that in 1980, the average real wealth of top 0.01% families ($44 million in constant 2010 prices) was half its 1929 value ($87 million). It took almost 60 years for the average real wealth of the top 0.01% to recover its 1929 value — which it did in 1988. . . . As these studies suggested, the most likely explanation is the drastic policy changes of the New Deal. The development of very progressive income and estate taxation made it much more difficult to accumulate and pass on large fortunes. . . . Part of these policies were reversed in the 1980s, and we find that top 0.01% average wealth has been growing at a real rate of 7.8% per year since 1988. In 1978, top 0.01% wealth holders were 220 times richer than the average family. In 2012, they are 1,120 times richer. . . .

The share of wealth owned by the middle class has followed an invert-ed-U shape evolution: it first increased from the early 1930s to the 1980s, peaked in the mid-1980s, and has continuously declined since then. . . . The large rise in the bottom 90% share from 16% in the early 1930s to 35% in the mid-1980s was driven by the accumulation of housing wealth, and more importantly pension wealth. Pension wealth was almost non -existent at the beginning of the twentieth century. . . . The decline in the bottom 90% wealth share since the mid-1980s owes to a fall in the net housing and fixed income (net of non-mortgage debt) components. The net housing wealth of the bottom 90% accounted for about 15% of total household wealth from the 1950s to the 1980s, while it now accounts for about 5-6% only. In turn, the decline in the net housing and net fixed income wealth of bottom 90% families is due to a rise in debts — mort-gages, student loans, credit card and other debts. . . . Since about 90% of (non-mortgage) debt belongs to the bottom 90% of the wealth distribu-tion, the upsurge in debt has had a large effect on the bottom 90% wealth share. . . .

Despite an average growth rate of wealth per family of 1.9% per year, for 90% of U.S. families wealth has not grown at all over the 1986-2012 period. This situation contrasts with the dynamics of the average wealth of the top 1%, which was almost multiplied by 3 from the mid-1980s (about $5 million) to 2012 ($14 million), fell by about 20% from mid-2007 to mid-2009, but quickly recovered thereafter.

As part of federal law and policy, Congress often discusses the federal tax rate. Consider how the historical tax rates influence the equalities discussed by Saez and Zucman.

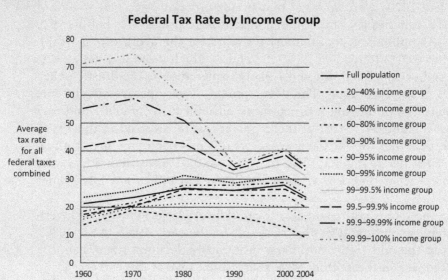

Federal Tax Rate by Income Group

The excerpt above indicates a disparity of wealth *within* the U.S. population. There is also a disparity of wealth among global populations. National percentages of populations living below the poverty line are much lower in North America and Europe than they are in Africa. A number of maps throughout this section reflect the distinction between these continents, implying a relationship between income/wealth and numerous social and environmental issues.

Selected additional information on the current state of income and wealth around the world includes:

- According to UNICEF [United Nations Children's Emergency Fund], 22,000 children die each day due to poverty.
- Number [of children] in poverty[:] 1 billion (every second child).
- More than 80% of the world's population lives in countries where income differentials are widening.
- A conservative estimate for 2010 finds that at least a third of all private financial wealth . . . is now owned by world's richest 91,000 people — just 0.001% of the world's population.
- An analysis of long-term trends shows the distance between the richest and poorest countries steadily worsened:
  - 3 to 1 in 1820
  - 11 to 1 in 1913

Demand in the rich world is satiated

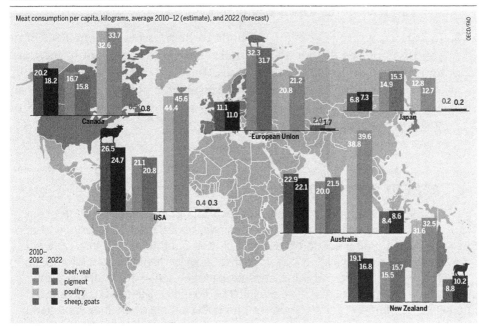

Figure 2-3

○ 35 to 1 in 1950

○ 44 to 1 in 1973

o 72 to 1 in 1992[17]

Consumption levels reflect income and wealth disparities. While a quarter of the global population (1.6 billion people) live without electricity,[18] overall consumption and consumption of fuel and meat in particular continue to increase in wealthier countries, as Figure 2-3 concerning per capita meat consumption indicates. In 2005, the wealthiest one-fifth of the world population accounted for 76.6% of total private consumption, while the poorest fifth accounted for only 1.5%.

Questions and Notes

1. What themes developed during the Industrial Revolution do you see in the Saez and Zucman article? What drives economic growth? Is it equality?

2. In the next two subsections we set forth some of the data on social and environmental challenges. Many of these challenges are direct and

---

[17] Anup Shah, *Poverty Facts and Stats*, GLOBAL ISSUES (Jan. 7, 2013), http://www.globalissues.org/article/26/poverty-facts-and-stats.
[18] *Id.*

indirect extensions of income inequality, reflecting policies that favor some systems at the expense of others.

3. In Part II, we review eight methods to help assess system R&S. Can you think of key economic indicators that you might want to measure and that will help identify and assess the R&S of a nation's economy? What information is important to measure for purposes of R&S in an economic system? How might the measures overlap with the R&S of social or ecological systems?

BENEFIT CORPORATIONS

Business can, and does, play a major role in the spheres of the economy, environment, and society. Businesses are generally very good at focusing on the economic aspects of their operations, but they may not have much incentive to consider their environmental or social impact. To the extent they consider the environmental or social implications of their business decisions, the primary incentive may still be financial, like the desire to avoid environmental or workforce scandals because bad publicity could result in decreased sales. In many instances, the impact of businesses may rival, or even eclipse, the impact of government. Because of the sheer magnitude of business in the world, the study of R&S is not complete without looking at it in the context of business.

With some limited exceptions, the law governing corporations has traditionally required corporate decisions to maximize the wealth of the shareholders.[19] This has effectively stood in the way of companies founded with the intention to work for the public good, whether that meant seeking to improve the environment or the local job market.[20] If shareholders did not like the decisions of the board, they could sue, and if they could prove that an alternative course of action would make more money, they could force the company to follow selfish policies, even if they were bad for the public. Lawmakers developed various policies that sought to provide a corporate board of directors with the flexibility to consider altruistic factors in their decisions, but each had its drawbacks. Constituency statutes permit a corporation to consider stakeholders outside those who owned the corporation's stock, but they didn't require such considerations, and courts did not give the statutes much weight.[21] Other options include the low-profit limited liability corporation ("L3C"), flexible purpose corporation, and hybrid nonprofits, which all have their own shortcomings.[22]

Enter the benefit corporation. Laws that authorize the creation of benefit corporations aim to give a company another option. A benefit corporation law has three primary rules: 1) requiring the corporation's decision-makers to consider the impacts of their decisions on society and the environment; 2) requiring the corporation to meet certain social and environmental accountability standards; and 3) requiring the corporation to

---

[19] Felicia R. Resor, *Benefit Corporation Legislation*, 12 Wyo. L. Rev. 91, 112 (2012); *see also* William H. Clark, Jr. et al., *The Need and Rationale for the Benefit Corporation: Why it is the Legal Form that Best Addresses the Needs of Social Entrepreneurs, Investors, and, Ultimately, the Public* (Jan. 18, 2013), http://benefitcorp.net/sites/default/files/Benefit_Corporation_White_Paper.pdf.
[20] Resor, *supra* note 19, at 112.
[21] Clark, *supra* note 19, at 10.
[22] *Id.* at 14.

publish annual reports on certain metrics.[23] The new parameters for decision-making permit mission-driven companies to declare the intention to prioritize goals other than profits. The reporting requirements, together with the accountability standards, aim to establish a trustworthy system for ensuring that benefit corporations are actually working toward the benefits they claim to advance.

As of the summer of 2015, 27 states have passed benefit corporation laws, and 14 more have a version in the legislative pipeline.[24] Delaware passed its benefit corporation law in 2013, which is of particular importance because more than half of publicly traded companies in the United States are incorporated in Delaware, including 64% of the Fortune 500.[25] Courts in other states often look to Delaware courts for guidance in corporate law decisions. Because the benefit corporation is a relatively new phenomenon, many courts have not had the occasion to review and interpret the laws that create them; thus uncertainty remains about how the requirements will be applied. Despite the lingering questions, the benefit corporation stands out as an appealing option for entrepreneurs and investors who seek to run businesses that generate a positive impact beyond the bottom line.

An example of a benefit corporation state law is Tennessee HB 0767 (2015) (effective Jan. 1, 2016) stating:

48-28-101. This chapter shall be known and may be cited as the "For-Profit Benefit Corporation Act." . . .

48-28-201. (a) A for-profit benefit corporation shall have a purpose of creating general public benefit. . . .

(b) The articles of incorporation of a for-profit benefit corporation may identify one (1) or more specific public benefits that it is the purpose of the for-profit benefit corporation to create. . . . The identification of a specific public benefit under this subsection (b) does not limit the purpose of a for-profit benefit corporation to create general public benefit under subsection (a).

(c) The creation of general public benefit and any specific public benefits under subsections (a) and (b) are in the best interests of the for-profit benefit corporation.

(d) A for-profit benefit corporation may amend its articles of incorporation to add, amend, or delete the identification of any specific public benefit that it is the purpose of the for-profit benefit corporation to create. . . .

(e) A professional corporation that is a for-profit benefit corporation does not violate [for-profit corporation statutes] by having the purpose to create general public benefit or any specific public benefit. . . .

48-28-301. (a) In discharging the duties of their respective positions and in considering the best interests of the for-profit benefit corporation, the board of directors, committees of the board, and individual directors of a for-profit benefit corporation:

(1) Shall consider the effects of any action or inaction upon:

(A) The shareholders of the for-profit benefit corporation;

---

[23] Resor, *supra* note 19, at 108-111.
[24] *See* BENEFIT CORP., http://benefitcorp.net/ (last visited Oct. 1, 2017).
[25] Christopher Wink, *64% of Fortune 500 firms are Delaware Incorporations: Here's Why*, TECHNICAL.LY (Sept. 23, 2014, 10:11 AM), http://technical.ly/delaware/2014/09/23/why-delaware-incorporation/.

(B) The employees and work force of the for-profit benefit corporation, its subsidiaries, and its suppliers;

(C) The interests of customers as beneficiaries of the general public benefit or specific public benefit purposes of the for-profit benefit corporation;

(D) Community and societal factors, including those of each community in which offices or facilities of the for-profit benefit corporation, its subsidiaries, or its suppliers are located;

(E) The local and global environment;

(F) The short-term and long-term interests of the for-profit benefit corporation . . . ; and

(G) The ability of the for-profit benefit corporation to accomplish its general public benefit purpose and any specific public benefit purpose.

2. SOCIAL OR EQUITY INDICATORS

Inequalities in wealth and consumption levels can also lead to a number of social challenges. While we touch upon some key social indicators below, there are obviously more social equity issues that we cannot cover in this brief section. For example, challenges related to discrimination, housing, war, social unrest, democratic participation, and healthcare (globally, "2.2 million children die each year because they are not immunized")[26] are all critical social issues not covered below. We are not trying to cover all key social challenges and systems. Rather, we want to provide a snapshot of the diverse challenges facing the resilience and sustainability of social systems. We begin with an excerpt that discusses several connections between economic and social indicators, highlighting the interconnectedness among these systems and how policy decisions often demand trade-offs.

Ichiro Kawachi & S.V. Subramanian, *Income Inequality*

IN SOCIAL EPIDEMIOLOGY 126-127, 134, 147 (2D EDITION, LISA F. BERKMAN, ICHIRO KAWACHI & M. MARIA GLYMOUR EDS., 2014)

Income poverty is bad for health. . . . The poor often cannot afford the means to lead a healthy life; for example, assuring adequate nutrition for their children, or paying the utility bills for heating during winter or air-conditioning in the midst of a heat wave. But in addition . . . being poor

---

[26] Shah, *supra* note 17.

also means lacking the income to participate fully in society. For example, to be able to participate as a citizen in a wealthy society like America, it is necessary to have access to additional goods and services such as means of communication (the Internet) and transportation (to get to jobs). . . .

Income inequality has risen during the past four decades within many societies, including the Unites States, prompting some scholars to raise the alarm concerning the corrosive effects of inequality on social cohesion. . . .

In *The Price of Inequality*, Joseph Stiglitz advances an argument for how the rent-seeking behavior of the top 1% imposes a tax on the rest of society. . . . The narrative unfolds in two steps. First, as the rich pull away from the rest of society, they literally "secede" from the mainstream of society — by segregating themselves in their own communities (sometimes gated communities that come equipped with 24-hour security), by sending their children away to private schools, by purchasing health services through boutique clinics, by arranging for their private trash collection, and so on. The result is that the rich begin to see less and less reason for why they should be subsidizing everyone else for public services (public education, public hospitals, public libraries) that they do not themselves use. In the second stage of the story, the rich begin to agitate for tax relief. As Stiglitz argues, when power is concentrated in one group, it generally succeeds in getting policies that benefit that group, at the expense of the rest of society. Indeed in the OECD [Organisation for Economic Co-operation and Development], the countries that have seen the largest increases in the shares of incomes at the top are also the countries that have passed the largest tax cuts to those at the top. This narrative neatly encapsulates what has happened in American society during the past two decades with regard to tax policy, regulatory policy, and public investment. Income inequality is therefore viewed as degrading the quality of life for all but the very richest in society. . . .

[T]he rise of neoliberal ideology starting around 1978-1980 — with its emphasis on economic liberalization, privatization, deregulation, de-unionization, and the retrenchment of the welfare state — seems to have tracked the global rise in income inequality rather closely. . . . Political and economic philosophy could be viewed as an attempt by the ruling elites to justify the existing social order; that is, the relation between ideology and income inequality is likely to be bidirectional. As income inequality has widened, power has become concentrated at the top, strengthening the ability of the top 1% to preserve their vested interests. Growing evidence from social psychology even suggests that the rich are less attuned to the sufferings of the poor; to put it bluntly, they can lack empathy. When the incomes of the rich and poor become polarized to the extreme degrees found in American society today, it gives rise to an empathy gap, creating a "careless" society in which some see no contradiction between cutting food stamps for the poor while advocating tax relief for the rich. The extreme concentration of wealth is already viewed (by some) as a threat to economic growth and the functioning of democracy.

Question

1. In Chapter 1, we raised the issue of *trade-offs*. What are some of the perceived and actual trade-offs involved with cutting social benefits to reduce taxes for the top 1% wealth holders? How might these trade-offs impact a community's resilience or sustainability?

Education gaps by income and country. In addition to life expectancy, the relationship between wealth, income, and levels of education present a significant social equity challenge. Figure 2-4 charts the relationship between individual income levels and education levels in 2010 in the United States. The image shows a dramatic increase in the likelihood of higher education as an individual's income increases.

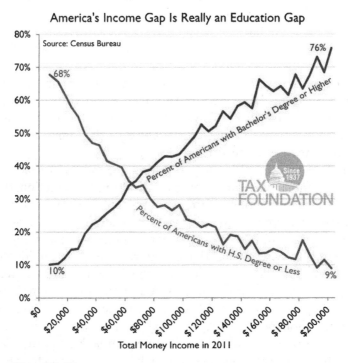

Figure 2-4[27]

[27] Richard Morrison, *Chart of the Day: America's Income Gap Is Really an Education Gap,* TAX FOUNDATION (Oct. 31, 2012), http://taxfoundation.org/blog/chart-day-americas-income-gap-really-education-gap.

Obesity and malnutrition. Obesity and malnutrition present major social equity challenges. The two images below show a great dichotomy in the world today concerning food. While millions of individuals are malnourished and thousands die from hunger, rates of obesity are increasing in most developed nations. Figure 2-5 illustrates an increase in obesity rates from 1990-2010 in the nine major economies and in the average of 34 Organisation for Economic Co-operation and Development (OECD) countries measured. Many of the countries experiencing increases in obesity rates are the same countries that have some of the lowest poverty rates and some of the highest income levels. Here again we see a correlation between economic challenges (disparities in wealth and income) and social challenges (obesity).

Obesity rates have increased substantially over the past 20 years and are highest in the US

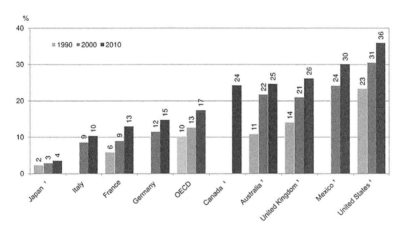

1. Data are based on measurements rather than self-reported height and weight.
Source: OECD Health Data 2012.

Figure 2-5[28]

Life Expectancy. Assessing the R&S of a system often requires gathering information from a number of interconnected disciplines. The excerpt above highlights the connections between social and economic systems and some of the trade-offs that can occur between the two. We now explore in more depth specific societal challenges facing the world today. Among the many challenges, we look at life expectancy, education, obesity and malnutrition, and computer and Internet access. Figure 2-6 indicates that citizens living in wealthier nations are more likely to live longer, raising significant social equity challenges. It illustrates that the higher a nation's per capita income, the more likely that nation is to have a higher average life expectancy.

[28] *U.S. Health Care System from an International Perspective*, OECD Health Data 2012, http://www.slideshare.net/OECD_Washington/us-health.

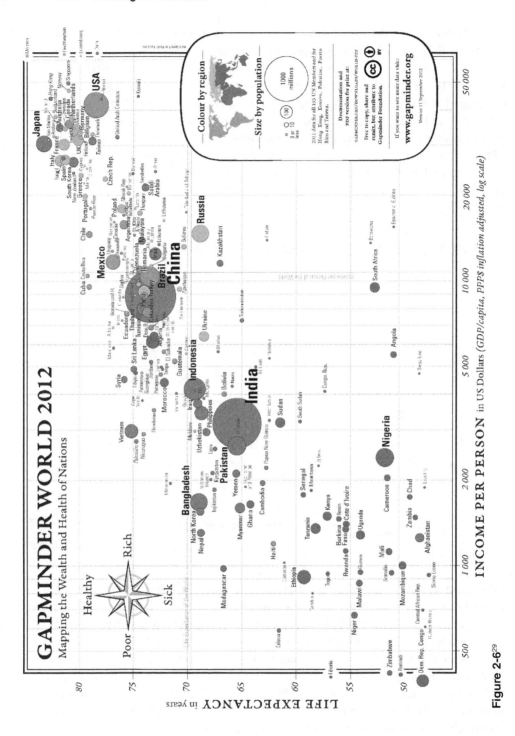

Figure 2-6[29]

[29] *See also Standard of Living in the Developing World*, GɪᴠᴇWᴇʟʟ, https://www.givewell.org/
international/technical/additional/Standard-of-Living#Summary (last visited Oct. 1, 2017).

In contrast to obesity rates, the United Nations Food and Agricultural Organization found that from 2011-2013 developed countries, like the OECD countries, experienced very low rates of undernourishment.[30] Over 65% of undernourished individuals worldwide live in Asia and over 26% live in sub-Saharan Africa, amounting to almost 800 million people

Internet Users (per 100 people):

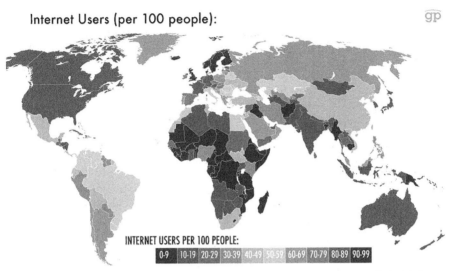

COUNTRIES WITH THE 1. Iceland (97) 2. Norway (95) 3. Sweden (95) 4. Denmark (95) 5. Netherlands (94)
MOST PEOPLE ONLINE 6. Liechtenstein (94) 7. Luxembourg (94) 8. Finland (92) 9. Bahrain (90) 10. U.K. (90)

Internet Users by World Region (per 100 people):

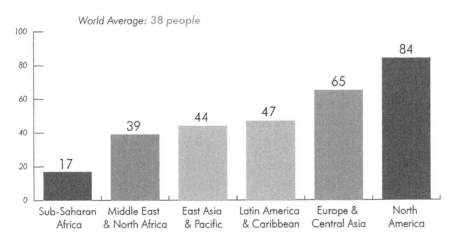

Source: World Bank (World Development Indicators), 2013   Simran Khosla / GlobalPost

Figure 2-7[31]

---

[30] *Hunger in Times of Plenty*, GLOBAL AGRIC., http://www.globalagriculture.org/report-topics/hunger-in-times-of-plenty.html (from FAO (2013), data for the period 2011-2013).
[31] World Bank World Development Indicators, *How Many People Are Online Around the World [map]*, LOCKERDOME (2013), https://lockerdome.com/6307866231448897/7350474508604692.

combined. Many of the countries in these areas also experience some of the highest poverty rates and lowest income levels.

Computer and Internet Access. As technology continues to advance and facilitates access to natural and economic capitals, an important social challenge is to provide equitable computer and Internet access. Figure 2-7 indicates that the use of and access to computers and the Internet is strongly correlated to education and economics. Note again that Internet use and cell phone availability seems to increase with increased wealth by individual and by nation.

Questions and Notes

1. R&S help us better understand social systems and policies that affect them. Look around your community. What are some of the key indicators you would use to measure whether your neighborhood is resilient or sustainable? Are individuals getting an equal education? What about healthcare? Nutrition and access to foods? What do your indicators tell us about the sustainability or resilience of systems in your neighborhood?

2. Some have criticized the concept of intergenerational equity on the ground that it does not pay sufficient attention to intragenerational struggles and equity. Critics argue that intergenerational equity de-emphasizes the current divisions among varying groups, such as the poor and rich. This division has been a major stumbling-block for international negotiations on a number of key issues such as climate change and deforestation.

3. What do the images above and the Adler and Newman excerpt below say about where we are and whether we are trending toward resilient or sustainable economic or social systems?

   Socioeconomic status, whether assessed by income, education, or occupation, is linked to a wide range of health problems, including low birthweight, cardiovascular disease, hypertension, arthritis, diabetes, and cancer. Lower socioeconomic status is associated with higher mortality, and the greatest disparities occur in middle adulthood (ages 45-65). . . .

   In addition to providing means for purchasing health care, higher incomes can provide better nutrition, housing, schooling, and recreation. . . .

   Socioeconomic status underlies three determinants [behaviors and lifestyles, quality of healthcare, and health insurance], which together are associated with an estimated 80 percent of premature mortality. The largest contribution is from behavior and lifestyle, accounting for about half of premature mortality, with environmental exposure accounting for another 20 percent, and health care, 10 percent. . . .

Access to, use of, and quality of health care vary by socioeconomic status. Among adults, 40 percent of those who have not graduated from high school are uninsured, compared with only 10 percent of college graduates; more than 60 percent of the uninsured are in low-income families. Persons who lack insurance receive less medical care, including screening and treatment, than those who are covered and may receive poorer-quality care. . . .

Nancy E. Adler & Katherine Newman, *Socioeconomic Disparities in Health: Pathways and Policies*, vol. 21, no. 2 HEALTH AFFAIRS 60-76 (Mar. 2002).

 The ice cream company Ben & Jerry's was one of the first companies in the world to place a social mission in equal importance to its product and economic missions. Ben & Jerry's overall mission is to make the best product so that the company can be both economically sustainable and replicable, as well as create positive social change both in their company and across the world.

Each year since 1989, Ben & Jerry's delivered a social performance report that tells people how they are doing on key social aspects. Ben & Jerry's believes that social performance is an important part of its business model. In addition to the social performance report, it also hires a third-party company to review the company's priorities and Social and Environmental Assessment Report (SEAR).

Ben & Jerry's Product Mission drives it to make ice cream by using locally sourced dairy, cage-free eggs, and fairly traded products, thus, promoting business practices that respect the Earth and the environment. Its ice cream production model also represents the company's intention to create positive change. Ben & Jerry's stores its ice cream in environmentally friendly freezers, sources the paper for its pints from a responsible supplier, and feeds its ice cream waste to pigs. The company has also created a "Lick Global Warming" campaign to help fight climate change. Ben & Jerry's actively recognizes the central role that business plays in society by initiating innovative ways to improve the quality of life locally, nationally, and internationally.

For its economic mission, Ben & Jerry's tries to manage for sustainable financial growth. The company is trying to increase value for the stakeholders and expand opportunities for development and career growth for its employees. Ben & Jerry's implements employer benefits, such as the "Ben & Jerry's Joy Gang," a group of employees whose mission is to "infuse joy into everything they do." This includes organizing companywide competitions and theme days, and providing comfort items like a hot cocoa machine for the freezer crew.

Ben & Jerry's states that the company believes in linked prosperity, which is that all stakeholders connected to its business should prosper while it prospers, from those who produce the ingredients, to employees who make the product, to the communities in which the company operates.

3. ENVIRONMENTAL INDICATORS

This subsection paints a bleak picture of where we are and where we are trending in relation to challenges facing ecological systems. We begin with one of the most pressing environmental issues today — a reduction in biodiversity.

Biodiversity. Several factors impact the loss of biodiversity: loss of habitats (such as forests, wetlands, and coral reefs — discussed below), invasive species, and overexploitation, to name only three. The excerpt below indicates that we are in the midst of a dramatic loss of biodiversity across the globe. The World Wildlife Fund's Living Plant Index (LPI), estimates the global loss of terrestrial, freshwater, and marine species to be 39%, 76%, and 39%, respectively, between 1970 and 2010. The LPI, "which measures trends in thousands of vertebrate species populations, shows . . . the number of mammals, birds, reptiles, amphibians and fish across the globe is, on average, about half the size it was 40 years ago."[32]

The drastic loss in biodiversity in recent decades has led several scholars to believe we are in the midst of a mass extinction — a position set forth in the piece below.

Gerardo Ceballos et al., *Accelerated Modern Human–Induced Species Losses: Entering the Sixth Mass Extinction*

SCI. ADV. 2015; 1:E1400253 JUNE 19, 2015

Arguably the most serious aspect of the environmental crisis is the loss of biodiversity. . . . This affects human well-being by interfering with crucial ecosystem services such as crop pollination and water purification and by destroying humanity's beautiful, fascinating, and culturally important living companions. . . .

Our analysis shows that current extinction rates vastly exceed natural average background rates. . . . We emphasize that our calculations very likely underestimate the severity of the extinction crisis because our aim was to place a realistic "lower bound" on humanity's impact on biodiversity. Therefore, although biologists cannot say precisely how many species

---

[32]*Living Planet Report 2014 Summary* 8 (2014), http://www.footprintnetwork.org/content/images/article_uploads/LPR2014_summary_low_res.pdf. For more information on additional fauna and flora at risk or extinct, see THE INTERNATIONAL UNION FOR CONSERVATION OF NATURE'S *Red List*, http://www.iucnredlist.org/.

there are, or exactly how many have gone extinct in any time interval, we can confidently conclude that modern extinction rates are exceptionally high, that they are increasing, and that they suggest a mass extinction under way—the sixth of its kind in Earth's 4.5 billion years of history. . . .

The evidence is incontrovertible that recent extinction rates are unprecedented in human history and highly unusual in Earth's history. Our analysis emphasizes that our global society has started to destroy species of other organisms at an accelerating rate, initiating a mass extinction episode unparalleled for 65 million years. If the currently elevated extinction pace is allowed to continue, humans will soon (in as little as three human lifetimes) be deprived of many biodiversity benefits. On human time scales, this loss would be effectively permanent because in the aftermath of past mass extinctions, the living world took hundreds of thousands to millions of years to rediversify. Avoiding a true sixth mass extinction will require rapid, greatly intensified efforts to conserve already threatened species and to alleviate pressures on their populations—notably habitat loss, overexploitation for economic gain, and climate change. . . . All of these are related to human population size and growth, which increases consumption (especially among the rich), and economic inequity. . . .

Deforestation. As the images below indicate, forest loss has been dramatic since the Industrial Revolution, resulting in, among other things, the destruction of key habitats for flora and fauna and the loss of numerous ecosystem services, including purification of water, soil retention, aesthetic beauty, and a variety of physical and mental health benefits. In addition, forests serve as a major carbon sink to mitigate climate change. "Nearly twenty percent of annual global carbon emissions result from forest loss and degradation, an amount greater than emitted by the global transportation sector each year."[33] When forests are burned or decomposed, not only is that portion of the forest no longer able to serve as a carbon dioxide sink, but also the burned or decomposing trees release some of the stored carbon dioxide back into the atmosphere, increasing atmospheric concentrations. "From 1850 to 1998, approximately one-third of man-made GHG emissions into the atmosphere came from releases due to land-use changes, mostly through deforestation . . . fully three-quarters of Brazil's GHG emissions, for example, come from deforestation."[34]

Figure 2-8 indicates a drastic reduction in U.S. forest canopy (tree cover) since 1620. While U.S. deforestation rates have decreased in recent years, other parts of the world continue to experience high rates of deforestation.[35]

---

[33] Blake Hudson, *Fail-safe Federalism and Climate Change: The Case of U.S. and Canadian Forest Policy*, 44 CONN. L. REV. 925, 930 (2012).

[34] Chris Wold et al., CLIMATE CHANGE AND THE LAW 11 (2d ed., 2013).

[35] The Green Market Oracle, *Global Deforestation/Reforestation and Climate Change* (Mar. 20, 2014), http://www.thegreenmarketoracle.com/2014/03/global-deforestationreforestation-and.html.

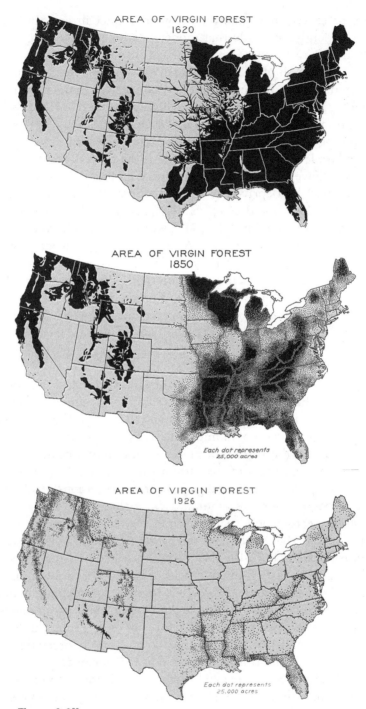

Figure 2-8[36]

[36] *Forests Return in the US*, Boston Globe (Sept. 1, 2013), https://www.bostonglobe.com/2013/08/31/forests-return/JnlculWuva7yGKcursuMWP/story.html.

ANTHROPOCENE

In 2000, the risks to and deterioration of natural environs by human dominance, led Nobel Prize-winning chemist Paul Crutzen and Eugene F. Stoermer to call for the end of the current geological epoch, known as Holocene, and the beginning of a new epoch marked by human control over natural environments, called *"Anthropocene."* In a short article published in *Nature* in 2002 entitled *Geology of Mankind*, Crutzen stated that the term "Anthropocene" was appropriate because of the heavy human imprint now on Earth, including increases in human population, methane and CO_2 emissions, energy use, damming and river diversion, alteration of 30-50% of the Earth's land surface, and depletion of tropical rainforest. Crutzen concluded that a "daunting task lies ahead for scientists and engineers to guide society towards environmentally sustainable management during the era of Anthropocene."

It is unsettled when the period known as Anthropocene began or whether it is possible or useful to identify a definitive date. Crutzen marks the Industrial Revolution as the starting point because of the unprecedented levels of human impact on the environment. Scientist and author James Lovelock agrees, marking the beginning date as 1712 when Thomas Newcomen invented the first reliable steam engine. Others place the date much earlier. Palaeoclimatologist, author, and professor, William Ruddiman marks the date as 8,000 years ago with the development of agricultural societies and clear-cutting for crops, and Smithsonian curators Bruce Smith and Melinda Zeder believe the relevant date to be 10,000 years or more ago.

The International Commission on Stratigraphy, Subcommission on Quarternary Stratigraphy considers whether we should officially recognize "Anthropocene" as a new epoch in 2017.

Wetlands loss. Wetlands across the globe have been drained, dredged, filled, damned, polluted, and diverted. In reviewing 189 reports analyzing changes in wetland areas, one scholar found:

> *[T]he reported long-term loss of natural wetlands averages between 54-57% but loss may have been as high as 87% since 1700 AD. There has been a much (3.7 times) faster rate of wetland loss during the 20th and early 21st centuries, with a loss of 64-71% of wetlands since 1900 AD. . . . Although the rate of wetland loss in Europe has slowed, and in North America has remained low since the 1980s, the rate has remained high in Asia, where large-scale and rapid conversion of coastal and inland natural wetlands is continuing.*[37]

Similar to deforestation, the loss of wetlands includes the loss of vital ecosystems supporting biodiversity and the loss of an important carbon sink helping to regulate the climate. Figure 2-9 illustrates the percentage of wetlands lost since the 1780s in each U.S. state. While rates of wetland loss may have slowed in recent years, some states such as California, Ohio, Illinois, Iowa, and Missouri, record over 85% wetland loss from the 1780s-1980s, leaving only a small fraction of wetlands left.

---

[37] *See* Nick C. Davidson, *How Much Wetland Has the World Lost? Long-term and Recent Trends in Global Wetland Area*, 65 MARINE & FRESHWATER RES. 934 (2014).

Percentage of Wetlands Acreage Lost, 1780s - 1980s

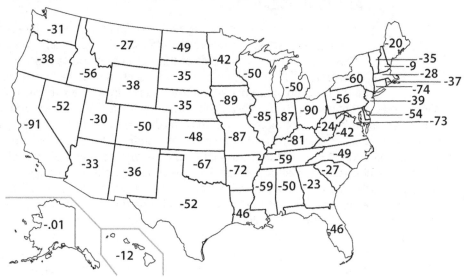

Figure 2-9[38]

Coral reef loss. Like forests and wetlands, coral reefs around the globe serve as vital habitats and local economic drivers, such as through tourism and fishing. Yet, they are disappearing at alarming rates. "Some scientists predict that all ocean corals may be dissolving by the year 2050."[39]

Below is a short excerpt on the current status of coral reefs and the economic benefits derived from coral reefs, authored by the U.S. National Oceanic and Atmospheric Administration. This excerpt connects economic and ecological systems and how decisions affecting one system can impact another.

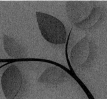

National Oceanic and Atmospheric Administration, *Value of Coral Ecosystems*

HTTP://CORALREEF.NOAA.GOV/ABOUTCORALS/VALUES/

Healthy coral reefs are among the most biologically diverse and economically valuable ecosystems on earth, providing valuable and vital ecosystem services. Coral ecosystems are a source of food for millions; protect

---

[38] For image, see William J. Mitch & James G. Gosselink, WETLANDS (2d ed. Van Nostrand Reinhold 1993). For table containing percentages and additional information, see U.S. Dep't of Interior, U.S. Fish & Wildlife Service, *Report to Congress, Wetlands Losses in the United States 1780's to 1980's*, Tbl.1, p. 6, https://www.fws.gov/wetlands/Documents/Wetlands-Losses-in-the-United-States-1780s-to-1980s.pdf.

[39] Wold et al., *supra* note 34, at 26.

coastlines from storms and erosion; provide habitat, spawning and nursery grounds for economically important fish species; provide jobs and income to local economies from fishing, recreation, and tourism; are a source of new medicines. . . .

In the US, coral reefs are found in the waters of the Western Atlantic and Caribbean (Florida, Puerto Rico, and the US Virgin Islands) and the Pacific Islands (Hawaii, Guam, American Samoa, and the Commonwealth of the Northern Mariana Islands). They are also found along the coasts of over 100 other countries.

While it is difficult to put a dollar value on some of the benefits coral ecosystems provide, one recent estimate gave the total net benefit of the world's coral reef ecosystems to be $29.8 billion/year. For example, the economic importance of Hawaii's coral reefs, when combining recreational, amenity, fishery, and biodiversity values, were estimated to have direct economic benefits of $360 million/year.

The global value above does not account for the economic value of deep-sea coral ecosystems, which . . . also provide important ecosystem services. Deep-sea corals serve as hot-spots of biodiversity. . . .

Yet coral reefs are in decline. . . . According to the Status of Coral Reefs of the World: 2008, 19 percent of the world's reefs are effectively lost, 15 percent are seriously threatened with loss in the next 10-20 years, and 20 percent are under threat of loss in the next 20-40 years.

Fresh water depletion. Fresh water resources are more heavily taxed now than ever. The combination of population increases, poor infrastructure, per capita consumption increases, pollution, and climate change is straining the availability of water, impacting local health, biodiversity, and economies. For example, of the "1.9 billion children from the developing world, there are . . . 400 million with no access to safe water [and] . . . 1.4 million [children] die each year from lack of access to safe drinking water and adequate sanitation."[40]

Figure 2-10 indicates the average level of "water stress" each country faces. The stress level is a product of total withdrawals and total renewable supply. The higher the withdrawal and/or the lower the renewable supply, the higher the level of stress. The researchers who assembled this map found, "that 37 countries currently face 'extremely high' levels of water stress, meaning that more than 80 percent of the water available to agricultural, domestic, and industrial users are withdrawn annually."[41] An excerpted UNESCO piece follows, describing the rapid increase in water usage, its impact on human health, and whether such usage is impacting the sustainability or resilience of the water system.

---

[40] Shah, *supra* note 17.
[41] Andrew Maddocks, *Water Stress by Country*, WORLD RESOURCES INST. (Dec. 2013), http://www.wri.org/resources/charts-graphs/water-stress-country.

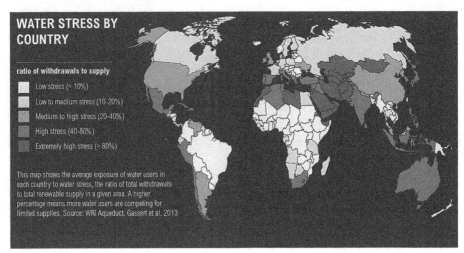

Figure 2-10[42]

WWAP (United Nations World Water Assessment Programme), *The United Nations World Water Development Report 2015: Water for a Sustainable World*

2015 UNESCO

Over the past century, the development of water resources has been largely driven by the demands of expanding populations for food, fibre and energy. Strong income growth and rising living standards of a growing middle class have led to sharp increases in water use, which can be unsustainable. . . .

Changing consumption patterns, such as increasing meat consumption, building larger homes, and using more motor vehicles, appliances and other energy-consuming devices, typically involves increased water consumption for both production and use. . . .

Population growth is another factor, but the relationship is not linear: over the last decades, the rate of demand for water has doubled the rate of population growth. . . .

Excessive water withdrawals for agriculture and energy . . . can further exacerbate water scarcity. Freshwater withdrawals for energy production, which currently account for 15% of the world's total . . . are expected to increase by 20% through 2035. . . .

[42] *Id.*

The agricultural sector is already the largest user of water resources, accounting for roughly 70% of all freshwater withdrawals globally, and over 90% in most of the world's least-developed countries (WWAP, 2014). . . .

Groundwater supplies are diminishing, with an estimated 20% of the world's aquifers being over-exploited . . . leading to serious consequences such as land subsidence and saltwater intrusion in coastal areas. . . . In the Arabian Peninsula, freshwater withdrawal, as a percentage of internal renewable water resources, was estimated at 505% in 2011. . . .

Water availability is also affected by pollution. Most problems related to water quality are caused by intensive agriculture, industrial production, mining and untreated urban runoff and wastewater. Expansion of industrial agriculture has led to increases in fertilizer applications. These and other industrial water pollutants create environmental and health risks. Excessive loads of nitrogen and phosphate, the most common chemical contaminants in the world's freshwater resources . . . contribute to the eutrophication of freshwater and coastal marine ecosystems, creating 'dead zones' and erosion of natural habitats. . . .

The disruption of ecosystems through unabated urbanization, inappropriate agricultural practices, deforestation and pollution is undermining the environment's capacity to provide basic water-related services (e.g. purification, storage). Degraded ecosystems can no longer regulate and restore themselves; they lose their resilience, further accelerating the decline in water quality and availability. . . .

A daily struggle for water is one of the terrible burdens of poverty, especially for women and girls who spend endless hours fetching water over long distances. . . . Not having sufficient and safe water means constant weakness and pain through recurrent diarrhea and other debilitating or fatal water related diseases. It leads to loss of time, educational and employment opportunities. Low incomes and limited access to water also means choosing between paying for water, food, school fees or medicines. Around the world, 748 million people lack access to an improved drinking water source, while billions more lack drinking water that is really safe. . . .

Climate Change and Other Types of Air Pollution. Climate change and greenhouse gases such as, carbon dioxide (CO_2), methane (CH_4), and nitrous oxide (N_2O), dominate the political discourse today concerning air pollution. However, there are numerous air pollutants that include chemical elements (e.g., mercury and lead), compounds (e.g., sulfur dioxide), and gases that also greatly impact the atmosphere and health, but only marginally or indirectly (as in the case of sulfur dioxide) contribute to climate change. To give one a sense of the scale and importance of air pollution, a 2014 World Health Organization Report found that 3.3 million people died from indoor air pollution and 2.6 million people died from outdoor air pollution in 2012 — approximately one death per every eight people.

We will discuss climate change and its impacts on systems' R&S in more detail in Chapter 10. As indicted in the images below (see Figures 2-11, 2-12, 2-13, and 2-14), and as stated in *Climate Change 2013: The Physical Science Basis*, increases are occurring in land surface, air, and sea surface temperatures (according to the National Oceanic and Atmospheric Administration (NOAA) 12 of the warmest 14 years on record occurred in the first 12 years of the twenty-first century), sea levels, and tropospheric temperatures, while decreases are occurring in Arctic sea-ice, glacier mass (80% of the glaciers on the Tibetan side of the Himalayan mountains have melted), and northern hemisphere snow cover.[43] The United States is also experiencing significant temperature increases, including some of the largest temperature anomalies in 2012 with 34,008 daily high records,[44] increased volume of rainfall in almost all areas,[45] and increases in the number of "extreme" weather events and billion-dollar disasters.[46]

The Intergovernmental Panel on Climate Change's (IPCC) 2014 Report tied many climate changes to anthropogenic activities, stating "[i]t is *extremely likely* that human influence has been the dominant cause of the

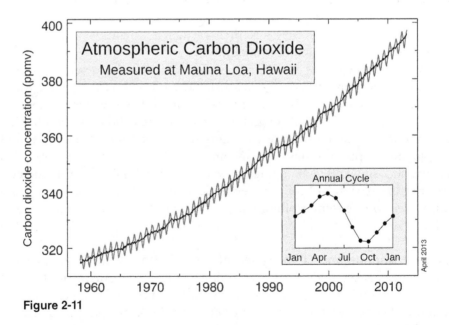

Figure 2-11

---

[43] *See* IPCC, *Summary for Policymakers. Climate Change 2013: The Physical Science Basis*, 9 (2013), https://www.ipcc.ch/pdf/assessment-report/ar5/wg1/WG1AR5_SPM_FINAL.pdf.
[44] RETHINKING SUSTAINABILITY TO MEET THE CLIMATE CHANGE CHALLENGE 68 (Jessica Owley & Keith H. Hirokawa eds., Envtl. L. Inst. 2015).
[45] *Id.*
[46] *Id.*

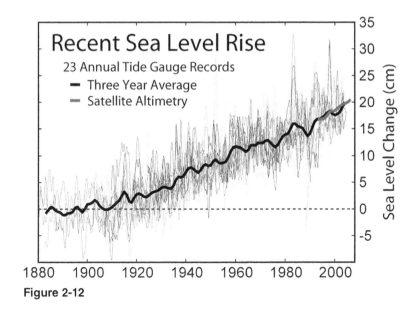

Figure 2-12

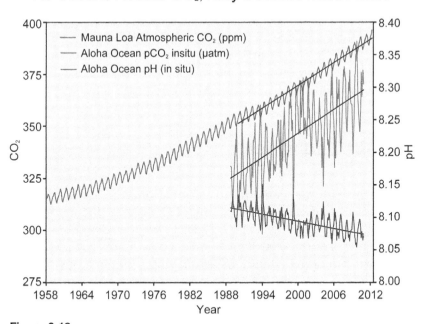

Figure 2-13

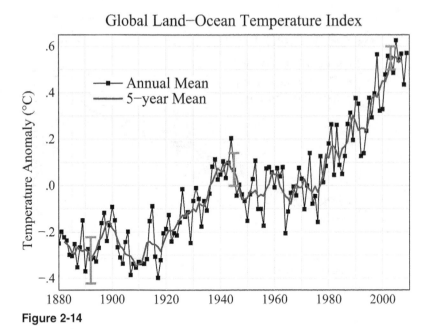

Figure 2-14

observed warming since the mid-20th century."[47] The IPCC's projections and other climate model projections forecast a dire situation in which we will continue to experience an increase in these climate patterns.[48] In addition, the increase in CO_2 contributes to ocean acidification, discussed in more detail in Chapter 10, in which the pH levels in the oceans decrease (increasing acidity) to levels not suitable for many species.

Questions and Notes

1. There is an enormous amount of information in this chapter. We cannot expect to understand fully many of the issues that are behind the information. However, you should start to see the complexity and interconnectedness of these issues, as well as how many systems are trending toward vulnerability and unsustainability. For purposes of assessing R&S, making sense of that complexity requires obtaining social and ecological information pertaining to those systems. This is often a very difficult task. The author David Orr highlights the interconnectedness and degradation of systems, noting:

> The "perfect storm" ahead, in short, is caused by the convergence of steadily worsening climate change; spreading ecological disorder (e.g., deforestation,

[47] *Id.*
[48] *Id.*

soil loss, water shortages, species loss, ocean acidification); population growth; unfair distribution of costs, risks, and benefits of economic growth; national and ethnic tensions; and political incapacity.[49]

2. The continued pursuit of economic growth and development in a manner started during the Industrial Revolution has had consequences. Many of those consequences manifest in social or environmental system degradations. As we begin our exploration of R&S, we not only want to be able to articulate the challenges facing the world today, but also the root of those challenges. The history of the Industrial Revolution highlights many of the root causes connected to economic growth. For example, many governments and private sector businesses today seek to promote economic growth with little discussion as to whether economic growth as a goal promotes a resilient or sustainable society. If so, at what cost to equity, the environment, or happiness?

3. How would you classify the following information, as indicators of economic, social, or environmental health? Or an overlap and how so?
   - Approximately 2.6 billion people in developing countries lack basic sanitation facilities.
   - Access to piped water into the household averages about 85% for the wealthiest 20% of the population, compared with 25% for the poorest 20%.
   - 12% of the world's population uses 85% of its water.[50]

4. Edith Brown Weiss' piece in Chapter 1 described three basic principles of intergenerational equity: "conserve the diversity of the natural and cultural resource base," "maintain the quality of the planet . . . in no worse a condition than the present generation received it," and "provide . . . conserve [equitable rights of] access for future generations." Based on the information in this chapter, are we meeting any or all of Weiss' three basic principles? Choose one subsection or system (for example, forest/deforestation) above and describe how, if at all, it meets Weiss' basic principles.

C. A View from the Future

In the following piece, the authors project what society might look like if we fail to alter policies relevant to the current conditions. They identify neoclassic economic theories (and their connection to social and environmental challenges) and positivism as core problems. Importantly, the authors ask "why"? Why, in the face of many of the concerns we covered

---

[49] David Orr, *Can We Avoid the Perfect Storm?*, *in* CREATING A SUSTAINABLE AND DESIRABLE FUTURE 215 (Robert Costanza & Ida Kubiszewski eds., 2014).
[50] Shah, *supra* note 17.

in this chapter, would we not adopt decisions and policies to alter course? This question is at the core of the remainder of this book, namely, how to incorporate R&S, as analytical frameworks, into law and policy to avoid catastrophic results and reverse unsustainable and vulnerable conditions.

Naomi Oreskes & Erik M. Conway, *The Collapse of Western Civilization: A View from the Future*

142 DÆDALUS, THE JOURNAL OF THE AMERICAN ACADEMY OF ARTS & SCIENCES 40 (WINTER 2013)

In the prehistory of "civilization," many societies rose and fell, but few left as clear and extensive an account of what happened to them and why as the twenty-first-century nation-states. . . . The case of Western civilization is different because the consequences of its actions were not only predictable, but predicted. . . . [T]he people of Western civilization knew what was happening to them but were unable to stop it. Indeed, the most startling aspect of this story is just how much these people knew, yet how little they acted upon what they knew.

A three-phase Industrial Revolution led to massive release of additional CO_2, initially in the United Kingdom (1750-1850); then in Germany, the United States, and the rest of Europe (1850-1950); and finally in China, India, and Brazil (1950-2050). At the start of the final phase, some scientists recognized that the anthropogenic increment of CO_2 could theoretically warm the planet, but few were concerned; total emissions were still quite low. . . .

In the 1970s, scientists began to recognize that human activities were changing the physical and biological functions of the planet in consequential ways–giving rise to the Anthropocene Period of Geological History. . . .

By the late 1980s, scientists had recognized that concentrations of CO_2 and other *greenhouse gases* were having discernible effects on planetary climate, ocean chemistry, and biological systems, threatening grave consequences if not rapidly controlled. . . .

In 1992, world nations signed the United Nations Framework Convention on Climate Change (UNFCCC) to prevent "dangerous anthropogenic interference" in the climate system. But there was backlash. Critics claimed that the scientific uncertainties were too great to justify the expense and inconvenience of eliminating greenhouse gas emissions, and that any attempt to solve the problem would cost more than it was worth. At first, just a handful of people made this argument. . . .

By the end of the millennium, denial had spread widely. In the United States, political leaders — including the president of the United States, members of Congress, and members of state legislatures — took denialist positions. . . .

By the early 2000s, dangerous anthropogenic interference in the climate system was under way. Fires, floods, hurricanes, and heat waves began to intensify. . . .

The year 2009 is viewed as the "last best chance" the Western world had to save itself, as leaders met in Copenhagen, Denmark, to try, for the fifteenth time since the UNFCCC was written, to agree on a binding, international law to prevent disruptive climate change. . . . But shortly before the meeting, a massive campaign (funded primarily by fossil fuel corporations . . .), was launched to discredit the scientists whose research underpinned the IPCC's conclusion. Public support for action evaporated; even the president of the United States felt unable to move his nation forward.

Meanwhile, climate change was intensifying. In 2010, record-breaking summer heat and fires killed more than 50,000 people in Russia and resulted in over $15 billion (in 2009 USD) in damages. The following year, massive floods in Australia affected more than 250,000 people. In 2012, which became known in the United States as the "year without a winter," winter temperature records, including for the highest overnight lows, were shattered. . . .

At the very time that the urgent need for an energy transition became palpable, world production of greenhouse gases *increased*. . . .

By 2012, more than 365 billion tons of carbon had been emitted into the atmosphere since 1751. Staggeringly, more than half of these emissions occurred *after* the mid-1970s — that is, *after* scientists had built computer models demonstrating that greenhouse gases would cause warming. Emissions continued to accelerate even after the UNFCCC was established: between 1992 and 2012, total CO2 emissions increased by 38 percent. . . . Less explicable is why, at the very moment when disruptive climate change was becoming apparent, wealthy nations dramatically increased their production of fossil fuels. . . .

To the historian studying this tragic period of human history, the most astounding fact is that the victims *knew what was happening and why*. . . . The thesis of this analysis is that Western civilization became trapped in the grip of two inhibiting ideologies: namely, *positivism* and *market fundamentalism*. . . .

Market fundamentalism — also known as free market fundamentalism, neoliberalism, laissez-faire economics, and laissez-faire capitalism — was a two-pronged ideological system. The first prong held that societal needs were served most efficiently in a free market economic system. . . . The second prong of the philosophy maintained that free markets were not merely a good or even the best manner of satisfying material wants: they were the *only* manner of doing so that did not threaten personal freedom. . . .

The toxic effects of DDT, acid rain, the depletion of the ozone layer, and climate change were serious problems for which markets did not provide a spontaneous remedy. Rather, government intervention was required: to raise the market price of harmful products, to prohibit those products, or to finance the development of their replacements. . . . The American people had been persuaded, in the words of President Reagan, that government was "the problem, not the solution." Thus, citizens slid into passive denial, accepting the contrarian arguments that the science was unsettled. . . .

[P]hysical scientists were chief among the individuals and groups who tried to warn the world of climate change, both before and as it happened. . . . Yet the idea of managing energy use and controlling greenhouse gas emissions was anathema to the neoliberal economists whose thinking dominated at this crucial juncture. Thus, no planning was done, no precautions were taken, and no management ensued until it was disaster management. . . .

III. SUMMARY OF THE CHALLENGES

Many of the indicators above illustrate a trend that challenges and implicates critical social-ecological systems. Some of the key themes we explored in this chapter include:

a. whether technology has made us better off, more moral, or virtuous;
b. whether technology can and should recreate ecosystems;
c. whether technology helps by providing access to more and better information on system functioning;
d. whether we can equate individual or per capita private wealth with general social welfare;
e. how population growth, economic development, and consumption impact system sustainability and resilience;
f. whether future generations will have the same ability to achieve like-minded goals of "happiness";
g. whether driving flora and fauna to extinction should matter;
h. whether there is an unrecognized value in biodiversity;
i. whether the rule of law should play a role in influencing systems R&S, and, if so, what that role might be; and
j. whether human decisions and values can be changed to alter the R&S of key systems.

As policymakers, chemists, geologists, biologists, planners, sociologists, executives, lawyers, and others continue to acknowledge the deterioration of social-ecological systems, we are increasingly employing R&S

to help guide decision makers. The information gained from assessing R&S can help challenge the underlying choices and behaviors behind the current wave of development and growth stemming from the Industrial Revolution. R&S help us question how and why we make certain decisions and whether long-lasting alternatives exist, in particular, alternatives that let us experience certain standards of living while ensuring that environment preservation and social equity are on equal footing with profit or economic progress. While we increasingly use resilience and sustainability as part of our lexicon, how we assess R&S and how we use that assessment to address the challenges set forth in this chapter is the focus of the remainder of this book.

Part II
Resilience
and Sustainability
in Context

The study of R&S would be little more than an exercise in theory without considering how to understand it, assess it, and then translate that assessment into policy to change behavior. This part facilitates the assessment of R&S by describing eight contexts where they play large roles. We divide these eight contexts into eight chapters that begin with basic needs:

- Water (Chapter 3)
- Food (Chapter 4)
- Shelter and Land Use (Chapter 5)

We then move to human activity, consumption, and production:

- Energy Production and Consumption (Chapter 6)
- Natural Resources (Chapter 7)

We conclude with the externalities and immediate and long-term challenges from both human and natural forces:

- Pollution (Chapter 8)
- Disasters (Chapter 9)
- Climate Change (Chapter 10)

To help assess R&S and ultimately make it part of the decision-making process we describe eight "Strategies to Facilitate Implementation":

1. Addressing Collective Action Challenges (Water, Chapter 3)
2. Precautionary Principle (Water, Chapter 3)
3. Ecosystem Services Management (Water, Chapter 3)
4. Systems Thinking (Energy, Chapter 6)
5. Baselines and Metrics (Energy, Chapter 6)
6. Adaptive Governance (Natural Resources, Chapter 7)
7. Life Cycle Sustainability Assessment (Pollution, Chapter 8)
8. Risk Analysis (Pollution, Chapter 8)

Many of the case studies described in Chapters 1 and 2 (Easter Island, the Atlantic cod, and Muscatine, Iowa) consist of human decisions that led to unsustainable and non-resilient systems and societies. At times, those decisions were based on a *lack of information* and at times, those decisions were based on *policies* notwithstanding the availability of relevant and accurate data. The Strategies to Facilitate Implementation are designed to help address both by providing mechanisms to obtain pertinent information and by establishing policy approaches that utilize that information. While we cannot cover all tools that help provide data and policy approaches relevant to R&S, the eight described in these chapters provide a foundation to explore questions necessary to obtain data relevant to R&S and help decision makers transform data into policy. By the end of this book, you should have a solid understanding of several approaches to help obtain data and transform it into policy in a way that considers systems' resilience and sustainability.

Many of the Strategies described below can be very complex and difficult to apply to a given situation and often require specific expertise. Our objective with the Strategies in Chapters 3 through 10 is to introduce them so that they can be integrated into law and policy. A few common characteristics you will find relevant to the Strategies include:

- They are *interdisciplinary* and *multiscalar* (private, public, international, national, subnational, and individual).
- They are *not designed to be normative*. The Strategies highlight critical data points, processes, or outcomes that help make decisions, but they do not dictate a particular decision. They do not prioritize specific goals or ideas. Rather, they highlight processes, fairness, and consequences

in an attempt to facilitate more informed decision making and indicate whether a specific policy does or will impact a given system's R&S.

- While not normative, they require *decisions that raise value judgments*. Utilizing the Strategies involves a determination as to which will be most useful — a decision that may heavily affect the outcome. If, for example, a Strategy produces only a piece of the relevant data, that data may assume a higher level of significance than it should because it may be the only data obtained. Similarly, each Strategy requires a determination of what to measure and how.

- Selecting a Strategy should be done in light of the *audience and available resources, including technology*. Questions relevant to each Strategy include: Who are the policy makers and stakeholders? What is the format in which the information collected will be delivered? Are the necessary expertise, finances, time, technology, and tools to implement properly accessible? Each Strategy requires some amount of expertise, finance, and time to properly assess and evaluate. If the sufficient resources are not allocated or available, the approach may provide false hope or may fail. *Technology* should also play a significant role in selecting the correct approach. As technology makes new data available and exposes new risks, the need and availability of approaches may change.

- Finally, when choosing the appropriate Strategy, it is important to consider *when in the decision-making process the Strategy will be implemented*. Each approach may be applied at numerous stages in the process, depending on objectives, audience, resources, technology, and effectiveness.

For each Strategy, we set forth a:

- *general description*;
- *specific description of its relevance to R&S*; and
- *illustration of its relevance to R&S*.

Water

3

I. INTRODUCTION

The history of Hawai'i land use illustrates how law and culture developed to manage land and water that people owned in common and that were subject to Collective Action Challenges (discussed in Section II.E below). In the traditional Hawaiian land system, the land was not subject to ownership but was instead, owned by the people.[1] The Kingdom of Hawai'i adopted its first written constitution in 1840 and declared that all land belonged to the King, not as private property, but to all the chiefs and common people over which the King was the head.[2] Each island was divided into a series of narrow wedge-shaped ahupua'a, which ran from the mountain (Makau) to the sea (Makai).[3] Each ahupua'a was governed by a local chief (ali'i) and administered by a local overseer (konohiki).[4] Thus, before the Great Māhele, a land division by the King in 1848, all land and the associated water were in the public domain.[5]

---

[1] Maivân Clech Lâm, *The Kuleana Act Revisited: The Survival of Traditional Hawaiian Commoner Rights in Land*, 64 WASH. L. REV. 233, 234-235 (1989) ("Until the passage of the Kuleana Act, the common people of Hawai'i had held . . . undivided interests in the land in common with the King and the chiefs. The first Constitution of Hawai'i, granted by Kamehameha III in 1840, described the traditional land system as follows: Kamehameha I, was the founder of the kingdom, and to him belonged all the land from one end of the Islands to the other, though it was not his own private property. It belonged to the chiefs and people in common of whom Kamehameha I was the head, and had the management of the landed property.").

[2] *Id.*

[3] *See Ahupua'a*, HAWAIIHISTORY.ORG, http://www.hawaiihistory.org/index.cfm?fuseaction=ig.page& CategoryID=299 (last visited Oct. 17, 2017).

[4] *Id.*

[5] Lâm, *supra* note 1, at 235-236.

Water, along with air, is a crucial resource required for survival. It is a common resource that is difficult to privatize and thus presents the **Collective Action Challenges**, discussed in Sections II.E and VII.B below. Water's importance to both human life and the critical eco-systems supporting fish, wildlife, and flora also presents challenges for **Ecosystem Services Management**, discussed in Section VI below. Finally, the **Precautionary Principle**, discussed in Section IV.C below, is evident in managing water resources for human consumption, agriculture, energy, transportation, instream and streamflow needs, and industry as this resource may be both abundant and scarce, depending upon geography and climate, and is subject to the destructive forces of pollution.

The physical size of the ahupua'a depended upon the resources available within the geographic area to support and sustain the people, and it generally followed the natural boundaries of the watershed.[6] Thus, the self-sustaining nature of the ahupua'a, governed by the availability of water and agricultural resources, was the basis for Hawaiian land division and control, as well as for Hawaiian culture and spirituality.[7]

THE GREAT MĀHELE

On January 27, 1848, the **Māhele**, or division of lands, began. With the Māhele, Hawai'i established the foreign concept of "land ownership." The traditional relationship Hawaiians had held with their āina (land) would never be the same. The Land Commission divided the land into equal thirds. One third would go to the ali'i (local chief), one third would go to the government, and the final third would go to the maka'āinana (people who lived on the land).

It did not take long for the aliens, or foreigners, to get what they wanted. **The Resident Alien Act of July 10, 1850**, gave them the right to buy land in fee simple. Fee simple means that land is owned rather than leased. It also means that individuals who own land may sell that land or pass it on to their heirs. This is the system the foreigners understood and wanted for Hawai'i.

As for the maka'āinana, the **Kuleana Act of August 1850** made it possible for them to own land in fee simple. Kuleana is the Hawaiian word for responsibility. Therefore kuleana also became the term for land that people had lived on and cultivated. The maka'āinana had to follow certain steps before they could own their land. First, they had to have their kuleana surveyed, or measured for size and boundaries. Then they had to present their claims to the Land Commission, showing that the land was cultivated to earn a living and that they had a right to those kuleana. They also needed to file their

---

[6] *See Ahupua'a, supra* note 3.
[7] *See id.*

claim by 1854. Unfortunately many maka'āinana did not do what the law required. They lacked the knowledge, experience, and money to pay for surveys. In addition, many missed the 1854 filing deadline. Hawaiians filed only 13,514 claims and the number of kuleana grants actually awarded was just 9,337. Maka'āinana ended up with less than 1% of the total land available.

Most Hawaiians did not own any land. Some of those who did own their kuleana lost it later because they did not pay land taxes. Then there were those who lost their land because they did not occupy, or live on, their kuleana. This was due to the "adverse possession" law. This law allowed a person to claim land that its owner had not occupied ten years or more. Once the law granted the kuleana lands, Hawaiians were no longer able to access the lands used in common by all inhabitants of an ahupua'a. They were forced to stay on their own kuleana, making survival dependent on fewer resources.

The **Great Māhele** and the **Kuleana Act**, virtually stripped Hawaiians of the lands they had owned for so long. Without land, many maka'āinana became part of an unpaid labor force used by chiefs and foreigners on large land holdings, worked on plantations, or became homeless. As Hawaiians lost their lands, foreigners took advantage of the **Resident Alien Act** and began buying and selling land in Hawai'i. A land division that once gave native Hawaiians claim to one third of the land of Hawai'i was now responsible for them ending up with virtually nothing. http://himonarchy. weebly.com/the-great-mahele.html; Source: Cachola, Jean Iwata. KAMEHAMEHA III: KAUIKEAOULI. Kamehameha Schools Press, Honolulu, 1995. From: http://www.ulu-kau.org/elib/cgi-bin/library?c=ks9&l=en.

Following the Great Māhele in 1848 and up until 1973, streams running through an ahupua'a were subject to private ownership by the konohikis (heads of a land division or ahupua'a who administered the land ruled by an ali'i chief) who derived title to their lands through the division. The konohikis could thus transfer surplus waters even if they did not remain appurtenant to the ahupua'a.[8] However, in 1973 the Hawai'i Supreme Court in *McBryde Sugar Co. v. Robinson*[9] held that water was not privately owned and was instead owned by the state according to the public trust doctrine. "We believe that the right to water is one of the most important usufruct of lands, and it appears clear to us that . . . the right to water was specifically and definitely reserved for the people of Hawaii for their common good in all of the land grants."[10] The court, in resolving the dispute between two sugar companies over water rights, concluded that while riparian landowners have the right to use the water, they do not have the right to transport water to another watershed. Instead, "title

[8] Hawaiian Commercial & Sugar Co. v. Wailuku Sugar Co., 15 Haw. 675, 680-681 (1904). Note that this case also involved two sugar companies, as was the situation in the *McBryde* decision of 1973.
[9] McBryde Sugar Co. v. Robinson, 504 P.2d 1330 (Haw. 1973).
[10] *Id.* at 1338.

to water was reserved to the State for the common good when parcels of land were allotted to the awardee under the mahele."[11]

Hawai'i's experience with water serves as a microcosm from which to view many of the water issues faced in the world that implicate the resilience and/or sustainability of water-based systems. Is water or any natural resource subject to ownership rights allowing sales and transfers? If it is a property right, is it privately owned or is it owned by the government in trust for the people? Did the Hawai'i Supreme Court in *McBryde* commit a judicial taking of property by changing its legal system governing water rights from one of private ownership by the konohikis to water protected by the public trust doctrine as a common good? For further discussion of the Public Trust Doctrine, see Chapter 5. How do we establish property or usage rights to water as among competing consumers when it is scarce? Are water rights based upon political boundaries, such as private land ownership, towns, states, and nations, or are they based upon natural boundaries, such as watersheds and other sustainable geographic boundaries, as illustrated by the ahupua'a divisions of land in Hawai'i? Which, if any, of these legal frameworks to regulate the use of water and associated resources are most likely to result in resilient and/or sustainable conditions? In this chapter, we will address these questions and others by exploring the current and variable legal frameworks governing water use and management and the impact these frameworks have on the sustainability and resilience of this essential resource.

In early 2016, Alexander & Baldwin (A&B), a company started in Maui by sugar-growing descendants of Protestant missionaries, announced that it "will phase out sugarcane farming on Maui at Hawaiian Commercial & Sugar Co. over the next 12 months and transition the 36,000-acre farm to a diversified crop model." The Star Advertiser article noted that although "[s]ugar and pineapple plantations run by big landowners once dominated Hawai'i's economy, tourism has become the economic machine." The article continued:

U.S. Sen. Brian Schatz said he was deeply saddened by the news. "For over 130 years, sugar production on Maui was more than a business, spawning a way of life and generations of hard working women and men who made our state remarkable and great," he said in a statement.

Maui Mayor Alan Arakawa said his heart goes out to workers who will lose their jobs, but the change was inevitable. "Fruit trees, taro, bio-mass, papayas, avocados and much more have all gone through trial testing, leaving us very confident that while sugar cane is dead, agriculture will remain very much alive here," he said in a statement.

---

[11] *Id.* at 1345.

Benjamin [A&B's president] said the company was providing enhanced benefits and one-on-one assistance to help those being laid off move into retirement or a new job.

Andrew Gomes, *Last Sugar Plantation in Hawai'i to Close this Year* Honolulu Star Advertiser (Jan. 6, 2016), http://www.staradvertiser.com/2016/01/06/business/business-breaking/last-sugar-plantation-in-hawaii-to-close-this-year/.

As we start to view R&S in context, consider the story of A&B. Is it an agriculture problem? A water rights problem? An economic problem? Which systems relevant to A&B are implicated in this story? Which might we consider resilient? Or sustainable? In Part I, we discussed *trade-offs*. What are some of the trade-offs at work in the story of A&B?

II. SURFACE WATER APPORTIONMENT SYSTEMS

In Chapter 2, we described a small sampling of the many social, economic, and environmental challenges facing water resources and their associated ecosystems:

- There is rapid depletion of the resource, in some cases, well in excess of renewable capacities.
- Species relying on water-based habits, such as wetlands, are threatened by the loss of these habitats.
- Globally, agriculture (a topic we turn to in Chapter 4) is responsible for 70% of freshwater use, while energy production (a topic we discuss in Chapter 6) is responsible for 15% of freshwater use.
- Numerous countries and millions of people live under conditions described as "water stressed."
- Saltwater intrusion threatens many freshwater sources and their associated ecosystems.
- Equity challenges concerning water arise in both quality and quantity across the globe.

In Chapter 2, we also looked closely at how overuse of a water-based resource—the Mississippi mussel—can result in unintended consequences that affect the resilience and sustainability of social-ecological systems. Further, when those resources are strained the social-ecological systems can collapse, leading to social, economic, and environmental ramifications.

Water use involves consumption, such as supplying municipal water needs and supporting agricultural activity, but uses such as energy production and instream ecosystem protection also extract or reserve water. In this section, we describe in more detail the legal frameworks that govern these uses of water. We then explore their relationship to the use or misuse of water and question how the frameworks impact the resilience and sustainability of water resources.

In the United States, there are three major legal frameworks for water apportionment: the riparian system, the prior appropriation system, and a hybrid of these two systems. States east of Kansas generally use the riparian system, which treats water as common property, because water is readily available.[12] However, as the demand for water has outpaced supply, some states have regulated the traditional common law of riparian rights to keep competing uses from interfering with each other and ensuring that all uses are reasonable.[13] States west of Missouri use the prior appropriation and hybrid systems because water is scarce and "the right to use water is carefully defined in terms of the location, duration, amount, and priority of use."[14] Prior appropriation systems operate as private rights with state agencies administering these rights based on the concept of first in time.[15]

A. The Riparian System

The riparian system, as adopted by the states from the English common law, is based upon real property ownership adjacent to a natural water body.[16] Riparian landowners were historically entitled to the "natural flow" of water, unimpaired in terms of quantity and quality, with the ability to withdraw water for domestic uses but not for off-tract uses.[17] This limitation on riparian rights to on-tract uses eventually resulted in a retreat from the natural flow doctrine of English common law to the "reasonable use" doctrine of riparianism in the United States.[18] Some states implemented this shift by statute while others relied upon judicial decision. The Restatement (Second) of Torts describes the prevailing U.S. rule of reasonable use riparianism as follows:

> *There is, in its strictest application, no primary right in anyone to have the natural integrity of a stream or lake maintained for its own sake. The primary right*

---

[12] Joseph W. Dellapenna, *The Evolution of Riparianism in the United States*, 95 Marq. L. Rev. 53, 53 (2011).

[13] *See id* at 53-54.

[14] *Id.* at 54.

[15] *See id.*

[16] *See id.* at 55-64. Riparian rights generally do not attach to artificial watercourses, such as canals, ditches, lakes formed from reservoirs and dams, or other waterways that are created by human intervention. *Id.*

[17] *See id.* at 58.

[18] *See id.* at 65-66. For an in-depth exploration of the history of riparianism and challenges to this general understanding of the development of riparian rights from natural flow, to reasonable use, and finally to regulation, see *id.*

of a riparian proprietor is to receive protection for his reasonable use of the stream or lake from an unreasonable use by another.[19]

The Restatement (Second) of Torts §850a lists the factors to determine whether a particular use of water is reasonable:

(1) purpose;
(2) suitability to the water body;
(3) economic value;
(4) social value;
(5) harm caused;
(6) potential to coordinate with competing uses;
(7) temporal priority in relation to competing uses; and
(8) the justice of imposing a loss on the use.[20]

Note the inclusion of economic and social considerations. Environmental considerations are not directly stated, however, they could be embedded in the consideration of "harm caused." Note, however, that the first sentence quoted from the Restatement states that there is no "primary right in anyone to have the natural integrity of a stream or lake maintained for its own sake."

Increased development, population growth, and water shortages from drought and climate change have strained the **quantity and quality of water resources**. Riparian law systems have shown resiliency in the face of these conflicts by changing from the "entitlement to natural flow" approach to the "reasonable use" doctrine in common law riparianism. In addition, many riparian states have established regulatory permit systems to replace or supplement common law riparianism to respond to the increasing concerns about the sustainability of our water supply for municipal use, agricultural use, and environmental and recreational uses. These changes in our legal regime of riparianism have shown the resilience of this system as our common law systems of distributing water give way to a regulatory scheme controlled by local, state, and federal government.

Traditional examples of riparian systems are found in New England states, such as Connecticut and Massachusetts. Both of these states at one point "recognize[d] the common-law doctrine that riparian owners have the right to the undiminished flow of the stream free from contamination or burden upon it."[21] Connecticut followed this natural flow theory of

---

[19] Restatement (Second) of Torts §850A (1979) as discussed in Joseph L. Sax et al., Legal Control of Water Resources: Cases and Materials 57-61 (4th ed. 2006).
[20] Restatement (Second) of Torts, *supra* note 19. Note that these factors are very similar to the factors suggested in the Restatement to determine whether there is an unreasonable use of property that results in nuisance liability.
[21] Connecticut v. Massachusetts, 282 U.S. 660, 662 (1931) (dismissing Connecticut's suit to enjoin Massachusetts from diverting water from the Connecticut river watershed to provide water for Boston and the surrounding area as there was no presently threatened injury to Connecticut).

riparian rights until 1982, when it switched to the reasonable use theory and a regulated riparian system by enacting a statutory diversion act.[22] Massachusetts follows the reasonable use theory for both streams and lakes,[23] as does Maine, which made the transition from the natural flow theory to reasonable use in 1885.[24] However, Maine has not transitioned to regulated riparianism, perhaps because of its abundant supply of water and relatively low population or overall demand on the water resource.[25] Midwestern farming states such as Iowa also adopted the riparian model and incorporated reasonable use into the common law,[26] and then evolved into regulated riparianism.[27]

IOWA CODE ANNOTATED §455B.265. PERMITS FOR DIVERSION, STORAGE, AND WITHDRAWAL—FEES AUTHORIZED

1. In its consideration of applications for permits, the department shall give priority in processing to persons in the order that the applications are received, except where the application of this processing priority system prevents the prompt approval of routine applications or where the public health, safety, or welfare will be threatened by delay. If the department determines after investigation that the diversion, storage, or withdrawal is consistent with the principles and policies of beneficial use and ensuring conservation, the department shall grant a permit. . . .

3. Permits shall be granted for a period of ten years; however, permits for withdrawal of water may be granted for less than ten years if geological data on the capacity of the aquifer and the rate of its recharge are indeterminate, and permits for the storage of water may be granted for the life of the structure unless revoked by the department. A permit granted shall remain as an appurtenance of the land described in the permit through the date specified in the permit and any extension of the permit or until an earlier date when the permit or its extension is canceled under section 455B.271. Upon application for a permit prior to the termination date specified in the permit, a permit may be renewed by the department for a period of ten years.

---

[22] *See* City of Waterbury v. Town of Washington, 800 A.2d 1102, 1155 (Conn. 2002).

[23] Howard J. Alperin, SUMMARY OF BASIC LAW 14C, §15.86 (4th ed.).

[24] *See* Lockwood Co. v. Lawrence, 77 Me. 297, 316 (1885) (citing the Massachusetts Supreme Court decision in Merrifield v. Lombard, 13 Allen 16 (Mass. 1866) in support of its transition).

[25] Bradford Bowman, *Instream Flow Regulation: Plugging the Holes in Maine's Water Law*, 54 ME. L. REV. 287, 288-289 (2002) (advocating for regulation of consumptive water uses to protect water resources); *see also* Dellapenna, *supra* note 12, at 86 n.178 (noting that "[a]s of 2011, [the author's] own compilation [of states adopting regulated riparianism] includes Alabama, Arkansas, Connecticut, Delaware, Florida, Georgia, Hawaii, Iowa, Kentucky, Maryland, Massachusetts, Michigan, Minnesota, Mississippi, New Jersey, New York, North Carolina, Virginia, and Wisconsin. In several of these states, the regulatory system has not been implemented or has only been partially implemented.").

[26] Willis v. City of Perry, 60 N.W. 727, 729 (Iowa 1894) (affirming the natural flow doctrine of riparian rights, but noting that if "a proprietor puts the water to an extraordinary or artificial use, he must do so in such a manner as not to interfere with its lawful use by others above or below him upon the same stream.").

[27] Iowa Code §455B.265 (2013).

4. Permits for aquifer storage and recovery shall be granted for a period of twenty years or the life of the project, whichever is less, unless revoked by the department. The department shall adopt rules pursuant to chapter 17A relating to information an applicant for a permit shall submit to the department. At a minimum, the information shall include engineering, investigation, and evaluation information requisite to assure protection of the groundwater resource, and assurances that an aquifer storage and recovery site shall not unreasonably restrict other uses of the aquifer. . . .

Question

1. As set forth above, those owning protected property interests along the water receive riparian rights. This system of allocating rights connects land ownership to the provision of water. What equity issues can arise in such a situation? Who can own land? Is it the same group of people who rely on water? Should we connect land ownership with water rights? Does riparianism promote the sustainable use of maintaining an adequate and healthy water system? Does it encourage a resilient water system in the face of supply variability?

B. The Prior Appropriation System

The prior appropriation system is based on the theory that, unlike the riparian system, land ownership is not required to obtain a right to use water. Instead, a person acquires a water right when water is taken from a natural watercourse and applied with due diligence to a "beneficial use" without waste. There are no limitations as to where the water is used, which can be outside of the natural watershed, but modernly most states require that a permit be obtained and that the proposed use is in the public interest. The water right cannot be held as a future investment, but must be applied to beneficial use or it will be abandoned or forfeited, unless such nonuse is allowed for conservation purposes by the regulating statutes. Priority over other users is based upon the date when the water was first beneficially used, and in times of scarcity, junior appropriators may be required to stop taking water from a watercourse so that the senior appropriators with the earlier appropriation dates will be able to meet their needs for beneficial water use.[28] The definition of "beneficial use" may vary from state to state. For example, Colorado statutorily defines

---

[28] Sax et al., *supra* note 19, at 124-126.

beneficial use as the "use of that amount of water that is reasonable and appropriate under reasonably efficient practices to accomplish without waste the purpose for which the appropriation is lawfully made."[29]

The more arid western states developed appropriative rights to meet "increasing demands to divert water for mining, irrigation, industrial, and municipal uses that could not be resolved satisfactorily even through recourse to the reasonable use theory" of riparianism.[30] Gold miners, unable to obtain title to land with expediency, instead trespassed and took the land and water needed to find gold.[31] The "first in time, first in right" concept settled disputes without the benefit of organized government and functioning laws in the Wild West.[32] Mining customs recognized these mining claims and launched the prior appropriation doctrine based on first possession.[33] Alaska, Arizona, Colorado, Idaho, Montana, Nevada, New Mexico, Utah, and Wyoming are pure appropriation states, while Kansas, North Dakota, Oregon, South Dakota, Texas, and Washington changed from riparianism to appropriation.[34] Colorado stands out as a prior appropriation state that has an extensive administrative structure with state water courts to manage water rights, whereas the other states use complex permit and management systems to orchestrate water usage. In addition, statutory class actions use the **general adjudication system** to establish the priority rights of appropriators of a particular watercourse resulting in a court decree to document "paper rights" and settle disputes over water rights to a water basin.[35]

COLORADO REVISED STATUTES ANNOTATED §37-92-203. WATER JUDGES—JURISDICTION

(1) There is established in each water division[36] the position of water judge of the district courts of all counties situated entirely or partly within the division. Said district courts collectively acting through the water judge have exclusive jurisdiction of water matters within the division, and no judge other than the one designated as a water judge shall act with respect to water matters in that division. . . .

---

[29] Colo. Rev. Stat. §37-92-103(4) (2017).
[30] See Dellapenna, *supra* note 12, at 76.
[31] Id. at 78.
[32] Id. at 79.
[33] Id. at 80.
[34] Sax et al., *supra* note 19, at 138.
[35] Id. at 132-133.
[36] Pursuant to Colo. Rev. Stat. §37-92-201 (2009), seven water divisions are defined by drainage basins in Colorado. For example, Division 1 "consists of all lands in the state of Colorado in the drainage basins of the South Platte river, the Big Laramie river, the Arikaree river, the north and south forks of the Republican river, the Smokey Hill river, Sandy and Frenchman creeks, and streams tributary to said rivers and creeks." Id. at (1)(a).

COLORADO REVISED STATUTES ANNOTATED §37-92-302. APPLICATIONS FOR WATER RIGHTS OR CHANGES OF SUCH RIGHTS—PLANS FOR AUGMENTATION

(1)(a) Any person who desires a determination of a water right or a conditional water right and the amount and priority thereof, including a determination that a conditional water right has become a water right by reason of the completion of the appropriation, a determination with respect to a change of a water right, approval of a plan for augmentation, finding of reasonable diligence, approval of a proposed or existing exchange of water . . . or approval to use water outside the state . . . shall file with the water clerk a verified application setting forth facts supporting the ruling sought. . . .

(b) Any person, including the state engineer, who wishes to oppose the application may file with the water clerk a verified statement of opposition setting forth facts as to why the application should not be granted or why it should be granted only in part or on certain conditions. . . .

New Mexico's experience with the **prior appropriation system** and the **pueblo rights doctrine** highlights the features of appropriation, also called the "Colorado doctrine," which was adopted by New Mexico and other western states instead of riparianism because of its suitability to arid regions.[37] In *State ex rel. Martinez v. City of Las Vegas*,[38] the New Mexico Supreme Court overruled its earlier case, *Cartwright v. Public Service Company of New Mexico*, which had adopted the pueblo rights doctrine.[39] The **pueblo rights doctrine** "entitles a municipality to take as much water from an adjacent water course as necessary for municipal purposes and permits expansion of the right to accommodate increased municipal needs due to population increases."[40] The dispute in *State ex rel. Martinez* arose from a **general adjudication** of the Pecos River system water rights involving pueblo settlements on the Gallinas River in the 1800s, which later consolidated in 1970 to form the City of Las Vegas.[41]

The "fundamental precepts" of the prior appropriation doctrine as established by New Mexico **exclude the equitable apportionment** of water rights and instead limit the right to use water to the amount of water an appropriator can apply to a **beneficial use**.[42] The concept of beneficial use promotes the efficient use of water and protects the

---

[37] Snow v. Abalos, 140 P. 1044, 1048 (N.M. 1914).
[38] State *ex rel*. Martinez v. City of Las Vegas, 89 P.3d 47 (N.M. 2004) (not to be confused with Las Vegas, Nevada).
[39] Cartwright v. Pub. Serv. Co. of N.M., 343 P.2d 654, 664-669 (N.M. 1958).
[40] State *ex rel*. Martinez, 89 P.3d at 48.
[41] *Id.* at 49 (noting that the pueblo of Nuestra Señora de Las Dolores de Las Vegas was established by a grant from the Republic of Mexico in 1835 and became part of the United States in 1848 based on the Treaty of Guadalupe Hidalgo, and another settlement on the river was established in 1841).
[42] *Id.* at 57-58.

conservation and preservation of water supplies.[43] After the initial appropriation, water users have a reasonable time to put the water to beneficial use and the use will "relate back" to the date of initial appropriation to establish priority. The pueblo rights doctrine does not require the municipality to use water beneficially within a reasonable time or forfeit the right, but instead allows indefinite expansion of the rights based on increasing the population. Because this indefinite expansion creates uncertainty, others may refrain from making beneficial use of water for fear they will invest in appropriating water, but future pueblo growth will interfere with their investment. Because municipalities cannot forfeit the pueblo right, public waters may be underutilized, and the efficient use of this precious resource in an arid region is thus incompatible with the pueblo doctrine.[44]

Every prior appropriation state, except Colorado, now requires appropriators to acquire rights using a regulated permitting system. While the main features of the system still allow unappropriated water from natural streams to be appropriated for beneficial use, permitting agencies play a much greater role in determining whether: such use is in the public interest; water needs to be reserved for instream use or future development; and how granting these permits may affect water quality and pollution control. In California, the State Water Resources Control Board, in determining whether there is unappropriated water available, will take into consideration "the amount of water needed for protection of instream uses and other public trust uses."[45]

Questions

1. As set forth above, in traditional prior appropriation states the first person to put a quantity of water to "beneficial use" has the protected legal right to continue to use that quantity of water for that use. When viewed as a "first in time, first in right" doctrine, what perverse incentives are created by the prior appropriation system when the sustainability of the water supply and the resilience of ecosystems depend upon a viable water source, particularly in arid regions? Does it depend on how "beneficial use" is defined? Consider Colorado's definition.

   Colorado Revised Statutes Annotated §37-92-103. Definitions

   (4) "Beneficial use" means the use of that amount of water that is reasonable and appropriate under reasonably efficient practices to accomplish without

---

[43] *Id.* at 59.
[44] *Id.* at 59-60.
[45] Sax et al., *supra* note 19, at 219.

waste the purpose for which the appropriation is lawfully made. Without limiting the generality of the previous sentence, "beneficial use" includes:

> *(a) The impoundment of water for firefighting or storage for any purpose for which an appropriation is lawfully made, including recreational, fishery, or wildlife purposes;*
>
> *(b) The diversion of water by a county, municipality, city and county, water district, water and sanitation district, water conservation district, or water conservancy district for recreational in-channel diversion purposes; and*
>
> *(c) For the benefit and enjoyment of present and future generations, the appropriation by the state of Colorado in the manner prescribed by law of such minimum flows between specific points or levels for and on natural streams and lakes as are required to preserve the natural environment to a reasonable degree.*

2. An important part of the prior appropriation doctrine is that subsequent users can take the remaining water for their own beneficial use, but they may not impinge on the rights of previous users. What if a subsequent user has a better use, but it would impinge on a previous user and both uses are "beneficial uses"? For example, what if a severe drought results in thousands of people not having adequate water because they have a junior interest to a prior appropriator, who has rights to extract water for intensive crop growth, such as almonds and pistachios? While the result may be clear pursuant to the prior appropriation doctrine, the doctrine is human-made law. We have to ask whether conditions may arise that require a rethinking of the law to sustain both the human population and the economic well-being of the agricultural enterprise. Other than first-in-time priority, how do we make these choices?

3. "Leaving water 'in place' would have been incomprehensible to almost all nineteenth-century westerners because it represented the waste of a valuable resource."[46] In addition, "[t]he prior appropriation doctrine encourages and rewards diversion and consumptive use of water, resulting in a failure to account for or protect instream flows during most of the first 100 to 150 years of western water law development."[47] How then should prior appropriation states sustain the instream flows necessary for ecosystem management?

---

[46] A. Dan Tarlock, *The Future of Prior Appropriation in the New West*, 41 Nat. Resources J. 769, 771 (2001).
[47] Janet C. Neuman, Protecting Instream Flows in Prior Appropriation States: Legal and Policy Issues, Water and Growth in the West §I.A. (2000).

4. Similar to many of the laws we cover, the prior appropriation doctrine is anthropogenic in its focus. In other words, humans are the appropriators. We have the protected ability to procure water rights pursuant to the prior appropriation doctrine. How do we protect flora and fauna? Should they also have protected rights to water? Water is necessary for ecosystems to survive — many of which pre-dated the prior appropriation doctrine. How, if at all, does this and should this fit into the prior appropriation doctrine?

C. The Hybrid System

The **hybrid system** exists in California, Oklahoma, and Nebraska and contains elements of both riparianism and appropriation that operate together in managing water use. The **development of a hybrid system** is illustrated by California's water system, which combines riparian rights with the prior appropriation doctrine. In 1967, the California Supreme Court in *Joslin v. Marin Municipal Water District*[48] addressed the conflict between a municipal water district, which appropriated water for municipal use by constructing a dam across a creek, and riparian owners adjoining the creek. The riparian owners complained that the dam disrupted the normal flow of water and reduced the rock and gravel deposited on their land.[49] The riparian owners operated a rock and gravel business on their land and alleged that the reduction in deposits negatively impacted the value of their land.[50] The *Joslin* court briefly reviewed the history of California water law, which began with the recognition of prior appropriation rights for gold miners, who did not own land adjoining streams, and riparian rights for landowners relying on adjoining streams for agriculture and domestic uses.[51] State regulations require that appropriators who obtained their rights after 1914 obtain a permit or license from the State Water Resources Control Board; however, those who obtained appropriative rights before 1914 and all riparian owners are not required to obtain a permit or authorization to exercise their water rights.[52]

California's prior appropriation and riparian rights came into conflict early it its history. In 1886, the court in *Lux v. Haggin* "declared 'that the rights of the riparian owners to the use of the waters of the abutting stream were paramount to the rights of any other persons thereto; that such rights were parcel of the land; and that any diminution of the stream against the will of the riparian owner by other persons was an actionable

---

[48] Joslin v. Marin Mun. Water Dist., 429 P.2d 889 (Cal. 1967).
[49] *Id.* at 890.
[50] *Id.* at 891.
[51] *Id.* at 891-892.
[52] Cal. Farm Bureau Fed'n v. State Water Res. Control Bd., 247 P.3d 112, 117-118 (Cal. 2011).

injury.'"[53] After the court reiterated its support of riparian rights seniority over appropriators in *Herminghaus v. Southern California Edison Co.* in 1926, legislators amended the California Constitution in 1928 to apply a rule of reasonable use to all water rights, either riparian or appropriative.[54] The *Joslin* court determined that even if the use of the riparian landowners of gathering rock and gravel was beneficial to their lands, "the use of such waters as an agent to expose or to carry and deposit sand, gravel and rock, is as a matter of law unreasonable within the meaning of the constitutional amendment."[55] Thus, California recognizes the reasonable use rule as applied to both riparians and prior appropriators. However, the determination of what constitutes reasonable use depends on the circumstances and may change over time. California courts have found that diverting water to flood land in order to dispose of gophers and squirrels is not a reasonable use,[56] nor is diverting water to protect crops from frost, if it results in sudden stream flow drops that harm fish and wildlife.[57]

Light v. State Water Res. Control Bd., 173 Cal. Rptr. 3d. 200, 205-206 (Ct. App. 2014)

In April 2008, a particularly cold month in a dry year, young salmon were found to have been fatally stranded along banks of the Russian River stream system, which drains Sonoma and Mendocino Counties. Federal scientists concluded the deaths were caused by abrupt declines in water level that occurred when water was drained from the streams and sprayed on vineyards and orchards to prevent frost damage. Following a series of hearings and the preparation of an environmental impact report, the State Water Resources Control Board (Board) adopted a regulation that is likely to require a reduction in diversion of water from the stream system for frost protection, at least under certain circumstances. The regulation itself contains no substantive regulation of water use, instead delegating the task of formulating regulatory programs to local governing bodies composed of the diverting growers themselves. The regulation declares that any water use inconsistent with the programs, once they have been formulated and approved by the Board, is unreasonable and therefore prohibited. The trial court granted a writ of mandate invalidating the regulation on several grounds. We reverse.

Foremost among plaintiffs' grounds for challenging the regulation is their contention the Board lacks the regulatory authority to limit water use by riparian users and early appropriators, whose diversion is beyond the permitting authority of the Board. Although the Board

---

[53] Joslin v. Marin Mun. Water Dist., 429 P.2d 889, 892 (Cal. 1967) (quoting Lux v. Haggin, 4 P. 919 (Cal. 1884)).

[54] *Id.* at 892-893 (citing Peabody v. City of Vallejo, 40 P.2d 486, 491 (Cal. 1935) (declaring that the amendment established that: "1. The right to the use of water is limited to such water as shall be reasonably required for the beneficial use to be served. 2. Such right does not extend to the waste of water. 3. Such right does not extend to unreasonable use or unreasonable method of use or unreasonable method of diversion of water. 4. Riparian rights attach to, but to no more than so much of the flow as may be required or used consistently with this section of the Constitution.")). *Id.* at 893.

[55] *Id.* at 895-897.

[56] Tulare Irrigation Dist. v. Lindsay-Strathmore Irrigation Dist., 45 P.2d 972, 1007 (Cal. 1935).

[57] Light v. State Water Res. Control Bd., 173 Cal. Rptr. 3d 200, 222 (Ct. App. 2014).

has no authority to require such users to obtain a permit to divert, there is no question it has the power to prevent riparian users and early appropriators from using water in an unreasonable manner. We conclude that, in regulating the unreasonable use of water, the Board can weigh the use of water for certain public purposes, notably the protection of wildlife habitat, against the commercial use of water by riparian users and early appropriators. Further, the Board may exercise its regulatory powers through the enactment of regulations, as well as through the pursuit of judicial and quasi-judicial proceedings. Because this is a facial challenge, our ruling is a narrow one, grounded in the general authority of the Board; we have no occasion to rule on the validity of any particular substantive regulation that might be approved by the Board in the process of implementation.

We also conclude the Board properly found the regulation to be necessary to enforce water use statutes and did not unlawfully delegate its authority by requiring local governing bodies to formulate the substantive regulations. Finally, we find no error in the Board's certification of the environmental impact report.

Questions

1. From which water source does your community access potable water? Which entity provides that water? Compare the riparian system with the prior appropriation system to explore which would best support the sustainability of the potable water system in your community and why.

2. How would you evaluate each of the three major legal structures in regards to the sustainability of existing and future human populations, agricultural and economic uses, and ecosystems that depend upon instream flows? What are some of the key indicators or metrics you would use to assess the sustainability of the water-based system(s) you are analyzing?

3. Which of the three legal structures has demonstrated resiliency to changing climate, population increase, and the growing consumption and withdrawal uses for social and economic well-being: riparian, prior appropriation, or hybrid? Would you recommend something else? What qualities or characteristics should the law governing water contain?

D. Global Water

Water law has been traced back 1,900 years with the discovery in Turkey of a marble block from 114 A.D. that describes an ancient city's water-use management system, including water measuring and penalties for unlawful use or water pollution.[58] Some countries, such as Australia, Chile, and Spain, treat water rights similar to the western United States in that they can obtain rights through prior appropriation and separate them from land ownership to create a water market system. In Chile, the 1980 Constitution established that water rights are property rights that can be transferred, sold, or purchased, and the 1981 Water Code reinforced that a water right is private property that can be freely transferred.[59]

 In Latin America, as in many other parts of the world, water availability and quality are suffering because of poor water management and regulation, increasing and competing demands on water resources, and the adverse impact of climate change and deterioration of our ecosystems.[60] Political favoritism and economic opportunities tend to guide Latin American governments, rather than enforcing existing water laws, managing water resources, and providing all the societal needs for water.[61] In Ecuador, not only is land ownership concentrated in the hands of a few, but large national and international agribusinesses have monopolized water resources to the detriment of small, local farmers and residents.[62] Water rights in Mexico have also been concentrated in industries and large landowners, excluding indigenous and rural communities from control over watersheds, equitable water availability, and sustainable water management.[63] Peru centralized control over water resources in government and industry in the 1970s, and the poor management of these resources increased water pollution and decreased water availability to indigenous and rural communities.[64] With the increasing stresses of climate change on water resources, rural and indigenous communities will face rising constraints on water access. The rights to these resources continue to be concentrated in the hands of the politically and economically powerful who will nevertheless face increasing costs for these resources.[65]

International water law disputes tend to be resolved by combining the prior appropriation doctrine with riparianism, similar to the water doctrines of the western United States. The Harmon doctrine — credited to the United States Attorney General who in 1895 stated that "[t]he

[58] *Ancient "water law" unearthed in Laodicea*, Hurriyet Daily News (Aug. 21, 2015), http://www.hurriyet dailynews.com/ancient-water-law-unearthed-in-laodicea-.aspx?pageID = 238&nID = 87259&News CatID = 375.

[59] Lindsay B. Masters, *Free Market Environmentalism: Desalination as a Solution to Limited Water Resources in Northern Chile's Mining Industry*, 23 Colo. J. Int'l Envtl. L. & Pol'y 257, 269 (2012).

[60] Rutgerd Boelens et al., *Threats to a Sustainable Future: Water Accumulation and Conflict in Latin America*, 12 Sustainable Dev. L. & Pol'y 41, 41 (2011).

[61] *Id.*

[62] *Id.* at 42.

[63] *Id.* at 43.

[64] *Id.* 43-44.

[65] *Id.* at 45; *see also* John Vidal, *As Water Scarcity Deepens Across Latin America, Political Instability Grows*, The Guardian (Mar. 1, 2017), https://www.theguardian.com/global-development-professionals-network/2017/mar/01/water-scarcity-latin-america-political-instability (discussing disputes over water scarcity in Bolivia, Ecuador, and Peru and noting that government policies are making climate change worse through the development of extractive industries and deforestation).

fundamental principle of international law is the absolute sovereignty of every nation, as against all others, within its own territory" — was used to resolve a legal dispute among water users in Colorado, New Mexico, and Mexico over the use of Rio Grande water.[66] While the United States eventually abandoned the Harmon doctrine and instead agreed to apportion the Rio Grande waters equitably, other nations have adopted this "absolute territorial sovereignty" principle from among the four alternative principles purported to govern waters that flow through more than one nation.[67] "[A]bsolute territorial integrity, community of property in water, and restricted territorial sovereignty" are the remaining three principles.[68]

The *absolute territorial sovereignty* principle allows a riparian to "freely dispose of waters flowing through its territory" without taking into consideration demands from other riparians for continued free flow.[69] The *absolute territorial integrity* principle requires a riparian to allow a watershed to follow its natural course and may not restrict the water flow into other nations, although it concomitantly has the right to demand the continued natural flow of water coming from other nations. The *community of property in water* principle requires cooperation among riparians to vest water rights in the communal unit of riparians or proportionately divide these rights among the individual riparians. And finally, the *restricted territorial sovereignty* principle, which is the most prevalent view adopted for international water rights, requires *equitable utilization* by all riparians on an international waterway such that "'each riparian's needs are to be considered on an equal basis in relation to the needs of the other states sharing the basin.'"[70] What principle would you identify as being the most sustainable for a nation based on the consequences of scarcity of water, competing interests of nations sharing a water resource, and economic realities? What factors influence your choice? What principle would you identify as being the most resilient for dealing with scarcity, competing interests, and economics? Does your choice address water supply only or what other factors should be researched and considered?

---

[66] Ian J. Silverbrand, *Israeli-Palestinian Water Literature's Misplaced Dependence Upon Customary International Law*, 37 Envt'l L. 603, 609 (2007) (quoting Judson Harmon, Treaty of Guadalupe Hidalgo — International Law, 21 U.S. Op. Att'y Gen. 274, 281-282 (1895)).

[67] Silverbrand, *supra* note 66, at 608-609.

[68] *Id.* at 609 (citing F.J. Berber, Rivers in International Law 12 (R.K. Batstone trans., London Inst. of World Affairs ed. 1959)).

[69] Silverbrand, *supra* note 66, at 609.

[70] *Id.* at 609-611 (quoting Daniel J. Epstein, *Making the Desert Bloom: Competing for Scarce Water Resources in the Jordan River Basin*, 10 Temp. Int'l & Comp. L.J. 395, 403 (1996)).

GOVERNING A SHARED RESOURCE: RHINE RIVER

Switzerland, Liechtenstein, Austria, Germany, France, and The Netherlands are situated on the Rhine River, which provides agricultural irrigation and drinking water for millions of people. The river ends at the sea in The Netherlands. Along the way, many companies discharge pollutants into the river. For years, MDPA, a French nationalized company running one of the biggest potash mines in Europe, deposited approximately seven megatons (million tons) of salt (sodium and potassium chloride wastes) into the river in Alsace, France. Originally, France stored the salt in underground tunnels, but rain caused the salt to pollute Alsace's pure groundwater supply. When the salt began altering the ecosystem associated with the Rhine River, the countries attempted to negotiate use of the resource under numerous agreements in a variety of forms, including the Berne Convention of 1963, which established the International Commission for the Protection of the Rhine against Pollution. By 1975, it was agreed—at the First Conference of Ministers of the Member States of the Rhine Commission—that France would store about half its salt and discharge the other half into the River. The cost for storing the salt was to be divided: 30% Germany and France; 6% Switzerland; and 34% Netherlands.

Because of great opposition to storing the salt from French citizens, the French government did not store it and continued discharging it into the river. The parties then agreed to the Rhine Chloride Convention in 1976, which would have injected the salt into the ground, however, the French refused to submit this treaty for ratification. International tensions rose as the Dutch pulled their ambassador from France, and Dutch citizens sued MDPA in both Dutch and French courts. After a number of rulings from several courts, both Dutch and French courts ruled that MDPA may be liable for having adverse effects outside French territory. In 1991, the countries finally agreed that France could discharge salt so long as the chloride levels did not reach a certain point. Shortly thereafter, the issue concerning salt became moot, as MDPA depleted the potash mine and closed it. For more information, see Jon Tinker, *Europe's Majestic Sewer*, New Scientist 194 (October 26, 1977).

Customary international law recognizes the ***doctrine of equitable utilization*** and the 1997 United Nations Convention on the Non-Navigation Uses of International Watercourses (Convention) affirmed this rule.[71] The doctrine allows multiple uses of international waters and equitably apportions these rights among different nations.[72] The International Law Association preceded the Convention and adopted general principles, called the Helsinki Rules, which entitled each nation to "a reasonable and equitable share in the beneficial uses of the waters of an international drainage basin."[73] This equitable apportionment system evolved from the western prior appropriation system as modified by the U.S. Supreme Court to resolve water disputes among states. The Court in *Kansas v. Colorado*[74] and in *Missouri v. Illinois*[75] required the states to equitably share interstate waters. In *Colorado v. New Mexico*,[76] the Court developed an approach to protect existing uses against new uses, but also to allow new valuable uses to displace existing inefficient uses by balancing the "comparative merits of different river uses over a long period of time."[77] While customary international water law recognized by the Convention is based on a property rights regime, the extent of these rights is uncertain because entitlement cannot be predicted. In addition, the Convention does not incorporate ecosystem protection within its rights regime, which will inhibit adaptation to changing climate conditions.[78] Disputes between states can be resolved by negotiation or by submitting the dispute to international tribunals or to arbitration.

In addition to using customary international water laws to resolve disputes as briefly described above, nations have also resolved disputes over international watersheds by ***international treaties***, such as the Berne Convention of 1963 and the Rhine Chloride Convention. These treaties may be used to allocate water resources and provide methods for resolving disputes in the future. For example, the United States and Mexico have entered into treaties to allocate water from the Rio

---

[71] A. Dan Tarlock, *How Well Can International Water Allocation Regimes Adapt to Global Climate Change?*, 9 J. TRANSNAT'L L. & POL'Y 423, 432-433 (2000).

[72] *Id.*

[73] *See* Sax et al., *supra* note 19, at 891 (quoting International Law Assn., Report of the 52nd Conference, Helsinki Rules on the Use of the Waters of International Rivers, art. IV (1966), and discussing the subsequent adoption of the Seoul Rules on the Law of International Groundwater Resources in 1986 and the adoption of the Berlin Rules to update and incorporate the previous rules in 2004).

[74] Kansas v. Colorado, 206 U.S. 46 (1907).

[75] Missouri v. Illinois, 200 U.S. 496 (1906).

[76] Colorado v. New Mexico, 459 U.S. 176, 190 (1982).

[77] Tarlock, *supra* note 71, at 431.

[78] *Id.* at 433-434.

Grande and the Colorado River, and the United States and Canada have used treaties to establish appropriate uses of the St. Mary River, the Milk River, as well as other shared basins such as the Great Lakes.[79] Palestine and Israel have entered into a formal agreement to resolve the distribution of water between these two territories.[80] The Declaration of Principles from 1993 endorsed a restricted territorial sovereignty principle by using the concept of "equitable utilization of joint water resources."[81] Jordan and Israel also reached agreement in a treaty that included sharing the Jordan River waters.[82] The Nile Waters Agreement of 1959 allocated water between Egypt and Sudan, but these two countries use 90% of water withdrawals.[83] Because Egypt and Sudan are desert countries, by necessity they must divert more water for irrigation and domestic use than countries to the south, which receive much more rainfall. However, the other nations within the Nile watershed (Burundi, Kenya, Rwanda, Tanzania, Uganda, Zaire, and Ethiopia) currently use less than 10% of the water, but with population growth, economic development, and global climate change, political conflict over this incomplete allocation will likely increase.[84]

E. Strategy to Facilitate Implementation #1: Addressing Collective Action Challenges

The legal frameworks governing water use and management encourage certain behaviors. These behaviors, in turn, affect water systems, disputes over water resources, and water systems' resilience and sustainability. Making the connection between laws, human behaviors, and impacts on natural resources is a key part of assessing and understanding resilience and sustainability.

Understanding how and why humans make decisions resulting in vulnerable and unsustainable conditions is made clearer by an understanding of collective action challenges ("CACs"). The CAC framework helps explain how social and ecological systems overlap to more completely predict and explain human behaviors. Understanding CACs also helps formulate decisions that can lead to resilient and sustainable

---

[79] Sax et al., *supra* note 19, at 893-902.
[80] Silverbrand, *supra* note 66, at 616-618.
[81] *Id.* at 618.
[82] *Id.* at 618-619.
[83] Tarlock, *supra* note 71, at 444-446.
[84] *Id.*

systems. Many disputes over water, whether concerning individuals or subnational governments as in *Joslin v. Marin Municipal Water District*[85] or nations as in the Rhine River dispute, involve some aspect of collective action challenges, which in some instances become intractable and lead to destruction of the resource. Understanding CACs can help identify problematic areas in the law that may encourage behaviors relative to CACs.

1. GENERAL DESCRIPTION OF COLLECTIVE ACTION CHALLENGES (CACs)

CACs arise when multiple individuals and/or entities—called "actors"—have equal access and rights to shared, depletable resources, called "common pool resources." A common pool resource is a shared resource. Typical common pool resources are part of many natural resources, such as fisheries,[86] forests,[87] and rivers.[88] A common pool resource can be distinguished from resources in an *open access regime* in which no one is excluded, for example, fish on the high seas.

According to some scholars, actors using common resources make choices for advancing their self-interest. Further, actors can be individuals, corporate entities, public governments, and others. When actors are encouraged to use a common pool resource for their short-term benefit, but to the long-term detriment of all actors, their use can lead to the deterioration of the common pool resource, to the point of complete depletion or ruin of the resource. This is commonly known as the "tragedy of the commons," popularized by Garrett Hardin's *The Tragedy of the Commons.* Hardin considered it a tragedy because individuals' actions collectively led to complete ruin of the resource. The excerpted book chapter below describes CACs, common pool resources, and Hardin's *The Tragedy of the Commons.*

---

[85] Joslin v. Marin Mun. Water Dist., 429 P.2d 889 (Cal. 1967).
[86] *See, e.g.,* Elinor Ostrom, GOVERNING THE COMMONS: THE EVOLUTION OF INSTITUTIONS FOR COLLECTIVE ACTION 144-146 (1990).
[87] *See, e.g.,* Clark C. Gibson et al., *Explaining Deforestation: The Role of Local Institutions, in* PEOPLE AND FORESTS: COMMUNITIES, INSTITUTIONS, AND GOVERNANCE 5-6 (Clark C. Gibson et al. eds., 2000).
[88] *See, e.g.,* Michael V. McGinnis, *On the Verge of Collapse: The Columbia River System, Wild Salmon and the Northwest Power Planning Council,* 35 NAT. RESOURCES J. 63, 75-76 (1995).

PUBLIC GOODS

"Public goods" are also a type of non-excludable resource. However, unlike common pool resources, public goods are *not depletable*. Thus, when one person uses the resource, it does not diminish the amount available to the others. Public good scholarship has characterized air as a form of public good, as well as "certain forms of knowledge and cultural resources. . . . [C]ommunities come together to share knowledge or culture with each other openly and freely, they create resources that are themselves public goods." Brigham Daniels, Blake Hudson, *Our Constitutional Commons*, 49 GA. L. REV. 995 (2015); *see also* Robert O. Keohane & Elinor Ostrom, *Introduction*, *in* LOCAL COMMONS AND GLOBAL INTERDEPENDENCE: HETEROGENEITY AND COOPERATION IN TWO DOMAINS (Robert O. Keohane & Elinor Ostrom eds., 1995); Margaret A. McKean, *Common Property: What Is It, What Is It Good for, and What Makes It Work?*, *in* PEOPLE AND FORESTS: COMMUNITIES, INSTITUTIONS, AND GOVERNANCE (Clark C. Gibson et al. eds., 2000).

Jonathan Rosenbloom, *Defining "Nature" as a Common Pool Resource*

IN ENVIRONMENTAL LAW AND CONTRASTING IDEAS OF NATURE: A CONSTRUCTIVIST APPROACH, (KEITH HIROKAWA ED. 2014)

One of the many ways in which we attempt to study resource use and conservation is to label nature and individual natural resources as "common pool resources." . . . Applying the common pool resource definition to [various parts of] nature incorporates several legal, societal, behavioral, and cultural concepts intended to capture the intricate and complex place where nature and the management of nature . . . meet. That intersection involves the coming together of two very different systems: one, a dynamic, diverse ecological system that includes many forms of natural capital, such as wetlands, forests, and water; and the other, a human-made, multijurisdictional, multilayered system of governance. . . .

Commons scholars have identified two key characteristics that are inherent in common pool resources: depletability and nonexcludability. . . . As a simple illustration of a depletable and nonexcludable resource, assume fisheries are labeled as a common pool resource. Assume also that any fish caught or consumed by one fisher[] is no longer available to the other fisher[]. This illustrates the *depletability* of the resource. Further, the open nature and largeness of the ocean make it very difficult to exclude any one fisher[] from continuing to consume the resource, exhibiting the *nonexcludability* of the resource. . . .

In *The Tragedy of the Commons*, Garrett Hardin described what he believed to be the inevitable result of allowing a common pool resource to be unregulated and not privatized. . . . Hardin theorized that the open nature of the commons allows each actor, or in the example, each fisher[], to make a rational calculation to continually consume the resource, or harvest the fish, in an effort to maximize personal economic gain. The rational actor will exploit the resource, Hardin stated, because he will gain the full benefit of utilizing the resource but will externalize, or transfer, almost all of the detriment from his use of the resource across the entire pool of users. On making a "short-term cost-benefit analysis," each appropriator perceives himself in competition with the other appropriators and makes a "rational" decision to take as much of the resource as quickly as possible or risk suffering from the other actors' overuse of the resource. . . . [T]he result, Hardin concluded, is destruction of the resource, as all actors will seek to improve their position and will overconsume the commons resource. . . .

"Externalities" are critical to a collective action analysis. When confronted with a common pool resource, one actor's utilization of the resource not only benefits that actor, but also negatively affects other actors. This shifting of costs is known as an "externality." According to Hardin, these externalities motivate actors to use the resource as quickly as possible or risk losing the resource to other's consumption.

———————

Identification of the relevant actors and designation of the resource as a "common pool resource" is important as it will influence the CACs analysis and the policies based on the analysis. The list of recognized resources in which CAC arise continues to expand and now includes sources beyond natural resources, including intellectual property, genomes, parking spaces, governance systems, economic systems, and many others. Brigham Daniels & Blake Hudson, *Our Constitutional Commons*, 49 GA. L. REV. 995 (2015) (citing numerous "new commons resources" including medical care, prisons, government budgets, email inboxes, federal systems of government, and presidential primaries).

2. SPECIFIC DESCRIPTION OF CAC's RELEVANCE TO R&S

An understanding of CACs helps address the complexities of assessing R&S by capturing some of the influences that motivate decisions relative to social-ecological systems. Laws often require certain behaviors or decisions. CAC analysis is valuable as it *helps explicate behaviors* and the reasons individuals or entities make certain decisions relative to common pool resources. It also helps us understand how those decisions can lead to brittle or unsustainable systems. For example, below we discuss the Rule of Capture and its influence over certain behaviors and decisions. We then connect those decisions to CAC as a way to understand the law and determine whether it encourages or discourages decisions that lead to resilient and sustainable systems.

In addition, the process of evaluating CAC analyses requires an *interdisciplinary approach* that mirrors the interdisciplinary nature of R&S. CACs account for a multitude of disciplines to understand how social and economic systems interrelate and potentially deteriorate ecological systems. Understanding potential CACs helps to project future behaviors and determine what might influence people to make certain decisions in the future.

Central to a CAC analysis is the idea that resources can be *depleted and exhausted*, making the systems based on them, in many cases, both unsustainable and non-resilient. Many areas around the world continue to experience an increase in population and per capita consumption, straining many resources. For example, one *Nature* report indicated that only 10% of all large fish, including tuna, swordfish, and marlin are left in the sea.[89] "Since 1950, with the onset of industrialized fisheries, we have rapidly reduced the resource base to less than 10 percent — not just in some areas, not just for some stocks, but for entire communities of these large fish species from the tropics to the poles. . . . The sustainability of fisheries is being severely compromised worldwide."[90] Understanding the prevalent CACs can help explain some of the motivations encouraging overfishing and depletion of the resource.

A CAC analysis may help explain why decisions were made that pushed a resource system over a threshold leading to a regime change. "Assessing sustainability involves considering what the limits to all systems, natural and human-built, are, and whether those limits can be changed to increase their ability to accommodate new needs and opportunities."[91] Surpassing a system's threshold often stems from structuring the law governing resource allocation in a way that raises CACs and encourages certain behaviors. Thus, understanding whether a system is subject to CACs and, if so, how those challenges are impacting system use and management may help explain why that system is trending toward unsustainability and vulnerability.

---

[89] Ransom A. Myers & Boris Worm, *Rapid Worldwide Depletion of Predatory Fish Communities*, 423 Nature 280 (2003).

[90] National Geographic News, *Big-Fish Stocks Fall 90 Percent Since 1950, Study Says*, Nat'l Geographic (May 15, 2003), http://news.nationalgeographic.com/news/2003/05/0515_030515_fish-decline.html; *see also* United Nations Food and Agriculture Organization (FAO), *General Situation of World Fish Stocks*, http://www.fao.org/newsroom/common/ecg/1000505/en/stocks.pdf (of the 600 marine fish stocks monitored by the United Nations Food and Agriculture Organization, 52% are "fully exploited" (meaning the fishery has "no expected room for further expansion"), 17% are "overexploited" (meaning "[t]he fishery is being exploited at above a level which is believed to be sustainable in the long term . . . and a higher risk of stock depletion/collapse"), and 7% are "depleted" (meaning "[c]atches are well below historical levels, irrespective of the amount of fishing effort exerted")).

[91] Wayne Feiden et al., Assessing Sustainability: A Guide for Local Governments 18 (APA Planning Advisory Service 2011).

GLOBAL FOOTPRINT

There are many ways to explore resource exhaustion. One, set forth by the Global Footprint Network, measures human impact on ecological systems. It measures both individual and country impacts to determine whether carrying capacities are being exceeded. In its National Footprint Accounts (2015 Edition) it noted that the global population has a total ecological impact per person of about 2.7 global hectares ("GHA") (GHA encompasses the average productivity of all biologically productive areas on Earth in a given year), while populations in the United Kingdom and the United States are about 4.2 and 6.8 GHAs, respectively, per capita. The Report also indicated that the total global biocapacity is about 1.7 GHA, while the United Kingdom and United States have about 1.4 and 3.7, respectively. These numbers led the Global Footprint Network to declare on August 13, 2015, "humanity has used up nature's budget for the entire year" in less than eight months.

Questions and Notes

1. A number of scholars on a number of fronts have challenged Hardin's projections as to the inevitable result of CACs and his solutions to avoid that result — higher-level government regulation and privatizing property rights. Some scholars identify additional influences that may alter actors' decisions when confronted with CACs. *See, e.g.,* Mark Granovetter, *Economic Action and Social Structure: The Problem of Embeddedness*, 91 Am. J. Sociology 481 (1985) (discussing embeddedness); Richard Thaler, The Winner's Curse: Paradoxes and Anomalies of Economic Life, 96-98 (1992) (noting the willingness of people to contribute to the public good despite motivations to consume resources); Elinor Ostrom, *A Behavioral Approach to the Rational Choice Theory of Collective Action*, 92 Am. Pol. Sci. Rev. 1 (1998) (seeking to "expand the range of rational choice models we use" including situational variables that affect the cost-benefit analysis); Elinor Ostrom, Governing the Commons: The Evolution of Institutions for Collective Action 58-103 (1990) (observing certain characteristics when individuals collaborate to successfully manage CAC); Daniel Kahneman et al., *Fairness as a Constraint on Profit Seeking: Entitlements in the Market*, 76 Am. Econ. Rev. 728 (1986) (finding that actors act contrary to self-interest due to concerns of fairness).

2. Consider CACs in the context of prior appropriation and riparian rights. What types of behaviors do those laws tend to encourage? Do they establish a framework in which CACs are more or less likely to occur? Answering these questions requires us to understand: the

legal frameworks; CACs; and how the legal frameworks help create or resolve CACs.

3. Consider Hardin's *The Tragedy of the Commons* in the context of subsidies. In Hardin's classic model, the commons is a closed system and each rational actor competes against the others for limited resources. What if a management body overseeing the system initiated some type of subsidy? Could it solve the CACs? The body could offer to pay money directly to any actor who exercises control, for example, limits their use of water. Or, if the actors are primarily interested in grazing animals to feed themselves, the government could offer to pay part of their grocery bill. Or, instead of trying to figure out what the actors are ultimately seeking, the government could focus on the health of the prairie grass by subsidizing grass planting, offering to pay anyone who will plant and tend the prairie.

4. As the following quote illustrates, calling a resource a "common pool resource" raises a number of issues:

> *Once the common pool resource definition is applied to nature, we commit to viewing nature through five distinct and specific lenses. . . . [The common pool resource label] (1) contextualizes our relationship with nature as one of appropriation in which the most beneficial, if not the only, use of nature is to extract from or consume it, (2) limits the value of nature to an economic quantification of the natural resource to the exclusion of other environmental or social benefits, (3) recognizes that natural resources may be depletable, (4) confines management of natural resources to traditional property law doctrines and assumes preservation of natural capital can be achieved principally through anthropocentric management, and (5) accounts for externalities and transboundary impacts. . . .*

> *[D]o the [five] commitments properly value nature's attributes? We see what the commitments give us; the next question is do we like what we see? Answering this question includes determining whether the common pool resource definition captures the critical aspects of nature and how we want to understand nature. And, perhaps most importantly, do[es] the definition . . . help us make informed decisions to sustainably manage nature for future generations in a way that gives us a better world?*

Jonathan Rosenbloom, *Defining "Nature" as a Common Pool Resource*, in ENVIRONMENTAL LAW AND CONTRASTING IDEAS OF NATURE: A CONSTRUCTIVIST APPROACH, (Keith Hirokawa ed. 2014).

5. How do various religious and spiritual beliefs impact how we value and treat nature? *See* Shelley Ross Saxer & Daryl Fisher-Ogden, *World Religions and Clean Water Laws*, 17 DUKE ENVTL. L. & POL'Y F. 63 (2006).

6. In the prior section, we set forth the ***absolute territorial sovereignty***, which allows a riparian to "freely dispose of waters flowing through its territory," and the ***restricted territorial sovereignty principles***, which require equitable utilization by all riparians on an international waterway. Analyze and compare the absolute territorial sovereignty and restricted territorial sovereignty principles in light of CACs. Do they help avoid CACs or exacerbate them?

7. In an ideal world, how would or should water be regulated under the law to avoid CACs? Would that result in a more resilient or sustainable system? What about the idea of treating water rights as a license instead of a property right? *See* Shelley Ross Saxer, *Managing Water Rights Using Fishing Rights as a Model*, 95 Marquette L. Rev. 91 (2011).

III. GROUNDWATER SUPPLY ALLOCATION SYSTEMS AND GROUNDWATER PUMPING, MINING, AND MANAGEMENT

At the time the rules were being formulated to allocate and manage groundwater resources, little was understood about the nature and movement of underground waters. Because this resource hides beneath our feet, its importance has been neglected and its overuse has led to unsustainable depletion, disputes among users, reduced and polluted surface water flows, sinking land, and infrastructure damage and destruction.[92] With modern science, we now have the hydrogeological knowledge and tools to obtain the needed information about groundwater supplies to allocate this resource among competing users. However, gathering this information is time-consuming and expensive so that even when states have an established regulatory scheme for groundwater, the resource monitoring and enforcement of these rules are weak.[93]

Five major groundwater regimes—the rule of capture/English rule, the American reasonable use rule, the correlative rights doctrine, the Restatement (Second) of Torts reasonable use rule, and prior appropriation rule—were established without knowing the complex interconnection of underground streams, percolating water, aquifers, and surface waters. We now understand that not all underground water is considered groundwater because only water located in the zone of

---

[92] Dave Owen, *Taking Groundwater*, 91 Wash. U. L. Rev. 253, 254-255 (2013).

[93] Joseph W. Dellapenna, *A Primer on Groundwater Law*, 49 Idaho L. Rev. 265, 290 (2013) (citing City of Los Angeles v. City of San Fernando, 537 P.2d 1250 (Cal. Ct. App. 1975) to illustrate the decade-long trial delay needed to gather information about the groundwater basins in dispute); *see also* Owen, *supra* note 92, at 257.

saturation, such as aquifers and water tables, are considered groundwater, while some of the water (not groundwater) exists in the zone of aeration and cannot be extracted by wells.[94] As agriculture, urban, industry, and ecological uses tap groundwater more extensively, the legal system needs to recognize the importance of hydrogeology in connecting surface and groundwater allocation systems that define the relationship among these competing water uses.

An example of the ***delayed legal response in addressing groundwater issues*** appeared in 2014 in the midst of the drought in the western United States when many were amazed to discover that California did not have a legal structure to manage groundwater rights. Although California uses one of the five common law groundwater allocation regimes—correlative rights (described in more detail below)—until the Sustainable Groundwater Management Act of 2014 (SGMA) was enacted, California, known for its environmental leadership, had one of the weakest systems in the United States to manage groundwater extraction.[95] It essentially created a massive collective action challenge, granting individuals rights to withdraw groundwater on a first come, first service basis. On the positive side, six of the seven water basins in Southern California are "adjudicated" basins because stakeholders have negotiated the rights to pump groundwater.[96]

The drought in California was one of the worst in decades. Water tables drastically dropped due to the mandatory reductions in surface-water use, which resulted in an increase in drilling and pumping of groundwater to maintain California agriculture. In some places, land surfaces sunk up to one foot a year, roads and other infrastructure suffered damage, shallow wells were sucked dry, and natural underground storage formations have been permanently damaged.[97] While California's new legislation will for the first time regulate pumping of underground aquifers, the new law relies on local agencies to develop groundwater plans over five to seven years and gives these agencies until 2040 to implement the plans.[98] This deferred reaction to the current reality of rapidly depleting aquifers, dry wells, land subsidence, disappearance of groundwater-fed surface streams, and ecological

[94] Dellapenna, *supra* note 93, at 265.
[95] *See* Todd Fitchette, *New California Law Seeks to Cap Groundwater Overdraft*, Western Farm Press (Jan. 20, 2015), http://westernfarmpress.com/irrigation/new-california-law-seeks-cap-groundwater-overdraft; Michelle Nijhuis, *Amid Drought, New California Law Will Limit Groundwater Pumping for First Time*, Nat'l Geographic (Sept. 18, 2014), http://news.nationalgeographic.com/news/2014/09/140917-california-groundwater-law-drought-central-valley-environment-science/.
[96] Sax et al., *supra* note 19, at 511, 514 (citing William A. Blomquist, Dividing the Waters: Governing Groundwater in Southern California (1992)); *See generally*, Sax et al., *supra* note 19 at 506-517.
[97] Justin Gillis & Matt Richtel, *Beneath California Crops, Groundwater Crisis Grows*, N.Y. Times (Apr. 5, 2015), http://www.nytimes.com/2015/04/06/science/beneath-california-crops-groundwater-crisis-grows.html?_r=0.
[98] *Id.*

damage may be too late, particularly in light of the fact that in 2011, one-third of California's water came from groundwater supplies and in 2014, groundwater constituted 75% of California's total water supply.[99]

In April 2017, Governor Jerry Brown of California declared that the five-year drought was officially over after precipitation from October through March almost reached the record of California's wettest year in 1983. However, Governor Brown warned that "[t]his drought emergency is over, but the next drought could be around the corner. . . . Conservation must remain a way of life." The Los Angeles Times reported that "on the whole, this intricately plumbed state proved to be surprisingly resilient in the face of what, by some measures, was the worst drought on record. 'We did remarkably well,' said Jay Lund, director of the UC Davis Center for Watershed Sciences. Despite water shortages, agriculture — the state's biggest water user — enjoyed record revenues in 2012, 2013 and 2014 thanks to soaring nut and dairy prices."[100]

The Los Angeles Times article described the California water system as being resilient, but is it sustainable? California residents had to take drastic measures — reducing water usage by 25% — thousands of acres of agricultural land were fallowed. Groundwater was pumped to make up for the reduced surface water supply. The California Department of Water Resources produced a Water Available for Replenishment report in January 2017, with a final report set for publication in early 2018 after public comments. One of its findings noted that "[g]etting groundwater basins into a sustainable regime of pumping and recharge will not be easy or painless. Regions that have, for years, pumped more groundwater than is replenished — in some cases to the point of causing land subsidence — must either find other sources of supply or do with less."[101]

California's new legislation, SGMA, requires most of California's ground basins to achieve sustainability by 2040, but the legislation does not define the term "sustainability." While other legislation regarding water usage has used the term "safe-yield," which has been defined by the courts, the legislature chose to use the undefined term "sustainability" which will likely result in either litigation or "clean-up" legislation. *See* Todd Fitchette, *New California law seeks to cap groundwater overdraft*, Western Farm Press (Jan. 21, 2015), http://westernfarmpress.com/irrigation/new-california-law-seeks-cap-groundwater-overdraft. Given our earlier discussion of "sustainability," how would you go about suggesting a "clean-up" of the legislative language?

---

[99] Colleen Shalby, *Even Scarier than California's Shrinking Reservoirs is its Shrinking Groundwater Supply*, PBS Newshour (Mar. 20, 2015), http://www.pbs.org/newshour/rundown/californias-groundwater-loss-mean-entire-u-s/.

[100] Bettina Boxall, *Gov. Brown Declares California Drought Emergency is Over*, L.A. Times (Apr. 7, 2017), http://www.latimes.com/local/lanow/la-me-brown-drought-20170407-story.html.

[101] DWR Sustainable Groundwater Management Program, *Water Available for Replenishment*, Cal. Dep't Water Resources (Jan. 2017), http://www.water.ca.gov/groundwater/sgm/pdfs/Draft_Water_Available_For_Replenishment_Report.pdf.

A. Groundwater Supply Allocation Systems

Underpinning any legislation managing groundwater extraction are the *five groundwater legal regimes* developed to define rights to groundwater as among more than one user. As we explore these legal regimes, ask what actions/decisions they encourage, and whether those actions/decisions will lead to resilient and/or sustainable conditions. The first legal regime is the absolute ownership rule, or the *rule of capture*, also called the *English Rule*, and it allows a landowner to withdraw an unlimited amount of water from his or her own property without liability to neighbors, no matter what the purpose of the water usage. The second legal regime is the *American Reasonable Use* doctrine, which allows a landowner to withdraw water, but limits the appropriation by requiring the use to be reasonable and beneficial, and not harmful to others. The third is the *Correlative Rights* doctrine. Developed in California, this legal regime requires that landowners over a common aquifer share the resource coequally and make beneficial use of the water. In times of scarcity, the water is apportioned based on the reasonable needs of the overlying landowners. The fourth legal regime, *Restatement (Second) of Torts Reasonable Use*, allocates groundwater usage based on an evaluation of several factors to determine the reasonableness of water use among landowners competing for the resource. Similar to the determination of what constitutes reasonableness of a defendant's conduct under a nuisance challenge for interference with the plaintiff's property interest, the Restatement approach evaluates on a case-by-case basis whether a landowner withdraws water for a beneficial purpose and whether the use is reasonable and not harmful to neighbors. The fifth and final doctrine is based on *prior appropriation* and allows a first-in-time withdrawing landowner to establish seniority over subsequent withdrawing landowners such that subsequent users will need to refrain from pumping water until the seniority rights have been fulfilled.[102]

The *five common law doctrines address groundwater allocation*, but do not generally interrelate to the surface water allocation schemes, even though groundwater and surface water are hydrologically connected. The Nebraska Supreme Court addressed the tension between the two allocation systems in *Spear T Ranch, Inc. v. Knaub* and adopted the Restatement (Second) of Torts §858(1)(c) to "govern conflicts between users of hydrologically connected surface water and ground water."[103] In Colorado, Montana, New Mexico, Washington, and Wyoming, prior appropriation is the doctrine used for both surface and groundwater. States should apply

---

[102] Sax et al., *supra* note 19, at 415-417; Spear T Ranch, Inc. v. Knaub, 691 N.W.2d 116 (Neb. 2005).
[103] *Spear*, 691 N.W.2d, at 122 (quoting the Restatement and holding "[a] proprietor of land or his or her grantee who withdraws ground water from the land and uses it for a beneficial purpose is not subject to liability for interference with the use of water of another, unless the withdrawal of the ground water has a direct and substantial effect upon a watercourse or lake and unreasonably causes harm to a person entitled to the use of its water."). *Id.*

the same legal doctrine to both groundwater and surface water that are hydrologically connected. Having them within the same framework will help resolve rights in one source when the other source is affected. Surface appropriators are typically senior to the groundwater users, so when conflict arises, groundwater pumpers may be restricted in order to protect surface water rights and regulators may refuse to grant a new groundwater permit unless the pumper agrees to maintain minimum surface flows of hydrologically connected streams.[104]

Many states do not apply the same allocation regime to both groundwater and surface water and instead use the *conjunctive use* doctrine "to coordinate the use of ground and surface waters in order to get the maximum economic benefits from both resources."[105] This is essentially a water management tool, but the underlying legal allocation systems must support this tool. For example, California is a hybrid state for purposes of surface water allocation and a *correlative rights* state for purposes of groundwater allocation, but it uses conjunctive management "to improve water supply reliability and sustainability, to reduce groundwater overdraft and land subsidence, to protect water quality, and to improve environmental conditions."[106] To facilitate conjunctive use, groundwater pumpers do not lose the right to extract water if they stop pumping for

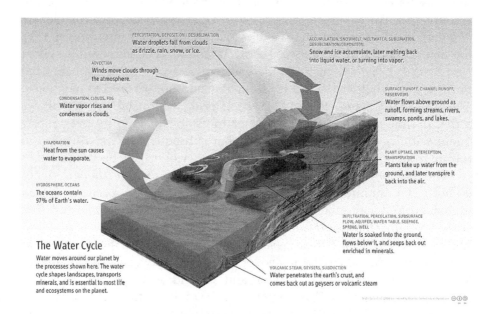

The Water Cycle

Water moves around our planet by the processes shown here. The water cycle shapes landscapes, transports minerals, and is essential to most life and ecosystems on the planet.

PERCIPITATION, DEPOSITION / DESUBLIMATION
Water droplets fall from clouds as drizzle, rain, snow, or ice.

ADVECTION
Winds move clouds through the atmosphere.

CONDENSATION, CLOUDS, FOG
Water vapor rises and condenses as clouds.

EVAPORATION
Heat from the sun causes water to evaporate.

HYDROSPHERE, OCEANS
The oceans contain 97% of Earth's water.

ACCUMULATION, SNOWMELT, MELTWATER, SUBLIMATION, DESUBLIMATION/DEPOSITION
Snow and ice accumulate, later melting back into liquid water, or turning into vapor.

SURFACE RUNOFF, CHANNEL RUNOFF, RESERVOIRS
Water flows above ground as runoff, forming streams, rivers, swamps, ponds, and lakes.

PLANT UPTAKE, INTERCEPTION, TRANSPIRATION
Plants take up water from the ground, and later transpire it back into the air.

INFILTRATION, PERCOLATION, SUBSURFACE FLOW, AQUIFER, WATER TABLE, SEEPAGE, SPRING, WELL
Water is soaked into the ground, flows below it, and seeps back out enriched in minerals.

VOLCANIC STEAM, GEYSERS, SUBDUCTION
Water penetrates the earth's crust, and comes back out as geysers or volcanic steam

[104] Sax et al., *supra* note 19, at 456-463.

[105] *Id.* at 467 (quoting Frank Trelease, *Conjunctive Use of Groundwater and Surface Water*, 27B Rocky Mtn. Min. L. Inst. 1853, 1854 (1982)).

[106] *California Water Plan Update 2009: Conjunctive Management and Groundwater Storage*, Resource Mgmt. Strategies Ch. 8 Vol. 2, 8-12, *available at* http://www.water.ca.gov/waterplan/docs/cwpu2009/0310final/v2c08_conjunctmgmt_cwp2009.pdf.

conservation purposes or temporarily switch to surface water use to allow for the recharge of an aquifer.[107]

Questions

1. As mentioned above, the five common law doctrines addressing ground-water typically do not interface with surface water doctrines, even though groundwater and surface water are part of the same hydrological system. How might we consider groundwater and surface water as more of a connected system? What would be the benefits and detriments to such a system? What would it take into consideration before allocating rights to water users? In Chapter 6 we introduce the concept of "Systems Thinking" in which systems are thought of holistically and not as individual parts.

2. Evaluate the five common law doctrines in light of collective action challenges. What decisions do the common law doctrines motivate users to make?

3. Given your analyses for questions 1 and 2 above, how would you describe the likelihood that any one or two of the common law doc-trines will achieve a resilient and/or sustainable water supply?

B. Groundwater Pumping and Mining

Groundwater pumping and mining has enabled those without access or rights to surface water to capture water beneath their land for domestic, agricultural, and urban use. These aquifers provide water for these uses and, at times, can help sustain surface water resources and associated eco-logical systems.[108] Underground water constitutes approximately 30% of global freshwater, although not all of it can be tapped because some of it is located in the zone of aeration and cannot be extracted. The need for this clean water source has grown as demand for water has increased and as sur-face waters have become more polluted, such that aquifers throughout the world are being depleted by pumping more water than is being recharged.

Extracting groundwater requires the drilling of wells and electricity to drive the pumps. Differentiating between pumping and mining ground-water is based on whether the groundwater can be recharged or whether replenishment is not possible so that the extraction is actually consid-ered mining of a non-renewable resource.[109] The use of groundwater has

---

[107] Sax et al., *supra* note 19, at 468.
[108] Owen, *supra* note 92, at 256.
[109] Sax et al., *supra* note 19, at 394-395.

increased dramatically since the invention of the high-speed centrifugal pump in 1937 and the growth of irrigated agriculture and urban populations in the latter half of the twentieth and twenty-first centuries.[110]

Think back to Chapter 2 where we discussed the role of technology in R&S. In addition to the impact groundwater mining has on interconnected surface waters, wells can interfere with each other and cause land subsidence. While oil and gas mining also contributes to damage from land subsidence, areas such as California and Texas are heavy users of groundwater and this mining impacts the sustainability of this resource for future generations. At some point, this mining will result in the reduction of available groundwater as well as the collapse of aquifers and recharge basins for storage purposes.[111]

In times of drought, groundwater depletion is a major concern as wells may be the only resource for farmers with junior surface water rights. During the western drought in the early part of the twenty-first century, California farmers drilled more wells and invested in more sophisticated and expensive drilling equipment in order to continue growing crops when they were cut off from surface water supplies.[112] Wells may go dry when there is a persistent drought, landowners drill more and deeper wells, aquifers are not replenished, and water tables shrink. As previously discussed, this over-pumping without recharging may also result in land subsidence, seawater intrusion, and water quality deterioration. While the five common law doctrines of groundwater allocation may help to determine water rights, we must manage existing groundwater resources on a broader basis to prevent a tragedy of the commons[113] where each landowner will extract water from a common aquifer until we completely deplete the resource.

C. Groundwater Management

In the United States, individual states have taken different approaches to managing groundwater within the state. Some have relied on the five common law doctrines, while others have created geographically relevant special districts to manage resources; enacted statutory controls; entered into interstate compacts; employed dispute resolution; and used general adjudications of groundwater rights. Groundwater management often uses the concept of *safe yield* to describe the water that can be extracted from an aquifer on an annual basis without adverse economic, ecological, and social costs. As noted above, new legislation in California does not use the term "safe yield"

---

[110] Sax et al., *supra* note 19, at 395.

[111] Sax et al., *supra* note 19, at 399-407, 494-497 (noting that aquifer storage may lie under several different landowners and recharging water may be considered a trespass or physical occupation of property resulting in a takings challenge).

[112] Matt Richtel, *California Farmers Dig Deeper for Water, Sipping Their Neighbors Dry*, N.Y. Times (June 5, 2015), http://www.nytimes.com/2015/06/07/business/energy-environment/california-farmers-dig-deeper-for-water-sipping-their-neighbors-dry.html.

[113] Dellapenna, *supra* note 93, at 317 (citing Garrett Hardin, *The Tragedy of the Commons*, 162 Science 1243 (1968)).

(which can in practice describe an aquifer that is continuing to be depleted), but instead uses the word "sustainability" without further definition. Senior well owners may also be restricted to "reasonable pumping levels" for purposes of protecting them against junior well owners. However, this is a vague standard that is difficult to monitor and creates uncertainty that can inhibit a functioning market for transferring water rights.[114]

Uncertainty about the hydrogeological conditions and the historic groundwater use has created complications in managing groundwater. Determining the behavior of water in aquifers is expensive and keeping track of groundwater extractions may require that wells be registered with the government using a permit system. It is difficult to understand and predict how pumping activities will impact groundwater resources, and it may be necessary to utilize complex groundwater models to determine the expected nature of these systems and their interconnectedness with surface water.[115] One way to manage the extractions and the interference with others is to require *well spacing*, a technique commonly used in oil and gas regulations, to mitigate these potential problems. Another management tool is *conjunctive use*, which "'coordinate[s] the use of ground and surface waters in order to get the maximum economic benefits from both resources.'"[116] California statutory law has instituted a legal framework to support the allocation of water rights using this method of managing both surface and ground waters.[117]

> **CALIFORNIA WATER CODE APP. §121-305.5. CONJUNCTIVE USE**
>
> Sec. 305.5. "Conjunctive use" means the coordinated operation of a groundwater basin and groundwater and surface water supplies. Conjunctive use includes increased groundwater use or decreased groundwater replenishment with surface supplies in years when surface supplies are less than normal and, in years of more abundant surface supplies, the increased use of surface water in lieu of groundwater, either to allow groundwater levels to recover or to replenish artificial groundwater supplies. Conjunctive use also includes long-term storage of water in a groundwater basin.

States have not typically used *general adjudications of groundwater rights* to resolve ongoing conflicts over shared aquifers, even though they have used them to resolve surface water conflicts in many areas. Basin-wide adjudications have been limited because of the lack of knowledge regarding water use and the need to join all landowners located over a common aquifer. On the other hand, Southern California has used this approach in

---

[114] Sax et al., *supra* note 19, at 476.
[115] Sax et al., *supra* note 19, at 407-411 (noting that expert testimony and admitting evidence of groundwater modeling may require adherence to the admissibility of scientific evidence standard under Daubert v. Merrell Dow Pharms., Inc., 509 U.S. 579 (1993)).
[116] Sax et al., *supra* note 19, at 467 (quoting Frank Trelease, *Conjunctive Use of Groundwater and Surface Water*, 27B Rocky Mtn. Min. L. Inst. 1853, 1854 (1982)).
[117] Sax et al., *supra* note 19, at 467-468.

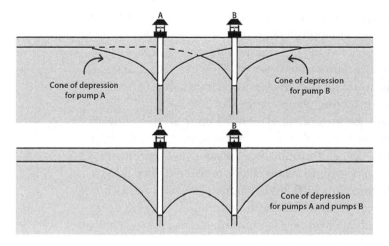

several water basins.[118] Negotiation, rather than litigation, has been used to limit pumping rights, impose pumping taxes, and import water replenishment as needed, in order to preserve groundwater basins for storage of surface and imported water, and prevent the contamination of these aquifers by saltwater intrusion.[119]

Groundwater management legislation is a modern approach to controlling groundwater usage and may take the same form as the regulated riparian approach for surface water, in which the state uses an administrative agency to grant or deny permits in light of either or both surface and groundwater resources and usage.[120] Courts have generally upheld this legislation, even when state groundwater law is changed to restrict rights that were formerly unrestricted. Courts have mostly rejected challenges to these water law changes based on takings law in favor of the government's right to exercise the police power to protect against the harms caused by unregulated extractions.[121] However, in the face of future groundwater scarcity and climate change, conflicts among users, including for ecological purposes, will necessarily require greater regulation of these resources along with the associated restrictions on private rights that will need protection.[122]

Question

1. As mentioned above, California's Sustainable Groundwater Management Act of 2014 did not define the term "sustainability." Given the definitions we explored in Chapter 1, how would you define sustainability in the context of groundwater management? What would you want it to include?

---

[118] Sax et al., *supra* note 19, at 443-444; *see also Groundwater*, Cal. Dep't of Water Res. (May 9, 2016), http://www.water.ca.gov/groundwater/.

[119] Sax et al., *supra* note 19, at 506-517 (discussing the management of southern California's groundwater basins).

[120] Dellapenna, *supra* note 93, at 304-310.

[121] Owen, *supra* note 92, at 284-292 (analyzing Edwards Aquifer Auth. v. Day, 369 S.W. 3d 814 (Tex. 2012) where the Texas Supreme Court held that landowners hold property rights to the groundwater beneath their land and that a regulatory restriction on groundwater use could constitute a taking of private property).

[122] Owen, *supra* note 92, at 306-307.

Would it incorporate intergenerational equity? Intragenerational equity? What about the three-legged stool? Or "safe yield"?

IV. MANAGING WATER QUANTITY AND QUALITY

While Sections II and III set forth the legal framework allocating the rights to use surface and ground waters, this section will address the economic, ecologic, and public health damages caused by too much water, not enough water, and/or the degradation of water quality. Efforts to manage flooding, divert water for hydropower, agriculture, and urban uses, and maintain water quality for ecological and human purposes may sometimes result in environmental and social impacts that are difficult to remedy. Managing water quantity can often affect water quality, and likewise, managing water quality will often have a direct impact on water quantity.[123] Traditionally distinct legal regimes have compartmentalized these efforts and different federal and state institutions and agencies have governed these laws. However, managing both water quantity and quality cooperatively could reduce the damage on both sides.[124] Recognizing that the distinction between water quantity and water quality can be an artificial one,[125] this section will nonetheless discuss these issues separately and describe the traditional law approaches to managing water quantity as well as the impact of hydrological alterations and the liability for damages from these efforts. Although we discuss water pollution in Chapter 8, we will also address water quality issues concerning safe drinking water and the pollution of waterways in this section.

A. Water Quantity

1. LAW OF DRAINAGE

Diffused surface water is the precipitation runoff before it finds its way to discrete water bodies. The United States has managed drainage under two traditional approaches — the *civil law approach* and *the common enemy doctrine*. These approaches, as well as the more modern reasonable use rule, apply to riparian jurisdictions as well as to prior appropriation and hybrid jurisdictions. The original civil law approach to drainage assigned tort liability for any diversion that interfered with the natural flow of surface water, although, over time, the approach has been modified to allow alterations to the flow so long as the damage to the affected land is

---

[123] Adam Schempp, *At the Confluence of the Clean Water Act and Prior Appropriation: The Challenge and Ways Forward*, 43 ENVTL. L. REP. 10138 (2013) (analyzing the conflicts between water quality and quantity and proposing solutions to achieve coordination of management efforts).

[124] *Id.* at 10138-10141 (addressing the issue and advocating coordination among state and federal agencies).

[125] *Id.* at 10144 (quoting "the oft-cited words of Justice Sandra Day O'Connor, herself an Arizonan, the separation of water quality and water quantity 'is an artificial distinction.'").

minimal and it is necessary for development of the altering parcel.[126] In contrast, the common enemy doctrine views diffused surface water as an enemy of all landowners so that each landowner is permitted to alter the natural flow to protect their own property from damage, even if it means that a neighbor's property will suffer.[127]

EXTERNALITIES AND THE LAW

How the law treats externalities affects systems' sustainability and resilience. This is particularly true with water law, where the regulation of quantity changes and quality changes can alter downstream uses. In *Ohrtman Revocable Trust v. Palo Alto Cty. Bd. of Supervisors,* litigants disputed whether a downstream user can limit upstream users to avoid the externalities created by the upstream use.

The case involved "Drainage District 80," established in 1916. Iowa law authorizes a drainage district to manage water runoff. It often does so through human engineered methods to control water, such as tiling or levees.[128] The county will create a drainage district when two or more contiguous landowners petition the county for formation. Drainage District 80 encompassed approximately 12,000 acres. However, the District claimed it received water from 57,000 acres through its tiling system and sought to annex those additional lands to compel the landowners to pay their share of addressing water runoff.

Landowners of 18,000 acres of the additional 45,000 acres sued to stop the annexation. On appeal, the court ruled that the District could not annex the land because it would not provide a benefit as required under Iowa law. Read the following quote from the appellate court and consider what, if any, effect a ruling like this might have on the R&S of the water system.

> The fallacy which seems to have operated upon the mind of the [county defendant] and of its engineer is one we encounter not infrequently; that is, that a landowner is under some continuing obligation to 'pay the freight' upon his own surface waters after they have left his lands and until they reach an ultimate outlet. . . . On the contrary, he may freely avail himself of the topography of his land, and may discharge his surface waters wherever gravitation naturally carries them, without further concern on his part as to where they go, for they are no longer his. There is no final outlet for the surface waters of this state this side of the gulf. . . . by the same logic it could be charged with benefits in the construction of the jetties at the mouth of the Mississippi.

Ohrtman Revocable Trust v. Palo Alto Cty. Bd. of Supervisors, 760 N.W.2d 210 (Iowa Ct. App. 2008).

---

[126] Sax et al., *supra* note 19, at 118.

[127] *Id.*

[128] Tiling is a practice that has been used for over 100 years and involves a subsurface drainage system designed to quickly remove water from one jurisdiction or site to the next. D.B. Jaynes & D.E. James, *The Extent of Farm Drainage in the United States, available at* https://www.ars.usda.gov/ARSUserFiles/50301500/theextentoffarmdrainageintheunitedstates.pdf.

About half of the states that formerly adhered to the two traditional approaches to drainage discussed above have adopted a ***reasonable use rule***, not to be confused with the reasonable use rule that manages conflicting riparian rights.[129] This rule views all circumstances to determine whether the defendant's conduct is reasonable in relation to the need for reasonable development of the property and the likelihood and degree of damage to neighboring landowners.[130] While the civil law approach and the common enemy doctrine may have the advantage of predictability for the defendant landowner, these approaches are harsh and may lead to unjust results, whereas the reasonable use rule allows the balancing of interests for all impacted landowners.[131]

2. HYDROLOGICAL ALTERATIONS

Dam construction, water diversion, stream channelization, tapping groundwater aquifers, and interbasin water transfers have greatly stressed the resilience and sustainability of water-based ecosystems.[132] Hydrological alteration is defined as "any anthropogenic disruption in the magnitude or timing of natural river flows[,]" with the major disruption being caused by dam construction to store water or raise the level of water to generate electricity or divert water into canals for supplying water to various users and assisting river navigation.[133] Studies of major river systems in the world have revealed that dams and river diversions have destroyed aquatic habitat and contributed to fishery destruction, species extinction, and loss of ecosystem services such as those provided by floodplains and wetlands in protecting water quality. In addition, some rivers, such as the Nile and Colorado, no longer provide freshwater and nutrient discharge into the sea, and some reservoirs emit greenhouse gases.[134]

In addition to dams and erosion of riverbanks and shorelines, ***channelization and channel modification*** are hydromodification activities that act as sources of nonpoint pollution (a point source is essentially a pipe that discharges into a water source, such as a municipal combined sewer outflow and an industrial pipe) to coastal waters. States must manage these nonpoint pollution sources under the guidance of the Environmental Protection Agency (EPA) and National Oceanic and Atmospheric Administration (NOAA).[135] In 2012, the U.S. Geological

---

[129] *Id.*

[130] *Id.* at 118-123.

[131] *Id.*

[132] David M. Rosenberg et al., *Global-Scale Environmental Effects of Hydrological Alterations: Introduction,* INTN'L RIVERS, https://www.internationalrivers.org/environmental-effects-of-hydrological-alterations (originally published in BIOSCIENCE, September 2000).

[133] *Id.*

[134] *Id.*

[135] *Management Measures for Hydromodification: Channelization and Channel Modification, Dams, and Streambank and Shoreline Erosion,* EPA (Jan. 1993), https://www.epa.gov/sites/production/files/2015-09/documents/czara_chapter6_hydromod.pdf.

Survey of the U.S. Department of the Interior, in cooperation with the U.S. Department of State, prepared "A Brief History and Summary of the Effects of River Engineering and Dams on the Mississippi River System and Delta."[136] This report presented a case study involving instream flows, competing and growing water consumption, dams, aquatic species, and watershed or river basin management.[137] The report's purpose was to summarize "the effects of dams and other engineering projects [in particular levees, dikes, and revetments], on large-river hydrology, sediment transport, geomorphology, ecology, water quality, and deltaic systems" on the Mississippi River system. The United States would provide information from the report to Laos, Thailand, Cambodia, and Vietnam, as these nations make management decisions about the Mekong River Basin, which is similar in scale and water discharges.[138]

The report concluded that dams and river engineering have afforded the United States "multiple benefits including navigation, flood control, hydropower, bank stabilization, and recreation."[139] However, these human interventions have also directly and indirectly impacted fish communities and caused a decline of approximately 25% of the fish species. By disconnecting the river distributary network from the delta plain, hydro-modification has caused wetland losses and the loss of the delta plain as protection against storm surges and global sea-level rise, enhanced saltwater intrusion and land subsidence, and reduced sediment deliveries from upstream. Lastly, nonpoint source nitrogen discharges have adversely affected the water quality in the Gulf of Mexico (known as the "Dead Zone" and described in more detail in the section on Watershed Management and Instream Flow Protections below).[140]

The Army Corps of Engineers (Corps) "refers to the [Mississippi] river as both 'beast' and 'benefactor'" and has participated in the human intervention designed to maintain this "vital waterway network" and control its cyclical flooding.[141] The Mississippi Water Basin drains nearly 40% of the continental United States and is "one of the most highly engineered river basins in the world."[142] In their brilliant book about the Mississippi and its century of unnatural disasters, Professors Klein and Zellmer present a compelling story of the triumphs and downfalls of the massive engineering projects that caused Mark Twain, when returning to the river some 30 years after he first traveled it, to remark that "the river seemed 'dead beyond resurrection.'"[143] Engineers digging channels deeper to enhance

---

[136] Jason S. Alexander et al., *A Brief History and Summary of the Effects of River Engineering and Dams on the Mississippi River System and Delta*, USGS (Jun. 6, 2012), https://pubs.usgs.gov/circ/1375/.
[137] *Id.*
[138] *Id.*
[139] *Id.*
[140] *Id.*
[141] Christine A. Klein & Sandra B. Zellmer, Mississippi River Tragedies: A Century of Unnatural Disaster 4 (2014).
[142] *Id.* at 2.
[143] *Id.* at 28.

commercial navigation caused more frequent and severe flooding. By constructing a system of floodwalls and levees to protect those settling in
the floodplain, engineers created a so-called "floodless floodplain" and
enticed agriculture, industry, and homeowners into areas dependent upon
the stability of artificial barriers.[144]

Early settlements of Native Americans on the Mississippi River delta
adapted to the natural and recurrent flooding of rivers by living up in
the hills and establishing easily movable communities to follow available
fishing and hunting resources.[145] Seasonal flooding enriched the already
fertile soil, but as European settlers established floodplain communities,
they would eventually call on government to protect these areas from the
major floods that occurred approximately every ten years. The flood of
1903 affected residents along the Missouri River and was the most devastating flood since European settlement began in the prior century.[146]
The waters spread across the floodplain, which then contained businesses,
homes, railways, stockyards, factories, and highly cultivated fields, killing
approximately 200 people and displacing about 22,000 others, as well as
destroying all but one of the 17 bridges over the lower Kansas River.[147]

Major floods and disasters continue to occur in the Mississippi
River basin over the years, but the engineering of the river and its flood

---

[144] *Id.* at 33-34.
[145] *Id.* at 36.
[146] *Id.* at 38.
[147] *Id.* at 39.

protection projects encourage communities to return, rebuild, and remain in the "floodless" floodplains. The 1917 Flood Control Act was an unsuccessful "levees-only" strategy of building higher and thicker levees, but after the great Mississippi River flood of 1927, Congress expanded the role of the federal government in flood prevention by enacting the 1928 Flood Control Act to build dams, spillways, and floodways.[148] Roosevelt's New Deal initiatives created the Tennessee Valley Authority in 1933 for management of the Southeast water resources and the Flood Control Act of 1936, which recognized federal responsibility for nationwide flood control.[149] During this time, the Corps used eminent domain to establish floodways by purchasing property from the affected landowners, or in many cases, purchasing only a "flowage easement" that would allow storage of floodwaters on the property when necessary.[150]

Following on the heels of the Flood Control Act of 1936, the Corps relieved the record-breaking Ohio River flooding in 1937 by blasting a hole in the levee and allowing the Mississippi River to escape into the Birds Point-New Madrid Floodway. The Corps' action spared the upstream city of Cairo, Illinois, but the Ohio River Valley experienced its worst flood in 175 years.[151] However, tempted by the rich soil, farmers returned to the floodway after the 1937 flood and farmed without much interruption from the intermittent flooding until 2011, when record floods on the Mississippi and Ohio rivers exceeded the 1937 levels and the Corps for a second time blasted open the Birds Point Floodway.[152] Farmers, damaged by the wall of water, brought suit against the Corps, but the court found that the flooding did not exceed the scope of the flowage easements purchased by the government and that government flood control projects had prevented such flooding for almost 75 years.[153]

The Midwest experienced severe flooding of the upper Mississippi and its tributaries, including the Missouri River, in 1993, and many of the federal and non-federal levees failed resulting in 48 deaths and property damages of almost $20 billion.[154] Only about 20% of the victims that were eligible for federal insurance had taken advantage of the National Flood Insurance Program of 1968 to insure against these losses. Cemeteries were unearthed and communities were submerged, but in 2000, Congress authorized federal levee improvements in the devastated community of Chesterfield, Missouri, and it was able to develop again in the floodplains.[155] However, Congress also passed the Hazard Mitigation and Relocation Assistance Act of 1993, which provided federal funds for disaster relief

---

[148] *Id.* at 58, 78-79.
[149] *Id.* at 81.
[150] *Id.* at 82-83.
[151] *Id.* at 87-88.
[152] *Id.* at 88.
[153] *Id.* at 89.
[154] *Id.* at 124.
[155] *Id.* at 130.

and hazard mitigation and resulted in buyouts of property located in flood-prone areas.[156] Congress enacted the National Flood Insurance Reform Act in 1994 to encourage insurance coverage and address the problem of repetitive loss (flooded property owners receiving multiple payments for repeated flooding). Congress reformed the program to prevent the moral hazard phenomenon (where there is no incentive for the insured party to avoid risk because protection is available through insurance) and reduce disaster relief funding that discourages property owners from paying for insurance because disaster relief will be free.[157]

Flooding due to hurricanes has also impacted communities in the lower Mississippi River Basin. Hurricane Betsy of 1965, a category 3 hurricane, struck Louisiana, with winds strong enough to push a storm swell up the Mississippi River to New Orleans, flooding homes in the low-lying city and in St. Bernard and Plaquemines parishes.[158] Flood victims sued the Corps, but the court found that the severe damages experienced by the plaintiffs were the result of the hurricane's fury, not the artificial construction built to enhance the navigation of the Mississippi.[159] With the increasing development of land in the floodplains and the resulting losses after floods and storms, the federal government enacted laws encouraging local governments to use land-use regulations to discourage new building in areas prone to flooding. However, landowners challenged state and local regulations that restricted or prohibited development of their property as regulatory takings under the Fifth and Fourteenth Amendments, requiring just compensation.[160]

In 1965, following Hurricane Betsy, Congress authorized the Lake Pontchartrain and Vicinity Hurricane Protection Project (LPVHPP) with a scheduled completion date of 2015. Hurricane Katrina, also a category 3, hit in 2005, well before the scheduled completion of the project but after billions had been spent on flood control and navigation structures. Again, the storm surge from Katrina hit the Gulf Coast, killed at least 1,800 people, and caused damages well over $100 billion.[161] The engineered shipping channels funneled the storm surge into New Orleans, while the city's levees crumbled and the floodwalls failed.[162] As it was with the victims of the Mississippi flood of 1927, the victims of Katrina were disproportionately

---

[156] *Id.* at 134.
[157] *Id.* at 137.
[158] *Id.* at 109.
[159] *Id.* at 111.
[160] *Id.* at 115-117 (discussing First English Evangelical Lutheran Church v. Los Angeles County, 482 U.S. 304 (1987). In *First English*, the Court held that the Takings Clause protects individuals from regulatory actions by the government that deprive individuals of all economically viable use of their property). Klein & Zellmer, *supra* note 141, at 118-120 (discussing Lucas v. South Carolina Coastal Council, 505 U.S. 1003 (1992), where the Court held that the state law deprived Lucas of all economically viable value, and therefore constituted a taking requiring just compensation).
[161] Klein & Zellmer, *supra* note 141, at 147.
[162] *Id.* at 148.

poor and black.[163] Courts held that the Corps was responsible for the negligence that resulted in unnecessary flooding from Katrina because navigability of the channel was elevated over the safety of the city. However, the Federal Tort Claims Act protected the government from liability.

Ten years after Katrina, the New York Times reported that in the aftermath Congress approved $14 billion to build protection around New Orleans with stronger levees, pumps, and gates to insure that a disaster of this magnitude will not occur again.[164] Analysts project that it will cost $50 billion to fund the master plan to restore the coast. Looking back on the history of the Mississippi River basin, the Times noted the levees that were built after the 1927 floods to make the region safer, also stopped the sand and silt that would have built up the land and kept it above water. The combination of hydromodification through levees, floodgates, pumps, and diversion, along with restoration of beaches, dunes, and marshes will help provide protection against hurricanes, floods, and sea rise. However, this might not be enough, and some have argued that we must move populations away from the riskiest areas.[165]

Professors Klein and Zellmer conclude their captivating story of the hydromodification of the Mississippi River Basin by stating three lessons learned from the U.S. efforts to manage floods: "1) Rivers *will* flood; 2) levees *will* fail; and 3) unwise floodplain development *will* happen if we let it."[166] Below, we return to the Mississippi watershed and explore collective action challenges among local governments in the watershed.

Question

1. As the hydrology of many rivers change due to human intervention, including climate change, what should be the response to areas that are increasingly at risk of flooding? Who should pay to remedy any damage incurred by flooding? Are there advantages to permitting flooding? If so, when? And when should rising waters be resisted?

3. LIABILITY FOR FLOODING

As discussed in the previous section, flooding caused by hydromodification and other water management techniques may generate damage

---

[163] *Id.* at 149-150; *see generally id.* at 161-172 (discussing environmental justice concerns).

[164] John Schwartz, *How to Save a Sinking Coast? Katrina Created a Laboratory*, N.Y. TIMES (Aug. 7, 2015), http://www.nytimes.com/2015/08/08/science/louisiana-10-years-after-hurricane-katrina.html.

[165] *Id.*

[166] Klein & Zellmer, *supra* note 141, at 187-189.

claims against those responsible for impacting private property. When the federal government is responsible, the Flood Control Act of 1938 and Federal Tort Claims Act may protect it from tort liability; however, claims of a Fifth Amendment taking may have more promise to secure compensation.[167]

In *Arkansas Game & Fish Commission v. United States*,[168] the state commission sued the United States alleging that the Army Corps of Engineers (Corps) authorized periodic flooding over a seven-year span of forestland owned and managed by the state. These temporary floodings destroyed 18 million board feet of timber and resulted in the invasion of harmful plants and the alteration of the character of the area.[169] The Court of Federal Claims found that a taking had occurred and valued just compensation at $5.7 million, but the Federal Circuit reversed the award holding that only permanent, not temporary, flooding induced by the government could give rise to a taking.[170] On certiorari, the U.S. Supreme Court addressed the issue as to "whether government actions that cause repeated floodings must be permanent or inevitably recurring to constitute a taking of property"[171] and held "that government-induced flooding temporary in duration gains no automatic exemption from Takings Clause inspection."[172] Instead, courts must evaluate on a case-by-case basis whether a flooding is a taking by considering facts such as the character of the land, the owner's "reasonable investment-backed expectations" as to use, the duration of the restriction, and the foreseeability of the government action.[173] Courts will likely assess temporary floodings using the case-specific takings test under *Penn Central Transportation Co. v. New York City*,[174] but they will probably consider permanent government invasions by flooding to be per se takings of property based on *Loretto v. Teleprompter Manhattan CATV Corp.*[175]

---

[167] *See, e.g.*, St. Bernard Parish Gov't v. United States, 121 Fed. Cl. 687, 690 (2015) (holding that takings claims were ripe for determining alleged temporary taking from flooding) (citing *In re Katrina Canal Breaches Litig.*, 696 F.3d 436, 444-454 (5th Cir. 2012), which resolved earlier claims stemming from the same lawsuit based on government immunity under the Flood Control Act and the Federal Torts Claim Act for alleged damages from the Hurricane Katrina canal breaches).

[168] Ark. Game & Fish Commn. v. United States, 568 U.S. 23 (2012).

[169] *Id.* at 26.

[170] *Id.* at 30.

[171] *Id.* at 31.

[172] *Id.* at 38.

[173] *Id.* at 39.

[174] Penn Cent. Transp. Co. v. N.Y.C., 438 U.S. 104, 124 (1978) (applying an ad hoc factual inquiry to determine whether or not a taking has occurred by looking at the character of the government action, the severity of the impact, and the interference with investment-backed expectations).

[175] Loretto v. Teleprompter Manhattan CATV Corp., 458 U.S. 419, 426 (1982) (taking found when there is a permanent physical occupation of property sanctioned by the government); *see also* Pumpelly v. Green Bay Co., 80 U.S. 166, 181 (1871) (holding "where real estate is actually invaded by superinduced additions of water, earth, sand, or other material . . . so as to effectually destroy or impair its usefulness, it is a taking").

PENN CENTRAL TRANSPORTATION CO. v. NEW YORK CITY, 438 U.S. 104 (1978).

In 1965, the City of New York passed one of the first comprehensive historic preservation laws. Pursuant to the Landmarks Preservations Act, the City's Landmarks Preservation Commission could designate and protect buildings as historic landmarks. Once a building was so designated, owners would need approval of the Commission to "alter the exterior architectural features of the landmark or to construct any exterior improvement on the landmark site."

Constructed in 1913, Grand Central Terminal, owned by Penn Central Transportation Company ("Penn Central"), was a "magnificent example of the French beaux-arts style." In 1967, the Commission designated the Grand Central Terminal as a landmark under the Act. In 1968, Penn Central entered into a renewable 50-year lease with UGP Properties, Inc. to (1) construct a multistory office building in the air space above the Terminal and (2) pay Penn Central $1 million in rent annually during construction and at least $3 million annually thereafter.

Penn Central and UGP submitted two separate plans for a modern office tower (one 53 stories and one 55 stories). When the Commission rejected both plans, Penn Central and UGP filed suit, claiming that the Act and rejection of their plans was a taking because it effectively deprived them of the use of the air space above the Terminal.

In upholding the Commission's decision, the U.S. Supreme Court applied a new test to determine whether a regulatory taking has occurred, which it called an "ad hoc, factual inquiry." In doing so, the Court identified three factors:

- The economic impact of the regulation on the claimant. This factor focuses on the extent of the economic loss experienced by a landowner as a result of the regulation.
- The extent to which the regulation interfered with distinct investment-backed expectations. This factor looks to the owner's reasonable "investment-backed" expectations.
- The character of the governmental action.

B. Water Quality

1. SAFE DRINKING WATER

Safe drinking water is critical throughout the world to address public health issues such as infectious diseases and sanitation.[176] In 2010, the United Nations Human Rights Council declared a human right to safe drinking water and sanitation.[177] Recognizing this human right has been viewed as an attack against the privatization and commodification of water; however

---

[176] Jonathan R. Eaton, *The Sieve of Groundwater Pollution Protection: A Public Health Law Analysis*, 6 J. HEALTH & BIOMEDICAL L. 109, 109 (2010) (quoting former Secretary-General of the United Nations Kofi Annan, "[w]e shall not finally defeat AIDS, tuberculosis, malaria, or any of the other infectious diseases that plague the developing world until we have also won the battle for safe drinking water, sanitation, and basic health care.").

[177] Sharmila L. Murthy, *The Human Right(s) to Water and Sanitation: History, Meaning, and the Controversy Over-Privatization*, 31 BERKELEY J. INT'L L. 89, 89 (2013).

"empirical studies suggest that involving the private sector in the delivery of water and sanitation services has been neither a ringing success nor a universal failure, as advocates of either side might suggest."[178] Humans consume both groundwater and surface water, but because groundwater is generally of higher quality than surface water, surface water quality has received more attention until recently.[179] Wells drilled by the United Nations Children's Emergency Fund (UNICEF) in Bangladesh to bring drinking water to that nation contaminated its groundwater, exposing millions of people to naturally occurring arsenic.[180] Seventy percent of China's freshwater supplies is polluted, so that nation has relied on bottled water for drinking; however, bottled water has become suspect because of contamination scandals.[181] Countries must provide its citizens with access to safe drinking water by addressing water quality issues in its freshwater resources and water delivery infrastructure in order to achieve social and economic progress.[182] Yet, as we set forth in Chapter 2, millions of individuals continue to have little or no access to safe drinking water on a daily basis.

The United States enacted the *Safe Drinking Water Act* (SDWA) in 1974 "to protect against both naturally-occurring and man-made contaminants that may be found in drinking water."[183] Under the authority of the SDWA, the EPA sets national health-based standards for drinking water and works with states and local agencies to meet these standards.[184] Unfortunately, even with several major amendments in 1986 and 1996, people have criticized this legislation as being relatively ineffective in addressing public health concerns. The SDWA does not regulate most private wells, and it has established health-based standards for only 89 of the hundreds, or even thousands, of chemicals — including "mutagens, carcinogens, and endocrine-disrupting chemicals," — that have been found in drinking water supplies and have known adverse health effects.[185]

Monitoring groundwater and surface water and enforcing SDWA standards is problematic because it is so difficult to trace the various sources of contamination.[186] For example, surface water runoff impacts drinking supplies and, as mentioned above in our discussion of riparian systems and below in Watershed Management and Instream Flow Protections, agriculture's impact on water quality can be severe. We must remedy the dangerous levels of nitrate in municipal drinking water because exposure

---

[178] *Id.* at 99.
[179] Eaton, *supra* note 176, at 110-111.
[180] *Id.* at 111-113.
[181] Abigail Barnes & Wei Cao, *Muddy Waters: The Public Health Risks and Sustainability of Bottled Water in China*, 38 Vt. L. Rev. 971, 971-974 (2014).
[182] *Id.* at 1025 (specifically discussing China's future).
[183] *Understanding the Safe Drinking Water Act*, U.S. EPA (June 2004), https://www.epa.gov/sites/production/files/2015-04/documents/epa816f04030.pdf.
[184] *Id.*
[185] Rachael Rawlins, *Planning for Fracking on the Barnett Shale: Soil and Water Contamination Concerns, and the Role of Local Government*, 44 Envtl. L. 135, 160-161 (2014).
[186] *Id.* at 159-160.

to nitrate-rich water can cause several environmental and health-related challenges.[187] Further,

> chemicals responsible for creating the Gulf of Mexico 'dead zone,' where most marine life cannot survive, come largely from agricultural sources. Midwest corn and soybean fields, such as those upstream from Des Moines, [Iowa] account for a quarter of the phosphorus and more than half of the nitrogen that enters the Gulf.[188]

The challenge in addressing nitrate pollution of surface and ground-water involves legal, social, economic, and cultural issues that we also discuss in the chapter on Pollution, the chapter on Food, and below in Watershed Management and Instream Flow Protections. Such concerns pit urban and rural populations against each other, but the economics of addressing nitrate pollution may eventually require more regulation of agriculture since "reducing a pollutant such as nitrogen or phosphorus is much cheaper in the field than in a treatment plant."[189] Ohio and Maryland have focused on upstream farming practices and stormwater runoff that may harm waterways.[190] California, with its severe drought and water quantity issues, must also deal with the pollution of its ground-water and waterways with dangerous levels of nitrates from agriculture.[191] In addition, the herbicide Atrazine has led to contamination of ground-water and drinking supplies in at least six states and has cost these states millions of dollars to remove this chemical from its drinking supplies.[192]

THE DRINKING WATER CRISIS IN FLINT, MICHIGAN

The Flint water crisis began in April 2014 after the city, which was under the supervision of a state-appointed emergency manager, switched its drinking water source from the Detroit Water and Sewerage Department, which draws its water from Lake Huron, to the Flint River. The more corrosive Flint River water was not treated with proper corrosion controls and caused lead to leach from pipes into homes and businesses.

---

[187] Daniel C. Vock, *Farmers and Cities Play the Water Pollution Blame Game*, GOVERNING (June 2015), http://www.governing.com/topics/transportation-infrastructure/gov-pollution-des-moines.html.
[188] *Id.* (noting that "[b]y comparison, urban areas contribute 12 percent of the phosphorus and 9 percent of the nitrogen that runs into it.").
[189] *Id.* (quoting Pat Sinicropi of the National Association of Clean Water Agencies and referencing a study conducted in the Chesapeake Bay watershed which "found that it would cost farmers $1.50 to $22 per pound to reduce nitrogen in the water. For wastewater utilities, the cost would be $15.80 to $47 per pound of nitrogen removed. For stormwater cleanup, the cost would be more than $200 a pound."). *Id.*
[190] *Id.*
[191] Susie Cagle, *After Water*, LONGREADS (Jun. 2, 2015), https://blog.longreads.com/2015/06/02/after-water/ (discussing the significant health risks of nitrate-rich well water that is relied upon by some of Central Valley's residents, particularly in East Porterville).
[192] Associated Press, *Syngenta pays millions in settlement to farming states*, CJ ONLINE (Jan. 25, 2013, 3:48 PM), http://cjonline.com/news/2013-01-25/syngenta-pays-millions-settlement-farming-states.

Residents began complaining almost immediately about discolored and smelly drinking water, but nothing changed until a Flint doctor discovered high lead levels in many of the city's children. The state began to take action to remedy the situation in September 2015, delivering bottled water and filters to the city and ultimately sending nearly $250 million there to address a variety of problems created by the contaminated water.

The state also settled a $97-million lawsuit that requires the state to replace all the city's lead or galvanized steel water lines over the next three years. The federal government approved $100 million for the city to help pay for that replacement.

Kathleen Gray, *On 3-year Anniversary, Change is Slow for Flint,* Detroit Free Press Lansing Bureau (Apr. 25, 2017), http://www.freep.com/story/news/local/michigan/flint-water-crisis/2017/04/25/flint-water-crisis-lead/100900478/.

Following the death of Robert Skidmore from Legionnaires' disease, prosecutors charged "five officials in Michigan, including the head of the state's health department [Nick Lyon]" on June 14, 2017. "It is the closest investigators have come to directly blaming officials for the deaths and illnesses that occurred when a water contamination crisis enveloped this city." Scott Atkinson, Monica Davey, *5 Charged With Involuntary Manslaughter in Flint Water Crisis*, N.Y. Times (June 14, 2017), https://www.nytimes.com/2017/06/14/us/flint-water-crisis-manslaughter.html.

Contamination from hydraulic fracking of shale is also of great concern to those who fear that the chemicals injected during the fracking process may enter into drinking water supplies through ground and surface water.[193] These chemicals "include carcinogens and endocrine-disrupting chemicals that may have latent long-term health effects . . . [and] may not surface for decades and could affect future generations."[194] At least one state agency in Texas has stated that regulating the structure and depths of the fracking wells protects groundwater against contamination from oil and gas operations. However, EPA reports on several occasions have linked groundwater contamination to hydraulic fracking operations.[195] The natural gas industry claims that groundwater contamination is not a result of hydro-fracking; but concerns about this possibility should encourage greater efforts in monitoring all drinking water sources, including both surface water and groundwater.[196]

Drinking water supplies in the United States contain trace amounts of pharmaceuticals and personal care products (PPCPs), which in isolation may not be sufficiently harmful to require regulation, but when combined with multiple chemicals in the long term such low-exposure may

---

[193] Rawlins, *supra* note 185.
[194] *Id.* at 137.
[195] *Id.* at 139-141.
[196] *Id.* at 194-197.

have adverse public health consequences.[197] Nonpoint sources, rather than the easier-to-regulate point sources as discussed in the Pollution chapter, release the majority of these PPCPs into the water supply. "The myriad nonpoint sources of PPCPs include: usage by individuals, pets, and livestock; excretion of un-metabolized drugs; drain disposal of unused medication; sewage system infrastructure leakage; land application of biosolid waste; agricultural releases; dung from concentrated animal feeding operations (CAFOs); and direct releases from bathing and swimming."[198] Higher levels of contamination from PPCPs are required before triggering regulation, and EPA may not have the authority "to regulate a substance based solely on its potential adverse *cumulative* effects when combined with other substances, if neither substance is intrinsically hazardous."[199]

Protecting water quality is a challenge to all nations, from those who face dealing with too much water, which exacerbates contamination from runoff and sewage overflow, and too little water, which creates ecological instability and reduces the dilution advantages of regular flows by increasing the strengths of contamination already present. The laws governing water allocation also affect safe drinking water supplies, such that the more powerful players may receive unfair allocations of water to the detriment of those living in poverty.[200] In the United States, the Clean Water Act regulates direct sources of water pollution from point sources; however, nonpoint sources, mainly in the form of runoff continue to be largely unregulated. Even with water being "one of the few essential requirements for life," the availability of safe drinking water is not the global norm, but is instead only the norm in developed countries, while "approximately half of the developing world's inhabitants suffer from illnesses caused by contaminated water supplies."[201]

2. POLLUTION OF SURFACE WATER AND GROUNDWATER

Returning briefly to the Hawaiian Islands, we observe the fragile nature of a self-sustaining geographical location that adjacent states or countries do not impact, except for the direct damages to its beaches, levels of

---

[197] John Wood, *Can We Teach Old Laws a New Risk? Federal Environmental Law, Risk Management Theory, and Contamination of U.S. Water Supplies with Pharmaceutical and Personal Care Products,* 21 N.Y.U. ENVTL. L.J. 193, 200-202 (2014).

[198] *Id.* at 200.

[199] *Id.* at 202 (emphasis in original).

[200] Janet Neuman, *Chop Wood, Carry Water: Cutting to the Heart of the World's Water Woes,* 23 J. LAND USE & ENVTL. L. 203, 204 (2008) (noting that "[t]he water gap is just one of the many differences between the rich and poor countries — just one variation on the age-old theme of the haves and the have-nots.").

[201] James Salzman, *Is It Safe to Drink the Water,?* 19 DUKE ENVTL. L. & POL'Y F. 1, 4-8 (2008) (also noting "[w]hile climate change has taken hold of the media as the greatest threat facing humanity, many environment ministers would disagree. To them, unsafe drinking water is clearly the single greatest threat facing their citizens, particularly children."). *Id.* at 8.

precipitation, and coral reefs wrought by global climate change. Drinking water is "Hawai'i's preeminent natural resource, upon which life and the economy depend," but unlike other states and countries, Hawai'i's constitution and legislature mandate conserving natural resources for future generations and self-sufficiency.[202] Indeed, Hawai'i has established an environmental court to address legal issues involving water pollution, aquifer depletion, shrinking forests, destabilization of ecosystems, climate change impacts, the public trust, and other challenges that threaten to diminish every citizen's state constitutional "'right to a clean and healthful environment.'"[203] However, as is the case with federal law, Hawai'i's Water Pollution Law does not require a permit for discharges from irrigated agriculture, and other discharges found to originate from "nonpoint sources." Thus, irrigation return flows containing pesticides and fertilizers that have been used extensively in Oahu's pineapple fields for decades, as well as in other agricultural regions, impact both surface water and groundwater.[204] The federal Total Maximum Daily Load (TMDL) program, as implemented by the states to regulate nonpoint sources of water pollution under the Clean Water Act, is just the first step to address the issue that "[t]he majority of inland waters are presently impaired mainly by nonpoint sources of pollution, primarily sediments, nutrients, heavy metals, and pesticide residues."[205]

A few examples of water pollution might illustrate how the law can help or hinder efforts to improve resilience and sustainability. First, the story of the Thames River in London is instructive as to the ability of a nation to restore water quality through long-term regulatory policies. In 1957, the Thames River, also known as the "Great Stink," was determined to be biologically dead after decades of Victorian sewage flows and chemicals from laundries that operated along the banks in the 1800s killed most of the fish and other aquatic life.[206] The government's Environment Agency began overseeing the river in 1996, and regulated water quality and wastewater treatment. The Environmental Agency instituted new regulations that were partially responsible for dramatic results (see Figure 3-1), leading the Zoological Society of London in 2015 to declare that the Thames now supports fish as well as seals and porpoises.[207]

---

[202] Hon. Michael D. Wilson, *The Hawaii Environmental Court: A New Judicial Tool to Enforce Hawaii's Environmental Laws*, HAW. B.J. 4, 5-7 (Aug. 19 2015).

[203] *Id.* at 5 (quoting HAW. CONST. art. XI, §9).

[204] Aarin F. Gross, *When Nobody Asks: The Toxic Legacy of Oahu's Pineapple Lands*, 29 U. HAW. L. REV. 553, 560-561 (2007).

[205] June F. Harrigan-Lum & Arnold L. Lum, *Hawaii's TMDL Program: Legal Requirements and Environmental Realities*, 15 NAT. RESOURCES & ENV'T 12, 14 (2000).

[206] Cassie Werber, *Once Dead, London's Thames River is now Teeming with Seals, Porpoises, and even a Whale or Two*, QUARTZ (Aug. 20, 2015), http://qz.com/483977/once-dead-londons-thames-river-is-now-teeming-with-seals-porpoises-and-even-a-whale-or-two/; *see also* Paul Krugman, *Michigan's Great Stink*, N.Y. TIMES (Jan. 25, 2016) https://www.nytimes.com/2016/01/25/opinion/michigans-great-stink.html (comparing the water crisis in Flint, Michigan with the Great Stink of 1958).

[207] Werber, *supra* note 206.

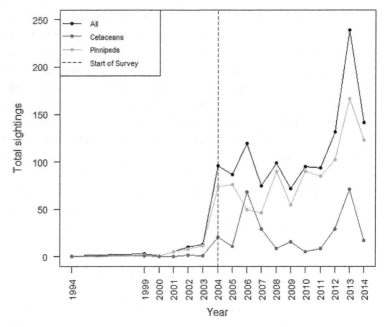

Figure 3-1[208]

The Cuyahoga River in Ohio was one of the most polluted rivers in the United States and reportedly caught on fire 13 times between 1868 and 1969.[209] However, it was the fire in 1969 that ignited the public's attention to environmental concerns and helped lead to the enactment of federal environmental laws in the 1970s, including the Federal Water Pollution Control Act Amendments of 1972 and the Clean Water Act of 1977. The damage from the 1969 fire was less than the damages caused by some of the previous fires. There were no fatalities in the 1969 fire as compared to the five peopled killed in the 1952 fire. However, the regulatory and remediation reactions to the 1969 fire, which received wide media coverage, have prevented subsequent fires, and, similar to the Thames River recovery, the Cuyahoga River is now supporting 60 different species of fish.[210]

Rivers and other water bodies are also susceptible to pollution from cleanup activities necessitated by the abandonment of mineral mines. Approximately 500,000 abandoned U.S. mines continue to pose a threat to rivers from toxic spills.[211] Additionally, many abandoned mines pollute waters through a phenomenon called "acid mine drainage," which acidifies water and adds heavy metals to it, and can result in streams that are devoid

---

[208] Rebecca Morrelle, *Marine Mammals Thriving in Thames*, BBC (Aug. 20, 2015), http://www.bbc.com/news/science-environment-33996020.

[209] *Cuyahoga River Fire*, OHIO HISTORY CONNECTION, http://www.ohiohistorycentral.org/w/Cuyahoga_River_Fire?rec = 1642 (last visited Oct. 9, 2017).

[210] *Id.*

[211] Joel A. Mintz, *Animas River Spill: Root Causes and Continuing Threats*, THE HILL (Sept. 2, 2015, 6:00 AM), http://thehill.com/blogs/congress-blog/energy-environment/252426-animas-river-spill-root-causes-and-continuing-threats.

of aquatic life and unsuitable for municipal water supplies.[212] State agencies and the EPA are responsible for cleanup of these unremediated sites. The EPA provides for cleanup by designating these abandoned mines as Superfund sites (land contaminated by hazardous waste and identified by the EPA as a candidate for cleanup under the Comprehensive Environmental Response, Compensation, and Liability Act) whenever possible and attempts to obtain some of the needed funding from potentially responsible parties, who are usually mining companies. However, mining companies often abandon a site and later declare bankruptcy. Bankruptcy laws then shield these companies from liability.[213] Therefore, while original mine operators profited from the mineral extractions, often from public lands, the public must now pay for their externalized costs through tax dollars funding both cleanup and water treatment. Acid mine drainage can potentially pollute in perpetuity, raising concern over how to treat the water in the long term.[214]

THE ANIMAS RIVER AND THE GOLD KING MINE CONTAMINATION

In August 2015, an EPA contractor responsible for cleaning up the abandoned Gold King mine in Colorado mistakenly caused a discharge of 3 million gallons of gold-mine wastewater into the Animas River near Silverton, Colorado.[215] Although the EPA had previously requested Superfund designation to clean up the Upper Animas River Basin and particularly Cement Creek where the Gold King Mine is located, local business interests blocked the designation.[216] Even though the Animas River was already suffering from existing mine waste and other pollutant contamination that has been occurring for decades,[217] the 2015 spill that turned the color of the river to mustard yellow was a visible reminder of the vagaries of mine reclamation activities that are still sorely needed.[218] While it is yet unclear what the long-term ecological impacts from the latest spill will be, it is important to remember that cleanup of existing toxic sites will be with us long into the future, likely into perpetuity. Further, as population centers expand closer to what were once remote mining sites, addressing the challenges of abandoned mines will become more critical to the health of communities.[219]

---

[212] Reclamation Research Grp., Acid Mine Drainage and Effects on Fish Health and Ecology: A Review 5 (June 2008), http://reclamationresearch.net/publications/Final_Lit_Review_AMD.pdf.

[213] In re Idaho Conservation League, No. 14-1149, 2016 WL 37443, at, *9-10 (D.C. Cir. 2016).

[214] See Polluting the Future: How Mining Companies are Contaminating Our Nation's Waters in Perpetuity, Earthworks 12 (May 2013), https://www.earthworksaction.org/files/publications/PollutingTheFuture-FINAL.pdf.

[215] Mintz, supra note 211; see also Kelly Roberts, A Legacy That No One Can Afford to Inherit: The Gold King Disaster and the Threat of Abandoned Hardrock Legacy Mines, 36 J. Nat'l Assn. Admin. L. Judiciary 361, 373-378 (2016), available at http://digitalcommons.pepperdine.edu/naalj/vol36/iss1/8.

[216] Chase Olivarius-Mcallister, Superfund: A dirty word to some in Silverton, Durango Herald (Aug. 3, 2013 1:14 PM), http://www.durangoherald.com/article/20130803/NEWS01/130809831/Superfund:-A-dirty-word-to-some-in-Silverton.

[217] Upper Animas Mining District, EPA, http://www.epa.gov/region8/upper-animas-mining-district (last updated Aug. 2015).

[218] Mintz, supra note 211.

[219] See Roberts, supra note 215, at 387.

Question

1. As mentioned above, Hawai'i established an environmental court to address legal issues involving water pollution, aquifer depletion, shrinking forests, and other challenges. Unlike the federal Clean Water Act or California's Sustainable Groundwater Management Act of 2014, Hawai'i's creation of the court is procedural and non-substantive in nature. In other words, creating the court did not enact new standards to protect Hawai'i's water supply. That said, can you make the argument that the court could help achieve more resilient and sustainable use of water? Can you make the opposite argument that it might not and why?

C. Strategy to Facilitate Implementation #2: Precautionary Principle

What should decision makers do when confronted with the potential that a policy will result in water quantity or quality challenges that stress system resilience and sustainability? Should they halt the policy? How severe should the risk be and how certain should they be that the threat will come to fruition before halting the policy? Should the policy commence until the threat actually arises? For example, at what point should we regulate chemicals in water streams? Which chemicals should be regulated and in what order? What evidence is needed before allowing the chemicals to be put in the water in the first instance? What evidence should be produced before halting ongoing discharge of chemicals into the water? And how do we determine the most effective regulatory approach to help achieve a more resilient and sustainable water-based system and management strategy?

The Precautionary Principle (PP) helps answer these questions by establishing a process in which policy makers have the opportunity to obtain more reliable and informative data before enacting a policy. When faced with uncertainty as to whether a new policy will lead to unforeseen consequences, such as polluting a water resource, the PP helps move policy forward in a way that accounts for uncertainty. Accommodating uncertainty is particularly important for R&S because social-ecological systems are complex. That complexity leads to unknowns and uncertainty. In addition, climate change and other anthropogenic impacts on systems are having cascading effects throughout Earth systems in unforeseen ways. The PP provides policymakers an opportunity to integrate this process into law and policy in order to address uncertainty.

Often thought to derive from the German concept of *Vorsorgeprinzip*, meaning "fore-caring" or "caring in advance" principle, Benjamin Franklin's well-known quote encapsulates the PP: "an ounce of prevention is worth a pound of cure." Pursuant to the PP, policy makers stall proposed actions when those actions present potential, but uncertain, risk. How much risk and uncertainty are necessary to postpone a proposed action or require alternative solutions and what level of proof is necessary are open questions and are discussed in more depth below.

1. GENERAL DESCRIPTION OF THE PRECAUTIONARY PRINCIPLE

A common understanding of the PP is that *when there is uncertainty as to the risks associated with a policy, alternative policies should remove those risks prior to exposing humans and the environment to such risks.* Pursuant to this characterization of the PP, policy makers need not wait for absolute certainty in the science before taking steps to remove risks.

Central to the PP is a trade-off between averting potential damage (stemming from short- and long-term risks) and delaying potential benefits. On the one hand, the PP can avoid years of harmful and, at times, lethal impacts, by delaying a policy until data is available to prove that the impacts will not occur. On the other hand, the PP may delay economic benefits and the protection of human health and the environment stemming from beneficial policies. The PP may slow down policies that could prove to be beneficial but will not take effect until the policies satisfy the requisite PP burden of proof.

The trade-off between risks and benefits depends on three key undefined terms embedded in the definition of the PP: *uncertainty*, *risk*, and *alternative policy*. As to uncertainty, what level of *uncertainty* is necessary for the PP to be relevant? For example, is one expert's projections sufficient to show uncertainty or do we require more? And how should the level of uncertainty be illustrated or proven? As to risk, how much *risk* can we tolerate before the PP is initiated? Any risk? Serious risk? Minor risk? And who has the burden to prove this level of risk? Finally, what does *alternative policy* mean? Does it mean scrapping the original policy in total or keeping core aspects and only making slight alterations to limit the risk to an acceptable level? Who is responsible for drafting alternative policies? And who should bear the costs?

Understanding the role of uncertainty, risk, and alternative policies is necessary to apply the PP in a meaningful way. As an example, Principle 15 of the Rio Declaration[220] states:

> *In order to protect the environment, the precautionary approach shall be widely applied by States according to their capabilities. Where there are threats of*

---

[220] Conference on Environment and Development, Rio Declaration on Environment and Development, A/CONF.151/26 (Vol. 1) (Aug. 12, 1992) [hereinafter Rio Declaration].

serious or irreversible damage, lack of full scientific certainty shall not be used as a reason for postponing cost-effective measures to prevent environmental degradation.

When we dissect Principle 15, we see there are several core parts that make up the PP:

1. *Lack of full scientific certainty shall not be used as a reason for postponing.* The failure to have **"full scientific certainty" (uncertainty)** that the threats will come to fruition should not prohibit preventative action to curtail the threats. That said, the more facts indicating a threat, the more likely policy makers are to postpone the policy in question.
2. *Threats of serious or irreversible damage.* Pursuant to this definition, the **risks** involved with the proposed action must involve "serious or irreversible" damage. Importantly, these are risks, not scientifically proven facts or actual occurrences.
3. *Cost-effective measures to prevent environmental degradation.* This requires policy makers to adopt only **alternative policies** when those alternatives are cost-effective and prevent environmental degradation.

Two other aspects of Principle 15 are worth noting. First, it states that the *PP shall be widely applied by States according to their capabilities.* This limits the PP's applicability to only those nations that have the ability to apply the PP. Presumably this provision mostly addresses financial ability. Second, with any application of the PP it is helpful to know who has the burden of proof. Who, for example, is or should be responsible for setting forth clear scientific data indicating that the policy will not result in serious or irreversible damage?

Once we decide to integrate the PP as a standard or requirement for policy implementation, the question then becomes *how to incorporate it into law and policy?* Several national agencies in Switzerland collaborated on a report to set forth useful considerations when applying the PP. Those considerations identified by the report include:

1. Principle of proportionality (the alternative policies are designed to avoid the risks, but must be proportional to the level of risk avoidance);
2. Requirement of coherence (assessing the viability of alternative options should use the same metrics and baselines);
3. Prohibition of discriminatory practices (the PP is not to be applied differently without factual reasons);
4. Alternative policies are not to aid and abet any disguised trade interests (this is to ensure that the PP is used to protect the environment

and humans and not used as a tool to create an unfair market advantage);

5. Alternative policies are to be based on the most comprehensive scientific assessment possible;
6. Alternative policies are well-founded and intelligible;
7. Alternative policies are provisional in character insofar as they are regularly reviewed in the light of new scientific findings and adapted where necessary (this latter portion is akin to Adaptive Governance, discussed in Chapter 7); and
8. Transparency (each step in applying the PP should be transparent and alternative policies should be clearly communicated).[221]

 Professor and International Environmental Law scholar Sumudu A. Atapattu has set forth the following steps as relevant to establishing a process that incorporates the PP into law and policy:

 a. Identify possible threats;
 b. Identify what is known and what is not known about such threats;
 c. Reframe the challenge by describing the purpose of the proposed activity in light of the impacts;
 d. Identify available alternatives to achieve the purpose without the risks;
 e. Assess alternatives, including political, technical, and economic feasibility;
 f. Determine a course of action; and
 g. Monitor and follow-up.[222]

2. SPECIFIC DESCRIPTION OF THE PRECAUTIONARY PRINCIPLE'S RELEVANCE TO R&S

The PP helps policymakers address uncertainty. Preparing for and addressing uncertainty is a critical part of R&S. Not only because social-ecological systems are complex and difficult to fully understand, thus, leading to uncertainty, but also because climate change and other anthropogenic impacts on systems are having cascading effects throughout Earth systems in unforeseen ways.

By providing policymakers with a method to address uncertainty, the PP facilitates their consideration of system resilience and sustainability in crafting law and policy. It does so by providing an opportunity to identify uncertainties (or unintended consequences that can lead to unsustainable and vulnerable systems) and make decisions in light of those uncertainties.

Assessing R&S requires a reliance on scientific information pertaining to social-ecological systems and resource exhaustion. However, many aspects of social-ecological systems and resource systems remain a mystery. The PP provides policy makers with

---

[221] Interdepartmental Working Group on the Precautionary Principle, *The Precautionary Principle in Switzerland and Internationally* 1, 16 (2003), http://www.who.int/ifcs/documents/forums/forum5/synthesepaper_precaution_ch.pdf.
[222] Sumudu A. Atapattu, EMERGING PRINCIPLES OF INTERNATIONAL ENVIRONMENTAL LAW 228-229 (2007).

guidance on how to move forward in the face of social-ecological system and resource exhaustion uncertainty in a way that can support R&S or, at a minimum, provides an opportunity to do so.

The PP may also help avoid decisions that result in vulnerable and unsustainable conditions. By accounting for scientific uncertainty concerning environmental or social degradation the PP helps avoid making decisions that have unintended consequences. The PP helps policy makers consider the lack of scientific certainty pertaining to environmental degradation and human health as social-ecological systems that are complex. The ramifications of failing to use precaution in the face of potential threats can lead to catastrophic conditions, leaving communities vulnerable. The PP addresses this concern by encouraging and/or requiring policy makers to alter course in the face of some risk that falls short of scientific certainty.

The PP is particularly relevant to resilience. The PP can help policy-makers move toward a decision aimed at enhancing system resilience, if so desired by ensuring that we manage risk to a system's characteristics appropriately and avoid risk where possible. If a decision is projected to threaten a system (for example, there is a risk of surpassing a system's threshold), decisions relative to those risks can be altered pursuant to the PP such that the system's resilience is strengthened.

PRECAUTIONARY PRINCIPLE AND PLANETARY BOUNDARIES

In Chapter 1, we described Planetary Boundaries, as a way of assessing the performance of eight systems. Below, Will Steffen, co-founder of Planetary Boundaries, and others describe the connection between the Precautionary Principle and Planetary Boundaries.

The precautionary principle suggests that human societies would be unwise to drive the Earth System substantially away from a Holocene-like condition. A continuing trajectory away from the Holocene could lead, with an uncomfortably high probability, to a very different state of the Earth System, one that is likely to be much less hospitable to the development of human societies. The [Precautionary Principle] framework aims to help guide human societies away from such a trajectory by defining a "safe operating space" in which we can continue to develop and thrive. It does this by proposing boundaries for anthropogenic perturbation of critical Earth System processes. Respecting these boundaries would greatly reduce the risk that anthropogenic activities could inadvertently drive the Earth System to a much less hospitable state. . . .

Will Steffen et al., *Planetary boundaries: Guiding Human Development on a Changing Planet*, Science (Jan. 15, 2015), http://www-ramanathan.ucsd.edu/files/pr210.pdf.

The interdisciplinary approach embedded in the PP may be reflective of sustainability. While some mistakenly think that the PP applies only to ecological systems, it can equally apply to social, such as human health, and economic systems. The primary goal of the PP is to allow policy makers to avoid making a decision that results in harm whether environmental, social, or economic in nature. Stop for a moment and think about the Flint, Michigan, water crisis, mentioned above. At what different decision-making points did the state, local, and federal actors fail to apply the precautionary principle? Could it have made a difference?

When defined as intergenerational equity, sustainability is also deeply embedded in the PP as the risks are indicative of projections and potential impacts on future generations:

> *Precautionary approaches are inherent in the concept of sustainable development, presumably because precaution is part of the burden of proof necessary to establish that particular development decisions meet the needs of today while simultaneously satisfying present environmental constraints and preserving the ability of future generations to meet their own needs.*[223]

If precautionary steps are not taken and known threats come to fruition (for example, the threats associated with the persistent use of fossil fuels and climate-changing impacts), we cannot maintain a resilient or sustainable system.

> *Instead of assuming that important natural systems are resilient or invulnerable, the precautionary principle presumes their vulnerability. By giving the benefit of the doubt to the environment when there is scientific uncertainty, the precautionary principle would shift the burden of proof from those supporting natural systems to those supporting development.*[224]

3. ILLUSTRATION OF THE PRECAUTIONARY PRINCIPLE'S RELEVANCE TO R&S

Located in the northern part of India, the state of Haryana formerly hosted two lakes, Badkhal and Surajkund (the lakes dried in 2014). The natural lakes served as catchment areas that absorbed surface water from the surrounding areas. Throughout the latter half of the twentieth century, excessive mining, which blocked the natural flow of water, mineral water companies' withdrawal, which diverted water from the lakes, and other

---

[223] David A. Wirth, *The Rio Declaration on Environment and Development: Two Steps Forward and One Back, or Vice Versa?*, 29 Ga. L. Rev. 599, 634 (1995).
[224] John C. Dernbach, *Sustainable Development as a Framework for National Governance*, 49 Case W. Res. L. Rev. 1, 61 (1998).

industrial and commercial uses led to an increase in pollution levels and a decrease in water levels in the lakes.

In order to reduce pollution and preserve the environment, the state government's pollution control board recommended that a 5 km radius around the lakes be deemed "sensitive" and construction be prohibited. Landowners, developers, and a local government sued, challenging the board's recommendation, and claiming, "buildings are under construction, plots have been allotted/sold . . . and the plot-holders have even started construction. . . . [V]ested rights of several persons are likely to be adversely affected causing huge financial loss to them."[225]

When the lawsuit reached the Supreme Court of India, the legal issue was whether economic activities, such as mining operations and housing development, may be stopped in order to preserve the environment, human health, and ecology, even though the risks to the environment, human health, and ecology were uncertain. In supporting development, the proponents argued that the 5 km radius was not based on technical or scientific rationales.

In ruling against the proponents of development, the court based its decision on the PP. The parameters of the PP, as found by the court, were: If a government entity finds that there are threats of serious and irreversible damage, the lack of scientific certainty should not be a reason to postpone measures to prevent the damage. The court ruled that the government had the affirmative obligation to *anticipate, prevent and attack the causes of environmental degradation.* This, in essence, gave the government the responsibility to identify risks to the environment and abate them. Those advocating actions that present threats to the environment, humans, or the ecology have the burden to show that those threats did not involve serious and irreversible damage.

After describing the applicability of the PP, the court found there was "no doubt" large-scale construction would impact the local ecology. Even though the precise impact was unclear, "[l]arge-scale construction . . . *may* disturb the rain water drains which in turn *may* badly affect the water level as well as the water quality. . . . It *may* also cause disturbance to the aquifers. . . . The hydrology of the area *may* also be disturbed." Notwithstanding the uncertainty of these findings, the court and the local government had an obligation to protect the environment, ecology, and human health in the face of threats. In short, the court was not certain that the impacts would come to fruition, however, the threats were significant enough to justify limiting construction in zones around the lakes.

While mindful that the ban would have economic impacts, the court stated: "This would undoubtedly cause hardship . . . but it is a price that has to be paid for protecting and safeguarding the right of the people to

---

[225] M.C. Mehta v. Union of India, para. 2, Nov. 10, 1996.

live in a healthy environment with minimal disturbance of ecological balance and without hazard to them. . . . Life, public health and ecology have priority over unemployment and loss of revenue."[226]

Questions and Note

1. The Supreme Court of India in the *M.C. Mehta* case above, paid great attention to development's impact on the ecosystems, particularly the water-based ecosystems. The challengers' counsel argued that it was arbitrary and unfair to place a buffer zone around these two lakes when other lakes in the country did not have bans. In response, the court ruled "[t]he functioning of ecosystems and the status of environment cannot be the same in the country. Preventive measures have to be taken keeping in view the carrying capacity of the ecosystems operating in the environment surroundings under consideration."[227] What is it about ecosystems—discussed in more detail in Section VI below—that makes the PP important for policy decisions?

2. The PP also works closely with Adaptive Governance (AG), discussed in Chapter 7. The successful application of AG calls for the availability of requisite data reflecting an accurate picture of system changes. Changes in a system based on proposed decisions, however, are not always readily, clearly, or scientifically available. PP informs how policy makers should proceed when the necessary data is not available. But once a policy is in place, AG can help policymakers establish a process to obtain information and assess systems' resilience and/or sustainability on an ongoing basis and make alternative policies moving forward.

3. As mentioned above, historical management of surface runoff water has been through the common enemy doctrine or the reasonable use doctrine. Analyze both of these from the perspective of the Precautionary Principle. Do either of them help policy makers consider risks or uncertainty in a way that could help achieve resilient or sustainable use of water resources? If not, what would?

4. Recall that the Safe Drinking Water Act has been criticized for establishing health-based standards for only 89 of the hundreds, or even thousands, of chemicals. What might a federal statute, like the Safe Drinking Water Act, look like if it adopted a Precautionary Principle approach?

---

[226] *Id.* at paras. 9-10.
[227] *Id.* at para. 6.

V. PROPERTY RIGHTS AND HUMAN RIGHTS TO WATER

The Precautionary Principle can help decision makers adopt policies that conserve or avoid damage to water resources. Another way to conserve water resources is to create a legal framework to protect water. Traditional legal frameworks view water as either a property right or as a human right. If it is considered a human right, there are questions as to how much water each individual is entitled to use and who administers this right. If it is viewed as a property right, then we need to determine who owns it, how much they own, does it have the same bundle of rights as land ownership (including the right to transfer), and how may these property rights be limited by the government without such limitations constituting a taking requiring just compensation in the United States.

It is surprising how unsettled the law is as to whether there is a legally cognizable **property right** in water. We have treated water as a private property right using the same approach we apply to private landowner-ship. However, the public trust doctrine has established that water rights are resources the government holds in trust for the people such that water rights constitute a "right to use" or a "mere license" instead of a private property right.[228] As the demand for water increases, public rights to nat-ural resources are pitted against private rights to water for agriculture, urban uses, and fishing. State, federal, and international jurisdictions recognize some measure of private property rights in water, but public rights to protect endangered or threatened species and ecological habitat by maintaining instream water flows may directly compete with these private property rights.[229]

There is historical support for the idea that water belongs to the pub-lic and that the government holds water resources in trust for the people. The public trust doctrine, federally reserved rights, and the navigation servitude are all concepts in the United States that limit the scope of pri-vate property rights. We should protect water interests obtained by private parties based upon allocation principles, such as prior appropriation or riparianism, against claims from other private parties, so long as this pro-tection is not adverse to the public good. Nevertheless, in order to meet sustainability goals for human survival, equity, and ecological health as water demand increases, it may be necessary to change our concept of water rights from private property rights to public resources that govern-ments must manage for the public benefit.[230]

---

[228] Shelley Ross Saxer, *The Fluid Nature of Property Rights in Water*, 21 DUKE ENVTL. L. & POL'Y F. 49 (2010).
[229] *Id.* at 50-51.
[230] *Id.* at 110-111.

The public trust doctrine provides that the state has an obligation to preserve water resources for the people, as well as certain other natural resources that may be determined to be "held in trust" for the benefit of the public. Originally an English common law doctrine with Roman Law roots, the doctrine was adopted by the United States in the 1800s, and provided that the public had rights to tidal lands and land beneath navigable waters. Several states adopted the federal common law view of the public trust to primarily address navigation and commerce; however, a few states in both the eastern and western regions of the United States have expanded the natural resources subject to this public trust to include wildlife, public lands, ecological resources, as well as navigable and non-navigable surface water and groundwater. As states respond to increasing demands on water resources produced by scarcity, development, and climate change, the government may more frequently apply the public trust doctrine to allocate water rights among existing private property water rights holders and public and ecological necessities.[231]

Federal reserved rights in water arise from the creation of Indian reservations and the withdrawal of lands from the public domain for a federal purpose such as the national forest system. Federal reserved rights allow the government to retain the water rights needed to manage these resources and create an exception to the general rule that state law defines water rights. A federal reserved right is not a specially created right but is instead a declaration of existing rights to the natural resources, such as forests, water, and minerals, that were attached to federal government lands before they were privatized.[232] *Indian water rights* provided the genesis for the federal reserved rights doctrine, which was created by the Supreme Court in *Winters v. United States*[233] to recognize that the federal government had reserved necessary water rights when it set aside tribal land reservations before western statehood occurred.[234]

State-defined water rights may be limited if the federal government retains instream flows sufficient to protect navigability, hunting, fishing, and aquatic habitat, as well as to provide for reasonable irrigation rights and biodiversity protection under the Endangered Species Act.[235] The federal government has a claim to large amounts of water based on federal reserved rights in Indian lands, national parks, and federal projects. Therefore, private and state claims to waters reserved by the federal government will be subject to federal involvement in determining water rights

---

[231] *Id.* at 64-68.
[232] Michael C. Blumm, *Federal Reserved Water Rights as a Rule of Law*, 52 IDAHO L. REV. 369 (2016).
[233] Winters v. United States, 207 U.S. 564, 577 (1908).
[234] Michael C. Blumm et al., *The Mirage of Indian Reserved Water Rights and Western Streamflow Restoration in the McCarran Amendment Era: A Promise Unfulfilled*, 36 ENVTL. L. 1157, 1159, 1162 (2006) (concluding that tribes have been largely unsuccessful in asserting their water rights because their claims have been "dominated by state law and state courts").
[235] Saxer, *supra* note 228, at 68-70.

and water resource allocation.[236] However, in early water rights adjudications involving federal reserved rights, the federal government could not be joined because of sovereign immunity. The McCarran Amendment of 1952[237] addressed this concern by "waiv[ing] federal sovereign immunity for the joinder of the United States as a defendant in general stream adjudications."[238] Subsequent Supreme Court decisions clarified the scope of this waiver, leading to state court control over the adjudication of water rights, including federal reserved rights.[239] Tribal water rights have not necessarily fared well under these state controls, and western stream flows have not improved as expected to support rights such as a tribe's treaty fishing rights.[240]

The navigation servitude also limits state-defined water rights by prohibiting riparian owners from obstructing navigation, based on the federal government's power over navigation under the Commerce Clause of the U.S. Constitution. So long as the federal government is acting to protect the public's interest in navigable waters, it can abrogate private property interests and the government is not required to pay just compensation to landowners or holders of water rights adversely impacted by navigation projects.[241]

The United Nations (UN) General Assembly in 2010 recognized a **human right to water** in a resolution that "declared that the 'right to safe and clean drinking water . . . [is] a human right that is essential for the full enjoyment of life and all human rights.'"[242] While some countries have recognized such a right, most nations do not have a constitutionally protected right to water and fundamental questions remain as to how such a right can be maintained.[243] In the United States, a few states have identified a human right to water and some local governments have done so as well, but this right is largely "undefined as the policies were designed to protect drinking water resources from over-extraction by corporations bottling water for commercial purposes."[244] Indeed, framing water as a human right is a response to concerns about the economic and environmental

---

[236] *Id.* at 70.

[237] The McCarran Amendment, 43 U.S.C. §666 (1952); *see also The McCarran Amendment*, U.S. Dep't of Justice (May 12, 2015), http://www.justice.gov/enrd/mccarran-amendment.

[238] U.S. Dep't of Justice, *supra* note 237.

[239] *Id.*

[240] Blumm, *supra* note 234, at 1203.

[241] *Id.*; Saxer, *supra* note 228, at 70-72.

[242] Rhett B. Larson, *The New Right in Water*, 70 Wash. & Lee L. Rev. 2181, 2184 (2013) (quoting 2010 UN Resolution).

[243] *Id.* (noting that there are unanswered questions as to "who owns water, how to price water, whether to subsidize water services, and whether such a right is sustainable and enforceable").

[244] Patricia A. Jones, *Complexity of Protections and Barriers in the Implementation of the Human Right to Water in the United States*, 106 Am. Soc'y Int'l L. Proc. 46, 48-49 (2012) (suggesting that we can use "economic studies and models that address affordability and access to water and sanitation services" and "identify financing mechanisms that will make the human right to water achievable — and sustainable").

challenges of water management and fears regarding the privatization of water.[245]

> In 2002, the UN Committee on Economic, Social and Cultural Rights recognized a human right to water in General Comment No. 15 to the International Covenant on Economic, Social and Cultural Rights ("Covenant"). The Covenant is a binding treaty to the over 162 countries that ratified the treaty, including China, Russia, and almost all of Africa and South America. It is not binding for those that have not, including the United States, which signed the treaty in 1979, but has never ratified it through the Senate.
>
> Article 11 of the Covenant states:
>
> > The States Parties . . . recognize the right of everyone to an adequate standard of living for himself and his family, including adequate food, clothing and housing, and to the continuous improvement of living conditions. The States Parties will take appropriate steps to ensure the realization of this right. . . .
>
> The clarifying General Comment No. 15 states:
>
> > The human right to water entitles everyone to sufficient, safe, acceptable, physically accessible and affordable water for personal and domestic uses. An adequate amount of safe water is necessary to prevent death from dehydration, to reduce the risk of water-related disease and to provide for consumption, cooking, personal and domestic hygienic requirements.

If governments must *provide* a right to water, such a right would be difficult to administer and enforce because of the difficulty in evaluating "the adequacy of water quality, quantity, and pricing" and may lead to increased consumption and inadequate funds for water infrastructure.[246] Instead of viewing the right as a "provision" or positive right such as education, framing the right as a "participation" or negative right such as access to the judicial system would give citizens a right to *participate* in water policy and water management based on the state's fiduciary duty under the public trust doctrine.[247] It should be possible for both the private and public sectors to participate in assuring "that everyone, without discrimination, has access to adequate amounts of good quality, accessible, and affordable water."[248]

---

[245] Murthy, *supra* note 177, at 147-148.
[246] Larson, *supra* note 242, at 2191-2193 (proposing instead a "participation right in water based on the public trust doctrine [which] would promote transparency, accountability, and experimentation in the development of water policy."). *Id.* at 2193.
[247] *Id.*
[248] Murthy, *supra* note 177, at 148.

Question

1. For purposes of R&S, does it matter whether we view water as a property right or as a human right? Would one more than the other tend to lead to resilient or sustainable water usage or systems? If so, how? Does the answer depend on how we interpret that right? Who grants and to whom is that right granted?

VI. STRATEGY TO FACILITATE IMPLEMENTATION #3: ECOSYSTEM SERVICES MANAGEMENT

Establishing a legal regime to regulate water and other natural resources often involves trade-offs. At times, those trade-offs involve the balancing of human health, health of the environment, and economic benefits. Helping to identify and assess trade-offs relevant to assessing R&S is ecosystem services management (ESM). At its core, ESM is about calculating and accounting for the benefits ecosystems provide to humans. These benefits often do not have a recognized monetary value. ESM helps reflect the true costs of policies and behaviors and more accurately reflects trade-offs by accounting for impacts to ecosystems. This information, in turn, helps policymakers develop decisions that are more informed.

A. General Description of Ecosystem Services Management

In the nineteenth century, Jules Dupuit, Alfred Marshall, and others introduced cost-benefit analysis (CBA) to help balance the pros and cons of a project. CBA assesses the strengths and weaknesses of a project by reviewing the various *economic costs* associated with the project, including time, labor, and materials. Throughout the twentieth century, lawmakers and business owners regularly integrated CBA into policy decisions. The result was that lawmakers wrote economic analyses into law and policy and it continued to rise in importance and drive policy decisions.

Missing from the archetypal CBA is an accounting of environmental and social costs. In fact, "natural ecosystems are greatly undervalued by society . . . [and] few people are conscious of the role natural ecosystem services play."[249] In response to the "near total lack of public appreciation of societal dependence upon natural ecosystems,"[250] scientists and ecological

---

[249]Gretchen C. Daily et al., *Ecosystem Services: Benefits Supplied to Human Societies by Natural Ecosystems*, 2 Issues in Ecology 1, 2 (1997).
[250]NATURE'S SERVICES: SOCIETAL DEPENDENCE ON NATURAL ECOSYSTEMS xv (Gretchen Daily ed., 1997).

economists in the 1990s formed an alternative to the CBA, called "ecosystem services management." Derived from a 1935 article in which ecologist and biologist Sir Arthur Tansley first detailed the concept of "ecosystems," ESM identifies a monetary value for ecosystem services.[251] Gretchen Daily, one of the leading scholars on ESM, defines ecosystem services as a "wide range of conditions and processes through which natural ecosystems, and the species that are part of them, help sustain and fulfill human life."

ESM focuses on two primary questions: "(1) what services do natural ecosystems provide society, and (2) what is a first approximation of their monetary value?"[252] In answering the first question, we typically divide human reliance on ecosystem services into four categories:

Provision of Goods or Products, such as:	Cultural Services, such as:
• Food and water • Fuel • Fiber	• Spiritual • Educational • Recreational
Regulating Services, such as: • Climate control • Water filtration • Flood control	**Supporting Services, such as:** • Nutrient cycling • Soil formation • Primary production

These four categories of services provide vital benefits we rely upon every day, including clean and regular flows of water, carbon sequestration and storage (for example from wetlands, forests, and oceans), production of fertile soil, relatively predictable weather, pest and disease control, species diversification and habitat protection, detoxification and decomposition of waste, and plant pollination.

Once we identify the ecosystem services and their associated anthropogenic benefits, the second question asks us to quantify the value of those benefits. This step should result in the production of a numerical value that reflects a system's benefits to humans. We can then compare this value to other values to help us make informed decisions and more completely understand the ramifications and trade-offs of a decision or policy.

For example, in 1997, a group of ecologists and economists collaborated on an effort to estimate the worldwide annual value of ecosystems. They concluded that ecosystem services provide an annual anthropogenic

---

[251] Robert Costanza et al., *The Value of the World's Ecosystem Services and Natural Capital,* 387 NATURE 253, 259 (1997).
[252] J.B. Ruhl & James Salzman, *The Law and Policy Beginnings of Ecosystem Services,* 22 J. LAND USE & ENVTL. L. 157, 159 (2007).

benefit of approximately $33 trillion.[253] At that time, the global gross national product was approximately $18 trillion.[254]

Economists struggling with how to quantify ecosystem services have devised a number of methodologies, including contingent valuation, hedonic pricing, and replacement cost. While economists have lauded each methodology for its pros and cons, they are different and focus on alternative means of evaluating ecosystem services:

- *Contingent valuation* surveys the value people place on an ecosystem service. It asks how much one *would* pay or would accept payment for the loss of a given service.
- *Hedonic pricing* is based on the premise that ecosystems and their services alter economic pricing. For example, hedonic pricing may look at the market value of a piece of real estate with and without ecosystem services (for example, trees provide shading, water retention, and food that can increase a property's value). The difference in these two values reflects the hedonic pricing value.
- *Replacement cost* explores how much it would cost to replace a given ecosystem. For example, how much would it cost to replace the pollination provided by bees or protection humans get from harmful ultraviolet B radiation shielded by the ozone layer?

B. Specific Description of Ecosystem Services Management's Relevance to R&S

ESM helps policymakers understand and account for the complexities embedded in assessing R&S by providing critical—and often neglected—information pertaining to ecosystems. This information helps more accurately weigh the true costs associated with decisions. While those costs do not dictate a particular law, policy, or course of action, the costs do help explain the potential ramifications decisions can have and provide a basis for making decisions that have positive impacts:

> *One cannot begin to understand flood control, for example, without realizing the impact of widespread wetland destruction on the ecosystem service of water retention; nor can one understand water quality without recognizing how development in forested watersheds degrades the service of water purification. The costs from degradation of these services are high[.]*[255]

---

[253] Costanza et al., supra note 251, at 259 (noting that an ecosystem services analysis such as this is often theoretical in that "it ignores the fact that many ecosystem services are literally irreplaceable.").

[254] *Id.* at 254, tbl. 1.

[255] Blake Hudson, *Federal Constitutions: The Keystone of Nested Commons Governance*, 63 ALA. L. REV. 1007, 1022-1023 (2012) (quoting David Hunter et al., INTERNATIONAL ENVIRONMENTAL LAW AND POLICY 11 (4th ed. 2010)).

As the above quote implies, making informed decisions includes hav-ing a clear understanding of the relevant ecosystems and the benefits humans gain from those systems. It is difficult to base law and policy on an assessment of R&S without knowing how a specific decision will affect ecosystems and the services they provide.

"The continued generation of ecosystem services depends on a social-ecological system's resilience."[256] If the system is not resilient, we risk losing the system and incurring inefficiencies and costs, and poten-tially harming other systems and losing their services as well. Climate change, for example, is stressing many ecosystem services. Changes in those services, in turn, affect human health and economies, stressing the resilience and sustainability of social-ecological systems ties to those services.

Incorporating R&S into law and policy benefits from an assessment and understanding of how much pressure an ecosystem can withstand before it changes and alters the services from which humans benefit. Kenneth Arrow, 1972 Nobel Memorial Prize Laureate in Economic Sciences, states the connection between R&S and ecosystems, as follows:

> The loss of ecosystem resilience is potentially important for at least three reasons. First, the discontinuous change in ecosystem functions as the system flips from one equilibrium to another could be associated with sudden loss of biological productivity, and so to a reduced capacity to support human life. Second, it may imply an irreversible change in the set of options open both to present and future generations (examples include soil erosion, deple-tion of groundwater reservoirs, desertification, and loss of biodiversity.) Third, discontinuous and irreversible changes from familiar to unfamiliar states in-crease the uncertainties associated with the environmental effects of economic activities.
>
> If human activities are to be sustainable, we need to ensure that the ecolog-ical systems on which our economics depend are resilient.[257]

While ESM is not a panacea, "[w]e cannot fully address the unsustain-able effects we are having on ecosystems and make the necessary behav-ioral alterations if we fail to adequately account for and acknowledge the impacts and look to properly allocate the costs of those impacts."[258]

---

[256] Hannah E. Birge et al., *Social-Ecological Resilience and Law in the Platte River Basin*, 51 Idaho L. Rev. 229, 240 (2014).

[257] Kenneth Arrow et al., *Economic Growth, Carrying Capacity, and the Environment*, 15 Ecological Econ. 91, 93 (1995).

[258] Jonathan D. Rosenbloom, *A Framework for Application: Three Concrete, Contextual Strategies to Accelerate Sustainability in* Rethinking Sustainable Development to Meet the Climate Change Challenge 13 (Keith Hirokawa & Jessica Owley eds., ELI Press 2014).

In *Economic Returns from the Biosphere*, Graciela Chichilnisky and Geoffrey Heal describe an example of ecosystem service management being used in law and policy to enhance the sustainability and resilience of water-based systems in New York City. New York City integrated an ESM approach to protecting the upstate watershed it relied on for water. In 1905, when New York City began accessing water from the watershed, 95% of the land was native old growth forest. That forest provided some of the cleanest drinking water in the country. Over time, however, the ecosystem was destroyed by the cutting of timber, increasing of roads, fertilizing of lawns, seeping of septic systems, and others.

By the turn of the millennium, New York City's water quality had diminished. The federal government informed New York City that it would have to install a major water treatment facility estimated to cost between $6 and 8 billion and about a half billion a year to operate. Essentially, the City was going to pay approximately a billion dollars a year (maintenance and debt service) for an ecosystem service it had once received for free.

Instead of building the plant, the City decided to invest $2 billion purchasing property rights in the watershed. This action supported and protected the ecosystem, rather than fought it. Today, New York City has improved water quality and saves approximately $1 billion a year. Graciela Chichilnisky & Geoffrey Heal, *Economic Returns from the Biosphere*, 391 NATURE 629 (Feb. 1998).

Question and Notes

1. One criticism of ESM is that ESM only recognizes the monetary value of ecosystem services, however, ecosystems have a "value" that goes beyond economic value to humans. Although not commenting on ESM, in *A Sand County Almanac — And Sketches Here and There*, Aldo Leopold sets forth the basis for this argument:

   > One basic weakness in a conservation system based wholly on economic motives is that most members of the land community have no economic value. Wild-flowers and songbirds are examples. Of the 22,000 higher plants and animals native to Wisconsin, it is doubtful whether more than 5 percent can be sold, fed, eaten, or otherwise put to economic use. Yet these creatures are members of the biotic community, and if (as I believe) its stability depends on its integrity, they are entitled to continuance.

   What do you think about this argument as it applies to ESM?

2. Although related to ESM, "Ecosystem Management" is a more normative-based concept. Ecosystem Management is a "strategy for the integrated management of land, water and living resources that promotes conservation

and sustainable use in an equitable way."[259] Professor R. Edward Grumbine detailed ten dominant themes of Ecosystem Management in his 1997 article, *Reflections on "What Is Ecosystem Management?."* In *Ecosystem Services and Ecosystem Management—How Good a Fit?*, J.B. Ruhl compares ESM and Ecosystem Management based on Grumbine's ten themes, creating the following table:[260]

Summary of Themes of Ecosystem Management and Ecosystem Services Theory

Ecosystem Management Theme	Fit with Ecosystem Services	Explanation
Hierarchical context	Strongly complementary	Ecosystem services flow at many scales and thus require sound understanding of cross-scalar and systems effects of management decisions
Ecological boundaries	Strongly complementary	Ecosystem services flow from natural capital to human beneficiaries across political and administrative boundaries
Ecological integrity	Potential conflicts	Managing for particular ecosystem services could undermine ecological integrity, depending on how ecological integrity is defined
Data collection	Strongly complementary	Ecosystem services management will demand intensive data collection to inventory natural capital and trace flows to human beneficiaries
Monitoring	Strongly complementary	Ecosystem services monitoring will demand robust monitoring of natural capital capacity and flows of services
Interagency cooperation	Strongly complementary	Ecosystem services could flow across land units managed by many different agencies and landowners
Organizational change	Potential conflicts	Organizational changes required for ecosystem management may or may not be compatible with management for ecosystem services
Humans as a part of nature	Potential conflicts	Ecosystem services theory is inherently anthropocentric, but recognizes the importance of natural capital to achieving ecosystem service values
Values	Potential conflicts	Values of ecosystem management regime may or may not be compatible with management for ecosystem services

---

[259] Convention on Biological Diversity, COP 5, Decision V/6, Ecosystem approach s.7(A)(1) (2000).
[260] J.B. Ruhl, *Ecosystem Services and Ecosystem Management—How Good a Fit?, in* The Laws of Nature: Reflections on the Evolution of Ecosystem Management Law and Policy 102 (Kalyani Robbins ed., 2013).

3. Developed in the late 1980s and 1990s, Biosphere 2 (the Earth was thought of as "Biosphere 1") was an attempt to recreate the Earth's biosphere—the sum of all ecosystems. Mission 1, which was funded by billionaire Edward Bass and lasted almost two years, consisted of eight people living in the biosphere, a three-acre, glassed structure located in Oracle, Arizona. The idea was that these eight people would recreate life on Earth inside a controlled setting.

Professor, ecologist, and biologist John Avise summarized an example of quantifying ecosystem services based on Biosphere 2:

> *The cost of the man-made technosphere that (marginally) regulated life-support systems for eight Biospherians over two years was about $150 million, or $9,000,000 per person per year. These services are provided to the rest of us more-or-less cost-free by natural processes, but if we were being charged, the total invoice for all Earthospherians would come to an astronomical three quintillion dollars for the current generation alone!*

Aside from making the point that ecosystem services provide an enormous amount of economic value, Avise's statement also raises the question of whether we have the technology to accurately replace those services.

VII. WATERSHED MANAGEMENT AND INSTREAM FLOW PROTECTIONS

ESM is a strategy that law and policy can incorporate to help decision makers account for externalities and the mismatch between political or legal boundaries and the boundaries of natural resources.[261] One such mismatch involves watershed boundaries verses the governmental jurisdictional boundaries touching the watershed. In this section, we explore watersheds and how they correspond to the geographic scale required to efficiently and effectively manage human activities in regard to the physical and biological organization of the environment and natural resources.[262]

A. Watershed Management

Watersheds are an ecological and geographic unit that can address human activities with regard to water. The ahupua'a divisions of land in Hawai'i, discussed at the beginning of this chapter, are an excellent illustration of how ESM can play a role to help achieve more R&S water-based systems.

---

[261] Craig Anthony (Tony) Arnold, *Adaptive Watershed Planning and Climate Change*, 5 ENVT'L & ENERGY L. & POL'Y J. 417, 422-423 (2010).
[262] *Id.* at 423.

In this case, the state restructured the political boundaries to respond to the ecological features of the watershed in a way that better aligns political decisions with the water resource.

Watershed management is critical to addressing the increasing demand on water resources as populations increase in drier parts of our world and climate change has the potential to disrupt historical patterns of rainfall and capture. Watershed management can help increase the resilience and sustainability of water-based systems by helping overcome many of the collective action challenges described earlier in this chapter and explored further in the next subsection.

We should manage water resources "at watershed scales, as watersheds are the ecological systems of water."[263]

> *Watersheds provide a range of ecosystem services, including provisioning services (e.g., food, water, wood, biomass), regulating services (e.g., water filtration, flood control, aquifer recharge, carbon sequestration), cultural services (e.g., recreation, aesthetic enjoyment, spiritual fulfillment), and supporting services (e.g., soil formation, nutrient cycling, habitat).*[264]

Adaptive watershed management is described as "a blend of ecosystem management and adaptive management in aquatic ecosystems."[265] Managers can use this approach to develop a watershed-resource management strategy that facilitates decision making based on an ongoing science-based process. This process includes "continual testing, monitoring, evaluating applied strategies, and revising management approaches continuously to incorporate new information, science, and societal needs."[266] Professor Craig "Tony" Arnold has suggested that adaptive watershed management be used because it discards planning methodologies in favor of responding to uncertainty and complexity by encouraging experimentalism to address changing conditions and evolving knowledge. Instead of focusing on planning to deal with allocating, conserving, preserving, and restoring natural resources, institutions tasked with these duties can concentrate on managing these resources with flexibility and experimentation.[267] In this way, watershed management incorporates Adaptive Governance (discussed in Chapter 7) and ESM and attempts to avoid collective action challenges.

---

[263] *Id.* at 420.
[264] Jonathan Z. Cannon, *Sustainable Watersheds*, 107 MICH. L. REV. FIRST IMPRESSIONS 74, 75 (2008).
[265] Melissa Mitchell, *Scholar of the Month: Craig Anthony Arnold*, CENTER FOR L., ADAPTION, AND RESOURCES (Jan. 6, 2014), http://www.law.unc.edu/documents/clear/scholars/20132014/arnold-scholar.pdf.
[266] *Draft*, TRES PALACIOS WATERSHED PROTECTION PLAN (Aug. 2016), http://matagordabasin.tamu.edu/media/639419/tresp_wpp_2016-08-29_final_draft.pdf.
[267] Arnold, *supra* note 261 at 420.

In advocating for adaptive watershed management, Professor Arnold succinctly describes the characteristics and processes of watersheds as follows:[268]

> *Watershed functions and processes include water drainage, water storage, flood mediation and management, filtration of sediment and pollutants, support of biological life, sediment load, evapotranspiration, and energy generation and flows, among others. A truly comprehensive effort to conserve and protect the health and integrity of all of a watershed's functions is a large and potentially overwhelming task. The range of human activities affecting watersheds is quite broad and includes: (1) the diversion, pumping, and consumptive uses of water; (2) water development projects and waterway alterations: (3) instream flow programs, including ecological and species protection, dredging for commercial navigation, fishing operations, and opportunities for recreational boating; (4) flood and runoff control; (5) land use and development patterns; (6) forestry, mining, and agricultural methods; and (7) introduction of pollutants into waterways, either directly or indirectly. Likewise, natural events that can substantially alter a watershed's hydrology, perhaps in synergy with human-created effects, include floods, major storms, hurricanes, and drought. Moreover, watershed characteristics selected for management may be defined, at least partly, with respect to social phenomena. These phenomena might include local culture and the ways by which a particular community defines itself with respect to waters; political objectives within or among particular units of government; and the available resources, expertise, or legal authority to address particular aspects of a watershed.*

B. Challenges Involved with Managing Watersheds

1. COLORADO RIVER WATERSHED

The Colorado River watershed has been heavily impacted by population growth (discussed in Chapter 2) and a long-term drought. As the only major river in the southwestern United States, the Colorado River supports the water needs of seven U.S. states—the upper-basin states of Colorado, New Mexico, Utah, and Wyoming and the lower-basin states of Arizona, California, and Nevada—along with two states in Mexico.[269] In the early 1900s, the Colorado River was heavily engineered to yield electricity, support agriculture, and control flooding. Studies have shown that the twentieth century was at least 15% wetter in the Colorado basin

---

[268] *Id.* at 427.

[269] Michael Wines, *Colorado River Drought Forces a Painful Reckoning for States*, N.Y. Times (Jan. 5, 2014), http://www.nytimes.com/2014/01/06/us/colorado-river-drought-forces-a-painful-reckoning-for-states.html.

than it had been in the previous 1,300 years and that in the future, global warming will reduce the river's average flow by 5-35% after 2050.[270] Attempts to share the Colorado River among the seven states and Mexico began in the 1920s by splitting the water 50-50 between the upper-basin states and the lower-basin states.[271] Even though these negotiations underestimated the water needs of the lower-basin states, during the twentieth century the water supplies were generally sufficient to offset shortages. However, after 16 years of drought, the growing populations that depend on the Colorado River can no longer tolerate the diminishing flow, particularly when even successful conservation efforts are not enough.[272] We will need to find new sources of water, such as through desalination, and even greater conservation efforts will be needed.[273]

Watersheds in the eastern United States do not necessarily face the disruptive factors of scarcity and drought experienced in the western water basins, but they do require adaptive watershed management to cope with pollution, flooding, and runoff.[274] A study of the Anacostia River basin located in Maryland and Washington, D.C., illustrates the complexity of the issues involved in adaptively managing an eastern watershed for resiliency. Seven key variables were identified as requiring continuing study, monitoring, and adaptive management:

> (1) land cover and land use; (2) the quantity, velocity, and quality of stormwater runoff; (3) streamflow; (4) pollutant loading, adjusted for changing ecological conditions, not merely a measure of compliance with TMDLs; (5) performance of green infrastructure; (6) the interactions between social values/norms and political forces, including not only measures of public attitudes and values towards the Anacostia and the environment but also trends and patterns in environmental, natural-resource, and land-use politics at various governance scales; and (7) institutional capacity and change.[275]

The study concluded that "the greatest opportunities for a more resilient, climate-adaptive Anacostia River watershed require continued and improved changes in watershed governance, restoration and green infrastructure initiatives, land use regulation, public engagement, integration of social justice into watershed decision making, and monitoring and feedback loops."[276]

---

[270] *Id.*

[271] *Id.*

[272] *Id.* (noting that Arizona "consumes essentially as much water today as in 1955, even as its population has grown nearly twelvefold.") *Id.; see also Drought in the Colorado River Basin*, U.S. DEP'T OF INTERIOR, https://www.doi.gov/water/owdi.cr.drought/en/ (last visited Oct. 11, 2017).

[273] Wines, *supra* note 269 (concluding that we will all have to use less water in the twenty-first century).

[274] Craig Anthony (Tony) Arnold et al., *The Social-Ecological Resilience of an Eastern Urban-Suburban Watershed: The Anacostia River Basin*, 51 IDAHO L. REV. 29 (2014).

[275] *Id.* at 89 (internal citations omitted).

[276] *Id.* at 90.

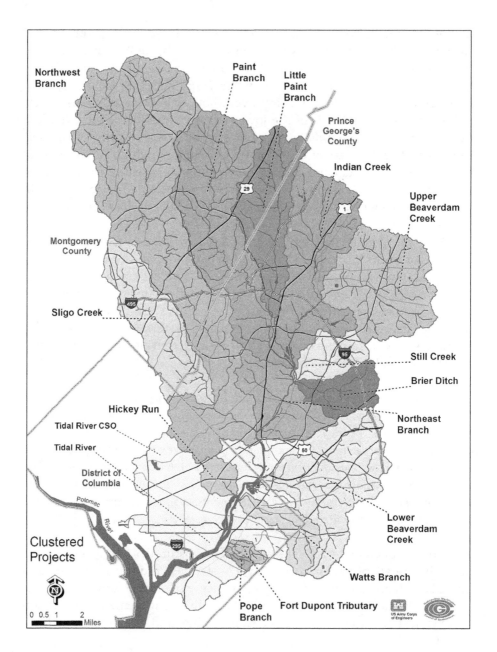

2. JORDAN RIVER BASIN AND COLLECTIVE ACTION CHALLENGES

Watershed management is particularly difficult when nations share geographic boundaries because collective action challenges arise. Management of the *Jordan River basin*, for example, has a great potential for failure because of the served nations' political, religious, and socio-economic differences as well as the scarcity of water resources and growing populations. There are five co-riparian nations served by the Jordan River:

Israel, Jordan, Lebanon, Palestine, and Syria.[277] Syria and Jordan draw water from the Yarmouk River, which is a tributary of the Jordan River, and Israel draws water from Lake Tiberias (the Sea of Galilee), which receives water from the Jordan River and conveys it to coastal cities and farms via its National Water Carrier.[278] Below Lake Tiberias, the Jordan River "trickles" into the Dead Sea, along with saline springs, agricultural runoff, and wastewater from the city of Tiberias in Israel.[279] The Dead Sea's historic salinity has thwarted the survival of aquatic life, save for some microscopic life forms, but serves as a habitat for bird populations and other animal life around the lake.[280] Dramatic shrinkage, 30% in the past 50 years caused by the heavy demand for Jordan River waters due to population increases in the basin, threatens its survival.[281]

Both the quantity and quality of the Jordan River have deteriorated, particularly in the lower section of the basin where the water has high salinity and pollution rates. While Israel and Palestine also rely on the **West Bank Aquifer** as a freshwater resource, the aquifer is being overdrawn by approximately 25% each year.[282] Officials have proposed various plans for sharing this scarce resource over the years, beginning in modern times after the 1948 Arab-Israeli War when American President Dwight Eisenhower appointed Eric Johnston in 1953 as a Special Ambassador to negotiate a regional plan for water resource development of the Jordan River Valley.[283] Riparians of the Jordan River have not committed to any of the regional agreements contained in the Johnston Plan, the Cotton Plan, or the Israel-Jordan Peace Treaty.[284] Part of the problem is that each of these plans has allocated fixed amounts of water to the riparians, calculated with the assumption that there will be a constant supply of water.[285] This over-commitment of water resources in the face of declining freshwater supplies will ultimately add to existing regional tensions, and water sharing in the Jordan River basin will be tied to ongoing conflicts among these nations.[286]

Conflicts over water, such as those in the Jordan River basin, involve numerous issues. One of those issues concerns collective action challenges (CACs). CACs arise due to the institutional arrangements and their corresponding jurisdictional boundaries and laws. One method to help avoid a

---

[277] Stephen C. McCaffrey, *The Shrinking Dead Sea and the Red-Dead Canal: A Sisyphean Tale?*, 19 Pac. McGeorge Global Bus. & Dev. L.J. 259, 261 (2006).

[278] *Id.*

[279] *Id.*

[280] *Id.* at 259-260.

[281] *Id.* at 260-261.

[282] Ian J. Silverbrand, *The History and Potential Future of the Israeli-Palestinian Water Conflict*, 44 Stan. J. Int'l L. 221 (2008).

[283] *Id.* at 228-229.

[284] *Id.* at 243-44.

[285] *Id.* at 245.

[286] *Jordan River Basin*, Inventory of Shared Water Res. in W. Asia, http://waterinventory.org/surface_water/jordan-river-basin (last visited Oct. 11, 2017).

potential tragedy and the destruction of the water resource is for actors to self-regulate by collaborating on the sustainable management and use of the watershed:

> *However sustainability is defined, it will require collaboration to address the fragmentation of governance structures and the broad impact ecosystems have across those structures. . . . [Many] challenges and ecosystems "are amorphous and multi-jurisdictional—freely flowing in and out of borders." Jurisdictional borders are rarely drawn or redrawn to respond to the proper management and operation of [commons resources]. . . .*
>
> *[I]nefficiencies arise out of collective action problems and are exacerbated by the mismatch between jurisdictional boundaries and [commons resources]. . . . Collaboration may help overcome the inefficiencies relevant to collective action problems [by] . . . incentiviz[ing] and more equitably allocate[ing] risks and costs among the relevant parties—regardless of the context—to encourage sustainable actions. Brought to life by the late Elinor Ostrom's Nobel Prize-winning work, collaborations . . . help shift the dynamic so that individuals and entities with a stake in an ecosystem and its services have the ability to measure, use, and protect that ecosystem in a sustainable manner. Instead of fragmenting and acting individually, collaboration offers the opportunity to control and alter the fate of a given ecosystem.*[287]

3. MISSISSIPPI RIVER WATERSHED AND COLLECTIVE ACTION CHALLENGES

An illustration of collective action challenges in watersheds and its implications on system R&S. Many ecosystem services associated with watersheds are essential to human health. Some of those services include clean air and water, soil retention, predictable weather patterns, and carbon dioxide absorption. Notwithstanding the importance of these services, many decisions concerning water resources result in unsustainable and non-resilient water-based systems. Unresolved collective action challenges may partially explain the stress on these systems. The Mississippi watershed, encompassing 41% of the continental United States and touching 31 states, provides such an example.

The watershed completely or almost completely encompasses the geographic area of 11 of the 31 states (listed in the left-hand column below). According to the U.S. Census, these 11 states have over 27,000 local governments.

---

[287] Rosenbloom, *supra* note 258.

State	General Purpose (city, town, county)	Special Purpose (ex. sch. dist., water dist.)	Total
Arkansas	577	979	1,556
Illinois	2,831	4,132	6,963
Iowa	1,046	901	1,947
Kansas	1,997	1,829	3,826
Kentucky	536	802	1,338
Louisiana	364	165	529
Missouri	1,380	2,388	3,768
Nebraska	1,040	1,541	2,581
Oklahoma	667	1,185	1,852
South Dakota	1,284	699	1,983
Tennessee	437	479	916
		TOTAL	**27,258**

Accounting for only part of the relevant geographic area illustrates the vast number of local governments that have some regulatory authority in the watershed. Some common ways in which these 27,000 local governments impact or use the water resource are:

- *Extracting volume from the watershed.* Local governments often provide for the provision of potable water or the use of water to irrigate agricultural land. For example, the Des Moines Water Works provides potable water to approximately 500,000 people in Central Iowa. It withdraws millions of gallons daily from the Raccoon and Des Moines rivers, which flow to the Mississippi.
- *Adding volume to the watershed.* Municipal sewer water discharges and a number of land use practices contribute to stormwater runoff, ranging from large parking lots in urban areas to tiling in rural areas. Tiling is the laying of PVC piping between four to six feet below agricultural land to expedite the removal of water and direct it to a stream or river. In Iowa, for example, about 20-26% of the land is tiled, pushing that water downstream, instead of absorbing it into the ground.
- *Adding pollutants to the watershed.* Discharges from combined sewer outflows, in which a city discharges raw sewerage and/or untreated stormwater runoff into a river upon certain rain events, pollute waterways. Over 700 cities throughout the United States use this

practice. Another example might be runoff from agricultural land in which a local government allows farmers to plant, fertilize, and use pesticides adjacent to the river's edge. Upon certain rain events, water running off farmland carries that fertilizer and pesticide into the river.

The daily decisions of thousands of local governments to extract, add to, or pollute the water resource results in a classic tragedy of the commons problem involving thousands of actors. Many actors (local governments, in this case) have access to the common pool resource — clean water — and are using it in a way that externalizes harm to others. That harm is experienced downstream and comes in many forms, including fishkills, non-potable or swimmable water, hypoxia, and the dead zone in the northern Gulf of Mexico.

The U.S. Geological Survey and the EPA estimate that nitrogen and phosphorus originating on agricultural lands throughout the watershed are in part responsible for the "dead zone" in the Gulf of Mexico. In some estimates, runoff from agricultural land is 70% responsible for an increase in nutrients in the watershed. When nutrients enter the watershed, algae feed off the nutrient-rich water. When the algae die, they sink to the floor of the Gulf, and are decomposed by bacteria, which deplete the water of oxygen. As the oxygen is depleted, marine life can no longer survive — leading to the dead zone, shown in Figure 3-2. In this scenario, upstream cities externalize harms stemming from their use of the resource, shifting those costs to New Orleans and other downstream cities along the Louisiana gulf coast.

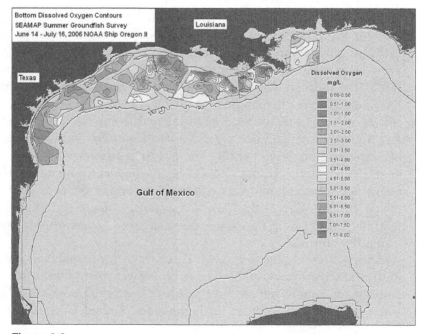

Figure 3-2

Garrett Hardin might suggest one way to correct this CAC is to have the federal and/or state governments regulate local governments' use of the resource. The federal government, however, appears to be unwilling or unable to regulate agricultural runoff as the Clean Water Act specifically exempts agricultural "nonpoint sources." No court has yet ruled that agricultural runoff is a point source, even when directed through a tiling system.

State governments too have been slow to respond. In Iowa, for example, where officials estimate that 90% of nitrogen runoff in the state originates from non-regulated sources ("nonpoint sources"), the state government has opted for a voluntary nutrient reduction strategy that does not require local governments to limit nutrient runoff from farms in their respective jurisdictions. Further, state governments throughout the watershed prohibit local governments from regulating fertilizer use. For example, Iowa's Code provides:

> *A local governmental entity shall not adopt or continue in effect local legislation relating to the use, sale, distribution, storage, transportation, disposal, formulation, labeling, registration, or manufacture of a fertilizer or soil conditioner, regardless of whether a statute or rule adopted by the department applies to preempt the local legislation. Local legislation in violation of this section is void and unenforceable. . . .*

I.C.A. §200.22

PESTICIDES AND STATE PREEMPTION

In addition to regulating fertilizer use, state governments throughout the Mississippi River watershed limit the ability of local governments to regulate the use of pesticides. Agriculture applies about a billion pounds of pesticides each year. Many of these pesticides run off agricultural land, find their way into the Mississippi watershed, deteriorate the ecosystem, and challenge the ability of governments to provide basic services and citizens' rights to use the watershed.

Notwithstanding the importance of pesticide runoff, 29 states explicitly preempt local governments from sustainably managing pesticide use in the watershed; 14 more allow local governments to regulate only upon approval from state agencies; and five continue to allow local governments to regulate pesticide use in their local communities. None of those five states is in the Mississippi River watershed. As an example, Iowa's law states:

A local governmental entity shall not adopt or continue in effect local legislation relating to the use, sale, distribution, storage, transportation, disposal, formulation, labeling, registration, or manufacture of a pesticide, regardless of whether a statute or rule adopted by the department applies to preempt the local legislation. Local legislation in violation of this section is void and unenforceable. . . .

I.C.A. §206.34

Based on the statutory language above, into which group does Iowa fall?

Throughout the watershed, local governments struggle with this CAC. Des Moines, Iowa, for example, sits at the confluence of the Raccoon and Des Moines rivers. The watersheds for these rivers lie within the Mississippi River watershed and extend up to Minnesota. Within this area is some of the richest farming soil in America. It is also some of the wettest. Once the Raccoon and Des Moines rivers join in downtown Des Moines, the Des Moines River continues out of the city and connects with the Mississippi River about 120 miles north of St. Louis.

Today, to keep the moisture out of the soil much of the farmland in these sub-watersheds is tiled. This bypasses the natural absorption and the denitrification processes that would otherwise protect the watershed. It also leads to flooding in Des Moines and a spike in nutrients in the primary source of potable water. It is common for the nutrient levels in one or both of the rivers to be in excess of the EPA limit for nitrates (10 parts-per-million).

At an additional cost of $6,000-$7,000 a day, the Des Moines Water Works is able to remove the nitrates through a sophisticated reverse osmosis system and distribute potable water. In a further illustration of the collective action challenges in the watershed, the Water Works obtains an EPA permit to discharge the nitrates back into the Des Moines River, working their way to the Mississippi and potentially the Gulf.

Notwithstanding the current practices, we are beginning to see some collaboration in sustainably managing water within the watershed. In 2010, Iowa, for example, authorized the creation of Watershed Management Authorities (WMA). WMAs are comprised of cities, counties, or soil and water conservation districts in a watershed. The government authorizes WMAs to assume a regional and holistic approach to watershed management, addressing issues such as flood risk, water quality, land use planning, education, and funding.

Local government's role in managing watershed resources and protecting instream flows has become increasingly important as we reach the limits of what state and federal levels can accomplish to manage water resources.[288] While local governments may not be able to address all

---

[288] Cannon, *supra* note 264, at 75-76 (noting that the lack of regulation over runoff is the greatest reason we have not met water management goals).

aspects of watershed degradation, they can work together in partnership with other local units, as well as with state and federal authorities, to play a major role in promoting sustainable development and watershed protection.[289] Organizing watershed policies along hydrological boundaries, rather than political ones, is not a new concept, but is instead a concept that has flowed in and out of favor over the history of the United States as both law and science have continued to disconnect rivers from their watersheds.[290]

Beginning in the 1990s, watershed management emerged again as the basis to control point and nonpoint sources of water pollution that affect water quality, ecosystems, wetlands and flood control, and endangered species.[291] Watershed management includes three common characteristics: "(1) well-integrated partnerships; (2) a specific geographic focus; and (3) action driven by environmental objectives and by strong evidence."[292] Local governments may be in the best position to promote watershed conservation because they are starting to integrate land use and water planning when reviewing land development that may adversely impact environmental features of a watershed, long-term water supplies (including groundwater), and instream water flows.[293]

Local government typically regulates many of the threats to watershed viability such as land development, paving activities that increase impervious surfaces, nonpoint source pollution from development activities on hillsides, floodplains, and other sensitive land.[294] Because water allocation doctrines have conceptually severed water rights from land use, watershed management has suffered from the independent regulation of these interrelated components.[295] Instead, watershed protection will need to involve local government units as vital partners in collaborative management of common resources across political boundaries.[296] Local autonomy is key to empowering those closest to these ecological services to prioritize and coordinate efforts to control misuse of these resources as they experience the benefits of restored and improved watershed services.[297]

---

[289] A. Dan Tarlock, *The Potential Role of Local Governments in Watershed Management*, 20 PACE ENVTL. L. REV. 149, 175 (2002).

[290] A. Dan Tarlock, *Reconnecting Property Rights to Watersheds*, 25 WM. & MARY ENVTL. L. & POL'Y REV. 69, 71-72 (2000).

[291] *Id.* at 75-76.

[292] Tarlock, *supra* note 289, at 155.

[293] *Id.* at 168.

[294] Keith H. Hirokawa, *Driving Local Governments to Watershed Governance*, 42 ENVTL. L. 157, 167-168 (2012).

[295] *Id.* at 167-168.

[296] *Id.* at 199.

[297] *Id.*

THE HYPOXIA TASK FORCE

Twelve states, five federal agencies, and several tribes in the Mississippi watershed have joined to form the Hypoxia Task Force under the auspices of the EPA. In 2015, the Task Force issued a new non-binding strategy to reduce nutrient levels in the watershed. It also

announced that it would retain its goal of reducing the areal extent of the Gulf of Mexico hypoxic zone to less than 5,000 km2, but that it will take until 2035 to do so. The [Task Force] agreed on an interim target of a 20 percent nutrient load reduction by the year 2025 as a milestone toward achieving the final goal in 2035. The Task Force also agreed to adopt quantitative measures to track progress in reducing point and nonpoint source inputs.[298]

These collaborative models and others represent policy decisions that are responding to CAC in a way that seems to create more resilient and sustainable ecological systems in the Mississippi watershed.

4. INSTREAM FLOW

Meeting instream flow needs is also a significant challenge in allocating waters in regions of water scarcity, as illustrated by the challenges experienced in the western United States.[299] The prior appropriation doctrine adopted by the western states encouraged first-in-time use of water to establish allocation rights. Aquatic habitat, environmental needs, and recreational uses were not taken into account in this legal regime focused on incentivizing settlers to put the water to economic use. As a result, many of the water bodies were over-appropriated and diminishing stream flows have threatened fish, other aquatic life, and recreation due to unnaturally low flows.[300]

Restoring instream flows is challenging in the western states because of population increases, agricultural uses, and climate change. State and federal protection of ecosystems and instream flows developed in the 1960s and 1970s with the federal enactment of the Clean Water Act and the Endangered Species Act and the recognition by states that instream uses constitute a beneficial use under prior appropriation. Western states have also allowed appropriative rights to be transferred so that rather than divert the water to a beneficial use, it can be left instream and receive protection against junior appropriators.[301] In addition to these formal legal protections, which may require a longer administrative process, states can use short-term informal agreements called "irrigation forbearance agreements" to provide immediate protection of instream flows. These agreements allow "environmental groups [to] pay a water right

---

[298] EPA, Mississippi River/Gulf of Mexico Watershed Nutrient Task Force, 2015 Report to Congress at 1 (2015), https://www.epa.gov/sites/production/files/2015-10/documents/htf_report_to_congress_final_-_10.1.15.pdf.
[299] Leon F. Szeptycki et al., *Environmental Water Rights Transfers: A Review of State Laws*, WATER IN THE WEST 1 (Aug. 31, 2015), http://waterinthewest.stanford.edu/sites/default/files/WITW-WaterRightsLawReview-2015-FINAL.pdf.
[300] *Id.*
[301] *Id.*

holder to leave water in the stream without changing the water right itself."[302]

Water organizations play an important role, particularly in the western United States, to control and allocate water resources, as well as manage watersheds, and monitor instream flows. These organizations typically consist of water districts, mutual water companies, and municipalities, which supply water to users and consolidate the storage and delivery of water from multiple sources.[303] The history of supplying water began with public wells, but as demand increased, private water companies took over.[304] However, many were concerned about conflicting motives between water quality and profit and encouraged municipalities to take responsibility for domestic water delivery.[305] Irrigated agriculture initially depended on community organizations that later developed into commercial "carrier ditch companies."[306] Again, concerns about profit-centered incentives eventually led to replacing these for-profit ditch companies with cooperative nonprofit companies called "mutual water companies."[307]

Mutual water companies involved farmers and shareholders in building the necessary infrastructure to supply and control irrigation water and, in some cases, domestic water.[308] Water districts (initially called irrigation districts) furnish water to agricultural, domestic, commercial, and industrial users.[309] Officials organize these districts according to need and include large regional districts to import and deliver water to smaller water districts or cities, conservancy districts to manage individual watersheds, and even districts to manage groundwater.[310] The state may grant governmental powers to these districts and consider them subdivisions of the state with discretion to control and distribute water.[311]

Federal and state agencies are also involved in water development and distribution. The federal government's role includes the construction of water projects for improving water transportation and flood control under the direction of the Army Corps of Engineers and the Reclamation Act of 1902, which gave the Bureau of Reclamation authority to construct irrigation projects for supplying western farmers. While the original intent of Congress was to furnish water to farmers who would then pay for the

---

[302] Julia Forgie, *California and Other Western States See Barriers to Protecting Streams: A New Report Highlights Twelve Western States' Efforts to Restore Stream Flows Using Environmental Water Transfers*, LEGALPLANET (Oct. 7, 2015), http://legal-planet.org/2015/10/07/california-and-other-western-states-see-barriers-to-protecting-streams/ (noting two risks that arise from these agreements — "[a]nother user could withdraw the water that has been left in the stream, or after five years the water right holder might forfeit the water right due to non-use."). *Id.*

[303] Sax et al., *supra* note 19, at 681.

[304] *Id.* at 682.

[305] *Id.*

[306] *Id.* at 683-684.

[307] *Id.* at 684-685.

[308] *Id.*

[309] *Id.* at 685-687.

[310] *Id.*

[311] *Id.* at 686-687.

costs of these projects without interest, farmers have not paid these costs and taxpayers subsidize reclamation water to farmers. In addition, many of these reclamation projects caused irreparable environmental damage.[312] State water projects may also serve an important role in developing and distributing water supplies, although they are generally secondary to the federal government.[313]

There are many *legal issues* confronting water organizations. These issues include the degree to which they can exercise the power to: allocate water and charge for water; decide who will be included or excluded from the district for purposes of taxation; and determine who is entitled to vote on the organization's representatives and decisions.[314] Municipal water suppliers have several advantages over other types of water organizations. First, domestic water use is generally favored over other water uses as a highly beneficial use. Second, in prior appropriation states that discourage speculation before the actual beneficial need is shown, municipal water suppliers are allowed to appropriate water in anticipation of reasonable future needs, while irrigation users and others are not. California has used the doctrine of "pueblo rights" to expand municipal water supplies as a city's population grows.[315] Original settlements by the Spanish and Mexicans called pueblos were entitled to water rights within their borders, superior to riparian and appropriative rights. These rights could not be forfeited by nonuse.[316] Thus, in some southwestern states, municipalities have asserted these greater "pueblo rights" if the city originated from an early settlement.[317] Finally, municipalities are also entitled to use their eminent domain power to condemn existing riparian claims in the eastern United States, both within and without their borders to obtain needed water supplies.[318]

Questions and Note

1. Above we introduced the concept of Ecosystem Services Management (ESM). How might an ecosystem services management approach to governing the Mississippi River watershed alter the collective challenges facing actors in the watershed?

2. Conflicts over the Colorado River continue today. Would an ESM approach to management of the Colorado River help address some of those disputes?

---

[312] *Id.* at 687-688.
[313] *Id.* at 688.
[314] *Id.* at 688-704.
[315] *Id.* at 705.
[316] *Id.* at 356.
[317] *Id.* at 356.
[318] *Id.* at 705.

3. Responses focused on the resiliency and sustainability of water-based systems require communities to plan for uncertainty, adapt to new challenges, overcome collective action issues, and leverage ecosystem services. Rebuilding New Orleans after Hurricane Katrina required both hard/gray infrastructure solutions (sea walls and pumps) as well as green infrastructure remedies (parks and rain gardens) to address the continuing need to address future climate-related disasters.[319] States and communities will need to rebuild in smarter ways to adapt to changing flood risks and change existing legislation that govern disaster recovery to allow more flexible and innovative approaches to be more resilient.[320] Miami Beach, Florida, has invested in re-engineering its streets by installing pumps and raising streets, sidewalks, and sea walls in order to adapt its landscape to rising sea levels.[321] The cost to preserve this tourist city against rising seas is estimated to exceed $400 million and some claim "pumping water without chemical treatment will cause problems for marine life in Biscayne Bay."[322] Nevertheless, construction continues in an effort to preserve this prime real estate as predictions of seawater rises vary from two to five feet by 2060.[323] The United States will need to address the impact of sea level rise on its coastal communities as flooding, water quality, and other issues will result.[324]

[319] Vicki Arroyo, *Lesson Learned from Rebuilding New Orleans: Consider Our Changing Climate*, HUFFINGTON POST, http://www.huffingtonpost.com/vicki-arroyo/lesson-learned-from-rebuilding-new-orleans-consider-our-changing-climate_b_8051028.html (last updated Aug. 27, 2015, 5:57 PM).

[320] *Id.*

[321] Joey Flechas & Jenny Staletovich, *Miami Beach's Battle to Stem Rising Tides*, MIAMI HERALD (Oct. 23, 2015, 5:00 AM), http://www.miamiherald.com/news/local/community/miami-dade/miami-beach/article41141856.html#storylink = cpy.

[322] *Id.*

[323] *Id.*

[324] *Lights Out? Storm Surge, Blackouts, and How Clean Energy Can Help*, UNION OF CONCERNED SCIENTISTS, http://www.ucsusa.org/global-warming/global-warming-impacts/lights-out-storm-surge-and-blackouts-us-east-coast-gulf-of-mexico#.VkfOx3arQgs (last visited Oct. 11, 2017).

VIII. MOVING FORWARD

Water resources and their associated ecosystems face a number of challenges, many of which continue to evolve in uncertain ways. In this chapter we introduced three concepts that can help decision makers integrate system R&S into policies, while accounting for uncertainties. Those concepts — ecosystem services management, collective action challenges, and the precautionary principle, are applicable to many disciplines. Keep them in mind as tools to help identify, analyze, and incorporate R&S into decision making.

We end this chapter with a brief introduction to **Green Infrastructure** and **Low Impact Development** (LID) — two methods that help achieve a more resilient and sustainable water system. Green infrastructure and LID can also increase groundwater discharge and treat infiltrated water.[325] Studies have shown that cities can recognize cost benefits by incorporating these infrastructure strategies, along with watershed health initiatives to achieve "future economic sustainability benefits in the form of lower energy costs, reduced emissions, improved air quality, increased property values, as well as a greater distribution of operations and maintenance costs leading to the potential for more employment opportunities."[326]

GREEN INFRASTRUCTURE

Stormwater runoff is a major cause of water pollution in urban areas. When rain falls in undeveloped areas, the water is absorbed and filtered by soil and plants. When rain falls on our roofs, streets, and parking lots, however, the water cannot soak into the ground. In most urban areas, stormwater is drained through engineered collection systems and discharged into nearby waterbodies. The stormwater carries trash, bacteria, heavy metals, and other pollutants from the urban landscape, polluting the receiving waters. Higher flows also can cause erosion and flooding in urban streams, damaging habitat, property, and infrastructure. Green infrastructure uses vegetation, soils, and natural processes to manage water and create healthier urban environments. At the scale of a city or county, green infrastructure refers to the patchwork of natural areas that provides habitat, flood protection, cleaner air, and cleaner water. At the scale of a neighborhood or site, green infrastructure refers to stormwater management systems that mimic nature by soaking up and storing water. These neighborhood or site-scale green infrastructure approaches are often referred to as low impact development. EPA encourages the use of green infrastructure to help manage stormwater runoff.

U.S. EPA, *Green Infrastructure*, http://water.epa.gov/infrastructure/greeninfrastructure/upload/CNT-Lancaster-Report-508.pdf.

---

[325] *What Is Green Infrastructure?*, EPA, https://www.epa.gov/green-infrastructure/what-green-infrastructure (last visited Oct. 11, 2017).

[326] *The Economics of Low Impact Development: Economics and LID Practices*, Univ. of New Hampshire Stormwater Ctr. 3-39 (July 2011), http://www.unh.edu/unhsc/sites/unh.edu.unhsc/files/docs/FTL_Chapter3%20LR.pdf.

Green infrastructure incorporates ecosystem services and adaptive governance to help the resilience and sustainability of water resources, both in terms of water quantity and quality. Green infrastructure has been described as "a network of decentralized stormwater management practices, such as green roofs, trees, rain gardens and permeable pavement, that can capture and infiltrate rain where it falls, thus reducing stormwater runoff and improving the health of surrounding waterways."[327] Additional green infrastructure practices include tree planting, bioretention and infiltration, and water harvesting. Through these practices, the ecological, economic, and social benefits obtained can enhance a community's health and viability, particularly as communities need to adapt their infrastructure to deal with climate change challenges.[328]

Traditionally, land use practices rely heavily on gray infrastructure to address water issues. Gray infrastructure is human-made and engineered solutions often involving steel and concrete. One of several challenges with gray infrastructure is it often enhances vulnerabilities by exacerbating the rigidity of the built environment. Gray infrastructure is not prepared for uncertainty and changes in ecosystems and is not able to adapt when changes occur. Green infrastructure incorporates an element of adaptive governance as the ecosystem adapts or transforms as systems are impacted.[329]

Similarly, *low impact development* (LID) is a helpful approach to reduce pollution and manage stormwater runoff more sustainably by providing natural landscapes, reducing the amount of impervious surface in a development, managing stormwater runoff on the site, and causing less of a land disturbance on the site, including staying out of wetlands and flood plains.[330] Not only is LID effective at managing the environmental impacts of land development, it is also economically advantageous for individual projects, as shown by LID case studies in New Hampshire, Rhode Island, Oregon, Illinois, Missouri, and New York.[331] Green infrastructure and low impact development address the challenges raised by gray infrastructure and incorporate more dynamic and flexible water systems to prepare for the future.

---

[327] *The Value of Green Infrastructure*, CTR. FOR NEIGHBORHOOD TECH. 7 (2010), http://www.cnt.org/sites/default/files/publications/CNT_Value-of-Green-Infrastructure.pdf.
[328] *Id.*
[329] *What Is Green Infrastructure?*, EPA, *supra* note 325.
[330] *The Economics of Low Impact Development, supra* note 326.
[331] *Id.*

Food

4

I. INTRODUCTION

Steve loved cooking for his friends and family. Being invited to dine with Steve was an experience to be anticipated and was never disappointing. Steve's friend Monty remembers that, "at Steve's dinner parties, there was always a lot of braising meats, duck confit, roasts. So one time I said, 'What are we having?' and he said, 'Burritos.' I remember being extraordinarily disappointed, because how good can a burrito be? My dad and I went to his house with a number of other people, and that's where I ate the first Chipotle burrito. It was absolutely delicious."[1] After earning his undergraduate degree in art history from the University of Colorado, Steve Ells graduated from the Culinary Institute of America before taking his first culinary job as a sous chef at Stars Restaurant in San Francisco. Steve's dream was to open a fine-dining restaurant, but instead, he opened Chipotle Mexican Grill in Denver and he has never looked back.[2]

Chipotle's focus has been on using naturally raised ingredients and the now-public company has had great success. Steve explains that his passion for culinary excellence is satisfied by bringing Chipotle's "food with integrity" approach to mainstream versus only high-end restaurants so that he can supply "the best quality, sustainably raised ingredients to everyone: chicken without antibiotics; beef without hormones."[3] The company went public in 2006, and with almost 2,000 stores throughout the United States,

---

[1] Kyle Stock & Venessa Wong, *Chipotle: The Definitive Oral History*, BLOOMBERG (Feb. 2, 2015), http://www.bloomberg.com/graphics/2015-chipotle-oral-history/ (quoting Monty Moran, former CEO of Chipotle).

[2] Colleen Debaise, *Starting Chipotle from Scratch*, WALL ST. J. (Sept. 22, 2009, 5:40 PM), http://www.wsj.com/articles/SB125319598236119629.

[3] *Id.*

has enjoyed tremendous success while cutting its carbon footprint, using local ingredients, carefully choosing its food and meat farmers, and promoting humane animal practices.[4]

Disaster for the company struck in the fall of 2015 when scores of customers across the country suffered from foodborne illnesses directly connected to some of Chipotle's restaurants.[5] This could be expected, particularly when the company itself recognized that "its use of 'fresh produce and meats rather than frozen,' and 'reliance on employees cooking with traditional methods rather than automation,' puts it at a higher risk for outbreaks of foodborne illnesses."[6] Even a company that emphasizes food safety and quality is susceptible to food safety problems that can occur at multiple points in the process of food production practices, distribution, and preparation.[7] Given the commitment of its founder to serving "food with integrity," Chipotle will likely recover from its bout with food safety issues and may help lead the way in improving food safety practices throughout the industry.

II. A BRIEF HISTORY OF AGRICULTURE

Agriculture began approximately 10,000 years ago during the Mesolithic period, which existed between 12,000 and 9,600 years B.C.[8] Archeology is the vehicle for researching the origins of agriculture since plant and animal domestication occurred before explicit writing systems were developed.[9] Techniques such as radiocarbon analysis of plant and animal remains have provided a framework for determining the times and places that various plants and animals were domesticated.[10]

---

[4] Roberto A. Ferdman, *What in the World is Happening to Chipotle*, WASH. POST (Dec. 9, 2015), https://www.washingtonpost.com/news/wonk/wp/2015/12/09/what-in-the-world-is-happening-to-chipotle/.
[5] Lisa Fickenscher, *Turns out Chipotle's Been Making People Sick for Months*, N.Y. POST (Dec. 11, 2015, 12:37 AM), http://nypost.com/2015/12/11/turns-out-chipotles-been-making-people-sick-for-months/.
[6] Ferdman, *supra* note 4.
[7] Katie Little, *Chipotle Just Got More Bad Food Safety News*, CNBC (Dec. 11, 2015), http://www.cnbc.com/2015/12/11/chipotle-just-got-more-bad-food-safety-news.html.
[8] K. Kris Hirst, *Climate Change and the Origins of Agriculture*, THOUGHTCO., http://archaeology.about.com/od/historyofagriculture/qt/History-Of-Agriculture.htm (last updated Feb. 9, 2017). Others, such as palaeoclimatologist and professor William Ruddiman, mark the date approximately 8,000 years ago. *See* William F. Ruddiman, *The Anthropogenic Greenhouse Era Began Thousands of Years Ago*, 61 CLIMATIC CHANGE 261-293 (2003).
[9] George Edwin Fussell et al., *Origins of agriculture*, ENCYCLOPEDIA BRITANNICA, http://www.britannica.com/topic/agriculture (last updated Mar. 10, 2017).
[10] *Id.*

As mentioned in Chapter 2, some mark the beginning of agriculture as the beginning of "Anthropocene," a new epoch marked by human dominance over natural environments. Some, such as paleoclimatologist and Professor William Ruddiman, mark the beginning of agriculture at 8,000 years ago.[11]

Plant domestication, defined as when its "native characteristics [are] altered such that it cannot grow and reproduce without human intervention[,]" was one of the first steps toward farming and began in the ancient Near East in approximately 9,000 B.C. with the domestication of fig trees, wheat, flax, peas, and barley.[12] In Northern Europe, people began to fish, hunt in groups, and domesticate animals and plants during the Mesolithic period—a period characterized by climate instability. Land management practices such as cutting trees and burning wetlands began to take place during the Mesolithic period. Sustained farming began during the Neolithic period when farming communities were established approximately 7,000 years ago.[13]

Animal domestication benefitted people by allowing them to use cattle for milk, meat, and plowing; horses for plowing or riding; dogs for

---

[11] *See* Ruddiman, *supra* note 8, at 261-293.
[12] K. Kris Hirst, *Plant Domestication—Table of Dates and Places*, ThoughtCo., http://archaeology.about.com/od/domestications/a/plant_domestic.htm (last updated Mar. 17, 2017).
[13] K. Kris Hirst, *Mesolithic Period*, ThoughtCo., http://archaeology.about.com/od/mesolithicarchaic/qt/Mesolithic.htm (last updated Sept. 5, 2017).

guardians and companions; and other animals for food, wool, transportation, and other uses.[14] Dogs were the first animals domesticated, in an undetermined area of origin between 14,000 and 30,000 B.C. Sheep, goats, and pigs were domesticated in Western Asia during the period between 7,000 and 8,500 B.C., and cats were domesticated in the Fertile Crescent (the "cradle of civilization," comprising Western Asia, the Nile Valley, and the Nile Delta) in approximately 8,500 B.C.[15]

Rice is one of the three major crops in the world, along with wheat and corn, and has a long history of importance for food sustenance and cultural heritage, dating back to approximately 4,600 B.C. in the Lower Yangtze region of China.[16] Rice has "fed more people over a longer period of time than any other crop" and is integral to folklore and religious celebration.[17] As the world's most productive crop, rice sustains much of the world's highest density populations in Southern and Eastern Asia. However, rice growing also contributes to greenhouse gas emissions as rice paddies produce methane in higher levels than dry or rain-fed rice fields. As paddy farming has increased globally over thousands of years, archaeobotanical research on rice agriculture can help inform climate science about the impact of humans on greenhouse gases.[18]

Wheat is a combination of several different kinds of grass that occurred in approximately 10,000 B.C. in Turkey.[19] During the Stone Age, in approximately 6,700 B.C., humans began to grind wheat with rocks to make flour and by 5,500 B.C. millstones were used. Communities formed as the need to hunt and gather dissipated because of the ability to reap and sow cereals. Wheat was the oldest and most widespread staple of humans until it fell from first to third place behind rice and corn in global production at the beginning of the twenty-first century.[20] About 20% of global human calorie consumption is still derived from wheat, a staple food in many countries, even though it is also used for livestock feed. The wheat plant is the only one that contains the gluten protein, which enables leavened dough to rise. Wheat is also high in carbohydrates, valuable minerals, and vitamins, and serves a variety of purposes.[21] However, recent

---

[14] K. Kris Hirst, *Animal Domestication — Table of Dates and Places*, THOUGHTCO., http://archaeology.about.com/od/dterms/a/domestication.htm (last updated Jan. 28, 2017).

[15] *Id.*

[16] Dorian Q. Fuller & Alison Weisskopf, *The Early Rice Project: From Domestication to Global Warming*, 13 ARCHEOLOGY INT'L 45 (2011), *available at* http://www.ai-journal.com/articles/10.5334/ai.1314/.

[17] *Where Rice Came From*, U.C. DAVIS, http://www-plb.ucdavis.edu/labs/rost/Rice/introduction/intro.html (last visited Oct. 11, 2017).

[18] Fuller & Weisskopf, *supra* note 16.

[19] *Ears of Plenty: the Story of Man's Staple Food*, ECONOMIST (Dec. 20, 2005), http://www.economist.com/node/5323362.

[20] *Id.*

[21] Lance Gibson & Garren Benson, *Origin, History, and Uses of Oat (Avena sativa) and Wheat (Triticum aestivum)*, IOWA STATE UNIV., DEPT. AGRONOMY (Jan. 2002), http://agron-www.agron.iastate.edu/Courses/agron212/Readings/Oat_wheat_history.htm.

trends such as the Atkins diet and concerns about gluten allergies have damaged wheat's reputation for wholesomeness.[22]

Norman Borlaug received the Nobel Peace Prize in 1970 for starting the Green Revolution by breeding fungus-resistant wheat. Borlaug's seeds yielded six times the wheat harvest in Mexico by 1963. Borlaug brought his Mexican wheat seeds to India in 1965, and by 1974, he tripled the wheat yield and India avoided mass famine and became self-sufficient in food production.[23] Borlaug's wheat breeding used natural mutants, but those who followed him used artificial mutants. These mutants damaged or altered DNA to produce mutant cereals through genetic modification (GM). While GM crops have at times increased yield and biodiversity, and decreased pesticide use and cost, most environmentalists have strenuously opposed genetic modification.[24]

Corn, or more properly, maize (Zea Mays), supplies approximately 21% of global nutrition and has existed in domesticated form for about 9,000 years. Native Americans in southern Mexico cultivated maize from a grass called Teosinte through a domestication process that probably took several hundred to a few thousand years to complete.[25] Maize did not reach the New England region of North America until approximately 1,000 years ago and the colonists in the 1600s learned the importance of it as a food source.[26] While it is unclear exactly when corn was exported to Europe, Christopher Columbus and his men reportedly discovered it in 1492 in Cuba. It quickly spread as a valuable food crop "throughout France, Italy, and all of southeastern Europe and northern Africa. By 1575, it was making its way into western China, and had become important in the Philippines and the East Indies."[27] Today, corn has a wide variety of uses including livestock feed, human foods, ethanol production, and industrial uses such as packing materials, chemicals, pharmaceuticals, and much more.[28] However, there is concern that one particular corn product, corn syrup, may be "linked to the high rates of obesity and diabetes in children and adults in the United States."[29] This link is disconcerting because corn syrup is found "in virtually every processed food."[30]

Maize is one of the "Three Sisters" of Native American food staples, joining beans and squash. Just as rice is bound to folklore and religious

---

[22] ECONOMIST, *supra* note 19.

[23] *Id.*

[24] *Id.*

[25] Sean B. Carroll, *Tracking the Ancestry of Corn Back 9,000 Years*, N.Y. TIMES (May 24, 2010), http://www.nytimes.com/2010/05/25/science/25creature.html?_r = 0.

[26] *Native American History of Corn*, NATIVETECH (1994), http://www.nativetech.org/cornhusk/cornhusk.html.

[27] Lance Gibson & Garren Benson, *Origin, History, and Uses of Corn (Zea mays)*, IOWA STATE UNIV. (Jan. 2002).

[28] *Id.*

[29] Mary Jane Angelo, *Corn, Carbon, and Conservation: Rethinking U.S. Agricultural Policy in a Changing Global Environment*, 17 GEO. MASON L. REV. 593, 596 (2010).

[30] *Id.*

celebrations, maize is culturally tied to Native American myths and legends.[31] The "Three Sisters," according to native belief, should never be separated. While this belief was grounded in cultural myth and legend, there were also practical reasons for growing these "sisters" together: "The stalk of the maize plant was strong and tall. It could provide support for growing bean vines in search of sunshine. Squash, gourd, and pumpkin vines grew thick around the base of the maize stalks and helped control the growth of weeds and the loss of moisture in the mound."[32] It has been suggested that these "traditional foods must be thought of as an important tool in healing the physical and emotional damage that a largely commodity foods-based diet has done to the American Indians of the Southwest." By reviving these traditional food systems, the hope is to rebuild food security and food sovereignty through improving "individual and community health and overcoming the most negative socio-cultural impacts of colonialism."[33]

In England, an agricultural revolution took place in the century following 1750, as an expanding population required a transition from a "low-intensity agricultural system based on fishing and fowling" to a "high-intensity system based on arable crops."[34] This transition involved new farming systems, such as the rotation of crops to increase production from the same land parcel, and land reclamation by draining marshes, clearing woodlands, and converting pastures. Nitrogen levels in the soil were also crucial to increasing the cereal crop yields and planting legumes, clover, and distributing manure where needed helped to maintain these levels. Agriculture was sustainable at this point, with a significant increase in food output that did not threaten the long-term viability of the soil. However, farming systems dependent upon chemical fertilizers and energy-intensive farming practices eventually replaced this organic agriculture.[35]

---

[31] Terry L. Sargent, *The Importance of One Simple Plant*, LEARN NC, http://www.learnnc.org/lp/editions/nchist-twoworlds/1874 (reprinted from 38(1) TAR HEEL JUNIOR HISTORIAN 11 (Spring 1984)).
[32] *Id.*
[33] Julia Guarino, *Tribal Food Sovereignty in the American Southwest*, 11 J. FOOD L. & POL'Y 83, 86-87 (2015) (citing Nancy J. Turner & Katherine L. Turner, *Traditional Food Systems, Erosion and Renewal in Northwestern North America*, 6 INDIAN J. OF TRADITIONAL KNOWLEDGE 57, 58-59 (2007)).
[34] Mark Overton, *Agricultural Revolution in England 1500-1850*, BBC, http://www.bbc.co.uk/history/british/empire_seapower/agricultural_revolution_01.shtml (last updated Feb. 17, 2011).
[35] *Id.*

The potato is the fifth most significant crop in the world, following rice, corn, wheat, and sugarcane. Originally from the Andes in Peru and Bolivia, it was brought by Spanish explorers from South America, first to the Canary Islands in the late 1500s and then to Spain and the rest of Europe in the 1600s and 1700s. It was carried back to North America in the 1600s and 1700s, finding its way to Jamestown and New Hampshire.[36] Some historians argue that the potato fueled the domination of European empires and the rise of western influence because of its ability to feed expanding populations.[37] Cultivation of the potato in Europe and North America led to the adoption of modern agricultural systems and the resulting transformation of agricultural productivity in the 1940s and 1950s. The use of chemical pesticides, fertilizers, and seed breeding created the Green Revolution.[38]

The potato has been dubbed history's most important vegetable because of its adaptability to different climates and topographies, its nutritional value, and its ability to yield more food per acre than any other crop. Indeed, wherever the potato was introduced, populations expanded.[39] In Ireland, the population doubled between 1780 and 1841 following the widespread cultivation of the potato.

The **Irish potato famine** from 1845-1850 was precipitated by the heavy dependence on this crop and the decimation of potato crops by a fungal blight.[40] Historians estimate that 1,500,000 people died from the effects of famine and that one to two million people emigrated.[41] While the Irish potato famine has received much attention in the western world, in terms of the numbers of people affected by famine, other global famines dwarf its size. The largest famine in history occurred

---

[36] Charles C. Mann, *How the Potato Changed the World*, Smithsonian (Nov. 2011), http://www.smithsonianmag.com/history/how-the-potato-changed-the-world-108470605/.

[37] *Id.*

[38] *Id.*

[39] Jeff Chapman, *The Impact of the Potato*, Hist. Mag., http://www.history-magazine.com/potato.html (last visited Oct. 11, 2017).

[40] *Irish Potato Famine*, The Hist. Place (2000), http://www.historyplace.com/worldhistory/famine/after.htm.

[41] *Id.*

in China between 1959 and 1961 and resulted in the death of 30 to 40 million people. Other famines have occurred throughout history in places such as North Korea, India, Vietnam, Africa, and Russia. Famines have been a result of extreme weather, political decisions, natural disasters, but mostly the combination of several of these factors.[42] As noted above in the discussion of wheat, Norman Borlaug's work with the Mexican wheat seeds that he brought to India in 1965 helped avoid a mass famine predicted to hit India because of the inability to feed the expanding population.[43]

Questions

1. Agricultural practices have been criticized for both supporting the growth of the human population and the development of modern technological societies. If agriculture has spurred human population, does it promote the unsustainability of some ecological systems? Or maybe the food system itself? Or is agricultural improvement critical to the sustainability of modern human societies? Does it matter whether you take an anthropocentric or a biocentric perspective on that question?

2. In Chapter 2, we describe the tension between rising populations and sustainability. In the context of food, that tension involves the ability to feed people and the steps we should take to feed people. If it is necessary to import food to feed people, is this a resilient food system? What about a resilient social system?

III. PRODUCTION AND PRACTICES

Agriculture in the United States will be the focus of the remainder of this chapter as we examine the modern transition from an agrarian society to large-scale commercial farming through the relatively short history of the United States. Upon its independence from England in 1776, the United States was an agrarian nation with more than 95% of its citizens involved in the farming economy. With the invention of agricultural tools such as the steel plow, the harvester, and the cotton gin, commercial agriculture became more significant and following the Civil War, with the South losing slave labor to support its agriculture, farm sizes increased and commercial crop yields expanded. By 1910, this increase in commercial agriculture, along with the

---

[42] Vaclav Smil, *China's Great Famine: 40 Years Later*, 319 BMJ 1619 (Dec. 18, 1999), *available at* http://www.ncbi.nlm.nih.gov/pmc/articles/PMC1127087/; Andrew Fitzgerald, *10 Terrible Famines in History*, LISTVERSE (Apr. 10, 2013), http://listverse.com/2013/04/10/10-terrible-famines-in-history/.
[43] ECONOMIST, *supra* note 19.

expanded opportunities for employment in the industrial economy, resulted in a drop in farming from 95% of the citizens to approximately 40%.[44]

The **Great Depression** that occurred after the 1929 stock market crash and lasted for ten long years until 1939, put additional strain on family farms when bank foreclosures and natural disasters impacted nearly one in four Americans who still lived on a farm. However, the primary cause of the "farm crisis" was the oversupply of food that resulted from agricultural improvements over the previous decade, which then caused prices to fall below the farmer's cost of production. Congress reacted by passing the Agricultural Adjustment Act of 1933 to control overproduction, provide crop insurance and credit to subsistence farmers, fight hunger with surplus crops, and implement soil and land conservation strategies. The nation did not return to Jeffersonian agrarianism, but instead, these agricultural market supports for over 100 crops became a long-term commitment for artificial market supports in the 1948 Agricultural Act.

Following **World War II**, military technology led to improvements in farming through new mechanization, pesticides, herbicides, and fertilizers. These modern advances, in addition to new plant breeding and hybridization techniques, ushered in the Green Revolution with its increased yields, economies of scale, and planting single crops (monoculture) instead of a diversity of crops. Overproduction in the late 1950s and early 1960s again caused prices to drop and, when the government declined to step in and support the small farmer, large farms became larger and consolidated "with other large farms and food processors to create modern agribusiness."[45] The Secretary of Agriculture, appointed by President Richard Nixon in the early 1970s, broke away from the ideals of the 1933 farm bill and instead encouraged farmers to become a big business with maximized yields and efficiency, exporting any overproduction. The resulting 1973 farm bill emphasized crop production at all costs and eliminated the conservation portion of the 1933 farm bill. The Food and Agriculture Act of 1977 encouraged maximum crop yields and assumed that the United States would continue to push surpluses into the international market.[46]

Another **farm crisis**, similar to the one experienced during the Great Depression, arose in the 1980s when the United States suspended exports to the Soviet Union for political reasons and a global recession caused a decline in agricultural exports. Congress stepped in with the Food Security Act of 1985, which continued to emphasize high production and exportation of surplus crops but also included marketing loan subsidies to farmers and reintroduced conservation programs to address soil erosion problems created in the 1970s.[47] The 1990 farm bill created additional conservation

---

[44] Mary Jane Angelo et al., Food, Agriculture, and Environmental Law 1-2 (Envt'l L. Inst., 2013).
[45] *Id.* at 5.
[46] *Id.* at 5-6.
[47] *Id.* at 7.

programs to encourage farmers to conserve wetlands and reduce water pollution. It also attempted to reduce the government's farm budget, by separating a farmer's planting decisions from federal subsidy payments, but the agricultural budget has continued to increase.[48]

RESILIENCE AND AGRICULTURE

Note how some systems can be sensitive (vulnerable) to change. The resilience of U.S. agriculture was tested not by supply or demand or changes to ecology that may have limited crop growth, but rather by external law and policy changes.

The Federal Agriculture Improvement and Reform Act of 1996 persisted in emphasizing a policy to decouple planting decisions from financial incentives, and many of the reforms it adopted have continued into the 2002 and 2008 farm bills. These reforms, along with changes in international trade resulting from the negotiations on the General Agreement on Tariffs and Trade (GATT) and the formation of the World Trade Organization (WTO) in 1995, have contributed to the increasing impact that U.S. decisions regarding agricultural supply and demand will have on global food markets and economies.[49]

In 2009, food scholar William S. Eubanks II described the U.S. Farm Bill as

> *legislation that affects* all *aspects of the natural environment. . . . The statute drives public health policy; . . . implements policies that result in severe malnutrition and hunger, both domestically and abroad; . . . encourages overproduction, trade distortion, and depression of world market prices, which directly and immediately drive immigration toward the United States from the developing world; and . . . strips rural communities of their senses of identity, cultural values, and traditional heritage.*[50]

Eubanks has also pointed out that farm bill subsidies increasingly benefit the largest agricultural producers rather than the family farms and that agribusiness receives billions of tax dollars even while these mega farms achieve record profits.[51] The 2014 farm bill may have responded to at least

---

[48] *Id.* at 8.

[49] *Id.* at 9-12.

[50] William S. Eubanks II, *The Sustainable Farm Bill: A Proposal for Permanent Environmental Change,* 39 ENVTL. L. REP. 10493, 10493 (2009) (emphasis in original).

[51] William S. Eubanks II, *A Rotten System: Subsidizing Environmental Degradation and Poor Public Health With Our Nation's Tax Dollars,* 28 STAN. ENVTL. L.J. 213, 227 (2009) (noting that "[i]n 2005 alone, when pretax farm profits were at a near-record $72 billion, the federal government handed out more than $25 billion in aid [to farms], almost 50 percent more than the amount it pays to families receiving welfare [in the United States]."). *Id.*

some of these concerns as the U.S. Department of Agriculture (USDA) states that the legislation

> will enable USDA to further expand markets for agricultural products at home and abroad, strengthen conservation efforts, create new opportunities for local and regional food systems and grow the biobased economy. It will provide a dependable safety net for America's farmers, ranchers, and growers. It will maintain important agricultural research, and ensure access to safe and nutritious food for all Americans.[52]

Question and Note

1. As noted above, almost all U.S. families in the early nineteenth century farmed. Today, "[f]arm and ranch families comprise just 2 percent of the U.S. population."[53] As indicated in Figure 4-1 below, "[s]mall family farms dominate the total U.S. farm count and occupy more than half of U.S. farmland, but midsize and large-scale family farms account for the bulk of agricultural production" and land operated.[54] How is the resilience or sustainability of the U.S. food system affected by an increase or decrease in the number of family farms or individuals who farm?

A. Large-Scale Farming

Agricultural law is "the study of the network of laws and policies that apply to the production, marketing, and sale of agricultural products, i.e., the food we eat, the natural fibers we wear, and increasingly, the bio-fuels that run our vehicles."[55] However, many are calling for the expansion of agricultural law to embrace a discipline that not only focuses on industrial agricultural production, but also agriculture's impact on the environment, human health, and food safety in the face of climate change.[56] A food-based agricultural law should be centered upon three basic understandings: 1) food should be safe and healthy; 2) ecological and moral issues should govern the production of living things that we eat; and 3) food

---

[52] *Secretary's Column: Ready to Help Pass a Food, Farm, and Jobs Bill*, USDA (May 3, 2013), https://www.usda.gov/media/blog/2013/05/3/secretarys-column-ready-help-pass-food-farm-and-jobs-bill.
[53] *Fast Facts about Agriculture*, Am. Farm Bureau Fed'n, http://www.fb.org/newsroom/fastfacts/ (last visited Oct. 11, 2017).
[54] Robert Hoppe, *U.S. Farms, Large and Small*, USDA (Jan. 13, 2015), http://blogs.usda.gov/2015/01/13/u-s-farms-large-and-small/.
[55] Susan A. Schneider, *A Reconsideration of Agricultural Law: A Call for the Law of Food, Farming, and Sustainability*, 34 Wm. & Mary Envtl. L. & Pol'y Rev. 935 (2010).
[56] *See, e.g., id.* at 935.

Most U.S. farms are small family farms

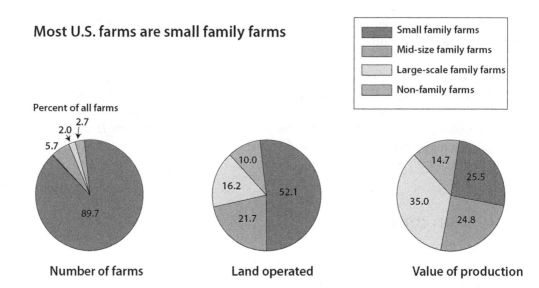

Small family farms
Mid-size family farms
Large-scale family farms
Non-family farms

Percent of all farms

2.7
2.0
5.7
89.7

Number of farms

10.0
16.2
52.1
21.7

Land operated

14.7
25.5
35.0
24.8

Value of production

Note: Small family farms have gross cash farm income less than $350,000, mid-size family farms $350,000-$999,999, and large-scale family farms $1,000,000 or more.

Source: USDA, National Agriculture Statistics Service and Economic Research Service.

Figure 4-1

production is heavily dependent upon natural resources, including land, water, and human resources.[57]

The **industrialization of agriculture** that occurred during the twentieth century resulted in increased efficiency and yields in farming. Individual farms increased in size, while the overall number of farms dropped significantly. Farm operations were specialized and large-scale commodity crops such as corn, soybean, and wheat now occupy approximately one-third of U.S. farmland.[58] These modern

---

[57] *See id.* at 946-948.
[58] Linda Breggin & D. Bruce Myers, Jr., *Subsidies With Responsibilities: Placing Stewardship and Disclosure Conditions on Government Payments to Large-Scale Commodity Crop Operations*, 37 HARV. ENVTL. L. REV. 487, 489 (2013).

farming techniques produce the food necessary to feed the world, but they also have a detrimental impact on water quality, air quality, and species habitat. Unfortunately, the alternatives to large-scale farming may increase costs and make it difficult to supply the global need for food. For example, some allege that organic farming "produces yields that are '25% lower than conventional farming methods.'"[59] Balancing the positive aspects of large-scale farming against the negative externalities it generates may require a revamping of our federal regulations that address pollution and a reassessment of the way we apply subsidy and incentive programs. While the agricultural industry as a whole has been favored over other polluting industries in the Clean Water Act (CWA), the Clean Air Act (CAA), the Federal Insecticide, Fungicide, and Rodenticide Act (FIFRA), and the Toxic Substances Control Act (TSCA), farm bill subsidies and incentives have, in effect, historically favored large-scale farming over smaller, diversified farms.[60]

Questions

1. Do modern agricultural practices help or undermine the sustainability of species diversification? Why and how?

2. Do modern agricultural practices promote the sustainability of soils? Why or why not?

Monoculture and genetically modified organisms (GMOs), in addition to the concerns about agricultural pollution, have been the most controversial large-scale farming methodologies in recent times. Monoculture, or the growing of one crop over a large area, is cost effective and maximizes productivity in the short term, yet it can also threaten the viability of future crops by causing topsoil erosion and depleting the soil of nutrients and biodiversity.[61] It is considered to be one of the hallmarks of industrialized agriculture, along with separating plant and animal agriculture, relying on chemical inputs, and changing out human resources for fossil fuel resources that impact global climate change.[62] As we seek to add more farmland, changing from monoculture to diverse crop fields could help "limit the impacts to wildlife and biodiversity resulting from

---

[59] Kelsey Peterson, *Farming in the Modern Era: Feeding the World with an Environmental Conscience,* 5 SEATTLE J. ENVTL. L. 139, 140 (2015).

[60] *Id.* at 141.

[61] Margot J. Pollans, *Regulating Farming: Balancing Food Safety and Environmental Protection in a Cooperative Governance Regime,* 50 WAKE FOREST L. REV. 399, 400 (2015).

[62] Mary Jane Angelo et al., *Small, Slow, and Local: Essays on Building a More Sustainable and Local Food System,* 12 VT. J. ENVTL. L. 353, 356-357 (2011).

the conversion of nature to farmland."[63] Diverse crops and crop rotation also help prevent the buildup of monoculture crop pests so that pesticides and fertilizer inputs do not need to increase and the farm field becomes more resilient to infestation as it becomes more diverse.[64]

Biotechnology and GMOs dramatically changed the agricultural landscape in the mid-1990s when scientists used recombinant DNA to genetically modify plants and animals instead of relying on the conventional breeding of desirable traits that had taken place for thousands of years. Conventional breeding allowed humans to domesticate plants and animals and develop better seed and food sources. Biotechnology transforms seeds to include beneficial traits such as drought tolerance, herbicide tolerance, or insect or disease resistance.[65] Genetic engineers manipulate DNA molecules and introduce a piece of DNA from another existing organism or a laboratory-synthesized one into the organism targeted to receive the beneficial trait. The U.S. Department of Agriculture's Animal and Plant Health Inspection Service (APHIS) regulates GMO plants as a "plant pest" under the Plant Protection Act (PPA). The agency oversees field tests, licenses GMO growth and sale, and may require the evaluation of environmental impacts under the National Environmental Policy Act (NEPA).[66]

Food sources such as cows, pigs, and salmon are also being genetically engineered (GE) and this practice has been justified on the grounds of protecting the health of the animals; providing new sources of medicine and transplant tissue for humans; and producing animals that have a reduced environmental impact and provide healthier food products. The Food and Drug Administration (FDA) regulates GE animals as a "new animal drug" because "it is intended to change the structure or function of the body of the GE animal."[67] The FDA also considers GE substances added to food, either plant or animal, as "food additives" so that it "has general jurisdiction over GMO foods to prohibit foods or food additives from being adulterated with 'any poisonous or deleterious substance which may render it injurious to health.'"[68] Finally, the EPA has authority to regulate GMOs under FIFRA or TSCA if they are a pesticide substance, including a pesticide-resistant plant, or if they are toxic. The EPA must assess human safety risks, environmental risks, and "safe" levels of exposure and food residue.[69]

---

[63] *Id.* at 363.
[64] *Id.* at 367.
[65] Brandon W. Neuschafer, *The Role of Biotechnology in Sustainable Agriculture*, 15 ABA Agric. Mgmt. Comm. Newsl. 13, 14 (2011), *available at* https://www.americanbar.org/content/dam/aba/publications/nr_newsletters/am/201105_am.authcheckdam.pdf.
[66] Stephanie Tai, *The Rise of U.S. Food Sustainability Litigation*, 85 S. Cal. L. Rev. 1069, 1094 (2012).
[67] *FDA Releases Final Guidance on Genetically Engineered Animals*, U.S. FDA, https://wayback.archive-it.org/7993/20161022072502/http://www.fda.gov/ForConsumers/ConsumerUpdates/ucm092738.htm (last visited Oct. 11, 2017).
[68] Tai, *supra* note 66.
[69] *Id.* at 1095.

In 2010, farmers planted GMO crops in more than 29 countries and of the 15 million farmers using these crops, 90% of them were small-scale farmers. While consumer and environmental groups have opposed GMO crops, the European Commission has "recognized that GMO crops are at least as safe for consumers and the environment as conventional crops and that biotechnology could help developing countries meet food pressures."[70]

Those who oppose GMOs express concerns about "possible human health risks, such as the potential toxicity of GMO food, potential allergenicity of such food, potential instability of the inserted gene, and potential detrimental nutritional impact." Opponents point to "environmental risks, including 'unintended effects on non-target organisms, ecosystems and biodiversity,' increased use of herbicides due to crop herbicide resistance, and unintended outcrossing of genes into the environment."[71] A report by the National Academy of Sciences (NAS) in 2010 noted that GMO crops have less adverse environmental impacts than conventional crops so long as pests do not evolve resistance to GMO crops and there remains limited gene flow from GMO crops to wild species. Caution, however, is still in order. Assessing GMO crops is an ongoing task as we learn more about the environmental, economic, and social impacts, and as these impacts adjust over time with adapting environments and changing farm practices.[72]

Questions and Notes

1. "In 2013, Chipotle made headlines for becoming the first national restaurant chain to voluntarily disclose the presence of GMOs in [its] food. In 2015, [it] succeeded in [its] quest to switch to serving food made only with non-GMO ingredients." https://chipotle.com/food-with-integrity.

2. Note the trade-offs involved with modern farming techniques. How would you define the interests that legislators must weigh when considering whether to support those techniques?

3. In Chapter 3, Section IV.C, we explored the Precautionary Principle (PP). The PP has garnered a fair amount of attention in the context of genetically modified foods. Genetic engineers make genetically modified foods from genetically modified organisms (GMOs), which are organisms (living things) whose genetic material, or genes or part of a gene, is altered using genetic engineering techniques. GMOs can be altered with plants, animals, or even viruses. Based on concerns

---

[70] Neuschafer, *supra* note 65, at 14.
[71] Tai, *supra* note 66, at 1091 (citing a 2005 World Health Organization study).
[72] *Id.* at 1092-1093.

stemming from the use of GMOs, some nations have limited the importation of GMOs until more research is completed. The European Union, Japan, Russia, and China, for example, all have some restrictions on the use of genetically modified foods, ranging from labeling requirements to bans. Several U.S. states, such as Vermont, Maine, and Connecticut, enacted some form of GMO labeling laws. However, on July 29, 2016, President Obama signed the first U.S. federal law requiring food manufacturers and distributors to label products that contain GMOs and preempted the state laws. S. 764, 114th Cong. (2016) (amendment to Agricultural Marketing Act of 1946, 7 U.S.C. §§1621 *et seq*). Within two years from the date the law goes into effect, the U.S. Department of Agriculture must create a new "national mandatory bioengineered food disclosure standard" for "any bioengineered food and any food that may be bioengineered." 7 U.S.C. §1639b(a)(1).

4. Assume you represented a country that wanted to ban or severely restrict GMOs based on the PP. What would be the policy arguments supporting your use of the PP in the context of GMOs? How significant should the risks be? What level of uncertainty? And who should have the burden of proof?

B. Raising Livestock

Concentrated Animal Feeding Operations (CAFOs) are a product of industrializing farming operations to increase yields and reduce costs by concentrating the raising of livestock in a reduced footprint. For example, while hog farming was common in U.S. rural environments beginning with the introduction of this domesticated animal to Florida in 1539 and Jamestown in 1607, the invention of the refrigerated train car in the twentieth century encouraged concentrated production of livestock in proximity to grain food stocks. The nuisance conditions created by these industrialized practices compelled lawmakers to include CAFOs as point sources subject to federal regulation under the Clean Water Act.[73]

CAFOs are controversial for those who are part of the sustainable food movement as well as for those who view such operations as animal mistreatment and cruelty. The percentage of all U.S. animals raised in CAFOs increased from 22% in 1982 to 43% in 2002. While CAFOs are generally known to generate more waste than can be safely disposed of without the risk of contamination to nearby ground and surface water and the emission of air pollutants, scientific evaluation of these impacts has been complicated and uncertain. Nevertheless, concerns about CAFOs

---

[73] Michelle B. Nowlin, *Sustainable Production of Swine: Putting Lipstick on a Pig?*, 37 Vt. L. Rev. 1079, 1081-1083 (2012).

include "excessive size, disregard for animal welfare, misuse of pharmaceuticals, mismanagement of waste, and socially irresponsible corporate ownership" as well as threats to the environment and public health "[b]y concentrating too much manure on too little land" resulting in water and air pollution that impacts the surrounding community.[74]

CAFO production practices breed and raise animals in confinement and focus on rapid growth to reduce the time between birth and slaughter and on the use of antibiotics to suppress disease. Operations separate animal production from crop production, which breaks the cycle of nutrients found on small diverse farms because the animals excrete the nutrients from feedstock raised in far-away operations and the subsequent CAFO waste disposal creates public health issues for neighbors.[75] These operations depress local land values, pollute local air and water, impair the public health, and emit greenhouse gases, including methane and nitrous oxides that contribute to climate change.[76] In addition, animal welfare supporters have objected to the care, transport, and slaughter practices that they allege constitute inhumane treatment of farm animals. Efforts to restrict these practices have failed at the federal level, but animal welfare supporters have been successful "in several states to impose some care requirements on animal producers."[77]

 Chipotle founder, Steve Ells, visited a McDonald's chicken farm in Arkansas during Chipotle's partnership with McDonald's between 1998 and 2005. Steve, committed to buying good, fresh food, had never visited the farms and returned from the chicken farm visit saying "it was absolutely the most disgusting thing he'd ever seen in his life."[78] As Steve developed his "food with integrity" approach, he switched to small pig farms

[74] Tai, *supra* note 66, at 1086.
[75] Nowlin, *supra* note 73, at 1083-1084.
[76] *See id.* at 1085-1091.
[77] Tadlock Cowan, *Humane Treatment of Farm Animals: Overview and Issues*, Cong. Res. Serv. (May 9, 2011), http://nationalaglawcenter.org/wp-content/uploads/assets/crs/RS21978.pdf.
[78] Stock & Wong, *supra* note 1.

to supply the pork for his carnitas burrito.[79] Chipotle refused to buy pork from conventional farms that did not meet its "Responsibly Raised" standards based on concerns that included the living conditions of the pigs.[80] In fact, the company stopped serving pork for several months in 2015 rather than serving it from animals not raised humanely.[81]

Pressure from the food industry, as well as state initiatives to encourage meat suppliers to use more humane approaches to meat production will likely be the main mechanism for changing current CAFO practices as farm animals have few, if any, legal rights. The Animal Welfare Act does not include birds and "only applies to farm animals used in animal testing for non-agricultural research." In addition, most states exempt factory-farming practices from animal cruelty statutes.[82] In 2008, California voters passed a ballot initiative by a 63% majority to prohibit certain farm animals from confinement in a manner that does not allow them to lie down, stand up, fully extend their limbs, or turn around. This ban on battery cages for chickens took effect in 2015 to cover all eggs sold in California. The movement against concentrated animal feedlot operations has continued to spread to other states such as Massachusetts, as well as to big restaurants and grocers, which have committed to switch entirely to cage-free eggs in the next decade, representing an estimated 70% of the demand for eggs in the United States. As of now, it is uncertain whether consumers will demand cage-free eggs, even if it means that they will need to pay almost double the price for these eggs.[83]

In addition to concerns about the humane treatment of farm animals, adding antibiotics into our food chain through animal feed has created a great deal of concern. Therapeutic and growth promotion methods use antimicrobials in food-producing animals and such uses constitute approximately 80% of all antibiotic sales in the United States. Antimicrobial use increased by 16% between 2009 and 2012, prompting the FDA to issue guidelines in 2013 to implement voluntary initiatives to restrict and eventually eliminate antimicrobial use for growth promotion purposes in animal feedstocks.[84] Unfortunately, voluntary compliance outside the regulatory system may not be a sufficient response to decades of evidence

---

[79] *Id.*

[80] Jillian Berman, *Chipotle Pork Shortage Is Proof of a Larger Problem Facing the Food Industry*, Huffington Post, http://www.huffingtonpost.com/2015/01/15/chipotle-pork-shortage_n_6473964.html (last updated Jan. 15, 2015).

[81] Craig Giammona & Shruti Date Singh, *Chipotle Has a Pork Problem*, Bloomberg, http://www.bloomberg.com/news/articles/2015-04-08/chipotle-s-carnitas-shortage-reflects-broader-supply-woes (last updated Apr. 8, 2015).

[82] Susan Adams, *Legal Rights of Farm Animals*, 40 Md. B.J. 19, 20 (2007).

[83] Vanessa Wong, *Egg Makers are Freaked out by the Cage-Free Future*, BuzzFeedNews (Mar. 22, 2017), https://www.cnbc.com/2017/03/22/egg-makers-are-freaked-out-by-the-cage-free-future.html.

[84] Diana R.H. Winters, *The Inadequacy of Voluntary Measures to Reduce the Use of Antimicrobials in Animal Feed*, Harvard L. Bill of Health Blog (Oct. 4, 2014), http://blogs.harvard.edu/billofhealth/2014/10/04/the-inadequacy-of-voluntary-measures-to-reduce-the-use-of-antimicrobials-in-animal-feed/.

showing human health risks associated with using antibiotics in food-producing animals.[85]

Concerns about large-scale biothreats follow the use of industrialized meat production techniques. In 2002, a Newcastle disease outbreak in commercial poultry took 11 months to resolve and required California farmers to destroy more than 3 million birds. Mad cow disease surfaced in the western United States in 2003 and cost the country $6 billion in lost export sales because of the fear of the human disease it causes, which killed 122 people in Great Britain between 1995 and 2013. The foot-and-mouth animal disease has not arisen in the United States since 1929, but an epidemic in Great Britain in 2001 cost the country $11 billion. The Department of Homeland Security is responsible for protecting "the agriculture and food system against terrorism attacks, major disasters and other emergencies" and the USDA tracks diseases. Farms are vulnerable to outbreaks—either natural or deliberately caused by humans—and our national security depends on our economic and food security.[86]

The avian ("bird") flu epidemic that occurred in the U.S. Midwest in 2015 is the worst animal disease outbreak in U.S. history. The bird flu typically comes from wild birds as they drop waste containing the virus in their migration patterns. Millions of birds fly across the United States every season and it is impossible to test every one of them. Following their wild migration patterns and taking various samples allows scientists to detect the virus. Unfortunately, the pattern of contagion in 2015 did not match the bird migration patterns and scientists have not yet been able to verify the disease source and how it spread. The avian flu epidemic cost the United States $2.6 billion in lost sales, $400 million in forgone taxes, and 15,693 jobs. The USDA and trade associations are taking efforts to plan how to protect farms from diseases and to prevent diseases from spreading between farms. Federal procedures are being increased "to detect viruses earlier and cull chickens faster" because the "[n]ext time it could be even worse."[87]

The production of animals for consumption continues to grow throughout the world. However, the confinement production model and the shift to industrialization by intensifying and consolidating animal agriculture is responsible for the increase in accessibility and the decrease in costs associated with this growth.[88] This shift to intensive production systems has resulted in 1) adverse impacts on the environment such as air and water pollution, land degradation, climate change, a decrease in biodiversity;

---

[85] Diana R.H. Winters, *Intractable Delay and the Need to Amend the Petition Provisions of the FDCA*, 90 IND. L.J. 1047, 1064-1065 (2015).
[86] Maryn McKenna, *The Looming Threat of Avian Flu*, N.Y. TIMES (Apr. 13, 2016), https://www.nytimes.com/2016/04/17/magazine/the-looming-threat-of-avian-flu.html.
[87] *Id.*
[88] Hannah M.M. Connor, *The Industrialization of Animal Agriculture: Connecting a Model with Its Impacts on the Environment*, in Angelo et al., *supra* note 44, at 65-67.

2) human health risks associated with the overuse of antibiotics in animal feedstocks; and 3) concerns about the mistreatment of animals. Concerns about the resilience and sustainability of many social-ecological systems associated with CAFO operations and large-scale farming may drive local communities to encourage small-scale farms that have externalities more capable of management.[89]

Questions

1. Chipotle's decision to serve only meat that meets its "Responsibly Raised" standards, strengthens which systems' resilience or sustainability? (As stated on Chipotle's website, "We set minimum space requirements for the animals producing the meat and dairy products that end up in our restaurants. We work with our suppliers to ensure the highest possible animal welfare standards, and are always setting the bar higher.")

2. Has agriculture made human health more resilient to disease? Why or why not? What do you make of the fact that many modern flu epidemics and pandemics start in domesticated farm animals like swine and chickens?

3. What are the ecosystem services management trade-offs we might want to consider when exploring whether and how to regulate CAFOs?

C. Seafood

Food from the waters and oceans has long provided sustenance for humans beginning with hunting, gathering, and fishing activities, and evolving into aquaculture — the farming of fish and plants in water. Despite the importance of this food source, the destruction of habitats and overfishing has exacerbated seafood scarcity, and food insecurity.[90] Seventy percent of the world's fisheries are suffering from overexploitation, and ocean ecosystem destruction threatens global health. We must better manage wild fisheries by accurately monitoring fish populations, regulating fishing to reduce bycatch, controlling dredging, and reducing other destructive fishing practices.[91] We must also operate fish farms, which produce more than half of

---

[89] Nowlin, *supra* note 73, at 1140-1141.
[90] Nell Green Nylen, *Why Federal Dietary Guidelines Should Acknowledge the Food-Choice/Environment Nexus: Examining the Recommendation to Eat More Seafood*, 40 ECOLOGY L.Q. 759 (2013).
[91] *Sustainable Seafood*, NAT'L GEOGRAPHIC (Apr. 27, 2010), http://ocean.nationalgeographic.com/ocean/take-action/sustainable-seafood/.

the world's seafood, in a manner designed to "minimize environmental impacts like pollution, disease, and other damage to coastal ecosystems on which wild species depend."[92]

Different parts of the world have practiced aquaculture for thousands of years, but the United States has a relatively new aquacultural history.[93] Nevertheless, "aquaculture is the fastest-growing agricultural sector in the nation" as the United States pushes to reduce its reliance on importing this source of protein, while simultaneously promoting the health benefits of this food source.[94] Sustainability of the seafood industry is problematic as government health guidelines urge people to consume this healthy food choice without understanding the environmental impacts of this consumption.[95] The U.S. Department of Agriculture (USDA) and the U.S. Department of Health and Human Services (HHS) are jointly responsible for publishing the Dietary Guidelines for Americans every five years. Recent guidelines encourage American adults to increase their consumption of seafood by more than twice the current consumption levels. However, government guidance about nutritional food choices has been divorced from information about the sustainability of these suggested choices.[96]

The major environmental impacts of harvesting wild-catch seafood are overfishing, bycatch, and habitat destruction. Ineffective monitoring, lack of scientific understanding, weak regulations, and failed enforcement worsen overfishing. Most of the illegal, unreported, and unregulated (IUU) fishing practices involve fishing companies based in developed countries. These companies are the ones mostly responsible for exploiting the waters of developing countries by "ignoring rules for permissible fishing gear, failing to report or misreporting catch composition and numbers, and fishing in off-limits areas."[97] Fishing practices such as bottom trawling while perhaps efficient also result in wasteful and unsustainable harvesting. Incidental bycatch and the discard of sea life, not targeted by fishing, intensify the effects of overfishing as bycatch may include "the capture of ecologically important species and juveniles of economically valuable species."[98] Fishing methods that target individual fish, such as pole/troll fishing, trolling, and harpooning, produce low bycatch and cause minimal habitat damage. Using traps and pots that do not drag fishing gear along the bottom also produce low bycatch and minimal habitat damage. Purse seining, gillnetting, and longlining are likely to lead to high bycatch;

---

[92] *Id.*
[93] Kristen L. Johns, *Farm Fishing Holes: Gaps in Federal Regulation of Offshore Aquaculture*, 86 S. Cal. L. Rev. 681, 683 (2013).
[94] *Id.*
[95] Nylen, *supra* note 90, at 764-765.
[96] *Id.* at 761-762.
[97] *Id.* at 767.
[98] *Id.* at 768.

however, trawling, dredging, and blast fishing produce high bycatch *and* cause significant habitat destruction.[99]

Significant environmental impacts can also result from aquaculture, which now produces more than one-third of the global seafood supply and provides for almost half of human seafood consumption worldwide. Consumers in the United States prefer fish such as tuna and salmon that are at the top of the food chain and thus require a much greater exploitation of species that are lower on the food chain.[100] Depending upon the type of fish farmed, the weight of the food input required to produce the desired edible seafood may greatly exceed the weight of food produced. In addition, marine or freshwater farming in open pens risks contaminating wild fish with parasites or disease, interbreeding or competing with escaped farm fish, destroying habitat, and polluting land and water with fish waste, pesticides, and antibiotics that produce algal blooms and dead zones from the anoxic water.[101] Finally, farmed seafood may contain more polychlorinated biphenyls (PCBs) than wild-caught seafood and be more hazardous to human health.[102]

Contamination of either wild-catch or farmed seafood by toxic pollutants such as methylmercury, dioxins, and PCBs, can offset the nutritional benefits of seafood consumption. The Dietary Guidelines warn pregnant and nursing women to avoid certain varieties of fish—the top predators that contain the highest levels of methyl mercury. This toxin continues to accumulate at each point in the food chain and can cause devastating impacts to embryos and young children. Pesticide residues from insecticides, herbicides, and fungicides also make their way into rivers, lakes, and oceans from agricultural stormwater and irrigation return flow and accumulate in the tissues of seafood. Chemicals and endocrine disruptors from household products, pharmaceuticals, and industry pass through wastewater treatment processes and bioaccumulate in fish, posing health hazards to consumers.[103]

Question

1. In Chapter 1, Section II.B.2.a.i, we examined the exploitation of the Atlantic cod and in Chapter 2, Section I, we examined the exploitation of the Mississippi mussels. Also in the last chapter, we introduced Collective Action Challenges (CAC). How would you characterize the CACs that arise around fishing, like the Atlantic cod and Mississippi mussels? What would motivate fishers to harvest a fish rapidly? Does

---

[99] *Id.* at 769.
[100] *Id.* at 772.
[101] *Id.* at 771.
[102] *Id.*
[103] *Id.* at 774-776.

this analysis help illustrate how or whether the laws regulating fish are enhancing the resiliency or sustainability of aquatic life systems?

IV. AGRICULTURAL POLLUTION FROM FERTILIZERS AND PESTICIDES

The Green Revolution in agriculture during the last half of the twentieth century resulted in high crop yields and improvements in production that helped to feed a growing global population. It also required the use of **fertilizers, pesticides** (see Chapter 3, Sections II.E and VII.B.3 for a discussion of some of the collective action challenges involving fertilizers and pesticides), water, and fossil-fueled technology to replace human labor. Environmental and health risks increased after adding new chemicals developed during World War II to the soil to produce these high yields. The pesticide DDT was effective in controlling some short-term insect-borne diseases and providing long-term effective pest control. However, there were trade-offs. The long-term consequences of DDT accumulation in living tissues as it moved through the food chain led to the severe restriction and banning of this pesticide in the 1970s and 1980s.[104]

While **pesticides** developed from wartime nerve gases are effective to kill insects and other pests rapidly, they are also highly toxic to humans, fish, and wildlife. In the United States, they remain the pesticide of choice, however, because they are less persistent in the environment than DDT. Additional categories of chemical pesticides that are not toxic to mammals effectively fight harmful insects, but they have also proven toxic to beneficial insects, fish, and other aquatic life. Biotechnology methods genetically modify both microbes and crops to produce pesticidal effects, but concerns persist about ecological risks.[105]

A. Risks of Using Pesticides and Fertilizers

The threat of pesticides to non-target wildlife remains despite the ban and restriction of DDT over the last several decades. Even EPA-approved pesticides present risks to hundreds of threatened or endangered species because of pesticide spray drift, pesticide contamination of waterways and soils, and endocrine-disrupting pesticide effects. Pesticides directly affect aquatic life, birds, amphibians, and those invertebrates most closely related to the targeted pests, such as butterflies and bees, with resulting ecosystems damage such as the loss of pollination services. In addition to these direct acute effects, there are chronic effects of pesticides that do not kill an organism but instead affect its reproduction, behavior, physiology, growth, and life

---

[104] Angelo et al., *supra* note 44, at 35-37.
[105] *Id.* at 37-38.

span. Finally, the ability of certain synthetic pesticides to mimic hormones and cause harm to humans and wildlife; the uncertainty of the effects on microorganisms that provide critical ecological services such as decomposition; and the tendency for certain pesticides to bioaccumulate and adversely affect organisms, are all reasons why EPA-approved pesticides continue to adversely affect numerous forms of wildlife.[106]

HOW MUCH WOULD IT COST TO REPLACE BEES?

In the last chapter, we introduced Ecosystem Services Management. (ESM) Imagine what the world would be like if humans had to pay the costs to pollinate. Farmers would be required to carry pollen from one plant to another or maybe use a yet-to-be-designed contraption to pollinate billions of flora. Could we afford the cost of such an action? Could we afford the cost of fruits, vegetables, and other plant products that bees currently pollinate free of charge, such as alfalfa, apples, beets, eggplants, guavas, kiwis, mangos, nectarines, onions, peaches, pears, plums, pomegranates, strawberries, and dozens of others?

Pesticides that kill bees and other insects providing this crucial ecosystem service are used regularly. As a 2015 report noted:

In North America, annual [honeybee] colony losses averaged 29.6% between 2006 and 2013. In some cases, colony failure has been so rapid that outwardly healthy colonies lost most of their adult bees in a matter of weeks. . . . Many stressors are contributing to bee colony failure, most with a strong anthropogenic component. These include parasites and pathogens, pesticides, and nutritional stresses. . . .[107]

How would an ESM approach, described in Chapter 3, Section VI, to the regulation of pesticide use, for example, provide information relative to bees and potentially be useful for the regulation of pesticides? Would an ESM approach help assess the resilience of the social-ecological system built around the services associated with bees? "Translated into dollars, the pollination services delivered by bees are valued around $23.5 billion a year in Europe and roughly $18 billion per year in the United

---

[106] *Id.* at 39-43.
[107] Clint J. Perry et. al., *Rapid Behavioral Maturation Accelerates Failure of Stressed Honey Bee Colonies*, Proceedings of the National Academy of Sciences, 112 Proc. Nat.'l Acad. Sci. 3427, 3427 (2015).

States." Madeline June Kass, *The Buzz: EU Steps Up on Bee Protection*, 32 Nat. Res. & Environ. 52 (Summer 2017).

In 2015, the U.S. Court of Appeals for the Ninth Circuit held that farmers could not apply pesticides with sulfoxaflor (a neonicotinoid chemically related to nicotine) to crop-land without further scientific testing and verification. The plaintiffs in the case, primarily organizations representing honey and beekeeping industries, sued Dow Agrosciences LLC and the U.S. Environmental Protection Agency (EPA), claiming the EPA improperly approved the use of sulfoxaflor without reliable studies concerning the impact on honeybee colonies. In agreeing with the plaintiffs, the court "vacate[d] the EPA's unconditional registration of sulfoxaflor and remand[ed] for the EPA to obtain further studies and data regarding the effects of sulfoxaflor on bees."[108]

Pesticidal GMOs create new risks in addition to the risks they share with traditional chemical pesticides. Most significantly, there is great uncertainty as to the nature and scale of such new risks. For example, a plant that produces pesticidal substances through genetic modification has the potential to cross-fertilize with other plants and spread these pesticides throughout agricultural or natural ecosystems. If the pesticidal GMOs pollinate with another species or wild relatives, there is the potential for "superweeds" that radically disrupt agricultural and natural ecosystems.[109]

Farmers historically used natural **fertilizers** such as animal wastes (manures) and compost to increase the nutrient level of the soil to increase crop yields. However, with the industrialization of agriculture, large-scale farms separated the animals from the plants. Instead of the small-scale farming practices of using animal wastes to feed the crops that provided the animal feed, concentrated animal feeding operations (CAFOs) now create vast amounts of waste that greatly contribute to water pollution, while fossil-fuel fertilizer is used to enhance soil nutrients.[110] Pesticide and fertilizer use has greatly increased over the last 50 years, as population growth has demanded greater crop yields and farmers have discarded traditional crop rotation practices.

Pollution resulting from this increased use is found in the runoff from agricultural land into waterways, which contains both pesticides and two of the three major components of fertilizer, nitrogen, and phosphorous. Agricultural runoff is a nonpoint source under the Clean Water Act because it does not meet the definition of a point source, which requires that the pollutant is discharged from a "discernible, confined and discrete conveyance" and because agricultural stormwater discharges and irrigation return flows are expressly excluded from the definition. Nonpoint water pollution has had a major impact on water quality, wetlands, and

---

[108] Pollinator Stewardship Council v. U.S. E.P.A., 806 F.3d 520, 533 (9th Cir. 2015).
[109] Angelo et al., *supra* note 44, at 43-44.
[110] *Id.* at 38.

the contamination of groundwater, with one-third of the waters in the United States having a high concentration of phosphorous or nitrogen from agricultural operations.[111] In Chapter 3, Section B.3, we described some of the challenges involved with nutrient runoff in the Mississippi River watershed.

Nutrient pollution from excess phosphorous and nitrogen stimulates plant growth in water bodies and results in the overgrowth of algae and the concurrent depletion of oxygen and sunlight penetration leading to eutrophication. Eutrophication is "the process by which a body of water becomes enriched in dissolved nutrients [as phosphates] that stimulate the growth of aquatic plant life usually resulting in the depletion of dissolved oxygen."[112] Eutrophication, with its increase in algae and aquatic plant life, can permanently damage aquatic resources because of its impact on phytoplankton, the loss of coral reefs, oxygen depletion, reduced water transparency, fish kills, and the loss of fish species. For example, the northern portion of the Gulf of Mexico is the largest "dead zone" in the United States, where it is likely that the nutrients from the agricultural operations in the Mississippi River basin have fed the massive growth of algae and resulted in the depletion of oxygen, known as hypoxia, essentially eliminating fish, shrimp, crab, and other aquatic wildlife. Agricultural fertilizers have adversely impacted other aquatic ecosystems in the United States, including the Chesapeake Bay and the Florida Everglades.[113]

In addition to the environmental risks posed by pesticides and fertilizers, these products pose risks to human health and well-being.

Gulf of Mexico Dead Zone

Agriculture is one of the largest sources of greenhouse gases in the world because of the use of fossil fuels in the production of pesticides and fertilizers as well as in the transport and use of these products. Groundwater contamination from pesticides and fertilizers leaching into aquifers can also impact drinking water supplies and create health risks for humans and animals. The use and overuse of

---

[111] *Id.* at 44-45.
[112] *Eutrophication*, MERRIAM-WEBSTER DICTIONARY, https://www.merriam-webster.com/dictionary/eutrophication (last visited Oct. 11, 2017).
[113] Angelo et al., *supra* note 44, at 44-47.

pesticides and fertilizers can cause serious environmental and human health damages, particularly because of the toxicity of the chemicals involved and the poor use and application management practices. We must balance the benefits of increased crop yields to ensure affordable and healthy food for our population against the environmental and economic impacts of our current food systems to achieve sustainable and resilient farming practices into the future.[114]

B. Regulating Agricultural Pesticides and Fertilizers

In the United States, the regulatory schemes of states and the Federal Insecticide, Fungicide, and Rodenticide Act (FIFRA) and the Toxic Substances Control Act (TSCA) control the **production, sale, and use** of agricultural pesticides and fertilizers. While pesticides are subject to FIFRA, but exempt from regulation under TSCA, Congress finds that "among the many chemical substances and mixtures which are constantly being developed and produced, there are some whose manufacture, processing, distribution in commerce, use, or disposal may present an unreasonable risk of injury to health or the environment."[115]

FIFRA requires any pesticide to be sold, distributed, or used in the United States to be reviewed before it is marketed and to be registered by the EPA to assure that when the pesticide is "used in accordance with widespread and commonly recognized practice[,] it will not generally cause unreasonable adverse effects on the environment."[116] The federal government began regulating pesticides under the Insecticide Act of 1910 and enacted the first version of FIFRA in 1947 to require registration before marketing. However, Congress made major changes to the statute in 1972 following the extensive controversy over environmental protection engendered by Rachel Carson's publication of *Silent Spring* in 1962.

Under the current statute, the EPA must conduct a premarket review of pesticides before registration to determine that it will not cause "unreasonable adverse effects on the environment." However, the EPA does not need to determine before registration that there are any economic or social benefits provided by the pesticide. Even if the pesticide lacks efficacy or other pesticides serving the same use are available, the EPA cannot deny registration based on these facts.[117] The applicant for premarket review and registration must submit the data necessary for the EPA to determine "unreasonable adverse effects." The EPA mostly directs data requirements to human health effects, but, to a lesser extent, also requires data related

---

[114] *Id.* at 48-50.
[115] *Toxic Substances Control Act*, 15 U.S.C. §2601 (2016).
[116] Angelo et al., *supra* note 44, at 130 (citing 7 U.S.C. §136a(c)(5) (2007)).
[117] *Id.* at 130-131.

to adverse impacts on wildlife, aquatic life, ecological systems, and non-target insects.[118]

Once registered, the EPA regulates the pesticide's use by requiring producers to label the product with any precautionary statements or warnings about its use along with the directions for the use and the ingredients contained. So long as pesticide users follow all label directions, the EPA has no further role in regulating user behavior — leaving regulation predominantly to the states. Realistically, however, monitoring individual users is not feasible and pesticide users may not understand or may fail to follow the labeling directions designed to reduce environmental risk.[119] The EPA also has authority to require the classification of higher-risk pesticides as "restricted-use pesticides" with their use supervised by a certified applicator. States work with the EPA to certify applicators, but applicators do not require training as to local ecological systems and their susceptibility to pesticides, nor do they require instruction on integrated pest management.[120]

FIFRA authorizes the EPA to register pesticides conditionally if there is insufficient data to support a registration determination, but the pesticide or the proposed new use is substantially similar to existing registered pesticides. The EPA may grant an emergency exemption under specified conditions to control pests that present significant risks or to issue an experimental use permit to allow field-testing necessary for gathering the data needed for registration. Registered pesticide producers have a continuing obligation to report to the EPA any information they may have about unreasonable adverse environmental effects. FIFRA also requires reregistration of pesticides registered before the more rigorous 1972 revisions. Finally, FIFRA gives the EPA authority to cancel or suspend registrations if it finds that the risks of the pesticide outweigh the benefits.[121]

In 1976, Congress enacted **TSCA** "to regulate chemical substances and mixtures which present an unreasonable risk of injury to health or the environment, and to take action with respect to chemical substances and mixtures which are imminent hazards."[122] It serves as the primary regulation for toxic chemical substances and requires registration of the chemical components in fertilizers. In contrast to FIFRA, which regulates the use of pesticides, TSCA does not restrict in any way the actual use of fertilizers. This limited regulation of the chemical substances in fertilizers results in the need to use other federal environmental regulations, such as the Clean Water Act, and state regulations to deal with the adverse effects caused by fertilizer use and runoff.[123] The Frank R. Lautenberg Chemical

---

[118] *Id.* at 131-132.
[119] *Id.* at 132-133.
[120] *Id.* at 133.
[121] *Id.* at 133-136.
[122] 15 U.S.C. §2601(b) (2016).
[123] Peterson, *supra* note 59, at 153.

Safety for the 21st Century Act amended TSCA, effective June 22, 2016. The new law received bipartisan support and improved the original Act by including a mandatory requirement that the EPA must "evaluate existing chemicals with clear and enforceable deadlines; [n]ew risk-based safety standard; [i]ncreased public transparency for chemical information; and [c]onsistent source of funding for EPA to carry out the responsibilities under the new law."[124] The EPA reported in the fall of 2017 that it has "successfully addressed the backlog of manufacturers' new chemical requests or pre-manufacturing notices (PMNs) under review by the Agency so that the number of cases under review is back to historically typical levels."[125]

V. REGULATING AGRICULTURAL PRODUCTION AND PRACTICES

A. Clean Water Act

The Clean Water Act (CWA) is the primary federal statute for regulating the environmental impacts on water resources from agricultural production and practices. Agricultural activities not only impact the quality of water resources, but they also impact the quantity of water available for other human and environmental needs. The CWA requires a permit under the National Pollutant Discharge Elimination System (NPDES) for any addition of a pollutant from a point source into navigable waters. Nearly all states administer the NPDES program themselves. However, states and the federal government have struggled with controlling pollution from nonpoint sources (NPS), which include agricultural runoff.[126]

Agricultural runoff from animal feeding operations and the mismanagement of irrigation and pesticide and fertilizer application not only affects the quality of the water bodies to which it drains but is also responsible for the degradation of the nation's wetlands.[127] As explained in more detail in Chapter 3, regulators set a total maximum daily load (TMDL) for each pollutant and each water body according to the water quality standards established by states for specific water bodies within each jurisdiction. These TMDLs are used to maintain or reduce pollutants entering water bodies by regulating both NPDES permits for point sources and urban, stormwater, and agricultural runoff.[128]

[124] *The Frank R. Lautenberg Chemical Safety for the 21st Century Act*, EPA, https://www.epa.gov/assessing-and-managing-chemicals-under-tsca/frank-r-lautenberg-chemical-safety-21st-century-act (last visited Oct. 12, 2017).
[125] *Statistics for the New Chemicals Review Program Under TSCA*, EPA, https://www.epa.gov/reviewing-new-chemicals-under-toxic-substances-control-act-tsca/statistics-new-chemicals-review.
[126] Angelo et al., *supra* note 44, at 147-148.
[127] *Id.* at 148-149.
[128] *Id.* at 156.

CWA provisions specifically directed to agricultural activities include Animal Feeding Operations (AFOs), identified by the EPA as "concentrated" Animal Feeding Operations (CAFOs) and potentially regulated as a "point source," requiring an NPDES permit. CAFOs are not exempt as agricultural stormwater discharges and are required to prepare comprehensive nutrient management plans (CNMPs) to control soil erosion and runoff pollution. A CAFO that discharges from its operation is required to obtain an NPDES permit and submit a nutrient management plan (NMP) under EPA rules.[129] Aquaculture in the form of fish farms and hatcheries may also be subject to CWA regulation as a point source discharge if they are defined by the EPA as a "concentrated aquatic animal production facility" (CAAP) because they significantly contribute to water pollution.

Finally, wetlands that are "waters of the United States" are subject to regulation under Section 404 of the CWA, which requires individuals dredging or filling material in a wetland to obtain a permit from the Army Corps of Engineers. There are agricultural exemptions under Section 404(f) for ongoing "normal" farming and harvesting activities that occur in wetlands, so long as the activity does not bring a wetland into new farming production. However, these exemptions allow existing farming practices to continue to degrade wetlands. The Swampbuster provisions of the Food Security Act of 1985 (FSA) are intended to be consistent with CWA §404 and operate to at least reduce the rate at which wetlands are converted into agricultural uses.[130]

Questions

1. In Chapter 3 you learned about the many pressures on freshwater resources. In many places, irrigated agriculture is one of those pressures. Is there a fundamental trade-off between the sustainability of agriculture in arid places and the sustainability of water resources in those same places? What are those trade-offs? How could an evaluation of agricultural irrigation practices through a policy lens of wanting to promote the sustainability of freshwater resources for future generations lead to changes in certain agricultural practices? For example, should we allow farmers to grow rice in a desert, regardless of how profitable rice can be as a crop? Do we need to increase the price of water to encourage efficient use of resources?

2. How could an evaluation of a water system's resilience in an arid agriculturally rich area lead to changes in agricultural practices?

---

[129] *See Compiled CAFO Final Rule*, U.S. EPA (July 30, 2012), https://www.epa.gov/sites/production/files/2015-08/documents/cafo_final_rule2008_comp.pdf.
[130] Angelo et al., *supra* note 44, at 158-161.

3. Has agriculture made human societies more resilient to drought and food shortages? Why or why not? As you think about that question, think about the issue from the opposite perspective as well: Are most modern communities vulnerable to widespread crop failure? Why or why not?

B. Clean Air Act

The Clean Air Act (CAA) regulates air pollution from industry and other emissions that cause human health and environmental impacts. The EPA has not held the factory farm industry to the same standards as other regulated emitters, even though concentrated factory farms emit toxic and conventional air pollutants harmful to humans and the environment. However, as states are beginning to address greenhouse gas emissions from factory farms, such as nitrous oxide and methane, the EPA must reexamine its initial position not to apply the traditional CAA permitting requirements to factory farms.[131]

As discussed in Chapter 8, the CAA establishes National Ambient Air Quality Standards (NAAQSs) for air pollutants the EPA designates as criteria pollutants. Thus far, the EPA has designated ozone, particulate matter, nitrogen oxides, sulfur dioxide, carbon monoxide, and lead as the six criteria air pollutants. However, agricultural operations emit fine and coarse particulate matter (PM)—ozone, hydrogen sulfide, methane, nitrous oxide, and ammonia—but the EPA has not designated either hydrogen sulfide or ammonia as a criteria pollutant. In addition, very few states have placed controls on the factory farm pollutants that are criteria pollutants. Instead, most states have developed State Implementation Plans (SIPs) to control emissions from industries other than factory farming.

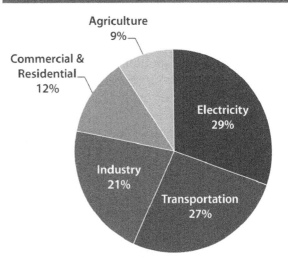

Total U.S. Greenhouse Gas Emissions by Economic Sector in 2014

Agriculture 9%
Commercial & Residential 12%
Electricity 29%
Industry 21%
Transportation 27%

U.S. Environmental Protection Agency (2017). Inventory of U.S. Greenhouse Gas Emissions and sinks: 1990-2015

---

[131] *Id.* at 163.

In addition to controlling air pollution through SIPs that address the attainment of NAAQSs, the CAA requires states to implement permitting programs for new "major sources" or for "major modifications" to existing major sources. These changes require new source review (NSR), and in areas already attaining the NAAQSs, a prevention of significant deterioration (PSD) permit is also required. The NSR program includes designated pollutants, as well as criteria pollutants, so agricultural operations that qualify as a new or modified major source will be subject to using the "best available control technology" (BACT) to control emissions of hydrogen sulfide, methane, nitrous oxide, ammonia and volatile organic compounds (VOCs) as precursors to ozone. Title V of the CAA also requires that existing major stationary sources of air pollution obtain a permit that incorporates the BACT standards.[132] PSD and Title V permits under the CAA do not exempt factory farms (including CAFOs) from regulation. However, the EPA and states have not actively enforced these requirements against agricultural operations.

Under the New Source Performance Standard (NSPS) the EPA establishes emission performance standards for different industries based on the "best-demonstrated technology" (BDT) for each particular industry category. These standards apply to designated and criteria pollutants emitted by new and modified sources, although existing sources may also be regulated by the states. The NSPS program regulates some agricultural facilities, such as fertilizer and pesticide manufacturers. Factory farms are not currently subject to regulation by the EPA, but the NSPS program has the potential to establish uniform and nationwide standards for emissions of pollutants from these facilities.[133]

The hazardous air pollutant (HAP) program of the CAA is administered by the EPA, not the states, and requires that pollutants anticipated to be "carcinogenic, mutagenic, teratogenic, neurotoxic, which cause reproductive dysfunction, or which are acutely or chronically toxic" be designated by the EPA as HAPs. The EPA must then determine maximum achievable control technology (MACT) standards for those industries emitting HAPs. The HAP program has not yet regulated factory farms, even though they emit hazardous pollutants. The EPA, however, has established MACT standards for other agricultural industries, such as manufacturers of fertilizers, pesticides, and other agricultural products.[134]

Factory farms with concentrated animal confinement facilities have increasingly violated CAA provisions and reporting obligations for the release of hazardous substances under the Emergency Planning and Community Right-to-Know Act (EPCRA) and the Comprehensive Environmental Response, Compensation, and Liability Act (CERCLA).

---

[132] *Id.* at 164-167.
[133] *Id.* at 166-168.
[134] *Id.* at 168.

Thousands of factory farm owners and operators negotiated a voluntary Consent Agreement with the EPA in 2005 to delay compliance obligations and stall enforcement actions. Although this agreement was challenged in federal court by public health and environmental advocates, it remains in place as the EPA works to conduct emission-monitoring studies of over 14,000 farms and issue penalties for violations that occurred after the monitoring studies were completed and the emission factors were issued. As a result, the EPA is not enforcing air pollution requirements for the farms covered by this agreement. Instead, some individual states have taken limited steps to protect public health and the environment from factory farm emissions by enforcing CAA state permitting requirements that the EPA Consent Agreement did not cover. In addition, most states have adopted hydrogen sulfide air quality standards, which along with ammonia, cause the odor and human health threats from factory farm emissions.[135]

A majority of states have established planning and operational requirements for factory farms to control odor and air emissions by requiring setbacks, waste handling procedures, and best-management practices. Controls over greenhouse gas emissions have also increased after the Supreme Court ruled in 2007 that the EPA could define greenhouse gases as air pollutants under the CAA and a few states have adopted state and regional regulation of greenhouse gas emissions to address global warming concerns. Methane and nitrous oxide are greenhouse gases emitted from factory farms and, as a result, large factory farms may eventually be required to obtain PSD and Title V permits and be subject to NSPS regulation for greenhouse emissions.[136] We explore greenhouse gases and climate change in more detail in Chapter 10.

C. Endangered Species Act

The Endangered Species Act (ESA) protects wildlife species against threatened extinction and, unlike other federal environmental law statutes that exempt agricultural activity from regulation, farmers and landowners are subject to ESA mandates to conserve and protect wildlife and ecosystems. As discussed in Chapter 7, the ESA requires that endangered or threatened species be listed and, once listed, these species are protected against being "taken" by an action that would "harass, harm, pursue, hunt, shoot, wound, kill, trap, capture, or collect" any member of such listed species. The Fish and Wildlife Service (FWS) or the National Marine Fisheries Service (NMFS) may authorize the "take" of a listed species in limited circumstances. Listed plant species are not subject to the

---

[135] *Id.* at 171-181.
[136] *Id.* at 181-183.

"take" provision, but the ESA protects them against import, transport, sale, or removal from federal lands.[137]

Agricultural activity may impact listed species in several different ways. First, there are studies indicating increased mortality of wildlife and insect species when consuming pollen from genetically engineered (GE) seeds. Therefore, when the ESA lists plant or animal species, it must analyze the impact of GE seeds on the threatened or endangered species' continued existence. The U.S. Department of Agriculture (USDA) also reviews seed company applications for using GE seeds under the Animal and Plant Health Inspection Service (APHIS) to determine, in consultation with the FWS and/or the NMFS, if the application complies with the ESA and whether the Plant Protection Act (PPA) allows them to plant the seeds commercially.[138]

Fertilizers and pesticides used in farming, as well as the irrigation processes that impact water quantity and quality, also potentially affect protected species. During the ESA's listing process, the EPA must analyze these impacts to determine the adverse effect on a particular threatened species. Fertilizers have long been known to contribute to the decline of wildlife and plant species by reducing biodiversity, impacting natural habitats, and causing harm to aquatic species through nutrient loads and eutrophication in water bodies. FIFRA regulates pesticides more strictly than it regulates fertilizers. Under FIFRA, the EPA is required to consult with the FWS and/or the NMFS before it approves the registration of a pesticide that may have adverse impacts on listed wildlife and plant species. Water quality and quantity issues will continue to impact threatened and endangered aquatic, plant, and wildlife as water scarcity and polluted runoff from agricultural and CAFO activities adversely affect critical water bodies.[139]

D. National Environmental Policy Act

The National Environmental Policy Act (NEPA) requires federal agencies to ensure that they have informed decision making as to the environmental impacts of a proposed federal action. As discussed in Chapter 8, federal agencies must prepare either an Environmental Assessment (EA) or an Environmental Impact Statement (EIS) before taking agency action if such action will "significantly affect . . . the quality of the human environment." If the agency determines that an EIS is not required, it must issue its EA to the public and prepare a finding of no significant impact (FONSI) to explain why an EIS is not necessary. If an EIS is required, the federal agency will prepare a detailed statement reflecting the

---

[137] *Id.* at 185-189.
[138] *Id.* at 192-194.
[139] *Id.* at 194-203.

environmental impact of the proposed action, unavoidable adverse environmental impacts, and alternatives to the proposed action.[140]

In addition to proposed federal actions, NEPA also applies to "every recommendation or report on proposals for legislation . . . significantly affecting the quality of the human environment." Federal legislation enacted to regulate agricultural practices in the form of "farm bill" programs has not been consistently subject to NEPA review in the past, although some have argued that a legislative EIS (LEIS) should be required for farm bills as implemented by the USDA. While the USDA's Farm Service Agency has prepared an EIS analyzing the impacts of the Conservation Reserve Program before implementation, other agencies implementing farm bill programs with significant environmental impacts have not applied NEPA to their actions.[141]

VI. FOOD SAFETY

After enjoying a nice dinner out at a local restaurant the night before, long-time friends Chiamaka and Nicolas each woke up experiencing nausea, vomiting, diarrhea, and stomach cramps. Although they scheduled to meet for an early tennis game, Chiamaka sent Nicolas a text explaining that she needed to cancel because she was not feeling well. Nicolas immediately responded, texting "food poisoning? Me too!" Angry, Nicolas called the restaurant to report that both he and his friend were suffering from a foodborne illness most likely caused by a problem at the restaurant. The manager on duty denied the accusation and said that they had served a large crowd the night before and had not received any complaints. After spending a very uncomfortable day at home, Nicolas recovered from his illness by late evening. Chiamaka, on the other hand, was in such pain that she called an ambulance and spent the next day in the hospital on an intravenous drip for hydration and nausea control.

Foodborne illness affects one in six Americans each year and there are more than 250 different foodborne diseases, which are infections caused by bacteria, viruses, and parasites or poisonings caused by toxic or chemical food contamination. While the symptoms may vary, the microbe or toxin enters the gastrointestinal tract and causes the first symptoms, such as those Chiamaka and Nicolas experienced, described as the "stomach flu," or diagnosed as gastroenteritis.[142] The Centers for Disease Control (CDC) estimates that approximately 48 million people each year become ill from domestically acquired foodborne illnesses, 128,000 of these illnesses

---

[140] *Id.* at 207-210.
[141] *Id.* at 211-217.
[142] *Foodborne Germs and Illnesses*, CTRS. FOR DISEASE CONTROL & PREVENTION, http://www.cdc.gov/foodsafety/foodborne-germs.html (last updated Aug. 31, 2017).

result in hospitalization and approximately 3,000 people die from the illness. The eight known pathogens that are responsible for the majority of these illnesses, hospitalizations, and deaths in the United States are *Norovirus, Salmonella* (nontyphoidal), *Toxoplasma gondii, E.coli* (STEC) O157, *listeria monocytogenes, Clostridium perfringens, Campylobacter spp.,* and *Staphylococcus aureus.*[143]

As discussed in the introduction to this chapter, Chipotle experienced several serious incidents with food safety in 2015-2016 that adversely impacted its reputation for fresh, responsible, and quality food, its business operations, and its stock price. Chipotle is transparent in reporting on its website the following information regarding the food illnesses experienced after 20 years in business without these issues. The two outbreaks of norovirus at Chipotle in 2015 involved a single restaurant in Simi Valley, California, sickening 243 people, and a single restaurant in Boston, Massachusetts, sickening 143. The company believes that "both cases were likely caused by a Chipotle employee who worked while sick, in violation of strict policies designed to discourage this." The *Salmonella* cases at Chipotle in Minnesota and Wisconsin reportedly sickened 64 people and "were linked to a batch of tomatoes that was served in 22 restaurants." *E. coli* reportedly sickened 60 people in 11 states, even though testing in the restaurants was not able to detect its presence after the fact. Founder, Chairman, and CEO of Chipotle, Steve Ells, has apologized and been proactive in addressing these concerns. He noted, "in 2015, we failed to live up to our own food safety standards, and in so doing, we let our customers down. At that time, I made a promise to all of our customers that we would elevate our food safety program."[144]

The Food Regulatory System for food safety in the United States arose directly from the public's vociferous outrage in reaction to Upton Sinclair's novel, *The Jungle,* published in 1906 about the meatpacking industry.[145] Although some have argued that regulatory inspections were already taking place before this novel and that Sinclair presented his story as factual when it was not, there is no doubt that *The Jungle* led to greater regulation of the food industry when President Roosevelt signed the Federal Food and Drugs Act in 1906.[146]

---

[143] *Burden of Foodborne Illness: Findings*, CTRS. FOR DISEASE CONTROL & PREVENTION, http://www.cdc.gov/foodborneburden/2011-foodborne-estimates.html (last updated July 15, 2016).

[144] Steve Ells, *Our Food Safety Advancements*, CHIPOTLE, https://chipotle.com/founderletter (last visited Oct. 12, 2017).

[145] Adam Cohen, *100 Years Later, the Food Industry Is Still "The Jungle,"* N.Y. TIMES (Jan. 2, 2007), http://www.nytimes.com/2007/01/02/opinion/02tue4.html.

[146] *See* Lawrence W. Reed, *Upton Sinclair's "The Jungle" Proved Regulation Was Required*, FOUND. FOR ECON. EDUC. (Oct. 31, 2014), https://fee.org/articles/29-upton-sinclairs-the-jungle-proved-regulation-was-required; *see also Part 1: The 1906 Food and Drugs Act and Its Enforcement*, U.S. FDA, http://www.fda.gov/AboutFDA/WhatWeDo/History/Origin/ucm054819.htm (last updated Oct. 5, 2017) (noting that this novel was "the final precipitating force behind both a meat inspection law and a comprehensive food and drug law").

The current regulatory food system is primarily administered by the Food and Drug Administration (FDA) and is encompassed to a large degree in the Federal Food, Drug, and Cosmetic Act (FFDCA), the Food Quality Protection Act (FQPA), and the Food Safety Modernization Act of 2010 (FSMA). The FDA is the agency responsible for ensuring that food products are "safe, nutritious, wholesome, and accurately labeled" although it is not responsible for the safety of meat and poultry.[147] The FSMA directed the FDA to promulgate rules for safe production and harvesting of raw

---

[147] Angelo et al., *supra* note 44, at. 223-224 & n.2.

fruits and vegetables that address "soil amendments, hygiene, packaging, temperature controls, animals in the growing area, and water."[148]

The enactment of the FSMA in 2011 shifted the FDA's focus from responding to food contamination, to preventing food safety hazards. The three major provisions of the Act seek to 1) prevent contamination using procedural safeguards and regulations on sanitary food transportation; 2) detect and respond to food safety issues by identifying high-risk facilities, upgrading testing methods, disposing of contaminated foods, and improving food safety training for officials; and 3) improve imported food safety.[149] Some have criticized the FSMA for several different reasons, including the concern that the program "focuses only on microbial food contamination and ignores farming's many environmental harms."[150] The conflicting goals of food safety and environmental protection produce at least three inconsistencies:

1. farmers must choose between applying food safety practices and observing environmental practices because of limited resources;
2. food safety practices such as keeping crops away from wildlife may actually have adverse impacts on the environment by incentivizing habitat destruction; and
3. there is a direct conflict between environmental programs to protect wildlife habitat under the USDA's Conservation Stewardship Program and the California Leafy Green Marketing Agreement that prohibits these same practices because of food safety.[151]

Responding to concerns about the burden on small producers and the access to fresh, local produce from farmers' markets, Congress passed the Tester-Hagan Amendment to the FSMA to exempt eligible small farms and businesses. The FDA also retained great discretion under the FSMA to design rules that were flexible in how they would apply to the production and harvesting operations of small businesses and entities selling directly to consumers. In addition to other adopted rules, the FDA promulgated the "Produce Rule" to provide standards for growing, harvesting, packing, and holding produce for human consumption and the "Preventive Controls Rule" to regulate food handling and preventive controls for bagging and canning foods.[152] In addition, the National Sustainable Agriculture Coalition (NSAC) was concerned that family farms would have a difficult time surviving and consumers would not be able to obtain safe, healthy,

---

[148] Samuel R. Wiseman, *The Implementation of the Food Safety Modernization Act and the Strength of the Sustainable Agriculture Movement*, 41 Am. J.L. & Med. 259, 260 (2015) (citing 21 U.S.C. §350h(a)(3)(B)).

[149] Angelo et al., *supra* note 44, at 226.

[150] Pollans, *supra* note 61, at 400.

[151] *Id.* at 403, 421-423.

[152] Wiseman, *supra* note 148, at 261-262.

and accessible fresh food. The FDA revised its rules in 2014 to address these concerns and some contend that this action shows the influence of the small farms' movement.[153]

The EPA establishes **maximum residue limits for pesticides in food**. The Food Safety and Inspection Service of the U.S. Department of Agriculture (USDA) is then responsible for monitoring and enforcing these pesticide tolerance levels in meat and poultry and the FDA is responsible for enforcing these maximum limits in fruits and vegetables.[154] Pesticide overuse on products may occur in meeting the "cosmetic standards" established by the USDA grading standards and the FDA defect action levels (DALs) to control the "maximum levels of natural or unavoidable defects in foods," which do not present significant health hazards. The U.S. marketplace has also demanded the availability of products without defects, but consumers need to be aware that there is a connection between better cosmetic appearance and increased pesticide use.[155]

Consumer awareness of the chemicals used to produce food generated a growing market for organic agricultural products. Concerns about personal health, as well as concerns about the adverse environmental impacts caused by pesticide use, drive the organic food market. Organic products are generally more expensive than conventional ones and consumers rely upon the regulatory system under the Organic Foods Production Act (OFPA) of 1990 and the National Organic Program (NOP) to establish production, handling, and labeling standards for these products.[156] The next section will address the labeling standards for organic products along with other types of dietary and production labeling and nutritional guidance.

Question

1. What should be the goal of food safety regulators? In answering this question, what trade-offs do you make and what interests do you weigh? Can you propose a goal that enhances the food system's sustainability or resilience such that we have adequate and safe food?

VII. NUTRITION, FOOD JUSTICE, AND LABELING

This chapter has thus far focused on food production, practices, regulation, and environmental externalities, but as with the food safety issues

---

[153] *Id.* at 262-263.
[154] Angelo et al., *supra* note 44 at 224.
[155] *Id.* at 225-226.
[156] *Id.* at 228.

discussed in the previous section, we must consider food consumption and its impacts on human health as a part of the food system. With rising rates of obesity and other dietary illnesses such as diabetes and heart disease, the United States must address nutritional guidelines, availability of healthy food for all, and appropriate food labeling regulation to provide people with informed choices about which foods to consume.

Nutrition. Obesity rates in the United States are more than twice what they were in 1980 and some are calling for a major revamping of our food laws and regulatory structure to respond to this public health challenge. While some might view this challenge as a matter of personal choice and responsibility, it is also the result of farm subsidies, industrial commodity crops, overly processed foods, and the lack of healthy food choices in some communities and schools.[157] As mentioned earlier, the farm bills have prioritized corn, wheat, rice, cotton, and soybeans through subsidies and thus farmers are encouraged to produce these commodity crops rather than fruits and vegetables. This system also creates regional growing patterns as states in the Midwest produce these commodity crops more readily, while states such as Florida and California produce fruits and vegetables. Regionalization of agriculture thus makes it more difficult for those individuals of lesser means to obtain healthy and balanced food choices from a local market. Farm subsidies of commodity crops have also stimulated the production and use of corn-based and soy-based food products, which add cheap and unhealthy sugars and fats to the food market.[158] Some argue that obesity in the United States has increased because food consumers have purchased food that is artificially cheap and nonnutritious as farmers focus on the commodity crops and ignore healthy crops such as fruits, grains, and vegetables.[159]

In addition to environmental challenges, obesity raises economic and social challenges. On the economic side, the Centers for Disease Control and Prevention estimate that the per capita cost of obesity is $1,723 per year.[160] On the social side, "[o]ne population-based study sample of 5-17-year-olds showed 70% of obese youth had at least one risk factor for cardiovascular disease. In addition, obese children have a greater likelihood to become obese adults. One study tracked two groups of high school graduates comprising a population sample of 5,000; one group graduated at a normal weight and the other group was chronically overweight since age 19. The

[157] See Emily Broad Leib, *The Forgotten Half of Food System Reform: Using Food and Agricultural Law to Foster Healthy Food Production*, 9 J. Food L. & Pol'y 18 (2013); *see also* Eubanks, *supra* note 51, at 213.
[158] Eubanks, *supra* note 51, at 280-284 (noting that rates of obesity have doubled since 1980 "due in part to the abundance of high-calorie, high-fat processed foods on supermarket shelves that are supported by Farm Bill subsidies."). *Id.* at 284; *see also* Angelo et al., *supra* note 44, at 123.
[159] Eubanks, *supra* note 51, at 284-285.
[160] *Childhood Obesity Facts*, Ctrs. for Disease Control & Prevention, http://www.cdc.gov/healthyyouth/obesity/facts.htm (last updated Jan. 25, 2017).

results of the study showed that those that were chronically overweight were "50 percent more likely to be unemployed, on welfare and single." David Albrecht & John Hardy, *Healthy Helpings: Harnessing the Power of School Nutrition*, http://www.law.drake.edu/newsEvents/docs/2014-sustainability-reportE.pdf (citations omitted).

The farm bill subsidies to commodity crops, particularly corn and soybeans, compel industrial agriculture to produce excessive crop yields (supported by the increased use of pesticides and herbicides) and convert them into highly processed food additives and ingredients. Almost every processed food contains high fructose corn syrup (HFCS) and many products contain hydrogenated fats and salts as well.[161] The processing of these commodity crops produces greenhouse gases and other air pollutants, wastewater pollution, and environmental damage from the materials used in food packaging that are eventually disposed of in landfills after use. Finally, processed food production expands the food supply chain across the United States and globally. Transportation of food increases carbon emissions and both conventional and organic foods may travel great distances to get to a store shelf. We calculate food miles for food traveling within the United States, but we do not count food miles for imported foods.[162]

Under the commodity program, the 2008 farm bill limited direct payments to farmers to a maximum of $40,000 a year per farm or other eligible entity. Farmers received direct payments, whether or not they actually grew crops. The 2014 farm bill stalled in Congress for more than two years and eliminated direct payments—saving $5 billion per year. By cutting direct payments, the bill increased contributions to the $9 billion-a-year government-subsidized crop insurance program. The bill "authoriz[ed] nearly $1 trillion in spending on farm subsidies and nutrition programs" and is "expected to save about $16.6 billion over the next ten years." While the new bill included $8 billion in cuts to food stamps, it also increased payments to food banks by $200 million to offset partially the demand for food.[163]

One possible solution to the over-subsidization of monoculture crops is to incentivize sustainable agriculture through subsidies to farmers who practice sustainable farming as defined in the 1990 farm bill:

> [A]n integrated system of plant and animal production practices having a
> site-specific application that will, over the long term, satisfy human food and

---

[161] Angelo et al., *supra* note 44, at 123.
[162] Angelo et al., *supra* note 44, at 124-128.
[163] Ron Nixon, *House Approves Farm Bill, Ending a 2-Year Impasse*, N.Y. TIMES (Jan. 29, 2014), http://www.nytimes.com/2014/01/30/us/politics/house-approves-farm-bill-ending-2-year-impasse.html?_r = 0.

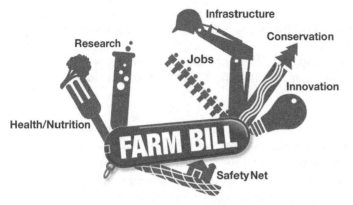

Infrastructure

Conservation

Research

Jobs

Innovation

Health/Nutrition

FARM BILL

SafetyNet

"It's like a Swiss Army knife."
- President Obama 2/7/14

fiber needs; enhance environmental quality and the natural resource base upon which the agricultural economy depends; make the most efficient use of nonrenewable resources and on-farm/ranch resources; integrate, where appropriate, natural biological cycles and controls; sustain the economic viability of farm/ranch operations; and enhance the quality of life for farmers/ranchers and society as a whole.

By shifting a portion of the farm bill subsidies to farms employing sustainable farming methods, rather than directing them to only the large commodity crop growers, more farmers who grow vegetables, fruits, and nuts will be incentivized to produce healthy crops by receiving subsidies previously unavailable to them.[164]

Childhood nutrition has been of great concern in the United States leading to the National School Lunch Act of 1946 (NSLA) and continuing with the enactment of the Healthy, Hunger-Free Kids Act (HHFKA) in 2010 and the Child Nutrition Reauthorization Act (CNA) that authorizes the USDA to administer nine federal nutrition programs. The 2010 program expired in September 2015, but while Congress debated the details of the CNA reauthorization in 2016, the school breakfast and lunch programs continued because they are permanently authorized. In addition to providing food stamps to families, now formally called the Supplemental Nutrition Assistance Program (SNAP), providing school food is an important part of children's lives and plays a large role in establishing good eating patterns for the future. Therefore, it is critical to offer healthy choices in our schools in order to keep children from developing bad eating habits that will need to be broken later in life to stay healthy.[165]

Originally signed by President Harry S. Truman "as a measure of national security, to safeguard the health and well-being of the Nation's children" in 1946, the NSLA program served 7.1 million students annually and now serves more than 30 million students.[166] This federal welfare program now costs more than $10 billion annually and has the potential

---

[164] Angelo et al., *supra* note 44, 298-299.
[165] Chef Ann Cooper, *What Is the Child Nutrition Act, and Why Should We Care?*, U.S. NEWS (Mar. 19, 2015), http://health.usnews.com/health-news/blogs/eat-run/2015/03/19/what-is-the-child-nutrition-act-and-why-we-should-care.
[166] *See* CONG. REC. E776-05 (daily ed. May 24, 2016) (Speech of Hon. Ruben Hinojosa of Texas on H.R. 5003).

to guide food policy and the agricultural supply market because schools often purchase surplus corn and soy commodity crops and the food processed from these crops. The original program was set up as a nonprofit with the purpose of offering free and reduced-price lunches that met minimum nutritional standards and used surplus commodity crops whenever possible. Schools offered competitive, non-NSLA approved food, such as soft drinks, candy, cookies, chips, etc., on campus. While the program introduced new guidelines and amendments to reduce the availability of highly processed food on school grounds, less than one-third of U.S. schools were able to meet these guidelines.[167]

The 2010 Healthy, Hunger-Free Kids Act reauthorized the Child Nutrition Reauthorization Act and gave the USDA greater authority to regulate competitive foods by applying the nutrition standards to all foods offered on school premises during the school day. It also encouraged the use of organic food and "farm to school" programs to foster local food system operations. The average school lunch uses 15-20% USDA food. However, the USDA is responsible for spending funds on food purchases and they are able to purchase commodity crops more cheaply than other food products. Thus, schools may be tempted to use commodity items and highly processed food products with long shelf lives, rather than local food sources and less-processed food products that cannot be recycled. In addition, many schools no longer have full-facility kitchens to prepare fresh food because they have relied for decades on prepackaged and prepared food items.[168] Reforms to our school food programs will require attention to food safety, nutritional content, and regulatory structures so that our most needy and vulnerable children will not be subject to administrative burdens that create unnecessary barriers to accessing healthy foods.[169] As noted above, while the CNA expired in 2015, the programs have continued to operate.[170]

Dietary Guidelines for Americans provide information to consumers about general health and nutrition associated with their food choices. In the Eighth Edition of these guidelines for 2015-2020, the U.S. Department of Health and Human Services (HHS) and the U.S. Department of Agriculture (USDA) acknowledged that the rates of chronic diseases have increased, with half of all American adults suffering from one or more diet-related ailments such as type 2 diabetes, heart disease, and overweight and obesity. However, they also noted that healthy eating and physical activity reduce the risk of chronic disease. This joint report, required by the 1990 National Nutrition Monitoring and Related Research Act, focused its five

---

[167] Angelo et al., *supra* note 44, at 233-235.
[168] *Id.* at 235-240.
[169] Cong. Rec., *supra* note 166.
[170] Food Research and Action Center, CNR, http://frac.org/action/child-nutrition-reauthorization-cnr (last visited Nov. 11, 2017).

major guidelines on "eating patterns and their food and nutrient character-istics" and emphasized an adaptable framework for these patterns to allow individuals to make personal choices.[171]

These guidelines do not currently take into consideration the environmental impacts of adhering to their suggestions. For example, the Dietary Guidelines released in 2011 called for American adults to double their seafood intake even though U.S. and global fisheries were already unsustainable.[172] Much of the debate about including sustainability goals in the 2015 Dietary Guidelines centered on meat production because of the land and water required to grow grain to feed livestock and the methane emissions that contribute to greenhouse gases. Perhaps the 2020 Dietary Guidelines will include sustainability goals to ensure long-term food security by adjusting our dietary patterns to lessen the impact that food production has on the environment.[173]

Questions

1. What issues relevant to the sustainability of the food system and the health system are raised by rising obesity? Does framing the obesity issue around assessing sustainability help formulate solutions? If so, with what limitations?

2. In terms of resilience, can you think of systems that show signs of weakening during times of rising obesity? What about strengthening or becoming more resilient? Does framing the obesity issue around assessing resilience help formulate solutions? If so, with what limitations?

Food Justice. Food justice is the "equitable access not only to healthy, culturally appropriate food, but also to the benefits of food production and distribution for all communities."[174] The U.S. EPA describes environmental justice as "the fair treatment and meaningful involvement of all people regardless of race, color, sex, national origin, or income with respect to the development, implementation and enforcement of environmental laws, regulations, and policies." The common element in both of these social movements is the fair treatment of communities in terms of public

---

[171] *Dietary Guidelines 2015-2020*, U.S. DEP'T OF HEALTH & HUMAN SERVS. & USDA, https://health.gov/dietaryguidelines/2015/guidelines/executive-summary/ (last visited Oct. 12, 2017).

[172] Nylen, *supra* note 90, at 761-762 (2013).

[173] Allison Aubrey, *New Dietary Guidelines Will Not Include Sustainability Goal*, NPR (Oct. 6, 2015, 6:16 PM), http://www.npr.org/sections/thesalt/2015/10/06/446369955/new-dietary-guidelines-will-not-include-sustainability-goal.

[174] Danielle M. Purifoy, *Food Policy Councils: Integrating Food Justice and Environmental Justice*, 24 DUKE ENVTL. L. & POL'Y F. 375, 375-376 (2014).

health and safety, environmental wellness, and social justice. If integrated, these two movements could enhance "the inclusion and empowerment of minority and low-income communities in the process and outcomes of improving food and the environment."[175]

Just as the traditional environmental movement began in the 1960s, largely supported by white environmentalists, experts, and lawyers focusing on ecological conservation and preservation, the sustainable food movement relied on those with sufficient disposable income to support expensive fresh food markets, backyard cultivation, and easy access to the resources needed to change food practices and policies. While these efforts are certainly laudable, environmental justice and now food justice are departures from the traditional movements because they focus on "achieving equality for low-income and low-access communities."[176] The food justice movement, in particular, is concerned with increasing "opportunities for moving toward a more just, healthy, democratic, and community-based system."[177]

The food justice movement in the United States has focused on domestic food law and policy, particularly the Farm Bill because it provides farm subsidies for commodity crops and federal funds for school meals and food banks, as discussed above. School meal programs are problematic because they should provide food to low-income children, but underfunded public schools do not have access to local, healthy food choices and must instead rely on the commodity crops supported by federal subsidies. These commodity foods are low in nutritional value and typically take the form of highly processed food products.[178]

The Farm Bill has contributed to obesity and other dietary illnesses by distorting domestic prices such that unhealthy food products containing the corn-based HFCS have decreased in price by almost 25%, while the unsubsidized fresh fruits and vegetables increased in price by 40%.

---

[175] *Id.* at 376.
[176] *Id.* at 379.
[177] Robert Gottlieb & Anupama Joshi, FOOD JUSTICE 10 (MIT Press 2010).
[178] Purifoy, *supra* note 174, at 380-382.

Consumers looking to find the most cost-effective means of securing the calories necessary for survival must find them in unhealthy foods because of the Farm Bill price distortion. The USDA issues Dietary Guidelines for healthy eating patterns, but the Farm Bill creates a discounted market for unhealthy processed foods by subsidizing commodity crops.[179]

It is interesting to note the link between USDA Dietary Guidelines and the impact these guidelines have on the market for products subsidized by the USDA. For example, the USDA guidelines discouraging the consumption of high-fat dairy products resulted in a 30-year decline in milk sales. In response to this decline, the USDA, which is responsible for the health of the dairy industry, funded milk marketing campaigns using fees levied on dairy farms, and sold high-fat milk surplus to fast food companies to create new products containing more cheese. The USDA policies of selling high-fat milk surplus to fast-food consumers, while warning general consumers against the product, has been referred to as food oppression because such policies disproportionately impact the health of low-income minorities who live in urban centers. Food oppression arises "from institutionalized, food-related policies and practices that undermine the physical strength and survival of socially marginalized groups."[180]

Food insecurity affects 12% of all U.S. households and approximately 40 million Americans who miss meals on a regular basis and are, at times, unable to purchase food. Low-income children eat unhealthy subsidized commodity crops at school and families buy the cheaper, low-nutrient processed foods at the grocery store. The government subsidizes corn "for fuel, livestock feed, and processed low-nutrient foods instead of cultivating fresh fruits, vegetables, and other food products that could assist those struggling to survive in a healthful manner." These subsidies produce surplus yields sold internationally to the developing world and contribute to world hunger because of the products' low nutritional value. Government policies favoring the production of ethanol from corn have resulted in the increase in price of other U.S. staple foods.[181]

The effects of climate change will contribute to food insecurity, particularly for the more vulnerable communities, and will widen the inequality gap based on race, ethnicity, and income. As state and local governments develop climate-resilient adaptation plans to address food security issues, they must also work toward eliminating this inequality gap by encouraging agricultural development of urban land that is suitable for growing crops. "Meaningful and equitable access to land and water for affordable

---

[179] Eubanks, *supra* note 51, at 285-289.
[180] Andrea Freeman, *The Unbearable Whiteness of Milk: Food Oppression and the USDA*, 3 UC IRVINE L. REV. 1251, 1254 (2013).
[181] Eubanks, *supra* note 51, at 293-295.

food production is essential to ensuring climate resiliency for environmental justice communities."[182]

Food deserts are areas disproportionately made up of poor and minority individuals, where fresh and healthy food is scarce and unaffordable. The USDA published a study in 2012 "that, in general, the higher the percentage of minority population, the more likely the area is to be a food desert."[183] Approximately 30% of low-income individuals in low-income communities have reduced access to supermarkets and must instead shop and eat at convenience stores and fast-food restaurants. While suburban dwellers rely on cars to get to supermarkets, urban dwellers typically do not have access to transportation to take them out of the city to shop. As a result, individuals living in these food deserts must purchase prepackaged, highly processed food or fast food known to be high in calories, fat, and sodium.[184]

Federal initiatives have attempted to address the issue of obesity and health-related problems associated with food deserts by allocating some of the USDA's budget "to bring grocery stores and other healthy food retailers to underserved communities." In addition to providing federal funding to incentivize supermarkets to locate in neglected neighborhoods, non-profits working with community members have established community gardens, farmers' markets, and food policy councils to address food deserts.[185] Although some research has found that "proximity to supermarkets does not reduce obesity, and that proximity to fast food does not increase it," national efforts to reduce obesity must, at a minimum, provide access to healthy foods as well as address other causes such as how various factors affect eating patterns.[186]

State and local attempts to combat food deserts include taxing sugary soda and fruit drink "-ades," placing moratoria on building new fast-food restaurants in disadvantaged urban communities and requiring calorie counts to be posted. However, strong opponents such as the American Beverage Association have generally thwarted these efforts on the basis that soda taxes and moratoria hurt job growth and interfere with personal freedom.[187] Some have criticized efforts to restrict the use of food

---

[182] Liza Guerra Garcia, *"Free the Land": A Call for Local Governments to Address Climate-Induced Food Insecurity in Environmental Justice Communities*, 41 Wm. Mitchell L. Rev. 572, 573 (2015).

[183] Lawrence F. Dempsey, *Feeding the Racial Disparity in Disease: How Federal Agricultural Subsidies Contribute to a Racial Disparity in the Prevalence of Diet Related Illness*, 7 Biotechnology & Pharmaceutical L. Rev. 109, 129-130 (2014) (discussing the report *Characteristics and Influential Factors of Food Deserts* and concluding that "[g]iven the racial disparity in income and poverty rates among white Americans and racial minorities, the influence of agriculture subsidies on food prices, as well as diet and public health, has created a far greater burden for racial minorities than it has for white Americans").

[184] *See* Thomas P. Ziehnert, *Food Deserts: Is the Let's Move Campaign an Oasis for the Urban Minority Community?*, 7 Mod. Am. 22, 22-24 (2011).

[185] *Id.* at 30-31.

[186] Paul A. Diller, *Combating Obesity With a Right to Nutrition*, 101 Geo. L.J. 969, 988-989 (2013).

[187] Avi Brisman, *Food Justice as Crime Prevention*, 5 J. Food L. & Pol'y 1, 2-6 (2009).

stamps, now called SNAP benefits, to purchase unhealthy food as targeted paternalism that may reduce program enrollment. However, some of the anti-hunger advocates who have opposed these restrictions have also received contributions from processed food and fast-food corporations.[188]

Local governments have been leading the way in addressing food concerns in their communities as increasing food access has improved public health, educational outcomes, and even crime statistics. More than 130 cities and counties in the United States and Canada have established food policy councils and local governments have enacted reforms to improve access to school food, amended zoning codes to allow urban agriculture, and improved transportation routes for healthy food sellers. Because each locality has its own food system challenges, local responses to these challenges may more meaningfully address the needs of neighborhoods and individuals, both in identifying food deserts and reducing their pervasiveness in disadvantaged communities.[189] The key to success in these local efforts is seeking community input and engaging different cultures to empower individuals and groups to develop successful policies that address the actual community needs and goals.[190]

Questions

1. How would you describe the connection between food justice and sustainability, as it relates to the triple bottom line and/or intergenerational equity?

2. Does viewing the food system through the lens of sustainability help address issues relevant to food justice? If so, how?

3. How are the resilience of our food system and supply and our vulnerabilities to drought and food shortages linked to modern agriculture, as well as to modern transportation and information capabilities? For example, if Los Angeles were cut off from transportation services (a possible scenario caused by a major earthquake), could it feed itself?

Foodshed planning on a regional basis, similar to watershed planning may promote access to locally grown produce and foster healthy eating patterns and sustainable agriculture. Planning regional food networks to lower delivery costs, reduce greenhouse gas emissions, and provide

---

[188] Rebecca L. Goldberg, *No Such Thing as a Free Lunch: Paternalism, Poverty, and Food Justice*, 24 STAN. L. & POL'Y REV. 35, 42 (2013).
[189] Emily M. Broad Leib, *All (Food) Politics Is Local: Increasing Food Access Through Local Government Action*, 7 HARV. L. & POL'Y REV. 321, 321-323 (2013).
[190] *Id.* at 329-330.

fresh and healthy food for regional residents may strengthen communi-ty-based efforts to "address issues of food security, public health, social justice, and ecological health in local communities and regions." Because foodsheds, like watersheds, are regional in nature and may cross local, state, and federal boundaries, the challenge to foodshed planning is the coordination of multiple local governments, state, and federal agencies to achieve food management goals that may be in competition or conflict with existing goals.[191]

As land use planners already know, regional planning may be the ideal, but it is difficult to achieve from the bottom up when you sit at the municipal level. Nevertheless, communities are forming food policy councils to explore food policies and strategies for regional food planning and incorporate these policies into the municipality's comprehensive plan. These policies recognize the importance of sustainable food systems and the need "to support local, organic, and grass-fed agriculture, small-scale diversification, local processing, distribution, and marketing, and public education about food security." Plans should also "acknowledge[ ] that increasing regional food production reduces transportation-related greenhouse gases, supports the local economy, and provides health ben-efits through the increased access to locally available, fresh and organic food."[192]

Labeling. Food labeling provides consumers with informed choices regarding the food they purchase and eat. In the United States, state and local law regulated food until the enactment of the Federal Food and Drugs Act of 1906, which "prohibited the sale of adulterated or misbranded food, but contained no labeling requirements." With the passage of the Federal Food, Drug, and Cosmetic Act (FDCA) in 1938, certain labeling was required to prevent adulteration, misbranding, and false advertising to consumers. The Fair Packaging and Labeling Act (FPLA) in 1966 enhanced the labeling requirements to allow consumers to gain accurate knowledge as to the quantity of food in order to enable value comparisons among products.[193]

In the 1970s and 1980s, the FDA began focusing labeling regulations on the nutritional content of food and its connection to public health. In 1990, Congress passed the Nutrition Labeling and Education Act (NLEA), which amended the FDCA to require standard nutrition facts labeling and to regulate the food industry's claims about nutrient content and the sci-entific links between diet and disease prevention.[194] Because of political pressure and Michelle Obama's *Let's Move!* campaign to end childhood obesity, the FDA issued new labeling rules in 2016, which update serving

---

[191] Patricia E. Salkin & Amy Lavine, *Regional Foodsheds: Are Our Local Zoning and Land Use Regulations Healthy?*, 22 FORDHAM ENVTL. L. REV. 599, 600-601, 605-607 (2011).

[192] *Id.* at 612.

[193] Diana R. H. Winters, *The Magical Thinking of Food Labeling: The NLEA as a Failed Statute*, 89 TUL. L. REV. 815, 819-821 (2015).

[194] *Id.* at 818-821.

sizes and most importantly distinguish between natural sugar in food and sugar added during processing.[195] Overall, the first part of the NLEA has been successful in providing consumers with nutrition facts such as calories, fat, and salt, but the second part, which regulates health claims about food, appears to have failed. Some have called for either a complete revamping of the NLEA or a repeal of the second part, which regulates health and nutrient content claims, resulting in a return to state control.[196]

Consumers have sued food manufacturers for misleading the public about nutrient content, ingredients, and health benefits, such as suing a grocery store for not disclosing that its farm-raised salmon was artificially colored or suing a food company that has included ingredients such as GMOs, but has labeled the product "all-natural." Because the FDCA does not provide for a private cause of action, plaintiffs have brought state claims under consumer protection statutes or common law theories. The food manufacturer defendants argue that federal statutes preempt state law or that the administrative agencies should have primary jurisdiction over claims, rather than the courts. The judicial results in these food-labeling cases differ as courts struggle to enforce these laws within a complex regulatory framework of NLEA preemption requirements, the FDCA, and state law.[197]

In addition to federally mandated labeling requirements for nutrient content and health claims under the NLEA, there are other labeling schemes designed to give consumers information about food product origin, production practices, allergies, and the product's impact on the environment. The United States and the European Union established comprehensive labeling requirements for the **organic food market**. In the United States, the 1990 Organic Foods Production Act (OFPA) launched a certification and labeling program for food produced and handled without using synthetic substances. OFPA "prohibits using synthetic fertilizers, growth hormones, and antibiotics in livestock, or adding synthetic ingredients during processing."[198]

The National Organic Program (NOP), under the authority of OFPA, created a four-tiered labeling system for organic foods that identifies: 1) "100% organic"; 2) "organic" if 95% organic; 3) "made with organic ingredients" if at least 70% organic; or 4) the organic ingredients may be listed, but cannot use the seal or the word "organic" if product contains less than 70% organic ingredients. The European Union organic product legislation is more ambitious than the U.S. version and covers "animal welfare, environmental pollution, biological diversity, and renewable energy" in

---

[195] Marion Nestle, *The FDA's New Rules for Food Labeling Are Finally Here*, Sci. Am. (May 24, 2016), http://blogs.scientificamerican.com/guest-blog/the-fda-s-new-rules-for-food-labeling-are-finally-here/.

[196] Winters, *supra* note 193, at 818-821.

[197] *Id.* at 846-850.

[198] Angelo et al., *supra* note 44, at 306.

addition to consideration of chemical and synthetic inputs included under OFPA.[199]

Congress enacted the **Food Allergen Labeling and Consumer Protection Act (FALCPA)** in 2004 to improve food labeling information for those suffering from food allergies caused by eight major food allergens. The major food allergens covered by the FALCPA include milk, eggs, fish, Crustacean shellfish, tree nuts, peanuts, wheat, and soybeans. The FDA held public meetings on allergens and **gluten** in 2005 to help define and permit voluntary food labeling using the term "gluten-free." In 2013, the FDA issued a final rule defining "**gluten-free**" for packaged food labeling. Approximately 3 million people in the United States suffer from celiac disease and the ingestion of foods that contain gluten can activate antibodies that attack and damage the intestinal lining. The FDA Gluten-Free Labeling Rule, effective in 2014, applies to food labeling regulated by the FDA, but not to food regulated by the USDA.[200]

The USDA had regulated labeling requiring the identification of **Country of Origin Labeling (COOL)** for beef and pork products. However, Congress repealed COOL in 2015 after the World Trade Organization (WTO) found that such labeling caused harm to Canada and Mexico and these countries could impose $1 billion in tariffs against the United States as punishment. Although the USDA continues to conduct rigorous food safety inspections on imported and domestic meat, it will not enforce Country of Origin Labeling requirements and Congress will amend the labeling requirements.[201]

GMO labeling in the United States is now required for food containing genetically modified ingredients after legislation was passed in 2016. The USDA will determine the genetically modified ingredients and require the labels to display the GMO content with words, pictures, or a barcode that smartphones can read. This national standard will override state law, and will preempt a more stringent Vermont law, scheduled to go into effect. According to one commentator, consumers are grateful for the transparency, farmers are happy because the labeling requirements will be uniform across the country, and the food manufacturers are satisfied with a nationwide, instead of a state-by-state, standard, even though they would have preferred voluntary labeling.[202]

---

[199] *Id.* at 306-307.

[200] *Food Allergens Guidance Documents & Regulatory Information*, U.S. FDA, www.fda.gov/Food/GuidanceRegulation/GuidanceDocumentsRegulatoryInformation/Allergens (last updated Nov. 29, 2016); Tricia Thompson, *Foods Labeled Gluten-Free Must Now Be in Compliance with the FDA Gluten-Free Labeling Rule*, GLUTEN FREE WATCHDOG (Aug. 5, 2014), https://www.glutenfree-watchdog.org/news/foods-labeled-gluten-free-must-now-be-in-compliance-with-the-fda-gluten-free-labeling-rule/.

[201] News Desk, *USDA Ends COOL Enforcement with President's Signature on Omnibus Bill*, FOOD SAFETY NEWS (Dec. 25, 2015), http://www.foodsafetynews.com/2015/12/usda-ends-cool-enforcement-with-presidents-signature-on-omnibus-bill/#.V6TMV_krLX4.

[202] Dianne Lugo, *U.S. Senate passes GM food labeling bill*, SCIENCE (July 8, 2016, 3:45 PM), http://www.sciencemag.org/news/2016/07/us-senate-passes-gm-food-labeling-bill.

The GMO labeling debate continues, as some believe that consumers will have difficulty determining whether a product contains GMOs or whether GM technology produced it. The various forms of disclosure — barcode, symbol, words, website, or toll-free number — may prove cumbersome for shoppers purchasing multiple products.[203] Others believe that a "non-GMO label" is based on a false assumption because "virtually all the foods we eat have been 'genetically modified,'" as evidenced by crops that were genetically modified in the 1960s and '70s using the "mutagenesis breeding" method.[204] Finally, some question the value of GMO labeling, as they prefer to see additional evidence showing adverse effects from GMOs.[205]

The public generally embraces mandated food labeling as an effective form of regulation. As discussed above, we use labeling to identify nutrient content, health benefits, product origin, production processes, the presence of allergens, and the presence of GMOs. Labeling also identifies foods as "low-fat," "non-fat," "trans-fat," "vegetarian," "vegan," "paleo," "locally grown," "natural or all natural," "safe-handling," "food justice," and "activity equivalent" (to inform consumers about the minutes of activity they need to burn the calories consumed).[206] Consumers feel empowered to make choices based on the labeling, but studies have shown "that labels have failed to promote even modest dietary improvements."[207] While food labeling may impact individual dietary choices to a degree, these choices are not reflected in health improvements.

Eco-labeling that evaluates the product's ecological and carbon footprint may be helpful in changing consumer purchasing preferences and promoting a sustainable food system. Environmental policy needs to focus on changing individual behavior. Even if we cannot show that nutritional labeling has improved our health because of the complexity of our eating patterns, individual choice based on labeling may be successful as a political tool to achieve sustainability, food justice, positive climate change impacts, and life-cycle best practices.[208] However, the proliferation of food labels has created challenges such as consumer confusion, the need for better information, and the lack of oversight of first-party self-declared food eco-labels. Government and industry will need to improve labeling

---

[203] Jane Kolodinsky, *Why the GMO Food Labeling Debate Is Not Over*, Observer (June 28, 2016, 12:24 PM), http://observer.com/2016/06/why-the-gmo-food-labeling-debate-is-not-over/.

[204] Steven Savage, *The Non-GMO Food Label Is a Lie*, Forbes (June 11, 2016, 12:21 PM), http://www.forbes.com/sites/stevensavage/2016/06/11/the-non-gmo-food-label-is-a-lie/#7a01a8e133fa.

[205] Omri Ben-Shahar, *The GMO Labeling Fight Has Nothing to Do With Information — On Either Side*, Forbes (Mar. 21, 2016, 11:46 AM), http://www.forbes.com/sites/realspin/2016/03/21/the-gmo-labeling-fight-has-nothing-to-do-with-information-on-either-side/#6f154237288c.

[206] Omri Ben-Shahar, *The Surprising Failure of Food Labeling*, Forbes (Apr. 18, 2016, 8:13 AM), http://www.forbes.com/sites/omribenshahar/2016/04/18/the-surprising-failure-of-food-labeling/#3beb0fe058c1.

[207] *Id.*

[208] Angelo et al., *supra* note 44, at 301-320.

oversight through regulation, enforcement, and third-party certification in order to help move the U.S. food system into a sustainable future.[209]

VIII. CONSERVATION AND PRESERVATION

Conservation. The history of agricultural conservation in the United States began in the 1930s. After the Great Depression and the Dust Bowl in the Midwest, the United States prioritized conservation by enacting programs designed to assist farmers in soil conservation practices to protect the soil and environment, while also increasing financial security and the quality of life for rural citizens. However, economic prosperity and criticism of programs such as the Soil Bank created by the Agricultural Act of 1956 fueled the decline of agriculture conservation programs during the 1940s, '50s, and '60s.[210] As incorporated into the early farm bills, conservation programs targeted assistance to the farmer for controlling soil erosion and increasing land productivity. Later farm bills focused on controlling the food supply to protect prices. In the early 1970s, the Secretary of Agriculture dispensed with conservation efforts and instead encouraged high yield farming to meet world demand — urging farmers to "plant fence row to fence row." These efforts greatly damaged any gains in conservation made in the prior four decades.[211]

Environmental conservation as part of U.S. farm policy began to take hold in the 1980s and the 1985 Farm Bill was the first one to have a title provision dedicated solely to conservation. Congress promoted soil conservation for reasons other than commodity productivity and added several new programs: Sodbuster, Swampbuster, Conservation Compliance, and the Conservation Reserve Program (CRP). The Sodbuster program required a conservation plan before developing highly erodible land (HEL). The Swampbuster program prohibited wetland conversion into agricultural production. The Conservation Compliance program established penalties and enforced compliance and the Conservation Reserve Program (CRP) funded the placement of 36.4 million acres into the CRP to conserve HEL and other biologically sensitive and ecologically important land. As a result, the average erosion rate of the acreage enrolled in the CRP decreased from 21 tons per acre per year to less than 2 tons.[212]

Progressive conservation programs continued to develop through the end of the twentieth century and into the beginning of the twenty-first century. These new programs addressed wetlands protection, ground

---

[209] Jason Czarnezki et al., *Creating Order Amidst Food Eco-Label Chaos*, 25 Duke Envtl. L. & Pol'y F. 281, 311 (2015).
[210] Eubanks, *supra* note 51, at 240-241.
[211] Zachary Cain & Stephen Lovejoy, *History and Outlook for Farm Bill Conservation Programs*, Choices (2004), *available at* http://www.choicesmagazine.org/2004-4/policy/2004-4-09.htm.
[212] *Id.*

water pollution, water quality, sustainable agriculture, and the importance of natural systems such as landscapes, watersheds, and ecosystems. The Wildlife Habitat Incentives Program (WHIP) encouraged the reclamation of wildlife habitat from existing agricultural land and the 2002 Farm Bill increased funding for "green payments" from the Conservation Security Program (CSP) to pay "producers to adopt or maintain practices that address resources of concern, such as soil, water, and wildlife." Land retirement programs expanded, Congress created the Grassland Reserve Program to help landowners conserve and restore grasslands, and the Farmland Protection Program received increased funding to allow state, tribal, local government, and nonprofits to purchase easements to protect against the development of productive farmland.[213]

The Food, Conservation, and Energy Act of 2008 provided incentives to conserve natural resources through such programs as voluntary land retirement, farmland protection, working lands, and mandatory conservation requirements. The bill reauthorized a majority of the programs discussed above from previous bills, amended some programs, and created new programs. The Conservation Stewardship Program (CSP) modified the previous Conservation Security Program to provide "green payments" for meeting stewardship goals to "improve and conserve the quality and condition of at least one resource concern." Resource concerns include issues such as "water quality, wildlife habitat, biodiversity, soil quality, soil erosion, water quantity, energy, and air quality" and actual installation costs for the conservation measure, the farmer's foregone income, and the anticipated environmental benefit determine the payments.[214]

While the **Agricultural Act of 2014** continues to financially protect and reward farmers for their efforts, Congress restructured it to consolidate the Wetlands Reserve Program, Grasslands Reserve Program, and Farm and Ranch Land Protection Program into the Agricultural Conservation Easement Program (ACEP). ACEP's purpose is to protect the sustainability of the nation's food supply by preventing the conversion of lands used for agriculture into lands used for non-agricultural purposes. In addition, Congress intended that this program improve environmental quality, provide for historic and wildlife habitat preservation, and protect open space. Given that the U.S. population is projected to increase by 50% by 2050 and that the acreage devoted to cropland, pasture, and grassland has decreased over the past six decades, "ACEP's policy reflects the government's knowledge of what is to come by protecting the long-term viability of in-use agricultural land and conserving such other arable land as it can."[215] "An agricultural easement is a form of conservation easement.

---

[213] *Id.*

[214] Angelo et al., *supra* note 44, at 21-24.

[215] Brian Wood, *Does the 2014 Farm Bill's New ACEP Program Really Benefit America, Or Does a Lack of Funding Stymie Any Good Works?*, 7 KY. J. EQUINE, AGRIC. & NAT. RESOURCES L. 537, 538-539 (2014-2015).

A conservation easement is a voluntary, legal agreement between a land-owner and a non-profit land trust that permanently protects land by restricting it for open space, recreation, wildlife habitat, or agricultural production."[216] The 2014 Farm Bill provides significantly less funding for agricultural conservation easements (ACEs) as was provided in the 2008 Farm Bill.[217]

Farm-bill conservation programs have failed to reduce significantly the environmental harms caused by industrial commodity farming. Commodity farming is unsustainable based on high fossil fuel inputs, adverse impacts caused by pesticides and fertilizers, and biodiversity loss because of large-scale monoculture, yet the government spends approximately $42 billion on commodity subsidies as opposed to $24 billion for conservation programs.[218] In addition to these programs being severely underfunded, the program structure ties conservation payments to subsidies that affect only commercial mega farms and there is little public involvement in the approval of farm bill legislation. The public assumes that existing environmental laws will protect the environment against agricultural harms, but many of these laws provide major exemptions for farmers.[219]

Since the first farm bill in 1933, the United States has sought to conserve agricultural land. Unfortunately, when adjusted for inflation, Congress in 1999 appropriated only half as much money for agricultural conservation as it did in 1937.[220] In order to return conservation to the heart of U.S. agricultural policy, the public and their elected policymakers must recognize that they are not sufficiently regulating the harmful impacts to the environment from commercialized commodity farming.[221] We need to increase funding for ACEP if we expect to solve the continuing agricultural and environmental issues, such as soil erosion and water pollution, which farm bills throughout the decades have failed to resolve.[222]

Farmland preservation encompasses different purposes and different perceptions. In the section above, we discussed agricultural conservation in terms of securing a future food supply, protecting sensitive lands, and addressing environmental harms created in particular by industrialized agricultural use. Farmland preservation, similar to agricultural conservation, may seek to protect farmland from development and the loss of arable land. However, we may use preservation for both admirable and not

---

[216] *Agricultural Easements*, Maine Farmland Trust, https://www.mainefarmlandtrust.org/farm-land-protection-new/agricultural-easements/ (last visited Oct. 12, 2017).

[217] *Agricultural Conservation Easement Program*, Ntn'l Sustainable Agric. Coalition, http://sustainab leagriculture.net/publications/grassrootsguide/conservation-environment/agricultural-conservation-easement-program/ (last updated Oct. 2016).

[218] Angelo et al., *supra* note 44, at 25.

[219] Eubanks, *supra* note 51, at 245-249.

[220] *Id.* at 245.

[221] *Id.* at 250-251.

[222] Wood, *supra* note 215, at 558-559.

so admirable purposes. For example, preservation may perpetuate cultural and historical ideals, but it may also serve as an exclusionary zoning technique under the guise that we must maintain "community character."[223]

Right to Farm Statutes are state-level enactments to preserve agrarian life and protect small-scale farmers against nuisance actions based upon the externalities farms generate. These statutes arise from the "coming to the nuisance" defense and protect small farms against residential development that brings landowners into regions formerly occupied only by agricultural operations. These statutes take different forms, but "there appears to be a presumption that farming operations that are not considered nuisances when they commence do not become such simply because someone later moves near the operation." In addition, the courts have generally interpreted these statutes as only being relevant in suits between farmers and nonfarmers. States have also adopted statutes to deal with liability issues resulting from "agritourism" — an activity that allows the public to view or enjoy rural activities for recreational, entertainment, or educational purposes. These laws create an assumption of the risk defense against those who claim injury while engaging in an agritourism activity.[224]

Cultural and historical preservation of agrarian life is an essential part of world history as most societies, including Europe, the United States, Africa, Mesopotamia, and the Mayans, progressed based on developments in agriculture and agricultural techniques such as irrigation, canals, and terracing to grow crops on slopes. "Agrarian culture is just that: an entire culture whose identity is tied to working the land. Through song, dance, food, visual art, and religious traditions, agrarian communities celebrate their connection with the earth in unique and invaluable ways."[225] Preserving agrarian culture requires maintaining soil resources, promoting sustainable farming, and supporting small-scale farmers such that family farmers can continue to earn a living from the land and find value added through a sense of place.[226] Some have even called for international support in the form of a global treaty so that nations will pursue the progressive policies needed to address the impact of industrial agriculture "on our soil and the cultures that depend upon it."[227]

Preserving agricultural lands fulfills an important aspiration of the U.S. population — to maintain our shared cultural heritage of not only urban life but also of rural life. Rural resources to be preserved may include country roads, bridges, views, traditional farm structures, such as farmhouses and barns, and other features of a rural landscape. Local governments

---

[223] Jesse J. Richardson, Jr., *Beyond Fairness: What Really Works to Protect Farmland*, 12 Drake J. Agric. L. 163, 182-183 (2007).

[224] Julian Conrad Juergensmeyer & Thomas E. Roberts, Land Use Planning and Development Regulation Law §13:3 (3d ed., Westlaw 2016).

[225] Nicholas A. Fromherz, *The Case for a Global Treaty on Soil Conservation, Sustainable Farming, and the Preservation of Agrarian Culture*, 39 Ecology L.Q. 57, 73-74 (2012).

[226] *Id.* at 77-78, 82.

[227] *See, e.g., id.* at 121.

have fostered preservation historic district zoning, as have states and the federal government through funding and coordination. While most of the preservation efforts have focused on urban areas, conservation easements could serve as an important tool for incentivizing rural resource preservation. In order to promote increased cultural and historical preservation of agricultural lands, we can modify existing laws and policies by "adjusting incentive programs to allow for the increased use of easements to protect agricultural historic resources, expanding historic rehabilitation tax credits to address more modest structures, and utilizing the agricultural policy framework to incorporate more meaningful consideration of heritage assets."[228]

IX. CONCLUSION

The Green Revolution dramatically altered the agricultural system in the United States and other nations by replacing human labor with machines requiring large amounts of fossil fuel and resulting in the industrialization of agriculture defined by "monocultures; few crop varieties; reliance on chemical and other inputs; and the separation of animal and plant agriculture."[229] This modern industrialized agriculture generated harmful impacts to both the quantity and quality of the nation's water supply, both surface water and groundwater, through irrigation and pollution. It was also responsible for harms to wildlife, habitats, and biodiversity from pesticide use and other chemicals. Its dependency on fossil fuel inputs has increased emissions of greenhouse gases contributing to climate change. Modern industrialized agriculture has impacted human health due to exposure to pesticides and other chemicals and consumption of highly processed foods from subsidized commodity crops leading to the obesity and diabetes epidemics. Finally, rural communities have suffered from the loss of jobs due to machines, the exodus from farming communities to the city, and the loss of connection to a community and to a place.[230]

Many farming practices can lead to more sustainable conditions and more resilient, food-based systems. Farming practices that promote sustainability by reducing environmental pollution and producing healthier food include

> *no-till farming, cover cropping, crop rotation, residue mulching, elimination of most or all agrochemical fertilizers, significant water usage reduction, nitrogen*

---

[228] Jess R. Phelps, *"A Tinge of Melancholy Lay Upon the Countryside": Agricultural Historic Resources Within Contemporary Agricultural and Historic Preservation Law*, 33 Va. Envtl. L.J. 56, 59-60, 100-101 (2015).

[229] Mary Jane Angelo, The Law and Ecology of Pesticides and Pest Management 52 (Routledge 2016).

[230] Angelo et al., *supra* note 62, at 355-368 (2011).

fixing through on-farm manure use, measurable energy reduction per acre farmed, non-use of pesticides and herbicides that break down slowly in the environment, greater use of integrated pest management, contour farming, and local market sales to reduce transportation.[231]

Local and regional food systems are key to sustainable agriculture. Michael Pollan has argued that a "regional food economy" will be essential to building a more sustainable agricultural system because it will allow for diversified farming and shorten the food chain, thus reducing the fossil fuel needed for food distribution. The benefits of a local system include access to fresher food and less processing when food is not shipped long distances. Food safety issues are easier to contain because we are not distributing large quantities of contaminated food throughout the United States so that tracking and recalling food will not require a widespread response. Diversification will also contribute to ecological resilience.[232] In addition, "[w]hen individuals are connected to their surroundings they are more interested in promoting sustainability."[233] Thus, connecting food to community members through local and regional systems will enhance sustainability efforts and "reconnect people with place."[234]

Resilience as applied to agricultural systems measures "an agricultural system's ability to continue to function and provide yield despite changes or perturbations such as increased pest populations, disease, or changed rainfall patterns."[235] The greater functional diversity there is in an ecosystem, the greater possibility that there will be sufficient redundancy in the ecosystem to deal with unexpected disturbances. Industrialized agriculture, which produces large-scale commodity monocultures, drastically reduces crop variety and biological diversity such that modern farming systems are vulnerable to changes. In order to become more resilient to unexpected changes, agricultural systems must become more biodiverse and redundant. In addition, these ecosystems must have the ability to respond to new conditions and the food distribution systems must provide food accessibility.[236]

Eco-agriculture offers a path to agricultural system resilience by promoting the diversity necessary to respond to disruption. There are three strategies used that center on agricultural production by 1) minimizing agricultural wastes and pollution; 2) managing resources to conserve water, soils, flora, and fauna; and 3) using vegetation that imitates the ecological structure and function of the surrounding habitat (i.e., ecosystem services).

---

[231] Eubanks, *supra* note 51, at 300-302.
[232] Angelo et al., *supra* note 62, at 369.
[233] *See* Sam Kalen, *Agriculture, Food, and Environmental Policy*, 26 NAT. RESOURCES & ENV'T 3 (2011).
[234] *Id.*
[235] Mary Jane Angelo, *Building a Sustainable and Resilient Agricultural System for a Changing Global Environment*, 43 ENVTL. L. REP. 11079, 11082 (2013).
[236] *Id.* at 11082-11083.

An additional three strategies manage the landscape around the agricultural production areas by: 1) minimizing the natural areas converted; 2) protecting and expanding "large natural habitat areas of high ecological quality"; and 3) developing and maintaining "effective ecological networks and corridors." We can achieve these strategies by employing farming techniques that enhance biodiversity and preserve ecosystem services.[237]

New Agriculture, as viewed by Professor Neil D. Hamilton, links to at least eight key forces "especially relating to the continuing development of a food system more responsive to concerns over healthy foods, creating opportunities for new farmers, and the impact on land stewardship." These eight forces are:

1. the increasing interest in becoming involved in farming;
2. the growing interest in food policy and the role of law;
3. the expanding forms of direct farm marketing;
4. continued growth of consumer interest in eating "better" foods;
5. the growth in urban agriculture;
6. renewed attention to childhood obesity, nutrition, and school food;
7. food artisans and using food for rural economic development; and
8. the relation between farmland ownership and sustainable land tenure.

Professor Hamilton is living localism in farming after working with his wife for the past 15 years to produce and sell food locally. Professor Hamilton concludes:

> *Efforts to build local and regional markets make good economic sense, help reestablish connections, and increase America's understanding of farming. Local markets put a face on our food and benefit all the farmers. Our farm may be different than my parents' farm, but they are both farms. It is important that we as a nation recognize all farms, regardless of their size, and all consumers, regardless of their means, as deserving both of our support and of equal treatment under the law. In the words of St. Paul etched on USDA's Whitten Building, "The husbandman that laboreth must be the first partaker of the fruits." I have written about many of the forces described in this essay as being part of the movement toward a food democracy, a powerful social force I believe is at work in our country creating more opportunities for farmers, eaters, communities, and rural residents alike.*[238]

---

[237] Mary Jane Angelo, *Whole-System Agricultural Certification*, 85 U. Colo. L. Rev. 689, 724-726 (2014).

[238] Neil D. Hamilton, *Farms, Food, and the Future: Legal Issues and Fifteen Years of the "New Agriculture,"* 26 J. Envtl. L. & Litig. 1 (2011).

Shelter and Land Use

5

I. INTRODUCTION

In a 1943 paper titled "A Theory of Human Motivation," American psychologist Abraham H. Maslow presented the idea that humans direct their behavior to obtain certain goals in order to meet five levels of human needs.[1] Maslow's hierarchy of needs starts with the lower-order physiological needs of food, water, warmth, and sleep, which must be satisfied before higher-order needs such as safety, belongingness, esteem, and self-actualization can influence behavior.[2] See Figure 5-1.

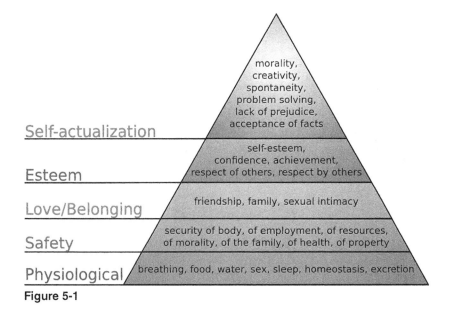

Figure 5-1

[1] *Maslow's Hierachy of Needs*, LEARNING THEORIES (July 18, 2014), https://www.learning-theories.com/maslows-hierarchy-of-needs.html.
[2] Saul McLeod, *Maslow's Heiarchy of Needs*, SIMPLY PSYCHOLOGY, http://www.simplypsychology.org/maslow.html (last updated 2016).

In Chapters 3 and 4, we focused on the resilience and sustainability of the systems that supply the physiological human needs for food and water. In this chapter, we continue our discussion of the physiological need for warmth and sleep as we address the human need for shelter, which has its legal home in the law of land use planning and control. We discuss resilience and sustainability in the examination of systems relevant to private property ownership and private and public controls over land use. In addition, we explore how common law principles, developed to help humans survive in a community and address the externalities of using land in close proximity to others, alter system resilience and sustainability.

Imagine living in a tent in a Kenyan refugee camp for your entire adult life where you meet your husband, marry, and have five children. Then imagine traveling to the United States and trying to find shelter when you arrive. Somali refugees have faced this challenge in great numbers as they have gravitated to existing pockets of Somali settlements in Minnesota, which is the state with the largest Somali population. Homeless shelters are the landing place for those families who do not have relatives already settled in a Minnesota community. While Somali immigrants before 2008 were able to rely on the hospitable Somali community to open their homes indefinitely, these longer-term residents are no longer able and willing to welcome complete strangers after the recession. In addition, recent newcomers have spent much of their lives in tent camps with limited access to formal education.[3]

"On any given night in the United States, half a million people are homeless. Some of them sleep in shelters, others on the streets; roughly one-quarter are children."[4] The homeless population in the United States is aging. Some of

---

[3] Mila Koumpilova, *New Somali Refugee Arrivals in Minnesota are Increasing*, STAR TRIBUNE (Nov. 1, 2014), http://www.startribune.com/new-somali-refugee-arrivals-in-minnesota-are-increasing/281197521/#1.

[4] Alana Semuels, *How Can the U.S. End Homelessness?*, THE ATLANTIC (Apr. 25, 2016), http://www.theatlantic.com/business/archive/2016/04/end-homelessness-us/479115/ [hereinafter *End Homelessness*].

these individuals, especially the baby-boomers, have been on the streets
and in and out of jail and rehabilitation centers since the late 1970s, early
1980s. The loss of jobs in the latest economic downturn has forced recent
arrivals of retirement age into homelessness. Solutions to reduce homelessness have generally been futile, although some states have recently
made progress in reducing the homeless veteran population.[5] While some
states have seen modest reductions in homelessness, many large cities
have experienced an increase of epidemic proportions resulting in cities,
such as Los Angeles, Seattle, and Honolulu, declaring a state of emergency.[6] Further, millions of people, although not technically homeless, live
in housing with deplorable conditions.

The U.S. Department of Housing and Urban Development (HUD)
administers **federal programs** to provide emergency, transitional, and
permanent housing each year. These programs serve over 1 million people. Individuals and families may qualify as homeless if they are actually
homeless, at imminent risk of homelessness, homeless under other federal
statutes, and fleeing or attempting to flee domestic violence. HUD's Office
of Special Needs Assistance Programs (SNAPs) provide funding to nonprofit
organizations, as well as state and local governments, to help find homes
for homeless individuals and families and link housing to other social and
medical needs.[7]

**State and local
programs** are allocat-
ing millions of dollars
to help eradicate home-
lessness by declaring a
"state of emergency."
For example, some say
that Los Angeles County
in California has a hous-
ing crisis rather than a
homeless crisis. This is
due to the need for hun-
dreds of thousands of
affordable rental units
for both the homeless

---

[5] *Id.*

[6] Adam Nagourney, *Old and on the Street: The Graying of America's Homeless*, N.Y. TIMES (May
31, 2016), http://www.nytimes.com/2016/05/31/us/americas-aging-homeless-old-and-on-the-street.
html?_r=0.

[7] David Callies, Robert H. Freilich & Shelley R. Saxer, LAND USE: CASES AND MATERIALS, 819-824
(West Academic Publishing 7th ed. 2017) [hereinafter LAND USE].

and residents who live in poverty and are falling into homelessness each month.[8]

Solving homelessness in the United States is complex and related to many complex social-ecological systems, but some believe it is not impossible. Affordable housing (discussed in more detail later) will certainly be critical to any long-term solution. It has been suggested that a housing-first approach, which means placing homeless people into long-term housing, even before dealing with drug and alcohol treatment issues, mental health, and job training, is more effective than homeless shelters with rehabilitative services. After settling the homeless in a stable home, they can receive rehabilitative services in a supportive environment. The homeless who suffer from mental illness and/or addiction need permanent supportive housing. This housing can successfully combine with low-income participants in a mixed-use housing development.[9]

Experts on homelessness have solutions, but housing costs are increasing, as are the program costs to fight homelessness. We need additional funding to tackle this challenge, but one possibility is to create more affordable housing to help both the chronically homeless and those who are only temporarily homeless. By solving the homeless crisis, society may save money overall by fixing other problems stemming from homelessness, such as, "truancy from schools, food insecurity, drug and alcohol abuse, and unemployment."[10]

FOOD AND LAND USE

As discussed in Chapter 4, food and food security heavily influence the R&S of many social-ecological systems. The following ordinances begin to incorporate a number of aspects of R&S at the local level.

MINNEAPOLIS STAPLE FOOD ORDINANCE

The staple foods ordinance . . . requires licensed grocery stores (including corner stores, gas stations, dollar stores, and pharmacies) to sell a certain amount of basic food items including fruits and vegetables, whole grains, eggs, and low-fat dairy.[11]

---

[8] West Bausmith, *How Should L.A. Spend Its $100-million Homelessness Emergency Fund?*, L.A. TIMES (Oct. 29, 2015), http://www.latimes.com/opinion/op-ed/la-oe-1023-homeless-100-million-fund-20151022-html-htmlstory. html.

[9] *End Homelessness*, *supra* note 4.

[10] *Id.*

[11] *Staple Foods Ordinance*, CITY OF MINNEAPOLIS, MN, http://www.minneapolismn.gov/health/living/eating/staple-foods (last updated Jan. 25, 2017).

SUSTAINABLE FOOD SERVICE WARE ORDINANCE, MILLBRAE ORDINANCE NO. 717

Millbrae municipal code prohibit[s] the use of polystyrene foam and solid disposable food service ware and require[s] the use of biodegradable, compostable, reusable or recyclable food service ware by food vendors in the city.[12]

ORDINANCE PROMOTING RESIDENTIAL FOOD SALES

The [Denver Sustainable Food Policy] supports an amendment to the Denver Zoning Code to allow the sale of raw agricultural goods and homemade food products on residential properties. This will help to promote the cultivation of backyard and community gardens for personal use while also increasing the availability of fresh produce for sale in all Denver neighborhoods. The amendment would only apply to fruits, vegetables and herbs and any food products made from plants grown on the same site. All raw food and products must be tied directly to the person selling it, and must be sold directly to the consumer.[13]

The remainder of this chapter focuses on issues regarding land use, assuming that all members of the community have a place to live. In doing so, we explore the role of resilience and sustainability in understanding and assessing systems relevant to improving the health, safety, and general welfare of the community. We examine whether and how R&S can help us understand challenges in a way that addresses potential land use conflicts and transportation needs to help meet our basic need for a safe and healthy place to call home.

II. THE TRADITIONAL TOOLS

The Traditional Tools. Prior to using government regulation to address conflicting land uses, private individuals traditionally used common law nuisance, restrictive covenants, and defeasible estates to control land use. While nuisance and restrictive covenants are still used modernly to supplement government regulation of land use, defeasible estates are problematic, as described in more detail below.

Estates in land rules allow grantors of an interest in land to condition ownership based on land use by conveying a defeasible estate. For example, the owner of a parcel of land could convey that parcel using the words of grant as follows: "to the purchaser and his heirs so long as the premises are used for residential purposes only, and if not so used, the land shall revert to the seller and his heirs." Modernly, this would be an inefficient method to control land use because:

[12] MILLBRAE, CA., ORDINANCE NO. 717 (2008).
[13] *Policy Issues*, DENVER SUSTAINABLE FOOD POLICY COUNCIL, https://web.archive.org/web/20160330002616/http://denversfpc.com/policy-issues/ (last visited Nov. 16, 2017).

- purchasers would pay a lesser price for the property because, if the premises are used for something other than residential, their property interest would be forfeited completely; and
- lenders would likely not be willing to finance such a purchase or loan against the property because the potential forfeiture would impact their security interest.

Instead, restrictive covenants more effectively regulate land use by using damages or injunctive relief, rather than forfeiture, to enforce these controls.[14]

Restrictive covenants are private promises involving the use of land that private citizens can enforce at law or in equity against current or future owners of the property encumbered by the promises. These promises are real covenants if enforced at law, typically through money damages. These same promises are equitable servitudes, if enforced through equitable remedies, typically injunctive relief. Landlord-tenant law uses real covenants based upon the promises in the lease related to the land, such as the promise to pay rent. Homeowner associations (HOA) typically use equitable servitudes to establish covenants, conditions, and restrictions (CC&Rs) to control how members of a particular residential neighborhood use their property and to obtain fees to fund the HOA's provision of private services to the residents.[15]

Nuisance is a common law action in tort that allows either a private individual or a public official to stop (or obtain damages or both) for the unreasonable and substantial interference with a property interest because of the activities of a neighbor. The maxim that encapsulates this idea is *sic utere tuo ut alienum non laedas* or "one must so use his property as not to injure that of another." Some have described nuisance as a form of "judicial" or "common law" zoning. A private nuisance is nontrespassory conduct that unreasonably interferes with a landowner's use and enjoyment of land. Public nuisance is an activity that: 1) endangers the health, safety, or property of a number of people; 2) offends public morals; or 3) interferes with the comfort or convenience of a number of people.[16]

Nuisance litigation focuses on the reasonableness of the defendant's behavior and, in determining whether the interference is unreasonable such that it constitutes a nuisance, we weigh the gravity of the harm caused by the behavior against the utility of the defendant's conduct. The Restatement (Second) of Torts requires that the interference is intentional and unreasonable in order for the defendant to be liable. We evaluate unreasonableness based on the *gravity of harm* using five factors: 1) the extent of the harm; 2) the character of the harm; 3) the social value of the use or enjoyment

---

[14] *See* Grant S. Nelson, Dale A. Whitman, Colleen E. Medill & Shelley R. Saxer, Contemporary Property, Chapter 4 (West, 4th ed. 2013) [hereinafter Property].
[15] *Id.* at Chapter 9.
[16] *Id.* at Chapter 10.

interfered with; 4) the suitability of the plaintiff's use to the locality; and 5) the burden on the person harmed to avoid the harm. We also evaluate unreasonableness based on the *utility of the conduct* using three factors: 1) the social value of defendant's conduct; 2) the suitability of the conduct to the locality; and 3) the impracticability of preventing or avoiding the interference. If *the gravity of the harm outweighs the utility of the actor's conduct*, the defendant's behavior is unreasonable and thus establishes nuisance liability.[17]

Nuisance law and zoning are similar in that they both regulate conflicting and disturbing uses of land. While planning and zoning attempt to anticipate problematic land uses and regulate them in advance, nuisance is reactive in nature because it applies only after a substantial and unreasonable interference occurs or is imminently anticipated. Even though environmental laws and local zoning regulations now provide the major controls over conflicting and harmful land uses, nuisance remains a valuable tool in circumstances where zoning permits or environmental regulations do not address the harmful activity.[18]

III. COMPREHENSIVE PLANNING AND ZONING

The Power to Plan and Zone. Nearly all planning and zoning for cities and counties is carried out at the local level. The state delegates the power, typically through enabling acts, allowing local government to promote the health, safety, morals, or the general welfare of the community. **The Standard State Zoning Enabling Act (SZEA)**, developed originally in 1922, is a model act promulgating general principles of American planning and zoning. All states have adopted an enabling act, authorizing local planning and zoning. However, several states have also authorized local governments to plan and zone under a doctrine called "home rule," which provides certain local governments with broad authority to act, including planning and zoning.[19]

The Standard City Planning Enabling Act (SCPEA) was also promulgated in the 1920s and "[was] intended to be adopted by the States and to form the legal basis for the future of American planning and development."[20] It was enacted "[t]o provide for city and regional planning; the creation, organization, and powers of planning commissions; the regulation of subdivision of land and the acquisition of the right to keep planned streets free from buildings; and providing penalties for violation of this act." Some of its purposes included that

---

[17] *Id.*

[18] Merrick v. Diageo, 805 F.3d 685, 692 (6th Cir. 2015).

[19] PROPERTY, *supra* note 14, at 1066-1067.

[20] Paul Knight, *Rediscovering the Master Street Plan: The Critical Missing Component in City Planning Today*, CONGRESS FOR THE NEW URBANISM 1, 1 https://web.archive.org/web/20150326020159/https://www.cnu.org/sites/www.cnu.org/files/rediscovering_the_master_street_plan_-_knight_0.pdf (last visited Nov. 16, 2017).

[t]he plan shall be made with the general purpose of guiding and accomplishing a coordinated, adjusted, and harmonious development of the municipality and its environs which will, in accordance with present and future needs, best promote health, safety, morals, order, convenience, prosperity, and general welfare, as well as efficiency and economy in the process of development.[21]

By the 1930s, almost all states had statutes allowing cities and counties to plan and zone. Demographic changes attributable to the growth of cities and the eventual exodus from the cities to the suburbs required local governments to plan for and respond to the impacts of these changes in human settlement patterns. Local government must plan for infrastructure such as roads, schools, and commercial and industrial facilities in order to balance impacts on the natural and existing physical environment with the demands of urbanization.[22] A plan that is properly developed can be valuable to a community seeking to improve its quality of life by providing a cleaner environment and building its economic health through the efficient use of its available resources.[23]

 WASTE AND LAND USE

Public health considerations are deeply integrated into waste disposal. The following ordinance addresses the waste aspect of public health and begins to illustrate one way local governments are integrating R&S into waste management.

GRANT COUNTY CODE OF ORDINANCES CHAPTER 37: ANIMAL WASTE STORAGE AND NUTRIENT UTILIZATION ORDINANCE

Animal waste storage and nutrient utilization is regulated through Chapter 90 of the Grant County Code of Ordinances. The purpose of this ordinance is to regulate the location, design, construction, installation, alteration, closure and the utilization of animal waste from these facilities in order to prevent water pollution and protect the water resources of Grant County. A permit is required before any construction activity takes place. Each application for a permit under the Ordinance shall include a complete set of detailed construction plans and a Nutrient Management Plan. Applications are reviewed by the Grant County CSZD to ensure compliance with NRCS standards and specifications.[24]

---

[21] LAND USE, *supra* note 7, at 39-40.
[22] John R. Nolon & Patricia E. Salkin, LAND USE IN A NUTSHELL 38 (Thomas/West, 2006).
[23] *See* 11 *Planning and Zoning Officials Academy* No. 5, *in* BASIC TRAINING, MICHIGAN ASS'N OF PLANNING, http://www.planningmi.org/downloads/the_zoning_ordinance.pdf (last visited Nov. 16, 2017).
[24] *Chapter 90: Animal Waste Storage & Nutrient Utilization Ordinance*, GRANT COUNTY, WI, http://www.co.grant.wi.gov/localgov_departments_details.asp?deptid=415&locid=147 (last visited Nov. 16, 2015).

The Comprehensive Plan (also called the General Plan or Master Plan) is the product of formal studies by planning professionals with input from the community. The comprehensive plan addresses the inevitable change and progression of a local community and plan for anticipated compatibility issues with various land uses, the management and preservation of natural resources and historically significant property, and the adequacy of the infrastructure to meet current and future development needs. The comprehensive plan typically contains an overall map of the community in addition to the narrative comprising the plan document.

The plan should address a wide range of planning issues, including but not limited to transportation patterns, population trends, schools, recreation, and housing.[25] Given the importance of planning in the ongoing development of a community, it is surprising that the majority of states do not require local governments to have a comprehensive plan in place as a prerequisite to administrative zoning. In fact, only 15 states make planning a mandate and many require an updated plan after a decade or more.[26]

Successfully implementing a comprehensive plan requires the plan to include recommendations and short-term, mid-term, and long-term strategies that the city and others involved with future development constantly review and execute.[27] This type of adaptive governance (adaptive governance is described in more detail in Chapter 7, Section II) helps guide the adoption of ordinances, development orders, proposed measures, programs, etc., that are used to implement the goals and objectives of the comprehensive plan. Many states require that actions taken in regard to land that is covered by the plan are "in conformance with" or "consistent with" the plan adopted, but most courts treat comprehensive plans only as guidance.[28]

Communities that wish to make resilience and sustainability a clear part of their goals must **develop a comprehensive plan that incorporates R&S**. Some communities have created entire new elements in their comprehensive plan to incorporate these goals, while others have integrated sustainability or resilience assessments or sought to enhance system resilience or sustainability. For example, a city might seek to enhance the resilience of its infrastructure system by promoting a combination of

---

[25] *See Comprehensive Planning*, UNIVERSITY OF ILLINOIS EXTENSION, http://extension.illinois.edu/lcr/comprehensiveplanning.cfm (last visited Nov. 16, 2017); *see also Zoning and the Comprehensive Plan*, NY DEP'T OF STATE DIV. OF LOCAL GOV'T SERV, http://www.saratogastormwater.org/Municipal-govt-ED/on%20line%20resc/Additional%20Resources/Zoning%20&%20Comprehensive%20Plans.pdf (last visited Nov. 16, 2017).

[26] Nolon & Salkin, *supra* note 22. *See, e.g.*, R.I. GEN. LAWS 1956 §45-22.2-6(a) (requiring a minimum 20 years); 53 P.S. §10301(c) (requiring minimum 10 years).

[27] *City of Roswell Frequently Asked Questions*, ROSWELL GEORGIA, https://www.roswellgov.com/i-want-to/browse-frequently-asked-questions/-selcat-19 (last visited Nov. 16, 2017).

[28] LAND USE, *supra* note 7, at 47.

gray infrastructure, such as pipes and ditches, and green infrastructure, such as bioswales.[29]

In updating a plan to include aspects of R&S goals, the community should first decide what resilience and sustainability mean in the context of their goals for future growth and development.[30] The American Planning Association (APA) has developed standards to prepare and assess sustainable comprehensive plans. The APA has identified six principles to provide a framework for the goals and objectives of a sustainable plan:

- **Livable Built Environment** — ensure that all elements of the built environment, including land use, transportation, housing, energy, and infrastructure, work together to provide sustainable, green places for living, working, and recreation, with a high quality of life.
- **Harmony with Nature** — ensure that the contributions of natural resources to human well-being are explicitly recognized and valued and that maintaining their health is a primary objective.
- **Resilient Economy** — ensure that the community is prepared to deal with both positive and negative changes in its economic health and to initiate sustainable urban development and redevelopment strategies that foster green business growth and build reliance on local assets.
- **Interwoven Equity** — ensure fairness and equity in providing for the housing, services, health, safety, and livelihood needs of all citizens and groups.
- **Healthy Community** — ensure that public health needs are recognized and addressed through provisions for healthy foods, physical activity, access to recreation, healthcare, environmental justice, and safe neighborhoods.
- **Responsible Regionalism** — ensure that all local proposals account for, connect with, and support the plans of adjacent jurisdictions and the surrounding region.[31]

Note the APA's use of "resilient" in refining "economy." How would you describe the overlap between achieving a "sustainable plan" and the necessity of a "resilient economy"? Adopted in 2016, Des Moines, Iowa's comprehensive plan vision statement provides an example illustrating core substantive values embedded in comprehensive plans. The city

---

[29] For an analysis of existing land use laws and infrastructure, see Jonathan Rosenbloom, *Fifty Shades of Gray Infrastructure: Land Use & the Failure to Create Resilient Cities*, 91 Wash. L. Rev. ___ (2018).

[30] APA Policy Guide on Smart Growth, American Planning Association, https://www.planning.org/policy/guides/adopted/smartgrowth.htm (last visited Nov. 14, 2017).

[31] *Comprehensive Plan Standards for Sustaining Places*, American Planning Ass'n, https://www.planning.org/sustainingplaces/compplanstandards/pdf/compplansustainabilitystandards.pdf (last visited Nov. 14, 2017).

characterizes the values in a way that makes the triple bottom line and intergenerational equity central to the plan:

In 2040, Des Moines will have . . .

- *Vibrant, healthy, and walkable neighborhoods with a mixture of housing, recreational opportunities, public spaces, schools, and mixed-use commercial centers.*
- *Housing that offers a diversity of choices in housing styles and affordability that meets the needs of residents throughout their lives.*
- *A complete transportation system providing safe and efficient infrastructure for walking, bicycling, mass transit, and automobiles.*
- *A resilient economy with a robust job environment and the provision of necessary land and infrastructure for business development.*
- *Protected natural resources and sensitive ecosystems, and clean air and water.*
- *Enhanced opportunities for urban agriculture.*
- *Compassion and inclusion for the physically, intellectually, and economically disadvantaged through programs to ensure accessibility to City services and facilities that are available to the public.*
- *Sustainable governance recognizing that policies and decisions have environmental, social, and economic impacts on the overall quality of life.*
- *A vibrant and creative cultural and recreational environment that inspires us as a community, educates us, promotes health and wellness, and is available for all residents.*
- *A strong and supporting environment for global residents from all heritages.*
- *Investment in the youth of the City to ensure equal opportunities for education and job training.*[32]

TRANSPORTATION AND LAND USE

Transportation, land use, and the resilience and sustainability of many social-ecological systems are closely intertwined. As illustrated below, numerous local governments are attempting to address transportation-based impacts, such as increased greenhouse gas emissions, by focusing on land use laws, such as Complete Streets.

"Complete streets" is a relatively new concept that means designing and operating streets to enable safe access for all users, including pedestrians, motorists and transit riders of all ages and

---

[32] City of Des Moines Community Development Department, *City of Des Moines Comprehensive Plan*, CITY OF DES MOINES, 1, 9 (Apr. 2016), https://plandsm.dmgov.org/system/resources/W1siZiIsIjIwMTYvMDUvMjMvNTRpbzRlc2l0al9GSU5BTF9QbGFuRFNNX3dlYi5wZGYiXV0/FINAL_PlanDSM_web.pdf?sha=127d17d7a35c505a.

ability. Provisions that make up a complete street include sidewalks, bike lanes (or wide paved shoulders), comfortable and accessible transit stops, frequent crossing opportunities, median islands, accessible pedestrian signals, curb ramps, etc. A complete street in the more rural parts of the County will look very different from the urban and even suburban areas, but both should be designed to ensure safety and convenience for everyone using the road.

Complete Streets Policy Template 2015, Des Moines Area Metropolitan Planning Organization, https://dmampo.org/complete-streets/ (last visited Jan. 16, 2018).

Starting over from the beginning is not an option for most communities as land patterns have already been set, buildings are standing, roads and other infrastructure networks are established, and people have an expectation of continuity. However, what if you could start over, as was the case with the small town of Greensburg, Kansas?

> *Greensburg is a small rural farming town in south Kansas, which, over the past forty years, experienced a decline in population and resulting economic struggles.*[33] *Then, in 2007, an EF5 tornado, with winds in excess of 200mph, struck Greensburg, destroying everything in its path. Eleven lives were lost and the storm destroyed 961 homes and businesses.*[34]

After the storm, it was apparent to city officials that significant changes would have to occur to spur redevelopment of a town that was already in a long period of decline before this catastrophe.[35] Greensburg adopted a Long-Term Community Recovery Plan (LTCRP) that was prepared through the Federal Emergency Management Agency's (FEMA) Long-Term Community Recovery (LTCR) program. The LTCRP was the product of steering committee meetings, stakeholder interviews, and discussions with citizens, civic groups, business owners, and local, state, and federal officials. There was a general feeling among Greensburg residents, business owners, and leaders that sustainability and resilience were noble causes and that support from the community for R&S goals would lower the risk of implementing green technologies and energy efficiency measures.[36] As a result, the LTCRP recommended that the town adopt a new general plan to serve as a blueprint for sustainable redevelopment of Greensburg. Ultimately, the residents of Greensburg developed the Greensburg Sustainable Comprehensive Master Plan. The plan states that: "[a] truly sustainable community is one that balances the economic, ecological, and social impacts of development."[37]

---

[33] Patrick Quinn, *After Devastating Tornado, Town is Reborn "Green,"* USA Today, (Apr. 25, 2013) http://www.usatoday.com/story/news/greenhouse/2013/04/13/greensburg-kansas/2078901/.

[34] *Facts About the May 4, 2007 Greensburg Tornado*, NOAA (Apr. 25, 2008), http://www.crh.noaa.gov/Image/ddc/News/Greensburg/Greensburg_Facts.pdf.

[35] *See* Al Letson, *Town Rebuilds Green After Devastating Tornado*, NPR (May 4, 2010), http://www.npr.org/templates/story/story.php?storyId=126833862.

[36] *Rebuilding It Better: Greensburg, Kansas*, U.S. Dep't of Energy (Apr. 2012), http://www.nrel.gov/buildings/assets/pdfs/53539.pdf.

[37] *Sustainable Comprehensive Master Plan*, Greensburg, KS, http://www.greensburgks.org/residents/recovery-planning/sustainable-comprehensive-master-plan/view (last visited Nov. 16, 2017).

PLANNING FOR UNCERTAINTY AND RESILIENCE JUSTICE

Comprehensive plans provide a process for local governments to take a step back and consider the unforeseen possibilities facing communities and their future. As climate change and its ramifications enhance the uncertainty in ecosystems, planning for an uncertain future is imperative for communities. In a brief blog post following Hurricane Harvey, Tony Arnold expounded on this point, noting:

this is a tragic, heart-wrenching example of what I've been teaching, speaking, and writing about for the past several years . . . plan for the unprecedented. This is fundamental to adaptive planning for resilience. The predictions of 30 inches of rain and advice to shelter in place have now been replaced by predictions of up to 50 inches and regret that there wasn't mandatory evacuation. Why can we not seem to learn and apply core lessons from Katrina and so many other climate disasters? . . . It's very difficult to get public officials and members of the public to accept and plan for extreme and unprecedented shocks and changes, but, time and again, we face the consequences of minimizing risk and instability in complex multi-system dynamics. Moreover, why can't we think in terms of Resilience Justice? Resilience justice is about the structural inequities in adaptive capacities and vulnerabilities of marginalized communities, such as low-income communities of color. It is about addressing these inequities through policy analysis and reform. . . . The need for policy and planning reform to address the vulnerabilities and capacities of marginalized communities is critical, yet we make so little progress and advance so slowly—too slowly for events like Harvey.

Craig (Tony) Arnold, *Adaptive Planning for Resilience, Harvey, & the Gulf Coast Region* (Aug. 27, 2017), http://lawprofessors.typepad.com/land_use/2017/08/adaptive-planning-for-resilience-harvey-the-gulf-coast-region.html.

Greensburg Today. Greensburg is now a model for green building, and a destination for eco-tourism. Groups are looking toward Greensburg's successes to generate new ideas for other communities. The city's master plan included the development of a new downtown area, improvements in walkability of the town, many green building projects, and related economic development plans.[38] Municipal buildings are all LEED certified and reduce energy costs to the city by 42%. New light-emitting diode streetlights reduce operating costs by 70% by being both more energy efficient and requiring less maintenance. Greensburg's business community has also rebuilt with an eye toward energy conservation. The local LEED certified John Deere dealership is even serving as a model for other dealerships nationwide.[39] Furthermore, Greensburg has made a commitment to creating green infrastructure. The city will be the first in the nation to run on "100% renewable energy, 100% of the time" through the creation

---

[38] *Advancing Sustainable and Resilient Communities*, U.S. Local Solutions (Sept. 14, 2017), http://sustainablecommunitiesleadershipacademy.org/resource_files/documents/greenburg-kansas-rebuilding-green-in-wake-of-disaster.pdf.
[39] Shanti Pless, Lynn Billman & Daniel Wallach, *From Tragedy to Triumph: Rebuilding Greensburg, Kansas, to Be a 100% Renewable Energy City*, National Renewable Energy Laboratory (Apr. 15, 2010), http://energy.gov/sites/prod/files/2013/11/f5/48300.pdf.

of a large wind farm.[40] Despite "a tragic disaster, the town of Greensburg was able to hold on to its sense of community and forge a greener, more sustainable new way of living and doing business in the Midwest."[41]

Questions

1. What parts of Des Moines' Comprehensive Plan vision statement (quoted above) incorporate aspects of resilience and/or sustainability? Does the vision statement overlap with definitions for R&S we explored in Chapter 1? If so, how or where?

2. Does the Des Moines' Comprehensive Plan mission statement rely on any of the Strategies for Implementation that we covered thus far (Ecosystem Services Management, Collective Action Challenges, or Precautionary Principle)?

3. What aspects of Greensburg's post-tornado development will enhance the resilience of its energy system? Water system? Food system?

IV. ZONING

Planning and zoning law involve all three branches of government — legislative, administrative, and judicial. The local legislative body is typically the city council or county commission. A board of adjustment, planning and zoning commission, and/or a board of zoning appeals generally handle administrative actions and the local court of general jurisdiction serves as the judicial function. The municipality may also have a city attorney's office with a land use planning section, or in many cases, the city will hire outside counsel by employing a firm that specializes in municipal law and serves several cities.[42]

  The level of deference a court gives to a local decision depends on whether the decision was legislative or administrative/quasi-judicial. The standard of judicial review for legislative decisions is a *presumption of validity* under the rational basis standard. Unless there has been an abuse of discretion, the action will be upheld if it is *fairly debatable*. Administrative or adjudicative actions receive more intense judicial review and require that *substantial evidence* support these decisions. *Substantial evidence* is

---

[40] *Building Green in Greensburg: Wind Farm*, U.S. Dep't of Energy, http://apps1.eere.energy.gov/buildings/publications/pdfs/corporate/ns/greensburgsign_windfarm.pdf (last visited Nov. 16, 2017).
[41] Tara Copeland, *Greensburg's Green Start*, Save on Energy (May 4, 2015), https://www.saveonenergy.com/green-energy/greensburgs-green-start/.
[42] Land Use, *supra* note 7, at Chapter 2.

such relevant evidence that a reasonable mind might accept as adequate to support the decision.[43]

The process of zoning is a legislative action that establishes regulations. Those regulations traditionally included height and bulk restrictions, as well as use designations. **Height and bulk regulations** generally direct overall height and size of buildings. They define the allowable density based on occupation and the proximity of the buildings. Zoning may also limit what part of

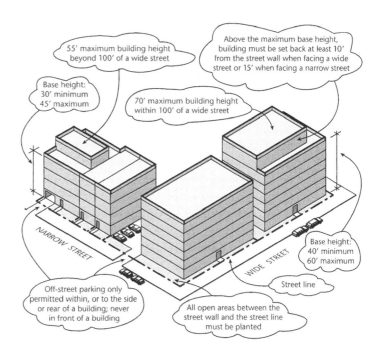

the area of a building lot may contain structures, the minimum parking areas for a commercial site, and requirements for garages and driveways for a home. Minimum lot size, setback and side yard requirements to control the distance between a building and the front, back, and side property lines, and floor area ratio (FAR) to regulate the intensity of the use are other examples of zoning ordinance bulk requirements.[44]

Use zoning requirements control how the property is used. Typical categories include residential, commercial, industrial, agricultural, and recreational. These categories usually break down into subcategories such as single family and multi-family residential uses and retail and light commercial uses. Zoning may also establish "buffer zones" that serve to gradually increase use density such as by zoning multi-family residential uses between commercial uses and single-family residential uses. Performance zoning controls for dust, noise, etc., in industrial zones and overlay zoning allows the community to establish historic districts to preserve economic and social stability and revitalize neighborhoods by encouraging tourism. The floating zone concept creates a use zone such as a residential planned unit development (PUD). If the city's plan calls for eventual residential development, the zone permitting it floats above the zoning map until the city determines where the development will actually take place. Finally, as a result of the New Urbanism movement (described in more detail below),

---

[43] *Id.*
[44] Will Van Vactor, *Zoning Ordinances and Regulations*, LAWYERS.COM, http://zoning-planning-land-use.lawyers.com/zoning-ordinances-and-regulations.html (last visited Nov. 16, 2017).

form-based zoning codes may be encouraged to place the form of the development above the actual use for a return to Traditional Neighborhood Development (TND), mixed use, and Transit-oriented development (TOD) (described in more detail below).[45]

Rezoning occurs when officials amend the original zoning to allow a landowner or group of landowners to develop land or make some substantial change in its use. It may affect whole zones or only a single parcel. Changes in zoning policy or updates in the comprehensive plan to reflect changes in the community require rezoning to implement. Although zoning is considered to be legislative, some states treat rezoning as administrative because it typically affects a smaller group of landowners and courts will subject the action to increased scrutiny under the substantial evidence standard.

If the rezoning affects only one landowner and a small parcel of land within the zone, litigants can challenge the action as "spot zoning" and even in a jurisdiction that treats rezoning as legislative, the court will more strictly scrutinize the action. Spot zoning will benefit the individual landowner whereas "reverse spot zoning" is detrimental and appears to single out a landowner for adverse treatment. Local officials may counter challenges of spot zoning by showing that the rezoning conforms or is consistent with the legislatively adopted comprehensive plan. Some states will not give deference to rezoning unless it is in response to a change in circumstances or a mistake in the original zoning.[46]

Variances and special exceptions, also called conditional use permits, allow flexibility in zoning and land use activity. A variance is a permit to do something the zoning code does not allow without such a permit; it is a waiver of some zoning requirement. A "**bulk**" or "**area**" variance waives a zoning regulation and grants the landowner an exception from complying with strict physical standards, such as a "setback" or building height. This type of variance is generally easier to obtain than a "use" variance and courts may apply the "**practical difficulties test**" which balances the benefit of the variance to the landowner against the harm to the public. Factors used in this balancing include the magnitude of the variance sought, the effect on neighborhood infrastructure by allowing the variance, the degree of change to the neighborhood, whether there were other feasible means for the landowner seeking the variance to avoid the difficulty, whether justice is served, and whether the need for the variance was self-created by the landowner.[47]

Use variances allow a property owner to use the property in a manner that the zoning ordinance forbids. Because use variances tend to have a more extensive impact on the area, courts may apply the more stringent "**unnecessary hardship**" test. A landowner requesting a use variance must show that the land cannot yield a reasonable return without the variance, the landowner's plight is due to the unique circumstances of the property, the new

---

[45] LAND USE, *supra* note 7, at Chapter 2.
[46] *Id.*
[47] *Id.*

use will not alter the locality's character, and the difficulty is not self-created. Both area and use variances cannot be self-created and the landowner's situation must be unique because otherwise land use officials should be recommending rezoning for everyone, rather than granting a variance. Granting or denying a variance request is an administrative or adjudicative action subject to the substantial evidence standard because the government makes an individualized decision that does not affect the public generally.[48]

Conditional use or special use permits are other tools for zoning flexibility when the municipality recognizes that certain uses are valuable within a zone, such as schools and churches in a residential area, but also realizes that these uses can create traffic, noise, and parking concerns. The zoning ordinance will allow these special uses, but those seeking to make such use of their property will be required to obtain a permit by showing that their use will not adversely affect adjacent properties. In addition, the city will be able to "condition" their use by establishing hours of operation, parking requirements, etc., to deal with the anticipated externalities of the operation.[49]

Nonconforming uses exist when local government zones or rezones after the use in question has already been in operation. Communities have several options as to how to deal with these uses. One option is to require the *immediate cessation* of the nonconforming use. Such an approach will likely be unconstitutional and challenged as a Fifth Amendment taking or as a violation of due process. Courts would likely find that this means of eliminating nonconforming uses would be either confiscatory or not reasonably related to a legitimate state interest.

Amortization ordinances give the nonconforming use a reasonable time to stay in operation before being required to close down. Cities and counties regulating for aesthetic purposes have frequently amended zoning codes to eliminate billboards and other signs but have established amortization periods for their eventual removal. When challenged, the reasonableness of the time period for these amortization ordinances is evaluated based on several factors: 1) whether the structure or use is nonconforming; 2) investment factors such as the life expectancy of the structure (depreciation), the investment realized to date, lease obligations; and 3) whether the nonconforming aspect is a nuisance. If the use constitutes a nuisance, the government may immediately stop the nonconforming use. A few jurisdictions find that either cessation (the complete stoppage of nonconforming uses) or amortization methods are unconstitutional. Finally, if the landowner abandons the use voluntarily with an overt act of *abandonment* and the intent to abandon, the nonconforming use will terminate. A *change in the character* of the use or an *expansion* or *reconstruction* of the nonconforming use may also serve to terminate the use.[50]

[48] *Id.*
[49] *Id.*
[50] *Id.*

Municipalities generally allow **home occupations** and **accessory uses** of the family home if they are necessary or convenient to the permitted use. Home occupations may include in-home offices for telecommuters, daycare offerings, dog kennels, hair salons, "granny" flats, music lessons, art activities, professional offices, sewing and alterations, and much more. However, when these uses become objectionable to neighbors who then challenge them, the homeowner may find that their use does not qualify as a home occupation allowed under the applicable ordinance.[51]

Initiatives and referenda are mechanisms used by voters as a form of direct democracy to curb alleged legislative abuse. While not all states recognize these electorate powers, where permitted, they can be used to carry out or veto zoning changes. At times, local citizens have used "ballot box zoning" to prevent growth or stop proposed uses that are more intensive in nature. The initiative allows voters to take legislative action to rezone before the landowner acquires a vested right to develop. The referendum process is reactive by allowing citizens to place an issue on the ballot to either approve or rescind legislative zoning action. The state constitution or enabling statute may reserve these powers to the people such that courts will uphold their use against a challenge of invalid delegation of legislative power by the state. A majority of states do not allow zoning by initiative, but there is an even split among the states as to whether zoning by referendum is allowed. Zoning by referendum is favored over initiative because the initiative arguably does not give notice and an opportunity to be heard, but the legislative act of rezoning before the referendum is triggered provides adequate procedural due process.[52]

The initiative and referenda processes have been criticized not only for potential procedural due process failures but also because they can mask discriminatory exclusionary zoning and negate the advantages of planning by allowing "piecemeal" zoning.[53] In California, some projects have used the initiative process to avoid environmental review of projects under the California Environmental Quality Act (CEQA). The California Supreme Court in *Tuolumne Jobs & Small Business Alliance v. Superior Court of Tuolumne County* confirmed that an initiative is not subject to CEQA, even if the initiative is not on the ballot and a local elected body instead adopts it.[54] Builders and developers in California have used the initiative process to avoid CEQA review for NFL football stadiums and other popular projects such as shopping complexes.[55]

---

[51] Anna Barbara Hantz, *Home Occupations and Accessory Uses: Zoning Considerations When You or Your Employees Work from Home*, Sheehan Phinney Bass and Green PA (June 25, 2013), https://www.sheehan.com/publications/good-company-newsletter/Home-Occupations-and-Accessory-Uses--Zoning-Considerations-When-You-or-Your-Employees-Work-From-Home.aspx.

[52] Land Use, *supra* note 7, at Chapter 2.

[53] *Id.*

[54] 59 Cal. 4th 1029, 1043-1044 (2014).

[55] Ian Lovett, *Builders Pierce California's Environmental Shield with New Weapon: The Ballot*, N.Y. Times (Jun. 7, 2016), http://www.nytimes.com/2016/06/08/us/builders-pierce-californias-environmental-shield-with-new-weapon-the-ballot.html?_r = 0.

General challenges to zoning include both procedural claims regarding the authority of government officials to regulate or the unlawful delegation of power, and substantive claims that the zoning action taken is unfairly favoring special interests, anticompetitive in nature, or bargaining away the police power. Zoning that does not conform to the comprehensive plan may be challenged as beyond the authority of local officials. Residents may also retain the police power necessary to promote initiatives or referenda. If the city council delegates authority to another body, it must establish standards to guide decisions and avoid favoritism or arbitrariness; otherwise, the city may face a challenge for an impermissible delegation of legislative authority. If the city abandons its authority by binding itself contractually with a landowner, a charge of contract zoning levied against the city may be successful unless the jurisdiction has statutorily authorized development agreements. Finally, if the sole purpose of the zoning ordinance is to suppress competition, the ordinance will be invalidated. However, it is acceptable for local officials to protect existing businesses if it does so through planning and not through ad hoc zoning.[56]

Questions and Note

1. In Chapter 3, we described the Precautionary Principle (PP) as a method to help understand and assess R&S. In addition, it can help operationalize it in law and policy. In some ways, zoning adopts a PP to land use. How would you describe that approach?

2. If you were advising state and local officials about rising concerns regarding the use of drones, what are some of the potential legal issues you might consider? *See* Troy A. Rule, *Drone Zoning*, 95 N.C. L. Rev. 133 (2016); Wendie L. Kellington & Michael Berger, *Why Land Use Lawyers Care About the Law of Unmanned Systems*, 37 Zoning & Plan. L. Rep. (2014); National League of Cities, What Cities Need to Know About Unmanned Aerial Vehicles (UAVs) (2016).

V. SUBDIVISION REGULATION

Subdivision regulation controls the typical process that allows a developer to divide land into parcels, tracts, or lots for sale after receiving approval from local officials. Subdivision regulation has evolved into a

---

[56] Land Use, *supra* note 7, at Chapter 2.

sustainability approach that incentivizes walkable mixed-use developments, green buildings, and the shift to renewable energy use. Sustainable development encompasses smart growth, new urbanism, green development, and renewable energy (described below).[57]

Under the authority of the Standard City Planning Enabling Act (SCPEA), the local planning commission regulates subdivision approval. Subdivisions must be in harmony with the master plan and should take into account conditions and facilities on property adjoining the subdivided land. In addition to guiding the subdivision by reference to the master or comprehensive plan, the SCPEA provides for the establishment of the **"Official Map"** to preserve major street rights-of-way and plat future streets. Mapping present and future streets gives direction and pattern to the community's future growth. Cities and counties have widened the scope of the Official Map to include "mapping of parks, trails, habitat corridors, environmentally sensitive lands, open spaces and public buildings."[58] Where the government uses the Official Map to prevent land development that would increase the cost of acquiring such land in the future through eminent domain, the landowner may be able to claim successfully that a regulatory taking under the Fifth Amendment has occurred. However, courts will uphold reasonable Official Map regulations and the government will not need to pay compensation until it actually condemns the land needed for public use.[59]

HABITAT PRESERVATION

Some local jurisdictions have increasingly turned to land use to help preserve biodiversity. The following two ordinances from Portland, Oregon illustrate some of the ways in which land use laws can help enhance the resilience and sustainability of some ecological systems by recognizing the impact land use has on flora and fauna. Can you identify the Ecosystem Services Management approach embedded in these ordinances?

TITLE 33: PORTLAND ZONING CODE SECTION 33.440 GREENWAY OVERLAY ZONES—03/01/15

The Greenway regulations are intended to:

1) Protect, conserve, enhance, and maintain the natural, scenic, historical, economic, and recreational qualities of lands along Portland's rivers;
2) Establish criteria, standards, and procedures for the development of land, change of uses, and the intensification of uses within the greenway;
3) Increase public access to and along the Willamette River for the purpose of increasing recreational opportunities, providing emergency vehicle access, assisting in flood protection and control, providing connections to other transportation systems, and

---

[57] *Id.* at Chapter 4.
[58] *Id.*
[59] *Id.*

helping to create a pleasant, aesthetically pleasing urban environment; implement the City's Willamette Greenway responsibilities . . . which include: providing a vegetated corridor to separate protected water features from development; maintaining or reducing stream temperatures; maintaining natural stream corridors; minimizing erosion, nutrient and pollutant loading into water; filtering, infiltration and natural water purification; and stabilizing slopes to prevent landslides contributing to sedimentation of water features.

There are five greenway overlay zones, each with its own focus and purpose. The purpose of each of the overlay zones is stated below.

1) River Natural. The River Natural zone protects, conserves, and enhances land of scenic quality or of significant importance as wildlife habitat.
2) River Recreational. The River Recreational zone encourages river-dependent and river-related recreational uses which provide a variety of types of public access to and along the river, and which enhance the river's natural and scenic qualities.
3) River General. The River General zone allows for uses and development which are consistent with the base zoning, which allow for public use and enjoyment of the waterfront, and which enhance the river's natural and scenic qualities.
4) River Industrial. The River Industrial zone encourages and promotes the development of river-dependent and river-related industries which strengthen the economic viability of Portland as a marine shipping and industrial harbor, while preserving and enhancing the riparian habitat and providing public access where practical.
5) River Water Quality. The River Water Quality zone is designed to protect the functional values of water quality resources by limiting or mitigating the impact of development in the setback.[60]

TITLE 33: PORTLAND ZONING CODE SECTION 33.630 TREE PRESERVATION—7/24/15

The land division process provides the flexibility and opportunity to promote creative site design that considers multiple objectives, including integration of trees. The regulations of this chapter require that trees be considered early in the design process with the goal of preserving high value trees and mitigating for the loss of trees. Desired benefits of trees include:

1) Protecting public health through the absorption of air pollutants, contamination, and capturing carbon dioxide;
2) Buffering from noise, wind, and storms;
3) Providing visual screening and summer cooling;
4) Reducing energy demand and urban heat island impacts;
5) Filtering stormwater and reducing stormwater runoff;
6) Reducing erosion, siltation, and flooding;
7) Stabilizing slopes;
8) Enhancing property values;
9) Providing fish and wildlife habitat, including support for native species biodiversity through the preservation and planting of native trees;
10) Providing food for people and wildlife; and
11) Contributing to the beauty of the City, its natural heritage, and the character of its neighborhoods.[61]

---

[60] PORTLAND, OR, PLANNING AND ZONING §33.440.030 (2015).
[61] PORTLAND, OR, PLANNING AND ZONING §33.630.010 (2015).

The **subdivision approval process** is adjudicative in nature, requiring that developers receive procedural due process. The first step in a traditional three-step process is the submission of the sketch plat, which is a rough design map of the proposed subdivision. Second, a preliminary or tentative plat or map, showing the detailed plan of the subdivision, is the first formal step of subdivision approval. Submission of the preliminary plat may begin the running of a "deemed-approved" statute, which requires the planning commission to act within the statutory period or forfeit the right to deny the application. Approval of the preliminary plat is discretionary in nature and sets the parameters against which officials judge the final plat. So long as the third step, submitting the final plat, meets all of the conditions imposed at preliminary approval, officials must grant final approval as a ministerial act.[62]

Vested rights theories will protect a developer from being subject to subsequent land use decisions that will negatively affect a project once it has begun. States adopting an **early vesting** approach to subdivision approval, grant the developer vested rights against subsequent zoning changes once the preliminary plat or tentative map receives approval. Vesting rights based on the common law theory of **estoppel** may also protect developers against subsequent zoning changes based on the landowner's substantial expenditures in good faith reliance on an act or omission of the government agency. Finally, some states have provided for **development agreements** by statute or judicial decision. These agreements have been challenged as contract zoning based upon claims that the city is "bargaining away its police power" by entering into these contracts. However, when recognized by the state, these agreements give assurance to a developer that officials will apply existing policies, rules, and regulations once they approve the project. Furthermore, the state authorizes these contracts so long as they are reasonably related to public health, safety, morals, and general welfare.[63]

Planned unit development (PUD) can authorize mixed residential use and provide for cluster or conservation subdivisions that integrate land development and uses, densities, and intensities to regulate project development, land use regulations, open space, and circulation systems. A planned unit development review is a discretionary process that substitutes for the traditional zoning system. "Planned unit developments first became popular as a development option for residential development because of gaps and flaws in land use ordinances. Planned unit development regulations are usually included in zoning rather than subdivision ordinances because a discretionary approval process that can consider the requirements contained in zoning ordinances is necessary."[64]

---

[62] *Id.*
[63] LAND USE, *supra* note 7, at Chapter 2.
[64] Daniel R. Mandelker, *Legislation for Planned Unit Developments and Master-Planned Communities*, 40 URB. LAW. 419, 422 (2008).

98.3.10 PLANNED UNIT DEVELOPMENT. FORT MYERS, FLORIDA

A. Purpose and intent. The planned unit development district (PUD) is created to provide an alternative method of land development not available within the framework of the other zoning districts. The standards and procedures of this district are intended to promote flexibility of design and allow for planned diversification and integration of uses and structures while at the same time retaining in the city council the authority to establish such limitations and regulations as it deems necessary to protect the public health, safety and general welfare. In doing so, the PUD district is designed to achieve the following objectives:

1. To accommodate a mixture of uses on a single parcel of land, which mixture is compatible both internally and externally through the limitations, sign control, building orientation, buffering or other techniques which may be appropriate to a particular development proposal.
2. Provide flexibility to meet changing needs, technologies, and economic and consumer preferences.
3. Permit the combining and coordinating of architectural styles, building forms and building relationships within a planned unit development.[65]

Ensuring completion of the public improvements generated by the subdivision is necessary so that the municipality does not become responsible for "finishing the job." Planning commissions often require developers to complete public improvements before final plat approval, but otherwise, the developer will need to provide security for the promise to complete. The subdivider may be required to post a **performance bond**, which ensures that the improvements are actually completed. However, this type of bond does not assure that the subdivider has paid all of the labor and material costs and the municipality may be subject to mechanic or materialman liens if it accepts dedication of the public improvements. Therefore, the performance bond may accompany a **payment bond**, which requires that any dedication of improvements after construction be free and clear of all liens and encumbrances. Finally, the city or county may require a **maintenance bond** in addition to performance and payment bonds to cover the cost of maintaining improvements until the city or county has accepted them by dedication.[66]

Financing Infrastructure. Finding the necessary funds to support current municipal and county needs while also providing for growth is a challenge for local governments. Local governments can raise revenues through taxes, public improvement district assessments, bonding, public utility rate structures, excise taxes, mitigation fees, impact fees, dedications of land and money-in-lieu-of-land dedications.[67] The focus of this chapter as it relates to subdivision controls will be on new development

---

[65] Fort Myers, Fla., Code of Ordinances §98.3.10 (2015).
[66] LAND USE, *supra* note 7, at Chapter 4.
[67] *Id.*

that produces the need for new or upgraded infrastructure. Some communities attempt to control unwanted growth by refusing to upgrade their infrastructure in order to justify denying approval for new development.[68]

Exactions constitute a regulatory tool used by the government to condition permit approval on the property owner's willingness to grant an entitlement, promise, or fee relating "to the expected external costs to the community of the owner's new use of her land."[69] Exactions typically fall into two different categories: on-site improvements required to support the physical infrastructure of the development and off-site improvements to upgrade other parts of the community to support the new development. Exactions can be "physical," when actual land is dedicated or "monetary in-lieu," when the developer pays money to offset the adverse impact of the development in lieu of dedicating land. The municipality may use in-lieu exactions when the developer's land is not useful in size or where there is a more suitable location for the needed infrastructure.[70] Exactions are typically the result of an individualized assessment by government officials as to the specific impact a proposed project will have on the community.

Local government may assess **impact fees** based upon legislative guidelines and formulas as to how a typical project that increases residential density or commercial activity will likely affect the community's infrastructure and ongoing needs. The distinction between impact fees and exactions may become an issue if a state statute specifically identifies legal differences based on this distinction, such as applicable statutes of limitation, or if these regulatory tools are challenged and subject to judicial review.[71]

Special assessments may be used for local improvement to confer some special benefit to the property assessed and must be in proportion to the benefit received from the improvement. Examples where special assessments are used include installing sewer systems in place of septic tanks in a particular part of the city or county or the creation of a business improvement district (BID).

Mandatory set-asides and companion **density bonuses** are financing mechanisms used to meet affordable housing needs impacted by residential development.

---

[68] Arthur Augustyn, *Wastewater Treatment Facility Breaks Ground, Dreams*, Malibu Times (June 30, 2016), http://www.malibutimes.com/news/article_69e107dc-3dba-11e6-8d84-4b01e2b0d870.html.

[69] Mark Fenster, *Regulating Land Use in a Constitutional Shadow: The Institutional Contexts of Exactions*, 58 Hastings L.J. 729, 734 (2007).

[70] Patrick J. Rohan, Zoning and Land Use Controls §1.03 (Eric Damian Kelly ed., Matthew Bender & Company, Inc. 2015) (1988).

[71] *See* Shelley Ross Saxer, *When Local Government Misbehaves*, 2016 Utah L. Rev. 105, 110-113.

The City of Burlington, Vermont, explains its affordable housing program as follows:

The program applies to all new market-rate developments of 5 or more homes and to any converted non-residential structures that result in at least 10 homes. The affordable housing set aside is 15 to 25% of the units, depending on the average price of the market-rate homes—with the higher percentage placed on the most expensive developments. The ordinance does not allow fee in-lieu payments or land donations, but will allow developers to provide the affordable housing off-site at 125% of the on-site obligation. The ordinance provides a range of incentives including fee waivers and a 15-25% density and lot coverage bonus. Affordable homes are targeted to households earning 75% or less area median income (AMI) and rented at 65% or less AMI. Developers can sell or rent the homes for more as long as the average of affordable homes sold or rented are at or below the target household income. Affordable homes are price controlled for 99 years.[72]

Communities may use **linkage fees** to meet neighborhood challenges of low-cost housing and job opportunities resulting from large-scale commercial development.

The City of Boston, Massachusetts, describes its linkage fee program as follows:

The Neighborhood Jobs Trust, along with Neighborhood Housing Trust, is supported by linkage fees from large-scale real estate development projects as a means of providing benefits to Boston residents who may be affected by development in their neighborhoods. Linkage fees are levied on non-residential developments, normally upon receipt of the building permit or prior to construction. The proceeds are used to fund the construction of affordable housing residential developments and to fund Job Training Programs. Confronted with the challenge of balancing large-scale commercial development with residential construction and an existing workforce in need of new job skills, the City of Boston established the Neighborhood Housing Trust (NHT) in 1986. As stated in its Declaration of Trust: "This Trust is established to promote the public health, safety, convenience and welfare by mitigating the extent to which Boston's low or moderate income households are unable to afford decent, safe and sanitary housing within the City of Boston."[73]

Municipalities inevitably face judicial challenges to their use of these various financing tools. Litigants challenge them as unreasonable or in excess of the police power; a regulatory taking under the Fifth Amendment; or an invalid tax if they do not confer some special benefit to the property assessed that is different from benefits enjoyed by all members of the community. These fees also face equal protection challenges if they

---

[72] *Inclusionary Zoning*, City of Burlington, Vermont, https://www.burlingtonvt.gov/CEDO/Inclusionary-Zoning (last visited Nov. 16, 2017).
[73] Michael Anderson, *Boston Linkage Fee for Large-Scale Developments Produces Jobs and Housing*, Center for Community Change (Fall 2014), http://housingtrustfundproject.org/boston-linkage-fee-for-large-scale-developments-produces-jobs-and-housing/.

discriminate against new residents and exclude them by raising the cost of housing. When challenged as a regulatory taking, exactions are subject to heightened scrutiny under the *Nollan/Dolan* test. However, the level of scrutiny applied to impact fees, special assessments, mandatory set-asides, and linkage fees is subject to ongoing debate.[74]

Two U.S. Supreme Court decisions provide the basis for the **Nollan/Dolan test for exactions** that subjects physical exactions to a heightened judicial review instead of the rational basis review standardly applied to land use regulations.[75] The *Nollan v. California Coastal Commission* case involved a beach house in Ventura whose owners needed permission from the California Coastal Commission (CCC) to renovate and enlarge their home. The CCC required that, in exchange for receiving the permit, the Nollans would grant an easement to the state allowing the public to use the dry sand portion of the beach in front of their home. The public trust doctrine allows the public to use the water and the shore up to the median high tide line, in other words, the wet sand portion of the beach. However, the dry sand portion of the beach is subject to private ownership and so the Nollans claimed that the condition of the permit was a taking of their property without just compensation. The Court decided that because the CCC could deny the permit outright due to the proposed development's adverse impacts, it could condition the grant of the permit on the home-owners' willingness to offset the impact with an exaction. Nevertheless, the Court required that there be some causal connection between the exaction demanded by the CCC for an easement and the harm caused to the public interest by the proposed renovation of the beach house. Finding no nexus between the two, the Court determined that the easement exaction was unconstitutional.[76]

The second Supreme Court case, *Dolan v. City of Tigard*, answered the remaining question as to the degree of causal connection (or essential nexus) between the exaction sought and the impact predicted. In *Dolan*, the landowner sought permission to expand her hardware store and parking lot. The City conditioned the permit approval on her agreement to dedicate a strip of land for use as a bike path to relieve traffic congestion and to dedicate a public greenway on the flood plain portion of her property to prevent flooding by keeping it as open space. The Court found that both of these requested exactions had a nexus to the project's potential impact, but it determined that the City must also show that the dedications were roughly proportional to the project's harm, which it failed to do. The resulting two-part test requires the court to employ heightened scrutiny to ensure that 1) exactions imposed by the government have an *essential nexus* to the adverse

[74] *See* Saxer, *supra* note 71, at 106.
[75] *See* Nollan v. Cal. Coastal Commn., 483 U.S. 825 (1987); *see also* Dolan v. City of Tigard, 512 U.S. 374 (1994).
[76] L AND U SE, *supra* note 7, at Chapter 4.

impacts caused by the proposed project, and 2) exactions be *roughly proportional* to the degree of the impact caused by the project.[77]

The Supreme Court in *Koontz v. St. Johns River Water Management District* later extended the *Nollan/Dolan* test to *proposed*, not just imposed, exactions and to demands for *monetary exactions* in lieu of physical property.[78] The *Koontz* case involved a landowner in Florida who wanted to build on a portion of his property designated as protected wetlands. To offset the environmental damage from this project, the landowner offered to dedicate a conservation easement over 75% of his remaining property. The water district rejected this offer and gave him the choice of either reducing the size of his development or paying to make improvements to wetlands owned by the water district that were located several miles away. The Court found that the proposed condition that Koontz pay money to mitigate wetlands on property located miles away was an exaction subject to the *Nollan/Dolan* test and reversed and remanded the decision for scrutiny under this heightened standard. While some believe that the *Nollan/Dolan* test, as extended by *Koontz*, applies to legislatively determined impact fees, others, including one of the authors, would evaluate impact fees, mandatory set-asides, and other legislatively determined fees under existing state standards, such as rational basis or the dual rational nexus test, rather than under *Nollan/Dolan* scrutiny.[79]

Questions

1. How would you describe the potential to impact economic systems' resilience through linkage fees, such as Boston's, or set-asides, such as Burlington's? What about food systems? Alternatively, what about water-based systems?

2. In Chapter 3 we described ecosystem services management (ESM). Is there an element of ESM in linkage fees or set-asides? If so, how would you describe it?

VI. GROWTH MANAGEMENT

Sprawl is the term used to "describe development that is an inefficient use of land (i.e., low density); constructed in a 'leap frog' manner in areas without existing infrastructure, often on prime farmland; auto-dependent

---

[77] *Id.*
[78] 133 S. Ct. 2586, 2599, 2602 (2013).
[79] *See* Saxer, *supra* note 71.

and consisting of isolated single-use neighborhoods requiring excessive transportation."[80] Sprawl is responsible for six major problems found in U.S. metropolitan areas:

1. deterioration of cities and nearby suburbs;
2. damage to environmentally sensitive land and degradation of water resources (quality and quantity);
3. global warming caused by GHG emissions from excessive vehicle travel and nonrenewable energy sources;
4. transportation congestion, infrastructure deficiencies, and fiscal difficulties in trying to provide for citizen services;
5. loss of agricultural and open space; and
6. lack of affordable housing.

In response to these challenges, many people are seeking to move to new, urban communities that are walkable. Drought in the Southwest has also slowed suburban sprawl in those regions impacted as state and local authorities demand more proof of sustainability from developers and the demand for suburban housing decreases with concerns about water, transportation, and energy costs.[81]

The four fundamental movements identified under the "umbrella of sustainability" to control sprawl are smart growth, new urbanism, renewable energy, and green development, which are discussed below.[82] The hope for proponents of these combined movements is that "America can become a better place to live, with clean air, walkable quality communities, and more vibrant cities and suburbs, replacing our deficient infrastructure, reducing our impact on global warming, and creating millions of jobs through new industries for renewable energy and a sustainable environment."[83]

A. Smart Growth

The main idea behind this movement is to channel development to areas that have existing infrastructure, such as urban and older suburbs, in order to reduce land consumption for new infrastructure and preserve green space, wetlands, and agricultural land. The goal of smart growth is to allow development for purposes of jobs and tax revenues while reducing the harmful externalities of this growth such as environmental damage,

---

[80] Robert H. Freilich et al., From Sprawl to Sustainability 173, 179 (ABA Publishing 2d ed. 2010) (quoting *In re* Petition of Dolington Land Grp., 839 A.2d 1021 (Pa. 2003)).
[81] *Id.* at 179-182.
[82] Robert H. Freilich & Neil M. Popowitz, *The Umbrella of Sustainability: Smart Growth, New Urbanism, Renewable Energy and Green Development in the 21st Century*, 42 Urb. Law. 1, 4 (2010).
[83] Freilich et al., *supra* note 80, at 182-183.

local tax increases, and traffic congestion.[84] Suburban neighborhoods are patterned after denser urban communities and developers are encouraged to revitalize and infill existing urban areas. However, the smart growth movement, by promoting redevelopment and increased density in existing cities, may also increase the risk from disasters as "many of our existing cities are located in risky locations, such as in low-lying coastal areas, along major earthquake faults, and along major rivers."[85] Proper planning supported by detailed studies is the most effective approach to building a growth management system that will survive a legal challenge.[86]

Growth control techniques may include interim development controls, moratoria, timing and phasing regulations to tie development approvals to public facility capacity, quotas and population caps, and tiered growth at the city, county, regional, state, and federal levels. Statewide programs may also provide for sustainable planning and development by mandating plans for open space; food supply; environmentally sensitive lands; infrastructure for utilities, roads, and capital facilities; and transportation by public transit and rail.[87]

Interim development controls are regulations that may prohibit local government from issuing development permits in a certain region that is under study or review for land use and planning concerns. These interim controls have been used to limit development and maintain the status quo until the local government has had a chance to assess public safety, health, and welfare concerns such as reviewing planning needs, amending or updating zoning regulations, determining flood risk, assessing soil and hillside stability, or preventing environmental damage in sensitive areas. The duration of these controls is a critical factor in determining whether the interim measure is reasonable. Courts will generally decide reasonableness on a case-by-case basis. Landowners may be entitled to notice and a hearing before local government enacts interim controls, but some jurisdictions treat these regulations as emergency zoning measures to preserve the status quo without a hearing. Courts are more likely to strike down interim development controls as bad faith action when officials unfairly direct them at a specific project.[88]

Local authorities use **moratoria** to protect the environment and the public health, safety, and welfare when inadequate or failing infrastructures such as sewer or water treatment facilities require corrective action. The general police power authorizes moratoria whereas the zoning enabling authority supports interim development controls so long as

---

[84] LAND USE, *supra* note 7, at Chapter 7.
[85] Lisa Grow Sun, *Smart Growth in Dumb Places: Sustainability, Disaster, and the Future of the American City*, 2011 B.Y.U. L. REV. 2157, 2163-2166.
[86] Fred P. Bosselman, David L. Callies & John Banta, COUNCIL ON ENVTL. QUALITY, THE TAKING ISSUE: AN ANALYSIS OF THE CONSTITUTIONAL LIMITS OF LAND USE CONTROL 290 (1973).
[87] LAND USE, *supra* note 7, at Chapter 7.
[88] *Id.*

they do not prevent the vesting of development rights. Similar to interim development controls, moratoria must be reasonable and in good faith as judged by whether they are temporary, necessary, and directed to community needs rather than individual landowners. Cities or counties that fail to address the adequacy of their infrastructure over time may not be able to deny a landowner's request for reasonable use of her land. Public utilities may also act as growth management when they deny service to new development. However, they must justify their refusal to serve new users with a utility-related reason such as a water shortage or financial crisis.[89]

In 1972, the seminal case of *Golden v. Planning Board of the Town of Ramapo*[90] upheld **timing and phasing controls** adopted by the Town of Ramapo, New York as statutorily and constitutionally valid. These regulations comprehensively linked local capital improvements with local planning and regulation "by coordinating the timing and phasing of development with the provisions of public facilities." The influential Ramapo Plan encouraged other jurisdictions throughout the United States to incorporate adequate public facilities requirements and infrastructure planning in growth management plans. Florida was the first state to require that "public facilities and services needed to support development shall be concurrent with the impacts of such development" and every "city and county [in Florida] has adopted a local comprehensive plan that incorporates the fundamental principles of the Ramapo Plan." The level of service (LOS) standards have also been used to tie development approvals to public facility capacity by taking into account existing demand and the anticipated population growth from the proposed development.[91]

Quotas and population caps limit the number of building permits issued based on an annual quota system with a formula to test and score the development applications. Such quota systems must be justified by solid scientific and statistical data supporting the rate of development and the validity of limiting permits in light of the burden imposed on the infrastructure. The Rate of Growth Ordinances (ROGOs) using a set percentage, such as 3%, have been upheld as related to a city's welfare in slowing growth until a city is equipped to sustain a higher rate of growth. Convincing evidence must support population caps on the absolute number of residents by a showing that the public facilities and services are not capable of supporting some growth.[92]

Tiered growth in urban areas involves planning for "transportation networks, water availability, topography, and historic development of the region." The pattern for tiered growth is a three-tier concept beginning

---

[89] *Id.*
[90] 30 N.Y.2d 359, *appeal dismissed*, 409 U.S. 1003 (1972).
[91] LAND USE, *supra* note 7, at Chapter 7; *see also* John R. Nolon, *Golden and Its Emanations: The Surprising Origins of Smart Growth*, 35 URB. LAW. 15, 15-16 (2003).
[92] LAND USE, *supra* note 7, at Chapter 7.

with Tier I, the existing urban area. Tier II, referred to as the "urbanizing tier," deals with timed and sequenced development over a 20-year period and can be accomplished using a concentric growth pattern, linear transportation corridors pattern, or freestanding "new towns" and "major mixed use centers." Tier III is typically a rural and agricultural, non-development tier.[93]

The Tier II concentric pattern is at work in the Minneapolis and St. Paul, Minnesota region, Alameda County, California, and Ventura County, California. This pattern may also incorporate urban growth boundaries as the mechanism to encourage urban development and preserve rural-agricultural uses and the environment. Washington, D.C., Montgomery County, Maryland, and Central Puget Sound, Washington have used transportation corridors to provide the framework for regional growth management. Freestanding urban centers and "new towns" is a growth management program illustrated by Maryland's "Smart Growth" initiative that emphasizes transportation mobility and encourages redevelopment in major urban areas. San Diego, California chose to manage growth by adopting a combined transportation corridor and "new town" mixed-use approach to encourage building in older areas already supported by public services rather than in new growth areas requiring infrastructure financing.[94]

State solutions may include state planning and sustainability legislation using regional "tiered" growth strategies to control sprawl by combining growth management, environmental sustainability, and new urbanism. California adopted the State Planning Act (AB 857) in 2002 to establish state planning policies for growth and development based on sound infrastructure planning. The legislature then enacted the California Global Warming Solutions Act of 2006 (AB 32) to set limits on greenhouse gas (GHG) emissions from stationary sources. The Sustainable Communities and Climate Protection Act of 2008 (SB 375) amended transportation planning and environmental quality legislation to develop GHG emission targets for automobiles and trucks and to achieve sustainable smart growth land use planning and development at the state, regional, and local level. The state determined that it could not meet long-term GHG emission targets without improved land use and transportation policies. Many other states, including Hawaii, Oregon, Washington, and Florida, have enacted comprehensive smart growth legislation using urban growth boundaries, tiered development, regional planning, transportation needs, concurrency of public facilities and services, and environmental protection.[95]

---

[93] *Id.*
[94] *Id.*
[95] *Id.*

In recent years, state and local governments have recognized the large impact land use can have on climate change (climate change is discussed in more detail in Chapter 10). The following examples illustrate two ways in which local governments are seeking to address climate change through land use laws: 1) general planning, and 2) specific zoning and building code regulations.

MULTNOMAH COUNTY CLIMATE ACTION PLAN

On October 14th, 2010, the Multnomah County Board of Commissioners adopted an ordinance formally establishing the Advisory Committee on Sustainability & Innovation [ACSI]. Appointed members have expertise in a range of sustainability-related issues facing the community. Members of the ACSI will provide recommendations on implementing [the county's] Climate Action Plan [which attempts to address climate change by aspiring to the following objectives]:

1) Reducing the total energy of building
2) Achieving zero carbon emissions in new buildings and homes
3) Supplying more energy used in buildings from renewable resources, with more produced on-site renewable sources, such as solar
4) Increasing access to transit, sidewalks, bike lanes and other transportation options
5) Reducing pollution exposure
6) Improving access to parks and other natural resources
7) Reducing burdens of housing and energy costs[96]

PLAN NYC—LL87: ENERGY AUDITS & RETRO-COMMISSIONING

Local Law 87 (LL87) mandates that buildings over 50,000 gross square feet undergo periodic energy audit and retro-commissioning measures, as part of the Greener, Greater Buildings Plan (GGBP). The intent of this law is to inform building owners of their energy consumption through energy audits, which are surveys and analyses of energy use, and retro-commissioning, the process of ensuring correct equipment installation and performance.

In addition to benchmarking annual energy and water consumption, energy audits and retro-commissioning will give building owners a much more robust understanding of their buildings' performance, eventually shifting the market towards increasingly efficient, high-performing buildings.

In summary, LL87's energy audit and retro-commissioning process requires the following:

1) Determine if a building needs to comply, and what year it is due.
2) Conduct an energy audit and retro-commissioning of base building systems and complete an Energy Efficiency Report (EER) electronically.
3) Submit the EER once every ten years to the City by December 31.[97]

---

[96] *Advisory Committee on Sustainability & Innovation*, MULTNOMAH COUNTY, OR., https://multco.us/sustainability/advisory-committee-sustainability-innovation (last visited Nov. 16, 2017).
[97] *LL87: Energy Audits & Retro-Commissioning*, NYC MAYOR'S OFFICE OF SUSTAINABILITY, http://www.nyc.gov/html/gbee/html/plan/ll87.shtml (last visited Nov. 16, 2017).

Questions

1. Growth control techniques, especially moratoria, are often controversial. How would you describe the effects a moratorium can have on growth? How do those effects impact the community's resilience, and to which disturbances?

2. Is a moratorium always sustainable or unsustainable?

3. What characteristics of a moratorium would tend to make a community more or less sustainable or less resilient? Which systems might be impacted and how?

B. New Urbanism

New urbanism was a movement begun mostly by architects and planners in response to a perceived decline in quality of life and loss of community. Euclidean zoning aimed at segregating residential development is one of the reasons behind the development of sprawl and the resulting unsustainable standards of living and quality of life. Advocates for new urbanism believed that it could restore declines in the quality of life and loss of community by looking to pre-World War II models of development.[98]

There are three primary patterns of development in new urbanism: 1) traditional neighborhood development (TND); 2) transit-oriented development (TOD); and 3) freestanding mixed-use centers. TND is the primary goal of new urbanism based on mixed-use development, diverse land uses, and walkable communities similar to European cities. The TOD pattern of new urbanism is to build mixed-use centers at station stops along transportation corridors.[99]

Smart growth and new urbanism, working together with green development and renewable energy can eliminate sprawl by building more compact, mixed-use, walkable, traditional communities and locating such communities within and adjacent to existing neighborhoods and cities to limit the length and number of vehicle trips and reduce greenhouse gas emissions and global warming. Once smart growth principles are in place, new urbanism determines the use, type, design, and community character of development that will occur within the different smart growth priority development areas.[100]

---

[98] Land Use, *supra* note 7, at Chapter 2.
[99] *Id.*
[100] *Id.*

Cities throughout the United States have included in their land use regulations provisions to promote this type of development. Generally, these types of regulations have been of two types: 1) some municipalities have amended existing regulations or enacted new ordinances to incorporate new urbanist principles; and 2) some have enacted special districts for this purpose. Even if the comprehensive plan requires the implementation of new urbanist principles, some would choose to implement the principles on the ground, making new urbanism the "default setting" for all the development in that district while others may advocate allowing applicants to propose landing a flexible floating or planned district zone.[101]

The characteristics of new urbanism that are reflected in these regulatory approaches include vertical and horizontal mixed use; a mix of housing types; compact design; walkability; and design standards for open space, streets, and form-based development. Form-based codes work in conjunction with new urbanism to elevate the importance of the physical form of development over the conventional land development regulations monitoring individual land uses. A new urbanist architectural firm developed the SmartCode as a comprehensive model form-based code based on a physical organizing system of high to low density from the urban core to the rural areas. [102]

Question

1. What is it about pre-World War II models of development that could help a community become more resilient to disturbances related to climate change?

C. Renewable Energy

We explore issues relevant to renewable energy and R&S in Chapter 6. Here, we explore more narrow land use issues that arise when considering renewable energies. Using renewable forms of energy such as solar, wind, geothermal, nuclear, hydroelectric, and biofuels will help improve the quality of life in communities in conjunction with smart growth, new urbanism, and green building by reducing GHG emissions and addressing climate change. Biofuels are a renewable energy source that can help diversify transportation fuels in the United States and often do not have

---

[101] *Id.*
[102] *Id.*; Robert H. Freilich & S. Mark White, 21st CENTURY LAND DEVELOPMENT CODE §2.6, 50 (Am. Planning Assn. 2008); Freilich et al., *supra* note 80, at 175-186.

the same challenges faced by the siting of wind and solar farms. Federal and some state goals (particularly those developed in agricultural states) have targeted biofuel use as a preferred energy security strategy, although the production of ethanol as the primary biofuel produced has generated concerns about food security and water use. Most biofuel refineries are located in the Midwest, so states such as California will demand more bio-refineries and their products as the nation moves away from fossil fuel energy through market demand or climate change legislation.[103]

The increasing availability and affordability of hybrid or completely electric cars will significantly affect traffic congestion, air pollution, and energy consumption in the future. Entrepreneur Elon Musk founded Tesla Motors in 2003 with the vision to commercialize electric vehicles in competition with GM, BMW, Ford, and Mercedes. Led by Musk, the company produced a high-priced sports car in 2007, a medium-priced sedan in 2012, and an SUV in 2015. By 2020, Tesla expects to be at full capacity to produce 500,000 electric vehicles every year with a dramatically reduced cost.[104]

Massachusetts Institute of Technology's (MIT's) Mobility-On-Demand project is developing and testing concepts such as the CityCar to replace traditional cars in dense urban neighborhoods. The CityCar is a foldable, electric two-passenger vehicle weighing less than 1,000 pounds that achieves 150-200 miles per gallon. Entrepreneur Mark Frohnmayer founded Arcimoto in 2007 to produce an electric car. In 2016, the company announced a three-wheeled prototype that has two seats, two electric motors weighing 1,000 pounds, and a top speed of 85 mph.[105] Viable electric vehicles are needed, but long-term sustainability requires a combination of smart growth, new urbanism, and more efficient public transportation systems, so that we no longer base sustainable personal mobility on the automobile.[106]

Solar energy has been encouraged at the federal, state, and local levels. States have enacted solar easement statutes to protect solar energy systems against private nuisance litigation and limit local government authority to exclude them. Some states have similar statutes to override private restrictions and covenants such as homeowner association rules. For example, Florida has a statute that provides:

> *A deed restriction, covenant, declaration, or similar binding agreement may not prohibit or have the effect of prohibiting solar collectors, clotheslines, or*

---

[103] Freilich & Popowitz, *supra* note 82, at 27-29.

[104] Ryan Bellinson, *Tesla's EV as Revolution in Sustainable Transportation?*, THE PROTOCITY (June 20, 2016), http://theprotocity.com/teslas-ev-revolution-sustainable-transportation/.

[105] *Electric Car Innovations Drive Sustainable Transportation Forward*, THE GUARDIAN, http://www.theguardian.com/sustainable-connections/ng-interactive/2016/may/17/electric-car-innovations-sustainable-transportation-emissions-vehicle (last visited Nov. 16, 2017).

[106] Bellinson, *supra* note 104.

other energy devices based on renewable resources from being installed on buildings erected on the lots or parcels covered by the deed restriction, covenant, declaration, or binding agreement. Fla. Stat. §163.04(2).[107]

In addition to ensuring access to renewable energy, all levels of government have been involved in financing and funding efforts to encourage green development and the use of solar and wind energy. In 2016, Congress passed the Omnibus Budget Bill to reauthorize investment tax credits for renewable solar and wind energy.[108] States, cities, and counties, in response to the high initial cost to retrofit buildings and install solar rooftop systems, have offered Property Assessed Clean Energy (PACE) Bonds. The proceeds from these bonds are used for loans to private commercial and residential property owners to finance the renewable energy retrofit and repay as a tax assessment over five, ten, or twenty years. Failure to repay the PACE loan may result in a tax foreclosure and because PACE uses local government assessments or taxes, these obligations have lien priority over other creditors. This lien priority caused the Federal Housing Finance Administration (FHFA) to stop making loans on residential properties with PACE assessments from 2009 until 2015. The problem was resolved by an agreement among the FHA, banks, and municipalities to make PACE loans subordinate to a first lien mortgage and allow borrowers with FHA loans to refinance or sell their properties without having to pay off the PACE loan.[109]

California has used **tax incentives and renewable energy credits (RECs)** to fund solar technologies for nonresidential and existing residential customers and to target the new residential construction mar-

ket. RECs represent the environmental benefits of solar rooftop power and owners of solar facilities can sell them to gain additional savings after using PACE to finance the initial installation. In addition to the federal tax incentives, which allow commercial building owners and residential property builders to receive tax credits or deductions for

---

[107] Land Use, *supra* note 7, at Chapter 8.
[108] *Id.*
[109] *Id.*

energy efficiency, California offers two tax incentives to encourage green building. The first incentive allows the property owner to exclude the cash value of a solar energy system from property taxes, even though it increases the appraised value of the property. Residential property owners may also "deduct interest paid on loans taken out with investor-owned utilities to purchase energy-efficient systems or products." California promotes small-scale renewable energy generation by allowing small generators to return surplus energy back to the grid and receive payment for this excess from the utility, thus reducing their electric bill. These net metering rules are available to customers generating up to one megawatt from solar or wind energy systems, but several programs specifically promote solar energy development.[110]

> ### FEDERAL AND STATE TAX INCENTIVES
>
> Robinson & Cole LLP has produced a comprehensive list of federal and state tax incentives promoting renewable energy and energy efficiency. The report separates the information by jurisdiction and includes the basic regulatory requirements for tax programs "which provide[] financial incentives for clean technology development through renewable energy and energy efficiency projects." *See* Jerome Garciano, *Green Tax Incentive Compendium* (July 1, 2017), http://www.rc.com/upload/RC-Garciano-Green-Tax-Incentive-Compendium-July-2017.pdf.

Wind energy in the western United States is viable in the deserts, as are solar facilities, but the electrical energy generated needs to be transmitted across the Rocky and Sierra Mountains to supply the urban areas along the Pacific Coast. The lack of federal government involvement, common law property rules, conflicting state and local regulations, and the environmental impacts to wildlife and plant habitats in remote areas impede the interstate electric transmission grid development that is required to convey renewable energy production. These issues pit those advocating for renewable energy to solve global warming against those who wish to preserve environmentally sensitive areas and protected wildlife and flora.[111]

The use of wind power in the United States has increased significantly since the 1990s. In 2012, 43% of all new capacity for electricity generation came from wind energy, which was greater than any other energy source. Wind power increases sustainability, reduces carbon emissions, and contributes to reducing the risks of climate change.

---

[110] *Id.*

[111] Hannah Wiseman, *Expanding Regional Renewable Governance*, 35 HARV. ENVTL. L. REV. 477 (2011); *see also* Alexa Burt Engelman, *Against the Wind: Conflict Over Wind Energy Siting*, 41 ELR 10549 (2011).

Wind power has increased 700 percent since 2002 and now represents more than 4 percent of the nation's total electrical output. It is expected to grow to 6 percent by 2020, and will probably reach 25 percent by 2020 to 2025. The cost of wind, wave and hydroelectric power is less than seven cents per kilowatt hour (kwh) and by 2020 will drop to four cents per kwh. Most of this growth surge comes from the federal Production Tax Credit and the Energy Investment Tax Credit.[112]

Nuclear power provides a relatively stable and reliable source of energy that emits only 1.6% of the GHGs of a similarly sized coal facility. It generates power at the lowest cost and is economically justifiable. However, state and local government regulations have presented major impediments to using advanced nuclear energy because of fears generated by the Three Mile Island accident and concerns about high-level waste disposal. Local land use approvals are valid regulatory controls over the location and siting of nuclear plants.[113]

Coal is a major fossil fuel that, when burned, produces approximately 25% of the world's electricity. In the United States, it is the second largest contributor to global warming based on carbon dioxide emissions. Emissions from coal generators contain pollutants regulated under the Clean Air Act, including sulfur oxides, nitrogen oxides, carbon oxides, and particulate matter. The EPA issued a final rule in 2015 to implement President Obama's Climate Action Plan by reducing GHG emissions from existing coal power plants. The rule also reduced GHG emissions from new or modified coal power plants in order to reduce state regional air pollution plans and achieve a 32% CO_2 emission reduction from 2005 emission levels by 2030 (climate change and the Clean Power Plan are discussed in more detail in Chapter 10). The coal industry is developing "clean coal" technologies that will allow for carbon capture and sequestration to remove pollutants from emissions and store them underground.[114] However, in 2017 the Whitehouse website documents the administration's position that "President Trump is committed to eliminating harmful and unnecessary policies such as the Climate Action Plan and the Waters of the U.S. rule."[115] Analysts at the Bonn climate talks in mid-2017 released a report finding that "the president's rollback of current climate regulations,

---

[112] LAND USE, *supra* note 7, at Chapter 8; *see also* Randy T. Simmons, Ryan M. Yonk & Megan E. Hansen, THE TRUE COST OF ENERGY: WIND POWER, INSTITUTE OF POLITICAL ECONOMY (2015), https://www.strata.org/wp-content/uploads/2015/07/Full-Report-True-Cost-of-Wind1.pdf.
[113] LAND USE, *supra* note 7, at Chapter 8.
[114] *See* Sean O'Hara, *The Importance of the United States Staying the Course While Implementing Environmental Policy in Accordance with the American Recovery and Reinvestment Act of 2009*, 17 U. BALT. J. ENVTL. L. 85, 88 (2009). *But see In Clean Coal We Trust . . . or Do We?*, PARIS TECH REVIEW (Oct. 15, 2014) (while CCS may be feasible, broader circumstantial considerations render resort to this technology infeasible); Christine Ehlig-Economides & Michael J. Economides, *Sequestering Carbon Dioxide in a Closed Underground Volume*, J. OF PETROLEUM SCI. & ENGINEERING 70, 130 (2010).
[115] The Whitehouse, *An America First Energy Plan*, https://www.whitehouse.gov/america-first-energy (last visited Nov. 17, 2017).

if successful, could cause the U.S. to release 0.4 gigatonne more carbon dioxide in annual emissions in the year 2030 than if those policies remained. That gap gets much larger when the report authors accounted for Trump's decision to dump the Climate Action Plan, which was created by the Obama administration but has not yet been fully implemented."[116]

D. Green Development

Sustainable or "green" development encompasses more than green building practices and includes development mechanisms such as transit-oriented development (TOD), regional energy systems, and environmental justice. Subsequent to the 1987 Brundtland Report (discussed in Chapter 1, Section II.B.1), nations have adopted various approaches to green or sustainable development. China, for example, has instituted a sustainable development framework that it refers to as "Ecological civilization," which is defined as "a resource efficient and environmental-friendly society, based on the carrying capacity of the environment, observing the law of nature and aimed at realizing sustainable development."[117] This concept was in response to the ecological and environmental challenges China has faced by following a traditional development path.[118] Developed countries, led by Europe, have promised to support poor, undeveloped countries in dealing with "the twin threats of climate change and poverty" by establishing a Green Climate Fund with the U.N.'s legal and political backing. This fund is intended to "support clean energy, low-carbon cities, low-emission agriculture, forestry and climate adaptation."[119]

While global and national attention to sustainable development is critical, state and local government may more effectively achieve these goals through incentives and neighborhood empowerment.[120] For example, the Tennessee Department of Environment and Conservation, in partnership with the Tennessee Stormwater Association, the Tennessee Valley Authority, and the Tennessee Department of Transportation, has

---

[116] Annie Sneed, Scientific American, *Analysis: How Much Carbon Will Trump's Climate Policies Add to the Atmosphere?*, Jun. 1, 2017, https://www.pbs.org/newshour/science/analysis-much-carbon-will-trumps-climate-policies-add-atmosphere (last visited Nov. 17, 2017).

[117] *China Investing Over U.S. $2 Billion in Its Transition to IGE*, PARTNERSHIP FOR ACTION ON GREEN ECONOMY, http://www.un-page.org/china-investing-over-us2-billion-its-transition-ige (Feb. 2016) (quoting "Hu Jintao (2012) [r]eport of the 18th National Congress of the Communist Party of China").

[118] *Multiple Pathways to Sustainable Development: Initial Findings from the Global South*, UNITED NATIONS SUSTAINABLE DEVELOPMENT (2015), https://sustainabledevelopment.un.org/index.php?page = view&type = 400&nr = 1986&menu = 35.

[119] Marc Gunther, *What Happened to the U.N.'s $100 Million Green Development Fund?*, GREEN BIZ (May 10, 2016), https://www.greenbiz.com/article/what-happened-uns-100-million-green-development-fund.

[120] Kenneth A. Stahl, *Local Home Rule in the Time of Globalization*, 2016 B.Y.U. L. REV. 177, 179; Edna Sussman, *Reshaping Municipal and County Laws to Foster Green Building, Energy Efficiency, and Renewable Energy*, 16 N.Y.U. ENVTL. L.J. 1, 3-4 (2008).

established a green development grant program "to help local governments fund green infrastructure and low-impact development projects," such as rain gardens, re-using stormwater runoff on site, green roofs, and education efforts.[121] At the local level, the City of Bellevue, Washington defines green development as "design, construction and operation practices that significantly reduce resource consumption and environmental impacts through site planning; energy efficiency; water conservation; waste reduction; pollution prevention; enhanced indoor environmental quality; and 'green' materials."[122] Furthermore, in Buffalo, New York, the People United for Sustainable Housing (PUSH) program has instituted a green development zone on the west side of the city to "bring neighborhood resources under community control and stewardship. . . . [including] land, homes, environmental assets, job opportunities, organizations, and carefully worked-out plans for the future."[123]

WATER AND LAND USE

Green development requires attention to the varying and complex aspects of local water use. As discussed in Chapter 3, resilience and sustainability can play critical roles in water resource management. For example, the following permit process addresses the diverse challenges facing local governments concerning water.

WINNEBAGO COUNTY—MS4 (MUNICIPAL SEPARATE STORM SEWER SYSTEM) PERMIT:

In 2007, the [Wisconsin Department of Natural Resources] issued a stormwater management permit to Winnebago County to monitor and improve stormwater quality running off county properties. The MS4 Permit requires Winnebago County to comply with the following . . . minimum steps:

a. Public Education & Outreach
b. Illicit Discharge Detection & Elimination
c. Post-Construction Site Stormwater Management
d. Public Involvement & Participation
e. Construction Site Pollution Control
f. Pollution Prevention[124]

---

[121] *Green Development Grants*, TENNESSEE DEP'T ENV'T & CONSERVATION, https://www.tn.gov/environment/article/grants-green-development-grants (last visited Nov. 16, 2017).
[122] *What Is Green and Sustainable Development?*, CITY OF BELLEVUE, WA, https://web.archive.org/web/20161130215610/http://www.ci.bellevue.wa.us/green-development-explained.htm (last visited Nov. 16, 2017).
[123] *Principles of the GDZ*, THE GREEN DEVELOPMENT ZONE, http://greendevelopmentzone.org/principles/ (last visited Nov. 16, 2017).
[124] *Stormwater Management*, LAND AND WATER CONSERVATION DEP'T, https://web.archive.org/web/20160409042139/https://www.co.winnebago.wi.us/lwcd/news/2011/1/11/stormwater-management (last visited Nov. 16, 2017).

Green buildings are a major component of sustainable development as traditional buildings use large amounts of energy, water, and other resources that contribute to global warming. Buildings that are shaded or have green roofs will use less energy for heating and cooling. In addition, local green infrastructure that incorporates more trees,

One Central Park, Sydney, Australia

parks, and less impermeable surfaces will help reduce urban temperatures. Bike paths and buildings with bike racks, as well as pedestrian pathways connected to transit services will help reduce the need for automobiles and parking requirements.[125] Green buildings are designed to use energy, water, and materials more efficiently and reduce the impact on the environment and human health by directing the activities of siting, building, operating, and maintaining these structures.[126]

Multiple approaches exist to encourage green building including the Leadership in Energy and Environmental Design (LEED) rating system, monetary and non-monetary incentives, and mandatory state or local requirements for green building standards, energy, and building codes, and specialized design elements. The LEED system rates buildings according to established sustainability standards and then certifies them as Certified, Silver, Gold, or Platinum. Many municipalities have committed to LEED certification for new or renovated public buildings and some have required private sector development to meet these standards for larger projects. Several communities are also requiring new residential construction to meet the Environmental Protection Agency's Energy Star Homes program that guides the construction of more energy-efficient houses.[127]

Energy and building codes are effective mechanisms to achieve green building by adopting and continually upgrading standards as new technologies emerge. State and local governments share the responsibility for developing and enforcing energy codes as specified under federal legislation and encouraged by the U.S. Department of Energy. States may enact

---

[125] Nolon & Salkin, *supra* note 22, at 279-280.
[126] Sussman, *supra* note 120, at 3-4.
[127] *Id.* at 8-14.

more stringent energy codes and in some jurisdictions, local governments may enhance local codes by adopting the International Building Code or developing their own supplemental code provisions. Municipalities that enact stringent codes may find that these requirements deter some developers and compel them to take their projects to less restrictive communities.[128]

Monetary incentives provided by federal tax law and state and local governments have been helpful in pushing developers to realize that green building not only helps the environment but may also yield financial benefits over time.[129]

> *While green building may have once been more expensive than traditional building techniques, this is no longer necessarily true. On the contrary, "[t]he financial payoff from green building will be multifaceted, comprising direct savings from reduced energy use, higher value in the real estate market (including resale value), increased employee retention and productivity, and potential carbon credits from reduced CO2 emissions." To realize these benefits, however, owners and developers must retain professionals who understand the many evolving options available for green building projects and can apply the appropriate choices to the project at hand.*[130]

Studies continue to show that green building does not cost substantially more than traditional building design and construction, but the costs are perceived to be higher and there is a disconnect between who pays for these additional costs and who benefits.[131]

The future of green development is bright because "[t]he overall costs of green development will come down as the supply of sustainable products and building materials increases and real estate service professionals — architects and designers, contractors, developers, and so on — become more familiar with green products, design, and construction practices." Mandated government compliance with green building standards, along with market demand for sustainable office and residential space and additional financial incentives, will coalesce to encourage sustainable development. Local, regional, and statewide efforts must strategically address the public infrastructure, services, utilities, and other resources required to support smart and sustainable growth.[132]

---

[128] *Id.* at 13-15.
[129] Jason R. Busch, Rosemary A. Colliver & Janet F. Jacobs, *Tax and Financial Incentives for Green Building*, 10 Los Angeles Law, 15 (2008).
[130] *Id.*
[131] Freilich et al., *supra* note 80, at 208-210.
[132] *Id.* at 210-211.

Sustainable development must also address the **sea level rise** resulting from climate change as it will likely severely impact cities, states, and even entire countries, such as the Maldives and the Marshall Islands. The Intergovernmental Panel on Climate Change has predicted that sea levels could rise more than three feet by century end, the U.S. Army Corps of Engineers predicts a five-foot rise, and the National Oceanic and Atmospheric Administration predicts up to a six and a half foot rise. Some estimate that a hundred million people in the world live within three feet of the mean high tide line and a hundred million more live within six feet of the line. Many of the world's largest cities are located along a coast and in the United States, many places now flood during high tides on both the East and Gulf coasts. Sea level rise will contribute to increasing flood risks and coastal erosion while development in floodplains will result in more devastating flood damage.[133]

Local governments along coastlines will need to prepare for long-term adaptation measures such as sea walls and natural buffers, but must also realize that, at some point, they must develop strategies for managed retreat. Most importantly, municipalities faced with coastal flooding must curb development in flood-prone areas and regulate the type of buildings allowed in case they require relocation.[134]

The [real] problem [facing government today] is the legacy of past local, state and federal flood control strategies. The country's investment in levees, dams and floodways have prevented damage, but they also have had a perverse effect: structural flood plain protection encourages more settlement, which in turn in-

creases the number of people and property impacted when a flood occurs. The result is a classic moral hazard problem. A moral hazard is a socially undesirable, often inefficient, behavior encouraged by the expectation that it will not be punished and often will be rewarded.

The moral hazard problem is especially acute in flood prone areas where

New Jersey after Hurricane Sandy

---

[133] Elizabeth Kolbert, *The Siege of Miami: As Temperatures Climb, So, Too, Will Sea Levels*, The New Yorker (Dec. 21 & 28, 2015), https://www.newyorker.com/magazine/2015/12/21/the-siege-of-miami.
[134] *Id.*

the existence of levees often leads to an illusionary sense of safety for flood plain residents. The illusion is a dangerous one, because our infrastructure is old and increasingly unsafe. . . . Post-flood compensation available through flood insurance and ad hoc disaster payments from the federal government feed the illusion and subsidize the cost of moral hazard behavior. The rub is that "since lump-sum government-relief payments usually do not relate to risk, no incentives are provided to potential victims to take effective preventative measures."[135]

Efforts by state and local governments to either retreat or protect threatened properties may require condemnation of property to benefit the property. The level of just compensation required under the Fifth Amendment may need to take into account the benefits provided as well as the property condemned. Landowners have challenged floodplain regulations as regulatory takings, but few state and federal decisions have invalidated these regulations.[136] Finally, some have postulated that a government that fails to act to protect private property from sea-level rise may violate the Takings Clause.[137]

Disaster response and recovery at the local level will be more effective if federal and state governments "have a pre-disaster 'picture' of local government capacity."[138] Scholars have proposed that a City Resilience Index could provide this insight by measuring multiple components relating to a local government's relative strengths and weaknesses in its ability to respond to ongoing challenges to viability. These components include essential systems and resources that are critical to daily life such as housing, healthcare, food, transportation, historical resources, and the local business economy as well as "cable television, fire, police, parks & recreation, planning & development, solid waste, wastewater, and water."[139] This City Resilience Index would function as "a policy tool that identifies components critical to a city's long-term resilience and establishes a framework to measure these components."[140]

---

[135] Debbie M. Chizewer & A. Dan Tarlock, *New Challenges for Urban Areas Facing Flood Risks*, 40 Fordham Urb. L.J. 1739, 1744-1746 (2013).

[136] Land Use, *supra* note 7, at Chapter 8.

[137] Christopher Serkin, *Passive Takings: The State's Affirmative Duty to Protect Property*, 113 Mich. L. Rev. 345, 345 (2014).

[138] John Travis Marshall & Ryan Max Rowberry, *Urban Wreckage and Resiliency: Articulating a Practical Framework for Preserving, Reconstructing, and Building Cities*, 50 Idaho L. Rev. 49, 57 (2014).

[139] *Id.* at 58.

[140] *Id.* at 53.

Questions

1. The prior four subsections describe new or advanced land use techniques to address issues that arise with traditional zoning, including sprawl. Select one of the techniques (for example, new urbanism). What impact might that technique have on the resilience of cities to the impacts of climate change?

2. How do any of the techniques affect the sustainability of the energy system? Water-based systems? Transportation systems?

3. Do any of the techniques rely on any of the Strategies for Implementation discussed thus far (Ecosystem Services Management, Collective Action Challenges, or Precautionary Principle)?

VII. URBAN REDEVELOPMENT

State and local governments control land development through subdivision regulation and growth management as communities expand beyond the urban core. However, government also regulates the redevelopment of the urban core as communities seek to revitalize their neighborhoods through rehabilitation, historic preservation, new urbanism, transit-oriented development, mixed use, infill, gentrification, and slum clearance. This revitalization may require consolidation of land through condemnation, incentives for private development such as tax increment financing, tax abatement, and density bonuses to entice development that will provide community benefits such as access to transit, open spaces, affordable housing, cultural facilities, and economic prosperity.[141]

A. Financing Redevelopment

Eminent domain is the major mechanism used by the government to eliminate blight and consolidate land holdings to make revitalization of the urban core viable for the developers and beneficial to the public good. *Berman v. Parker* was the landmark U.S. Supreme Court decision from 1954 that upheld the use of eminent domain for redevelopment.[142] *Berman* involved an urban renewal program to redevelop blighted property in

---

[141] LAND USE, *supra* note 7, at Chapter 6.
[142] 348 U.S. 26 (1954).

the District of Columbia. Michigan used eminent domain to allow for expansion of a General Motors (GM) facility that forced the relocation of 3,500 people in Detroit. In the 1981 Michigan Supreme Court decision in *Poletown Neighborhood Council v. City of Detroit*, the court found that, even though the city would convey the land it acquired through eminent domain to GM for an assembly plant, the project was constitutionally and statutorily valid as a "public purpose."[143] The Michigan Supreme Court later overruled *Poletown* in its 2004 decision in *County of Wayne v. Hathcock*,[144] but in 2005, the U.S. Supreme Court in *Kelo v. City of New London* continued its broad view of public purpose to allow the use of eminent domain to eliminate urban blight and advance private economic development and city revenues.[145]

Public reaction to the *Kelo* decision was fierce, and many states quickly enacted or amended redevelopment statutes. States required a finding of blight and defined or redefined blight so that local or state government could only use eminent domain for redevelopment to serve a valid primary public purpose.[146] Following the *Kelo* decision and the revision of many state statutes in response, courts have evaluated challenges to condemnation actions and some have upheld these actions for redevelopment so long as the purported economic benefits are not the sole justification for the taking. Other courts have established factors, in addition to finding blight, to determine whether public benefits substantially predominate over private gain when government uses eminent domain to transfer property from one private owner to another.[147]

Tax abatement and tax increment financing (TIF) are tax techniques used to facilitate "public-private" partnerships. These techniques combine the government powers needed to undertake large-scale projects with the private capacity to implement and oversee significant urban development projects. By offering monetary incentives through reduced taxes and issuing bonds secured by a pledge of payments in lieu of taxes, a municipality can promote private redevelopment of deteriorating or blighted areas. Tax increment financing encourages redevelopment projects and uses the proposed increase of the real property value in the redevelopment area to generate incremental taxes from the increased property tax assessment. Government deposits these incremental taxes in a fund

---

[143] 410 Mich. 616 (1981).
[144] 471 Mich. 445 (2004).
[145] 545 U.S. 469 (2005).
[146] LAND USE, *supra* note 7, at Chapters 3, 6.
[147] *Id.* at Chapter 6.

and uses them to pay directly for the redevelopment or to retire the bonds initially issued.[148]

Tax increment financing legislation exists in 49 states and the District of Columbia. Local government uses TIF primarily for shopping centers, multi-unit housing, office blocks, large-scale entertainment, and big box retail companies.[149] While TIF can serve as an excellent approach to creating new urbanism areas and downtown development, cities can also use it to compete with each other for jobs and retail development. Some have criticized the redevelopment agencies that control these funds for failing to develop affordable housing and for holding large sums of unused tax increments to support other local services such as schools.[150] Governor Jerry Brown essentially eliminated California redevelopment agencies in 2011 when he signed legislation "intended to stabilize school funding by reducing or eliminating the diversion of property tax revenues from school districts to the state's community redevelopment agencies."[151]

Business Improvement Districts (BIDs) provide another financing technique to redevelop the urban core by combining mandatory taxation with private sector business knowledge. Instead of relying on city governments to supply services such as trash collection, street cleaning, lighting, and security, a BID uses privately funded professional management to provide services similar to a suburban shopping mall. The projected benefits of BIDs include an increase in pedestrian foot traffic, a rise in business profitability, and an upsurge in property values. Through BIDs and the work that they do, cities and business owners hope to make the "public square" attractive and the urban core more readily competitive with suburban shopping malls, office parks, and gated communities.[152]

Increasing urban sustainability requires efforts such as green roofs, green buildings, walkability, transit-oriented development, mixed use, renewable energy, and maximizing resources while minimizing waste. BIDs can help these efforts by controlling carved-out areas within the urban core through nonprofit organizations that operate similarly to homeowners' associations. "Property owners in a BID pay special taxes

[148] *Id; see also* Richard Briffault, *The Most Popular Tool: Tax Increment Financing and the Political Economy of Local Government*, 77 U. Chi. L. Rev. 65 (2010).
[149] Land Use, *supra* note 7, at Chapter 6.
[150] George Lefcoe, *Competing for the Next Hundred Million Americans: The Uses and Abuses of Tax Increment Financing*, 43 Urb. Law. 424, 424 (2011).
[151] Cal. Redevelopment Assn. v. Matosantos, 267 P.3d 580, 602 (Cal. 2011) (upholding legislation that granted state the power to eliminate redevelopment agencies in California).
[152] Wayne Batchis, *Business Improvement Districts and the Constitution: The Troubling Necessity of Privatized Government for Urban Revitalization*, 38 Hastings Const. L.Q. 91, 91-94 (2010).

or assessments, which, in turn, the BID uses to fund various initiatives, such as special beautification efforts or extra security, as determined by the BID's board of directors."[153] However, some have questioned whether the privatization of cities through BIDs will violate constitutional principles by turning what was previously a public space into a privately controlled urban environment with profit as the primary goal. Concerns about free speech and the interests of the nonconsuming public, as well as equal protection and the BID's potential to divert funds and services away from urban areas not serving business interests, make BIDs subject to criticism for blocking true public discourse and creating intracity inequality.[154]

Enterprise zones (EZs) encourage businesses to stay, expand, or locate in specific geographic areas that need revitalization by offering corporate income tax credits, property tax abatements, and other incentivizing tax exemptions or subsidies. The federal government and most states have established "enterprise" or "empowerment" zones over the past 30 years to attract new investment and create jobs. State programs will generally identify what areas qualify for EZ subsidies based on the state definition of blight or distress, unemployment or job loss rates, education levels, population decline, and vacancy rates of commercial and residential buildings.[155] The federal EZ system began in 1993 with Empowerment Zone (EZ), Enterprise Community (EC), and Renewal Community (RC) initiatives to reduce unemployment and increase economic growth in distressed communities through grants and federal tax incentives. Congress reenacted these programs at various points in time, however, as of now, the Enterprise Community and Renewal Community programs have expired, and the only remaining federal designations are for Empowerment Zones.[156]

These incentive programs have been popular over the last three decades, but there is disagreement as to whether they have been effective in attracting new investment and creating jobs.[157] Several studies found that "there was no significant difference in economic growth or job creation inside the enterprise zones from the surrounding area."[158] Often incentive

---

[153] Kim Slowey, *Business Improvement Districts — Ready Proving Ground for Sustainability Technology,* FORBES (June 27, 2016), https://www.forbes.com/sites/kimslowey/2016/06/27/business-improvement-districts-ready-proving-ground-for-sustainability-technology/#381b5b2536f8.

[154] Batchis, *supra* note 152, at 97-100.

[155] *Enterprise Zones,* GOOD JOBS FIRST (Sept. 14, 2017), http://www.goodjobsfirst.org/accountable-development/enterprise-zones.

[156] *Community Renewal Initiative,* HUD EXCHANGE, https://www.hudexchange.info/programs/community-renewal-initiative/ (last visited Nov. 16, 2017).

[157] Diane Lupke, *As the US and UK Re-Up For EZs, What Lessons from the Past Hold Promise for the Future?,* 24 J. MULTISTATE TAX'N 28 (2014).

[158] Bruce Bartlett, *Enterprise Zones: A Bipartisan Failure,* THE FISCAL TIMES (Jan. 10, 2014), http://www.thefiscaltimes.com/Columns/2014/01/10/Enterprise-Zones-Bipartisan-Failure.

programs did not really create jobs but instead relocated them along with the associated business moving from just outside of the zone into the subsidized zone. In addition, high taxes in the urban areas do not discourage business investments as much as other factors such as the lack of an educated labor force, transportation, and consumer purchasing power. Even as President Obama endorsed a variation of enterprise zones as "promise zones" designated to receive significant federal support in 2014,[159] with a shift in financial markets, economic recession, and recovery, and a global marketplace, states are making changes to their EZ programs to remain competitive. For example, the California legislature repealed its Enterprise Zone Act in 2014 and eventually replaced it with three new tax incentives: the California Competes tax credit; a partial sales exemption; and the New Employment hiring tax credit.[160]

Question

1. TIFs and other economic development tools may foster unhealthy competition among local governments. Local governments use TIFs and other strategies to provide incentives to private companies to encourage the companies to relocate out of one jurisdiction and into another. In Chapter 3, we discussed Collective Action Challenges (CAC). How does this competition among local governments raise CAC? What could or should we do about it?

B. Community Benefits

Transit-oriented development (TOD), introduced earlier in the section on subdivision regulation and new urbanism, is an important aspect of urban redevelopment to efficiently bring people into the city for jobs, shopping, and entertainment. TOD brings together housing, jobs, and transportation by making it easier for people to walk, bike, drive, or take transit from affordable housing to potential employers and businesses. While transit and TOD are beneficial to urban environments, the infrastructure required is very expensive. Street networks, sidewalks, and parking are required to get drivers, transit users, bikers, and pedestrians

---

[159] *Id.*
[160] Max Shenker, *Performance Review for California's Enterprise Zone Replacements*, EZ Policy Blog (Mar. 23, 2016), http://www.ezpolicyblog.com/performance-review-for-californias-enterprise-zone-replacements/.

to their local destinations. Passenger rail and TOD projects are long-term transportation investments that can generate economic prosperity; however, they require massive funding or financing to implement. Innovative financing options use many methods and tools, but such projects will nevertheless involve long-term economic commitments and community or state will.[161]

The private sector has expanded its role in planning, designing, financing, and marketing redevelopment for transit-oriented and large-scale mixed-use projects. Public-private partnerships can be used to carry out joint development that provides the desired public amenities, a reasonable return on the investment for the developers, private sources of capital for the required infrastructure, and provisions for long-term maintenance of the infrastructure. When the private developer faces greater costs and more risk, the public sector will need to contribute to the creation of a longer and greater return on investment to encourage private participation in the venture.[162]

Communities desiring to revitalize the urban core and achieve successful TOD will need to incorporate this long-term vision in their comprehensive planning. Public funds and public investments in TOD will require prioritization to develop a broad funding base that attracts private investment and creates a stable revenue stream. Redevelopment should focus on areas that are in proximity to transportation corridors and transit stations and should accommodate mixed use for both residential and commercial users. Streamlining project approval can also incentivize urban infill and TOD. Environmental impact review in some states has been minimized by completely exempting such projects from state environmental quality acts, requiring less analysis of certain impacts or alternatives, shortening review periods, or requiring fewer documents for a project impact filing. Avoiding higher project costs and delays from environmental impact analysis may help promote environmentally and economically sustainable development.[163]

---

[161] LAND USE, *supra* note 7, at Chapter 6 (quoting *Report on Infrastructure Financing Options for TOD*, NATIONAL LEAGUE OF CITIES SUSTAINABLE CITIES INSTITUTE (2013)).

[162] *See* Robert H. Freilich & Brenda Nichols, *Public–Private Partnerships in Joint Development: The Legal and Financial Anatomy of Large-Scale Urban Development Projects*, 7 MUN. FIN. J. 5 (1986); Michael S. Bernick & Amy E. Freilich, *Transit Villages and Transit-Based Development: The Rules Are Becoming More Flexible — How Government Can Work with the Private Sector to Make It Happen*, 30 URB. LAW. 1, 14 (1998).

[163] LAND USE, *supra* note 7, at Chapter 6 (citing *Transit Oriented Development PowerPoint by Stefanos Polyzoides, Moule & Polyzoides*, PASADENA CALIFORNIA (2016)).

TRANSIT-ORIENTED DEVELOPMENT

Transit-oriented development is a type of mixed-use development that is centered around transit stops, not away from them. Housing, largely in the form of lofts or multi-family townhouse-style complexes are intermingled with commercial developments, particularly retail, all centered around transit stops. Creating jobs and housing within 1/4 to 1/2 mile of transit stops not only reduces congestion and transportation costs, but it also creates a more pedestrian-friendly environment as people are able to walk or bike to work and shopping. The key to transit-oriented development is to ensure that a sufficient stock of the available housing is affordable for the employees of that area, or else it defeats the purpose of a truly mixed-use, transit-oriented development.[164]

Transit-oriented development is an approach to development typically characterized by:

1) A mix of uses
2) Moderate to high density
3) Pedestrian orientation/connectivity
4) Transportation choices
5) Reduced parking
6) High quality design[165]

Common Zoning Techniques That Encourage TOD:

1) Mixed-use by-right within 1/4 mile of the main line of the railway with ground level retail or other active use
2) Increased densities
3) Maximum set-back standards or build-to-line requirements
4) Increased Floor to Area Ratio (FAR) above 1.0 at centers or along the main rail line through increased building height
5) Maximum, rather than minimum, parking requirement over minimum
6) Allow higher density if underground or structured parking is included
7) Transit Overlay Zones or Transit Corridor Overlay Zones
8) Maximum lot sizes for residential housing[166]

Historic preservation and the use of transferable development rights (TDRs) provide opportunities to revitalize the urban core while at the same time preserve the cultural and historical richness of the community. While there are different levels of government involved in historic preservation and different methods to advance these goals, the principal regulation of private owners of historic property takes place at the local level. Historic preservation does not require preservation of all

---

[164] *Sustainable Planning and Zoning Handbook*, Stark County, Ohio 1, 8 (June 2011), http://www.starkcountyohio.gov/StarkCounty/media/StarkCounty/StarkCountMain/Regional%20Planning%20Commission/Sustainable-Planning-and-Zoning-Handbook110112-1.pdf.
[165] Transit-Oriented Development (TOD), National League of Cities: Sustainable Cities Institute, http://www.nlc.org/resource/transit-oriented-development (last visited Jan. 3, 2018).
[166] *Case Your Key to TOD*, Pennsylvania Public Transportation Ass'n, https://web.archive.org/web/20151018180034/http://www.ppta.net/todtoolkit/zoning.html (last visited Nov. 16, 2017).

old buildings, but it does provide the standards and procedures to choose properties for "designation" and therefore subject them to preservation regulations. Historic preservation identifies individual properties as "landmarks" and groupings of buildings and associated features as "historic districts."[167]

Property designation requires a finding of historic significance, based on several criteria including such values as architecture, engineering, culture, setting, materials, and association with historical events or people. Because the extent of the criteria is so broad and mostly vague, some have used historic preservation devices to halt undesired redevelopment or, conversely, to contribute to urban revival. Historic preservation regulation will require designated property landowners to obtain a historic preservation permit in order to alter or add to a designated building, demolish it, or build on a vacant lot located in a historic district.[168]

Developers and architects are learning to respect preservation goals and have been able to design and build within the constraints of preservation standards. "The essence of this approach is to preserve the important visible features of historic buildings on a site and design additions that, while recognizably modern in flavor, are compatible in size and rhythms with the historic fabric. Developers have found that the market likes these structures."[169] Unfortunately, those who contributed cultural value to communities do not generally receive the benefits of revitalization. Instead, the marketplace commodifies these benefits and distributes them to groups and individuals external to the community. City officials should encourage developers to include more affordable housing in new projects to keep low-to-moderate-income minority residents in urban neighborhoods in order to equitably distribute the benefits of urban reform and achieve "long-term social, political, and distributional benefits for traditionally marginalized groups."[170]

TDRs are land use incentives that offer landowners the right to develop in other locations in exchange for not developing their own land that is historically significant or otherwise environmentally sensitive. TDR programs allow owners of particular buildings to transfer their unused development potential to other buildings they own or to another site in a receiving area. As part of a comprehensive land use plan, a city planning commission designates "sending areas" that are to be preserved from development and "receiving areas" that can accommodate the increased density or nonpermitted uses. The sending-area owners receive compensation by selling their unused development rights. Receiving-area owners

---

[167]J. Peter Byrne, *Precipice Regulations and Perverse Incentives: Comparing Historic Preservation Designation and Endangered Species Listing*, 27 Geo. Int'l Envtl. L. Rev. 343, 348-349 (2015).
[168]*Id.* at 350-351.
[169]*Id.* at 386-387.
[170]Lisa T. Alexander, *Hip-Hop and Housing: Revisiting Culture, Urban Space, Power, and Law*, 63 Hastings L.J. 803, 851-855 (2012).

obtain increased permission to develop.[171]

In *Penn Central Transportation Co. v. New York City*,[172] the U.S. Supreme Court upheld the validity of TDRs as a land use mechanism to reduce the economic impact inflicted on a landowner by restricting development rights through historic and landmark preservation law. Governments have used TDRs to preserve historic landmarks, preserve farmland, and preserve wetlands or other environmentally sensitive land. When used in conjunction with a highly restrictive land use regulation scheme, "TDRs create a

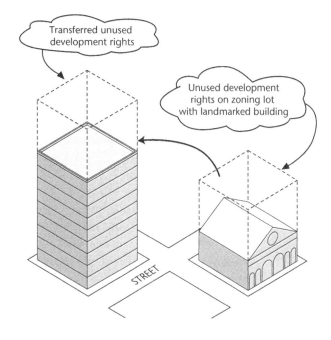

market for unused development potential and thus mitigate the economic impacts of governmental regulations that limit a property owner's development rights in the name of preservation."[173]

When revitalizing the urban core, a local government could offer TDRs to private owners of multi-family housing who agree to keep their buildings affordable. It could also offer a property-rehabilitation tax credit and time-limited property tax abatement to owners of small, owner-occupied historic homes to assist in rehabilitation. Finally, it could offer time-limited tax abatements and economic development funds to existing businesses in historic districts to encourage them to remain in place and serve existing communities. By preserving affordable housing in historic districts with cultural assets, existing and future low-income residents would be able to remain in place during revitalization so that "the gentrifying benefits of culture accrue to existing residents, rather than those external to the community."[174]

C. Revitalization of Vacant Property

Abandonment of properties that have changed from productive use to nonuse can heavily affect a community's resilience and sustainability.

---

[171] *Id.* at 857.
[172] 438 U.S. 104 (1978).
[173] Alexander, *supra* note 170, at 858.
[174] *Id.* at 857-860.

Abandonment is often a symptom of financial decline in the inner city and brings with it crime, decreased property values, the risk to health and welfare, and overall community decline. Foreclosures following the recession in the early twenty-first century exacerbated the problems in industrial cities and caused vacancy rates to grow nationwide. Problems with vacancies arise when property owners abandon ownership responsibilities, such as paying the mortgage and property taxes, and fail to perform routine maintenance of the building leading to public nuisance concerns. Local governments and communities struggle to address the challenge of reusing vacant and abandoned properties, but strategies to revitalize neighborhoods "may stimulate economic recovery and growth or, in the case of shrinking cities, manage decline in ways that improve the quality of life for the remaining residents."[175]

The foreclosure crisis and long-term urban decline have increased **vacancy rates** as residents moved to the suburbs and the number of households decreased leaving a gap between housing supply and demand. Job opportunities also moved to the suburbs and, as a result, left behind industrial and commercial sites. A reduced population and shrinking incomes make it difficult for communities to support urban revitalization and the presence of vacant and abandoned properties negatively impacts neighboring properties, communities, and cities. The "broken windows theory" posits that just one sign that a neighborhood is deteriorating will encourage further decline. This is because criminal activity increases with fewer neighbors to monitor the community and vacant buildings provide cover for illegal activity and become targets for theft. Arson is a problem that accompanies abandoned and vacant property and "[r]esearch also suggests that the longer a property remains vacant, the greater its impact on surrounding property values and the larger the radius of this effect."[176]

Detroit, Michigan used **nuisance abatement ordinances** in the 1980s to identify vacant and deteriorated dwellings that "create a public nuisance or exert a downgrading or blighting influence on the surrounding neighborhood, resulting in discouraging neighbors from making improvements to properties and thus adversely affecting the tax revenue of the city." Detroit allowed families to repair and move into abandoned homes to increase neighborhood stability and fulfill housing needs. Detroit City Ordinance No. 556-H was challenged as a taking of property requiring just compensation, but the court in *Moore v. City of Detroit* found that because the ordinance authorized "only a temporary physical possession of property for the purpose of abating a public nuisance" it did not constitute an unreasonable exercise of police power.[177] Unfortunately, these nuisance

---

[175] *Vacant and Abandoned Properties: Turning Liabilities into Assets*, HUD Uஸer, https://www.huduser.gov/portal/periodicals/em/winter14/highlight1.html (last visit Nov. 16, 2017).
[176] *Id.*
[177] 406 N.W.2d 488, 491 (Mich. Ct. App. 1987).

abatement measures and other efforts did not keep Detroit's population from shrinking by more than 200,000 residents in the first decade of the twenty-first century and from 1.8 million people in the mid-1950s to 713,000 city residents in 2010.[178]

Detroit residents continue to fight back against the "creeping" blight that has impacted their city by deploying 150 residents in 2015 to document abandoned properties that the Detroit land bank will strategically auction to revitalize neighborhoods with the best chance of recovery and to preserve homes worth saving.[179] The city's Housing and Revitalization Department is focusing on "creating a mixed-income neighborhood with both ownership and professionally managed rental housing and open space" by using landscape design and preserving existing homes to eliminate blight and support neighborhood revitalization. The city will redevelop some parcels into green space while rehabilitating adjacent vacant houses. In addition, the city and the Greening of Detroit organization are working to develop employment opportunities through green jobs training and by cleaning and clearing vacant lots to create "a greener, more walkable, more desirable community."[180]

Land banking is a state or local regulatory project that works to address abandoned and vacant property ownership. A government or nonprofit organization "land bank" receives the right of first refusal to acquire a private property that becomes tax-delinquent without having to make a cash payment before a sheriff's sale. Other city agencies, such as the department of revenue, may negotiate with the land bank to seek concessions such as unpaid taxes rather than have the land bank acquire the property. The goal of these acquisitions is to make productive use of vacant, abandoned, and tax-delinquent property by acquiring title, eliminating liabilities, and transferring the property to reliable new owners who are interested in using the property to achieve community-based plans. A local ordinance or programs developed within housing departments, planning departments, or redevelopment agencies based on state-enabling authority will create these land-banking programs.[181]

Land banks offer a direct response to a growing inventory of vacant and abandoned properties that the private marketplace has rejected, in some cases because the accumulated tax liability exceeds the property's market value and in others because the repairs required would exceed the

[178] LAND USE, *supra* note 7, at Chapter 6 (citing Detroit Free Press editorial, March 23, 2011).

[179] Emily Badger, *How Cities Are Starting to Turn Back Decades of Creeping Urban Blight*, WASH. POST (May 20, 2015), https://www.washingtonpost.com/news/wonk/wp/2015/05/20/how-cities-are-starting-to-turn-back-decades-of-creeping-urban-blight/.

[180] Roz Edward, *City of Detroit Releases RFPs for Revitalization of Fitzgerald Neighborhood*, MICHIGAN CHRONICLE, http://michronicleonline.com/2016/07/06/city-of-detroit-releases-rfps-for-revitalization-of-fitzgerald-neighborhood/ (last visited Nov. 16, 2017).

[181] *Frequently Asked Questions on Land Banking*, COMMUNITY PROGRESS, http://www.communityprogress.net/land-banking-faq-pages-449.php (last visited Nov. 16, 2017).

return on investment.[182] While developers and city officials see land banks as helpful programs to search title records for vacant and abandoned lots and make them available for sale and redevelopment, some community residents are concerned that developer efforts to revitalize the neighborhood will result in gentrification and higher taxes that will push out longtime homeowners. Land banking is just one tool to redevelop vacant and abandoned properties, however, community efforts to address revitalization of the urban core should ensure that the cultural assets of these urban neighborhoods are not lost and that the benefits of revitalization are shared with longtime residents.[183]

Brownfields are abandoned industrial or manufacturing sites that create urban blight and are in need of environmental cleanup action. "The Brownfield movement focuses on cleaning up these urban environmental sites and at the same time fights against urban blight by making already existing urban sites more attractive to developers."[184] Keeping companies from relocating outside the urban core can avoid urban sprawl by redeveloping vacant or abandoned land to create a larger tax base, more jobs, and a stable community. The Brownfield movement has resulted in the 2002 Brownfields Revitalization Act, which modified the Comprehensive Environmental Response, Compensation, and Liability Act of 1976 (CERCLA) to lower the EPA standards for cleaning up brownfields. This has encouraged developers to purchase and redevelop these polluted properties that they would have otherwise been responsible for cleaning up under CERCLA.[185]

Strategies to promote brownfields cleanup include federal, state, and local tax incentives, private ventures, and public-private partnerships.[186] Relief from liability under CERCLA established by the Brownfields Revitalization Act is a critical factor in encouraging cleanup and reuse although developers who purchase the polluted property must not do anything to disturb or release contaminants on the site. Lenders have also been encouraged to finance the development of these sites by the 1996 enactment of the Lender Liability Act, which limits the scope of lender liability for environmental costs and cleanup.[187]

Cities have received federal assistance from the HUD's 2015 Brownfields Economic Development Initiative (BEDI) to help with the redevelopment of abandoned or underused industrial and commercial facilities that are environmentally contaminated or suspected of being environmentally contaminated. Development grants, along with guaranteed Section

---

[182] *Id.*
[183] *See* LAND USE, *supra* note 7, at Chapter 6; Alexander, *supra* note 170, at 850-851.
[184] *See* LAND USE, *supra* note 7, at Chapter 6.
[185] LAND USE, *supra* note 7, at Chapter 6.
[186] *See* Andrea Wortzel, *Greening the Inner Cities: Can Federal Tax Incentives Solve the Brownfields Problem?*, 29 URB. LAW. 309 (1997).
[187] LAND USE, *supra* note 7, at Chapter 6.

108 loans under the Housing and Community Development Act of 1974, provide communities help to redevelop brownfields.[188] Through a combination of brownfields incentives, land banking, nuisance abatement, and other federal, state, and local funding programs designed to revitalize the urban core, there is hope that residents in the inner-city may continue to enjoy the cultural benefits of their neighborhoods while at the same time improve their quality of life through sustainable planning and building.

Question

1. What is it about abandoned or vacant buildings that can stress a community's resilience?

VIII. HOUSING

Decent, stable housing provides shelter, stability, health, physical safety and security, increased educational and job opportunities, and a sense of dignity and pride.[189] Internationally, the right to adequate housing is a basic human right to live in security, peace, and dignity. This human rights framework is critical when dealing with housing and land disputes following disasters and conflicts that displace people. Housing is more than providing shelter and the adequacy of the housing provided. We should evaluate housing adequacy based on the following criteria: security of tenure; cultural adequacy; affordability; availability of services; materials; facilities and infrastructure; habitability; and accessibility and location.[190] In the United States, home ownership is a major element of the "American Dream," and provides a place to live as well as a long-term investment.[191]

A. Exclusionary and Inclusionary Zoning

Local government has zoned for the purpose of either directly or indirectly excluding racial, religious, and economic minorities. Historically, local ordinances explicitly excluded these minorities or communities by

---

[188] *Id.*

[189] *Why Shelter?*, Habitat for Humanity, http://www.habitat.org/how/why.aspx (last visited Nov. 16, 2017).

[190] *The Importance of Addressing Housing, Land and Poverty (HLP): Challenges in Humanitarian Responses*, IFRC 1, 8 (2016), http://www.ifrc.org/Global/Documents/Secretariat/Shelter/IFRC-NRC%20HLP%20report%202016.pdf.

[191] Land Use, *supra* note 7, at Chapter 5.

using private restrictive covenants to accomplish exclusion. The courts eventually overturned these overt methods of exclusion as being unconstitutional, however, local governments began using facially inoffensive exclusionary techniques such as minimum lot size, minimum floor areas, restrictions on multi-family dwellings, bans on mobile homes, and growth controls. In addition to "snob zoning" and other discriminatory motivations, these communities have fiscal motivations to discourage larger families from locating in their neighborhoods, since larger families increase the municipal costs needed to service the schools.[192]

In the 1970s, state courts in Pennsylvania, New York, and New Jersey found that the regional effects of local zoning, using large lot, low-density housing with no zones available for multi-family housing and mobile homes, violated state constitutional guarantees of substantive due process and equal protection. The most famous case of exclusionary-inclusionary zoning was the New Jersey Supreme Court's decision in *Southern Burlington County NAACP v. Township of Mt. Laurel*, in which the court viewed the right to housing as fundamental and found that the zoning was exclusionary and unconstitutional.[193] Not only did the court invalidate the township's zoning, it ordered the township to affirmatively plan and to provide reasonable opportunities for a variety of housing.[194]

Federal reaction to exclusionary zoning has been both proactive and reactive because it created the interstate highway system, provided the mortgage interest tax deduction, and guaranteed mortgage loans, all of which contributed to urban sprawl and the resulting segregated living patterns. In addition, loan guarantees given by the federal government in the 1930s required that racially restrictive covenants be included in deeds to discourage the movement of minorities into all-white neighborhoods.[195] The U.S. Supreme Court invalidated a racially exclusionary zoning ordinance on due process grounds in *Buchanan v. Warley*,[196] but endorsed the use of zoning for economic segregation in *Village of Euclid v. Ambler Realty*.[197]

In *Village of Arlington Heights v. Metropolitan Housing Development Corp.*,[198] the U.S. Supreme Court upheld the Village's decision to deny rezoning that would allow a racially integrated, low-and-middle-income housing project, finding that although the decision might have had a discriminatory effect on racial minorities, there was no evidence of an intent

---

[192] *Id.*

[193] 336 A.2d 713 (N.J. 1975) (now known as *Mt. Laurel I*).

[194] Land Use, *supra* note 7, at Chapter 5.

[195] Robert F. Drinan, S.J., *Untying the White Noose*, 94 Yale L.J. 435, 437 (1984); *see also* James A. Kushner, *Apartheid in America: An Historical and Legal Analysis of Contemporary Racial Residential Segregation in the United States*, 22 Howard L.J. 547 (1979).

[196] *See* James W. Ely, Jr., *Reflections on Buchanan v. Warley, Property Rights, and Race*, 51 Vand. L. Rev. 953 (1998) (discussing Buchanan v. Warley, 245 U.S. 60 (1917)).

[197] 272 U.S. 365 (1926).

[198] 429 U.S. 252 (1977).

to discriminate and thus no violation of equal protection. Based upon the Court's earlier decision in *Washington v. Davis*,[199] "[p]roof of racially discriminatory intent or purpose is required to show a violation of the Equal Protection Clause."[200] Although the Seventh Circuit, on remand, found that the denial of rezoning constituted a violation of the Fair Housing Act, it was not until the U.S. Supreme Court decision in *Texas Department of Housing and Community Affairs v. The Inclusive Communities Project, Inc.*[201] that the Court recognized that discriminatory effect was a violation of the Fair Housing Act.

The New Jersey Supreme Court first recognized **inclusionary zoning** in *Southern Burlington County NAACP v. Township of Mount Laurel (Mount Laurel I)*.[202] The *Mount Laurel* doctrine requires land use regulations to "make realistically possible the opportunity for an appropriate variety and choice of housing for all categories of people who may desire to live there, of course including those of low and moderate income."[203] However, eight years after *Mount Laurel I* invalidated the Mount Laurel zoning, the parties returned to the same court, which noted, "Mount Laurel remains afflicted with a blatantly exclusionary ordinance. . . . [which] at its core is true to nothing but Mount Laurel's determination to exclude the poor." The *Mount Laurel II* court once again invalidated the ordinance and encouraged voluntary compliance by clarifying the constitutional obligation.

The court defined the *Mount Laurel* obligation to require municipalities to:

- "remove all municipally created barriers to the construction of their fair share of lower income housing";
- use affirmative measures, such as state and federal subsidies and incentives to encourage developers to set aside part of their developments for lower income housing, in order to make the opportunity for lower income housing real;
- allow zoning for mobile homes; and
- provide "least cost" housing, but only where there are conditions that make it impossible to meet the fair share obligation.[204]

In 1985, the New Jersey legislature enacted the state Fair Housing Act to codify the fair share obligation developed by the *Mount Laurel* court decisions. Some state courts and legislatures have also adopted similar fair share regulations modeled after the *Mount Laurel* doctrine. The affirmative measure outlined by the *Mount Laurel* court — incentivizing developer

---

[199] 426 U.S. 229 (1976).
[200] *Village of Arlington Heights*, 429 U.S. at 265.
[201] 135 S. Ct. 2507 (2015).
[202] 67 N.J. 151 (1975).
[203] *Id.* at 187.
[204] S. Burlington County NAACP v. Township of Mt. Laurel, 456 A.2d 390 (N.J. 1983).

set-asides for affordable housing ("mandatory set-aside") — is the principal technique municipalities use to achieve affordable housing. A local government may offer density, area, and other development bonuses to encourage construction of affordable housing, or it may require a developer to set aside a portion of the units to account for the impact the development has on the community. Litigants have challenged these mandatory set-asides as beyond the authority delegated by the state or as a taking of property without compensation.[205]

"**Housing trust funds** are distinct funds established by city, county, or state governments that receive ongoing dedicated sources of public funding to support the preservation and production of affordable housing and increase opportunities for families and individuals to access decent affordable homes."[206] Housing trust funds provide a repository for relocation fees imposed on developers who demolish or convert low-income housing to another use and most states fund these housing trusts through revenue obtained from real estate transfer taxes or recording fees. The National Housing Trust Fund (NHTF), enacted as part of the Housing and Economic Recovery Act of 2008 (HERA), "is a dedicated fund intended to provide revenue to build, preserve, and rehabilitate housing for people with the lowest incomes." The NHTF provides funds to states, who in turn allocate these funds to communities to assist extremely low-income (ELI) renters and homeowners with their housing needs.[207]

Affordable housing is still a challenge for most municipalities and while many of the efforts to address this issue are managed at the state and local level, a new federal law, the Housing Opportunity through Modernization Act of 2016, is intended to "increase access to affordable rental housing, provide assistance to low-income renters and facilitate homeownership."[208] Cities are also tackling "workforce housing" to subsidize public school teachers and municipal employees, particularly police and firefighters, who cannot afford to live in the communities they serve.[209] Linkage fees may be a technique used to provide housing in the community by charging nonresidential development for affordable housing needs generated by

---

[205] *See* Land Use, *supra* note 7, at Chapter 5; *see also* Cal. Bldg. Indus. Assn. v. City of San Jose, 61 Cal. 4th 435 (2015), *cert. denied*, 136 S. Ct. 928 (2016) (holding that mandatory set-aside adopted by the city to address affordable housing was a land use regulation, not an exaction subject to *Nollan/Dolan* heightened scrutiny).

[206] *What Are Housing Trust Funds?*, Center for Community Change, http://housingtrustfundproject.org/ (last visited Nov. 16, 2017).

[207] *See* Cecily T. Talbert, Nadia L. Costa & Alison L. Krumbein, *Recent Developments in Inclusionary Zoning*, 38 Urb. Law. 701, 706 (2006).

[208] 37 No. 9 Quinlan, Landlord Tenant Law Bulletin NL 6 (Sept. 2016).

[209] Tim Iglesias, *Our Pluralist Housing Ethics and the Struggle for Affordability*, 42 Wake Forest L. Rev. 511, 581 (2007); *see also* Len Ramirez, *$250K Per Year Salary Could Qualify for Subsidized Housing Under New Palo Alto Proposal*, CBS SF Bay Area (Mar. 22, 2016), http://sanfrancisco.cbslocal.com/2016/03/22/250k-per-year-salary-could-qualify-for-subsidized-housing-under-new-palo-alto-plan/.

the development.[210] As outlined in the *Mount Laurel II* decision, municipalities may use many affirmative measures to "provide a realistic opportunity for low and moderate income housing." Cities and states across the nation have employed additional innovative measures and by emphasizing sustainable communities, affordable housing may eventually be a "dream come true."

Questions

1. What is it about exclusionary zoning that tests a community's sustainability? Can a community meet the triple bottom line while implementing exclusionary zoning?

2. Which social-ecological systems' resilience will exclusionary zoning stress?

B. Discrimination and the Fair Housing Act

The Fair Housing Act (FHA) responds to the denial of housing opportunities based on race, color, religion, national origin, familial status, and handicap. Both intentional acts of discrimination and acts that have a discriminatory impact will generate liability.[211] The FHA covers most housing but exempts owner-occupied buildings with four units or less, single-family housing sold or rented without using a broker, and housing operated by organizations that limit occupancy to members.[212]

A violation of the FHA may be found if there is discrimination against any of these protected groups in the rental or sale of housing, setting terms or conditions, providing services or facilities, falsely denying housing availability, interfering with someone exercising a fair housing right, or advertising a preference based on these classifications, even though otherwise exempted from FHA liability. If there is a physical or mental disability, the landowner must make reasonable accommodations for the use or allow the tenant to make reasonable modifications at their own expense. Housing for older persons is exempt from familial status discrimination liability if the housing qualifies as housing for elderly persons or meets other criteria under the Act.[213]

---

[210] *See* William W. Merrill & Robert K. Lincoln, *Linkage Fees and Fair Share Regulations: Law and Method*, 25 URB. LAW. 223 (1993).

[211] *See* LAND USE, *supra* note 7, at Chapter 5.

[212] PROPERTY, *supra* note 14, at 400-403.

[213] *Id.*

HOUSING DISCRIMINATION AND REDLINING

Home ownership rates in the United States steadily increased between World War II, when national rates were 43.6%, and 2004, when national rates were 69.2%. Following the housing crisis, rates consistently dropped and were at 63.5% in 2016. Robin Malloy & James Smith, REAL ESTATE TRANSACTIONS: PROBLEMS, CASES, AND MATERIALS (5th ed. Aspen Pub. 2017).

Home ownership, however, is not equal. In 2004, prior to the housing market collapse, 48% of African-Americans owned homes, 46% of Hispanics, 60% of Asian-Americans, and 75% of whites.

Redlining is one way in which discrimination against various groups has occurred. Redlining is the denial of financing and insurance in certain areas due to the predominant demographics in the area. Essentially, banks and insurers refuse to offer services in a particular area. Relatedly, reverse redlining is the practice of extending credit on unfair terms to those same areas. Reverse redlining has been associated with predatory lending in which companies offer loans with unfair, impractical, and often illegal terms to individuals living in a particular area.

Land use and environmental justice concerns arise when local, state, or federal agencies site Locally Undesirable Land Uses (LULUs) in communities of color or in poor communities. Equal protection claims are not likely to work as poverty is not a suspect class and discrimination based on race will require the community to show discriminatory intent. Challenges to discriminatory siting of adverse environmental activities under Title VI of the Civil Rights Act of 1964 have also faced difficulty after the Supreme Court in *Alexander v. Sandoval* held that there is no private right of action under Title VI.[214] While litigation may not have succeeded in bringing environmental justice concerns to light, "[p]ublicity about the issue has led to an increased level of consciousness in regulators, industry, and residents about the potential adverse health effects of living near waste facilities and the unfairness of subjecting communities of color to a disproportionate burden."[215]

C. Non-Traditional Living Arrangements and Group Homes

Zoning has historically protected the single-family home as the highest use and has traditionally defined the family as the mother, father, and

---

[214] 532 U.S. 275 (2001). *See generally* Tara Ulezalka, *Race and Waste: The Quest for Environmental Justice*, 26 TEMP. J. SCI. TECH. & ENVTL. L. 51 (2007) (assessing federal, state, and common law remedies); Melissa A. Hoffer, *Closing the Door on Private Enforcement of Title VI and EPA's Discriminatory Effects Regulations: Strategies for Environmental Justice Stakeholders after Sandoval and Gonzaga*, 38 NEW ENG. L. REV. 971 (2004).

[215] LAND USE, *supra* note 7, at Chapter 5.

biological and adopted children. Non-traditional living arrangements have entered the traditional single-family neighborhood as college students, religious orders, foster families, and group homes for independent living, disabled, and halfway houses have chosen to locate in these neighborhoods. Neighbors have resisted these living arrangements and used zoning rules, nuisance, and private covenants to exclude these unwanted arrangements.[216]

The U.S. Supreme Court first confronted the issue of group homes in *Village of Belle Terre v. Boraas*.[217] The village served the homeowners with an order to remedy violations of the ordinance, which defined family as "(o)ne or more persons related by blood, adoption, or marriage, living and cooking together as a single housekeeping unit, exclusive of household servants." The renters, a group of college students, challenged the ordinance as an interference with the right to travel, and the right of privacy and it was "said that the Belle Terre ordinance reeks with an animosity to unmarried couples who live together."[218] The Court upheld the definition of family and its adverse application to the college students on the basis that the police power could validly be used "to lay out zones where family values, youth values, and the blessings of quiet seclusion and clean air make the area a sanctuary for people."[219]

In the *City of Ladue v. Horn*, a Missouri court upheld a zoning ordinance against constitutional challenge even though it excluded unmarried men and women in order to promote marriage and family values.[220] However, in *Moore v. City of East Cleveland*,[221] the ordinance defined "family" to allow individuals to have their unmarried children living with them only if there were no grandchildren. An exception allowed the dependent children of the dependent child of the head of the household to live with them. As a consequence of this definition, Mrs. Moore, who lived with her son Dale, and Dale's son, Dale, Jr., was prohibited from having her second grandson, John, come to live with them following his mother's death. John did not qualify as "family" because he had a different parent than Dale, Jr. The lower court convicted Mrs. Moore and fined her for failing to evict her grandson, John. It then sentenced her to five days in jail. The Court held that when the freedom of personal choice in matters of marriage and family life is involved, it will examine carefully the importance of the government interest and cannot override the grandmother's choice to live with her grandson.[222]

---

[216] *Id.*
[217] 416 U.S. 1 (1974).
[218] *Id.* at 2-4, 8.
[219] *Id.* at 9.
[220] 720 S.W.2d 745 (Mo. App. 1986).
[221] 431 U.S. 494 (1977).
[222] *Id.* at 499.

Group homes were again before the U.S. Supreme Court in *City of Cleburne v. Cleburne Living Center.*[223] In *Cleburne*, the zoning ordinance required a special use permit for a group home for the mentally disabled but did not require one for other similar uses. If the discrimination asserted in an equal protection challenge involves a "suspect" classification or a fundamental right, the level of judicial review requires that a court give "strict scrutiny" to the government's action, otherwise the court evaluates the action on a "rational basis" standard. In *Cleburne*, the Court concluded the mentally disabled were not a "suspect" class requiring heightened scrutiny of the alleged government discrimination. However, the Court found that "requiring the permit in this case appears to us to rest on an irrational prejudice against the mentally retarded," which violates the Equal Protection clause of the U.S. Constitution.[224]

In both the *Belle Terre* case and in *Cleburne*, the group home occupants were not part of a "suspect" classification under the Constitution, nor was there a "fundamental right" such as the family relationship involved in the *Moore* case. However, under the rational basis standard, the Court found a rational basis for the discrimination in *Belle Terre* against college students, but no rational basis for the discrimination against the mentally disabled. Some have called the *Cleburne* rational basis standard "rational basis with a bite" because courts uphold most all government action evaluated under the standard rational basis test.

The Federal Fair Housing Act (FHA) was amended in 1988 to protect the physically and mentally disabled from discrimination in housing. Ten years after its decision in *Cleburne*, the U.S. Supreme Court once again reviewed a city ordinance that affected a group home, but this time, it evaluated the ordinance under the 1988 FHA, rather than the Equal Protection clause. In *City of Edmonds v. Oxford House, Inc.*,[225] the Court held that the city's ordinance defining single-family as those related by "genetics, adoption, or marriage" or a maximum of five unrelated individuals did not meet the FHA's exemption for ordinances that contain a maximum occupancy restriction. Therefore, the government's criminal action against a group home for 10 to 12 adults recovering from alcoholism and drug addiction would be subject to the FHA provisions protecting persons who are "handicapped" against discrimination.

While current, illegal use of or addiction to a controlled substance does not constitute a "handicap" under the FHA, the individuals in the Oxford House group home "are recovering alcoholics and drug addicts and are handicapped persons within the meaning of the Act." The only question before the Supreme Court was whether the City of Edmond's ordinance was exempt from the FHA. Finding it was not exempt, the Court stated

---

[223] 473 U.S. 432 (1985).
[224] *Id.* at 450.
[225] 514 U.S. 725 (1995).

that "[i]t remains for the lower courts to decide whether Edmonds' actions against Oxford House violate the FHA's prohibitions against discrimination." The Court also noted in its decision that discrimination includes "a refusal to make reasonable accommodations in rules, policies, practices, or services." Oxford House had asked Edmonds to make a "reasonable accommodation" by allowing the 8 to 12 residents it needed to make the group home "financially and therapeutically viable." However, Edmonds refused to allow the Oxford House to stay in a single-family residential zone but did pass an ordinance permitting group homes in multi-family and general commercial zones.[226]

D. Public Housing Assistance

Congress enacted the first Housing Act in 1937 with the goal of providing safe and decent rental housing to low-income families, the elderly, and the disabled. Public Housing Authorities (PHAs) sold bonds to buy land and build public housing projects. Between 1937 and 1970, the federal government working with local PHAs built segregated and dense high-rise public housing projects as part of urban renewal efforts. These federally built projects began declining in the late 1960s and at the same time, the federal Fair Housing Act prevented discrimination in the siting of public housing projects. Subsequent court decisions and legislation barred continuing efforts to site high-rise public housing projects in urban neighborhoods with concentrated minority populations. The Dallas Housing Authority (DHA) in conjunction with HUD continued to build public housing projects in segregated African-American minority neighborhoods and a series of court decisions held them responsible for racial segregation in low-income public housing because of the manner in which they selected the sites. The federal district court required the city of Dallas to develop low-income family housing units in surrounding suburban cities to further desegregation efforts. When HUD selected a site in 1997 that was located in a non-minority area of North Dallas, the area homeowners filed suit to stop the construction. The Fifth Circuit rejected these attempts and approved two small public housing apartment buildings.[227]

In its latest housing discrimination decision, *Texas Department of Housing and Community Affairs v. Inclusive Communities Project, Inc.,*[228] the

---

[226] *Id.* For more information about the impact of the 1988 FHA amendments on local land use, see Peter W. Salsich, Jr., *Federal Influence on Local Land Use Regulations: The Fair Housing Act Amendments*, 9 J. Affordable Housing & Community Dev. L. 228 (2000); see also Robert L. Schonfeld, *"Reasonable Accommodation" Under the Federal Fair Housing Amendments Act*, 25 Fordham Urb. L.J. 413, 413-441 (1997); Laurie C. Malkin, *Troubles at the Doorstep: The Fair Housing Act of 1988 and Group Homes for Recovering Substance Abusers*, 144 U. Pa. L. Rev. 759 (1995).

[227] Walker v. Dep't of HUD, 169 F.3d 973 (5th Cir.1999), *cert. denied*, 528 U.S. 1131 (2000). *See generally* Land Use, *supra* note 7, at Chapter 5.

[228] 135 S. Ct. 2507 (2015).

U.S. Supreme Court recognized disparate impact claims under the FHA, in addition to intentional discrimination claims. The Court set aside a low-income housing tax credit program because it provided tax credits on a discriminatory basis. The Court noted that by recognizing liability for disparate impact claims it could prevent "segregated housing patterns that might otherwise result from covert and illicit stereotyping."[229]

Federal housing support no longer relies on building new housing, but instead provides rental, tax credit, grant, and loan assistance. The federal government established income guidelines for housing assistance, and state and local governments use these income limitations in their own affordable housing programs. In 1993, Congress enacted the Hope VI program to demolish all existing housing projects and replace them with smaller housing units. The goal of transforming public housing is supported by specific elements such as: changing the physical shape of public housing; establishing positive incentives for resident self-sufficiency and empowerment; reducing concentrations of poverty by placing public housing in non-poverty areas and promoting mixed use; partnering with other agencies and groups to gain support and resources; and demolishing existing distressed projects.[230]

The Section 8 program provides for rental assistance to those who qualify for public housing, but assistance is also available for privately owned housing. HUD manages the program. The biggest portion of the program, the Housing Choice Voucher program, pays a large portion of the rents and utilities for approximately 2.1 million households. The voucher program provides rental assistance that is "tenant-based" so that a tenant may move from one unit of housing, such as a public housing project demolished under Hope VI, to the private housing sector. Section 8 housing must comply with health and safety standards under the Public Housing Authority and income assistance is limited to families with income below 50% of the median income for the urban area.

Landlords are eligible for low-income housing tax credits if they participate in housing support programs and rent some or all of their apartments to low-income tenants at a restricted rent. State and local agencies have the authority to allocate these credits to encourage the acquisition, rehabilitation, or new construction of low-income rental housing. Very low-income homeowners in rural areas receive services from a program that provides loans and grants for repair, improvement, or home modernization to remedy health and safety issues. Finally, the federal Community Development Block Grant provides grants to local governments to subsidize interest rates, enforce the housing code, demolish buildings, and for urban renewal and rehabilitation.[231]

---

[229] LAND USE, *supra* note 7, at Chapter 5.
[230] *Id.* at Chapter 6.
[231] *Id.* at Chapter 6.

Questions

1. How did federal programs between 1937 and 1970 impact the resilience of the housing system?

2. What is critical about low-income housing for purposes of creating a sustainable community?

E. Housing Codes and Statutory Housing Requirements

Local ordinances set minimum housing standards and local government enforces these standards. The Housing and Urban Development Act of 1965 and the Housing and Community Development Act of 1974 incentivized "housing code" adoption across the country. Housing codes prevent neighborhood deterioration by establishing standards for healthy and safe housing. The three main areas addressed by housing codes are the supplied facilities in the structure, the level of structural and sanitary maintenance, and the occupancy features of the interior space.

When an inspection reveals **code violations**, the owner is required to repair to current code standards or be subject to the possible receivership of the property, city repair, and foreclosure to collect costs or demolition.[232] Repairing to current standards may be especially difficult for older buildings and some have argued that housing codes should be more flexible to limit repairs to what is economically affordable in specific areas of a city.[233]

In communities that use conventional building codes, the level of building upgrades required in a rehabilitation project depends on the estimated cost of the project, rather than the type or scope of work proposed. The more expensive the project, the greater the degree to which the building must comply with current standards. Use of this system can trigger requirements for extensive renovation in rehabilitation projects that make only minimal structural changes — a scenario that increases costs and may discourage the redevelopment of affordable homes.[234]

Mandatory inspection may be required when selling or renting an apartment or the building, otherwise, the city must rely on tenant

---

[232] *Id.* at Chapter 6.
[233] *See* Robert Hickey, *A Framework for Addressing Local Affordability Challenges*, CENTER FOR HOUSING POLICY (Aug. 21, 2014), http://www.mayorsinnovation.org/images/uploads/pdf/2_-_Hickey.pdf; *see also* Peter W. Salsich, Jr., *Housing and the States*, 2 URB. LAW. 40 (1970); Georgina Landman, *Flexible Housing Code — The Mystique of the Single Standard: A Critical Analysis and Comparison of Model and Selected Housing Codes Leading to the Development of a Proposed Model Flexible Housing Code*, 18 HOWARD L.J. 251, 255 (1974).
[234] *See* Hickey, *supra* note 233.

London complex with code violations

complaints in order to have the authority to enter and inspect the building interior.[235] Litigants have challenged mandatory inspections under the Fourth Amendment search and seizure protections. The Seventh Circuit, in reviewing such a challenge, stated "'Point of sale' ordinances such as this one are common and have withstood constitutional attack in all cases that we know of in which the ordinance avoided invalidation under the Fourth Amendment by requiring that the city's inspectors obtain a warrant to inspect a house over the owner's objection." Because the city's ordinance, in this case, provided for obtaining a warrant over objection, the court upheld the ordinance against the Fourth Amendment challenge.[236]

Remedies for housing code violations include: requiring the property owner to correct the violations; appointing a receiver to collect the rents and make the necessary repairs; allowing the city to make the repairs and use foreclosure, if necessary, to collect the costs; and demolishing the property. Cities may abate or condemn buildings that are public nuisances, without facing liability for destruction or damages. One suggested approach is to treat the code violations as a continuing public nuisance and seek civil injunctive relief. The court can then customize the remedy to the situation and enforce the adapted remedy by civil contempt.[237] Major cities have also used specialized "housing" courts to identify chronic violators. Particularized remedies, such as fines, supervised probation, and close coordination with the local housing code agencies, are then available to address recidivist offenders.

Demolition is a particularly important remedy for housing code violations, as well as for abandoned and vacated buildings. However, any city-ordered demolition should give owners the opportunity to make repairs

---

[235] *See generally* Otto Hetzel, *The Search for Effective and Cost-Efficient Housing Strategies: Enforcing Housing Condition Standards through Code Inspections at Time of Sale or Transfer*, 36 Wash. U. J. Urb. & Contemp. L. 25 (1989).
[236] Mann v. Calumet City, 588 F.3d 949 (7th Cir. 2009).
[237] Land Use, *supra* note 7, at Chapter 6.

or rehabilitate and occupy the buildings. The Fourteenth Amendment prohibits the government from depriving any person of life, liberty, or property, without due process of law, a fundamental requirement of which is the opportunity for a hearing. The opportunity "must be granted at a meaningful time and in a meaningful manner."[238] The city should hold a pre-deprivation hearing before depriving the person of her property. Where there is a public health or safety threat that requires prompt action, the government may need to act quickly to eliminate the threat and a pre-deprivation hearing may not be possible. Therefore, in certain emergencies, providing a meaningful post-deprivation process may satisfy procedural due process requirements.[239] It is critical that local governments have the power to condemn unsafe, unhealthy, or nuisance-creating buildings without paying just compensation in order to ensure adequate housing and blight reduction in the urban core.

Questions

1. Improving housing helps a community build resilience to which disturbances? Does it depend on the type and cost of housing? If so, which type of housing would increase a community's resilience to what type of disturbance?

2. Based on the above, are we achieving a sustainable system of housing in the United States? What is working? What is not?

3. Should it be the role of governments to ensure safe and adequate housing?

IX. LIMITATIONS ON LAND USE REGULATION

The U.S. Constitution, state constitutions, federal and state statutes that control land use, state common law, intergovernmental conflicts, federal and state environmental statutes, and governmental land ownership all impose limitations on land use regulation. We discuss some of these limitations below, starting with the greatest deterrent against government interference with private property rights—the Fifth Amendment Takings Clause.

---

[238] Armstrong v. Manzo, 380 U.S. 545, 552 (1965).
[239] Elsmere Park Club, L.P. v. Town of Elsmere, 542 F.3d 412 (3d Cir. 2008).

A. The Fifth Amendment Takings Clause

The Fifth Amendment to the U.S. Constitution provides in part "nor shall private **property** be **taken** for **public use** without **just compensation**" and is designed to keep the government from "forcing some people alone to bear public burdens which, in all fairness and justice, should be borne by the public as a whole."[240] In order to appreciate the U.S. Supreme Court's jurisprudence in interpreting this constitutional protection of property rights, the bolded terms above in the "takings clause" of the Fifth Amendment are examined below.

In a claim under the Fifth Amendment, we must first determine what is the private **property** involved. It is typically real property, but personal property and any vested right or entitlement may be subject to a takings claim. At times, it may not be clear that the interest claimed is actually a property right subject to a takings claim. For example, water rights may be property rights or merely "rights to use." Grazing rights for cattle, fishing licenses, and liquor licenses may or may not be property for purposes of the takings clause.

The "denominator" issue is also at play in deciding the property at issue when a property owner owns multiple parcels, but only one of the parcels is subject to government interference. When evaluating the severity of the government's interference with the property owner's interests, the question is whether the parcel subject to interference is the only property interest involved in the analysis (the denominator) or whether the parcel subject to interference is evaluated against all of the parcels owned (the denominator). The U.S. Supreme Court in *Murr v. Wisconsin*[241] addressed this issue after noting that

> no single consideration can supply the exclusive test for determining the denominator. Instead, courts must consider a number of factors. These include the treatment of the land under state and local law; the physical characteristics of the land; and the prospective value of the regulated land. The endeavor should determine whether reasonable expectations about property ownership would lead a landowner to anticipate that his holdings would be treated as one parcel, or, instead, as separate tracts. The inquiry is objective, and the reasonable expectations at issue derive from background customs and the whole of our legal tradition.[242]

If we use the single parcel as the denominator, then interfering with that parcel constitutes a complete taking, whereas if all of the parcels owned constitute the denominator, then interfering with only one parcel

---

[240] Armstrong v. United States, 364 U.S. 40, 49 (1960).
[241] 137 S. Ct. 1933 (2017).
[242] *Id.* at 1945.

is a partial taking. This determination becomes important in deciding whether a takings claim is a *per se* taking under *Lucas* (see below) because it deprives the landowner of all economically beneficial or productive use of the one affected parcel. Alternatively, if we use all of the parcels as the denominator, the taking will only be a partial one and be subject to the *Penn Central* test (see below).

The second determination is whether the government has **taken** the property identified. The government has the power to use **eminent domain** to condemn (take) property so long as it is for a public use and the government pays just compensation. In *Pennsylvania Coal v. Mahon*,[243] the Supreme Court recognized the concept of a **regulatory taking** in a case involving a state statute that required coal companies to keep enough pillars of coal in the ground to support surface rights and prevent subsidence involving structures. The Court stated that "[t]he general rule at least is, that while property may be regulated to a certain extent, *if regulation goes too far* it will be recognized as a taking."[244] Determining whether a regulation has gone too far has continued to occupy the Court's takings jurisprudence from 1922 until the present time.

The Court has identified **two *per se* takings tests**. First, if the government permanently physically occupies your property, or causes someone else to occupy your property, you have lost the most important stick in your bundle of ownership rights—the right to exclude. A **permanent physical occupation** no matter how small, unless it is de minimis, constitutes a Fifth Amendment taking and the government must pay just compensation. The Court applied this *per se* taking test to real property in *Loretto v. Teleprompter Manhattan CATV Corp.*[245] The Court held that a New York City ordinance requiring property owners to allow the installation of a half-inch cable on the outside of buildings constituted a *per se* taking of the landowner's property requiring the City to pay just compensation.[246] The Court also applied this *per se* takings test to personal property in *Horne v. Department of Agriculture.*[247] In *Horne*, the Court determined that a California Raisin Marketing Order demanding that raisin growers turn over a percentage of their crop based on the federal Agricultural Marketing Agreement Act of 1937 was a *per se* taking of personal property because it confiscated private property.[248] As discussed above in the section on subdivision regulation, physical and in-lieu exactions are exceptions to the *Loretto per se* taking test. Instead, exactions are subject to the *Nollan/Dolan* heightened scrutiny test.

---

[243] 260 U.S. 393 (1922).
[244] *Id.* at 415 (emphasis added).
[245] 458 U.S. 419 (1982).
[246] *Id.* at 441.
[247] 135 S. Ct. 2419 (2015).
[248] *Id.* at 2428.

The Court in *Lucas v. South Carolina Coastal Council*[249] identified the second *per se* takings test, "**where regulation denies all economically beneficial or productive use of land**," unless the government can "identify background principles of nuisance and property law that prohibit the uses [the landowner] now intends in the circumstances in which the property is presently found."[250] The Court rejected analyzing a takings claim based on whether the regulation was intended to "prevent a harmful use" (not a taking) or instead "confer a benefit" (a taking). The Court noted "the distinction between 'harm-preventing' and 'benefit-conferring' regulation is often in the eye of the beholder" and "[s]ince such a justification can be formulated in practically every case, this amounts to a test of whether the legislature has a stupid staff."[251]

If the alleged regulatory taking is not a *per se* taking under either *Loretto* or *Lucas*, it is because the landowner has some remaining value in the property as burdened by the government regulation or action. Such **"partial" takings** are subject to an ad hoc, factual inquiry, which uses the following factors: the character of the government action, the economic impact of the regulation, and the interference with investment-backed expectations. The Court developed these "***Penn Central* factors**" in *Penn Central Transportation Co. v. New York City.*[252]

In *Penn Central*, the owners of Grand Central Terminal challenged the application of New York City's Landmarks Preservation Law to the parcel occupied by a railroad station within one of New York's most famous buildings that is also "a magnificent example of the French beaux-arts style."[253] Penn Central wanted to construct an office building on top of the Terminal and submitted two separate plans in order to obtain permission. The Landmarks Preservation Commission rejected these plans and Penn Central did not submit alternate plans in order to obtain permission.[254] After it analyzed the factual situation under the factors identified, the Court held that applying New York City's Landmarks Law to the parcel occupied by the Terminal was not a taking of property because the restrictions substantially relate to promoting the general welfare and permit reasonable beneficial use of the landmark site. In addition, the law also gives Penn Central opportunities to enhance the Terminal site, as well as other property, through Transferable Development Rights (TDRs). To the extent the landmarks law denied Penn Central the right to build in the airspace above the Terminal, Penn Central could transfer these air rights to other sites near the Terminal to allow new office buildings.[255]

---

[249] 505 U.S. 1003 (1992).
[250] *Id.* at 1031.
[251] *Id.* at 1024, 1025 n.12.
[252] 438 U.S. 104 (1978).
[253] *Id.* at 115.
[254] *Id.* at 118-119.
[255] *Id.* at 138.

The Court's jurisprudence has developed the *Penn Central* factors over time. First, the Court refined the **character of the government action** in the *Loretto* case, which determined that if there was a permanent physical occupation a *per se* taking would result. This factor may still identify government regulation or action that appears to target a particular parcel or landowner, such as occurs with landmark designation and regulation. The character of the government action in shutting down a nuisance may also be important in determining whether the action constitutes a taking.

Second, the Court incorporated the **economic impact of the regulation** factor into the *Lucas per se* taking analysis by finding that a taking results if the government denies all economically beneficial or productive use of the property. Economic impact takes into account whether the landowner is still able to earn a **reasonable rate of return** on the property when burdened by a regulation or government action. Courts also continue to consider the **reciprocity of advantage** that one landowner enjoys by having other properties subject to similar regulation that is intended to benefit the public as a whole when evaluating the economic impact on a single landowner. Using transferable development rights has been controversial because if TDRs are viewed as just compensation for a taking, they are likely not sufficient compensation. However, if courts use TDRs to determine the economic impact of the government action, the TDRs will reduce the impact and possibly force a *Penn Central* analysis of the partial takings claim, rather than a *Lucas* analysis for a denial of all economically viable use of the targeted property.

Third, the **interference with investment-backed expectations** of the landowner will take into account whether the landowner obtained the property by inheritance or gift. The landowner's expectations may depend on when she purchased the property — before or after the government enacted the challenged regulation. The Supreme Court in *Palazzolo v. Rhode Island*[256] reviewed a landowner's takings claim based on wetlands regulation that precluded him from developing his ocean-side property, except for an upland portion valued at $200,000. The Court found that the state court applied a rule that "a purchaser or successive title holder like the petitioner is deemed to have notice of an earlier-enacted restriction and is barred from claiming that it effects a taking." The Court rejected the rule because "the post-enactment transfer of title would absolve the State of its obligation to defend any action restricting land use, no matter how extreme or unreasonable." It noted that such a rule would also preclude heirs or successors from asserting a right to compensation, which would be a windfall for the state.[257] The Court remanded the case to state court to evaluate the landowner's claim under a *Penn Central* analysis because

---

[256] 533 U.S. 606 (2001).
[257] *Id.* at 626-627.

"[t]hat claim is not barred by the mere fact that title was acquired after the effective date of the state-imposed restriction."[258] However, when analyzing these factors, "the regulatory regime in place at the time the claimant acquires the property at issue helps to shape the reasonableness of those expectations."[259]

The third determination required under a Fifth Amendment takings claim is whether the taking was for a **public use**. The traditional type of eminent domain action was to condemn private property in order to build public roads or public buildings such as schools, parks, and libraries, which the public would actually use. Over time, public use became synonymous with a **public purpose**. The Court in *Berman v. Parker*[260] upheld as constitutional the use of eminent domain under the District of Columbia Redevelopment Act of 1945. The Act provided that "the acquisition and the assembly of real property and the leasing or sale thereof for redevelopment pursuant to a project area redevelopment plan . . . is hereby declared to be a public use." The property condemned was both blighted and unblighted, but the Court recognized that "[i]t was important to redesign the entire area to eliminate the conditions that cause slums."[261] The *Berman* Court permitted the government to use eminent domain for redevelopment, even though the project would not be a public one and would instead involve private enterprise. The Court equated public use with the police power to promote the public health, safety, morals, and general welfare and declared that "the role of the judiciary in determining whether that power is being exercised for a public purpose is an extremely narrow one."[262]

In *Kelo v. City of New London*,[263] the Court relied on its holding in *Berman* and a later case, *Hawai'i Housing Authority v. Midkiff*,[264] as well as other precedent, to find that economic redevelopment qualifies as a public use under the Fifth Amendment. The City of New London expected the development plan to create more than 1,000 jobs and revitalize the economically distressed city by increasing tax and other revenues. The Court upheld the city's right to use eminent domain to assemble the land needed for the project through voluntary purchase and condemnation. It noted

---

[258] *Id.* at 630.

[259] *Id.* at 633-635 (O'Connor concurring) (noting that "the state of regulatory affairs at the time of acquisition is not the only factor that may determine the extent of investment-backed expectations. For example, the nature and extent of permitted development under the regulatory regime vis-a-vis the development sought by the claimant may also shape legitimate expectations without vesting any kind of development right in the property owner. We also have never held that a takings claim is defeated simply on account of the lack of a personal financial investment by a post-enactment acquirer of property, such as a donee, heir, or devisee. Courts instead must attend to those circumstances which are probative of what fairness requires in a given case").

[260] 348 U.S. 26 (1954).

[261] *Id.* at 34.

[262] *Id.* at 32.

[263] 545 U.S. 469 (2005).

[264] 467 U.S. 229 (1984).

that "[f]or more than a century, our public use jurisprudence has wisely eschewed rigid formulas and intrusive scrutiny in favor of affording legislatures broad latitude in determining what public needs justify the use of the takings power."[265]

Regardless of whether the taking is by eminent domain or a regulatory taking, the government must show that its action promotes the public health, safety, morals, and general welfare. Although the interpretation of public purpose under the police power is so broad that courts will inevitably find a valid public purpose, if the government action does not rationally tie to the police power, the government cannot use its eminent domain power or any other regulation or action because such action will violate substantive due process (see below).

The final determination under the Fifth Amendment is the award of **just compensation**, but only if a taking or a temporary taking has been found. Just compensation is the fair market value of the property at the time of the taking, which is what a willing buyer would pay to a willing seller based on the highest and best use of the property.[266]

Questions

1. How does providing just compensation to individuals who have had a taking tend to impact system resilience? Which systems are or could be affected by takings jurisprudence? In addition, are those systems made more resilient or less resilient?

2. Pick a system that land use impacts (for example, transportation, water, or food). Can you think of a scenario where that system's resilience is made more vulnerable by the takings jurisprudence? Can you think of a scenario where that system's sustainability is enhanced?

B. Other Constitutional Limitations

In addition to takings claims under the Fifth Amendment takings clause, the government may face constitutional challenges for interfering with private property rights. Under the Fifth Amendment and Fourteenth Amendment, challengers may assert both procedural due process and substantive due process claims when the government has deprived them of a property interest. First Amendment challenges under both the free

---

[265] *Id.* at 483.
[266] LAND USE, *supra* note 7, at Chapter 3.

expression and religion clauses are available when the government seeks to regulate community noise, adult businesses, billboards and signs, and religious uses. Equal protection claims are viable where it appears that the government is discriminating against individual landowners based on a suspect classification such as race or nationality or interfering with a fundamental right such as privacy.[267]

The **due process clause** of the Fifth and Fourteenth Amendments provides that no one shall be "deprived of life, liberty, or property, without due process of law." A property interest must exist before there can be a deprivation. In land use situations, this may present a problem if a landowner complains that the government denied her a permit. Some courts view the requested permit as an expectation and not an entitlement or vested property right if there is any discretion used to grant or deny the permit. Other courts use the landowner's interest in the underlying property to establish the property interest required for either a substantive or procedural due process challenge.[268]

Procedural due process requires that administrative actions, but not legislative actions, give the affected landowner the appropriate notice and a hearing. The nature of the hearing provided does not need to duplicate a hearing in a court of law and jurisdictions differ as to whether such hearings should allow cross-examination of witnesses. In legislative actions, the public nature of the legislative process satisfies procedural due process requirements.[269]

Government regulation or action that is "unfair" or is outside the scope of the police power authority to promote the public health, safety, morals, and general welfare of the community is subject to **substantive due process** challenge. If a landowner can show that the government's action is an arbitrary or irrational exercise of power, the action is invalid. Substantive due process claims litigated in federal court may require a higher standard of irrationality such as it "shocks the conscience of the court" or is "truly irrational" before the court will invalidate a state or local regulation. However, state standards for evaluating such claims vary between a searching standard, where the court will balance the hardships of the regulation on the landowner against the benefits to the public, and a deferential standard, where the court will uphold the regulation if its rationality is debatable or if there is any basis to support the legislative decision.[270]

Equal protection challenges brought under the Fourteenth Amendment are successful if the plaintiff "alleges that she has been intentionally treated differently from others similarly situated and that there is no rational basis for the difference in treatment."[271] These claims are

---

[267] *Id.*

[268] *Id.*

[269] *Id.*

[270] *Id.*

[271] Village of Willowbrook v. Olech, 528 U.S. 562, 564 (2000).

subject to judicial review under the rational basis standard, which means that almost any government action is valid so long as it relates to the police power. In *Village of Willowbrook v. Olech*, the plaintiff alleged "the Village intentionally demanded a 33-foot easement as a condition of connecting her property to the municipal water supply where the Village required only a 15-foot easement from other similarly situated property owners."[272] Equal protection claims typically address discrimination among classes of individuals, but the Supreme Court in *Olech* held that a class may consist of only one person and that "irrational and wholly arbitrary" government action will be sufficient to state a claim for relief.[273]

Government regulation that intentionally targets a suspect class or a fundamental right is subject to heightened judicial scrutiny. Some of the housing issues, discussed above, have had either intentional discrimination or a discriminatory impact on protected classes. Poverty is not a suspect classification and housing is not a fundamental right. In *Village of Arlington Heights v. Metropolitan Housing Development Corp.*,[274] the Court evaluated an equal protection challenge to the Village's denial of a request to rezone a parcel from a single-family to a multi-family designation. The Court held that even though the rezoning denial did result in a discriminatory impact on racial minorities, an equal protection claim requires a showing of discriminatory intent in order to succeed.[275] The Court remanded the Fair Housing Act (FHA) claim to resolve whether showing discriminatory impact would be sufficient to state a claim under the FHA. We discussed FHA claims of discrimination in more detail in the Housing section above.

First Amendment challenges may be appropriate when government regulation or action restricts expression or religion. The First Amendment **freedom of expression** clause protects against government interference with freedom of speech, press, assembly, the right to petition the government for a redress of grievances, and the implied rights of freedom of association and belief. Regulations that are based on the **actual content** of the expression are presumptively unconstitutional and the government must show that the regulations are necessary to serve a compelling state interest and narrowly drawn to achieve the desired end. In addition, the government must show that it cannot achieve the desired end by a less restrictive means. This judicial examination of the government's right to regulate based on speech content is called the "**strict scrutiny**" standard of review.[276]

Billboards and signs are particularly problematic for local government to regulate. Cities may wish to regulate signs for aesthetic and perhaps safety purposes if they are too distracting to drivers. However, cities

---

[272] *Id.* at 565.
[273] *Id.* at 564-565.
[274] 429 U.S. 252 (1977)
[275] *Id.* at 269-271.
[276] LAND USE, *supra* note 7, at Chapter 3.

may also wish to allow "For Sale" signs, directional signs, retail identification signs, and political signs during election periods. The difficulty is that cities cannot regulate on the basis of the sign content, even by category, unless they can demonstrate that the regulation is necessary to serve a compelling state interest and narrowly drawn to achieve the desired end. Although the Court in *Reed v. Town of Gilbert, Arizona*[277] insisted that its decision "will not prevent governments from enacting effective sign laws,"[278] some fear that local governments will face more uncertainty and restrictions in regulating signs.[279]

In *Reed*, the Court found that the sign code regulations distinguished based on the content of the signs regulated and that the Town had the "burden to demonstrate that the Code's differentiation between temporary directional signs and other types of signs, such as political signs and ideological signs, furthers a compelling governmental interest and is narrowly tailored to that end."[280] The *Reed* Court determined that the Town did not meet its burden and held that the regulations "are facially content based and are neither justified by traditional safety concerns nor narrowly tailored."[281]

In some situations, the government wishes to control only the **time, place, or manner** of communication without regard to the content of the expression. This type of **content-neutral** regulation was at issue in *Ward v. Rock Against Racism*[282] where New York City attempted to regulate the volume of amplified music at the bandshell in Central Park so as not to disturb others in the vicinity. A rock concert sponsor challenged the noise control regulation and the Court noted that the First Amendment protects music as one of the oldest forms of human expression. The Court explained that "even in a public forum the government may impose reasonable restrictions on the time, place, or manner of protected speech, provided the restrictions 'are justified without reference to the content of the regulated speech, that they are narrowly tailored to serve a significant governmental interest, and that they leave open ample alternative channels of communication of the information.'"[283] After applying the time, place, or manner test, the *Ward* Court held that "[t]he city's sound-amplification guideline is narrowly tailored to serve the substantial and content-neutral governmental interests of avoiding excessive sound volume and providing sufficient amplification within the bandshell concert ground, and the guideline leaves open ample channels of communication."[284]

---

[277] 135 S. Ct. 2218 (2015).
[278] *Id.* at 2232.
[279] Brian J. Connolly & Alan C. Weinstein, *Sign Regulation after* Reed: *Suggestions for Coping with Legal Uncertainty*, 47 Urb. Law. 569 (2015).
[280] Reed v. Town of Gilbert, Ariz., 135 S. Ct. at 2231.
[281] *Id.* at 2232.
[282] 491 U.S. 781 (1989).
[283] *Id.* at 791.
[284] *Id.* at 803.

Adult businesses have long been the target of municipal regulation as cities seek to rid their communities of these unwanted uses. However, adult films, books, videos, and nude dancing are all protected expression under the First Amendment. In *Young v. American Mini Theatres*, Inc.,[285] adult theaters challenged Detroit zoning ordinances that "differentiate between motion picture theaters which exhibit sexually explicit 'adult' movies and those which do not" in order to disperse adult uses as impermissible content-based regulation. The Court held that the government's use of the content of these materials as a basis for putting them in a classification different from other films was permissible.[286] The Court followed the *American Mini Theatres* decision in *City of Renton v. Playtime Theatres, Inc.*,[287] where it developed the **"secondary effects"** test for adult businesses.

In *Renton*, the Court relied on *American Mini Theatres* to assign a lower value of First Amendment protection to non-obscene, sexually explicit expression. The *Renton* Court noted that the ordinance prohibiting adult theaters "from locating within 1,000 feet of any residential zone, single- or multiple-family dwelling, church, park, or school" does not "fit neatly into either the 'content-based' or the 'content-neutral' category."[288] However, the Court concluded that because the Renton ordinance targets the **secondary effects** caused by adult theaters, not the content of the films, any ordinances regulating these uses are **content-neutral time, place, or manner regulation**.[289] Subjecting Renton's ordinance to the test of "whether it is designed to serve a substantial governmental interest and allows for reasonable alternative avenues of communication," the Court found that the ordinance clearly met this standard and that "the Renton ordinance represents a valid governmental response to the 'admittedly serious problems' created by adult theaters."[290]

Freedom of religion is located in two different clauses in the First Amendment, made applicable to the states by the Fourteenth Amendment. The **free exercise clause** provides that the government cannot prohibit the free exercise of religion, including the right to believe and profess the religious doctrine of choice. The establishment clause provides that the government "shall make no law respecting an establishment of religion." Most of the land use conflicts involving religious freedom turn on the free exercise clause, although at times, efforts to protect religious exercise are subject to claims that they establish a religion.[291]

---

[285] 427 U.S. 50 (1976).
[286] *Id.* at 71.
[287] 475 U.S. 41 (1986).
[288] *Id.* at 43, 47.
[289] *Id.* at 47-50.
[290] *Id.* at 50, 54.
[291] LAND USE, *supra* note 7, at Chapter 3.

In *Employment Division v. Smith*[292] the Court examined "whether the Free Exercise Clause of the First Amendment permits the State of Oregon to include religiously inspired peyote use within the reach of its general criminal prohibition on use of that drug, and thus permits the State to deny unemployment benefits to persons dismissed from their jobs because of such religiously inspired use."[293] The Court reaffirmed that "the right of free exercise does not relieve an individual of the obligation to comply with a 'valid and neutral law of general applicability on the ground that the law proscribes (or prescribes) conduct that his religion prescribes (or proscribes).'"[294] The *Smith* Court held that because ingesting peyote was prohibited in Oregon and the prohibition is constitutional, Oregon may deny unemployment compensation to those who are dismissed from their job because they used the drug.[295] The outcome of this decision meant that neutral laws of general applicability can curtail religious activities without triggering strict scrutiny unless there is a system of individualized exemptions or the challenge is based on a hybrid of religious exercise violations along with other First Amendment violations.[296]

The Court subsequently decided *Church of the Lukumi Babalu Aye v. Hialeah*,[297] holding that laws targeting a specific religion, such as the Santeria religion, require strict scrutiny. In the *Lukumi* decision, the Court found that the City of Hialeah's prohibitions against animal slaughter and sacrifice failed to satisfy the *Smith* requirements because the ordinances were not neutral and instead targeted the Santeria religion.[298] In addition, the "ordinance represents a system of 'individualized governmental assessment of the reasons for the relevant conduct'" and therefore a compelling reason must be shown by the government for singling out a religious practice for discriminatory treatment.[299] Congressional action, including the Religious Freedom Restoration Act (RFRA) of 1993 and the Religious Land Use and Institutionalized Persons Act (RLUIPA) of 2000, followed the *Smith* case, and we discuss them below.

Litigants may use **Section 1983 of the Civil Rights Act** as the vehicle for bringing federal constitutional challenges as it provides that every person who, under color of law, deprives any citizen of any constitutional right should be liable. "Person" includes municipalities and government officials, although there are some situations where absolute immunity or qualified immunity may restrict liability. To assert a claim under Section 1983, there must be a deprivation of a federal right by a government action. A major advantage of bringing constitutional challenges under

---

[292] 494 U.S. 872 (1990).
[293] *Id.* at 874.
[294] *Id.* at 879.
[295] *Id.* at 890.
[296] *Id.* at 881-884.
[297] 508 U.S. 520 (1993).
[298] *Id.* at 534-537.
[299] *Id.* at 537-538.

Section 1983 is that, under Section 1988, prevailing plaintiffs are entitled to attorney's fees.[300]

Question

1. Many of the U.S. Constitutional provisions above establish minimum standards protecting individuals from a variety of land use decisions. Pick one of the provisions. How does that provision that protects individuals from land use decisions implicate a community's sustainability? This question asks you to understand the potential implications law and policy can have on sustainability.

C. Other Federal and State Limitations on Land Use

There is a myriad of local, state, and federal laws that impact land use decisions in addition to what we have already discussed. State common law, including nuisance, trespass, adverse possession, and restrictive covenants are historical property concepts, along with lateral and subjacent land support rights, water rights, and similar doctrines establishing the relationship of people as to real property and its associated rights. In addition, local, state, and federal statutes control land use and the externalities associated with activities that take place on land. As mentioned above in discussing First Amendment protections, Congress took action to protect religious exercise in land use decisions.[301]

The **Religious Land Use and Institutionalized Persons Act of 2000 (RLUIPA)** is a federal act that restricts local land use authorities from substantially burdening religious exercise in an individualized action unless the government shows a compelling state interest and that the zoning action is the least restrictive means of furthering such interest. The statute defines "religious exercise," but it does not define "substantial burden." Religious exercise is "any exercise of religion, whether or not compelled by, or central to, a system of religious belief" and includes the use, building, or conversion of real property for the purpose of religious exercise.[302]

A **substantial burden** is one that actually inhibits religious practice by virtue of a land use decision. In addition to the substantial burden prohibition in the statute, the government may not impose or implement

---

[300] LAND USE, *supra* note 7, at Chapter 3.
[301] *Id.*
[302] 42 U.S.C.A. § 2000cc-5(7)(A)&(B).

a land use regulation that treats a religious assembly or institution on **less than equal terms** than a nonreligious assembly or institution. Under this "equal terms" provision, it is not necessary that the religious proponent shows a "substantial burden." Finally, the government may not act unreasonably in limiting or excluding religious uses from its community.[303]

RLUIPA was enacted to protect religious land uses and institutionalized persons after a prior federal statute, the Religious Freedom Restoration Act of 1993 (RFRA), inspired by protest against the *Smith* decision (discussed above), was struck down by the Supreme Court in *City of Boerne v. Flores.*[304] The City of Boerne denied a church a building permit because of their building's historic significance and the church challenged the denial under RFRA. The Court found that RFRA, as applied to state and local actions, was invalid because Congress exceeded its authority under the Enforcement Clause of the Fourteenth Amendment.[305] RFRA is still valid as applied to federal action and was used in *Burwell v. Hobby Lobby Stores, Inc.*[306] to exempt a closely held for-profit corporation from the so-called "contraception mandate" of the Affordable Care Act based on the religious exercise of the owners.[307] In addition, several states enacted state RFRAs to require religious exemptions to state and local laws and there is the controversial possibility that federal or state RFRAs will provide religious exemptions from discriminatory actions based on sexual orientation in employment and public accommodations.[308]

The **federal and state environmental statutes** that impact land use development include:

- the federal and state environmental quality acts (NEPA),
- wildlife habitat and the Endangered Species Act (ESA),
- the Clean Water Act (CWA) for dredging and filling wetlands and local controls over discharges into local water bodies,
- environmental justice concerns,
- Coastal Zone Management (CZM) programs,
- floodplain development restrictions,
- hillside protection,
- water resource availability, and
- global warming legislation.

---

[303] Land Use, *supra* note 7, at Chapter 3.
[304] 521 U.S. 507 (1997).
[305] *Id.* at 536.
[306] 134 S. Ct. 2751 (2014).
[307] Martin S. Lederman, *Reconstructing RFRA: The Contested Legacy of Religious Freedom Restoration,* 125 Yale L.J. F. 416, 417-419 (2016).
[308] Zachary A. Bray, *RLUIPA and the Limits of Religious Institutionalism,* 2016 Utah L. Rev. 41 (2016); *see also* Craig v. Masterpiece Bakeshop, 370 P.3d 272, (Colo. App. 2015); *cert. granted,* Masterpiece Cakeshop, Ltd. v. Colo. Civil Rights Commn., 137 S. Ct. 2290 (2017).

The National Environmental Policy Act (NEPA) and its state counterparts, require that proposals for legislation or other major government actions significantly affecting the quality of the human environment must include a detailed statement on the environmental impact of the proposed action, any unavoidable adverse environmental effects, and alternatives to the proposed action.[309] Unless a statute exempts the project from such review, the agency must conduct an Environmental Assessment (EA) to determine whether to require an Environmental Impact Statement (EIS). If the EA process finds that there is no significant effect, a Finding of No Significant Impact (FONSI) statement is prepared. If, however, an EIS is required, the EIS must discuss whether there are any alternatives to the proposed action or legislation and whether the project can avoid or mitigate any significant impacts. Parties may challenge the adequacy of the EIS and a court will review the sufficiency of the information in the document, not the correctness of the EIS's conclusions. Under the "rule of reason," the EIS must be specific enough to permit informed decision making, but it does not prohibit unwise agency action.[310]

The Endangered Species Act (ESA) prohibits activities that may affect endangered or threatened species and may be part of the NEPA process to examine environmental impacts of government legislation or action. Section 4 of the ESA requires the Fish and Wildlife Service (FWS) to designate critical habitat and Section 7 requires federal agencies to consider the impact that proposed actions may have on protected species and work with FWS to conduct a biological assessment to determine whether to issue a Biological Opinion. Section 9 of the ESA makes it unlawful for any person to take, harass, harm, pursue, and hunt any endangered species and includes significant habitat degradation.[311] In some situations, the FWS may grant an "incidental take" permit under Section 10, if the "take" is for a lawful purpose and the permit request includes a habitat conservation plan that provides for mitigation, alternatives, and a showing of financial ability to complete the plan.[312]

The Clean Water Act (CWA) has authority to regulate "navigable waters" and this authority applies broadly to "waters of the U.S," including wetlands that have a nexus to a navigable waterway. Section 404 of the CWA requires those who wish to dredge and fill "navigable waters" to obtain a permit from the Army Corps of Engineers. Therefore, if a land parcel is going to be developed and it is a wetland under the regulations, the developer will be required to obtain a permit. Thus, to some degree, Section 404 of the CWA protects wetlands so long as they are "waters of the U.S."[313]

---

[309] 42 U.S.C. §4321 (1970).
[310] LAND USE, *supra* note 7, at Chapter 8.
[311] 16 U.S.C. §§1533, 1536, 1538 (1973).
[312] 16 U.S.C. §1539 (1973).
[313] 33 U.S.C. §§1251-1387 (1972).

The CWA also protects the water quality of local water bodies. Point sources for the discharge of pollutants into a water body are required to obtain a National Pollutant Discharge Elimination System (NPDES) permit unless specifically exempted by Congress. Point sources are "any discernible, confined and discrete conveyance, such as a pipe, ditch, channel, tunnel, conduit, discrete fissure, or container" and include discharges from vessels and Concentrated Animal Feeding Operations (CAFOs).[314] Local regulations limit discharges from nonpoint sources, such as urban, agricultural, or stormwater runoff into water bodies with poor water quality. Officials use Total Maximum Daily Loads (TMDLs) to calculate the maximum amount of a pollutant that can exist in a water body and reduce the amounts entering it by allocating reductions to one or more sources of that pollutant.[315]

Coastal zone management is a function handled at both the federal and state level. The Federal Coastal Zone Management Act of 1972 (CZMA) recognized that the coastal zones of the United States were under significant stress and that federal assistance would be needed to help states "manage the complexities of the coastal zone."[316] Congress stated that the national policy under this Act and its amendments in 1980 and 1990 is

> (1) to preserve, protect, develop, and where possible, to restore or enhance, the resources of the Nation's coastal zone for this and succeeding generations; (2) to encourage and assist the states to exercise effectively their responsibilities in the coastal zone through the development and implementation of management programs to achieve wise use of the land and water resources of the coastal zone, giving full consideration to ecological, cultural, historic, and esthetic values as well as the needs for compatible economic development.[317]

The Act provides federal funding to states to manage their Coastal Management Plans (CMPs) and requires federal agencies to follow these state CMPs whenever possible. Recognizing that coastal zone management is primarily a local land use function, the CZMA does not create federal rules that govern a state or local action.[318] However, it does protect national interests by requiring that the National Oceanic and Atmospheric Administration (NOAA) only approve state CMPs that conform to certain requirements as specified by the CZMA. In addition, Section 307 of the CZMA provides that "federal agencies must ensure that all actions they

---

[314] *NPDES Permit Basics*, EPA, https://www.epa.gov/npdes/npdes-frequent-questions#pane-5 (last visited Nov. 15, 2017).

[315] *Clean Water Act Section 303 (d): Impaired Waters and Total Maximum Daily Loads (TMDLs)*, EPA, https://www.epa.gov/tmdl (last visited Nov. 16, 2017).

[316] Lt. Commander Joseph Romero, *Uncharted Waters: The Expansion of State Regulatory Authority Over Federal Activities and Migratory Resources Under the Coastal Zone Management Act*, 56 NAVAL L. REV. 137, 140 (2008).

[317] 16 U.S.C. §1452.

[318] Romero, *supra* note 316, at 141-142.

conduct, fund, or permit, and that have a direct or indirect environmental, economic, or social impact on a state's coastal zone, are consistent with the enforceable policies contained in that state's management program." This so-called "consistency review" essentially allows a potential preemption of federal law by state coastal law.[319]

States have great flexibility in structuring their coastal programs so long as they involve all relevant state agencies and local governments in coastal management. State programs vary as to "(1) what tools are used to allocate the coast among alternative uses; (2) who actually makes which decisions; and (3) which parties, including developers, environmental organizations, local governments, and individual citizens, have standing to participate in the deliberations or otherwise to influence the decision."[320]

For example, California has the largest Coastal Zone Management Act in the nation that extends 1,100 miles from Mexico to Oregon and 5 miles outward from the shoreline. The Coastal Commission's jurisdiction extends only 1,000 yards inland in developed urban areas and the implementation of the Act lies with the creation of Local Coastal Plans (LCPs) and Zoning Regulations. After an LCP is certified, the Coastal Commission reviews all regulations and development approvals for consistency with coastal policies under the Act.[321] Members of the California Coastal Commission are unpaid and receive their appointment from the governor, the state Senate Rules Committee, or the speaker of the Assembly. While the Commission cannot stop building on coastal private property, they do have a great deal of authority over the size and scope of the development.[322]

The two main features of coastal zone authority are delineating the coastal zone and managing the permit process for allowing coastal development. To restrict development in a coastal zone, the coastal zone authority must show an adverse impact on the coastal zone's environment.[323] Some of the important policies at issue in coastal law include controlling devices that protect upland property against erosion, but damage productive ecosystems such as marshes; maximizing public access to the dry sand portion of the beach; and protecting special areas such as "wetlands, floodplains, estuaries, beaches, dunes, barrier islands, coral reefs, and fish and wildlife and their habitat."[324] The 1990 amendments to the CZMA included another important policy in requiring coastal states to improve water quality in their coastal zones by reducing nonpoint source pollution from the various runoff sources.[325]

---

[319] Josh Eagle, COASTAL LAW, Chapter 5 (Aspen 2011); Robert G. Healy & Jeffrey A. Zinn, *Environment and Development Conflicts in Coastal Zone Management*, 51 J. AM. PLANNING ASSN. 299 (1985).
[320] *Id.* (citing Healy & Zinn, *supra* note 319).
[321] LAND USE, *supra* note 7, at Chapter 9.
[322] Jack Dolon, *U2's The Edge and His Decade-Long Fight to Build on a Pristine Malibu Hillside*, L.A. TIMES (May 13, 2016), http://static.latimes.com/the-edge/.
[323] LAND USE, *supra* note 7, at Chapter 9.
[324] Eagle, *supra* note 319 (citing 16 U.S.C. §1452(2)(A)).
[325] *Id.* at Chapter 6.

Floodplain and hillside protection are important aspects of local land use control. Floodplains, which include wetlands, provide protection against flooding. Development in floodplains is problematic and regulation, condemnation, and incentivizing legislation can limit this use. The Federal Emergency Management Agency (FEMA) administers the National Flood Insurance Program and Federal Disaster Protection Act, which discourage development in flood-prone areas. Similarly, the Coastal Barrier Resources Act of 1982 does not provide insurance in high-hazard flood areas. The National Landslide Hazards Program regulates and mitigates hillside protection and development. Local steep slope ordinances control the degree of slope and allowable density in order to restrict inappropriate hillside development.[326]

Water supply and global warming concerns can also restrict development by requiring developers to show a sufficient and sustainable water supply for the proposed project and that the development would not significantly affect greenhouse gas emissions. California has been at the forefront of these issues as it faces challenges of water supply, deteriorating infrastructure, and insufficient transportation corridors.[327]

Questions and Note

1. The regulation of land by Congress raises important issues involving democracy, representation, and centralization. Is there anything specific to land that would make the regulation of it more or less sustainable at the local versus state versus federal level? For purposes of sustainability, what are the pros and cons of regulating land at the national level? Can it help address collective action challenges among local governments, discussed in Chapter 3?

2. What are the pros and cons of regulating land and the ecology on the land at the local level? Is there a difference between regulating the forest and regulating the stream where all our family and friends go to swim and fish? If so, what are those differences? Do they involve a community's values and identity? How do those differences implicate sustainability and resilience?

3. Consider local land use regulation in light of the following quote:

   In places, it becomes clear that there is a moment at which community and ecology become indistinguishable. An exercise may help to introduce the

---

[326]LAND USE, *supra* note 7, at Chapter 9.
[327]Jeanette Brown, *State of the State: Assessing the Effects of California's Infrastructure Challenges,* CALIFORNIA REAL ESTATE 21, 21 (Mar./Apr. 2015), http://www.car.org/ccre/pdf/Summit_Magazine_Article.pdf.

clues that evidence perspective: which of the following descriptions of places might be better found in a local government declaration, and which are more uniquely characteristic of a federal perspective? . . .

*   * We are a destination community . . . for innovation, education, commerce, and living—a place where you belong. [local vision statement]*

*   * Our children have inherited a livable, vibrant and economically diverse community. [local vision statement]*

*   * [This law declares a] policy which will encourage productive and enjoyable harmony between man and his environment; to promote efforts which will prevent or eliminate damage to the environment and biosphere and stimulate the health and welfare or man. (NEPA). . . .*

There is a notable difference between local vision statements . . . and the statements made by Congress in the NEPA. The divergences are not random, and they are not oversights. Throughout NEPA, the environment is portrayed as an object. In stark contrast, the local statements talk about "we" and "our place." These are local statements, made in the course of local governance of the surroundings, of the community, of home and of place. . . . This is an important observation. "We" is important to how the environment is governed. "We" can emerge from communities—as it pertains to people, ecology, industry or other. "We" means something different when it comes from the federal government. There is no "here" in the federal "there."[328]

---

[328] Keith Hirokawa, *Environmental Law from the Inside: Local Perspective, Local Potential*, 47 Envtl. L. Rep. 11050 (2017).

Energy Production and Consumption

6

I. INTRODUCTION

Humans produce and consume resources, goods, and services to be able to perform numerous activities, including those required for basic survival, such as food, water, and safe shelter.[1] Transportation, for example, provides us with many opportunities, including the ability to change our location to support ourselves through employment, maintain community and family connections, distribute goods and services, and facilitate recreational and aesthetic activities. To support activities, such as transportation, we require the production of energy and the use of natural resources. Increased consumer demands have placed increased demands on the energy sector and on critical natural resources necessary for the production and distribution of energy. In addition, there are unintended consequences stemming from the use, production, and distribution of energy, such as pollution and climate change that present ongoing and uncertain challenges. These challenges and others illustrate an increasingly urgent need to consider resilience and sustainability in energy and associated systems.

This chapter and Chapter 7 provide an overview of the law regulating resources needed to obtain the requested energy, including the extraction of raw materials and production of goods and services.[2] In addition to discussing energy and associated natural resources, we will introduce the systems that use energy for transportation, electricity, and to produce consumer goods. We will then examine the resilience and sustainability of the resources and systems.

---

[1] *See, e.g.,* Steven Ferrey, *In from the Cold: Energy Efficiency and the Reform of HUD's Utility Allowance System,* 32 HARV. J. ON LEGIS. 145, 145-146 (1995).
[2] As an introductory piece, see Kenneth A. Manaster, *An Introductory Analysis of Energy Law and Policy,* 22 SANTA CLARA L. REV. 1151 (1982).

Figure 6-1 sets forth the total amount of energy produced in the United States since 1949. The chart divides the production of energy into three individual and primary areas we will discuss below: fossil fuels (Section III), nuclear electric power (Section V.A), and renewable energy (Section V.B). Figure 6-2 shows where the United States used that energy during the same timeframe. As you read this chapter, refer to these charts to help better understand how the United States uses various energy sources.

By Source, 1949–2016

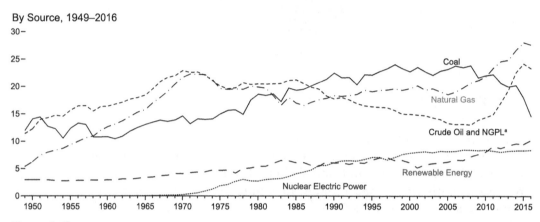

Figure 6-1[3]

WHAT IS A BTU?

A British thermal unit (Btu) is a measure of the heat content of fuels or energy sources. It is the quantity of heat required to raise the temperature of one pound of liquid water by 1 degree Fahrenheit at the temperature that water has its greatest density (approximately 39 degrees Fahrenheit).

One Btu is approximately equal to the energy released by burning a match. A single Btu is insignificant in terms of the amount of energy a single household or an entire country uses. In 2016, the United States used about 97.4 quadrillion (written out, one quadrillion is a 1 followed by 15 zeros) Btu of energy.

U.S. Energy Information Administration, *British Thermal Units (Btu)*, https://www.eia.gov/energyexplained/index.cfm?page=about_btu (last visited Nov. 16, 2017).

---

[3]U.S. Energy Information Administration, *Monthly Energy Report* (Sept. 2017), Tbl. 2-1, https://www.eia.gov/totalenergy/data/monthly/pdf/mer.pdf.

As you work through this chapter and Chapter 7, consider the fictional story of Amir and Juan, which highlights many of the ways in which behaviors and consumption patterns use energy. You will be asked to answer questions in some of the sections below based on this story.

Amir and Juan met up in Organic Chemistry class at California State University Northridge on a Friday morning in early June and decided to take a weekend trip to Las Vegas, Nevada to celebrate Juan's twenty-first birthday. Juan told Amir that Juan's Uncle Hank drove his Volkswagen "Bug" to Las Vegas back in 1968 to celebrate his birthday with friends. Juan promised Uncle Hank that he would stop by the Las Vegas Paiute Tribal Smoke Shop on Main Street and pick up one of Hank's favorite cigars. Amir volunteered to drive his 1999 Toyota Prius and Juan agreed to share the gasoline cost for the trip. When they passed through Mojave, California at about 3:00 p.m., they noticed the vast Tehachapi wind farm stretching as far as they could see. Amir and Juan also passed by signs indicating the construction of the Beacon solar thermal project along the California State Route 15 corridor.

They arrived in Las Vegas just as the sun was setting and the sparkling neon lights were beginning to light up the darkening streets. The heat hit them like a furnace blast as they exited their car and entered the cheap hotel where they had booked a room. Although the gaudy lobby smelled of stale smoke, it was cool, almost cold, as the air-conditioning pumped. As soon as they got to their room, they took turns jumping into a long, refreshing shower before beginning their evening adventures at the rich, red-oak blackjack tables. After gambling for the better part of the night, Amir and Juan returned to their room for a few hours of sleep. The next day, they set off around noon for a quick overnight trip with a tour company specializing in canoe trips on the Colorado River, tours of the Hoover Dam, and ATV off-road vehicle adventures.

Questions and Notes

1. At what point did Amir and Juan consume some form of energy or witness the production or consumption of energy? What decisions led them to use energy? Could there have been alternatives?

2. What types of energy did Amir and Juan use? For example, Amir and Juan needed gasoline for their Prius to transport them to Las Vegas for a weekend of entertainment. Oil, coal, and natural gas are fossil fuels needed to fuel combustion engines and other mechanical processes needed for heating and cooling. As a hybrid automobile, the Prius uses

Overview, 1949–2016

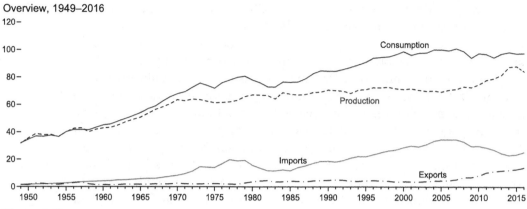

Figure 6-2[4]

both a combustion engine and a battery for power. Japan produces the battery for a Prius using rare earth minerals such as nickel, cobalt, and lanthanum. Currently, China is the only country that mines these rare earth minerals. Extracting those materials requires energy and has a number of environmental and social effects.

3. Upon their arrival in Las Vegas, Amir and Juan enjoyed a neon display and much-needed air-conditioning. The energy for both the air-conditioning and the neon lights likely came from NVEnergy, a power company that supplies Nevada's electrical energy needs through natural gas plants, renewable energy sources (such as solar and wind), and by importing nuclear energy from California's San Onofre plant and Arizona's Palo Verde plant. In addition to the risks inherent in nuclear power production, nuclear energy is a "nonrenewable resource" because of its reliance on uranium. Nuclear plants produce approximately 20% of the energy used in the United States. Nevada's energy grid relies upon natural gas and coal to provide most of the state's energy needs, but NVEnergy's goal is to use renewable resources for 25% of its power by 2025.[5] Further, Amir and Juan's tour took them to the Hoover Dam,

---

[4] *Id.*

[5] Other states have passed laws that require their utility companies to obtain a percentage of their electricity from clean sources. For example, under the Renewable Energy Program, California's utilities were required to obtain 20% of their electricity from clean sources by the end of 2010, although they were also given an extra three years to comply before assessing penalties. For further information on these initiatives and the struggles the energy companies are undergoing to comply, see *California Renewable Energy Overview and Programs*, The Cal. Energy Comm'n, http://www.energy.ca.gov/renewables (last visited Nov. 18, 2017); *see also* Tiffany Hsu, *California Utilities Struggle to Meet Renewable-Power Requirement*, L.A. Times (July 10, 2010), http://articles.latimes.com/2010/jul/10/business/la-fi-clean-power-20100710.

the Colorado River trip, and the ATV experience, which all have consequences on energy use and natural resources.

4. Fossil fuels predominantly provide the recent U.S. energy consumption levels: petroleum at 36%; natural gas at 25%; and coal at 20%. Renewable energy and nuclear electric power provide 9% and 8%, respectively. In Sections III and V, we describe the law concerning these major sources of energy, beginning with fossil fuels (Section III) and then non-fossil fuels (Section V).

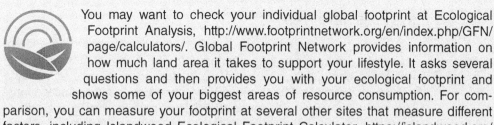

You may want to check your individual global footprint at Ecological Footprint Analysis, http://www.footprintnetwork.org/en/index.php/GFN/page/calculators/. Global Footprint Network provides information on how much land area it takes to support your lifestyle. It asks several questions and then provides you with your ecological footprint and shows some of your biggest areas of resource consumption. For comparison, you can measure your footprint at several other sites that measure different factors, including Islandwood Ecological Footprint Calculator, https://islandwood.org/footprint-calculator/, Center for Sustainable Economy, http://myfootprint.org/, and EPA's Carbon Footprint Calculator, https://www3.epa.gov/carbon-footprint-calculator/.

II. STRATEGY TO FACILITATE IMPLEMENTATION #4: SYSTEMS THINKING

A Systems Thinking (ST) analysis can help us more completely understand the energy system, including the extraction of raw materials, production, distribution, and use. Assume you are a mechanic. If you want to know how an electric car works, you would not disassemble the vehicle and investigate the rechargeable batteries, electric motor, controller, and other parts in isolation. Instead, you would need to know how the parts interact as a whole, which parts operate to convert stored electrical energy to mechanical energy to propel the car forward, which parts support that process, and how the system responds to stresses from starting, accelerating, stopping, and so on. This contextualized view of the car as a single system provides a complete picture of how the car works, how the parts interact, and what role each part performs. This type of holistic approach is Systems Thinking.

General Description of Systems Thinking. ST provides a complete understanding of an entire "system" (defined in the box below), each part's role in that system, and the overall functioning of the system. ST helps more accurately predict how the system will behave under both stable and changing circumstances, how it accomplishes its functions, and whether it exhibits inefficiencies. When policy makers more completely understand how the overall system and the various parts of a system work, they are less likely to make decisions that unintentionally impact part or all of a system in a way that negatively affects system functioning. ST helps highlight and avoid these unintended consequences.

SYSTEMS REVISITED

In Chapter 1, we defined systems. Systems are all around us and are constantly intertwining and overlapping. For purposes of ST, "system means a configuration of parts connected and joined together by a web of relationships. The [Special Integration Group of the International Society for the Systems Sciences (ISSS)] defines system as a family of relationships among the members acting as a whole."[6] In *Systems Effects: Complexity in Political and Social Life*, Professor Robert Jervis stated "[w]e are dealing with a system when (a) a set of units or elements is interconnected so that changes in some elements or their relations produce changes in other parts of the system, and (b) the entire system exhibits properties and behaviors that are different from those of the parts."[7]

Part of an ST approach includes the difficult task of defining the relevant system. Systems may be environmental or natural resource based, such as ecosystems in which subparts (for example, soil, atmosphere, water, fauna, and flora) work to sustain life together. Systems may be economic and/or social, such as energy production and distribution, transportation, manufacturing, urbanization, and communications. In addition, systems may be a combination of environmental, economic, and societal factors, such as forests, fish, and wildlife (all explored in the next section). Understanding the overlap between natural and human-made systems is something we explore in more depth in Chapter 3 on addressing Collective Action Challenges.

---

[6] Bela Banathy, *A Taste of Systemics*, THE PRIMER PROJECT, http://www.isss.org/taste.html (last visited Nov. 18, 2017).
[7] *See generally* Robert Jervis, SYSTEM EFFECTS: COMPLEXITY IN POLITICAL AND SOCIAL LIFE (Princeton Univ. Press, 1997).

Once we identify the appropriate system, finding the proper scale or boundaries to define and analyze the system can be challenging. For example, the bluehead wrasse, a saltwater fish, is a system in and of itself in terms of its physiology. This system consists of how the various anatomic pieces function together, such as how the bluehead wrasse

uses gills to extract oxygen from water. The bluehead wrasse is also part of progressively larger systems. It is part of a larger water-based food web cascading down to zooplankton (part of the bluehead wrasse's primary diet) and phytoplankton (part of zooplankton's primary diet) and cascading up to the roughtail stingray (a predator of the bluehead wrasse) and the great hammerhead shark (a predator of the roughtail stingray). In addition to being a part of a larger food-based system, the bluehead wrasse is also part of a larger ecological system that includes coral reefs (part of the bluehead wrasse's habitat) and oceans generally. It is also part of societal and economic systems, consisting of fishers, their families, and their fishing heritage based on a number of species related to the bluehead wrasse, including roughtail stingrays.

Determining where the relevant system pertaining to the bluehead wrasse begins and ends will affect the system analysis, the resources necessary for ST, and the potential results. The example illustrates the difficulty in identifying the parts of a system that are likely to be relevant and likely to provide important information for purposes of ST.

Once we define the system's boundaries, the next critical aspect of ST is **systems analysis**, which identifies and examines a system's **inputs** and **outputs**. Inputs are external factors that contribute to a system and outputs are what the system produces. For example, if the life process of a tree is the system, then carbon dioxide and water would be two inputs and oxygen would be an output, as the tree converts CO_2 and water into glucose and breathes out oxygen.

A critical part of systems analysis is aligning inputs and outputs with system parts. This helps elucidate changes and predict outcomes stemming from internal and external stimuli. This also helps policy makers understand how changes to specific parts may irreparably alter the functioning of the larger system. As technology and our understanding of systems improve, so too will systems analysis as we will have better access to data on inputs and outputs and their impacts on specific parts of a system.

Specific Description of ST's Relevance to R&S. Because R&S typically involve system-wide analyses to system-wide challenges, ST is particularly useful as it provides a system process. Chapter 1 quotes Professor Humby as saying: "resilience thinking is foremost systems thinking." When a system's resilience is strained (for example, nearing a threshold), ST helps to identify weaknesses in the system, which can then help develop possible solutions and predict potential consequences (changes in inputs and outputs). ST provides a means to translate data into healthy and viable solutions that minimize unintended consequences.

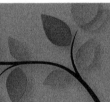

Joseph Fiksel, *Sustainability and Resilience: Toward a Systems Approach*

VOL, 2, NO. 2 SUSTAINABILITY: SCIENCE, PRACTICE, & POLICY (2006)

Our premise is that the effective pursuit of global sustainability requires a systems approach to the development of policies and intervention strategies. Absent a full understanding of system implications, there is a risk of unintended consequences. . . .

It has become increasingly unrealistic to perform a self-contained analysis of sustainability in a particular industry without touching upon the broader questions of energy, transportation, climate change, and urban planning. . . .

Interdisciplinary research teams are studying the links among industrial systems (energy, transportation, manufacturing, food production), societal systems (urbanization, mobility, communication,) and natural systems (soil, atmospheric, aquatic, biotic), including the flows of information, wealth, materials, energy, labor, and waste. The complexity, dynamics, and nonlinear nature of these interdependent systems imply that the notion of "sustainability" as a steady-state equilibrium is not realistic. Forces of change, such as technological, geopolitical, or climatic shifts will inevitably disrupt the cycles of material and energy flows. Therefore, achieving sustainability will arguably require the development of resilient, adaptive industrial and societal systems that mirror the dynamic attributes of ecological systems. . . .

The U.S. Environmental Protection Agency's (EPA) Office of Research and Development is now embracing a systems view of environmental progress. Its draft Sustainability Research Strategy proposes a new scientific framework for a more systematic and holistic approach to environmental protection that considers the complex nature of environmental issues and the welfare of future generations. The EPA has come to understand that designing sustainable systems encompasses several important challenges:

- Addressing multiple scales over time and space.
- Capturing system dynamics and points of leverage or control.
- Representing an appropriate level of complexity.
- Managing variability and uncertainty.
- Capturing stakeholder perspectives in various domains.
- Understanding system resilience relative to foreseen and unforeseen stressors. . . .

In the piece above, Dr. Fiksel states the importance of ST in understanding and assessing system R&S. He begins by noting the impracticality of trying to sustain industrial and societal systems in a "steady state." Maintaining a steady state is challenged, he states, by the "complexity, dynamics, and nonlinear nature" of systems. Fiksel provides examples of stimuli that may alter systems, including technology, politics, and others. In order to sustain a system's *core functions in the face of changes*, Fiksel notes, a system must become resilient. ST can sustain a system's core functions by identifying: external and internal forces; how those forces alter a system's parts; and where weaknesses exist.

Questions and Notes

1. Because the study of R&S is in many ways the study of complex social-ecological systems, such as the energy system, ST is a useful tool. First, however, we have to identify the relevant system. Which systems (social, economic, and environmental) do you see helping to form the energy system? What are the subparts of that system? What about the inputs and outputs?

2. Where would you draw the boundary when considering ST and the energy system? Assume you were trying to improve efficiencies

concerning residential energy use. Where would you draw the relevant system's boundaries?

3. How does the Precautionary Principle (discussed in Chapter 3) overlap with Systems Thinking? Professor David Orr has stated, "systems thinking can lead to greater realism and precautionary public policies for the simple reason that most systems are nonlinear and therefore inherently unpredictable. . . ."[8] How does Professor Orr characterize the connection between the Precautionary Principle and Systems Thinking?

4. Keep ST in mind as you consider natural resources, consumption, and energy in the next sections. Consider how ST might alter decisions people make relevant to natural resources.

III. ENERGY RESOURCES: FOSSIL FUELS

We begin this section by describing the legal structure regulating some of the major fossil fuels used to produce energy. We then turn to how those laws implicate the resilience and sustainability of systems relevant to the energy sector.

A. Oil and Natural Gas

Mining and Production.   Oil and natural gas are natural resources formed by the decay of plants and animals, deposited millions of years ago in a sea or lake, which were covered by multiple layers of sand and sediment, and eventually liquefied and gasified by pressure and heat.[9] These fossil fuels are hydrocarbons found beneath the Earth's surface as petroleum ("rock oil") in the form of a liquid crude oil and gaseous natural gas (mostly methane). The oil and gas are contained within minute spaces in sedimentary rock, in many cases trapped within impermeable rock layers, and are located by geologists before a well is drilled to extract the resource using pressure-differential pumps or steam, water, or gas injection. We produce natural gas along with oil and then send it into gas pipelines, or from gas-only fields with no oil production.

---

[8] David Orr, *Systems Thinking and the Future of Cities*, 5 SOLUTIONS 54 (Jan. 2014), https://www. thesolutionsjournal.com/article/systems-thinking-and-the-future-of-cities/.
[9] *See What Is Energy? Explained*, U.S. ENERGY INFORMATION ADMINISTRATION, https://www.eia.gov/ energyexplained/index.cfm?page = about_home (last visited Nov. 18, 2017).

Oil and Gas Laws in the United States.   U.S. laws differ from most other countries since the United States, along with Canada, allows private ownership of oil and gas, whereas most of the world treats them as government owned. Common law or statutory tort and property law govern mining and production activities in the United States, so states predominantly regulate these activities.[10] Ownership of oil and gas in the United States is based upon the surface land ownership unless the subsurface ownership interests have been severed. Most drilling and producing is performed by companies that have leased the rights from the owner of the land or the mineral rights, typically in exchange for royalty payments based upon production. Regulation of property rights and severance of mineral rights is under state control.[11]

Courts used the state law rule of capture doctrine typified in the 1805 New York case *Pierson v. Post*, which involved a dispute over the ownership of a dead fox's carcass, to resolve early ownership disputes about oil and gas in the United States.[12] The rule of capture awards ownership to the first person who brings a previously unowned (wild) resource into their certain control unless the resource escapes. For example, in *Pierson* the court held that once an individual catches or kills a wild animal, bringing it within the control and dominion of the hunter and making escape impossible, that individual gains protected property rights. By doing so, the court essentially created a race to take, appropriate, or kill something as quickly as possible to assure the procurement of property rights.

Modernly, the rule has determined ownership of common resources, as well as previously unowned or abandoned property, including a disputed baseball hit into the stands by Giants' player Barry Bonds for a record-breaking home run.[13] The rule of capture has been applied to all kinds of oil and gas extraction, including hydraulic fracturing to extract natural gas by horizontal drilling of productive oil or gas strata.[14] However, a pure rule of capture does not apply in every state. Some states have modified the rule of capture by adopting the common law doctrine of correlative rights, designed to promote shared legal rights and duties among owners of a common source.[15]

---

[10] *See generally 2012 Oil and Gas Survey*, 18 Tex. Wesleyan L. Rev. 443, 447-702 (2012) (discussing a survey of oil and gas law in 23 states).
[11] *See* Nw. Cent. Pipeline Corp. v. State Corp. Commn. of Kan., 489 U.S. 493, 512 (1989).
[12] 3 Cai. R. 175 (N.Y. 1805).
[13] Popov v. Hayashi, No. 400545, 2002 WL 31833731, at *1 (Cal. Super. Ct. Dec. 18, 2002).
[14] For a discussion of the relationship between property rights and natural resources, see Edella Schlager & Elinor Ostrom, *Property-Rights Regimes and Natural Resources: A Conceptual Analysis*, 68 Land Econ. 249 (1992).
[15] For a very thorough discussion on the rule of capture as it pertains to drilling and natural gas, see Coastal Oil & Gas Corp. v. Garza Energy Trust, 268 S.W.3d 1 (Tex. 2008), excerpted below and holding that a royalty holder of a natural gas lease could not recover for trespass due to the rule of capture. *See also* Lightning Oil Co. v. Anadarko E&P Onshore, LLC, 520 S.W.3d 39, 50-51 (2017) (citing *Coastal Oil* for rule of capture and concluding that mineral lessee's injury of a small loss of minerals suffered from a surface owner's drilling was not sufficient to support a trespass claim given the "longstanding policy of this state to encourage maximum recovery of minerals and to minimize waste").

RULE OF CAPTURE AND COLLECTIVE ACTION CHALLENGES

In Chapter 3, we describe Collective Action Challenges (CAC). These are challenges that arise over the competition of resources when numerous individuals or entities attempt to use the same resource. Part of our focus in this book is on laws that encourage or compel actors to either not act for the common good or make decisions in the actor's self-interest to the detriment of the common good.

The rule of capture has been criticized as being one such law. The Rule has long been recognized as encouraging actors to inefficiently consume resources, such as oil and gas, as quickly as possible, often to their depletion (for example, the consumption of fish stocks). The Rule does so by providing each actor with a privately held protected right to extract, use, or pollute a resource. In this way, the Rule recognizes that the actors collectively have common ownership over the resource, until one actor seizes a part or unit of the resource. Further, none of the actors has the right to exclude others from extracting, using, or polluting the resource. When one actor uses the resource, she prevents the other actors from doing so. In theory, each actor views herself in competition with the others to utilize the resource and thus, is motivated to consume the resource quickly before it is depleted and she is left with nothing.

The United States regulates onshore production of petroleum resources at the state level and typically involves a split estate such that an entity distinct from the owner of the surface will own or lease the subsurface mineral, oil, and gas rights. The surface owner and the oil and gas or mineral developer may manage conflicts through agreements and private covenants restricting the use of surface land. In the absence of such agreements, the law has historically treated the mineral estate as dominant and has allowed free use of the surface land.[16] Government attempts to reduce this dominance through state legislation or local zoning ordinances in order to protect health and safety, or to require mineral owners to compensate surface owners for damages, have generated constitutional challenges based on the Takings Clause of the Fifth Amendment.[17] Courts have at times managed

---

[16] *See* Hunt Oil Co. v. Kerbaugh, 283 N.W.2d 131, 135 (N.D. 1979) ("The above cases recognize the well-settled rule that where the mineral estate is severed from the surface estate, the mineral estate is dominant.") (citing 53 A.L.R.3d 16; 4 Summers, Oil and Gas §652; 58 C.J.S. Mines and Minerals §159b).

[17] For an illustration of the constitutional challenges and a discussion of the Takings Clause, see Keystone Bituminous Coal Assn. v. DeBenedictis, 480 U.S. 470 (1987) (where coal companies challenged Pennsylvania law under the Takings Clause, which required a portion of the underground coal be left intact so as to preserve the integrity of the surface structure and structural integrity of houses and other buildings; the Court held that there was no unconstitutional taking of property rights, and that the right of surface land owners to be free from concerns about the integrity of their house or buildings outweighed the interest in the coal company's need to mine *all* of the coal under the surface).

to modify the dominance of the mineral estate by requiring that any use of the surface must be reasonable and non-negligent for the development of oil and gas, and must reasonably accommodate existing use of the surface land, such as raising crops.

Ownership and Regulatory Jurisdiction.   Ownership may also be at issue where extracting a subsurface resource will damage or destroy the surface estate. Surface destruction is not generally an issue with conventional oil and gas withdrawal, but mineral extraction requiring strip mining, open-pit mining, or fracking can lead to litigation. States have attempted to resolve this ownership issue through various common law approaches, but mineral extraction developers continue to face conflicts between surface and mineral estate owners, coal developers, and coal bed methane (CBM) developers. Developers have also experienced frustration in dealing with the multiple layers of regulation at the federal, state, and local level when obtaining permits for resource development and shutting down sites after production ceases.[18]

Because mining, production, and private ownership of oil and gas resources are regulated by states, the only federal regulations applied to drilling operations are for offshore drilling, which may also be regulated by states when located within three miles from shore. State and federal law have come into conflict in three-mile coastal zones when the Department of the Interior leases offshore oil fields, and such leases do not comply with state coastal zone requirements developed under the Coastal Zone Management Act (CZMA).[19] The U.S. Supreme Court in *Secretary of the Interior v. California* held that the "sale of outer continental shelf oil and gas leases is not an activity 'directly affecting' the coastal zone within the meaning of the statute."[20] However, the Ninth Circuit in *California v. Norton* later held that California had the authority to review oil lease activity under the state's coastal management program pursuant to the CZMA.[21] The Ninth Circuit found that a 1990 amendment to the CZMA specifically overturned the Supreme Court's earlier decision.[22]

Federal and state authorities have also clashed when states attempt to protect their citizens against adverse impacts of federal actions, such as the

---

[18] Jan G. Laitos & Elizabeth H. Getches, *Multi-Layered, and Sequential, State and Local Barriers to Extractive Resource Development*, 23 Va. Envtl. L.J. 1, 2-4 (2004).
[19] 16 U.S.C. §§1451-64 (2012).
[20] 464 U.S. 312, 315 (1984).
[21] 311 F.3d 1162, 1165 (9th Cir. 2002).
[22] *Id.* at 1173.

destruction of Alaskan native subsistence resources caused by federal leasing of public lands in Alaska for oil exploration.[23] State regulations may prescribe minimum facility maintenance standards to require industry to detect leaks, prevent corrosion, inspect and clean tanks, and maintain gauges and valves. Rig operators may be required to submit a spill contingency plan to state authorities.[24] Most states have extensive environmental regulations, particularly where oil or natural gas production is a large state industry.

International Aspects.   International drilling began with large private oil companies receiving concessions from oil-bearing countries, which allowed them to develop oil fields in return for paying royalties to the host governments, similar to the early leasing agreements used domestically in the United States. Disputes between host countries and oil companies have typically been resolved through a process called arbitration. Arbitration is the major dispute resolution approach for international agreements, as the litigation of claims against host governments or state-owned oil companies faces substantial barriers. These jurisdictional barriers include the "act of state" doctrine (precluding courts from judging the legality of a foreign state's sovereign act), the doctrine of *forum non conveniens* (to prevent plaintiffs from purposefully filing suit in a forum that is inconvenient for defendants), and international comity (one nation must recognize the legislative, executive, or judicial acts of another nation).[25]

---

[23] For courts' discussion on the issue of conflicts involving federal and state laws, see Mobil Oil Exploration & Producing Se., Inc. v. United States, 530 U.S. 604 (2000) (oil companies sought restitution from U.S. government under breached lease due to conflicting state and federal regulations; Supreme Court held, among other things, that the regulation authorizing suspension to conduct an environmental analysis did not incorporate the requirements of future statutes excluded by the contracts' provisions, and suspension was not authorized pursuant to the Outer Banks Protection Act, which was enacted after execution of the contracts, where the Department of the Interior had determined that oil companies' exploration plan fully complied with the OCSLA); Amoco Prod. Co. v. Vill. of Gambell, Alaska, 480 U.S. 531 (1987) (Alaskan native villages brought action to enjoin offshore drilling, and the Supreme Court held that the Alaska National Interest Lands Conservation Act section setting forth procedures to be followed before allowing lease, occupancy, or disposition of public lands that would significantly restrict Alaskan natives' use of lands for subsistence did not apply to outer continental shelf, thus precluding an injunction); California v. Norton, 311 F.3d 1162 (9th Cir. 2002) (challenging the suspension of leases, the Ninth Circuit held that approval of lease suspensions was subject to consistency review by state, and agency did not adequately document its reliance on claimed categorical exclusion to review requirements of National Environmental Policy Act).

[24] For cases that deal specifically with issues of state regulations, see Hermosa Beach Stop Oil Coal. v. City of Hermosa Beach, 103 Cal. Rptr. 2d 447 (Ct. App. 2001) (coalition of environmental organizations sought declaratory and injunctive relief requiring city to apply to particular oil drilling and production project ballot initiative prohibiting oil and gas exploration, drilling and production on sites previously excepted from otherwise comprehensive ban; court held that the initiative applied, and it was not an unconstitutional impairment of contract); Wells Fargo Bank v. Goldzband, 61 Cal. Rptr. 2d 826, 841-850 (Ct. App. 1997) (discussing California codes that pertain to the cleanup of abandoned oil wells).

[25] For illustration of these doctrines, see *In re* Refined Petroleum Prods. Antitrust Litig., 649 F. Supp. 2d 572 (S.D. Tex. 2009) (act of state doctrine); Carijano v. Occidental Petroleum Corp., 643 F.3d 1216 (9th Cir. 2011) (forum non conveniens); Delta Air Lines, Inc. v. Chimet, S.P.A., 619 F.3d 288 (3d Cir. 2010) (forum non conveniens); Jota v. Texaco Inc., 157 F.3d 153 (2d Cir. 1998) (forum non conveniens and international comity).

The New Zealand Resource Management Act of 1991, one of the first environmental management schemes requiring sustainability, defines sustainable management as, "managing the use, development, and protection of natural and physical resources in a way, or at a rate, which enables people and communities to provide for their social, economic, and cultural wellbeing and for their health and safety."[26]

In the early 1970s, many host countries began exerting control over production, exportation, and pricing by creating state-owned oil companies through nationalization and participating in the Organization of Petroleum Exporting Countries (OPEC), whose member countries control over 70% of the world's oil reserves. In the 1990s, lower oil prices encouraged a trend back toward privatization and greater participation by private oil companies. This growth of transnational corporations resulted in a situation where the oil companies are essentially self-regulating because these countries do not have solid regulatory environmental standards and no comprehensive, effective body of international law governs sustainability.

Additionally, litigants have alleged that private oil companies have violated human rights for committing or aiding and abetting murder, rape, and torture to further forced labor. Oil companies have been subject to claims under the Alien Tort Claims Act of 1789, which allows an alien to sue in U.S. federal district court for a tort that violates "the law of nations" or a treaty with the United States[27] Claims of human rights violations are largely unsuccessful in the U.S. courts.[28] For example, in *Aguinda v. Texaco, Inc.*, residents of Ecuador and Peru brought two class action lawsuits against Texaco under the Alien Tort Claims Act, alleging that between 1964 and 1992 Texaco's oil operation polluted the rain forests and rivers in Ecuador and Peru.[29] The Second Circuit affirmed the district court's dismissal of the claims on the basis that "Ecuador was an adequate alternative forum and that the balance of private and public interest factors

---

[26] Bret C. Birdsong, *Adjudicating Sustainability: New Zealand's Environment Court*, 29 ECOLOGY L.Q. 1, 12 (2002) (internal quotation marks omitted).

[27] For a general discussion on this topic, see Judith Kimerling, *International Standards in Ecuador's Amazon Oil Fields: The Privatization of Environmental Law*, 26 COLUM. J. ENVTL. L. 289 (2001) (discussing the problem with privatization of the global oil market, in that few government regulations require companies to mitigate their negative impact on the environment, and specifically examining the Amazon Rainforest in Ecuador initiative and Occidental Petroleum's environmental self-regulation). For an overview of the suits against various oil companies under the Alien Tort Claim Act, see Flores v. S. Peru Copper Corp., 414 F.3d 233 (2d Cir. 2003) (personal injury claims for severe lung disease allegedly caused by pollution from mining company's operations in Peru brought by residents and survivors under Alien Tort Claims Act); Abecassis v. Wyatt, 785 F. Supp. 2d. 614 (S.D. Tex. 2011) (claims by survivors and relatives of those killed by suicide bombings in Israel against companies involved in the oil and gas business); Bowoto v. Chevron Corp., 557 F. Supp. 2d 1080 (N.D. Cal. 2008) (claims by Nigerian workers under Alien Tort Statute alleging oil company paid Nigerian military to carry out attacks on an oil platform).

[28] 10 Bus. & Com. Litig. Fed. Cts. §117:11 (3d ed.).

[29] Aguinda v. Texaco, Inc., 303 F.3d 470, 473 (2d Cir. 2002).

tilted in favor of dismissal."[30] A court in Ecuador adjudicated the case and in 2011, it ordered Chevron, as the successor to Texaco, to pay damages of approximately nine billion dollars.[31]

Some of the legal and policy issues surrounding oil and gas production pertain to ownership rights of the land and the exploited resource, taxation, leasehold rights, contract rights, tort claims for injury, royalty payments, production efficiency, pricing, resource sustainability through recycling and conservation, and environmental protection. Market-demand proration, which uses Maximum Efficient Rate of Recovery (MER) and the Market-demand Factor (MDF) to control the amount of field production, has controlled production efficiency and pricing. OPEC performs market-demand proration on an international level, while in the United States many states have voluntarily agreed to be members of the Interstate Compact to Conserve Oil and Gas, which estimates national market demand and assigns production quotas to stabilize pricing through proration. In 2011 and 2012, the United States imported a net of (imports minus exports) about 40% of its oil.[32] This dependency is a national security issue, which generated the need for a Strategic Petroleum Reserve (SPR) created in 1976 to store 90 days of crude oil in case of a national crisis caused by an embargo, a war, or high prices.

Transporting and Distributing Fuel. While mining, production, and intrastate transportation are regulated at the state level in the United States, the federal government has an interest in making sure that interstate pipelines for transport of these resources are properly maintained to protect land and people. The Secretary of Transportation must set forth the governing standards under the Pipeline Safety Act, 49 U.S.C. §60103. Federal rules also govern the transport and sale of natural gas in interstate commerce under the Natural Gas Act, 15 U.S.C. §717. The Federal Power Commission establishes the applicable rates and is responsible for approving a company's request to transport and sell natural gas.[33] This legislation explicitly preserves "production or gathering" for regulation by individual states.[34]

Oil tankers and oil pipelines are the two major methods to transport oil. Pipelines also transport natural gas. Trucks, rail, and barges transport some heavy forms of oil, such as asphalt. In 2008 in the United States,

---

[30] *Id.* at 476.
[31] Simon Romero & Clifford Krauss, *Ecuador Judge Orders Chevron to Pay $9 Billion*, N.Y. Times (Feb. 14, 2011), http://www.nytimes.com/2011/02/15/world/americas/15ecuador.html.
[32] *How Dependent Are We on Foreign Oil?*, U.S. Energy Info. Admin., https://web.archive.org/web/20130825061846/http://www.eia.gov/energy_in_brief/article/foreign_oil_dependence.cfm (last updated May 10, 2013).
[33] 42 U.S.C. §717(c) (2012).
[34] *See* 42 U.S.C. §717(b) (2012).

there was a natural gas pipeline grid of more than 305,000 miles and more than 173,000 miles of hazardous liquid pipelines.[35] Historically, oil pipelines were regulated as common-carrier open-access lines. The pipeline companies also owned natural gas pipelines, bought gas from the producer, transported it, and then sold it to a distributor for transmission to the end user. The natural gas industry began restructuring to allow competitive markets after the 1992 order of the Federal Energy Regulatory Commission (FERC), which required interstate natural gas pipeline companies to split off their sales functions from the transportation function.[36]

Oil and Gas Pipelines. In the United States, pipelines are subject to FERC regulations as well as to regulations under the Environmental Protection Agency (EPA) and the Department of Transportation's Office of Pipeline Safety (OPS). A tragic oil pipeline rupture near Carlsbad, New Mexico, which killed 12 campers in 2000, led to the Pipeline Safety Improvement Act of 2002, 49 U.S.C. §§60101–40.[37] This Act allowed for OPS reforms, greater state inspection and enforcement authority, better public information, industry oversight, and attention to potential terrorist concerns. The statute requires companies to inspect oil pipelines for cracks or corrosion to avoid leakage and ruptures. Natural forces such as floods, extreme temperatures, and hurricanes can contribute to disastrous consequences when pipelines rupture and cause fires, oil spills, and supply disruptions. These pipelines cross state lines and national borders, so regulation may be a mix of domestic and international law.

A natural gas wellhead or field produces natural gas. Pipelines then transport the gas to processing stations, which transport it directly to a mainline transmission grid unless contact with crude oil has contaminated the gas requiring further processing. Underground natural gas storage and Liquefied Natural Gas (LNG) facilities provide inventory management and act as a back up to help maintain balance within the system as large shifts in daily demand occur. Gas companies in urban areas distribute gas for heating, cooking, and industrial processes to homes and businesses using gas mains under the streets. These pipelines and storage facilities operate under intense pressure and require sufficient maintenance to prevent

---

[35] *About U.S. Natural Gas Pipelines*, U.S. Energy Info. Admin., https://web.archive.org/web/20170712192248/https://www.eia.gov/pub/oil_gas/natural_gas/analysis_publications/ngpipeline/index.html (last visited Nov. 18, 2017); *Annual Report Mileage for Hazardous Liquid or Carbon Dioxide Systems*, Pipeline & Hazardous Materials Safety Admin. (Sept. 1, 2016), http://www.phmsa.dot.gov/pipeline/library/data-stats/annual-report-mileage-for-hazardous-liquid-or-carbon-dioxide-systems.

[36] FERC Order No. 636 (April 9, 1992).

[37] Andrew Restuccia & Elana Schor, Pipelines Blow Up and People Die Politico (Apr. 21, 2015) https://www.politico.com/story/2015/04/the-little-pipeline-agency-that-couldnt-217227 (last visited Nov. 16, 2017).

explosions, which can cause devastating results.[38] For example, 50 homes caught fire when an underground gas line exploded in 2011, killing eight people in the unsuspecting San Francisco satellite neighborhood of San Bruno.[39]

DAKOTA ACCESS PIPELINE AND STANDING ROCK

Energy Transfer Partners is a Dallas, Texas, company that established a 2,000-mile pipeline to move oil from North Dakota, the second largest oil-producing state in the United States, through South Dakota and Iowa to an Illinois shipping point. The Standing Rock and Cheyenne River

Sioux tribes filed a lawsuit to stop the project claiming "that a rupture in the section that crosses under Lake Oahe would threaten their water supply and sacred sites and would prevent them from practicing their religion, which requires clean water." The tribes successfully pushed the U.S. government in December 2016 to prepare a full environmental study of the Lake Oahe crossing, but President Donald Trump rescinded the study after he took office in 2017. Protests and opposition against the Dakota Pipeline have continued, including "'coordinated physical attacks' on the pipeline."[40]

---

[38] Government websites contain a great deal of information pertaining to the process of natural gas extraction and the intricacies of how pipelines work. *See, e.g., About U.S. Natural Gas Pipelines, supra* note 35. For an example of a pipeline rupture and oil spill in Montana, see *Pipeline Rupture Spews Oil Down Yellowstone River: Discovery News,* SEEKERS (July 3, 2011), http://www.seeker.com/pipeline-rupture-spews-oil-down-yellowstone-river-discovery-news-1765287093.html; *Montana Oil Spill in Yellowstone River,* ABC NEWS (July 4, 2011), http://abcnews.go.com/GMA/video/montana-oil-spill-yellowstone-river-exxonmobil-guessing-extent-13992024 (video coverage).

[39] For extensive background on the California disaster, see Krista Mahr, *The San Francisco Explosion: Another Strike Against an Industry Under Scrutiny?,* TIME (Sept. 10, 2010), http://science.time.com/2010/09/10/the-san-francisco-explosion-another-strike-against-an-industry-under-scrutiny; Neal Karlinsky et al., *San Bruno Gas Explosion: Responders' Recordings Released,* ABC NEWS (Sept. 14, 2010), http://abcnews.go.com/US/san-bruno-gas-explosion-residents-return-destruction/story?id=11631344.

[40] Associated Press, *Dakota Access Pipeline Now Has Oil Beneath Missouri River, Company Says,* NBC NEWS (Mar. 28, 2017, 2:47 AM), http://www.nbcnews.com/storyline/dakota-pipeline-protests/dakota-access-pipeline-now-has-oil-beneath-missouri-river-company-n739296.

Oil Tankers.   Ships transport a great deal of oil, including 50% of U.S. oil imports. International treaties created the International Maritime Organization (IMO) in 1948, which regulates anything having to do with maritime transport. The IMO implemented safety regulations to ensure safe maritime oil transport following oil spills and the ensuing environmental consequences. The International Convention for the Prevention of Pollution of the Sea by Oil (OILPOL) implemented the first such regulation in 1954, which prohibited the dumping of oily wastes within a certain distance from land and in environmentally sensitive areas. After the ship Torrey Canyon ran aground in 1967 and spilled oil into the English Channel, the IMO established an international convention to regulate the transportation of oil to reduce the environmental impact. Following spills off the New England coast in 1977, the government more stringently regulated ships and discharges into the waters.

The Exxon Valdez spill in 1987 prompted the United States to implement the Oil Pollution Act of 1990 (OPA), 33 U.S.C. §§2701-2720, which requires that ships have double hulls. The IMO subsequently adopted the double hull requirement. The Oil Pollution Act also provides a liability trust fund for cleanups and specifies vessel and facility liability for damages resulting from discharged oil, requirements for evidence of financial responsibility, and planning and prevention activities. However, the OPA allows states to enforce some of the OPA requirements for addressing spill liability within the navigable waters of the state. As indicated in Figure 6-3, crude oil and oil products account for a large portion of

Number of oil spills from tankers worldwide, 1970-2016

The bars show the number of oil spills per year. Smaller oil spills (7-700 metric tons) in dark grey ■ and large oil spills (>700 metric tons) in light grey ■.

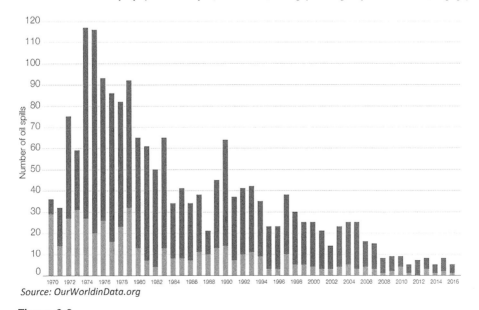

Source: OurWorldinData.org

Figure 6-3

the cargo transported by sea. However, even though maritime transport has increased since the IMO's inception, oil pollution from shipping has decreased.[41]

When ships transport oil, there are concerns about spills and environmental damage. In addition, there are international transit chokepoints, such as sea passages and pipelines, that may be affected by political uncertainty, potential piracy, and shipping accidents affecting the supply of oil. These major chokepoints include:

- Yemen, where the Red Sea connects with the Gulf of Aden and the Arabian Sea;
- the Bosporus/Turkish Straits in Turkey;
- the Panama Canal and Trans-Panama Pipeline;
- the Strait of Hormuz in Iran, connecting the Persian Gulf with the Gulf of Oman and the Arabian Sea;
- the Strait of Malacca in Singapore, connecting the Indian Ocean with the South China Sea and the Pacific Ocean; and
- the Suez Canal and Sumed Pipeline in Egypt, connecting the Red Sea and the Gulf of Suez with the Mediterranean Sea.[42]

Questions

1. In this section, we discussed the comparative federal and state authority to regulate oil extraction and transportation. What are the benefits of having one or the other regulate this industry? Would one tend to lead to a more sustainable energy system?

2. As mentioned above, the United States is one of only a few countries that recognize a private property right to oil. Does the recognition of private rights to oil tend to increase or decrease energy system resilience? What factors would you consider in answering this question? Does it increase some subsystems, while decreasing others? How so?

3. How do questions 1 and 2 above illustrate some of the differences between resilience and sustainability?

---

[41] For more information on the history of the IMO see *Oil Pollution Prevention: Background*, INTERNATIONAL MARITIME ORG., http://www.imo.org/OurWork/Environment/PollutionPrevention/OilPollution/Pages/Background.aspx (last visited Nov. 18, 2017).

[42] For a thorough report on the details and background of the chokepoints, see *World Oil Transit Chokepoints*, U.S. ENERGY INFO. ADMIN., https://www.eia.gov/beta/international/analysis_includes/special_topics/World_Oil_Transit_Chokepoints/wotc.pdf (last updated July 25, 2017).

B. Coal

Mining and Production. Coal, like oil and gas, is a fossil fuel created when decaying matter on land compacts and forms into a solid, rather than a liquid or gas. Coal is the largest energy source in the world for the production of electricity through combustion, but it is not a clean source. There are adverse environmental impacts from the extraction of the mineral and from the burning of coal, which is one of the leading contributors to smog, acid rain, toxic air quality, and global climate change (discussed in more depth in Chapter 10).[43] Coal has fueled the world for centuries, but the demand for this resource increased dramatically during the Industrial Revolution (discussed in Chapter 2). Modernly, China is the largest producer and user of coal, with coal constituting 70% of the nation's energy supply. The United States is the second largest coal producer, but it has the largest coal reserves in the world at approximately 22%, with Russia following at 14%, China at 13%, Australia at 9%, and India at 7%. World coal production is estimated to peak in 2025, and by estimating reserve life based on current production levels and proved reserves, China has approximately 35 years of reserve while the United States has approximately 240 years.[44] The Chinese have used gasification or liquefaction to convert coal into gasoline or diesel in order to be energy independent, as much as possible, from suppliers of oil.

There are two primary forms of coal mining: surface mining, such as open pit or strip mining; and underground mining, such as room-and-pillar and longwall mining. Mountaintop removal is surface mining that combines area and contour strip-mining to remove mountaintops and expose coal seams. Extraction processes involve removing overburden dirt and rock to expose coal seams near the surface, carving rooms into the coal seam and sometimes leaving coal pillars, to allow for extracting coal from beneath the surface.[45] "Huge machines, called 'draglines,' push rock and dirt into nearby streams and valleys, forever burying waterways. The massive dragline [. . .] , which can weigh up to 12 million pounds and be as big as an entire city block, is dwarfed by the scale of this devastation."[46]

related to shortage water resources

---

[43] *Environmental Impacts of Coal Power: Air Pollution*, UNION OF CONCERNED SCIENTISTS, http://www.ucsusa.org/clean_energy/coalvswind/c02c.html (last visited Nov. 18, 2017); CoalSwarm & The Center for Media and Democracy, *Environmental Impacts of Coal*, http://www.sourcewatch.org/index.php/Environmental_Impacts_of_Coal (last updated Mar. 16, 2015).

[44] For a survey of world energy resources, including coal, see *World Energy Resources: 2013 Survey*, WORLD ENERGY COUNCIL (2013), https://www.worldenergy.org/wp-content/uploads/2013/09/Complete_WER_2013_Survey.pdf.

[45] *Coal*, NAT. GEOGRAPHIC, https://www.nationalgeographic.org/encyclopedia/coal/ (last visited Nov. 18, 2017).

[46] *What Is Mountaintop Removal Mining?*, EARTHJUSTICE, http://earthjustice.org/features/campaigns/what-is-mountaintop-removal-mining# (last visited Nov. 18, 2017).

Surface Mining. Mountaintop removal mining presents environmental and health challenges because of its cumulative effects of deforestation, changes in habitats, and impacts on water quality due to increased run-off, stream thermal changes, and increased sediments. In the Appalachian region of the United States, these concerns about human health and the aquatic ecosystem have prompted the Environmental Protection Agency (EPA) to issue guidance for review of mountaintop removal mining permits.[47] This guidance provides for the EPA to exercise oversight authority to ensure that the holders of a Clean Water Act permit required for these mining operations are following the law. States are responsible, in coordination with EPA, for establishing state water-quality standards. The Department of the Interior (DOI) is also committed to making sure that the Office of Surface Mining Reclamation and Enforcement (OSM) effectively oversees individual state permitting and enforcement activities and engages in rulemaking to protect streams under the Surface Mining Control and Reclamation Act (SMCRA). The agency evaluates mining permits in light of the potential impacts on water quality for drinking water supplies and the aquatic ecosystems, fish and wildlife values, recreation, aesthetics, habitats, human health, and any disproportionate impact on low-income and minority populations.[48]

Managing Production Impacts of Surface Mining. In the United States, individual states are responsible for controlling coal mining.[49] While the SMCRA gives Congress the power to regulate the coal mining industry, states may create their own regulatory programs with approval from the federal government so long as the states demonstrate that their laws are

---

[47] Surface Mining Control and Reclamation Act of 1977 (SMCRA), 30 U.S.C. §§1201-1328 (2012); *Section 404 of the Clean Water Act: CWA Policy and Guidance*, EPA, http://water.epa.gov/lawsregs/guidance/wetlands/mining.cfm (last visited Sept. 24, 2017); *see generally Office of Surface Mining Reclamation & Enforcement*, U.S. Dep't of the Int., http://www.osmre.gov (last visited Nov. 18, 2017).

[48] *EPA Issues Comprehensive Guidance to Protect Appalachian Communities from Harmful Environmental Impacts of Mountaintop Mining*, EPA (April 1, 2010), http://yosemite.epa.gov/opa/admpress.nsf/e77fdd4f5afd88a3852576b3005a604f/4145c96189a17239852576f8005867bd!OpenDocument.

[49] State law governs most aspects of coal mining operations. Specifically, under the Surface Mining Control and Reclamation Act (SMCRA), 30 U.S.C. §§1201-1328 (2006), states are able to create their own regulatory programs, of which the federal government must approve. *See* Montco v. Simonich, 285 Mont. 280, 286-289 (1997) (providing an overview of coal mining permit requirements); Dep't of Envtl. Res. v. Croner, Inc., 152 Pa. Cmwlth. 144 (1992) (discussing SMCRA); Davis v. Eagle Coal & Rock Co., 220 W. Va. 18 (2006) (holding federal law does not preempt state tort law for coal mining accidents). Additionally, for an overview of various state statutes, see Tex. Nat. Res. Code Ann. §§131-135 (West 2010); W. Va. Code §§22-3-4 *et seq* (2017) (governing coal mining and reclamation). Federal regulations include the Federal Coal Mine Health and Safety Act of 1969, 30 U.S.C. §§951 *et seq.* (2006) (requiring two annual inspections of every surface coal mine and four at every underground coal mine, and otherwise increasing federal enforcement powers in coal mines; later amended to provide even more stringent safety regulations by the Coal Mine Act of 1977, 91 Stat. 1290 (1998)), and regulations of any mining operations taking place on Native American tribal lands. *See Laws and Regulations Applicable to Coal Mining*, Tribal Energy & Envtl. Info., http://teeic.indianaffairs.gov/er/coal/legal/index.htm (last visited Nov. 18, 2017).

as strict as the SMCRA. The SMCRA created the OSM (a bureau within the DOI) to oversee mining operations, enforce SMCRA provisions, and approve state programs. In addition, OSM works with various universities to research mining and reclamation methods that are environmentally sustainable. The regulatory program under the SMCRA sets minimum environmental standards for mining operations and requires companies to provide plans for cleanup of the land upon completion of mining operations, obtain permits before conducting surface mining, and post a bond to cover the cost of reclaiming the site. The SMCRA also provides authority to inspect and enforce regulations, prohibits surface mining on certain lands, such as in National Parks and wilderness areas, and creates an Abandoned Mine Land (AML) Fund[50] to clean up mines abandoned before the adoption of these regulations in the 1970s. The Mine Safety and Health Administration provides additional federal oversight of the safety regulations for workers in the mine.[51]

International Coal Consumption.   The United States recently reduced its reliance on coal, which reduces national air pollution, but U.S. coal exports to Germany, India, China, Japan, South Korea, and England have increased and contributed to overall global GHG emissions. The price of natural gas has fallen, which motivates U.S. companies to switch from coal but also discourages investment in renewable energy sources. Following the Fukushima disaster in Japan, several countries shut down nuclear plants and substituted coal burning to address their energy shortfall.[52]

China has been dependent on burning coal and is currently the world's largest carbon emitter. Coal will remain essential to supply global electricity demand for several more decades. Because coal is a cheap energy source, "[o]ver the last decade, global coal consumption has increased by more than the growth in oil, natural gas and hydro and nuclear power combined."[53]

Managing Emissions from Coal-Fired Power Plants.   Carbon dioxide emissions from coal-fired power plants contribute heavily to climate change. In 2015, at the United Nations Climate Change Conference,

---

[50] *See generally Abandoned Mine Land Reclamation Program*, U.S. Dep't Interior Natural Res. Revenue Data, https://useiti.doi.gov/how-it-works/aml-reclamation-program/#the-aml-fund (last visited Nov. 18, 2017).

[51] The Supreme Court has upheld the SMCRA as constitutional in Hodel v. Indiana, 452 U.S. 314 (1981) (holding that the "prime farmland" provisions of SMCRA establishing specific standards of mining for farmland did not violate the Commerce Clause, the Fifth Amendment or the Tenth Amendment, and neither was it an unconstitutional taking). For further information on mine safety and coal regulations, see U.S. Dep't of Labor: Mine Safety & Health Admin., http://www.msha.gov (last visited Nov. 18, 2015).

[52] Ann Carlson, *The Good, the Bad and the Ugly About Coal*, Legal Planet: Envtl. L. & Pol'y (June 19, 2012), http://legal-planet.org/2012/06/19/the-good-the-bad-and-the-ugly-about-coal/.

[53] Robert Bryce, *Dirty but Essential—That's Coal*, L.A. Times (July 27, 2012), http://articles.latimes.com/2012/jul/27/opinion/la-oe-adv-bryce-coal-epa-climate-20120727.

Conference of the Parties, 21 nations to the U.N. Framework Convention on Climate Change drafted an agreement to reduce greenhouse gas (GHG) emissions and move toward a sustainable future. The core part of the agreement, called the Paris Agreement, requires all parties ratifying the agreement to establish metrics and baselines for GHG emissions from their individual country, called "nationally determined contributions" (NDCs), and to strengthen those NDCs every five years. The agreement seeks to reduce GHG emissions such that global temperatures will not increase more than two degrees Celsius with a preference of not more than one and a half degrees.[54] As part of the United States' NDC, it proposed regulating existing and new coal-fired power plants. While complex and involving a series of Environmental Protection Agency regulations, the underlying goal is to reduce carbon emissions by about a third from 2005 levels by 2030. Dozens of state attorney generals have challenged these regulations and these disputes have been working their way through the court system.[55] However, in June 2017, U.S. President Donald Trump announced that the United States is withdrawing from the Paris agreement and said that the 2015 accord "imposed wildly unfair environmental standards on American businesses and workers . . . [and] vowed to stand with the people of the United States against what he called a 'draconian' international deal."[56]

---

[54] Paris Agreement, United Nations Framework Convention on Climate Change 14 (2015), https://unfccc.int/files/essential_background/convention/application/pdf/english_paris_agreement.pdf.

[55] In December 2009, Rocky Mountain Farmers Union, Redwood County Minnesota Corn and Soybean Growers, Penny Newman Grain, Inc., Growth Energy, Renewable Fuels Association, Rex Nederend, Fresno County Farm Bureau, Nisei Farmers League, and California Dairy Campaign sued the state of California and various California officials in federal court. Rocky Mountain Farmers Union v. Goldstene, 843 F. Supp. 2d 1042 (E.D. Cal. 2011). Plaintiffs alleged that the Low Carbon Fuel Standards (LCFS) promulgated by the California Air Resource Board in accordance with the California Global Warming Solutions Act would harm the corn ethanol industry (pushing Midwestern producers out of the California market) as well as violated the dormant Commerce and Supremacy Clauses. Through a series of orders, the district court rejected the defendants' arguments that Section 211(c)(4)(B) of the Clean Air Act authorized the LCFS to remove it from both preemption and Commerce Clause scrutiny, found that the LCFS violated the dormant Commerce Clause in its treatment of ethanol and crude oils, granted an injunction to enjoin defendants from further enforcing the LCFS, and directed the clerk to enter judgment in favor of the plaintiffs on their Commerce Clause claims. Rocky Mountain Farmers Union v. Goldstene, Nos. CV-F-09-2234 LJO DLB, CV-F-10-163 LJO DLB, 2012 WL 217653, at *1 (E.D. Cal. Jan. 23, 2012). On appeal, the Ninth Circuit affirmed in part, reversed in part, vacated in part, and remanded the case to the district court. Rocky Mountain Farmers Union v. Corey, 730 F.3d 1070, 1107 (9th Cir. 2013). On remand, the district court granted defendants' motion for partial summary judgment on plaintiffs' first claim that the original LCFS was an impermissible extraterritorial regulation in violation of the Commerce Clause. Am. Fuels & Petrochemical Mfrs. Assn. v. Corey, No. 1:09-CV-2234-LJO-BAM, 2015 WL 5096279, at *8 (E.D. Cal. Aug. 28, 2015). As to the amended LCFS, the court granted without leave to amend the defendant's motion to dismiss plaintiff's claim that it was an impermissible extraterritorial regulation. *Id.* at *12. As to the dormant Commerce Clause claim, the court concluded that the plaintiff could not state a discriminatory effects claim against the amended LCFS's crude oil provisions, and therefore granted without leave to amend defendant's motion to dismiss plaintiff's claim that the provisions discriminated in purpose and effect. *Id.* at *36.

[56] Michael D. Shear, *Trump Will Withdraw U.S. from Paris Climate Agreement*, N.Y. Times (June 1, 2017), https://www.nytimes.com/2017/06/01/climate/trump-paris-climate-agreement.html.

In *Massachusetts v. EPA*, 549 U.S. 497 (2007), the U.S. Supreme Court determined that GHG emissions were air pollutants subject to regulation under the Clean Air Act, §202(a), and directed the EPA to determine whether these emissions endanger public health or welfare. As the EPA has gone about its duties under the Clean Air Act, including making the requisite endangerment finding, litigation has ensued, resulting in decisions upholding EPA regulations and actions and in decisions striking down the EPA's attempts to address GHG emissions.[57]

"Syngas" is an alternative energy technology that may reduce GHGs through efficiencies and gasifying the coal rather than burning it. This technology exposes the coal to steam, air, or oxygen under high temperatures and pressures to break apart coal molecules and cause chemical reactions, which produce a mixture of gaseous compounds." Syngas consists mostly of hydrogen and carbon monoxide, which is cleaned and then (similar to natural gas) burned as fuel in a combustion turbine. Some of the alleged benefits of gasification include the ability to achieve higher power generation efficiencies approaching 60% as opposed to 33-40% efficiency in conventional coal plants and a corresponding reduction in GHG emissions, as well as a large reduction in sulfur oxides, nitrogen oxides, and particulate emissions.[58]

C. Unconventional Fossil Fuels

Shale oil, shale gas, and CBM are unconventional fossil fuels because of the distribution and permeability of the resource. Conventional oil and gas resources are highly permeable and easier to extract because of the higher flow rate.[59] "Hydrofracking," "fracing," or "fracking" is the process of expanding natural or manmade fractures in the rock layers using high-volume fluid injection to increase the extraction

---

[57] *See, e.g.*, Coal. for Responsible Regulation, Inc. v. EPA, 684 F.3d 102 (D.C. Cir. 2012) (upholding authority of EPA in setting GHG emission standards for motor vehicles), *rev'd and remanded*, E.P.A. v. EME Homer City Generation, L.P., 134 S. Ct. 1584 (2014); Util. Air Regulatory Grp. v. EPA, 134 S. Ct. 2427 (2014) (holding that CAA neither compels nor permits EPA to regulate stationary sources for GHG emissions under Prevention of Significant Deterioration (PSD) or Title V permitting programs); *see generally Clean Air Act Cases Vehicle and Engine Enforcement Case Resolutions*, U.S. ENVIRON. PROTECTION AGENCY, https://www.epa.gov/enforcement/clean-air-act-vehicle-and-engine-enforcement-case-resolutions (last visited Nov. 18, 2017).

[58] Office of Fossil Energy, *Gasification Technology R&D*, U.S. DEP'T OF ENERGY, https://web.archive.org/web/20140719105337/http://www.fossil.energy.gov/programs/powersystems/gasification (last visited Nov. 18, 2017); *see also* William G. Rosenberg, Michael R. Walker & Dwight C. Alpern, *A National Gasification Strategy*, FORTNIGHTLY MAG. (June 2005), http://www.fortnightly.com/fortnightly/2005/06/national-gasification-strategy.

[59] *Shale Gas and Coal Bed Methane: Potential Sources of Sustained Energy in the Future*, ERNST & YOUNG (2010), http://www.ey.com/Publication/vwLUAssets/Shale_gas_and_coal_bed_methane/$File/Shale_gas_and_coal_bed_methane_-_Potential_sources_of_sustained_energy_in_the_future.pdf.

and recovery rates of oil and especially natural gas from shale or other deposits.[60] The injection process uses fluid that is composed of water, sand (called the "proppant"), and fracking fluid. The water and fracking fluid open the rock, and the sand keeps the rock fractures open to release the oil or gas for capture at the surface. As discussed above, the rule of capture, sometimes modified by the correlative rights doctrine, applies to unconventional oil and gas mining by hydraulic fracturing. An excerpt from the Texas Supreme Court case explains the importance of these fossil fuel resources as well as illustrates the rule of capture as applied to the oil and gas industry.

Coastal Oil & Gas Corp. v. Garza Energy Trust

268 S.W.3D 1 (TEX. 2008)

The primary issue in this appeal is whether subsurface hydraulic fracturing of a natural gas well that extends into another's property is a trespass for which the value of gas drained as a result may be recovered as damages. We hold that the rule of capture bars recovery of such damages.

* * *

Respondents, to whom we shall refer collectively as Salinas, own the minerals in a 748-acre tract of land in Hidalgo County called Share 13, which they and their ancestors have occupied for over a century. At all times material to this case, petitioner Coastal Oil & Gas Corp. has been the lessee of the minerals in Share 13 and an adjacent tract, Share 15. Coastal was also the lessee of the minerals in Share 12 until it acquired the mineral estate in that 163-acre tract in 1995. A natural gas reservoir, the Vicksburg T formation, lies between 11,688 and 12,610 feet below these tracts.

* * *

The Vicksburg T is a "tight" sandstone formation, relatively imporous and impermeable, from which natural gas cannot be commercially produced without hydraulic fracturing stimulation, or "fracing", as the process is known in the industry. This is done by pumping fluid down a well at high pressure so that it is forced out into the formation. The pressure creates cracks in the rock that propagate along the azimuth of natural

---

[60] For additional information about this topic, see Amanda Cohen Leiter, *A Few Thoughts and a Reading List on . . . Fracking*, ENVTL. L. PROF BLOG (July 18, 2012), http://lawprofessors.typepad.com/environmental_law/2012/07/a-few-thoughts-and-a-reading-list-on-fracking.html; *see also Shale Gas Extraction in the UK: A Review of Hydraulic Fracturing*, ROYAL SOC'Y (June 2012), http://raeng.org.uk/shale.

fault lines in an elongated elliptical pattern in opposite directions from the well. Behind the fluid comes a slurry containing small granules called proppants — sand, ceramic beads, or bauxite are used — that lodge themselves in the cracks, propping them open against the enormous subsurface pressure that would force them shut as soon as the fluid was gone. The fluid is then drained, leaving the cracks open for gas or oil to flow to the wellbore. Fracing in effect increases the well's exposure to the formation, allowing greater production. First used commercially in 1949, fracing is now essential to economic production of oil and gas and commonly used throughout Texas, the United States, and the world.

* * *

[W]e find four reasons not to change the rule of capture to allow one property owner to sue another for oil and gas drained by hydraulic fracturing that extends beyond lease lines.

First, the law already affords the owner who claims drainage full recourse. This is the justification for the rule of capture, and it applies regardless of whether the drainage is due to fracing. If the drained owner has no well, he can drill one to offset drainage from his property. If the minerals are leased and the lessee has not drilled a well, the owner can sue the lessee for violation of the implied covenant in the lease to protect against drainage. If an offset well will not adequately protect against drainage, the owner (or his operator) may offer to pool, and if the offer is rejected, he may apply to the Railroad Commission for forced pooling. The Commission may also regulate production to prevent drainage. No one suggests that these various remedies provide inadequate protection against drainage.

Second, allowing recovery for the value of gas drained by hydraulic fracturing usurps to courts and juries the lawful and preferable authority of the Railroad Commission to regulate oil and gas production. Such recovery assumes that the gas belongs to the owner of the minerals in the drained property, contrary to the rule of capture. While a mineral rights owner has a real interest in oil and gas in place, "this right does not extend to specific oil and gas beneath the property"; ownership must be "considered in connection with the law of capture, which is recognized as a property right" as well. The minerals owner is entitled, not to the molecules actually residing below the surface, but to "a fair chance to recover the oil and gas in or under his land, or their equivalents in kind." The rule of capture makes it possible for the Commission, through rules governing the spacing, density, and allowables of wells, to protect correlative rights of owners with interests in the same mineral deposits while securing "the state's goals of preventing waste and conserving natural resources." But such rules do not allow confiscation; on the contrary, they operate to prevent confiscation. Without the rule of capture, drainage would amount to a taking of a mineral owner's property — the oil and gas below the surface of the property — thereby limiting the Commission's power to regulate production to assure a fair recovery by each owner. The Commission has never found it necessary to regulate hydraulic fracturing, a point to which we will return below, but should it ever choose to do so, permitting fracturing that extended beyond property lines, however reasonable in terms of industry operation, would be met with the objection that the Commission had allowed the minerals in the drained property to be confiscated. While "'all property is held subject to the valid exercise of the police power' and thus not every regulation is a compensable taking, . . . some are." "Physical possession is categorically, a taking for which compensation is constitutionally mandated." We need not hold here that without the rule of capture, all regulation of drainage would be confiscatory and thus beyond the Commission's power. We observe only that the rule of capture leaves the Commission's historical role unimpeded. "It is now well settled that the Railroad Commission is vested with the power and charged with the duty of regulating the production of oil and gas for the prevention of waste as well as for the protection of correlative rights." The Commission's role should not be supplanted by the law of trespass.

Third, determining the value of oil and gas drained by hydraulic fracturing is the kind of issue the litigation process is least equipped to handle. One difficulty is that the material facts are hidden below miles of rock, making it difficult to ascertain what might have happened. Such difficulty in proof is one of the justifications for the rule of capture. But there is an even greater difficulty with litigating recovery for drainage resulting from fracing, and it is that trial judges and juries cannot take into account social policies, industry operations, and the greater good which are all tremendously important in deciding whether fracing should or should not be against the law. While this Court may consider such matters in fashioning the common law, we should not alter the rule of capture on which an industry and its regulation have relied for decades to create new and uncertain possibilities for liability with no more evidence of necessity and appropriateness than this case presents. Indeed, the evidence in this case counsels strongly against such a course. The experts in this case agree on two important things. One is that hydraulic fracturing is not optional; it is essential to the recovery of oil and gas in many areas, including the Vicksburg T formation in this case. (This fact has recently been brought to the public's attention because of development in the Barnett Shale in north Texas, which is entirely dependent on hydraulic fracturing.) The other is that hydraulic fracturing cannot be performed both to maximize reasonable commercial effectiveness and to avoid all drainage. Some drainage is virtually unavoidable. In this context, common law liability for a long-used practice essential to an industry is ill-advised and should not be extended absent a compelling need that the Legislature and Commission have ignored. No such need exists.

Fourth, the law of capture should not be changed to apply differently to hydraulic fracturing because no one in the industry appears to want or need the change. The Court has received amicus curiae briefs in this case from the Railroad Commission, the General Land Office, the American Royalty Council, the Texas Oil & Gas Association, the Texas Independent Producers & Royalty Owners Association, the Texas Alliance of Energy Producers, Harding Co., BJ Services Co., Halliburton Energy Services, Inc., Schlumberger Technology Corp., Chesapeake Energy Corp., Devon Energy Corp., Dominion Exploration & Production, Inc., EOG Resources, Inc., Oxy Usa Inc., Questar Exploration and Production Co., XTO Energy, Inc., and Chief Oil & Gas LLC. These briefs from every corner of the industry — regulators, landowners, royalty owners, operators, and hydraulic fracturing service providers — all oppose liability for hydraulic fracturing, almost always warning of adverse consequences in the direst language. Though hydraulic fracturing has been commonplace in the oil and gas industry for over sixty years, neither the Legislature nor the Commission has ever seen fit to regulate it, though every other aspect of production has been thoroughly regulated. Into so settled a regime the common law need not thrust itself.

Accordingly, we hold that damages for drainage by hydraulic fracturing are precluded by the rule of capture. It should go without saying that the rule of capture cannot be used to shield misconduct that is illegal, malicious, reckless, or intended to harm another without commercial justification, should such a case ever arise. But that certainly did not occur in this case, and no instance of it has been cited to us.

AN ISSUE OF OWNERSHIP: AMOCO PRODUCTION CO. v. SOUTHERN UTE INDIAN TRIBE[61]

The extraction of CBM is regulated as natural gas rather than as coal, and in a challenge over ownership of CBM and coal reservations, the U.S. Supreme Court established ownership of CBM as separate from the ownership of the coal. In the Coal Lands Act of 1909, Congress authorized the federal government to issue land patents to settlers who had made good faith efforts at farming tracts identified later as coal lands. However, the patents were issued subject to a narrow reservation to the United States of all coal rights to prospect, mine, or remove the coal, with some exceptions for domestic use. The 1910 Coal Lands Act extended this authorization to all new entries under the homestead acts. However, some of the lands the government patented to settlers under these acts were reservation lands of the Southern Ute Indian Tribe that were ceded to the United States in 1880. The ceded reservation lands still owned by the United States were restored to the Tribe in 1938, including the reserved coal from patents issued under the 1909 and 1910 Acts. Over 20 million acres of land were patented under the 1909 and 1910 Acts and these lands contain large quantities of CBM gas.

---

[61] 526 U.S. 865 (1999).

Originally, we viewed CBM gas as a dangerous byproduct of mining coal. However, by the 1970s, CBM gas had become a significant energy resource. Oil and gas companies entered into leases with landowners who held title under 1909 and 1910 Act patents, relying on a government official's opinion in 1981 that CBM gas was not coal and therefore was not subject to the narrow reservation. The Tribe brought suit in 1991 against the royalty owners and producers under the leases seeking a declaration that the reservation of coal in the 1909 and 1910 Acts included CBM gas so that the Tribe owned the CBM gas, not the successors of the land patentees.

The U.S. Supreme Court determined that CBM is a gas and not coal.[62] Therefore, the Coal Lands Acts of 1909 and 1910, which conveyed public land to patentees but reserved the coal to the United States, did not reserve the CBM.[63] Thus, in 1938 when the United States granted title to the reserved coal to the Southern Ute Tribe, the Tribe did not succeed to ownership of the CBM.[64]

Mining and Production of Oil Shale.   Oil shale is a sedimentary rock that has not been under pressure or heat long enough to create petroleum. Shale oil can serve as a substitute for crude oil, but the process of converting this oil, found in the chemical compound mixture, kerogen, within the oil shale, is much costlier than producing conventional oil from wells and is more harmful to the environment. Oil shale is a hard mineral, which produces a vapor when heated. The vapor is cooled to produce liquid shale oil and, finally, this oil is separated from shale gas to create an unconventional oil, which can be burned to generate power or used as raw material for other manufacturing processes. Because it is a mineral, oil shale in the United States was originally subject to the General Mining Act of 1872.[65] However, the 1920 Mineral Leasing Act provided for regulation of oil shale leasing according to procedures used for oil and gas. When conventional oil and gas prices increased sufficiently to make oil shale production attractive, there was a spike in litigation over oil shale claims that predated the 1920 regulations.[66]

Fracking raises significant issues implicating resilience and sustainability. Although natural gas drilling in shale has used fracking for decades, this technology has been controversial because of concerns about chemical contamination of drinking water, the large volume of water used in the process, and the potential for generating earthquakes. Proponents of continued fracking claim that the process does not disrupt surface uses, other than for the three to six month drilling operation, and the shale gas

[62] *Id.* at 880.
[63] *See id.*
[64] *See id.* at 870.
[65] 30 U.S.C. §22 (2012).
[66] For more on this issue, see Cliffs Synfuel Corp. v. Norton, 291 F.3d 1250 (10th Cir. 2002).

is cheap to develop and produce.[67] The concerns over the environmental impacts of CBM production are similar to the concerns over conventional oil and gas production. The exception is that CBM wells are shallow, more closely spaced, and they need large amounts of water to pressure the release of CBM from coal. The result is groundwater depletion, water quality problems, and the need to dispose of excess water after completing the process. Air pollution caused by drilling operations in rural areas has affected visibility in national parks, exceeded air quality standards, and created acid rain.[68]

Oil shale production also has significant implications for many systems' resilience and sustainability. The United States, Russia, and Brazil have the largest global reserves of oil shale, which account for 86% of the world reserves.[69] Oil shale becomes more valuable when the price of conventional oil and gas increases, since the cost to produce oil from this rock greatly exceeds production costs for conventional resources. However, environmental concerns that surround mountaintop removal activities from surface mining are similarly present, such as the impact on local water quality, ecosystem damage, deforestation, fish, wildlife, and the health of local populations. In addition, the extraction process requires significant water use, which may present conflicts for reserves located in arid regions. Furthermore, the greenhouse gas emissions from burning oil shale are greater than conventional fossil fuel combustion.

Questions

1. The court in *Coastal Oil & Gas Corp.* upheld the rule of capture and affirmed its applicability to fracking. What are some of the actions

---

[67] For a complete discussion on the dangers of hydrofracking, and the particular view courts take on the subject, see Legal Envtl. Assistance Found. v. EPA, 276 F.3d 1253 (11th Cir. 2001) (challenging the EPA's approval of Alabama's program for the underground injection of hydraulic fracturing fluids to enhance the recovery of methane gas from coal beds). For an overview of how CBM is treated as a natural gas for purposes of regulation, see W. Org. of Res. Councils v. Bureau of Land Mgmt., 591 F. Supp. 2d 1206 (D. Wyo. 2008) (challenging the environmental impact statements concerning a project to develop thousands of coal bed methane wells in Wyoming and Montana); *see also* Lynch v. State Bd. of Equalization, 210 Cal. Rptr. 335 (Ct. App. 1985).

[68] For an illustration of courts' discussion on property rights concerning surface owners and mineral lease holders, see Amoco Prod. Co. v. S. Ute Tribe, 526 U.S. 865 (1999) (holding that Indian tribe did not hold equitable title to reserved coal in lands patented under Coal Lands Acts of 1909 and 1910); Gerrity Oil & Gas Corp. v. Magness, 946 P.2d 913 (Colo. 1997) (holding that a claim of trespass by a surface owner against oil and gas operator for excessive surface use requires a showing that the operator's use of surface was reasonable and necessary); Getty Oil Co. v. Jones, 470 S.W.2d 618 (Tex. 1971) (ruling that oil and gas lessee did not have the right to exclusive use of superadjacent air space above the limited surface area occupied by its pumping units, and lessee was limited to the use of the land that was reasonably necessary).

[69] Klaus Brendow, *Global Oil Shale Issues and Perspectives*, 20 OIL SHALE 81, 83 (2003), http://www.kirj.ee/public/oilshale/9_brendow_1_03.pdf.

encouraged by the rule of capture in the context of fracking? What are the actors motivated to do?

2. Based on your answer to question 1, do these actions lead to a more resilient energy system? A more sustainable one?

D. Resilience, Sustainability, and the Use of Fossil Fuels

The law regulating the use of fossil fuels and its use as a source of energy has resulted in numerous impacts to social-ecological systems, including the climate and financial systems. R&S provide frameworks with which to analyze systems and how law affects them. In particular, analyses of resilience and sustainability can help address negative impacts stemming from the law or absence thereof. From the extraction of resources regulated through the rule of capture, to the use of energy and associated GHG emissions, the energy produced with fossil fuels raises challenges stressing the resilience and sustainability of many systems.

Analysis of supply side R&S has included, among other things, a slow, but steady, migration away from fossil fuels. This migration is not new. We have witnessed energy source transformations in the past from using candles and fireplaces for light, to using whale oil, then kerosene extracted from tar and asphalt, and finally to petroleum oil and gas. After overfishing sperm whales depleted the whale oil supply, alternative energy supplies such as kerosene became more price-competitive and produced a higher quality illumination. After the discovery of greater sources of petroleum, the price of kerosene, a primary use of petroleum in the nineteenth century, dropped so that it was no longer a luxury and we used it extensively for lighting. The light bulb eventually replaced this use of petroleum, and in the twentieth century, we used petroleum for the automobile instead. With our current dependence on petroleum, we will eventually see another migration to new energy sources as technology makes these new sources price competitive. An understanding of the resilience and sustainability of the energy system can sometimes bring about these changes. Conversely, changes in the energy system can have profound effects on many systems' R&S. Further, those effects may vary whether one is assessing resilience or sustainability.

Many of the most significant challenges facing the energy sector today involve carbon emissions (and smaller amounts of methane and nitrous oxide, which are also greenhouse gases) stemming from the use, production, and distribution of fossil fuels. The combustion of fossil fuels to produce electricity emits greenhouse gases into the atmosphere. As depicted in Figure 6-4, instead of allowing heat radiating from the Earth's surface to pass through to the upper atmosphere, greenhouse gases trap some of the heat and re-radiate some of it back to the surface, causing

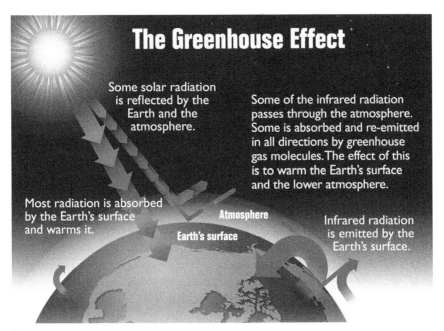

The Greenhouse Effect

Some solar radiation is reflected by the Earth and the atmosphere.

Some of the infrared radiation passes through the atmosphere. Some is absorbed and re-emitted in all directions by greenhouse gas molecules. The effect of this is to warm the Earth's surface and the lower atmosphere.

Most radiation is absorbed by the Earth's surface and warms it.

Atmosphere

Earth's surface

Infrared radiation is emitted by the Earth's surface.

Figure 6-4

the Earth's climate to change. Chapters 2 and 10 describe several climate change impacts including rising surface air temperatures, water temperatures, sea level, and precipitation levels.

We anticipate that developing countries will contribute to a substantial growth in carbon emissions and the global community has pledged to help these countries develop more sustainable practices by providing financial and technological assistance. However, little progress in this regard has been achieved, and the Clean Technology Fund, which is a Climate Investment Fund administered by the World Bank, has often been used to support carbon-intensive activities rather than non-fossil-fuel power plants. Using coal for energy is strategic for many developing countries with the largest supplies and allows them to have energy independence from oil-producing countries. Regions depending on coal for relatively inexpensive electricity may suffer economically as cleaner energy sources replace coal-fired power plants. Yet, coal mining, particularly surface mining and mountaintop removal operations, creates significant externalities such as poor water quality for drinking supplies and aquatic ecosystems, human health hazards from wastes, deforestation, damage to fish and wildlife, and the permanent destruction of beautiful natural landscapes (we describe "externalities" in more detail in a text box in Chapter 3, Section IV.A.1). Coal mining also results in thousands of worker deaths each year worldwide.[70] Most significantly, the carbon emissions from coal-fired

Brazil's Amazon

---

[70] Bryce, *supra* note 53.

power plants contribute to increased human mortality from sulfur dioxide, nitrogen oxides, and fine particulates, not to mention the impact on climate change.[71]

Reducing Production Waste. Recycling and conservation are some of the approaches used to sustain the use of fossil fuels. In this way, these actors increase the fossil fuel industry's resilience. Do they improve upon the overall resilience of the energy system? How is human health and the sustainability of communities affected?

In the United States, at least 30 states participate in the Interstate Compact to Conserve Oil and Gas. Originally created in 1935, the Compact requires that any company that produces oil must prevent and reduce oil waste. For example, the Compact restricts companies in California from operating a well with an inefficient gas-water ratio and it prohibits the sale of any oil produced in disregard of the Compact rules.[72] The blowing, release, or escape of gas is prima facie evidence of unreasonable waste, which necessarily violates the Compact.[73] California legislation may require that used oil be recycled and/or reused to the maximum extent possible, but companies suffer penalties only if oil is improperly disposed of.[74]

PRODUCTION WASTE OR POLLUTION? THE ALISO CANYON STORY

In 2015, the Aliso Canyon natural gas storage facility in Southern California suffered the largest methane—a potent GHG—leak in U.S. history from a ruptured well, which emitted tens of thousands of tons of gas over a four-month period. The leak forced approximately 8,000 families in the Porter Ranch community of the San Fernando Valley to leave their homes. Many complained of health issues including cancer, nosebleeds, and nausea.

The facility was eventually shut down, but officials announced in July 2017 that injections of methane for storage would resume to "stave off an energy shortage in Southern California." While the facility will operate at a 28% capacity and only store the minimum gas needed to supply the Los Angeles area, residents claim that "Aliso Canyon simply isn't needed, and that our utility system operates safely and reliably, and consumers are protected without it."

The chair of the California Energy Commission announced that his staff will work with other agencies to shut down the facility within the next ten years. He stated, "I am confident that through sustained investments in renewable energy, energy efficiency,

---

[71] Steve Herz, *The Clean Technology Fund and Coal: A Cautionary Tale for Copenhagen*, 9 SUSTAINABLE DEV. L. & POL'Y 21, 21-24, 63 (2009); Dan Farber, *Accounting for the Harm of Coal*, LEGAL PLANET (Sept. 28, 2011), http://legal-planet.org/2011/09/28/accounting-for-the-harm-of-coal ("On average, the harm produced by burning the coal is over twice as high as the market price of the electricity."); *see also* Coal. for Responsible Regulation, Inc. v. EPA, Nos. 09-1322, et al., 2012 WL 6621785 (D.C. Cir. Dec. 20, 2012), *aff'd in part, rev'd in part*, Util. Air Regulatory Grp. v. EPA, 134 S. Ct. 2427 (2014).
[72] *See* CAL. PUB. RES. CODE §§3275-78 (West 2008).
[73] CAL. PUB. RES. CODE §3300 (West 2008).
[74] Used Oil Recycling Act, CAL. PUB. RES. CODE §3463 (West 2008).

electric storage technologies and other strategies, we can make this transition a reality." However, political leaders and environmentalists claim that resuming operation of the facility without having determined what caused the blowout in the first place is "unnecessary and reckless."

Los Angeles City Councilman Mitchell Englander, who represents Porter Ranch, asserted that "[t]he gas leak 'showed the danger of operating such facilities near residential areas, . . . [a]nd while state regulatory agencies have taken steps to improve safety at the facility, the only way to ensure that history does not repeat itself is through permanent closure of the facility.'"[75]

The U.S. federal government legislatively encouraged the recycling and reuse of oil, and the reduction of environmental waste from discarded used oil by enacting the Recycled Oil Rule, 42 U.S.C. §6363 (2010) in 1988. Australia has similar legislation, the Product Stewardship (Oil) Act of 2000, but unlike the U.S. legislation, which merely legalizes recycling by allowing the refining and labeling of used oil as new oil, Australia's program provides financial incentives for oil recycling through both direct compensation and tax exemptions. Ideally, the market for used oil should sufficiently incentivize recycling as demand and pricing make this an attractive alternative for fueling power turbines or re-refining it into lubricating oil.

The cost of petroleum and coal extraction will likely expedite the migration to non-fossil fuels. Petroleum costs are expected to increase as demand forces industry to extract oil from more challenging environments, such as deep offshore drilling and impermeable locations. In 2000, the U.S. Geological Survey released the results of a thorough and comprehensive five-year study assessing the world crude oil and natural gas resources. The U.S. Energy Information Administration (EIA) analyzed these facts and projected that the long-term world oil demand would likely peak in 2037 at 53.2 billion barrels per year and that production would peak sometime in the middle of the twenty-first century. The United States currently consumes approximately 22% of the world's petroleum supply. The EIA report concluded that although it is unlikely that crude oil will run out, the prohibitive cost of producing oil should encourage industry to develop other energy resources. The EIA warns that we cannot be complacent about research and development of either the demand or the supply side of this energy resource because of the extensive lead time it will take for new technologies to penetrate the energy market.[76]

---

[75] Alene Tchekmedyian & Joseph Serna, *Aliso Canyon Natural Gas Facility that was Site of Massive Leak Can Reopen, State Says*, L.A. TIMES (July 19, 2017, 7:25 PM), http://www.latimes.com/local/lanow/la-me-ln-aliso-canyon-gas-20170719-story.html.

[76] For further detailed information and reading on the impact of these decreasing oil supplies, see John H. Wood, Gary R. Long & David F. Morehouse, *Long-Term World Oil Supply Scenarios: The Future Is Neither as Bleak or Rosy as Some Assert*, U.S. ENERGY INFO. ADMIN. (Aug. 18, 2004), https://web.archive.org/web/20170711082617/https://www.eia.gov/pub/oil_gas/petroleum/feature_articles/2004/worldoilsupply/oilsupply04.html.

Similar to oil, the cost of coal is likely to fluctuate. However, the reason for these fluctuations is different. The ability of countries to rely on coal-fired power projects will depend on the availability of coal supplies domestically and internationally, as well as the regulations over the burning of coal for power plants and their impacts on health and the environment. Shortages of domestic coal in India have affected Indian power projects. The coal mining industry in India has blamed these shortages on the following: new regulations in Indonesia, which increase coal prices by benchmarking domestic coal to international market prices; environmental delays for new mining projects because of litigation and regulation; and inadequate rail transportation to move coal stockpiled at mines. The International Energy Agency, which implements an international program of energy cooperation among 28 countries, has predicted that natural gas demand will increase as environmental regulations on coal increase and the uncertainty over nuclear power continues.[77]

Pricing will necessarily influence the sustainable supply of any particular energy resource. In the United States, natural gas prices became more competitive when the government lifted price controls in the late 1970s and repealed federal restrictions on the use of natural gas under the Powerplant and Industrial Fuel Use Act. Natural gas was an advantageous alternative to coal combustion because of its reduced greenhouse gas emissions. Natural gas is also important for the development of cost-effective fuel cells and for conversion to electricity by the combined-cycle gas turbine in modern power plants.[78] Cheap natural gas prices are influencing the domestic energy market.[79] Currently, low prices have altered the market demand for natural gas and oil. Natural gas prices will likely rise, however, the U.S. Energy Information Administration predicts a resulting increase in exports and corresponding price increases.

Gas produced from unconventional sources, such as CBM, shale gas, tight sands gas, stranded fields having no pipeline access, and other hard-to-reach deposits, will be an available resource for some time, although price, technology, and environmental impacts will dictate its use as an

---

[77] *See generally* Steven Macmillan, Alexander Antonyuk & Hannah Schwind, *Gas to Coal Competition in the U.S. Power Sector*, INT'L ENERGY AGENCY (2013), https://www.iea.org/publications/insights/insightpublications/CoalvsGas_FINAL_WEB.pdf.

[78] *See* Paul Nastu, *Switching 3.5M Commercial Trucks to Natural Gas Would Save 1.2M BBL of Oil a Day*, ENVTL. LEADER (Apr. 16, 2010), http://www.environmentalleader.com/2010/04/16/switching-3-5m-commercial-trucks-to-natural-gas-would-save-1-2m-bbl-of-oil-a-day.

[79] *See, e.g., Effect of Increased Natural Gas Exports on Domestic Energy Markets*, U.S. ENERGY INFO. ADMIN. (Jan. 2012), http://energy.gov/sites/prod/files/2013/04/f0/fe_eia_lng.pdf; *see also America's Cheap Gas: Bonanza or Bane*, ECONOMIST (Mar. 2, 2013), http://www.economist.com/news/finance-and-economics/21572815-natural-gas-prices-are-sure-riseeventually-bonanza-or-bane ("The rapid rush of gas onto the market has sent prices tumbling."); Bob Adelmann, *Cheap Abundant Natural Gas Is a Game Changer, Says the IMF*, NEW AM. (Mar. 22, 2013), http://www.thenewamerican.com/economy/markets/item/14878-cheap-abundant-natural-gas-is-a-game-changer-says-the-imf ("The impact in the United States is already being felt. Economist Mark Perry calculated that on an energy equivalent basis, natural gas is now almost 80 percent cheaper than oil, making it 'a real game changer.'").

alternative to oil and other energy sources.[80] The Energy Policy Act of 2005, Pub. L. No. 109-58, 119 Stat. 594, amended the Natural Gas Act to protect the public against manipulation and deception in the sale and transportation of natural gas, and to restore public confidence in the natural gas market. Comparisons of the effectiveness of gas restructuring with electricity restructuring are appropriate since energy resources are so analogous.[81]

The availability of liquefied natural gas (LNG), which is natural gas cooled to convert it into a liquid, impacts the sustainability and resilience of fossil fuel energy. As a liquid, the process stores LNG and tankers transport it outside the infrastructure of gas pipelines. The process regasifies the liquid at receiving terminals and returns it to existing or new gas pipelines. This technology allows shipping of natural gas throughout the world to address gaps in supply and demand. However, there are deep concerns about the emissions involved with LNG and storing what is already a dangerous substance in high concentrations. A terrorist attack, for example, could generate catastrophic damage in the form of intense fire and radiation.[82] Compressed natural gas (CNG) and LNG also have the ability to power motor vehicles, which could reduce reliance on oil.[83] For example, if the United States was able to replace 3.5 million medium and heavy vehicles with natural gas vehicles by 2035, it could avoid importing about 1.2 million barrels of oil a day.

Shipping and transportation of fossil fuels also present challenges relevant to resilience and sustainability. The European Union adopted the Integrated Maritime Policy (IMP) in 2007 to create sustainable practices for maritime transportation, fisheries, and the environment. The IMP follows the International Convention for the Prevention of Pollution from Ships (MARPOL) limitation on air emissions from ships to provide developing countries with better, greener ship-dismantling plants, limit

---

[80] *How Is Shale Gas Produced?*, Dep't. of Energy, https://energy.gov/sites/prod/files/2013/04/f0/how_is_shale_gas_produced.pdf (last visited Nov. 18, 2017).

[81] William A. Mogel & Shuchi Batra, *The New Balance of Power: Do States Have Any Rights in Siting LNG Terminals?*, Fortnightly Mag. (June 2007), https://www.fortnightly.com/fortnightly/2007/06/new-balance-power.

[82] For an overview of the dangers associated with LNG storage, see Richard A. Clarke, *LNG Facilities in Urban Areas: A Security Risk Management Analysis for Attorney General Patrick Lynch Rhode Island*, Good Harbor Consulting LLC (May 2005), https://web.archive.org/web/20160402163704/http://www.goodharbor.net/media/images/books/pdf-liquid-natural-gas-report.pdf (examining the potential security risks associated with the proposed construction of a liquid natural gas tanker offloading facility in downtown Providence). For courts' discussion of LNG, see New Jersey v. Delaware, 552 U.S. 597 (2008) (state of New Jersey brought suit against Delaware seeking a declaration that Article VII of the 1905 Compact gave it regulatory authority to construct a liquefied natural gas unloading terminal project that extended into Delaware's territory); *see also* Gulf Restoration Network v. U.S. Dep't or Transp., 452 F.3d 362 (5th Cir. 2006) (review of a license grant for storage of LNG).

[83] *See, e.g.*, Adelmann at *supra* note 79 ("At present, Ford has 10 different models of over-the-road tractors ready to use either liquefied petroleum gas (LPG) or compressed natural gas (CNG) with sales of such vehicles exploding 350 percent just in the last three years. When the vehicles are modified, their drivability is the same as with gasoline, but the savings can be huge. Over six years fuel savings can exceed $150,000, making the switch economically very attractive.").

competition over coastal fishing, and increase biodiversity. In 2007, the United States initiated Ocean Policy reform to address sustainable shipping practices and to work with the IMO to negotiate a new convention on ship recycling.[84]

Oil spills present a significant challenge to resilience and sustainability. Local, state, federal, and international authorities may become involved when production activity or transportation causes oil spills. These spills have devastated the sustainability and resilience of our environment. Some of the major spills include the Torrey Canyon spill in the English Channel in 1967, the Santa Barbara oil spill off the California coast in 1969, the Exxon Valdez spill in Alaska in 1989, the 2006 British Petroleum (BP) oil spill in Prudhoe Bay, and the 2010 BP Deepwater Horizon oil spill in the Gulf of Mexico.[85] We will discuss a case study of the BP Deepwater Horizon oil spill in Chapter 8. In the United States, the Oil Pollution Act of 1990 (OPA) (discussed above) creates strict liability for any oil company involved in a spill, but it caps the amount of damages for which a company can be liable. The OPA amended the Clean Water Act and established the Oil Spill Liability Trust Fund, which funds up to $1 billion to address a spill. The OPA does not preempt state liability law and states have the authority to enforce the OPA requirements for financial responsibility on the navigable waters of the state. The Trust Fund also provides states with fund access or reimbursement for costs incurred during oil spill response and cleanup efforts. However, the OPA does preempt any state laws concerning safety regulations for oil tankers.[86] Internationally, the IMO regulates maritime transport, and member governments enforce safety regulations to prevent pollution and injuries to people. The IMO developed a system to address liability and compensation for damages due to oil spills.[87]

Offshore oil spills are particularly problematic for the marine environment as well as coastlines.[88] In the United States, the federal Coastal Zone Management Act (CZMA) incentivizes states to develop a coastal

---

[84] Joan M. Bondareff, *The EU Adopts an Integrated Maritime Policy and Action Plan: Is the U.S. Far Behind or Ahead?*, 8 SUSTAINABLE DEV. L. & POL'Y 47, 47 (2007).

[85] For example, the BP oil spill in 2006 was a significant disaster, and it is an important example of how vital regulations are for controlling the transport of oil and natural gas. For insight into how Congress dealt with the situation, see *BP's Pipeline Spills at Prudhoe Bay: What Went Wrong?: Hearing before the Subcomm. on Oversight & Investigations of the Comm. on Energy & Commerce*, 109th Cong. 1-4 (2006). For further information about the BP Deep Horizon Oil Spill, see *Deep Water: The Gulf Oil Disaster and the Future of Offshore Drilling*, NAT'L COMM. ON THE BP DEEPWATER HORIZON OIL SPILL & OFFSHORE DRILLING (Jan. 11, 2011), https://www.gpo.gov/fdsys/pkg/GPO-OILCOMMISSION/pdf/GPO-OILCOMMISSION.pdf; *see also* Hari M. Osofsky, *Multidimensional Governance and the BP Deepwater Horizon Oil Spill*, 63 FLA. L. REV. 1077 (2011).

[86] *Oil Pollution Act Overview*, EPA, https://web.archive.org/web/20170604224523/https://archive.epa.gov/emergencies/content/lawsregs/web/html/opaover.html (last visited Nov. 18, 2017).

[87] *Marine Environment*, INT'L MAR. ORG., http://www.imo.org/ourwork/environment (last visited Nov. 18, 2017).

[88] *Oil Spills Along the Shore*, NOAA, https://response.restoration.noaa.gov/oil-and-chemical-spills/oil-spills/oil-spills-along-shore.html (last visited Nov. 18, 2017) (explaining the effects of oil spills to coastlines and the animals that live there).

zone regulatory system. However, federal and state officials have litigated to determine which entity has authority over oil and gas leases in the Outer Continental Shelf and whether the leases are subject to NEPA environmental standards.[89] The Outer Continental Shelf Lands Act attempts to regulate this drilling by relegating control to the Secretary of the Interior, who is also supposed to regulate inspections of oil drilling facilities.[90] However, a 1990 amendment to the CZMA made it clear that oil and gas leases by the Department of the Interior in the Outer Continental Shelf are subject to state approval and must be consistent with the state coastal management plans.[91]

The **institutional arrangements** governing the energy sector have significant effects on the resilience and sustainability of systems associated with fossil fuels for energy. The privatization of the global oil market has resulted in transnational corporations (TNCs) taking over the industry and minimal government regulations of negative impacts to the environment. Instead, contract provisions negotiated between the oil companies and government officials provide the environmental law regime applied to these TNCs. The discovery of oil in the Amazon has had dramatic environmental impacts. International oil companies acquired drilling rights from the Ecuadorian government, which eventually led to litigation over claims of rainforest destruction, biodiversity reduction, deforestation, damage to the health of the native people, and even human rights abuses.[92] This trend has generated calls for the international community to develop environmental standards for the TNCs so that these corporate entities do not privatize environmental law and we have an effective body of law to govern goals for resilience, sustainability, and corporate responsibility.[93]

Ultimately, reducing unsustainable production and consumption of oil and gas will be required to address humanity's impact on the environment, especially in regard to climate change. The private sector, the United States, the European Union, China, India, and the international community must continue to cut carbon emissions by recycling,

[89] *See* Sec'y of the Interior v. California, 464 U.S. 312 (1984); Amoco Prod. Co. v. Vill. of Gambell, Alaska, 480 U.S. 531 (1987).
[90] Outer Continental Shelf Lands Act, 43 U.S.C. §§1331-56 (2006).
[91] *See* Mobil Oil Exploration & Producing Se., Inc. v. United States, 530 U.S. 604 (2000); California v. Norton, 311 F.3d 1162 (9th Cir. 2002); *see also* G. Kevin Jones, *Understanding the Debate over Congressionally Imposed Moratoria on Outer Continental Shelf Oil and Gas Leasing*, 9 Temp. Envtl. L. & Tech. J. 117 (1990).
[92] Carlos Herrera, *Ecuador: Oil Exploration and Environment Rape*, Axis of Logic (Mar. 5, 2005), http://www.axisoflogic.com/artman/publish/Article_16093.shtml; *see also* Michael Isikoff, *Chevron Lobbyists Fight Ecuador Toxic-Dumping Case*, Newsweek (July 25, 2008), http://www.newsweek.com/chevron-lobbyists-fight-ecuador-toxic-dumping-case-93189 (Chevron lobbyists in Washington attempted to make the United States impose trade restraints on Ecuador when the judiciary would not dismiss the litigation); *Texaco/Chevron Lawsuits (re Ecuador)*, Bus. & Human Rights Res. Ctr., http://www.business-humanrights.org/Categories/Lawlawsuits/Lawsuitsregulatoryaction/Lawsuits Selectedcases/TexacoChevronlawsuitsreEcuador (last visited Nov. 18, 2017).
[93] Laitos & Getches, *supra* note 18; *see also* Judith Kimerling, *Disregarding Environmental Law: Petroleum Development in Protected Natural Areas and Indigenous Homelands in the Ecuadorian Amazon*, 14 Hastings Int'l & Comp. L. Rev. 849, 900-903 (1991).

conserving, reducing, and substituting cleaner forms of energy to meet economic demands, achieve energy stability, and create a more resilient and sustainable energy system.[94]

Questions and Notes

1. In Chapter 2, we discussed the potential conflicts between technology and the use of natural resources. In the context of fossil fuels, new technologies are developing new methods for extracting fossil fuels. For example, In-situ Conversion Process (ICP) separates kerogen from rock by essentially speeding up the natural processes of heating and pressure that took millions of years to produce the conventional oil and gas reserves. ICP involves slowly heating the subsurface for three to four years using electric resistance heaters inserted into holes drilled into the shale. Concerns about the effect of such new processes on surrounding land and ecosystems have arisen. What, if any, regulations should be in place prior to utilizing such techniques? Does it matter that the new technologies provide less expensive energy and other benefits?

2. In 2016, the State of Oregon became the first state to ban coal for the electric supply. The legislation also mandated 50% renewable sources for electricity by 2040. At the time Oregon passed the law, it received about 30% of its electricity from coal supplies. While Oregon had only one remaining coal-fired plant that anticipated closing in 2020 and it did not provide all of Oregon's coal-fired electricity (the bulk came from Utah, Wyoming, and Montana), can you see how the legislation will have impacts outside the state? Does Oregon's law help the energy system become more sustainable? Resilient? Are there parts of the system that become more resilient, while others become less resilient?

3. What are some issues you would consider if you were deciding between switching to renewable fuels (discussed in Section V below) and making fossil fuels more sustainable? Which would make the energy system more resilient?

---

[94] Zhong Xiang Zhang, *Assessing China's Energy Conservation and Carbon Intensity: How Will the Future Differ from the Past?* (May 24, 2010), *in* CHINA: THE NEXT TWENTY YEARS OF REFORM AND DEVELOPMENT 99, 99-100 (Ross Garnaut, Jane Golley & Ligang Song eds., 2010).

IV. STRATEGY TO FACILITATE IMPLEMENTATION #5: BASELINES AND METRICS

Measuring, tracking, comparing, and assessing key data greatly helps us understand and assess the R&S of the energy system and other systems. In the case of fossil fuels, for example, we may set metrics to measure carbon emissions or percentage of renewable energies (as in the case of Oregon above). Baselines and Metrics help access data that informs whether certain disturbances and laws impact R&S. We can then use such information to inform the decision-making process, track performance, and ensure that we move toward regulation in an intentional way. Baselines and Metrics, by themselves, will not increase or decrease system R&S. Instead, they help us tell a more complete story about how a specific decision generates impacts and how it affects systems. For example, they do not dictate a migration to non-fossil fuels, but they can provide information indicating the importance of that migration and progress being made in that direction and how that impacts system resilience and sustainability.

A. General Description of Baselines and Metrics

As a general matter, Baselines and Metrics are the means to gather information pertaining to the performance and status of a system or a part of a system. Together, they are a methodical way to measure system changes that we can use to help analyze a decision and monitor it over time. "While the strength of the success of any policy may always be debated, discernible metrics exist that can be assessed to help observers determine . . . whether the policy problem [failing to increase or decrease system sustainability or resilience] . . . has in fact been addressed."[95]

In *Assessing Sustainability: A Guide for Local Governments*, Wayne Feiden and Elisabeth M. Hamin divide metrics, also called "indicators," into three general forms:

- *Scientific/technical indicators.* These indicators are based on solid data that are likely gathered by professional staff, and they also likely measure the fairly specific, incremental sorts of things that are most amenable to validation. Examples might include literacy rates or parts per million of a pollutant in the water.
- *Publicly oriented indicators.* These indicators are what we might call "white tennis shoe" indicators. . . . They may not be as scientific as the previous examples, but they may better engage the community in data gathering and reporting. . . . Examples might include

---

[95] Blake Hudson, *Federal Constitutions: The Keystone of Nested Commons Governance*, 63 ALA. L. REV. 1007, 1034 (2012).

resident counts of how many people are walking in town on a given
day or reports of sightings of favorite bird species.

● *Headline indicators.* These indicators are well known to the general
public, and they include such measures as gross domestic product and the inflation rate. Media outlets headline these indicators
because the public can understand the story behind the indicator — for example, is the economy getting better or worse? Are our
streets getting safer or less safe?[96]

While metrics are the standard category of measurement, baselines
designate a point on a metric. Baselines serve as benchmarks for comparison to document change and to determine whether there has been
some movement in the system. This movement helps us assess a system's
resilience and determine whether it is trending toward vulnerabilities.
"Combined, the two provide a consistent method for tracking and assessing changes in a given []system and/or the impacts of a given decision.
'They help establish a point for which we can then measure improvement,
stagnation, or failure.'"[97]

As an example, assume a family implements a monthly budget to
save money (the desired result); the family may divide spending into categories, such as food. Relevant spending *metrics* to measure food expenditures might include the tracking of grocery bills, take out spending,
and use of coupons. As *baselines*, the family might choose the average
for each respective metric over the previous six months or last year's
corresponding monthly spending (for example, the amount of takeout
spending in January, year zero versus January, year two). Once the family sets Baselines and Metrics, it has begun the process of tracking key
information and relative performance that may help it better understand
its spending on food and help it identify ways to refine its strategy to
accomplish its goals.

In the following piece, the authors challenge the use of the gross
domestic product as an accurate metric to determine a nation's economic
well-being. In doing so, the authors set forth some of the key characteristics to consider when choosing metrics.

---

[96] Wayne Feiden & Elisabeth M. Hamin, Assessing Sustainability: A Guide for Local Governments
(2011).
[97] Jonathan Rosenbloom, *A Framework for Application: Three Concrete, Contextual Strategies to
Accelerate Sustainability, in* Rethinking Sustainable Development to Meet the Climate Change
Challenge 73 (Keith Hirokawa & Jessica Owley eds., 2014).

Robert Costanza, Maureen Hart, John Talberth, Stephen Posner, *Beyond GDP: The Need for New Measures of Progress*

PARDEE PAPER NO. 4, BOSTON: PARDEE CENTER FOR THE STUDY OF THE LONGER-RANGE FUTURE (JAN. 2009)

For more than a half-century, the most widely accepted measure of a country's economic progress has been the changes in its Gross Domestic Product (GDP). GDP is an estimate of market throughput, adding together the value of all final goods and services that are produced and traded for money within a given period of time. It is typically measured by adding together a nation's personal consumption expenditures (payments by households for goods and services), government expenditures (public spending on the provision of goods and services, infrastructure, debt payments, etc.), net exports (the value of a country's exports minus the value of imports), and net capital formation (the increase in value of a nation's total stock of monetized capital goods). . . .

Because GDP measures only monetary transactions related to the production of goods and services, it is based on an incomplete picture of the system within which the human economy operates. . . . [T]hat . . . economy draws benefits from natural, social, and human capital. . . . By measuring only marketed economic activity . . . GDP ignores changes in the natural, social, and human components of community capital on which the community relies for continued existence and well-being. As a result, GDP not only fails to measure key aspects of quality of life; in many ways, it encourages activities that are counter to long-term community well-being. . . .

Indicators are intended to provide information about a system — its current condition, how that condition has changed or will change over time, and the condition of and changes in the forces affecting the system. By choosing particular indicators, one is also defining what is important — one is defining goals. To be useful, an indicator needs to be reliable and the underlying data needs to be available in a timely fashion and at an appropriate scale and scope. In addition, an indicator needs to appropriately inform decisions or measure progress toward desired goals. . . .

Indicator *reliability* is whether a change in an indicator is an accurate signal of change in the system it is supposed to measure. . . .

Timeliness relates to the frequency with which the underlying data is available. . . .

Data scope is the breadth of the items that are measured. . . .

Data scale is the level of detail of the data collected and reported. . . .

Methodology *standardization* refers to the decisions underlying the construction of an indicator—which items are chosen, how items are measured, and how different items are combined. . . .

Indicators reflect *societal choices, values, and goals*. We measure what we think is important and our choice of indicators implicitly defines our goals. As society changes, what is most important also changes and indicators should change to reflect that. . . .

Two frequently stated axioms are "what gets measured, gets managed" and "what gets measured, gets done." . . .

All indicators are proxies and limited in scope. By themselves none can really measure all significant aspects of economic, social, and environmental well-being. However, there is a need for consensus on better indicators to set policy, inform decisions, and measure progress. . . .

Given the complexity of the problems confronting humanity, a single indicator will most likely not be sufficient; a comprehensive set of integrated indicators may be most effective . . . .

[T]he world is in need of new goals and new ways to measure progress towards those goals. . . .

· The excerpt above highlights six important characteristics to consider when choosing Baselines and Metrics. These are not the only six, but they begin to form the basis of justifiable metrics that can help measure and track system resilience and sustainability and thus, provide a basis for legal or policy action:

- Reliability
- Timeliness or frequency of measurement
- Scope of the data
- Scale or level of detail
- Standardization of measurement
- Societal choices, values, and goals embedded in the metrics

The process used to select metrics is not only important as it may focus attention and policy on areas that we may or may not have weighted properly, but also it may exclude or include key stakeholders, The absence of key stakeholders may also alter the measure's effectiveness and determine whether the measure accurately assesses system resilience or sustainability. Failure to determine the proper baseline or metric may skew results and lead to an absence of key information necessary to determine whether a particular action will lead to the intended effect on system resilience or sustainability. For example, in the United States, cutting carbon emissions 20% from a baseline set at 2007 levels is significantly easier than cutting emissions from a baseline of 1990 levels because GHG levels were much higher in 2007 than in 1990. Here, selecting a baseline at 2007 alters the ease of accomplishment and the potential impacts.

B. Illustration of Application of Baselines and Metrics to R&S

The following brief case study illustrates a community's use of Baselines and Metrics to help it move toward more resilient and sustainable systems that are relevant to the community. By measuring a mixture of complex and diverse aspects of social-ecological systems, including those relevant to the energy sector, the community establishes key metrics. The case study also illustrates how we can use Baselines and Metrics to facilitate R&S in diverse contexts, including a large urban area — Los Angeles, California — with a population of approximately 3,900,000.

In Chapter 1, to help define "sustainability," we introduced Los Angeles' vision for a sustainable city through its "pLAn." To help implement its vision, Los Angeles established 36 Baselines and Metrics that measure the progress the City makes over the next 20 years. Los Angeles grouped the metrics in four areas (environment, economy, equity, and "lead by example" (focusing on municipal functioning)). For each of these metrics, Los Angeles set a baseline goal it hopes to achieve and a strategy to achieve that goal.

Within the environment section, for example, the pLAn establishes three goals: reduce GHG emissions, improve efficiency, and divest coal-fired plants.

For each goal, except divestment, the City assigned corresponding Baselines and Metrics as follows:

- *Reduce GHG emissions*
  - Baseline: 45%, 60%, and 80% below 1990 levels
  - Metric: metric tonnes [a metric tonne is equivalent to approximately 2,205 pounds of CO_2 or what one car emits after driving] of city-wide CO_2 emissions produced annually
- *Improve efficiency*
  - Baseline: 55% of 2010 levels
  - Metric: metric tonnes of city-wide CO_2 emissions per million dollars of metro area Gross Domestic Product
- *Divest coal-fired power plants*
  - Baseline: not applicable due to goal of complete divestment
  - Metric: not stated nor tracked on pLAn's data website

On its website, http://plan.lamayor.org/our-progress/second-annual-report/, the City provides up-to-date data that helps inform whether the City is meeting its designated goals.

Carbon Visuals (http://www.carbonvisuals.com/) helps bring many of the difficult concepts involving the environment to life by depicting them in easily accessible imagery. Below is Carbon Visuals' depiction of one metric ton (tonne) of carbon dioxide.

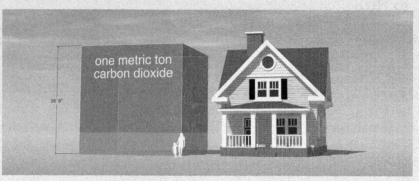

⤳ Other metrics associated with additional goals include: imported water purchases, local-sourced water, average daily water use per capita, sewer spills, water quality, solar capacity, transit-oriented new housing, rent-burdened households, average daily vehicle miles traveled per capita, green job growth, unemployment rate gap, air pollution, food access, childhood asthma, percentage of residents within a half mile of a park, and urban agriculture sites. The City states that it will create an annual report and adjust the "pLAn" based on what the City learns from tracking the metrics (adaptive governance is described in Chapter 7). By identifying and tracking these metrics, the City believes it can improve the quality of life for all residents of Los Angeles by "breaking through barriers, creating new tools, and connecting the dots of the City."[98]

Questions and Notes

1. Although not mentioned on its website, how could you track the status of Los Angeles' goal to divest coal-fired plants? What metrics could you use? Moreover, what would they tell you?

2. As presented, in the form of a tool to measure progress, Baselines and Metrics do not specify which impacts we measure. By doing so, they are applicable to many different contexts simultaneously. For example, the Baselines and Metrics we need to understand the R&S of commercial leasing may include tracking utility costs (including upfront capital

---

[98]*About the pLAn*, L.A. MAYOR'S OFFICE, http://plan.lamayor.org/about-the-plan/ (last visited Jan. 19, 2018).

for system upgrades and daily usage costs). Whereas, the Baselines and Metrics we use for procurement (the purchase of goods and services) may include life-cycle analyses or ecosystem services management (described in Chapter 3), which have little relevance to commercial leasing. What metrics would you use to track the R&S of life in a university dorm hall? What are your goals in selecting those metrics?

3. Since 2012, John F. Helliwell, Richard Layard, and Jeffrey Sachs have edited the *World Happiness Report* in which they use Baselines and Metrics to measure happiness as "a proper measure of social progress." In measuring happiness, they note that the "concepts of happiness and well-being are very likely to help guide progress towards sustainable development." For the full 2015 World Happiness Report, see http://www.theglobeandmail.com/news/national/article24073928.ece/BINARY/World + Happiness + Report.pdf.

4. In recent years, a number of groups have standardized Baselines and Metrics to help public and private sector entities measure various systems' R&S. Some of those include: B Impact Assessment (http://bimpact-assessment.net/); Ecolabel (http://www.ecolabelindex.com/); Ecological Footprint Analysis (http://www.footprintnetwork.org/en/index.php/GFN/page/calculators/); Genuine Progress Indicator (http://genuineprogress.net/genuine-progress-indicator/); Gross National Happiness (http://www.grossnationalhappiness.com/); Happy Planet Index (http://www.happyplanetindex.org/); Institute for Innovation in Social Policy (http://iisp.vassar.edu/defs_sources.html); Leadership in Energy and Environmental Design (http://www.usgbc.org/leed); Sustainability Tools for Assessing and Rating Communities (http://www.starcommunities.org/rating-system/); UN Human Development Index (http://hdr.undp.org/en/content/human-development-index-hdi); UN Multidimensional Poverty Index (http://hdr.undp.org/en/content/multidimensional-poverty-index-mpi); and many others.

V. ENERGY RESOURCES: NON-FOSSIL FUELS

A. Nuclear Energy

Nuclear energy originates in the core nucleus of an atom and the processes of fusion or fission release this energy. Nuclear fusion fuses atoms together to create a larger atom and this process releases the energy. The sun uses fusion to create energy, but research has not yet yielded a commercially viable way of using energy from nuclear fusion to generate electricity. In contrast to fusion, nuclear fission splits atoms apart in a nuclear reactor to release energy. Most nuclear power plants use non-renewable uranium fuel since it is easy to split atoms of the relatively rare uranium type, U-235. A neutron bombards the U-235 atom, which then splits to release heat, radiation, and more neutrons, causing a chain reaction that splits more U-235 atoms. Nuclear energy serves a variety of non-military purposes since its military beginnings at the end of World War II, when the United States invented and deployed the atomic bomb on the Japanese cities of Hiroshima and Nagasaki.[99]

1. NUCLEAR ENERGY PRODUCTION

The United States enacted the Atomic Energy Act of 1946 to control the use of nuclear energy and in 1954, new legislation allowed the nonmilitary, commercial use of nuclear energy for electrical power generation and other industrial, medical, and research applications. The Atomic Energy Commission (AEC) was responsible for the regulation of nuclear energy under the 1946 and 1954 Acts, but Congress disbanded the AEC in 1974 because it was concerned about the AEC's effectiveness in regulating the safe use of radiation. The Nuclear Regulatory Commission (NRC) replaced the AEC in 1974 when Congress enacted the Energy Reorganization Act. Congress tasked the NRC with protecting public health and safety from exposure to hazardous levels of radiation, preventing a major reactor accident, shielding nuclear materials from theft or diversion, and regulating the disposal of nuclear waste.[100]

A nuclear power plant generates electricity by using the heat released through the process of nuclear fission to produce power. Nuclear fission takes place within a nuclear reactor, which has a core made of uranium fuel that consists of ceramic pellets stacked into metal fuel rods. Hundreds of these fuel rods are bundled to create a fuel assembly, and there are many fuel assemblies within the reactor core. Fission involves splitting atoms into smaller atoms, which releases energy and creates heat. Instead of burning fossil fuel, the heat created from fission generates the heat necessary to create steam. The steam, produced in either a fossil fuel power plant or a nuclear plant, turns the turbine blades to drive the generators that make electricity. A separate cooling tower turns the steam back into reusable water. Nuclear energy is a clean energy source because nuclear plant operation does not release the air pollutants or carbon dioxide generated by power plants burning fossil fuels. Nevertheless, the energy needed to mine and process the uranium and build the plant and reactors requires burning fossil fuel, which results in polluting air emissions. In addition,

---

[99] *Nuclear Energy Is Energy in the Core of an Atom*, U.S. ENERGY INFO. ADMIN., https://www.eia.gov/energyexplained/index.cfm?page = nuclear_home (last updated Aug. 31, 2017).

[100] *See generally Governing Legislation*, U.S. NUCLEAR REG. COMM'N, http://www.nrc.gov/about-nrc/governing-laws.html (last visited Nov. 18, 2017).

uranium mining contributes to water pollution and nuclear waste storage and disposal is a continuing concern.[101]

In the United States, 104 nuclear reactors produce approximately 20% of the electricity and 8% of all energy the country consumes. As of 2010, the United States had more nuclear power capacity than any other nation, even though it has not ordered a new reactor since 1978.[102] France, Japan, and Germany are also leaders in nuclear capacity, and are all far more dependent on this energy source than is the United States. Other countries, such as Russia, India, China, and South Korea, are actively adding nuclear reactors to increase their nuclear energy capacity. With the dependence on this type of power comes local, national, and international concern and public anxiety about the danger created by nuclear power plant operations. Public anxiety peaks after any major accident occurs. While rare, several major accidents have occurred globally during the 50-plus years that nuclear power plants have been operating.[103]

2. RESILIENCE, SUSTAINABILITY, AND NUCLEAR ENERGY

The production and use of nuclear energy raise a number of issues relevant to resilience and sustainability. We must examine the impact nuclear energy will have on future generations, determine whether externalities from a potential accident or from storing dangerous waste can be minimized, consider the social equity of how we site nuclear plants and dispose of waste, and conclude whether nuclear energy disrupts the functioning and resilience ecosystems. Below we set forth some, but not all, of these issues, including those relevant to nuclear energy accidents, disposal of nuclear waste, and environmental justice.

a. Nuclear Energy Accidents

When a nuclear accident releases radiation, the devastation that can occur is wide-ranging and long-term. Immediate deaths, increases in cancer rates, and contamination of the surrounding environment are consequences that potentially affect future generations for hundreds of years. Further, nuclear accidents can have catastrophic impacts on a system's resilience and the resilience of related social-ecological systems.

The first major nuclear accident that garnered public attention occurred in 1979 at the Pennsylvania Three-Mile Island No. 2 nuclear reactor when

---

[101] See the following informative YouTube video on how nuclear energy works: ENECeducation, *How Nuclear Energy Works*, YOUTUBE (Dec. 30, 2009), http://www.youtube.com/watch?v = VJfIbBDR3e8.
[102] *See generally Nuclear Statistics*, NUCLEAR ENERGY INST., http://www.nei.org/Knowledge-Center/Nuclear-Statistics (last visited Nov. 18, 2017).
[103] *Nuclear Power Plant Accidents: Listed and Ranked Since 1952*, THE GUARDIAN, https://www.the-guardian.com/news/datablog/2011/mar/14/nuclear-power-plant-accidents-list-rank (last visited Nov. 16, 2017).

there was a partial meltdown of the plant reactor core that released radiation. The accident was rated a Level 5 (accident with wider consequences) on the seven-point International Nuclear and Radiological Event Scale (INES) established by the International Atomic Energy Agency.[104]

The second major accident occurred in Chernobyl, Ukraine, in 1986. The steam explosion released a significant amount of radiation into the environment, which caused immediate deaths and thousands of additional cancer deaths from exposure to the released radiation. The disaster was rated a Level 7 (major accident) and triggered a large-scale abandonment of the local population and the decimation of ecosystems. The Fukushima Daiichi nuclear disaster, also rated a Level 7, occurred in 2011 after an earthquake and the subsequent tsunami severely damaged the Japanese nuclear reactors.[105] The Fukushima disaster will be discussed in Chapter 9 as a case study.

Because of the potential for accidents, local and state governments in the United States have considered whether to use their power to shut down local plants when the federal permits expire. However, such local action may bring about preemption challenges by national policy makers who see nuclear energy as the answer to reducing our reliance on foreign fuel resources. In the past several decades, the United States has ordered few new nuclear plants because of safety concerns, radioactive waste disposal, and fear after the 2001 terrorist attack that such plants are a terrorist target. Groups that seek licenses to operate new reactors find that the application process is lengthy and costly. Europe continues to rely on nuclear power as a major energy source and operates almost twice as many nuclear reactors as the United States, even after the Chernobyl accident. Asia has also supported the building of nuclear reactors, although the Japanese disaster may hinder, at least temporarily, the widespread support nuclear energy enjoys in that region.[106]

b. Environmental Impact and Disposal of Nuclear Waste

Disposal of nuclear waste threatens future generations because it can remain hazardous for thousands of years. It can also damage or destroy social-ecological systems and their subsystems, stressing resilience. Nuclear energy appears to offer an ecologically friendly energy source, particularly since it produces limited greenhouse gases, as compared to

---

[104] Rejane Spiegelberg-Planer, *A Matter of Degree: A Revised International Nuclear and Radiological Event Scale (INES) Extends Its Reach*, INT'L ATOMIC ENERGY AGENCY, https://web.archive.org/web/20140901134656/http://www.iaea.org/Publications/Magazines/Bulletin/Bull511/51102744649.html (last visited Nov. 18, 2017).

[105] Shinichi Saoshiro & Yoko Nishikawa, *Japan Says Nuclear Crisis Stabilizing, Time to Rebuild*, REUTERS (Apr. 12, 2011), http://www.reuters.com/article/us-japan-fortimeline-apriltwelve-idUSTRE7 3B6FG20110413.

[106] *Nuclear Statistics, supra* note 102.

other major sources such as coal and natural gas. However, as mentioned above, the development of nuclear energy to meet increasing demand and consumption has slowed in the United States because of the ongoing fear of nuclear accidents, terrorist threats, and the difficulty in dealing with nuclear waste disposal. In addition to public perception issues, other challenges to increasing the development of nuclear energy include the availability of uranium, the world supply of which is estimated to be 80 years; the impact on water supplies used to cool the reactors; and the lack of a labor force properly trained in nuclear engineering.

Nuclear waste disposal encompasses both low-level radioactive waste and high-level radioactive waste. The wastes' radioactivity decreases over time through a process of radioactive decay. The term "half-life" is the amount of time required to reduce the radioactivity to one-half of its original level. Low-level radioactive waste results from exposing materials to nuclear fuel during power plant operation, and exposing medical and research materials to radioactive materials. This waste generally includes machine parts and tools, gloves and other protective clothing, lab supplies, and water purification filters and resins.

We classify low-level radioactive waste into four categories, with Class A containing the least hazardous waste and the Greater-Than-Class-C (GTCC), being the most hazardous classification. Ninety-five percent of low-level radioactive waste is classified as Class A, with its radioactivity diminishing within 100 years. We can dispose of it by using conventional waste disposal practices of shallow burial at three designated disposal sites in the United States, which we monitor to detect any release of radioactive material. In the United States, several federal agencies, as well as state regulators, manage and provide for safe transportation and disposal of these wastes including the Environmental Protection Agency (EPA), Department of Transportation (DOT), Nuclear Regulatory Commission (NRC), and the Department of Energy (DOE). Class B and C radioactive waste raise significant issues relevant to R&S because such waste does not decay for up to 500 years, even though we heavily regulate its storage and disposal. GTCC waste disposal is the responsibility of the DOE and may not be disposed using near-surface conventional methods.

High-level nuclear waste is the byproduct of reactions that occur within the reactors and this spent fuel no longer contains energy sufficient to fuel the reactor. Reprocessing spent fuel creates waste that may take thousands of years to decay to an acceptable level of safety. High-level nuclear waste is in solid form as fuel pellets contained within long metal rods. The NRC has authorized nuclear power plants to store spent nuclear fuel onsite until it finds a permanent geological repository. The fuel is stored in dry casks and in specially designed water-filled pools, which cool the fuel and shield the radiation. The NRC is responsible for securing these storage sites against either intentional or unintentional disturbance. Congress has also tasked the NRC with overseeing the decommissioning of nuclear plants to ensure that the removal of radioactive material and structures will not pose adverse health, safety, and environmental impacts.[107]

Finding a permanent offsite storage location has been extremely controversial. Congress approved a location at Yucca Mountain, Nevada, in 1987. The DOE submitted an application to the NRC in 2008 to obtain authorization to construct the permanent repository. The DOE withdrew its application in 2010 after the Obama administration announced in 2009 that the site was no longer an option for long-term storage. Extensive litigation against the DOE for breach of contract claims has been in play because utilities have paid fees to the DOE for many years to fund the DOE's permanent waste disposal. In the meantime, water-pool storage space has run out at a majority of nuclear sites and dry cask storage is used, albeit with some advantages, such as safety and cost.[108] European countries have also struggled with nuclear waste disposal, and many believe that permanent burial is the preferred solution. Nevertheless, some argue that if it is scientifically and technologically possible in the future to re-use the material, it might be better for the waste to be available onsite for recycling, rather than permanently buried.[109]

SAN ONOFRE NUCLEAR POWER PLANT CLOSURE AND WASTE STORAGE

In 2012, Southern California Edison closed its San Onofre plant located on the San Diego County coastline after newly installed replacement steam generators leaked radiation. State and federal officials approved a plan for onsite storage of the nuclear waste generated by the plant. The waste was stored for decades in cooling pools located between the twin reactors, but the waste will move to dry-storage canisters built within 100 feet of the ocean shore. "Opponents of the storage plan worry that the canisters may be vulnerable to earthquakes or tsunamis. They say the casks could leak or become unmovable to a federal nuclear waste repository if one is ever developed. Environmentalists sued the California Coastal Commission for issuing a permit to allow the waste to be stored within 50 miles of more than 8 million residents."[110]

---

[107] Citizens Awareness Network, Inc. v. U.S. Nuclear Regulatory Commn., 59 F.3d 284 (1st Cir. 1995) (laying out the regulatory framework for decommissioning or shutting down a nuclear power plant).

[108] See Kelley v. Selin, 42 F.3d 1501 (6th Cir. 1995).

[109] See generally Nuclear Energy Inst., Inc. v. EPA, 373 F.3d 1251 (D.C. Cir. 2004); Indiana Michigan Power Co. v. Dep't of Energy, 88 F.3d 1272 (D.C. Cir. 1996).

[110] Jeff McDonald, *Google Earth Images Alarm Critics of San Onofre Nuclear Waste Plan*, SAN DIEGO TRIBUNE (Mar. 13, 2017), http://www.sandiegouniontribune.com/news/watchdog/sd-me-nuclear-waste-20170313-story.html.

3. ENVIRONMENTAL JUSTICE ISSUES

Nuclear plant siting and waste disposal generate environmental justice concerns, as economically disadvantaged neighborhoods, minorities, and indigenous people often struggle to prevent externalities of nuclear energy production from being unfairly concentrated in their communities. For example, in 2012, indigenous people living near the Colorado River in Utah traveled over 600 miles to protest the proposed siting of a nuclear reactor near the Green River, which is the largest tributary of the Colorado River. A delegation from the Fort Mojave Indian Tribe reservation in Needles, California, also arrived to protest the siting.[111] This same tribe had previously defeated proposed plans for a nuclear waste dump near their tribal lands.[112] The Green River siting has generated concern about contaminating the Colorado River, as well as the need to withdraw 48 million gallons of water a day from the Green River to run the reactor. The Green River is the second-most endangered river in the country and such a large water diversion would further adversely affect native fish and local tourism.

The U.S. Environmental Protection Agency's Civil Rights Office (Office) investigates racial discrimination in environmental decision making. The Office gets its authority from Title VI of the Civil Rights Act of 1964, which prohibits discrimination by those receiving federal financial assistance.

A recent investigation by the Center for Public Integrity (Center) and NBC News indicated that the Office has "never once made a formal finding of a Title VI violation" in its 22-year history of processing environmental discrimination complaints:

Of the cases reviewed by the Center, the EPA:

- Rejected 162 without investigation;
- Dismissed 52 upon investigation;
- Referred 14 to other agencies, including the departments of Justice, Health and Human Services and Transportation;
- Resolved 12 with voluntary or informal agreements;
- Accepted 13 for investigations that remain open today, the oldest begun in 1996.

The Center noted that others have reviewed and criticized the Office in the past, including a 2011 Deloitte Consulting report that concluded that the Office complied with its 20-day statutory deadline in only 6% of the Title VI complaints reviewed.

The Center assembled an interactive analysis of the complaints originating from each state, which you can view at https://www.publicintegrity.org/2015/08/03/17668/environmental-racism-persists-and-epa-one-reason-why.

---

[111] *See generally No Nuclear Power Plant in Green River, Utah! — Citizen Protest Against Blue Castle Proposal*, NO GREEN RIVER NUKE, http://www.nogreenrivernuke.org (last visited Nov. 18, 2017).
[112] David F. Salisbury, *Indian Reservation Buries Plan for Hazardous-Waste Dump Site*, The CHRISTIAN SCI. MONITOR (June 25, 1982), www.csmonitor.com/1982/0625/062543.html.

4. WATER IMPACTS

Withdrawing water for nuclear power plant operation, as well as returning it to the flow, causes environmentally adverse effects. In addition to affecting aquatic life by diverting water needed for the power plant, the process returns water at a higher temperature that contains pollutants such as heavy metals, salts, and small amounts of radioactive elements, which also negatively affect water quality and aquatic life.

5. MINIMIZING NUCLEAR ENERGY EXTERNALITIES

Minimizing externalities is a key issue for sustaining nuclear power. Nuclear waste disposal difficulties and the potential for nuclear disasters such as the meltdown at Fukushima caution against a commitment to this energy source. However, other energy sources such as oil and gas are also dangerous, as we have seen with the *Exxon Valdez* and *Deepwater Horizon* oil spills and the natural gas explosion, which destroyed a Northern California neighborhood. National and international energy policies respond to energy disasters, but the approach varies depending on political forces, economic impacts, and public response. While disasters may provide opportunities to reassess reliance on particular sources of energy and implement changes to prevent future disasters, they are not necessarily a sound basis for energy policies going forward.[113] As with other environmental policies, energy policies involve an assessment of risks in light of benefits (we describe risk analysis in more detail in Chapter 8).[114]

Nuclear energy provides a partial response to the resilience challenges presented by coal and oil energy systems. Although uranium mining, enrichment, and transport emit some pollutants, nuclear energy in general produces few GHG emissions and few conventional air pollutants. However, the risks associated with safety, radioactive waste disposal, and potential disasters such as Chernobyl and Fukushima must be carefully weighed, as these trade-offs present additional challenges to the resilience and sustainability of deriving energy from nuclear sources.[115]

---

[113] *See* Ralph Vartabedian & Ian Duncan, *First New U.S. Nuclear Reactors in Decades Approved: The Nuclear Regulatory Commission Approves Construction and Licensing of Two New Nuclear Reactors at Plant Vogtle in Georgia, the First Such Approval in the U.S. Since 1978*, L.A. Times (Feb. 9, 2012), http://articles.latimes.com/2012/feb/09/nation/la-na-nuclear-20120210 (noting that approval came after meltdown at Fukushima as nuclear power supporters were able to successfully argue "that a new generation of reactors and strong U.S. regulations justify making it part of the mix to meet the nation's energy needs").

[114] *See* Lincoln L. Davies, *Beyond Fukushima: Disasters, Nuclear Energy, and Energy Law*, 2011 BYU L. Rev. 1937 (2011).

[115] *See* Arnold W. Reitze, Jr., *Electric Power in a Carbon Constrained World*, 24 Wm. & Mary Envtl. L. & Pol'y Rev. 821, 883-890 (2010).

B. "Renewable" Energy Sources

Recognizing that the term "renewable" may be a misnomer, we have grouped the water, wind, biomass, geothermal, and solar energy sources under the main title of "Non-Fossil Fuels." Because much of the literature thus far has focused on using the renewable category for these resources, our initial introduction to these is brief. For each of the following sub-sections, we describe the renewable resource, the law relevant to that resource, and how the law impacts the resilience and sustainability of the energy system and associated systems.

Renewables are used to varying degrees, depending upon the country, but it is projected that such sources can supply the world with 15% of its energy by 2020. While the United States has been slow to embrace renewable energy, several European countries generate a large portion of their electricity from renewable sources, and China actively promotes the use of renewables.

The Natural Resources Defense Council (NRDC) graded the Group of Twenty Finance Ministers and Central Bank Governors (also known as the G20) on how they used renewable energy. The G20 countries produced approximately 80% of the total electricity in the world in 2010 and produced more than 82% of electricity from renewable resources in the same year. The NRDC study examining global information from 2002 through 2011, found that Germany and the European Union, in general, had the highest use of renewable energy for electricity production, with the United States ranking seventh and Russia in the last place. However, all of the G20 countries were behind Spain, Portugal, New Zealand, and Iceland, which used more than 15% renewable sources for electricity production.[116]

Tracing its roots to the 1970s, the G20 was comprised of 19 countries and the European Union in 2016: Argentina, Australia, Brazil, Canada, China, France, Germany, India, Indonesia, Italy, Japan, Republic of Korea, Mexico, Russia, Saudi Arabia, South Africa, Turkey, the United Kingdom, the United States, and the European Union.

The five renewable sources used most often are water (hydropower), wind, geothermal, biomass (which includes wood and wood waste, landfill

---

[116] Jake Schmidt & Aaron Haifly, *Delivering on Renewable Energy Around the World: How Do Key Countries Stack Up?*, Nat. Res. Def. Council 1, 2 (May 2012), http://www.nrdc.org/energy/files/delivering-renewable-energy.pdf.

gas and biogas, municipal solid waste, ethanol, and biodiesel), and solar.[117]
However, tidal and wave energy also produce electricity by harnessing the
moon and sun's pull on large water bodies such as seas and great lakes. We
continue to explore these sources, recognizing that various parts of the world
use them to a minor degree already. In the United States, the five renewable
sources listed above are in the order of greatest to least use for electricity
generation. As you can see in Figure 6-5, the United States depends on non
-renewable energy for over 87% of its electrical energy needs and uses more
than 12% renewable energy for electricity generation.

Predominately renewable fuel for utility-scale electricity generation, 2011

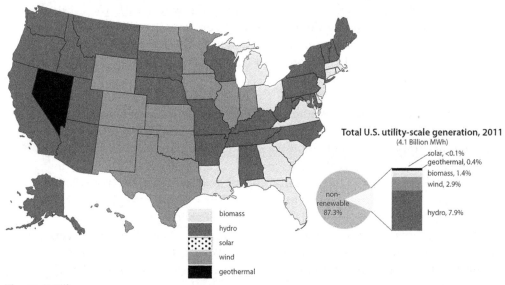

Figure 6-5[118]

Fossil fuels have provided more than 80% of total U.S. energy consumption for more than 100 years. Since 1928, when consumption of natural gas

---

[117] For more information about renewable energy, see generally *The Renewable Energy Reader*, U.
DENVER, STURM COLL. LAW, http://www.law.du.edu/the-renewable-energy-reader (last visited Nov. 18,
2017).
[118] U.S. ENERGY INFO. ADMIN., http://www.eia.gov/renewable/.
[119] Michael Mobilia, *Even as Renewables Increase, Fossil Fuels Continue to Dominate U.S. Energy Mix*,
U.S. ENERGY INFO. ADMIN. (July 3, 2017), https://www.eia.gov/todayinenergy/detail.php?id = 31892.

Energy consumption in the United States (1776-2016)
quadrillion British thermal units

Figure 6-6

surpassed that of biomass, the three fossil fuels—petroleum, natural gas, and coal—have been the most consumed fuels in the United States. In 2016, fossil fuels accounted for 81% of total U.S. energy consumption, the lowest fossil fuel share in the past century.

In 2016, the renewable share of energy consumption in the United States was 10.5%. This was the largest renewable share since the 1930s, when overall energy consumption was lower and the amount of biomass consumption (mainly wood) was relatively high. The greatest growth in renewables over the past decade has been in **solar and wind electricity generation**. **Liquid biofuel** consumption—more than half of which is ethanol blended into motor gasoline—has also increased in recent years, contributing to the growing renewable share of total energy consumption.

In addition to the increasing share of renewables, the decline in the fossil fuel share of consumption is attributable mainly to declines in coal consumption. U.S. coal consumption fell nearly 9% in 2016, following a 14% drop in 2015. Overall, U.S. coal consumption has declined almost 38% since 2005. In each of the past 20 years, the power sector has accounted for more than 90% of total U.S. coal consumption.

Petroleum, which encompasses nearly all transportation fuels and several petroleum-based fuels used in homes, businesses, and industries, continues to be the largest source of energy consumption in the United States. Petroleum consumption has increased in each of the past four years.

Consumption of natural gas has risen in 9 of the past 10 years. As recently as 2006, the United States consumed more coal than natural gas (in energy-equivalent terms), but as natural gas consumption has increased—particularly in the electric power sector—natural gas use in 2016 was about twice that of coal.

Current projections for global energy sources through 2040 show renewable energy as the fastest growing energy source, increasing by an average of 2.6% per year between 2012 and 2040, as seen Figure 6-7 from

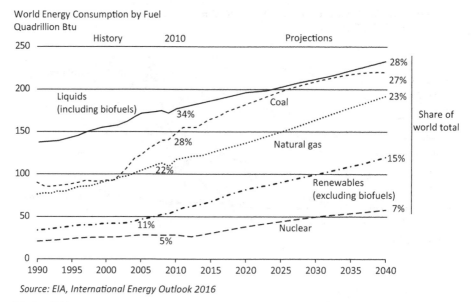

Source: EIA, International Energy Outlook 2016

Figure 6-7

the U.S. Energy Information Administration (EIA) report, International Energy Outlook 2016.[120]

Growth in Use of Non-Fossil Fuels.   We will need both international and national action to support this growth of renewable sources. In 1974, a treaty, the Agreement on an International Energy Programme, formed the International Energy Agency (IEA). The IEA serves as an energy forum for 28 member countries to allow them to take joint measures to deal with oil supply emergencies, share energy information, and coordinate energy policies. In addition, the forum encourages these countries to develop policies concerning energy efficiency, diversification of energy sources, and integrating environmental concerns. The IEA recognizes the role of renewable energy in responding to climate change, energy security, and access to energy. The IEA also analyzes these technologies, the associated policies, and markets as countries deal with the challenges of an unsustainable global energy structure.[121]

Encouraging Use and Investment in the United States.   In the United States, federal, state, and local governments use incentives and mandates to encourage us to use renewable energy and invest in renewable energy programs. The federal government helps increase renewables by requiring that we account for externalities such as carbon emissions in order to recognize the true cost of using fossil fuel energy. By enacting policies that require carbon reduction, capture, or storage such as establishing an emissions trading program (cap-and-trade) and regulating air pollutants

---

[120] *International Energy Outlook 2016*, U.S. ENERGY INFO. ADMIN. (May 11, 2016), https://www.eia. gov/outlooks/archive/ieo16/.
[121] For more information on the IEA, see generally *Our Mission*, INT'L ENERGY AGENCY, http://www. iea.org/about/ourmission/ (last visited Nov. 18, 2017).

more stringently, the government can discourage the use of fossil fuels. As we recognize the true costs of fossil fuels, renewable energy will become more economically viable. The federal government has also created financial incentives to use renewable energy by providing monetary incentives, establishing tax credits, offering federal grants, and directly funding efficient energy projects and smart grid technologies.[122] Financing renewable energy will require a combination of government incentives and private innovation to compete with cheaper energy sources.[123]

State governments have also adopted policies to encourage the use of renewable resources and have generally framed them as Renewable Portfolio Standards (RPS). These standards require that renewable energy generate a certain percentage of power sold within the state. Oregon has a renewable standard of 50% by 2040, Hawai'i 100% by 2034, California and New York 50% within 25 years, and Massachusetts requires a 1% annual increase indefinitely until it reaches a full renewable portfolio for electricity.[124] Even these goals are in flux as lawmakers struggle to enact ambitious targets. For example, the California Senate approved a bill that speeds up the state's goal of reaching 50% renewable energy by 2026, instead of the original target of 2030. In addition, by 2045 California's goal is to receive 100% of its power from renewable energy.[125]

There is no RPS program at the national level and litigants have challenged some state RPS programs as discriminating against interstate commerce, thus violating the Dormant Commerce Clause under the U.S. Constitution.[126] Thus far, both the Tenth Circuit and the Second Circuit have upheld challenged state RPS programs as constitutional under the Dormant Commerce Clause.[127] Some have criticized the lack of an effective national renewable energy policy in the United States, particularly when a number of countries in the European Union have become world leaders in renewable energy.[128]

---

[122] *See generally* Reitze, Jr., *supra* note 115.
[123] Paul Schwabe, Michael Mendelsohn, Felix Mormann & Douglas J. Arent, *Mobilizing Public Markets to Finance Renewable Energy Projects: Insights from Expert Stakeholders*, NAT'L RENEWABLE ENERGY LABORATORY iii (June 2012), http://www.nrel.gov/docs/fy12osti/55021.pdf.
[124] DeSmog Blog, *Oregon Becomes First State in Nation to Sign Bill That Phases Out Coal, Ramps Up Renewables*, EcoWatch (Mar. 14, 2016, 8:26 AM), http://www.ecowatch.com/oregon-becomes-first-state-in-nation-to-sign-bill-that-phases-out-coal-1882189350.html.
[125] Liam Dillon, *California Plan for 100% Renewable Energy by 2045 Clears Key Hurdle*, L.A. TIMES (May 31, 2017, 12:31 PM), http://www.latimes.com/politics/essential/la-pol-ca-essential-politics-updates-california-plan-for-100-renewable-1496258464-htmlstory.html.
[126] Daniel K. Lee & Timothy P. Duane, *Putting the Dormant Commerce Clause Back to Sleep: Adapting the Doctrine to Support State Renewable Portfolio Standards*, 43 ENVTL. L. 295, 326-328 (2013).
[127] *See* Allco Fin. Ltd. v. Klee, 861 F.3d 82, 102-104 (2d Cir. 2017) (finding no discrimination under the Dormant Commerce Clause and concluding that Connecticut's RPS program passes the more deferential *Pike* balancing test); Energy & Env't Legal Inst. v. Epel, 793 F.3d 1169, 1172 (10th Cir. 2015) (reviewing Colorado's renewable energy mandate under *Baldwin* test only and concluding it survived constitutional challenge).
[128] E. Donald Elliott, *Why the U.S. Does Not Have a Renewable Energy Policy*, 43 ENVTL. L. REP. 10095, 10100 (Feb. 2013), *available at* http://ssrn.com/abstract=1878616 (quoting a New York Times article from August 2010: "'If the United States is to catch up to countries like Portugal, the United States must overcome obstacles like a fragmented, outdated energy grid poorly suited to renewable energy, a historic reliance on plentiful and cheap supplies of fossil fuels, especially coal, powerful oil and coal industries that often oppose incentives for renewable development and an energy policy that is influenced by individual states.'").

DORMANT COMMERCE CLAUSE CHALLENGE AGAINST RENEWABLE PORTFOLIO STANDARD (RPS)

Allco Finance Limited v. Klee, 861 F.3d 82 (2d Cir. 2017)

Allco claims that a separate Connecticut program, the Renewable Portfolio Standard ("RPS"), Conn. Gen. Stat. §16-245a(b), violates the dormant Commerce Clause.

Connecticut's RPS program requires utilities to have an increasing percentage of their generation portfolios be "generated from" renewable energy. Conn. Gen. Stat. §16-245a(a). Connecticut's RPS program allows utilities to satisfy this requirement either by generating renewable energy themselves, or by purchasing renewable energy certificates ("RECs"). *See id.* §16-245a(b). (Each REC represents one megawatt-hour of renewable energy produced by a third-party generator.)

* * *

Plaintiff * * * argues that it has been injured by two different features of Connecticut's RPS program, both of which, Plaintiff claims, amount to discriminatory "regional protectionism" in violation of the dormant Commerce Clause. First, Allco alleges that it has a solar power facility in Georgia that has been discriminated against by Connecticut's RPS program insofar as Connecticut utilities cannot satisfy the RPS program's requirements by purchasing the Georgia RECs. Second, Allco argues that it has been injured by the fact that renewable energy generators in adjacent control areas—though able to sell qualifying RECs—must pay a fee to transmit their energy into the ISO-NE grid in order to sell their RECs to Connecticut utilities pursuant to NEPOOL GIS Rule 2.7(c). Allco asserts that it owns such a renewable facility in New York, and that it "will not deliver its electricity into the ISO-New England control area because of the additional cost burdens involved in doing so."

* * *

a. Alleged Discrimination Against Allco's Georgia Facility

Insofar as Allco argues that the RPS program discriminates against Allco's Georgia facility, and the RECs it produces, Connecticut responds by saying that: "RECs are inventions of state property law," Wheelabrator Lisbon, Inc., 531 F.3d at 186, and because the RECs produced by Allco's Georgia facility do not meet the legal requirements of Connecticut's RPS program, see Conn. Gen. Stat. §16-245a(b), the two types of RECs are different products. Connecticut's RPS program therefore does no more than treat different products differently in a nondiscriminatory fashion. As such, Connecticut asserts, there is no discrimination under the dormant Commerce Clause. We agree, and therefore apply the more deferential balancing test under *Pike*, concluding that the RPS program passes that test.

* * *

Following the Court's analysis in [Gen. Motors Corp. v. Tracy, 519 U.S. 278, 303 (1997)], we resolve this dilemma by asking whether the opportunity for increased competition between REC producers in the national market necessitates treating REC-producers in Georgia and New England alike for dormant Commerce Clause purposes, or whether the needs of Connecticut's local energy market permits treating the two types of REC producers differently. That is, should we give "controlling significance" to the market in which the two types of REC producers compete, or to the market served only by REC producers that can connect to Connecticut's power grid? *Id.* As in *Tracy*, we find that "[a]lthough there is no a priori answer, a number of reasons support a decision to give greater weight" to the market for RECs that are produced by generators able to connect to Connecticut's grid, *id.* at 304, and hence to treat those generators and Allco's Georgia generator as dissimilar for dormant Commerce Clause purposes.

It is here that the more general language in *Tracy* gives us guidance. Just as the *Tracy* Court recognized the importance of Ohio's interest in protecting the captive natural gas market from the effects of competition in order to promote public health and safety, *id.* at 306-07, so must we here recognize the importance of Connecticut's interest in protecting the market for RECs produced within the ISO-NE or in adjacent areas. Connecticut's RPS program serves its legitimate interest in promoting increased production of renewable power generation in the region, thereby protecting its citizens' health, safety, and reliable access to power.

* * *

And since, as the Court stated in *Tracy*, such "health and safety considerations [may] be weighed in the process of deciding the threshold question whether the conditions entailing application of the dormant Commerce Clause are present," 519 U.S. at 307, we conclude, analogously to the Court's decision in *Tracy*, that Connecticut's regulatory response to the needs of the local energy market has resulted in a noncompetitive REC product that is capable of being produced only by in-region generators, and that this distinguishes such generators from Allco's Georgia generator "to the point that the enterprises should not be considered 'similarly situated' for purposes of a claim of facial discrimination under the Commerce Clause." *Id.* at 310.

Having reached this conclusion, and for the same reasons discussed above, it is clear that the burden imposed by Connecticut's RPS program is also not "clearly excessive in relation to the putative local benefits," and therefore passes the more permissive *Pike* test. *Pike*, 397 U.S. at 142 * * * "We have consistently recognized the legitimate state pursuit of such interests as compatible with the Commerce Clause, which was 'never intended to cut the States off from legislating on all subjects relating to the health, life, and safety of their citizens,' even if that 'legislation might indirectly affect the commerce of the country.' " *Tracy*, 519 U.S. at 306-07 (quoting Huron Portland Cement Co. v. City of Detroit, 362 U.S. 440, 443–44 (1960)).

Allco's argument that Connecticut's RPS program discriminates between its Georgia renewable energy generator and in-region renewable energy generators therefore fails, and the district court's dismissal of this claim must be affirmed.

b. Alleged Discrimination Against Allco's New York Facility

With respect to Allco's claim that its New York facility has suffered discrimination because it has had to pay transmission fees in order for its RECs to qualify under the RPS program, we determine that Allco has failed sufficiently to plead that such charges are anything more than use fees, analogous to road tolls, which regularly pass constitutional muster. * * * Allco's conclusory allegations do not allow us to make any inferences of excessive burden. We therefore affirm the district court's dismissal of Allco's dormant Commerce Clause claim with respect to its New York facility.

Roadblocks to using renewable resources include cost relative to fossil fuels, reliability, storage, distribution, and environmental and aesthetic land use impacts.[129] Future constraints on carbon emissions may change the economics of using fossil fuel for energy production by increasing the cost of electricity from these sources. Combining these constraints with giving direct subsidies and other incentives to encourage renewable sources could make renewables cost competitive with coal and other carbon sources. We might be able to resolve the problem with the intermittent nature of renewables such as wind, solar, and tidal sources by developing commercially proven storage devices for excess electricity and improving the electrical distribution grid to deal with moving this energy from the production location to end users.

Improved technology for the design and operation of green energy devices will reduce environmental impacts to ecosystem, aquatic, and wildlife habitats. We must address the impacts caused from the siting of solar panels, tidal turbines, dams, and wind farms, as well as from the fracking and injection of water for geothermal energy capture in order to increase renewable energy sources.[130] Local residents sometimes object to the siting of these green devices as aesthetically displeasing, although they may have even stronger objections to a nearby coal-fired power plant.[131]

Questions and Note

1. As you work through the subsections below on individual renewable energies, consider our discussion from Chapter 1 and the definitions of resilience and sustainability. For example, what would a resilient energy system consist of? What is the significance of an energy system that resists, adapts, and transforms? Do renewable energies help accomplish this understanding of resilience? What about sustainability? Do renewable energies help achieve more sustainable conditions? What considerations do renewables raise relevant to the triple bottom line?

---

[129] Kristen Castaños, *Governor Brown Signs Two More Bills to Streamline Renewable Energy Development in California: SB 267 and SB 618*, Cal. Envtl. L. Blog (Oct. 10, 2011), http://www. californiaenvironmentallawblog.com/esa/governor-brown-signs-two-more-bills-to-streamline-renewable-energy-development-in-california-sb-267.

[130] Sara C. Bronin, *The Promise and Perils of Renewable Energy on Tribal Lands, in* Tribes, Land and the Environment 103 (Sarah A. Krakoff & Ezra Rosser eds., 2012).

[131] *See, e.g.*, Katheleen Conti, *Solar Projects Increasingly Meeting Local Resistance*, Boston Globe (May 5, 2013), http://www.bostonglobe.com/metro/regionals/south/2013/05/04/solar-farm-projects-hit-roadblocks-some-communities-solar-projects-meet-resistance-locally/jUFUAxSZEpK4swEc Ca9hPM/story.html (explaining how residents argued that the 3.3-megawatt installation on 50 acres of open farmland would "be ugly, devalue their properties, and cause health problems.").

2. Note the difference in objectives with the questions above. In terms of resilience, the question asks how we can create a resilient **energy system**; while in terms of sustainability, the question asks how we can achieve sustainable **conditions**. How we frame the objective and/or question may alter the results. For example, the steps we take to achieve a resilient energy system may be different from steps taken to achieve a resilient society. Can you see where they might diverge or overlap?

1. WATER

Waterpower is the largest "renewable" clean energy source for electric energy in the world. It includes hydropower, and more recently, wave, current, and tidal power. Hydropower use began in the late 1800s in the United States. By the early 1900s, hydropower constituted about 40% of the country's electric power supply; by its height in the 1940s, it provided 75% of the electricity in the West and Pacific Northwest, and one-third of the total U.S. electric power supply.[132] Its use later decreased in importance with the development of fossil fuel and nuclear power plants beginning in the 1950s.

a. Production and Regulation

Hydropower produces electricity by forcing water through a hydraulic turbine connected to a generator, which harnesses the kinetic energy created by water flowing downstream. Generating sufficient water flow requires precipitation and elevation changes, thus the U.S. Pacific Northwest, with its high rainfall levels and mountainous terrain, is an ideal geographic region for hydroelectric power plants. The U.S. federal government owns several hydropower facilities such as the Hoover Dam and the Glen Canyon Dam on the Colorado River, and the Grand Coulee Dam in Washington State. In addition to the 75 hydropower dams operated by the U.S. Army Corps of Engineers, the 58 hydropower dams operated by the Bureau of Reclamation, and the 29 hydropower plants operated by the Tennessee Valley Authority (the largest electric company in the United States), there are approximately 1,600 hydropower projects operated by nonfederal, private, state, or local government entities.[133]

the importance of steadily diversifying electricity production by region until we come to a full renewable energy use

---

[132] *Hydropower Program: The History of Hydropower Development in the United States*, Bureau of Reclamation, http://www.usbr.gov/power/edu/history.html (last updated Feb. 3, 2016).
[133] The Law of Clean Energy, Efficiency and Renewables 479-507 (Michael B. Gerrard ed., 2011) [hereinafter The Law of Clean Energy].

Hydropower Regulation.   In the United States, the federal government regulates hydropower plants. While states may have the right to participate in the federal licensing process, they can only regulate the water in these projects for irrigation or municipal uses. Federal law preempts any attempt by the state to directly license or regulate a hydropower project.[134] The Federal Energy Regulatory Commission (FERC) under the Federal Power Act (FPA) provides the major federal authority over hydroelectric projects. FERC is responsible for licensing, obtaining an exemption for small projects under the 1978 Public Utility Regulatory Practices Act (PURPA) and the 1980 Energy Security Act (ESA), and decommissioning — shutting down — a plant after its license has expired and is not renewed. However, FERC's authorized actions are subject to the requirements of the National Environmental Policy Act (NEPA), the Endangered Species Act (ESA), the Clean Water Act (CWA), the Coastal Zone Management Act (CZMA), and the National Historic Preservation Act (NHPA).[135]

International Hydropower.   Managing transboundary waters is one of the major international issues confronting the growth of hydropower as an energy source. China, for example, is building dams on the Mekong River to increase hydropower electricity to meet its industrial growth. Downstream riparian countries, which include Vietnam, Cambodia, Laos, Thailand, and Myanmar, suffer harmful effects from this dam building and operations. These downstream countries, except for Myanmar, are part of the Mekong River Commission, an intergovernmental organization designed to manage the transboundary waters of the Mekong Basin. This Commission would seem to provide an appropriate mechanism for resolving disputes regarding China's hydropower projects, except that China is not a member and has operated as a "dialogue partner" with limited involvement with the other countries.[136]

In 2010 after low water levels severely impacted the Mekong River, China was heavily criticized for its dam building activities and operations that were viewed as responsible for aggravating the severe drought conditions. Because of these challenges, China has started to take a more active and cooperative stance in managing water resources in the Mekong region. In late 2015, "the foreign ministers of China, Myanmar, Laos, Thailand, Cambodia, and Vietnam launched the Lancang-Mekong Cooperation Mechanism (LMCM) . . . [which] will cover five priority areas: interconnectivity, production capacity, cross-border economic cooperation, water resources and cooperation on agriculture and poverty reduction."[137]

---

[134] *See generally* California v. FERC, 495 U.S. 490 (1990).
[135] THE LAW OF CLEAN ENERGY, *supra* note 133.
[136] L. Waldron Davis, *Reversing the Flow: International Law and Chinese Hydropower Development on the Headwaters of the Mekong River*, 19 N.Y. INT'L L. REV. 1, 2 (Summer 2006).
[137] Sebastian Biba, *China Drives Water Cooperation with Mekong Countries*, THETHIRDPOLE. NET (Feb, 1, 2016), https://www.thethirdpole.net/2016/02/01/china-drives-water-cooperation-with-mekong-countries/.

Another challenge facing hydropower projects throughout the globe is climate change. Climate change threatens to make these projects less reliable as yearly flows of rivers, such as the Nile Basin in Africa and the Mekong Basin in Central Asia, experience severe droughts, which interrupt the electricity generated by these plants.[138]

Waves and Tidal Currents.   Waves and tidal currents have the potential to provide waterpower to generate electricity. In addition, ocean thermal energy can generate electricity through technology by using the difference in water temperature between deep cold waters and the warmer surface water. The U.S. Department of Energy (DOE) projects that water power could generate 15% of America's electricity by 2030. Strong tides exist on the West Coast and in Alaska and Hawai'i, while the East Coast also has great potential for wave energy development. The DOE has offered financial incentives through grants to encourage projects that "will advance commercial viability, cost-competitiveness, and market acceptance of new technologies that can harness renewable energy from oceans and rivers."[139]

Marine and hydrokinetic energy is an emerging field and there are only a few development projects in the United States[140] The Water Power Program (WPP) is responsible for developing these advanced technologies and encouraging market adoption. The WPP also works on finding ways to maximize the efficiency of these projects while reducing the potential for adverse environmental effects on marine life and aquatic ecosystems.

Canada has been a leader in harnessing wave and tidal power and hopes to determine through its Fundy Ocean Research Center for Energy (FORCE) project whether "tidal energy really and truly [is] viable from a social, environmental, economic perspective in Nova Scotia."[141] Other countries, including Australia, China, Denmark, Ireland, Portugal, and South Korea, have been exploring this resource, but few projects are commercially viable. In the United States, DOE grants, as well as support from several states and the military, have increased the interest in this new energy

[handwritten margin note: + for coastal countries & doesn't have to be just that. a combination of renewable resources. esp-Devlp Countries]

---

[138] A. Dan Tarlock, *Water Security, Fear Mitigation and International Water Law*, 31 HAMLINE L. REV. 703, 711 (2008) (citing INTERGOVERNMENTAL PANEL ON CLIMATE CHANGE, CLIMATE CHANGE 2001: IMPACTS, ADAPTATION & VULNERABILITY 496-497 (James J. McCarthy et al. eds., 2001)).

[139] *DOE Selects Projects for Up to $7.3 Million for R&D Clean Technology Water Power Projects*, U.S. DEP'T ENERGY (Sept. 18, 2008), http://energy.gov/articles/doe-selects-projects-73-million-rd-clean-technology-water-power-projects; *see also DOE Awards Up to $14.6 Million to Support Development of Advanced Water Power Technologies*, U.S. DEP'T ENERGY (Sept. 15, 2009), http://energy.gov/articles/doe-awards-146-million-support-development-advanced-water-power-technologies.

[140] *Maine Project Takes Historic Step Forward in U.S. Tidal Energy Deployment*, U.S. DEP'T ENERGY (May 4, 2012), http://energy.gov/articles/maine-project-takes-historic-step-forward-us-tidal-energy-deployment.

[141] Kelsey Power, *Tidal Power in the Bay of Fundy: A Dream Without Danger?*, NAT'L OBSERVER (June 6, 2017), http://www.nationalobserver.com/2017/06/06/analysis/tidal-power-bay-fundy-dream-without-danger; *see also* Bob Drogin, *Companies Tapping the Tides in Quest for Renewable Energy*, L.A. TIMES (Nov. 19, 2010), www.latimes.com/news/nationworld/nation/la-na-tides-20101120,0,5912157.story.

source. These projects require licenses regulated by the FERC that are subject to NEPA review and the DOI, which has leasing authority over the Outer Continental Shelf, governs the leases for the projects. The National Oceanic and Atmospheric Administration (NOAA) is responsible for ocean thermal energy projects and individual states have also enacted regulations for ocean energy development within the states' three-mile limit.

b. Resilience and Sustainability

Hydropower, as a non-fossil fuel energy resource, has many benefits but also has several detriments. While its production emits far fewer GHG emissions than fossil fuels, there is the potential for GHG emissions, such as methane emissions from reservoirs due to decomposing vegetation along flooded areas. The construction and operation of these plants will most likely require building dams, which can have a significant adverse impact on vulnerable communities and the environment. Once the dam is constructed, the flooding that occurs will destroy human and wildlife habitat. This flooding frequently affects indigenous peoples as their communities depend on the river for fishing, hunting, and navigation.[142]

Dams will interfere with water flows, alter ecosystems, and impact people and wildlife that rely on the waters. The process of releasing water from a hydropower plant into rivers does not cause pollution. However, the temperature and volume variability of the releases may harm fish, other aquatic life, and the associated ecosystems. Turbine blades may harm fish directly as they swim through the hydroelectric plants or indirectly by altering their life cycles if they can no longer return upstream to spawn.[143]

For example, in the mid-1900s, the Chief Joseph and Grand Coulee Dams in Washington State were built to provide hydroelectricity, flooding thousands of acres of land and permanently blocking hundreds of miles of salmon habitat (according to the U.S. Department of Energy, the Grand Coulee Dam is the largest electric power-producing facility in the United States). The decisions to construct these dams had profound and pronounced impacts on future generations. After living on ancient ancestral lands and creating a way of life around salmon runs for thousands of years, Native Americans lost their lands by the flooding caused by the dams and lost access to salmon runs, which were permanently blocked. These consequences strain the resilience and sustainability of several social-ecological systems. They deny access to the historical and cultural grounding for future generations and wreak havoc on ecosystems

---

[142] For discussion of tribes in Brazil fighting the construction of the Belo Monte Dam complex along the Xingu River in the Amazon, see *Amazonian Indigenous Leaders Call for Suspension of Construction License for Belo Monte Dam*, INT'L RIVERS (July 9, 2012), http://www.internationalrivers.org/resources/amazonian-indigenous-leaders-call-for-suspension-of-construction-license-for-belo-monte.

[143] John Harrison, *Fish Passage at Dams*, THE N.W. POWER & CONSERVATION COUNCIL (Oct. 31, 2008), https://www.nwcouncil.org/history/FishPassage.

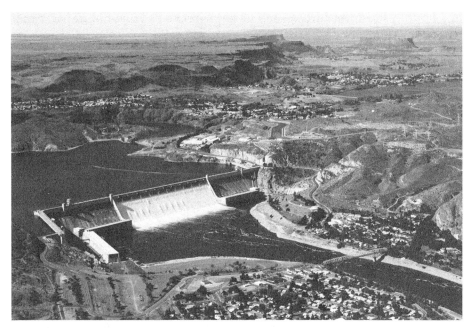

Grand Coulee Dam

involving the river, salmon, and other species. In an attempt to rectify this, some dams have been equipped with "fish ladders" to help salmon swim upstream to reproduce.

These environmental concerns and others have surfaced in the United States as many of the nonfederal projects seek to relicense after the expiration of a 50-year license given in the mid-1900s. New licenses are now subject to revised licensing regulations as well as to NEPA, ESA, and CWA requirements. NEPA environmental impact assessments and studies required for relicensing have shown that removing dams may have significant environmental benefits such as restoring ecosystems, promoting the recovery of endangered species, and improving recreation and tourism. However, removal is not necessarily the best solution and may negatively affect communities by reducing available power sources and changing the topography of the area, including losing the reservoir and increasing the size and flow of the river.[144] These trade-offs must be weighed prior to making the decision to remove a dam.

Marine and hydrokinetic energy generation also have the potential to cause adverse environmental effects. We are uncertain as to how wave power buoys, tidal power turbines, ocean currents, and rivers will impact marine life and aquatic ecosystems. While most of the equipment is underwater, the location of these projects may generate concerns from local communities about additional issues, including visual impacts or the

---

[144]Jackson Cty. v. FERC, 589 F.3d 1284 (D.C. Cir. 2009).

impact to historic resources such as shipwrecks.[145] Potential impacts that we must explore include entangling fish and wildlife, creating noise and vibration, releasing pollutants, and altering aquatic ecosystems, including marine life, the ocean floor, currents, sediments, and ocean temperature.[146]

The benefits of using waterpower in addressing climate change include reducing GHG emissions and protecting communities against water shortages and flooding. In addition to supplanting millions of barrels of oil each year (otherwise needed for generating electricity), these projects provide flood control, irrigation, water supply, and recreation. While some consider hydropower to be one of the least expensive power sources, initial development costs for major plants can run in the billions of dollars.[147] Water serves as the fuel and pumped storage projects help provide a stable energy source; however, droughts can cause major power outages in countries such as Norway and Brazil that rely heavily on hydropower. It should be noted that other energy sources, such as nuclear power, solar thermal plants, geothermal plants, and biomass, also rely on water, and droughts could severely impact these sources as well.[148]

At the national level, countries may be able to regulate and incentivize the use of waterpower while still addressing the environmental concerns and local community impact of power plants. Building a dam or installing energy capturing devices such as ocean or lake turbines will potentially create great harm in a local community. In the United States, as discussed above, the FERC, with input from other U.S. government agencies as well as state and local interests, controls the nation's hydropower. Tidal energy may also provide affordable, renewable energy in the future and it is projected that harnessing this source could provide up to 20% of the United Kingdom's electric power needs.[149] One of the advantages of this source is that it is more reliable than wind and solar power, which are not as predictable as currents and tides.

Internationally, there are organizations seeking to promote sustainable water power to generate energy while other organizations work to establish guidelines to address sustainable environmental and human rights concerns. The International Hydropower Association (IHA), a nonprofit organization with members in approximately 80 countries, represents the hydropower sector with the goal to promote the sustainable development

---

[145] *See Amazonian Indigenous Leaders Call for Suspension of Construction License for Belo Monte Dam*, *supra* note 142.

[146] THE LAW OF CLEAN ENERGY, *supra* note 133, at 516-522.

[147] *See generally Facts About Hydropower*, WIS. VALLEY IMPROVEMENT CO., http://www.wvic.com/content.cfm?PageID=686 (last visited Nov. 18, 2017).

[148] Sara Barczak, *Energy and Water Collisions: Drought Implications*, S. ALLIANCE FOR CLEAN ENERGY (July 31, 2012), http://blog.cleanenergy.org/2012/07/31/energy-and-water-collisions-drought-implications.

[149] *Wave and Tidal Energy: Part of the UK's Energy Mix: An Explanation of the Energy-Producing Potential of Wave and Tidal Stream Energy in the UK*, DEP'T FOR BUS., ENERGY & INDUS. STRATEGY (Jan. 22, 2013), https://www.gov.uk/guidance/wave-and-tidal-energy-part-of-the-uks-energy-mix.

of this energy source.[150] The IHA has developed a protocol to assess the sustainability of hydropower projects.[151] This protocol uses multiple factors to objectively assess a project during the different development phases. The protocol topics addressed during assessment include:

- climate change,
- downstream flow,
- resettlement,
- siting,
- design,
- financial viability,
- human rights,
- erosion and sedimentation,
- indigenous peoples,
- gender,
- water quality,
- public health,
- infrastructure safety,
- project benefits,
- livelihoods,
- biodiversity and invasive species,
- cultural heritage,
- asset reliability, and
- efficiency.

International Rivers (IR) is a nonprofit organization that "protects rivers and defends the rights of communities that depend on them." The organization attempts to "stop destructive dams and promote water and energy solutions for a just and sustainable world."[152] While IR does not dismiss hydropower as an energy source because of its adverse impacts, it does suggest that there be an open participatory process to assess the needs for water, food, and energy followed by a public process to determine how to meet those needs. IR takes into account social and environmental factors in addition to economic and financial factors.[153] The World Commission on Dams (WCD), created in 1997 by the World Bank and the World Conservation Union, issued a report in 2000 with guidelines for building dams that protect the environment and dam-affected people and ensure

---

[150] *See generally* Int'l Hydropower Ass'n (2014), http://www.hydropower.org.

[151] *See generally The Protocol Documents*, Hydropower Sustainability Assessment Protocol, http://www.hydrosustainability.org/Document-Library.aspx (last visited Nov. 18, 2017).

[152] *See generally Mission*, Int'l Rivers, http://www.internationalrivers.org/mission (last visited Nov. 18, 2017).

[153] *See generally Water and Energy Solutions*, Int'l Rivers, http://www.internationalrivers.org/campaigns/water-and-energy-solutions (last visited Nov. 18, 2017).

that dam benefits are more equitably distributed.[154] IR supports the work of the WCD, but criticizes the IHA protocol because it provides assessment guidelines, but does not require that the hydropower sector meets specific standards. Additionally, IR is concerned that the industrial sector controls IHA protocol and that affected people are not involved in the process.[155]

Questions

1. Because rivers often flow through national borders, when an upstream country dams a river it can have significant implications for the downstream country. Do you think it is possible for international organizations to set hydropower standards without legally binding treaty obligations? In other words, can upstream users be convinced that they should use the resource in a way that is more sustainable for downstream users? *See Case Concerning the Gabcikovo-Nagymoros Project (Hungary-Slovakia)*, Sept. 25, 1997, *Concerning the Gabcikovo-Nagymoros Project (Hungary-Slovakia)*, http://www.icj-cij.org/files/case-related/92/092-19970925-JUD-01-00-EN. pdf (international dispute concerning the development of hydroelectric dams on the Danube River, pitting environmental concerns against the need for electricity).

2. How might Baselines and Metrics assist nations in coming to agreements on hydroelectric dams?

3. How can local communities and national governments best address and balance the social and environmental concerns that arise with hydropower and the need to build or remove dams?

4. Based on the fictional story at the beginning of this chapter, do you think Amir and Juan's trip to the Hoover Dam and their overnight camping and canoe trip on the Colorado are sustainable forms of recreation? What information can you find out about the Hoover Dam? How much electricity is produced by the Hoover Dam? What is the status of its license? Can you find any information about whether it should be removed or how much longer it will operate before sedimentation reduces its efficiency?[156]

---

[154] *Dams and Development: A New Framework for Decision-Making*, WORLD COMM'N ON DAMS (Nov. 2000), https://web.archive.org/web/20160603103745/https://www.internationalrivers.org/files/attached-files/world_commission_on_dams_final_report.pdf.

[155] *See The Hydropower Sustainability Assessment Protocol*, INT'L RIVERS, http://www.internationalrivers.org/campaigns/the-hydropower-sustainability-assessment-protocol (last visited Nov. 18, 2017).

[156] According to the DOI, Bureau of Reclamation, the Hoover Dam has produced, on average (for the ten-year period from 1999-2008) about 4.2 billion kilowatt hours of electricity. *Hoover Dam Frequently Asked Questions and Answers*, U.S. DEP'T INTERIOR, BUREAU OF RECLAMATION, http://www.usbr.gov/lc/hooverdam/faqs/powerfaq.html (last updated Feb. 7, 2017).

2. WIND

Civilizations have used wind power from as early as 5,000 B.C. Windmills historically powered boats, produced food, pumped water, and generated electricity for homes and industry. With the increased use of fossil fuels and the ability to transport electricity, wind energy became less popular, that is, until the oil shortages in the 1970s. The search for alternative energy in the late twentieth century resulted in a dramatic increase in wind generation at the beginning of the twenty-first century (as shown in Figure 6-8), with the United States, China, India, and Western Europe leading this growth. In the United States, the Wind Energy Systems Act in 1980 encouraged wind energy systems, both large and small scale, and supported technology advancement. Individual states have also established agencies to promote wind energy systems and regulate wind-farm development.[157] Wind power is "the most rapidly growing method of generating electricity."[158]

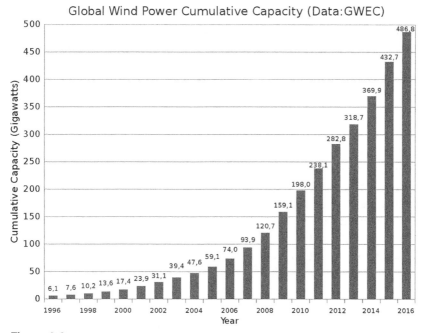

Figure 6-8

a. Production and Regulation

Wind is created by the uneven heating and cooling of the Earth as different surfaces such as land and water absorb and retain the sun's heat at

---

[157] *See, e.g.,* Sanya Carleyolsen, *Tangled in the Wires: An Assessment of the Existing U.S. Renewable Energy Legal Framework*, 46 NAT. RESOURCES J. 759 (2006).
[158] Reitze, Jr., *supra* note 115, at 867.

different rates. The temperature differences create airflows, which contain energy captured by a wind turbine. The Earth's rotation also adds to the wind, due in large part to the Coriolis effect, which is how moving objects like hurricanes veer right in the Northern hemisphere or left in the Southern hemisphere. The Coriolis effect is the deflection of circulating air into curved paths as the Earth rotates. If the Earth did not rotate, "the atmosphere would circulate between the poles (high-pressure areas) and the equator (a low-pressure area) in a simple back-and-forth pattern". Instead, the rotation deflects the air to the right in the Northern hemisphere and to the left in the Southern hemisphere.[159]

When the wind hits a turbine, the turbine blades spin a rotor connected to a generator that produces electrical energy.[160] Utility-scale wind farms consist of many wind turbines connected by electrical cables that move power from the turbines to transformer substations for grid delivery.[161] These wind farms are located both onshore and offshore, but even the world's largest wind farm in Texas has a generating capacity that is only equivalent to an average coal-fired plant.

Land Use Siting.   In the United States, federal, state, tribal, and local land use regulations govern onshore wind energy development. The Energy Policy Act of 2005 encourages the Secretary of the Interior, under the responsibility of the Bureau of Land Management (BLM) within the DOI, to locate non-hydropower renewable energy projects on public land. The BLM created a Wind Energy Development Program, which excluded some highly protected wilderness and scenic areas but encouraged wind energy projects that would allow other land uses as much as possible. The BLM, as a manager of public lands, issues permits as a right of way (ROW) to use a specific piece of government land for a project, such as for wind or solar development.[162] Federal agencies have also encouraged the development of wind energy on tribal lands by providing technical assistance and financial support.

State governments have significant amounts of control when it comes to who may distribute electricity in a state. They may require certain permitting prior to installation of turbines or may require extensive regulatory overview. In the United States, local governments also play a role in the development of turbines. Local governments have significant control over zoning and building codes, which can alter where and whether turbines may be developed. Local codes may prohibit the placement of turbines by

---

[159] *Surface Ocean Currents*, NOAA, http://oceanservice.noaa.gov/education/kits/currents/05currents1. html (July 6, 2017).

[160] Reitze, Jr., *supra* note 115, at 868.

[161] THE LAW OF CLEAN ENERGY, *supra* note 133, at 362-363.

[162] *See* Rebecca W. Watson, *Renewable Power Projects on Federal Lands: Wind and Solar and the FLPMA Right-of-Way—Is It Working?*, ROCKY MOUNTAIN MIN. L. FOUND. 1, 1 (Sept. 2009), http://www.wsmtlaw.com/cms-assets/documents/146239-674480.00228231.pdf.

banning them altogether or may use less direct methods (intentionally or not), including the prohibition of any structure over a certain height. We discuss land use control in more depth in Chapter 5.

Offshore Siting. Offshore wind energy projects in the United States require a state lease or permit when the project is located on state property within three miles of the shoreline. The U.S. Army Corps of Engineers also grants permits, which are subject to the CWA, ESA, and NEPA. The Bureau of Ocean Energy Management, (BOEM), under the Outer Continental Shelf Lands Act (OCSLA), governs offshore project leasing outside the three-mile state boundary. Similar to wave and tidal energy development offshore, FERC and the DOI share jurisdictional authority because the project affects the Outer Continental Shelf (OCS). The DOI approved plans for an offshore wind farm off the Massachusetts coast, but as of 2011, the United States had no viable offshore wind energy projects.

As offshore wind energy is developed, leases entered into by states for lakes and on coasts within the three-mile limit or by the DOI on the OCS are subject to challenge under the public trust doctrine. Public trust doctrine principles may require states and the federal government to protect navigation, recreation, and natural resources to promote the public interest.[163]

Wind Capacity Availability. Less than 2% of global wind capacity is located offshore, as opposed to onshore development because of the cost and technology requirements. Existing offshore wind capacity is primarily located off northern Europe; and Japan, China, South Korea, and Taiwan have begun developing offshore projects.[164] The IEA supports a database detailing national policies for renewable energy, including wind power energy generation.[165] China, the largest producer of wind power, has produced a technology roadmap to achieving a reduction of CO_2 emissions by 2050 that is equivalent to the combined total of emissions of Germany, Italy, and France in 2009.[166] However, China still has structural difficulties to resolve in connecting electricity generation to the grid. The European Union also has great ambition to increase significantly its wind energy capacity, as detailed in the member states' National Renewable Energy

[163] THE LAW OF CLEAN ENERGY, *supra* note 133, at 377-378.
[164] *Offshore Wind Power*, GLOBAL WIND ENERGY COUNCIL, http://www.gwec.net/global-figures/global-offshore/ (last visited Sept. 24, 2017); *How Much of the World's Electricity Supply Is Generated from Wind and Who Are the Leading Generators?*, U.S. ENERGY INFO. ADMIN., https://web.archive.org/web/20111019185656/http://www.eia.gov/energy_in_brief/wind_power.cfm (last visited Nov. 18, 2017).
[165] *IEA/IRENA Joint Policies and Measures Database*, INT'L ENERGY AGENCY, http://www.iea.org/policiesandmeasures/renewableenergy (last visited Nov. 18, 2017).
[166] *Technology Roadmap: China Wind Energy Development Roadmap 2050*, INT'L ENERGY AGENCY (Oct. 2011), http://www.iea.org/publications/freepublications/publication/china_wind.pdf.

Action Plans, which you can view at https://ec.europa.eu/energy/en/topics/renewable-energy/national-action-plans.[167]

b. Resilience and Sustainability

Wind turbines do not directly emit carbon, and the carbon emitted from the manufacture and construction of the turbines is only 2% of the carbon emitted from a natural gas plant and 1% of the carbon emitted by a coal-fired plant. However, there are other environmental impacts such as bird and bat deaths, noise pollution, "shadow flicker" from the turbine blade, aeronautical hazards such as aircraft collisions and degradation of radar performance, navigational safety of offshore wind turbines, and land use impacts from onshore turbines. The land use impacts are limited since there is little disruption of the surface except for the turbine structure, and other surface activities such as farming and grazing can continue.[168] Interference with the avian and bat populations is particularly troublesome when endangered species are impacted.[169]

Neighbors may also object to wind turbines because of the noise, the aesthetics, and the interference with natural scenery. Some have complained that the turbine blades affect television and radio reception. Technology may be able to mitigate these concerns by using non-metallic blades and appropriately placing the turbines in areas outside the reception paths.[170] Private nuisance suits by neighbors may be successful unless local, state, or national governments enact legislation protecting these uses, similar to what has been legislated to protect satellite dishes, cell towers, and solar panels.[171]

For the best efficiency, power generation from the wind requires that we locate the turbines as high as possible and that they have a large blade span. Buildings or other structures that interfere with airflow will affect this efficiency, and government regulation or private agreements in the form of covenants or easements may be required to protect capital investments.

Local ordinances under zoning laws and building regulations may also present barriers to development if communities protest these projects as locally undesirable land uses (LULUs). Because local government regulates land use based upon the delegation of authority from the state, local legislation will be key to developing sustainable energy sources. This is particularly true if legislation seeks to require distributed installation of renewable energy structures, such as wind turbines and solar panels.

---

[167] Irene Vos, *The Impact of Wind Power on European Natural Gas Markets*, Int'l Energy Agency (Jan. 2012), http://www.iea.org/publications/freepublications/publication/impact_of_wind_power.pdf.
[168] Reitze, Jr., *supra* note 115, at 871-872.
[169] *See* Tripp Baltz, *Wind Power Industry Seeks Review of Policy on Sage Grouse in Wyoming*, 40 Env't Rep. (BNA) 1728 (2009).
[170] Carleyolsen, *supra* note 157.
[171] *See, e.g.*, Rose v. Chaiken, 453 A.2d 1378 (N.J. Super. Ct. Ch. Div. 1982).

Local communities fear that wind turbine structures will reduce property values, create nuisances, and diminish local aesthetics.[172] If local regulations discourage wind turbines by regulating such use through height restrictions, we will need state or federal legislation to preempt such regulations in order to promote this renewable source. Alternatively, financial incentives such as tax credits, entitlements, and funding may be more effective to encourage sustainable land use without foregoing local autonomy.[173] However, as with locating any LULU, such as a waste facility, prison, factory, group home, etc., we must be careful not to unfairly burden the poorest communities, which will be the ones most likely to respond to compensation-based LULU siting.[174]

Wind power electricity is becoming more economically competitive with fossil fuel electricity, although the cost varies depending on the size of the turbine, the cost to build the facility, and the average wind speed.[175] The favorable production costs combined with the reduced lead-time to construct a facility,[176] in comparison with fossil fuel or nuclear plant construction, make this renewable energy a promising resource for the future. However, wind power is not reliable in that it is not predictable like the tides, and wind speed tends to decrease at night. Infrastructure will need to store this energy or to sell surplus electricity to the grid in exchange for purchases when wind energy is not available. Finally, the potential environmental and land use impacts discussed above must be resolved on the local, state, federal, and international level.

Questions

1. As mentioned above, one of the challenges facing the wind industry is local opposition to the siting of a wind farm and the use of the local zoning code to stop it. Who should have control over the location of wind projects? What type of siting for wind farms would increase the resilience and sustainability of the energy system? Should the decision be affected by where the energy flows to and from? For example, is the energy used locally or transferred hundreds of miles?

---

[172] *See id.*

[173] *See generally Wind Energy Technologies Office*, U.S. DEP'T ENERGY, http://energy.gov/eere/wind/wind-program (last visited Nov. 18, 2017).

[174] Troy A. Rule, *Renewable Energy and the Neighbors*, 2010 UTAH L. REV. 4 (2010), *available at* https://web.archive.org/web/20150113005955/http://epubs.utah.edu/index.php/ulr/article/viewFile/486/354.

[175] Reitze, Jr., *supra* note 115, at 871.

[176] *See 2014 Wind Technologies Market Report*, U.S. DEP'T ENERGY iv, 47 (Aug. 2015), http://energy.gov/sites/prod/files/2015/08/f25/2014-Wind-Technologies-Market-Report-8.7.pdf.

2. Earlier we introduced Baselines and Metrics. Which Baselines and Metrics concerning wind would help promote resilience and sustainability in the energy system?

3. Amir and Juan passed by the wind project in the Tehachapi Mountains in Kern County on their way to Las Vegas. How do you think they responded emotionally to the vast array of windmills in the desert? How would you respond to the siting of a wind project in your neighborhood?[177] What information about the project would be helpful for you to know in answering this question?

3. BIOMASS

Biomass, the oldest source of renewable energy, is produced by plants and animals and includes organic sources such as wood, crops, manure, and garbage. Carbon is the major component of biomass. Wood, generally burned to release heat, is the largest source of biomass energy. The energy originates from the sun and plants convert this energy into chemical energy through the process of photosynthesis. Animals eat the plants and produce waste containing this chemical energy. We can release the chemical energy from biomass by burning it for heat or converting it to other forms of energy such as methane gas, ethanol, and biodiesel fuel. Methane gas is the major ingredient of natural gas and landfills expel this gas in large quantities. Ethanol is created by fermenting crops such as corn and sugarcane and discarded vegetable oil and animal fat is converted to biodiesel fuel.

a. Production and Regulation

Biomass has three basic uses—biopower, biofuels, and bioproducts. Biopower is derived directly from burning biomass or converting it to a fuel to generate electricity. Biofuels are created through fermentation and oil reaction with alcohol to produce liquid transportation fuels. Bioproducts use chemicals created by biomass conversion to make plastics and other petroleum-based products.[178]

Biomass supplies approximately 4% of the U.S. energy needs and includes 45% from wood, 44% from biofuels, and 11% from landfill waste. While most of the biomass power plants are small, utility-scale plants are in the process of being developed. In Brazil, the United States, and other nations, biorefineries are producing power, fuels, and products all at the

---

[177] See Marc Lifsher, *California's Clean Energy Future Threatened by Federal Delays, State Officials Say*, L.A. Times (July 28, 2010), http://articles.latimes.com/2010/jul/28/business/la-fi-solar-energy-20100728.

[178] *Biomass Energy Basics*, Nat'l Renewable Energy Lab., https://www.nrel.gov/workingwithus/re-biomass.html (last visited Nov. 18, 2017).

same location. We use biofuels globally to heat residential and commercial buildings and supply alternative transportation fuels. Bioproducts constitute approximately 5% of global petrochemical sales. However, it is projected that 10% to 15% of petrochemicals can be replaced by bioproducts within the near future.[179]

Biopower.   Biopower uses biomass to generate electricity and/or heat using several different technologies. The most widely used technology for biopower plants is the process of *burning* biomass feedstocks to create steam, which drives the turbines to run the generator and convert the power to electricity. Biomass can also be mixed with fossil fuels in traditional power plants to reduce emissions, converted into syngas through *gasification* and used instead of natural gas in gas turbines, or converted to a liquid through a thermochemical process called *pyrolysis* that burns the liquid to generate electricity. When biomass decays without the presence of oxygen, it produces methane naturally. Drilling decaying biomass in landfills also releases this methane to produce electricity by burning it. Biomass in closed reactors produces methane suitable for power generation by using natural bacteria to decompose the feedstock through a process called *anaerobic digestion.*[180]

Biofuels.   A biorefinery produces biofuels by converting feedstock into common types of transportation fuels including cellulosic ethanol, ethanol, and biodiesel. There are many different types of materials used as feedstock including corn, grain, forest and crop residue, yard waste, municipal solid waste, soy, sugarcane, vegetable oil, and recycled grease. Cornstarch primarily produces ethanol, which we use as an additive to petroleum-based fuels, but we may also use it as an alternative fuel. Like other alcohol products, we produce ethanol by sugar fermentation, but we can also produce it through gasification, a process that converts the biomass into syngas. Biodiesel is made primarily from soybean oil and is blended with petroleum diesel.[181] The process to produce biodiesel requires the reaction of oil feedstocks with an alcohol, called "transesterification," and we then refine the biodiesel. We powered some of the first automobiles with biofuels, but cheap gasoline prices after World War II caused us to shift to fossil fuels. With increasing gas prices and concerns about GHG emissions, policy makers throughout the world are looking at the advantages and disadvantages of biofuels.[182]

---

[179] *See generally* Int'l Biomass Conf. & Expo, http://www.biomassconference.com (last visited Nov. 18, 2017).
[180] *Biomass Energy Basics, supra* note 178.
[181] The Law of Clean Energy, *supra* note 133, at 446.
[182] Alex Morales & Sally Bakewell, *U.K. Boosts Gas While Cutting Support for Wind, Biomass,* Bloomberg Businessweek (July 25, 2012), http://www.bloomberg.com/news/articles/2012-07-25/u-k-cuts-onshore-wind-support-10-percent-boosts-wave-power.

Bioproducts. Bioproducts use chemicals created from biomass to replace the fossil fuels used by the petrochemical industry to produce petroleum-based products. Some of the products created from biomass include plastics, glues, artificial sweeteners, textiles, and foam insulation. While there are challenges to creating products using biomass as a substitute for fossil fuels, most current petrochemical industry products can be produced using biomass. In addition, it may also be possible to make new products not currently available from petrochemicals.[183]

b. Resilience and Sustainability

Biomass can provide up to ten times more energy than wind and solar power can produce. It is an inexhaustible and renewable energy source, and we can generally produce and use it in the same location so that transportation through pipelines or other means is not required. Biomass also uses organic and agricultural waste to provide a plentiful feedstock supply. However, gathering, storing, and extracting biomass is more expensive than using fossil fuels, and a biomass power plant requires a large amount of space and water to recycle waste. Biomass production and use also release carbon dioxide, methane, and nitrous oxide into the atmosphere, contributing to global warming.

We make bioproducts from renewable sources and we can generally produce them using less energy than fossil-based products. Biopower, produced through biomass electrical generation, is the second most common renewable source behind hydropower. Biopower is also the safest and most economical energy source.[184] Burning biomass to create biopower may decrease GHG emissions, even though the process releases carbon dioxide in the same amount as burning fossil fuels. However, the release of carbon dioxide from biomass is roughly equivalent to the carbon dioxide it draws in during the process of photosynthesis for its own growth, leading some to claim it is carbon neutral.[185] Nevertheless, there is a carbon penalty if we clear forests to grow biomass. Accordingly, we should grow biomass on land we have previously cleared and are not currently using for other crops.

To calculate whether biofuels produce fewer GHG emissions than fossil-based fuels, a life cycle analysis (discussed in more detail in Chapter 8)

---

[183] *Biomass Energy Basics*, *supra* note 178.

[184] *But see How Biopower Works*, UNION OF CONCERNED SCIENTISTS (Nov. 12, 2015), http://www.ucsusa.org/clean_energy/our-energy-choices/renewable-energy/how-biomass-energy-works.html#.V8OyhWXe3dk (noting "[s]everal recent studies show little to no economic potential to increase biopower in the U.S. over the next two decades because of its relatively high costs compared with other renewable energy and low carbon technologies"; and "[i]f not managed and monitored carefully, biomass for energy can be harvested at unsustainable rates, damage ecosystems, produce harmful air pollution, consume large amounts of water, and produce net global warming emissions").

[185] *Carbon Neutral*, AM. ENERGY INDEPENDENCE, http://www.americanenergyindependence.com/carbonneutral.aspx (last visited Nov. 18, 2017).

is performed. This analysis takes into account: "land use change; electricity generation necessary for fertilizer production; feedstock production; soil emissions from the application of fertilizers (which contain nitrogen, and from which nitrogen oxides (NOx) are emitted); emissions from biorefineries; the transportation of refined fuel; and end-use combustion of fuel."[186] The analysis differs, of course, for ethanol versus biodiesel fuel. Direct land use changes, through tilling the soil or burning plants, and indirect land use changes, through displacing existing cropland and requiring native habitat to be converted to cropland somewhere else, both cause the release of GHG emissions.[187] Additionally, fuel crops replace food crops, reducing food supplies and increasing food prices.

Transportation primarily uses ethanol as an additive, constituting 5% to 10% of petroleum fuels, in order to reduce toxic emissions and increase octane.[188] Ethanol also serves as an alternative fuel, although the availability of fueling stations for flexible fuel vehicles capable of burning ethanol is limited. The most common type of biodiesel, called "B20," is blended with petroleum diesel at a 6% to 20% level.[189] As with the alternative fuel, ethanol, the number of fueling stations is limited. However, diesel vehicle fleets using biodiesel can get credit for using this alternative fuel without having to purchase new alternative fuel vehicles.

Because of concerns about ethanol production competing with food crops, current biofuel research focuses on developing cellulosic ethanol, which does not use cornstarch, but instead uses non-edible plant materials as feedstock. This fibrous material from plant cellulose and hemicellulose is converted to ethanol through fermentation and gasification. Dedicated energy crops that grow fast on land that does not support food crops will reduce the competition between biomass and food production. Researchers are also exploring using microalgae as a feedstock to produce transportation fuels.

Utilizing biomass as a resource requires a significant amount of water, straining the resilience and sustainability of several systems. The impact on both water supply and water quality, because of a large amount of water used and because of the runoff from soil erosion containing fertilizers, requires mitigation through advanced technology and changing the feedstocks used.[190] As discussed in Chapters 2 and 3, the water system is greatly stressed through overuse and pollution. Biomass, while potentially

---

[186] THE LAW OF CLEAN ENERGY, *supra* note 133, at 447.

[187] *See* Cymie Payne, *Local Meets Global: The Low Carbon Fuel Standard and the WTO*, 34 N.C.J. INT'L L. & COM. REG. 891 (2009) (discussing increased stresses on wetlands and forests (currently serving as carbon sinks) by converting these lands to grow corn and other biofuel crops).

[188] *Ethanol as a Transportation Fuel*, CAL. ENERGY COMM'N, https://web.archive.org/web/20141016191230/ http://www.consumerenergycenter.org/transportation/afvs/ethanol.html (last visited Nov. 18, 2017).

[189] *Biodiesel Blends*, U.S. DEP'T OF ENERGY ALTERNATIVE FUELS DATA CTR., http://www.afdc.energy.gov/ fuels/biodiesel_blends.html (last visited Nov. 18, 2017).

[190] THE LAW OF CLEAN ENERGY, *supra* note 133, at 447-448.

increasing the resilience of the energy system or parts thereof, may strain the resilience of an already stressed water system. In addition, biomass may be impractical in water-stressed places, such as those described in Chapter 3.

Government policies regarding the use of biomass as an energy source look to the goal of promoting energy security and reducing dependence on foreign fuel.[191] Supporting biofuels will require significant changes to infrastructure like distribution networks and pumps to dispense the fuel. Low carbon fuel standards (LCFS) reduce carbon emissions from transportation by increasing vehicle efficiency, reducing GHG emissions by using renewable fuels, and decreasing the use of vehicles by providing alternative transportation. In the United States, the federal government has not set nationwide LCFS, but some states, such as California, have adopted LCFS or are using California's LCFS as a model to develop their own program. California has set its LCFS with a goal to reduce carbon intensity from transportation fuels by 10% by 2020.[192]

— Indirect land use change (ILUC) is a particular concern for the corn ethanol industry. Taking into account land use change impacts when we analyze the benefits of biomass may decrease the value of using corn ethanol as compared to other renewable fuels. In the United States, local government typically controls land use so federal policies promoting biomass may run into conflict with local land use authorities or state regulations.[193] Local communities will likely object to the development of biorefineries and biomass power plants, and may use local zoning regulations to either encourage or discourage new construction.[194] However, policy makers will continue to face these same concerns with other renewable sources and must balance them against the benefits of biomass energy.

4. GEOTHERMAL

Geothermal energy, also known as subterranean energy, is harnessed from underground steam that produces geysers or hot springs from the heat rising from the Earth's core. The Earth's core continuously generates heat from the decay of radioactive particles that produce temperatures hotter than the sun's surface. As depicted in Figure 6-9, the Earth's inner core is solid iron and the outer core is composed of melted rock called magma.

---

[191] *See, e.g.*, U.S. policy under the Energy Independence and Security Act of 2007 (EISA), discussed in *id.* at 456.

[192] THE LAW OF CLEAN ENERGY, *supra* note 133, at 460-463.

[193] *See* Rocky Mountain Farmers Union v. Goldstene, 719 F. Supp. 2d 1170 (E.D. Cal. 2010); *see also* C & A Carbone, Inc. v. Town of Clarkstown, 511 U.S. 383 (1994) (discussing Commerce Clause issues when state or local government try to hoard a particular energy resource); THE LAW OF CLEAN ENERGY, *supra* note 133, at 464-465.

[194] *See* N. Iredell Neighbors for Rural Life v. Iredell Cty., 674 S.E.2d 436 (N.C. Ct. App. 2009); Step Now Citizens Grp. v. Town of Utica Planning & Zoning Commn., 663 N.W.2d 833 (Wis. Ct. App. 2003).

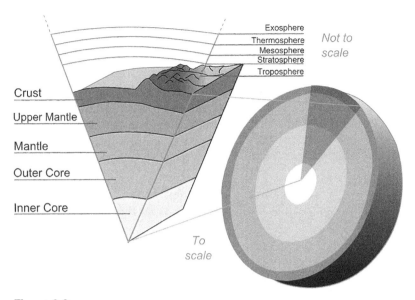

Figure 6-9

Rock and magma make up the Earth's mantle and the Earth's crust contains tectonic plates that move and collide at the boundaries. Magma can move through faults and reach the subsurface or, in the case of volcanoes, the surface. These same faults or weakness zones in the Earth's crust allow the water to sink into the subsurface, be heated by the magma, and then rise back to the surface. We can capture steam near the Earth's surface by drilling wells into geothermal reservoirs to bring hot water to the surface to spin turbines and generate electricity. Figure 6-10 illustrates:

1. Hot water is pumped from deep underground into a well under high pressure.
2. When the water reaches the surface, the pressure drops, which causes the water to turn into steam.
3. The steam spins a turbine, which connects to a generator that produces electricity.
4. The steam cools off in a cooling tower and condenses back to water.
5. The cooled water is pumped back into the Earth to begin the process again.

a. Production and Regulation

There are three types of geothermal power plants — dry-steam plants, flash power plants, and binary power plants. A dry-steam plant uses steam from a dry-steam reservoir that produces very little water and pipes it into the plant to force the turbine generator to spin and produce electricity. A flash power plant uses water that has been under high pressure, with temperatures between 300 to 700 degrees Fahrenheit (water boils at 212 degrees

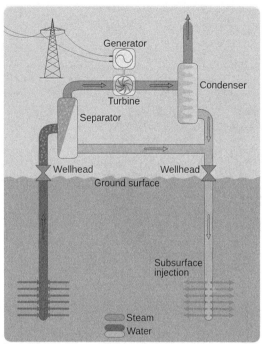

Source: *Geothermal Energy, U.S. EPA*

Figure 6-10

Fahrenheit, 100 degrees Celsius). Well production brings the searing water to the surface and releases it into a chamber where it "flashes" into steam and spins the turbines. A binary power plant uses water that has a temperature lower than 400 degrees Fahrenheit and that cannot flash into steam. The heat from this water passes via a heat exchanger to another liquid (such as pentane), which has a lower boiling point and can flash into a vapor, instead of steam, to spin the turbines. Finally, the working fluid from any of these three types of plants must be cooled, condensed, and either recirculated or reinjected into the ground.

Technologies called Enhanced Geothermal Systems (EGS) can also capture heat from dry rock. These technologies require the forcible injection of fluid into impermeable dry rock to fracture it. The dry rock heats the fluid, which we recover from a well and use for geothermal power production. This process has great potential for energy production. However, problems exist, such as the loss of large amounts of the injected fluids and increased seismic activity, which must be resolved before large-scale commercial use is viable.

Households and commercial buildings use geothermal energy that is not sufficient to produce electricity for heating and cooling. Low-temperature geothermal fluids are piped from a geothermal reservoir into a heat exchanger and space heating or agricultural processes use this heated secondary fluid. A geothermal heat pump (GHP) also provides direct use of geothermal technology by burying pipes containing refrigerant fluid into the ground to pull heat from the warm ground when the air temperature is colder and shift heat to the cooler ground in the summer.[195] These direct uses may be able to reduce the cost of heating and cooling by 50% of what it costs to use natural gas and reduce carbon emissions.[196]

Common Uses.   We have used geothermal energy for thousands of years. Ancient cultures such as Rome, China, and the Native Americans "used

[195] *See generally Renewable Energy: Geothermal FAQs*, Dep't of Energy, https://energy.gov/eere/geothermal/geothermal-faqs (last visited Nov. 18, 2017).
[196] The Law of Clean Energy, *supra* note 133, at 424-426.

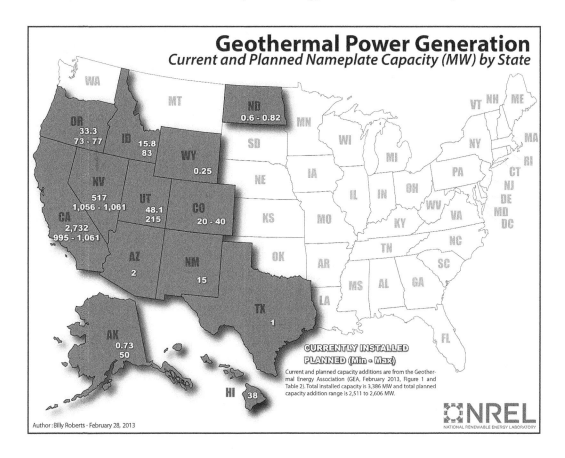

Geothermal Power Generation
Current and Planned Nameplate Capacity (MW) by State

CURRENTLY INSTALLED
PLANNED (Min - Max)

Current and planned capacity additions are from the Geothermal Energy Association (GEA, February 2013, Figure 1 and Table 2). Total installed capacity is 3,386 MW and total planned capacity addition range is 2,511 to 2,606 MW.

⬡NREL
NATIONAL RENEWABLE ENERGY LABORATORY

Author: Billy Roberts - February 28, 2013

hot mineral springs for bathing, cooking, and heating."[197] These were early direct hot water uses at or near the surface. We build electricity generation power plants near geothermal reservoirs and draw heat through drilled wells. Geothermal heat pumps help heat and cool buildings. The most common industrial use for geothermal energy is dehydration of fruits and vegetables. "Even if only 1% of the thermal (heat) energy contained within the Earth's uppermost crust (10 kilometers or less) were tapped for use, that output would be equivalent to 500 times the energy contained in all the known oil and gas resources known in the world."[198]

The United States is the largest producer of geothermal energy in the world, but geothermal plants in five western states provide less than 1% of its total electricity. The second largest producer is the Philippines, generating 16% of its power needs. Iceland is the seventh largest producer and generates 26% of its electricity from geothermal sources.[199]

[197] *Geothermal Energy*, EPA, https://web.archive.org/web/20170428122623/https://www3.epa.gov/climatechange/kids/solutions/technologies/geothermal.html (last visited Nov. 18, 2017).
[198] *Federal Interagency Geothermal Activities*, U.S. DEP'T ENERGY, GEOTHERMAL TECH. PROGRAM (June 2011), http://www1.eere.energy.gov/geothermal/pdfs/ngap.pdf.
[199] *Geothermal Explained: Use of Geothermal Energy*, U.S. ENERGY INFO. ADMIN., http://www.eia.gov/energyexplained/index.cfm?page=geothermal_use (last visited Nov. 18, 2017).

U.S. Regulation and Rights.   In the United States, the federal government and some states regulate geothermal resources as minerals. Depending upon the state's definition, geothermal resources are also treated as water, or as *sui generis* resources. If geothermal fluids are regulated as either groundwater or surface water, state water law will define how rights to these resources are governed. The regulation of water rights varies considerably from state to state, and states will apply these differing rules to geothermal resources. States regulating these resources as *sui generis* will treat them as closely related to, but not, water or minerals. Some states classify these resources as either groundwater or mineral, depending upon the water temperature.

The Geothermal Steam Act of 1970[200] governs rights to geothermal resources on federal land, treats them as minerals, and allows private development through leasing, similar to oil and gas leases on federal land. When ownership rights are split between surface rights and mineral rights, federal reservation of mineral rights includes geothermal resources.[201]

States treating these resources as minerals will recognize private ownership rights of the surface owner over the mineral estate. However, if the state treats these resources as groundwater, it may require that an appropriation permit be obtained. The private ownership interests of the surface owner will not necessarily govern rights to the geothermal resources. Leasing programs will administer the production of resources found on state-owned land. In Alaska, for example, the state owns even the geothermal resources found under private land.

Private property rights in geothermal resources are even more complex when we sever or reserve subsurface rights from surface estates when multiple owners hold undivided fractional interests in these resources and when rights are held in varying present and future estates or as executive rights or royalty interests. Ambiguous reservations in previous grants and varying state property rules applying to these shared interests encourage geothermal developers to gain control over all the geothermal rights before they begin development.[202] Adjudicating rights to these resources can involve resolving issues of federal law mineral rights that are in conflict with state law mineral rights or water rights.[203] Geothermal development of culturally significant or environmentally sensitive sites will require environmental impact analyses for federal leases, and cost-benefit analyses of the power produced versus the cost of energy transmission and land use conflict resolution.[204]

---

[200] 30 U.S.C. §§1001-1028 (2012).

[201] THE LAW OF CLEAN ENERGY, *supra* note 133, at 428-433; *see also* United States v. Union Oil Co. of Cal., 549 F.2d 1271 (9th Cir. 1977).

[202] THE LAW OF CLEAN ENERGY, *supra* note 133, at 428-433; *see also* Occidental Geothermal, Inc. v. Simmons, 543 F. Supp. 870 (N.D. Cal. 1982); Geothermal Kinetics, Inc. v. Union Oil Co. of Cal., 141 Cal. Rptr. 879 (Ct. App. 1977).

[203] *See* Rosette, Inc. v. U.S. Dep't of the Int., 169 P.3d 704 (N.M. Ct. App. 2007).

[204] THE LAW OF CLEAN ENERGY, *supra* note 133, at 438-440; *see also* Pit River Tribe v. U.S. Forest Serv., 469 F.3d 768 (9th Cir. 2006).

In the United States, federal lands may be leased for geothermal pro-duction over available reservoirs. The Geothermal Steam Act of 1970, as amended by the Energy Policy Act of 2005, governs these leases. Federal leasing regulations encourage cooperation of adjoining landowners or leaseholders to appropriately space injection wells and participate jointly in exploration and exploitation to protect geothermal resources under a process called unitization. Some states have also required unitization to protect resources for the public interest. State and federal permitting and leasing will typically be subject to NEPA (or the state equivalent), as well as other site-specific reviews under various federal and state laws. However, the Energy Policy Act, which mandated the processing of backlogged lease applications, encouraged the BLM and U.S. Forest Service (USFS) to pre-pare a Programmatic Environmental Impact Statement (PEIS) to deter-mine the environmental impacts of federal geothermal leasing. The PEIS substitutes for NEPA review, but agencies may be required to conduct additional reviews under the ESA, the Clean Water Act (CWA), the Clean Air Act (CAA), and the National Historic Preservation Act (NHPA).[205]

b. Resilience and Sustainability

Geothermal energy has enormous potential for supplying clean and sus-tainable power from a renewable source and as a relatively untouched source connected to the Earth's core, it has remarkable resilience. It pro-vides a continuous baseload source for electricity, and geothermal power plants are efficient, relatively inexpensive, and not subject to fluctuating fuel prices.[206] In comparison with other energy sources, the environmental impacts of geothermal energy are relatively minor.

There are, however, challenges in locating sufficient sources, designing the geothermal field, and controlling the large amount of land necessary to develop a geothermal resource. Geothermal energy is a clean renewable source with great potential, but there are several environmental concerns. First, geothermal steam causes air pollution by emitting SO_2 and mercury into the atmosphere. Second, geothermal fluids contain water pollutants such as silica precipitates and brine. Third, the cooling processes deplete the water supply. Fourth, the siting of geothermal plants interferes with endangered species, habitat, and historic cultural resources. Lastly, the noise and pipelines disrupt wildlife and other land uses. We can miti-gate some of these environmental impacts by converting gases to sulfur, reinjecting or capturing geothermal fluids to minimize emissions and dis-charges, consuming treated wastewater, and using a small land footprint to minimize habitat disruption.[207]

---

[205] THE LAW OF CLEAN ENERGY, *supra* note 133, at 433-436.
[206] *See Geothermal*, U.S. DEP'T ENERGY, https://energy.gov/eere/geothermal/geothermal-energy-us-department-energy (last visited Nov. 18, 2017).
[207] THE LAW OF CLEAN ENERGY, *supra* note 133, at 436-438.

Geothermal energy power plants are relatively small in comparison to conventional power plants and are located on top of the geothermal power source. Because the use is so localized and requires reservoirs that are close to the surface, conflicts between private property rights and the rights to energy access may exist.[208] Conflicting and differing state and federal laws regarding property rights make the legal aspects daunting at times, and site management through leasing, permitting, or ownership may be particularly challenging.[209]

We will need collaboration among governments, research universities, the geothermal industry, and venture capitalists to develop energy from hot dry rock.[210] Enhanced geothermal technology (EGS) will facilitate the full potential of geothermal energy. However, critics have charged that EGS technology, similar to hydraulic fracturing for fossil fuels, has the potential to induce earthquakes. We must address such concerns before wide-scale commercial use will be feasible. The United States, Australia, France, Germany, and Japan have research and development programs aimed at making EGS viable.[211] We will need to develop appropriate infrastructure to transmit geothermal power from the remote sites where many of the geothermal reservoirs are located to consumers in order to encourage greater use of this resource. Investments and improvements in technology should be able to resolve concerns about existing environmental impacts,[212] but conflicting jurisdictional rules over land use, land ownership, and rights to subsurface resources will continue to present resource development challenges in the near future.

5. SOLAR

Solar energy is a renewable source of energy harnessed from the sun shining on the Earth. "Every hour the sun beams onto Earth more than enough energy to satisfy global energy needs for an entire year."[213] We use four major methods to generate energy from the sun. The two main commercial technologies we use are **concentrated solar power** (CSP) and **photovoltaic (PV) panels,** and to a lesser degree, we use **solar thermal** and **solar lighting.** The level of solar radiation we receive on Earth depends on

---

[208] Fred Bosselman, Joel B. Eisen, Jim Rossi, David B. Spence & Jacqueline Lang Weaver, ENERGY, ECONOMICS & THE ENVIRONMENT 848 (3d ed. 2010) [hereinafter ENERGY, ECONOMICS & THE ENVIRONMENT].

[209] THE LAW OF CLEAN ENERGY, *supra* note 133, at 438.

[210] *Geothermal Technologies*, NAT'L RENEWABLE ENERGY LAB., http://www.nrel.gov/geothermal/publications.html (last visited Nov. 18, 2017).

[211] *Clean Energy: How Geothermal Energy Works*, UNION CONCERNED SCIENTISTS, http://www.ucsusa.org/clean_energy/our-energy-choices/renewable-energy/how-geothermal-energy-works.html (last visited Nov. 18, 2017).

[212] *See* Mathias Aarre Maehlum, *Geothermal Energy Pros and Cons*, ENERGY INFORMATIVE, http://energyinformative.org/geothermal-energy-pros-and-cons (last updated June 1, 2013).

[213] *Solar Energy*, NAT'L GEOGRAPHIC, http://environment.nationalgeographic.com/environment/global-warming/solar-power-profile (last visited Nov. 18, 2017).

geographic location, landscape, weather, season, and time of day. Air molecules, vapor, pollutants, and other atmospheric conditions diffuse some of the radiation, while some of the radiation is direct. The combination of diffused solar radiation and direct solar radiation constitutes **global solar radiation,** which we can measure to determine the amount of solar power we can generate at any particular location.[214] There is a growing global market for solar energy applications, particularly in developing countries that have plenty of sunlight but lack access to conventional electricity.[215] As solar energy costs become more competitive and technology advances make this source more efficient, solar energy use should continue to grow, as evidenced by a 20% increase in solar energy use per year over the past 15 years. Government policies such as tax incentives and investments in research and development will allow solar electricity to become cost-effective.[216] Morocco is a good example of how government support has allowed this African country, lacking in oil resources, to provide electricity using solar energy rather than the fossil fuels readily found in neighboring Arabian countries. Zimbabwe and other South African countries are investing in solar power to achieve sustainability, increase the resilience of the energy system, and reduce harmful emissions.[217]

a. Production and Regulation

Concentrated solar power (CSP) produces energy using mirrors to direct reflected sunlight to a receiver to heat a liquid and produce steam to run the turbines. CSP is a utility-scale operation that we can connect to the electrical grid. We can also use CSP systems for distributed power by locating smaller units directly where we need the energy. There are several different types of CSP systems including Linear Concentrator Systems, Dish/Engine Systems, Power Tower Systems, and Thermal Storage Systems.[218]

    Photovoltaic (PV) panels produce energy by changing sunlight directly into electricity. PV material consists of either individual solar cells or a layer of cells that create a panel. PV cells are made of semiconductor material, most commonly crystalline silicon, and when solar radiation collides with the atoms of the PV cell material, electrons are released from their atomic positions and become part of the electrical current in a circuit.[219] Once installed on the ground or a roof, PV panels require nominal

---

[214] *Energy Basics*, U.S. Dep't Energy, http://www.eere.energy.gov/basics/renewable_energy/solar_resources.html (last visited Nov. 18, 2017).

[215] *See generally Solar Energy Facts*, http://www.solarenergy-facts.org (last visited Nov. 18, 2017).

[216] Energy, Economics & the Environment, *supra* note 208.

[217] Brett Williams, *South African Solar Energy Project Receives $142 Million in Funding*, Hydrogen Fuel News (July 2, 2014), http://www.hydrogenfuelnews.com/south-african-solar-energy-project-receives-142-million-funding/8518514.

[218] *See generally Renewable Energy Technology Basics*, U.S. Dep't Energy, http://energy.gov/eere/energybasics/renewable-energy-technology-basics (last visited Nov. 18, 2017).

[219] *See generally Photovoltaic Technology Basics*, U.S. Dep't Energy, http://energy.gov/eere/energybasics/articles/photovoltaic-technology-basics (last visited Nov. 18, 2017).

upkeep and do not need special mechanisms or fluids to operate. Inverters are required to convert the DC electricity created by PV material to the AC electricity used in buildings.[220]

Solar heating and cooling processes use solar collectors to trap heat for building use. Solar collectors allow sunlight to come in through glass or plastic, where it is absorbed and changes into heat trapped inside the collector that we can use as a heat source for a building. The heat that the collectors gather during sunny weather is stored, sometimes in a storage device such as a battery, for future use as needed. **Passive** solar buildings use the building itself as the solar collector so that no special heat distribution equipment is required. These homes or buildings may also have greenhouses attached, which trap more heat by allowing more light. Walls and floors of the building absorb solar energy. In the winter, special shades over the windows keep the heat inside while in the summer, overhangs and awnings help cool the house.

Active solar buildings use special equipment to collect and distribute the heat. Solar collector boxes covered with glass absorb sunlight and change it into heat. The heat then transfers to air or water that flows through the collectors into a solar distribution system that functions the same as a conventional furnace. Hot water or air can also be stored in a tank or under the building so that it can be used when needed. With either active or passive solar heating systems, another energy source will serve as backup in case there are long periods without sunlight. These backup heating systems may include furnaces, wood burning stoves, or continued connection to the electrical grid.

Solar lighting uses a solar panel or PV cell to collect the sun's energy during the day and store it in a battery to provide lighting after dark using Light Emitting Diode (LED) lights. Residential and commercial applications of this technology for outdoor lighting are very popular, and after installation, there are no continuing costs for energy use and no carbon emissions.

Solar power in its various forms generates onsite and utility-scale electricity. Solar power provides heat, cooling, and hot water for buildings; supports outdoor residential and commercial lighting; powers satellites and handheld calculators; heats pools; and provides energy for cooking, power vehicles, and many additional applications—current and future. These various applications make solar energy a versatile energy source and it has the advantages of being an inexhaustible source that is noise free and pollution free.[221] Solar energy projects will vary in scale, with smaller scale projects installed for onsite usage referred to as distributed generation projects, and larger, more complex, projects built as utility-scale projects.

---

[220] The Law of Clean Energy, *supra* note 133, at 392.
[221] *See* Energy, Economics & the Environment, *supra* note 208.

Utility companies, as well as local and state governments, typically support distributed generation projects to encourage solar power use by homeowners and small business owners. These projects can connect to the local utility system to provide both power backup for the customer and the opportunity to sell excess power to the utility. Utility-scale projects require a larger land use footprint, which could involve obtaining site approval, solar easements, or covenants from neighbors, and meeting more intense regulatory standards at the local, state, and national level.[222] Some states and municipalities provide for the protection of solar devices against shading by neighbors.[223]

LOCAL GOVERNMENTS, DEVELOPMENT, AND SOLAR

As part of their building and zoning codes, some cities are requiring the incorporation of renewable or distributive energies, including solar. Two such cities, Sebastopol and Lancaster, California, require some new buildings and large retrofits to residential and/or commercial buildings to install solar power before issuing a certificate of occupancy. For example, Sebastopol's ordinance states:

15.72.030-40 . . . New commercial or residential buildings, and specific alterations, additions and remodels require the installation of a photovoltaic energy generation system. . . . The minimum system size utilizing the prescriptive method is two watts per square foot of conditioned building area including existing, remodeled and new conditioned space. . . . [Otherwise, t]he photovoltaic system must offset 75% of the electrical load of the building on an annual basis.

15.72.060 Prior to the issuance of a Certificate of Occupancy . . . the owner of record . . . shall certify in writing that the solar photovoltaic system is operational.

b. Resilience and Sustainability

Solar power is an inexhaustible energy source supplied by the sun. Solar installations, particularly utility-scale projects, will potentially affect land use, water resources, wildlife, and their habitats. While using solar energy avoids carbon emissions, there may be conflicts with the local community over project location,[224] agricultural land use, endangered species and habitats, and water availability. Solar thermal plants require approximately 800 gallons of water per megawatt-hour (MWh) of electricity generated, while nuclear plants typically require approximately 500 gallons

---

[222] THE LAW OF CLEAN ENERGY, *supra* note 133, at 404-406.

[223] *See, e.g.,* CAL. PUB. RES. CODE §§25980-25986 (1978) (California's Solar Shade Control Act, with the purpose of promoting all feasible means of energy conservation and all feasible uses of alternative energy supply sources in the state of California).

[224] *See, e.g.,* Rule, *supra* note 174; *see also* Sara C. Bronin, *The Quiet Revolution Revived: Sustainable Design, Land Use Regulation, and the States.* 93 MINN. L. REV. 231 (2008).

of water per MWh generated.[225] We often install these projects in desert areas where there is maximum sunlight, but these areas also lack water resources, may have fragile ecosystems, and may contain threatened and endangered species and Native American cultural resources. Utility-scale projects can easily have a land footprint that covers six square miles of desert. The installation of large numbers of reflector panels requires scraping or mowing of desert land and such activities may destroy habitat and displace native wildlife.[226]

MEGAWATTS

The Solar Energy Industries Association estimates that in the United States each megawatt of solar photovoltaics powers approximately 164 homes. The Association goes on to state that "the average number of homes powered per MW of PV varies from state to state due to a number of factors including: average sunshine (also called insolation), average household electricity consumption, temperature and wind."

Solar Energy Industries Association, http://www.seia.org/about/solar-energy/solar-faq/how-many-homes-can-be-powered-1-megawatt-solar-energy.

In 2016, the price for electricity generated by solar power was greater than the price for electricity from plants using fossil fuels or nuclear power. Leading up to 2016, however, the price difference has continued to shrink. Private market approaches through renewable energy credits or certificates (RECs) as well as loan guarantees, bonds, funding, subsidies, and other government incentives help offset the higher price of solar electricity. This subsidization might not be necessary if price comparisons took into account the full social and environmental costs of using fossil fuel power. If fossil fuel pricing incorporated externalities, such as the impact of GHG emissions through carbon legislation, solar power would be imminently more commercially competitive with carbon-based energy sources.

The sun provides a reliable and consistent energy source, but many of the solar power applications consume water. While the solar process of absorbing and heating can use other fluids, water has generally been the most efficient and least costly resource. However, droughts and historical water shortages in the desert areas may restrict the viability of large-scale projects. Technology innovations may provide a solution to the water requirement and allow smaller footprints from these operations, so as not to interfere with wildlife habitat or other sensitive resources.

---

[225] THE LAW OF CLEAN ENERGY, *supra* note 133, at 407.
[226] Julie Cart, *Sacrificing the Desert to Save the Earth*, L.A. TIMES (Feb. 5, 2012), http://www.latimes.com/news/local/la-me-solar-desert-20120205%2C0%2C7889582.story.

Questions and Notes

1. On their way to "Vegas," Amir and Juan passed signs indicating the construction of the Beacon solar farm along California State Route 15 corridor in Kern County. After two and one-half years of regulatory applications, the California Energy Commission in 2010 approved this large solar project. With a production capacity of 250 megawatts, it is the first large-scale solar thermal project in 20 years.[227] What makes an energy system resilient? Does solar energy make an energy system more or less resilient than one built on fossil fuels?

2. In June 2012, the National Renewable Energy Laboratory (NREL) released a study titled the Renewable Energy Futures Study (RES).[228] The RES concluded that by 2050, the U.S. could meet its demand for electricity with 80% of its needs generated from renewable electricity technologies, resulting in "deep reductions in electric sector greenhouse gas emissions and water use."[229] This future for renewable technologies will only be possible if every element of the electricity system grid transforms to increase the system's flexibility and expand the multi-state transmission infrastructure. Such a transformation will require "the development and adoption of technology advances, new operating procedures, evolved business models, and new market rules."[230] The RES noted that several international studies have also "explored the possibility of achieving high levels of renewable electricity penetration, primarily as a greenhouse gas (GHG) mitigation measure."[231]

3. As countries commit to reducing GHG emissions from fossil fuels, they are increasingly looking to several renewable resources simultaneously. In the United States, for example, public and private sectors are harnessing wind, solar, water, geothermal, and biomass to help reduce GHG emissions because of the ease of access to these resources often based on geography.

---

[227] Chris Meehan, *Beacon Solar Plant Is a Go!*, CLEAN ENERGY AUTH. (Aug. 26, 2010), http://www.cleanenergyauthority.com/solar-energy-news/california-s-beacon-solar-project.

[228] *See Renewable Electricity Futures Study: Exploration of High-Penetration Renewable Electricity Futures*, NAT'L RENEWABLE ENERGY LABORATORY, U.S. DEP'T ENERGY (M.M. Hand et al. eds., 2012), http://www.nrel.gov/docs/fy12osti/52409-1.pdf; *see also* Steven Weissman, *How Much of the Grid Can Be Renewable?*, LEGAL PLANET: ENVTL. L. & POL'Y (June 18, 2012), http://legalplanet.wordpress.com/2012/06/18/how-much-of-the-grid-can-be-renewable.

[229] *Renewable Electricity Futures Study*, *supra* note 228, at xvii.

[230] *Id.*

[231] *Id.* (noting in n.4: "[a]s examples, recent detailed studies include those prepared for Europe (ECF 2010) and Germany (SRU 2010), as well as a review of 164 global energy scenarios by the Intergovernmental Panel on Climate Change (IPCC 2011). Cochran et al. (2012) also describes several case studies of countries successfully managing high levels of variable renewable energy on their electric grids.").

VI. THE ELECTRICITY GRID

The electricity grid is an incredibly complex infrastructure. It operates under a simple truth—supply and demand must be equal at any given moment. If there is too much supply and not enough demand, the system is overloaded; if the converse is true, there is a blackout. To prevent either of these problems, the power source must deliver energy to the consumer in a manner that is reliable, efficient, and effective. The electricity grid infrastructure provides energy management, storage, and delivery. Smaller power generators, referred to as distributed energy (DE) technologies, supplement the grid.

Emerging energy storage technology will need to make the grid more flexible to energy demands and incorporate a larger portfolio of renewable resources, such as wind and solar. [232] Consumer demands are variable by time of day and by season, and energy power from wind and solar is inconsistent due to natural conditions. Energy storage technologies, in addition to the common battery, will need to "time-shift" electricity for use when needed, instead of when generated, which will enhance the electricity grid system and increase the use of renewable energy.[233] "Time shifting" refers to the ability to store energy during either low price times or high supply times and discharging that energy during high price times or low supply times. For example, it could include the storing of excess solar energy during daylight hours and utilizing that energy during evenings or low direct and diffused light times.

Energy management helps meet consumer demands for baseload power (minimum demand a power plant experiences), backup power (a reserve appliance such as a stand-by generator), and peaking power (power generated to meet short-lived and variable high demand periods). Energy distribution infrastructure has become a homeland security concern because of our extensive dependence on electricity supply. Transporting energy from alternative energy sources such as wind and solar, which may be suited to remote geographic areas, requires a more resilient energy grid.[234]

Transmission Efficiency, a Smart Grid, and Distributed Energy.   In the United States, the Department of Energy (DOE) modernizes the electricity grid infrastructure and has a short-term goal of a "smarter grid" and a long-term goal of achieving a robust "smart grid."[235] While the U.S. electricity system is 99.97% reliable, there are still "power outages and interruptions

---

[232] *See How Energy Storage Works*, Union of Concerned Scientists, http://www.ucsusa.org/clean-energy/how-energy-storage-works#.V8Jw92Xe3dk (last visited Nov. 18, 2017).
[233] *See* Ethan N. Elkind, *The Power of Energy Storage: How to Increase Deployment in California to Reduce Greenhouse Gas Emissions*, Berkeley L. Ctr. for L., Energy & Env't & UCLA Envtl. L. Ctr. (July 2010), http://www.law.berkeley.edu/files/Power_of_Energy_Storage_July_2010.pdf.
[234] Reitze, Jr., *supra* note 115, at 872.
[235] Litos Strategic Communication, *The Smart Grid: An Introduction*, U.S. Dep't Energy, http://energy.gov/sites/prod/files/oeprod/DocumentsandMedia/DOE_SG_Book_Single_Pages%281%29.pdf (last visited Nov. 18, 2017).

that cost Americans at least $150 billion each year — about $500 for every man, woman and child."[236] The Western State Energy Crisis of 2000 and 2001 demonstrated the vulnerability of the U.S. electricity infrastructure when the lack of power supply, resulting from a number of factors, created system instability and the need for "rolling blackouts."[237]

> *[The Federal Energy Regulatory Commission] concluded in a March 2003 final investigation report on the Western energy crisis that market conditions involving diminished power supplies due to drought conditions, inadequate infrastructure and a flawed power market design contributed to the market manipulation that prolonged and exacerbated the economic harm caused by the crisis.*[238]

Market manipulation by Enron, a Texas energy company, as well as other illegal and unethical behavior by corporate players led to the demise of the company and the criminal prosecution of some of its executives.[239]

Blackouts. Nations throughout the world have experienced problems with the electricity grids in their countries. For example, a huge blackout in India in August 2012 deemed to be "the worst blackout in world history," affected more than 600 million people and was caused by a failure in the overburdened and mismanaged electricity grid.[240] The United Nations has addressed energy security issues by defining when a nation is energy-secure as the degree to which "fuel and energy services are available to ensure: a) survival of the nation, b) protection of national welfare,[241] and c) minimization of risks associated with supply and use of fuel and energy services. The five dimensions of energy security include energy supply,

---

[236] *Id.* at 5.
[237] *Addressing the 2000-2001 Western Energy Crisis*, Fed. Energy Reg. Comm'n, http://www.ferc. gov/industries/electric/indus-act/wec.asp (last visited Nov. 18, 2017); *see also The Western Energy Crisis, the Enron Bankruptcy, and FERC's Response*, Fed. Energy Reg. Comm'n, http://www.ferc.gov/ industries/electric/indus-act/wec/chron/chronology.pdf (last visited Nov. 18, 2017); Litos Strategic Communication, *supra* note 235, at 8.
[238] *Addressing the 2000-2001 Western Energy Crisis*, *supra* note 237; *see also* Spencer Weber Waller, *Competition, Consumer Protection and Energy Deregulation: A Conference Introduction*, 33 Loy. U. Chi. L.J. 749 (2002); Jim Rossi, *The Common Law "Duty to Serve" and Protection of Consumers in an Age of Competitive Retail Public Utility Restructuring*, 51 Vand. L. Rev. 1233 (1998) (discussing the conflict between the electricity industry's duty to serve as a monopoly subject to federal regulation and the competition of public utilities, in the context of deregulation).
[239] *See Behind the Enron Scandal: Called to Account*, Time, http://content.time.com/time/specials/ packages/0,28757,2021097,00.html (last visited Sept. 24, 2017).
[240] Simon Denyer & Rama Lakshmi, *Huge Blackout Fuels Doubts About India's Economic Ambitions*, Wash. Post (Aug. 1, 2012), http://www.washingtonpost.com/world/asia_pacific/huge-blackout- fuels-doubts-about-indias-economic--ambitions/2012/08/01/gJQAtjeYOX_story.html.
[241] Litos Strategic Communication, *supra* note 235, at 9 ("When the blackout of 2003 occurred — the largest in US history — those citizens not startled by being stuck in darkened, suffocating elevators, turned their thoughts toward terrorism. And not without cause. The grid's centralized structure leaves us open to attack. In fact, the interdependencies of various grid components can bring about a domino effect — a cascading series of failures that could bring our nation's banking, communications, traffic, and security systems among others to a complete standstill.").

economic, technological, environmental, social and cultural, and military/ security dimensions."[242]

"Smart Grid" can incorporate a number of tools to gather information and technology to help with energy efficiency, use, and reliability. The U.S. federal statute Energy Independence and Security Act of 2007 (EISA-2007) sets forth ten characteristics that are helpful in considering a Smart Grid:

(1) Increased use of digital information and controls technology to improve reliability, security, and efficiency of the electric grid. (2) Dynamic optimization of grid operations and resources, with full cyber-security. (3) Deployment and integration of distributed resources and generation, including renewable resources. (4) Development and incorporation of demand response, demand-side resources, and energy-efficiency resources. (5) Deployment of "smart" technologies (real-time, automated, interactive technologies that optimize the physical operation of appliances and consumer devices) for metering, communications concerning grid operations and status, and distribution automation. (6) Integration of "smart" appliances and consumer devices. (7) Deployment and integration of advanced electricity storage and peak-shaving technologies, including plug-in electric and hybrid electric vehicles, and thermal storage air conditioning. (8) Provision to consumers of timely information and control options. (9) Development of standards for communication and interoperability of appliances and equipment connected to the electric grid, including the infrastructure serving the grid. (10) Identification and lowering of unreasonable or unnecessary barriers to adoption of smart grid technologies, practices, and services.

Improvements in transmission efficiency may supplement improvements in generation efficiency so that we more effectively manage the transmission grid.[243] In the United States, the transmission infrastructure has not kept up with the increasing energy demand, and grid reliability and efficiency has suffered from this lack of investment.[244] The DOE and FERC have helped form profit-neutral organizations[245] to coordinate supply and demand using a smart distribution system. These organizations will coordinate, control, and monitor the power system operation on a state or regional basis. According to the DOE's report on the Smart Grid:

> *Adoption of the Smart Grid will enhance every facet of the electric delivery system, including generation, transmission, distribution and consumption. It will energize those utility initiatives that encourage consumers to modify patterns of electricity usage, including the timing and level of electricity demand. It will*

---

[242] *Multi-Dimensional Issues in International Electric Power Grid Interconnections*, UNITED NATIONS SUSTAINABLE DEV. PROGRAMME 151 (2006), http://www.un.org/esa/sustdev/publications/energy/inter connections.pdf (last visited Nov. 18, 2017).

[243] ENERGY, ECONOMICS & THE ENVIRONMENT, *supra* note 208, at 961.

[244] Litos Strategic Communication, *supra* note 235, at 6.

[245] These organizations are called Independent System Operators (ISOs) or Regional Transmission Organizations (RTOs). *See Industry Activities*, FED. ENERGY REG. COMM'N (July 5, 2012), http://www. ferc.gov/industries/electric/indus-act.asp (last updated Nov. 4, 2016).

increase the possibilities of distributed generation, bringing generation closer to those it serves (think: solar panels on your roof rather than some distant power station). The shorter the distance from generation to consumption, the more efficient, economical and "green" it may be. It will empower consumers to become active participants in their energy choices to a degree never before possible. And it will offer a two-way visibility and control of energy usage.[246]

The DOE is working with states, cities, public utilities, research institutions, and private companies to develop the technologies needed for the Smart Grid, fund the needed infrastructure investments, and implement policies using political will to facilitate the changes needed to reach these goals.[247]

Energy Conservation. To create a resilient and sustainable energy system will require national energy policies that include energy conservation (use of less energy through the sacrifice of benefits derived from such use), energy efficiency (achieving the same benefits, but using less energy), and development of alternative energy sources from a variety of sources.[248] In the United States, Congress provided resources for energy conservation, energy efficiency, and renewable energy research as part of the American Recovery and Reinvestment Act of 2009.[249] In the United States, FERC has the overall responsibility for regulating the interstate transmission and wholesale sales of electricity, natural gas, and oil. FERC also has jurisdiction over public electric and natural gas utilities.[250] Therefore, the interstate infrastructure, the grid, and support for this transmission will be subject to FERC's regulations.[251] The Public Utility Regulatory Policies Act of 1978 (PURPA) also encourages electric energy conservation and efficiency, equitable retail rates, small dam hydropower development, and natural gas conservation by identifying "qualifying facilities" that generate electricity and meet certain standards to receive special regulatory treatment and rates from FERC.[252]

---

[246] Litos Strategic Communication, *supra* note 235, at 12.

[247] For more information on distributed energy, see *Distributed Energy Resources,* ELECTRIC POWER RESEARCH INST., http://www2.epri.com/Our-Work/Pages/Distributed-Electricity-Resources.aspx, (last visited Nov. 21, 2017); Kari Alanne & Arto Saari, *Distributed Energy Generation and Sustainable Development,* 10 RENEWABLE & SUSTAINABLE ENERGY REVS., 550 (2006), http://citeseerx.ist.psu.edu/viewdoc/download?doi = 10.1.1.131.9860&rep = rep1&type = pdf.

[248] *See* Reitze, Jr., *supra* note 115, at 890; *see also* THE LAW OF CLEAN ENERGY, *supra* note 133, at 43-45 (discussing international efforts to address energy efficiency through the IEA, the International Partnership for Energy Efficiency Cooperation, and the International Organization for Standardization (ISO)).

[249] Reitze, Jr., *supra* note 115, at 891 (citing American Recovery and Reinvestment Act of 2009, Pub. L. No. 111-5, §123 Stat. 115 (2009)).

[250] THE LAW OF CLEAN ENERGY, *supra* note 133, at 401.

[251] *See generally What FERC Does,* FED. ENERGY REG. COMM'N, http://www.ferc.gov/about/ferc-does.asp (last updated May 24, 2016).

[252] *See generally What Is a Qualifying Facility?,* FED. ENERGY REG. COMM'N, http://www.ferc.gov/industries/electric/gen-info/qual-fac/what-is.asp (last updated Nov. 18, 2016); *see also* New York v. FERC, 535 U.S. 1 (2002).

At the state and local levels, communities are taking a number of actions to enhance efficiency, many of which we set forth in Chapter 5 on land use. Those actions are directed at a variety of sectors, including transportation (requiring or incentivizing improved vehicular efficiency, mass transit, pedestrian and bike transit, and others), the building sector (requiring certain building and zoning standards), and power plants (requiring certain renewable energy portfolios, such as those described above).

Question

1. Can you make an argument that improving the energy grid through Smart Grid and Distributive Energy can help increase the resilience of the energy system? Which systems might be made more vulnerable through a Smart Grid approach?

Natural Resources

I. INTRODUCTION

Human production and consumption are part of a system that requires energy. Natural resources are often the raw materials required to develop energy and manufacture or produce consumer goods. In Chapter 6, we discuss the energy sector and its relation to the resilience and sustainability of systems connected to many natural resources. Some of the same natural resources we discuss in Chapter 6, we discuss here in the context of the production of consumer goods including forests, rangelands, and wildlife. We use many natural resources such as oil, gas, water, wood, minerals, to produce not only energy, but also consumer goods such as plastics, furniture, cars, and jewelry.

We can classify natural resources as private goods, public goods, or common goods. Private goods are those resources that are subject to property ownership because they have property characteristics, also described as the bundle of rights, including the right to possess, use, transfer, and exclude others. Minerals, timber, and contained natural gas are examples of private goods. Public goods are those resources that are not subject to capture and dominion and cannot be exclusive. Air, sunlight, and the wind are public goods. Common goods are migratory resources that are not subject to ownership until captured, and it is difficult to transfer them or exclude others from using them. Oil, natural gas, and water are common goods until captured.[1] Because public goods and common goods are not easily subject to private ownership, these resources are vulnerable to the concept of the "tragedy of the commons,"[2] discussed in Chapter 3, Section II.E. Legal and public policy approaches to these resources will vary based upon their property attributes and the need to limit or encourage economic market behavior.

---

[1] *See* Jan G. Laitos, NATURAL RESOURCES LAW 2-4 (2002) [hereinafter LAITOS HORNBOOK].
[2] *See* Garrett Hardin, *The Tragedy of the Commons*, 162 SCI. 3859, 1243 (1968), http://www.geo.mtu.edu/~asmayer/rural_sustain/governance/Hardin%201968.pdf.

Question

1. Based on what we have covered throughout this book, how does the concept of private ownership affect the way we allocate and use these resources in an economic enterprise to convert them from a natural state into a consumer product? How does regulation limiting these ownership rights impact human behavior such that particular public policies can be achieved? Should we allow private ownership of these resources? Do they instead belong to the public, state, nation, or world?

II. FORESTS, TIMBER, AND WATERSHED PROTECTION

Forests provide major anthropogenic-based ecosystem services, including timber harvesting for wood, watershed protection, soil retention, air purification, aesthetic beauty, recreational areas, carbon sequestration, and wildlife habitats.[3] Many of those services directly and indirectly relate to energy and energy conservation. In the United States, the Organic Act of 1897 recognized two services (timber harvesting and watershed protection) for purposes of national forests, but in 1960, Congress broadened the purposes to include "recreation, range, timber, watershed and wildlife and fish purposes" as supplemental to timber harvesting and watershed protection in the Multiple-Use Sustained-Yield Act (MUSYA).[4]

UNITED STATES FOREST SERVICE

The United States Forest Service (USFS) is a federal agency established in 1905, which manages national forests "for the sustained yield of renewable resources such as water, forage, wildlife, wood, and recreation" such that these resources "benefit the American people while ensuring the productivity of the land and protecting the quality of the environment."[5] The USFS manages the National Forest System and works with state and local governments, as well as private landowners and forest industries, to protect and develop natural resources. The USFS also works with other U.S. agencies, nonprofit organizations, and international organizations to protect and manage international forest resources.[6]

---

[3] LAITOS HORNBOOK, *supra* note 1.
[4] LAITOS HORNBOOK, *supra* note 1, at 359 (discussing MUSYA, 16 U.S.C. §§528-531).
[5] *See generally About the Agency*, U.S. FOREST SERV., http://www.fs.fed.us/aboutus/meetfs.shtml (last visited Sept. 26, 2017).
[6] *Id.*

A. Timber

Timber management requires decisions as to when to harvest, plant, and protect forests, as well as the harvesting methods used. Forests depreciate in value based on age, fire, and disease. Infestation and timber development may have substantial impacts on wildlife, water, and ecosystems.[7] State law including property, contract, and tort law govern private timberland development in the United States, while federal timberland development is under the jurisdiction of the USFS. The sale of national forests to private timber companies has historically been below the cost charged for private timberland harvesting and rarely includes or calculates the value provided by other forest services. Setting aside new national forests for wilderness and recreational purposes precludes logging activities.[8]

The United States legislatively requires forest management and planning, which projects future supply and demand; assesses renewability; prevents irreversible watershed damage; protects wetlands and water quality, and generally assures public benefits while maintaining environmental integrity over nationally designated forests.[9] The goal of forestry is to manage these resources to achieve "the greatest good, for the greatest number in the long run," a concept referred to as "sustained yield."[10] Federal statutes, such as NEPA, the ESA, the 1964 Wilderness Act, and the CWA, also help protect forestlands by addressing environmental and preservationist values impacted by USFS forest management and planning measures.

Timber harvesting methods are typically either selective cutting or clearcutting, although the harvesting methods of shelterwood cutting and seed-tree cutting are also used. Selective cutting harvests trees based on the age of the tree and the area, whereas clearcutting removes all trees, regardless of their age, which has the potential for adversely affecting wildlife and other resources.[11] Shelterwood cutting retains enough trees in place to protect immature trees and the seed-tree method leaves certain trees in place to seed the surrounding area. Without accounting for externalities, clearcutting is the most economically efficient method in the short-term for the timber industry. The industry uses this method for even-aged management where they harvest trees of a certain age all at once and the area is, in the best case, regenerated with a new stand of timber. The

---

[7] LAITOS HORNBOOK, *supra* note 1, at 338.
[8] *Id.* at 351; *see also* Sierra Club v. Hodel, 848 F.2d 1068 (10th Cir. 1988), *overruled by* Vill. of Los Ranchos De Albuquerque v. Marsh, 956 F.2d 970 (10th Cir. 1992); N. Spotted Owl v. Lujan, 758 F. Supp. 621 (W.D. Wash. 1991).
[9] LAITOS HORNBOOK, *supra* note 1, at 362-369 (describing these Acts and citing the Resources Planning Act of 1974, 16 U.S.C. §§1601-1613); *see also* Federico Cheever, *Four Failed Forest Standards: What We Can Learn from the History of the National Forest Management Act's Substantive Timber Management Provisions*, 77 OR. L. REV. 601 (1998).
[10] *See* Christine A. Klein, Federico Cheever & Bret C. Birdsong, NATURAL RESOURCES LAW 318 (2d ed. 2009) (discussing Gifford Pinchot's fundamental concept as the first Chief of the USFS).
[11] LAITOS HORNBOOK, *supra* note 1, at 355-356.

environmental impacts of clearcutting have generated litigation[12] and legislative responses over the years such that the USFS must limit clearcutting on national forest land to situations where it is the optimum method after the USFS has fully assessed the environmental impacts.[13]

Externalities associated with deforestation are too often not recognized. For example, logging in the Monongahela National Forest in West Virginia deforested much of the natural forest cover in this area of the United States and caused disastrous flooding in the early twentieth century because the soil could not hold the water within the watersheds of navigable streams. The federal government purchased the area for reforestation, but the National Forest Service (NFS) began allowing clearcutting again in 1964. In 1975, the Fourth Circuit upheld a challenge against this logging practice based upon the language of the Organic Act of 1897, which requires that timber is marked and designated before sale.[14] In its ruling, the Fourth Circuit in *Izaak Walton League v. Butz* expressed its concern that the National Forest System had changed its role from that of a protector of the national forests in the early twentieth century to that of a timber producer during World War II and after.[15] The U.S. District Court of Alaska in 1975 also required selective marking and cutting of trees in the Tongass National Forest to limit harvesting to those tree-by-tree standards specified by the Organic Act.[16] This litigation led to the enactment of the National Forest Management Act (NFMA) in 1976, a planning statute that requires land and resource management plans for the development of the National Forest System, which must include the principles of "multiple uses" and "sustained yield."[17]

B. Deforestation

As set forth in Chapter 2, there are grave international concerns about **deforestation**, particularly because of the importance of tropical forests in preserving biodiversity, watershed management, and offsetting global carbon emissions.[18] There is no existing international policy on deforestation, but developed nations can attempt to mitigate this destruction by providing incentives to private investors to encourage forest mitigation

---

[12] Curry v. U.S. Forest Serv., 988 F. Supp. 541 (W.D. Pa. 1997); Sierra Club v. Glickman, 156 F.3d 606 (5th Cir. 1998); Sierra Club v. Peterson, 185 F.3d 349 (5th Cir. 1999); Sierra Club v. Marita, 46 F.3d 606 (7th Cir. 1995).

[13] *See* 16 U.S.C. §1604(g)(3)(F) (2012); *see also* Laitos Hornbook, *supra* note 1, at 355-356.

[14] W. Va. Div. of Izaak Walton League of Am. v. Butz (The Monongahela Case), 522 F.2d 945 (4th Cir. 1975); *see also* Oliver A. Houck, *The Water, the Trees, and the Land: Three Nearly Forgotten Cases that Changed the American Landscape*, 70 Tul. L. Rev. 2279, 2309 (1996).

[15] *Id.* at 2294-2295.

[16] *See* Zieske v. Butz, 406 F. Supp. 258 (D. Alaska 1975).

[17] *See* Klein et al., *supra* note 10, at 341-342.

[18] Andrew Long, *Tropical Forest Mitigation Projects and Sustainable Development: Designing U.S. Law for a Supportive Role*, 36 Wm. Mitchell L. Rev. 968, 101 (2010).

projects through carbon credits and offsets.[19] Consumers can also encourage sustainable timber management by requiring sustainable wood and paper products, certified by an independent certification organization. For example, the Forest Stewardship Council will only certify products that meet the principle that "[f]orest management shall conserve biological diversity and its associated values, water resources, soils, and unique and fragile ecosystems and landscapes, and, by so doing, maintain the ecological functions and the integrity of the forest."[20]

With its natural forests 98% deforested, Haiti is one of the most deforested countries in the world. French colonists planted coffee trees and the Haitian people cut down trees for their main source of fuel leaving no forest canopies to shield the land against the rain and wind. Landslides have become a major concern as the soil and water flow downhill. Earthquakes, such as the one in 2010 (the strongest in Haiti in 200 years), contribute to soil destabilization and the possibility of landslides.[21] In addition to overpopulation, natural disasters, and corruption, deforestation has directly contributed to the nation's severe poverty because it has destroyed agriculture and all but eliminated Haiti's major fuel source.[22]

Other countries have also suffered the consequences of deforestation.[23] The population in Uganda, as with the Haitian population, uses wood or charcoal as the main energy source. The lack of good agricultural practices and the use of the forests for fuel have resulted in deforestation of almost 80% of Uganda. In addition, rapid population growth and political turmoil in the 1980s led to the conversion of forests for agricultural purposes; over-grazing and undisciplined timber harvesting increased to meet an increasing demand for charcoal.[24] Ninety-seven percent of Ugandans rely on firewood as an energy source, contributing to the destruction of nearly one-third of their nation's forests over the last 20 years and the release of harmful GHG emissions from the burning of wood and inefficient stoves. Uganda can only meet its environmental sustainability goals by either

---

[19] *See generally id.*

[20] *See* Jonathan Zasloff, *Lawyerly Greenwashing from the Sustainable Forestry Initiative*, LEGAL PLANET: ENVTL. L. & POL'Y (Nov. 7, 2011), http://legalplanet.wordpress.com/2011/11/07/lawyerly-greenwashing-from-the-sustainable-forestry-initiative (discussing the industry's certification organization, Sustainable Forestry Initiative as compared to the Forest Stewardship Council).

[21] Ker Than, *Haiti Earthquake, Deforestation Heighten Landslide Risk*, NAT'L GEOGRAPHIC NEWS (Jan. 15, 2010), http://news.nationalgeographic.com/news/2010/01/100114-haiti-earthquake-landslides/.

[22] Jon Henley, *Haiti: A Long Descent to Hell*, THE GUARDIAN (Jan. 14, 2010), https://www.theguardian.com/world/2010/jan/14/haiti-history-earthquake-disaster (discussing other historical reasons for Haitian poverty level).

[23] Mat McDermott, *10 Countries with the Highest Deforestation Rates in the World*, TREEHUGGER (Aug. 11, 2009), http://www.treehugger.com/corporate-responsibility/10-countries-with-the-highest-deforestation-rates-in-the-world.html.

[24] Charlotte Kanabahita, *Forestry Outlook Studies in Africa: Uganda*, FOOD & AGRIC. ORG. OF THE UNITED NATIONS (Dec. 2001), http://www.fao.org/docrep/004/AC427E/AC427E05.htm; *see also* Christine Echookit Akello, *Environmental Regulation in Uganda: Successes and Challenges*, 3/1 L., ENV'T & DEV. J. 20 (2007), http://www.lead-journal.org/content/07020.pdf; *Uganda*, LUTHERAN WORLD FED'N, https://www.lutheranworld.org/content/uganda (last visited May 9, 2016).

Estimates of GHG* Net Emissions in Brazil in 2015

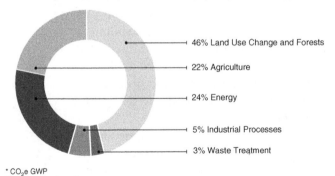

46% Land Use Change and Forests

22% Agriculture

24% Energy

5% Industrial Processes

3% Waste Treatment

* CO_2e GWP
Source: seeg.eco.br

Figure 7-1

turning to alternative energy sources such as solar energy or by using more energy-saving stoves.[25]

Deforestation in the Amazon of Brazil generates great international concern and attention because it involves such a large land mass and the Amazon forest contributes greatly to global biodiversity and carbon trapping. In 2012, deforestation of the Amazon fell to its lowest levels since 1988, when measurements began. Deforestation peaked in 2004, but the rates of clearance have since fallen by almost 75%. This reduction in deforestation has been attributed to changes in society, the political decision to inspect, punitive actions taken by government agencies, and enhanced enforcement of regulations through satellite monitoring. Brazil has also increased existing national parks, regularized land ownership and tenure, protected biodiversity areas, recognized indigenous land rights, and established initiatives to encourage sustainable practices.[26] Yet, as mentioned in Chapter 2 (and presented in Figure 7-1), deforestation remains responsible for the bulk of Brazil's average carbon emissions.

Sustainable forestry is critical for timber products as well as for protecting wildlife habitat, biodiversity, watershed, water quality, and carbon emission reduction. The International Tropical Timber Organization describes sustainable forest management as "the process of managing forest to achieve one or more clearly specified objectives of management with regard to the production of a continuous flow of desired forest products and services without undue reduction of its inherent values and future productivity and without undue undesirable effects on the physical and social environment."[27] To maintain a sustainable production level, "nothing should be done that will irreversibly reduce the potential of the forest to produce marketable timber — that is, there should be no irreversible loss of soil, soil fertility or genetic potential in the marketable species."[28] Nations that currently rely on forests for their energy needs must switch to alternative energy sources as soon as cost-effectively possible.

---

[25] *See generally id.*

[26] Jonathan Watts, *Amazon Deforestation at Record Low, Data Shows*, THE GUARDIAN (June 7, 2012), http://www.guardian.co.uk/environment/2012/jun/07/amazon-deforestation-illegal-logging-brazil.

[27] *See generally Sustainable Forest Management*, INT'L TROPICAL TIMBER ORG., http://www.itto.int/sustainable_forest_management (last visited Sept. 26, 2017).

[28] Sophie Higman, James Mayers, Stephen Bass, Neil Judd & Ruth Nussbaum, THE SUSTAINABLE FORESTRY HANDBOOK: A PRACTICAL GUIDE FOR TROPICAL FOREST MANAGERS ON IMPLEMENTING NEW STANDARDS 39 (2d ed. 2005).

Developed nations will need to assist developing nations in finding new energy resources and sustainably managing existing forest resources to preserve biodiversity and fight global climate change.

Some local governments are also taking steps to improve the tree canopy and take advantage of the many services forests provide. For example, trees assist local governments in reducing stormwater management costs. A University of New Hampshire study indicated that a residential street tree will save $10.80 in stormwater management costs and commercial street trees will save over $23.36.[29] Another study,[30] basing its research on the avoided stormwater construction costs measured by American Forests' CITYgreen, found that trees saved the following amounts in one-time stormwater-construction costs:

Houston, Texas	$1.33 billion
Atlanta, Georgia	$2.36 billion
Vancouver, Washington/Portland-Eugene, Oregon	$20.2 billion
Washington D.C. Metro Area	$4.74 billion
New Orleans, Louisiana	$0.74 billion
San Antonio, Texas	$1.35 billion
San Diego, California	$0.16 billion
Puget Sound Metro Area, Washington	$5.90 billion
Detroit, Michigan	$0.38 billion
Chesapeake Bay Region	$1.08 billion

Local governments also are taking advantage of the shading provided by trees to lower energy costs and to reduce the urban heat island effect.[31] Replacing removed trees and adding trees into the landscape will create shade that can reduce how much sunshine reaches heat-retaining materials, such as concrete. The reduction in the heat island effect can reduce heat stress-related illnesses and fatalities.[32] In addition, tree mitigation and planting more trees adds value to a community, including higher property values. Trees improve urban aesthetics and community livability.

---

[29] *The Economics of Low Impact Development: Economics and LID Practices*, Univ. of New Hampshire Stormwater Ctr. 3-1 (July 2011), http://www.unh.edu/unhsc/sites/unh.edu.unhsc/files/docs/FTL_Chapter3%20LR.pdf.

[30] ECONorthwest, *The Economics of Low-Impact Development: A Literature Review*, (Nov. 2007), http://www.econw.com/media/ap_files/ECONorthwest-Economics-of-LID-Literature-Review_2007.pdf (also noting that a single tree can remove 0.44 pounds of air pollution per year).

[31] *The Value of Green Infrastructure: A Guide to Recognizing its Economic, Environmental and Social Benefits*, Ctr. for Neighborhood Tech. 7 (2010), http://www.cnt.org/sites/default/files/publications/CNT_Value-of-Green-Infrastructure.pdf.

[32] *Id.*

Studies show that there are many economic incentives for communities that implement green infrastructure.[33]

Questions and Note

1. In Chapter 6, Section II, we describe Systems Thinking. What might some of the inputs and outputs concerning a forest be? Would identifying these inputs and outputs help draft policy to ensure a social-ecological forest system that is resilient and sustainable to climate change?

2. What are the pros and cons relative to achieving a more resilient and sustainable forest system based on the International Tropical Timber Organization's (ITTO) definition of sustainable forest management? Recall that ITTO defines this as "the process of managing forest to achieve one or more clearly specified objectives of management with regard to the production of a continuous flow of desired forest products and services without undue reduction of its inherent values and future productivity and without undue undesirable effects on the physical and social environment"; and "nothing should be done that will irreversibly reduce the potential of the forest to produce marketable timber — that is, there should be no irreversible loss of soil, soil fertility or genetic potential in the marketable species." What are the pros and cons of using the U.S. definition of "sustainable yield" and its potential interpretations?

   You may find it helpful to "skip ahead" and read Professor Craig's article about fisheries and sustainable yield found in the box following "Resilience and Sustainability of Fish Stocks." This will also help you answer the next question.

3. Given the large amount of deforestation in the United States and around the world, is the definition of "sustainable yield" working? Is the term equivalent with "sustainability"? Does it result in resilient or sustainable forests?

III. MINERALS

"[W]e are increasingly dependent on mineral materials to create products that support our way of life, our health, and the global economy,"

---

[33] *See generally The Economics of Green Infrastructure,* EPA, https://www.epa.gov/green-infrastructure/economics-green-infrastructure (last updated Sept. 26, 2017). Note that communities also face opportunity costs.

according to the U.S. Mineral Resources Program, a federal organization responsible for researching the potential, production, consumption, and environmental effects of minerals.[34] An average car contains more than a ton of iron and steel, 240 pounds of aluminum, 50 pounds of carbon, 42 pounds of copper, 41 pounds of silicon, 22 pounds of zinc, and more than 30 other minerals including titanium, platinum, and gold.[35] It is interesting to note that the hybrid battery used in the 1999 Prius driven to Las Vegas by Juan and Amir at the beginning of Chapter 6 contained 60 pounds of nickel, 24 pounds of lanthanum, and 3 pounds of cobalt—all considered rare Earth minerals, not readily available in many regions of the world. The Mineral Resources Program's studies show that every year each person in the United States requires more than 25,000 pounds of new nonfuel minerals to make everyday items and estimates that a person born in 2008 will use, over a lifetime, approximately 3.5 million pounds of nonfuel minerals.[36]

Minerals such as coal, oil shale, and uranium for nuclear power are energy sources. We also use them for building materials, industrial processes, manufactured products, and other purposes. In the United States, state and federal law controls mineral ownership and development, including conflicts between surface and mineral rights, mining of hard rock minerals, obtaining patents or leases for mineral resources on federal lands, and exploration and development of these resources. The General Mining Act of 1872 declares, "all valuable mineral deposits in lands belonging to the United States, both surveyed and unsurveyed, shall be free and open to exploration and purchase. . . ." The definitions of "valuable" and "mineral" do not include radon gas, shell rock, organic soil, and water, but do include bird guano.[37]

Mining and Production: In the United States, the General Mining Act of 1872 governs the location and mining of minerals such as gold, silver, tin, copper, uranium, building stone, and diamonds. Under this law, a person physically stakes a mining claim on public land, posts a location notice to mark the boundaries of the claim and comply with state and federal laws, and files notice of that location in the county records and with the Bureau of Land Management (BLM). The U.S. government maintains legal title to the land, but the holder of the mining claim receives exclusive possession of the surface for mining purposes and the right to mine and remove minerals.

---

[34] *Do We Take Minerals for Granted?*, U.S. GEOLOGICAL SURV., https://minerals.usgs.gov/granted.html (last visited Jan. 22, 2018).
[35] Note that Toyota boasts that 85% of the raw materials used to make Amir's 2010 Prius can be recycled. *See Prius and the Environment*, TOTOTA.CO.UK, http://media.toyota.co.uk/wp-content/files_mf/1319274453PriusEnvironmentalDeclaration.pdf (last visited Sept. 26, 2017).
[36] *See Mineral Resources Program*, U.S. GEOLOGICAL SURV., http://minerals.usgs.gov (last visited Sept. 26, 2017).
[37] Klein et al., *supra* note 10, at 446 n.1.

The Mineral Leasing Act of 1920 governs the development of coal, phosphate, potash, sodium, sulfur and other leasable minerals on public lands and on lands having federal reserved minerals. The BLM grants mining leases in exchange for rents or royalty payments to the government. Coal leases are subject to somewhat different standards and are regulated by the Office of Surface Mining Reclamation and Enforcement (OSM), which operates under the Department of the Interior (DOI). Prior to the enactment of the Mineral Leasing Act in 1920, oil shale was a mineral under the General Mining Act of 1872, but since 1920, a leasing procedure similar to that used for oil and gas governs oil shale. Oil shale claims existing prior to 1920 have been the subject of litigation, but generally only when oil prices rise substantially.[38]

Unlike most countries, which do not recognize private ownership of minerals, the United States allows fractional ownership of surface and mineral estates. In the absence of agreement as to how multiple owners of mineral estates share obligations and rights to these subsurface rights, the common law allows one concurrent owner to drill or lease without the consent of other cotenants but requires the developing cotenant to account for any profits and share with non-developing co-owners. This divided ownership presents a difficulty for companies interested in mining or drilling, which makes leasing of public land from the government a much more attractive and profitable approach.

To gain a legally protectable interest in minerals on federal land under the Mining Law, the claim must be "located" and a valuable mineral deposit "discovered."[39] If a qualified prospector enters the federal land and believes there is a valuable mineral deposit, the prospector must follow state and federal location procedures to "locate" the claim. There are two kinds of location — lode and placer. The lode location is a "vein or lode of rock in place bearing valuable mineral," while a placer location is some other form such as "scattered particles of gold found in the softer covering of the Earth."[40] The prospector is entitled to exclusive surface occupation, referred to as *pedis possessio* (possession by foothold),[41] and if a "valuable mineral deposit"[42] is then physically discovered, the prospector is entitled to an "unpatented mining claim."[43] These unpatented mining claims allow the miner to remove minerals and occupy the surface without payment to the United States, other than a $100 annual maintenance fee, or the miner

---

[38] *See Minerals and Mining Law*, FINDLAW, http://library.findlaw.com/1999/Jan/1/241491.html (last visited Sept. 26, 2017); *see, e.g.*, Cliffs Synfuel Corp. v. Norton, 291 F.3d 1250 (10th Cir. 2002).
[39] LAITOS HORNBOOK, *supra* note 1, at 281.
[40] Cole v. Ralph, 252 U.S. 286 (1920).
[41] *See* Union Oil v. Smith, 249 U.S. 337, 346-347 (1919).
[42] *See* United States v. Coleman, 390 U.S. 599, 600 (1968) (discussing the need to show that the deposits are valuable by passing the "marketability test" showing that "the mineral can be 'extracted, removed and marketed at a profit'").
[43] LAITOS HORNBOOK, *supra* note 1, at 281; *see also* United States v. Locke, 471 U.S. 84 (1985) (discussing the property contours of unpatented mining claims).

may pay for a patent to the mineral and surface estates for a low one-time payment of $5.00 an acre for lode claims and $2.50 an acre for placer claims.[44] Suggested amendments to the 1872 Mining Law include disallowing patent mineral claims, requiring royalty payments to the United States, requiring operation plans for mining, and imposing more stringent reclamation and bonding requirements.[45]

Not all federal lands are open to location, even though the Mining Law seems to indicate that its jurisdiction is extensive. Federal land may be appropriated, reserved, or withdrawn from location for other purposes such as prior mining claims, national parks, wildlife refuges, wilderness areas, wild and scenic rivers, oil-bearing lands, and also for certain classes of minerals such as onshore energy minerals and offshore oil and gas deposits.[46] Case law, statutes, and amendments have narrowed the Mining Law phrase "all valuable mineral deposits."[47] While coal was never locatable under the Mining Law, the 1920 Mineral Leasing Act[48] and the Geothermal Steam Act of 1970 removed other energy sources such as onshore oil, gas, geothermal resources, and oil shale. The Materials Act of 1947, as amended by the Common Varieties Act of 1955, removed stone, sand, cinders, and gravel from location.[49] Valuable minerals that are still locatable under the Mining Law include quartz, gold, silver, cinnabar [mercury], lead, tin, copper, gemstones, and diamonds.[50]

A. Resilience and Sustainability of Mining

Creating resilient and sustainable systems associated with mining and minerals requires action at all levels. While the objective depends on the specific situation and system, laws focusing on sustainability would likely "address the environmental, economic, health, and social impacts and benefits of mining, minerals and metals throughout their life cycle, including workers' health and safety."[51] The Plan of Implementation, adopted by the 2002 World Summit on Sustainable Development in Johannesburg, South Africa, declares that a resilient and sustainable mining system would:

---

[44] *See* Amoco Prod. Co. v. S. Ute Indian Tribe, 526 U.S. 865 (1999) (for value of patented rights).
[45] LAITOS HORNBOOK, *supra* note 1, at 281 (discussing potential for bogus unpatented mining claims); *see also* United States v. Zweifel, 508 F.2d 1150 (10th Cir. 1975).
[46] LAITOS HORNBOOK, *supra* note 1, 282-283.
[47] *Id.* at 283.
[48] *See* Duesing v. Udall, 350 F.2d 748 (D.C. Cir. 1965); *see also* Mobil Oil Exploration & Producing Se., Inc. v. United States, 530 U.S. 604 (2000).
[49] LAITOS HORNBOOK, *supra* note 1, at 283.
[50] *Id.*
[51] World Summit on Sustainable Development, *Plan of Implementation* ¶46(a), U.N. Doc. A/CONF.199/20 (Sept. 2002).

[e]nhance the participation of stakeholders, including local and indigenous communities and women, to play an active role in minerals, metals and mining development throughout the life cycles of mining operations, including after closure for rehabilitation purposes . . . [;] [and] [f]oster sustainable mining practices through the provision of financial, technical and capacity-building support to developing countries and countries with economies in transition, for the mining and processing of minerals. . . .[52]

The U.S. BLM and Forest Service have embraced the Plan of Implementation.[53] While these goals are laudable, there are many challenges facing sustainable mining including:

- the "large amounts of material involved in large-scale mining and minerals extraction,"
- the significant use of chemicals to treat raw materials,
- the long-term and irreversible decisions about where and how to dispose of the large volumes of waste, and
- the continuing environmental effects of past mining operations, including the irreversible loss of biodiversity.[54]

The Environmental Law Institute (ELI) Mining Center is a research institute dedicated to addressing the environmental and sustainable development challenges brought by the mining sector's global impact. The Center has collaborated with partners in Peru, Chile, Mexico, and Canada to improve community participation in environmental impact assessment. A 2000 study by ELI presented a comparative analysis of how eight countries use policy tools to promote pollution prevention in the mining industry.[55]

Intensive water usage remains a significant challenge to the resilience and sustainability of any mining system. Mining production and processing uses extensive water resources and many minerals are located in areas of water scarcity. Mining companies must secure water for mining needs, while not compromising the current and future needs of others. Unfortunately, dry processing minerals reduces water consumption but increases a mining company's energy consumption and carbon emissions. Companies must also recycle water and assess mining operations from

---

[52] *Id.* at ¶46(b).
[53] *Sustainable Development Minerals Application*, U.S. Bureau of Land Mgmt. (Oct. 22, 2003), http://www.fs.fed.us/geology/fs_blm_statement_of_support.pdf.
[54] James L. Hendrix, *Sustainable Mining: Trends and Opportunities*, U. Neb. Lincoln 51 (Feb. 2006), http://digitalcommons.unl.edu/chemengmining/3.
[55] Higman, *supra* note 28.

start to finish for improved efficiency in order to continue mining while not destroying or degrading the rights of other water users.[56]

The environmental impacts of mining are significant both during the actual mining operations and after ceasing the mining activity. The U.S. Forest Service regulates mining claims within national forests to address environmental protection of surface resources and the reclamation of mining sites after mining has ended.[57] These regulations support the resilience of the mining sector. The Bureau of Land Management (BLM) is also involved in regulating mining on federal lands to satisfy its duties under the Federal Land Policy and Management Act (FLPMA) to "take any action necessary to prevent unnecessary or undue degradation of the [public] lands."[58] Additional federal laws and their state equivalents, including the National Environmental Policy Act, the Clean Air Act, the Clean Water Act, the Resource Conservation and Recovery Act, and the Endangered Species Act, require that mining activities comply with protective environmental regulations.[59]

The mining industry faces environmental challenges on a global scale because extracting minerals disturbs land by removing large amounts of soil and rock. While mining companies find it economically beneficial to remove the least amount of material and recover the greatest amount of mineral, there will be some land imprint and waste generated from mining operations. In addition to land disturbance such as erosion and sinkholes, other environmental impacts of mining include energy use and emissions, water use and pollution, waste, and the potential effects on biodiversity. The environmental impact of mining operations will vary depending on the geographic location and the type of mining, such as open pit mining, underground mining, coastal mining, inland alluvial mining, and marine mining.

 "Ethical" minerals and metals are also of global concern, as highlighted by the "blood" diamond controversy that involves diamonds mined and traded to support insurgent weapons or armies.[60] The Global Witness organization, which "investigates and campaigns to prevent natural resource-related conflict and corruption, and associated environmental

---

[56] *Id.*
[57] *See, e.g.* United States v. Weiss, 642 F.2d 296 (9th Cir. 1981); *see also* Okanogan Highlands All. v. Williams, 236 F.3d 468 (9th Cir. 2000); Clouser v. Espy, 42 F.3d 1522, 1539 (9th Cir. 1994).
[58] Mineral Policy Ctr. v. Norton, 292 F. Supp. 2d 30, 33 (D.D.C. 2003) (quoting 43 U.S.C. §1732(b)); *see also* Native Vill. of Eklutna v. Alaska R.R. Corp., 87 P.3d 41 (Alaska 2004) (cultural significance of mining operations must be considered).
[59] Klein et al., *supra* note 10, at 486.
[60] BLOOD DIAMOND (Warner Brothers 2006).

and human rights abuses," exposed this issue in the 1990s.[61] The concern about these "conflict" diamonds led the United Nations General Assembly to adopt the Kimberley Process Certification Scheme (KPCS) in 2003. With a majority of the diamond trade originating in African countries, certification helps ensure that diamond purchases do not finance armed insurgents seeking to overthrow legitimate governments.[62] Participating countries are responsible for implementing these rules, and the United States, as the world's largest diamond consumer, enacted the Clean Diamond Trade Act in 2003 to stop the trade of conflict diamonds.[63] In response to international standards attempting to address the Congo's conflict minerals trade, the United States also enacted Section 1502 of the Dodd Frank Act, which requires minerals such as tin, tantalum, tungsten, and gold from the Congo to be labeled for consumers and reported publicly.[64] Another example of promoting "responsible minerals" is a campaign encouraging people to recycle their mobile phones, which contain the metal coltan, mined by clearing gorilla habitat in the Democratic Republic of Congo.[65]

Coltan Mining

---

[61] *See* GLOBAL WITNESS, http://www.globalwitness.org (last visited Sept. 26, 2017).

[62] *See generally About*, KIMBERLEY PROCESS, http://www.kimberleyprocess.com/en/about (last visited Sept. 26, 2017).

[63] Clean Diamond Trade Act, Pub. L. No. 108-19, 117 Stat. 631 (2003) (codified at 19 U.S.C. §§3901-3913), http://www.fas.org/asmp/resources/govern/108th/pl_108_19.pdf.

[64] Sophia Pickles & Mike Davis, *Renewed Fighting in Eastern Congo Highlights Urgent Need to End Conflict Minerals Trade*, GLOBAL WITNESS (May 30, 2012), http://www.globalwitness.org/library/renewed-fighting-eastern-congo-highlights-urgent-need-end-conflict-minerals-trade; *see also* Jim Puzzanghera, *SEC Takes Aim at "Blood Minerals,"* L.A. TIMES (Aug. 23, 2012), http://www.latimes.com/business/la-fi-sec-minerals-rule-20120823,0,5882198.story?track=lat-email-topofthetimes.

[65] Damien Giurco, *Sustainable Mining: A Vision for Australia to Lead the World*, CONVERSATION (Sept. 28, 2011), http://theconversation.edu.au/sustainable-mining-a-vision-for-australia-to-lead-the-world-3159; *see also* Sam Hoe-Richardson, *Making Anglo American Water-Resilient*, THE GUARDIAN (Aug. 13, 2012), https://web.archive.org/web/20120819044522/http://www.guardian.co.uk/sustainable-business/creating-sustainable-water-supply?newsfeed=true.

Countries use various regulatory approaches to control the environmental impact of mining operations. Environmental impacts include ground and surface water contamination from the improper use of chemicals or from uncontrolled runoff from mining waste, destruction of soils and vegetation leading to erosion and loss of habitat, and the emission of air pollutants from smelting activities. Some of the controls various countries use to deal with these impacts include:

- environmental impact assessment;
- planning for mining and post-closure;
- permitting based on imposing conditions;
- obtaining concessions from the mining companies;
- establishing, monitoring, and enforcing regulatory standards;
- requiring disclosure to the government and the public;
- obtaining financial assurances through bonds and other means;
- restricting land use;
- providing for public participation in environmental decision-making processes;
- establishing environmental management systems to guide organizations in meeting their environmental obligations;
- providing economic and other incentives to encourage pollution prevention;
- remining previously mined areas to remedy environmental problems; and
- assigning liability to mining companies to remedy harm and encourage pollution prevention.[66]

In the United States, the Environmental Protection Agency (EPA) has addressed the human health and environmental threats posed by mining by spending over $2.4 billion and placing 95 mining and mineral processing sites on the Superfund National Priorities list for cleanup under the authority of the Comprehensive Environmental Response, Compensation, and Liability Act (CERCLA, aka Superfund). The EPA has relocated families to avoid exposing them to asbestos and lead poisoning, inspected sites that pose a significant risk to communities, required alternative drinking water supplies or removal of lead-contaminated soil from residential yards, and attempted to bring mining and mineral processing facilities into compliance with the law to protect the environment and local communities. Local land use zoning regulation over quarry permits and quarry

---

[66] *See* Susan Bass, *Pollution Prevention and Mining: A Proposed Framework for the Americas*, Envtl. L. Inst. (Jan. 2000), http://www.eli.org/sites/default/files/eli-pubs/d10_02.pdf.

expansion also serves to protect local communities, but there are differing approaches depending upon the state.[67]

Concerns about the human health and environmental impact of mining on local communities have generated controversy, litigation, and even civil war in other countries. For example, in Papua New Guinea a civil war began after workers sabotaged gold and copper mines and residents of the island of Bougainville objected to environmental contamination from Rio Tinto LLC, a mining operation owned by a London-based mining company. The islanders sued Rio Tinto in U.S. federal court under the Alien Tort Statute of 1789, which allows foreign nationals to sue for violations of international law or treaties. The lawsuit alleged that Rio Tinto induced the country of Papua New Guinea to use military force to keep the mine open, resulting in 10,000 civilian deaths. There have also been allegations against an Australian mining company in the Philippines for human rights abuses, including forced relocation of indigenous peoples, harassment and intimation, and failing to provide accurate information for informed decision making by local communities.[68]

Finally, abandoned mines are the source of extensive pollution of soil, water, and ecosystems and create serious threats to human health and the environment. There are approximately 500,000 abandoned mines in the United States. These mines generate human health and environmental concerns including:

- radiation exposure from abandoned uranium mines;
- contaminated surface and ground water;
- an acidic aquatic environment that is not supportive of aquatic life and vegetation;
- the presence of metal in the water or in fish tissue;
- surface runoff of silt and debris that clogs streams and endangers fish;
- exposure to toxic dust blown from the sites; and
- endangering threatened species.

In Canada, a joint industry-government group and other stakeholders met in 2001 to address the problems posed by orphaned or abandoned mines where the owner is absent or is unwilling or financially unable to clean

---

[67] Hansen Bros. Enters. v. Bd. of Sup'rs, 35 Cal. Rptr. 2d 358 (1994), *review granted and opinion superseded sub nom.* Hansen Bros. Enterprises v. Bd. of Sup'rs of City of Nev., 889 P.2d 537 (Cal. 1995), *and rev'd sub nom.* Hansen Bros. Enterprises, Inc. v. Bd. of Supervisors, 12 Cal. 4th 533, 907 P.2d 1324 (1996); Twp. of Fairfield v. Likanchuk's, Inc., 644 A.2d 120 (N.J. Super. Ct. App. Div. 1994); Buffalo Crushed Stone, Inc. v. Town of Cheektowaga, 864 N.Y.S.2d 598 (App. Div. 2008), *aff'd*, 913 N.E.2d 394 (2009).

[68] *Rio Tinto Accused Over Bougainville "Genocide,"* ABC Newcastle (Oct. 26, 2011, 6:47 PM), http://www.abc.net.au/news/2011-10-26/us-court-revives-rio-tinto-lawsuit/3601136/?site = newcastle; *see also OceanaGold Under Renewed Scrutiny for Human Rights Abuses at Its Didipio Operation*, Oxfam Australia (July 11, 2008), https://www.oxfam.org.au/media/2008/07/ oceanagold-under-renewed-scrutiny-for-human-rights-abuses-at-its-didipio-operation/.

up the contaminated site. This National Orphaned or Abandoned Mines Initiative (NOAMI) reviewed the issues surrounding these mines and resolved to implement remediation programs to make significant progress in assessing, remediating, and reclaiming mine sites within a five- to ten-year period.

In the United States, the U.S. Geological Survey (USGS) conducted an Abandoned Mine Lands (AML) Initiative between 1997 and 2001 to help the Federal Land Management Agency (FLMA) remediate abandoned hard rock mining contamination. This was part of a larger effort by the U.S. Department of the Interior and the U.S. Department of Agriculture to clean up federal lands affected by abandoned mines. This cleanup effort used a watershed approach, based on the idea that contaminated sites that have the most profound effect on water and ecosystem quality within a watershed can be identified, characterized, and ranked for cleanup. These national programs represent small steps to enhance the resilience and sustainability of ecosystems impacted by mining.[69]

Questions and Notes

1. In Chapter 6, Section IV, we introduced Baselines and Metrics. If we tasked you with creating a legal system that supported the Plan of Implementation's objectives of a sustainable mining system, what baselines and metrics would you choose? This question requires understanding the Plan's idea of sustainable mining (set forth above) and determining which metrics would support the Plan or show progress toward the Plan's objectives.

2. As stated above, in the absence of an agreement in the United States, any concurrent owner may drill for minerals without prior consent. What might this motivate concurrent owners to do? Does that behavior support a resilient mining system? Does it support the resilience of related ecosystems? Can you think of an alternative way to structure legal rights around minerals?

3. Some have criticized the "sustained yield" standard for not furthering goals consistent with resilience. Can you see how "sustained yield" could be interpreted to strain the resilience of many ecosystems?

---

[69] *See About NOAMI*, Nat'l Orphaned/Abandoned Mines Initiative, http://www.abandoned-mines.org/en/ (last visited Sept. 27, 2017); *see also* Integrated Investigations of Environmental Effects of Historical Mining in the Basin and Boulder Mining Districts, Boulder River Watershed, Jefferson County, Montana (Nimick et al. eds., 2007), http://pubs.usgs.gov/pp/2004/1652; *Extent of Problem*, Abandoned Mine Lands Portal, https://web.archive.org/web/20151023002948/http://www.abandonedmines.gov/ep.html (last visited Sept. 27, 2015); *USGS Abandoned Mine Lands Initiative (AMLI)*, U.S. Geological Surv., http://amli.usgs.gov (last updated Dec. 16, 2016).

4. Is it possible to have a sustainable society with each person using 25,000 pounds of new nonfuel minerals a year? Does your answer depend on additional information? What information would be most helpful? Is it possible to have a resilient society with each person using 25,000 pounds of new nonfuel minerals a year? What are the different questions you ask when differentiating between resilience and sustainability?

IV. RANGELAND

Rangelands are "lands on which the indigenous vegetation is predominantly grasses, grass-like plants, forbs or shrubs and is managed as a natural ecosystem. They include grasslands, savannas, shrublands, deserts, tundras, marshes and meadows."[70] Rangelands supply goods such as food, forage for livestock grazing, substances used to produce pharmaceuticals, and biomass for energy. Rangelands also serve other functions such as purifying air and water, mitigating drought and flooding, decomposing waste, and supporting biodiversity.[71]

Private or Public Ownership: In the United States, more than half of rangelands, particularly those lands east of the Rocky Mountains, are privately owned.[72] Rangelands owned by the federal government are generally west of the Rocky Mountains and remained open to public grazing until 1934 when Congress enacted the Taylor Grazing Act (TGA) to address the problem of overgrazing on this open and unregulated land. The open lands policy preceding the TGA resulted in a true "tragedy of the commons,"[73] which destroyed large portions of public grazing lands and caused "lasting ecological damages — including sinking water tables, erosion, and invasions of non-native species."[74] This unrestrained grazing by cattle and sheep contributed to the Dust Bowl in the 1930s, which produced a ghastly dust storm in 1934 that blew from Montana and Wisconsin across the nation and "arrived in Washington as the Senate debated the TGA."[75] While many states have their own grazing rules, the TGA may preempt these rules.[76]

---

[70] Joel R. Brown et al., *Rangelands and Global Change*, Soc'y for Range Mgmt. 1, http://www.range lands.org/pdf/Global_Issue_Paper.pdf (last visited May 15, 2016).
[71] *Id.*
[72] *Id.*
[73] Hardin, *supra* note 2.
[74] Klein et al., *supra* note 10, at 387.
[75] *Id.*; *see also* Pub. Lands Council v. Babbitt, 529 U.S. 728 (2000) (for historical reference).
[76] Laitos Hornbook, *supra* note 1, at 266; *see also* United States v. Shenise, 43 F. Supp. 2d 1190 (D. Colo. 1999).

Resource Management: Unlike minerals and forests, federal rangeland has not been subject to private property ownership in the United States. Instead, grazing on federal land has been a privilege when lands were open, or a license,[77] subject to revocation after the TGA required grazing permits.[78] Control over grazing is governed by a concept known as "animal unit mouths" (AUMs), which is a measurement based on the amount of forage consumed in a month by a certain number of cows or sheep. Grazing fees have been relatively low on public lands as compared to private lands prompting some to argue that the government is subsidizing the livestock industry and that rangeland would better serve the public if instead it were used to conserve native biodiversity.[79] Ranchers have resisted permit reductions of the number of AUMs in order to restore rangeland sustainability because it diminishes the value of their land in the short term. Even though grazing permits are not property rights, calculations of ranch land value include these permits and the permits may serve as assets to secure bank loans.[80]

While reductions in grazing after Congress enacted TGA improved rangeland conditions, by the 1960s the rangelands had still not recovered sufficiently. As a result, the Secretary of the Interior increased grazing fees to try to capture the economic cost.[81] The Federal Land Policy and Management Act of 1976 (FLPMA) facilitated land use planning for all of the resources managed by the Bureau of Land Management (BLM) based on "multiple uses," including "recreation, range, timber, minerals, watershed, wildlife and fish, and natural and scenic, scientific, and historical usage."[82] The Public Rangelands Improvement Act (PRIA) of 1978 required more than the FLPMA land use planning and mandated that the BLM take action to assess and monitor the unsatisfactory condition of public rangelands and stop the decline of this resource, using measures such as discontinuing (either temporarily or permanently) the grazing uses on certain lands.[83]

---

[77] United States v. Fuller, 409 U.S. 488 (1973).

[78] Klein et al., *supra* note 10, at 386-388.

[79] *Id.* at 390 (citing Debra L. Donahue, THE WESTERN RANGE REVISITED: REMOVING LIVESTOCK FROM PUBLIC LANDS TO CONSERVE NATIVE BIODIVERSITY (1999); George Cameron Coggins & Margaret Lindberg-Johnson, *The Law of Public Rangeland Management II: The Commons and the Taylor Act,* 13 ENVTL. L. 1 (1982)).

[80] LAITOS HORNBOOK, *supra* note 1, at 271. *See also* Sacramento Grazing Assn., Inc. v. United States, 2017 WL 5029063 *32 (U.S.C.F.C. Nov. 3, 2017) (court determined that USFS's actions to restrict grazing rights in a national forest to protect endangered species effected a Fifth Amendment taking of SGA's right to beneficial use of stock water sources under New Mexico law).

[81] Pub. Lands Council v. Babbitt, 529 U.S. 728 (2000).

[82] *Id.* at 738.

[83] Public Rangelands Improvement Act (PRIA) of 1978, 43 U.S.C. §§1901, 1903 (2006).

Question

1. In Chapter 3, Section II.E, we described the tragedy of the commons. What is the connection between the tragedy of the commons and grazing? What laws contribute to the tragedy of the commons in grazing? How do the laws do so? How did those laws stress the resilience and sustainability of commons across the country in 1934?

A. Resilience and Sustainability of Rangelands

The ecological damage caused by grazing includes degradation of native species habitat, especially in riparian zones; water pollution; soil erosion; promotion of invasive species; and archeological and paleontological resources damage.[84] The Bureau of Land Management is responsible under the FLPMA for preparing land use plans that protect the ecological resources of federal rangeland and for administering the livestock-grazing program.[85] As a federal agency, BLM's actions are subject to the requirement that a "detailed environmental impact statement (EIS) be prepared for every major federal action significantly affecting the quality of the human environment."[86] In litigation over this NEPA requirement, the court in *Natural Resources Defense Council v. Morton* held that BLM's programmatic environment impact statement for the entire livestock-grazing program was insufficient and that the agency must assess the specific environmental effects of the permits.[87] BLM eventually agreed to prepare approximately 150 EISs, but not a separate EIS for each of its 24,000 grazing permits.[88] After Congress passed the FLPMA in 1976, the BLM merged the NEPA EIS requirements with the land use planning process required by FLPMA.[89] However, it appears that the BLM is still committed to grazing over other uses such as recreation, wildlife habitat, and watershed.[90]

Public rangeland may also support rights of way for transportation, energy transmission, and water pipelines, but the government may condition these rights of way to protect the environment and natural resources. Federal lands governed by the BLM may be accessible to citizens for

---

[84] Klein et al., *supra* note 10, at 435.
[85] NRDC v. Morton, 388 F. Supp. 829 (D.D.C. 1974), *aff'd*, 527 F.2d 1386 (D.C. Cir. 1976), *and aff'd sub nom.* Appeal of Pac. Legal Found., 527 F.2d 1386 (D.C. Cir. 1976).
[86] *Id.* at 832.
[87] *Id.* at 841-842.
[88] Klein et al., *supra* note 10, at 413-414.
[89] *Id.* at 414; *see also* NRDC v. Hodel, 624 F. Supp. 1045 (D. Nev. 1985), *aff'd*, 819 F.2d 927 (9th Cir. 1987).
[90] Laitos Hornbook, *supra* note 1, at 267.

outdoor recreation, but because of environmental damage caused by off-road vehicles (ORVs) such as snowmobiles, motorcycles, and four-wheelers, the BLM has authority to decide which areas will be open to such ORV usage. Finally, wild horses and burros compete with cattle and sheep grazing, but the Wild, Free-Roaming Horses and Burros Act of 1971 protects them against harm by private parties such as ranchers.[91]

Restoration: Secretary Bruce Babbitt of the Interior Department (DOI) made amendments to federal grazing regulations in the 1990s to hasten restoring federal rangelands. The ranching community opposed these amendments because they required increased accountability of permit holders, a change in the makeup of advisory boards to restrict the influence of the ranching community, and changes to the BLM's management practices. Ranchers challenged three of these amendments, but the Supreme Court in *Public Lands Council v. Babbitt* upheld the Secretary's change to the definition of "grazing preference," the removal of the requirement that a permit holder is "engaged in the livestock business," and the decision to grant the United States title to future permanent range improvements by agreement.[92]

Ranchers in the West continue to object to federal regulation of U.S. rangelands, which constitute approximately 80% of Nevada and half of Oregon. Ranchers argue that the federal government should release these holdings to the individual states. Some individual ranchers have directly challenged federal authority by obstructing federal officials, refusing to pay grazing fees, protesting, setting fires that spread onto land managed by the Bureau of Land Management (BLM), making death threats against managers of a National Wildlife Refuge in Oregon, and occupying with force the same refuge in early 2016.

Ammon Bundy is the son of Nevada rancher, Cliven Bundy, who owed over one million dollars in grazing fees and participated in a 2014 armed standoff with federal officials from the BLM in Nevada. Ammon was the alleged leader of the Oregon occupation in 2016, joined by his brother, Ryan, to protest the arson convictions and sentencing of father and son, Dwight and Steven Hammond. The Hammonds are Oregon ranchers with a history of obstructing federal authority and making death threats against managers of the wildlife refuge in Oregon. The court sentenced the Hammonds to five years in prison for setting fires in 2001 and 2006 that spread to federal land. Some considered this sentencing harsh, including the federal district court judge whose lighter sentence was overturned by the appellate court. The minimum five-year sentence was

---

[91] *Id.* at 276-277.
[92] *Id.* at 275-276.

the result of federal legislation enacted after the Oklahoma City bombing to increase penalties for arson committed against federal property.[93]

The armed occupation of the refuge lasted for almost six weeks and resulted in the fatal shooting of one of the protestors and the federal prosecution (and acquittals) of those involved. Such clashes are not new.[94] Although the federal government tries to "balance environmental protection and conservation with permitted uses[,] . . . ranchers, private land owners, and some local and state governments have fought for more control over how the land is used."[95] For example, the "Sagebrush Rebellion" in the late 1970s was an attempt by Western states to gain more control of federal lands within their borders.[96]

Rangeland sustainability requires that we treat these lands as more than just a resource to provide grazing for privately held livestock. We must manage them as ecosystems, providing a wealth of important benefits. We must assess and monitor the ecosystems supported by rangelands, particularly in the face of global climate change impacts on vegetation, soil, and water. Grazing livestock releases about 20% of U.S. methane emissions—a potent greenhouse gas (GHG). In addition, fecal-borne pathogens from livestock may contaminate freshwater drinking supplies unless we control access to certain areas. Globally, livestock production releases 18% of GHG emissions—more than the transportation sector releases.[97] Conversely, rangelands can trap carbon emissions and

[93] Colin Dwyer, *Or Ranchers and Rancor: The Roots of the Armed Occupation in Oregon*, NPR (Jan. 3, 2016, 6:25 PM), http://www.npr.org/sections/thetwo-way/2016/01/03/461831737/of-ranchers-and-rancor-the-roots-of-the-armed-occupation-in-oregon.

[94] The Associated Press, *Jury Acquits Leaders of Oregon Wildlife Refuge Occupation*, NBC News (Oct. 27, 2016), https://www.nbcnews.com/news/us-news/jury-acquits-leaders-oregon-wildlife-refuge-standoff-n674296.

[95] Brian Clark Howard, *Why Federal Lands Are so Wildly Controversial in the West*, Nat'l Geographic (Jan. 4, 2016), http://news.nationalgeographic.com/2016/01/160104-oregon-protest-malheur-national-wildlife-refuge/

[96] *Id.*

[97] Debra L. Donahue, *Elephant in the Room: Livestock's Role in Climate and Environmental Change*, 17 Mich. St. J. Int'l L. 95, 98 (2008).

forage can serve as biomass as well as grazing. Invasive species can also alter rangelands and change the ecosystem to encourage native weeds to replace native grasslands and habitats.[98] Because many in the developing world depend on small-scale, itinerant herding for survival, population growth is putting pressure on grazing lands, and farming interests are encroaching on these fragile lands, which may result in deforestation for livestock and agriculture needs. Commercial grazing in industrialized countries has also degraded public rangeland. Livestock production has adverse impacts on climate change and biodiversity, and unless we reduce consumption of these products, using rangelands to support grazing may not be sustainable.[99]

Questions

1. If you were in charge of establishing grazing fees on federal rangelands, what would you take into account when setting the fee? In other words, what is the true cost of grazing? In answering this question, consider the services rangelands provide and the cost of losing those services, including the potential consequences, such as the 1930s' Dust Bowl.

2. Should the federal government permit livestock grazing on federal land? If so, under what conditions? Are the current conditions sustainable or resilient?

3. Would the DOI regulations designed to assist restoration tend to increase or decrease system resilience? Does it depend on *which* system we are referencing? Which system(s)' resilience might increase? Which might decrease?

V. FISH AND WILDLIFE

The definition of wildlife typically includes only animals and excludes fish and plants. We have classified animals to denote their degree of wildness as wild, feral, tamed, or domesticated, although these categories are not always clearly defined or ascertainable in all circumstances.[100] Wildlife law and policy encompasses issues of ownership, consumption, conservation, recreation, preservation, ethical significance, and government jurisdiction.

---

[98] Brown et al., *supra* note 70.
[99] Donahue, *supra* note 97, at 120-121.
[100] Koop v. United States, 296 F.2d 53 (8th Cir. 1961).

Ownership and Scarcity: Property law and natural resources law govern ownership and establish both private and public rights to wildlife resources. The "rule of capture," best known to property law students from the *Pierson vs. Post* case (described earlier in Chapter 6, Section III.A), is about a fight over the carcass of a dead fox. The Rule provides that a person can gain ownership rights over an unowned wild animal by being the first to take it into possession by restricting its natural liberty and bringing it within certain control or dominion by mortally wounding or capturing the animal. We have also applied this Rule to other natural resources that are fugitive in nature such as oil and gas. Private land ownership limits the Rule in that we consider the landowner to have "constructive" possession of any wildlife captured on the landowner's private property, and thus the landowner has greater rights than the person who actually captures the wild animal.

As human populations have grown, wildlife resources in some areas have become scarce, and continued species survival has been threatened or endangered. Hunting, while still important for some native or developing country communities for subsistence or culture, is mainly a recreational sport for developed nations. Attempts by animal rights activists to interfere with hunting have engendered anti-hunting harassment legislation in some states. Some have successfully challenged this anti-hunting harassment legislation as an unconstitutional restriction on free speech.[101] Over time, the private property rules of capture and landowner possession have become subject to government regulation at the state, national, and international levels in order to attempt to control consumption and exploitation.[102]

Conservation and Preservation: Aldo Leopold's 1949 book of essays entitled *A Sand County Almanac* promoted conservation and preservation of wildlife and their habitats by encouraging humans to recognize a "land ethic" and relate to nature as just one member of the interwoven community of life. Animal rights proponents have challenged the view of animals as property or instruments for human utility and have argued that animals should have some degree of moral standing and significance.[103]

Wildlife provides many important functions, both consumptive and nonconsumptive. Wildlife provides food and other economic goods for local communities and for export, but it also provides ecological health, biodiversity, scientific research, and socio-cultural values such as aestheticism,

---

[101] *See* People v. Sanders, 696 N.E.2d 1144 (Ill. 1998).

[102] State v. Bartee, 894 S.W.2d 34 (Tex. App. 1994).

[103] *See generally The Moral Status of Animals*, STANFORD ENCYCLOPEDIA OF PHIL. (Sept. 13, 2010), http://plato.stanford.edu/entries/moral-animal/. *See, e.g.,* Richard L. Cupp Jr., *A Dubious Grail: Seeking Tort Law Expansion and Limited Personhood as Stepping Stones Toward Abolishing Animals' Property Status*, 60 SMU L. REV. 3 (2007); Richard L. Cupp, Jr., *Moving Beyond Animal Rights: A Legal/Contractualist Critique*, 46 SAN DIEGO L. REV. 27 (2009).

recreation, and tourism.[104] Indirect values of wildlife include sustaining ecosystems and their associated services, enabling scientific research, promoting the aesthetic appreciation of nature, and providing the existence value of wildlife for socio-cultural values. Therefore, the value of wildlife is both economically significant and nutritionally, ecologically, and culturally important.[105]

U.S. Regulation: The United States did not reference wildlife in its constitution and did not initially regulate wildlife on a national basis. Instead, states had primary jurisdiction over wildlife until the 1970s when the U.S. Supreme Court held that the federal government had power over wild animals under the Commerce Clause. However, the decision allowed states to protect and conserve wildlife so long as such regulation was consistent with national policies.[106]

The first federal act to conserve wildlife was the Lacey Act of 1900, which prohibited interstate shipments of wildlife taken in violation of state law; required labeling of interstate wildlife shipments; and required the federal government to conserve certain wildlife species.[107] The Lacey Act, as subsequently amended, provides federal regulation of wildlife commerce, which includes "any wild mammal, bird, reptile, amphibian, fish, mollusk, crustacean, arthropod, coelenterate, or other invertebrate."[108] In the early 1900s, there was also great concern about migratory bird populations and the United States enacted the Weeks-Mclean Migratory Bird Act in 1913 at the urging of the National Audubon Societies. States challenged this Act as infringing state rights to regulate wildlife, but the case became moot when Congress enacted the Migratory Bird Treaty Act in 1918 to enforce a 1916 treaty entered into by the United States and Great Britain (acting for Canada) to protect these birds.[109] The legislation authorized creating federal agencies, such as the U.S. Fish and Wildlife Services, and Congress enacted statutes to protect wildlife including, most notably, the Endangered Species Act (ESA) in 1973.

Under the Property Clause of the U.S. Constitution,[110] Congress has power over federal lands, which allows federal regulation of wildlife on

---

[104] Ph. Chardonnet, B. des Clers, J. Fischer, R. Gerhold, F. Jori & F. Lamarque, *The Value of Wildlife*, Rev. Sci. Tech. Off. Int. Epiz. 21 (1) (2002), http://www.oie.int/doc/ged/D510.PDF.

[105] *Id.*

[106] Hughes v. Oklahoma, 441 U.S. 322 (1979).

[107] Eric T. Freyfogle & Dale D. Goble, Wildlife Law: Cases and Materials 83 (2d ed. 2010).

[108] Lacey Act, 16 U.S.C. §3371(a); *see also* United States v. Butler, 694 F.3d 1177 (10th Cir. 2012); United States v. Place, 693 F.3d 219 (1st Cir. 2012); United States v. Reeves, 891 F. Supp. 2d 690 (D.N.J. 2012).

[109] Missouri v. Holland, 252 U.S. 416 (1920); *see also* Wild Bird Conservation Act of 1992, 16 U.S.C. §§4901-4916 (protecting birds not naturally found in the United States); Neotropical Bird Conservation Act of 1999, 16 U.S.C. §§6101-6109 (protecting U.S. bird species that winter in Latin America and the Caribbean); United States v. Boynton, 63 F.3d 337 (1995).

[110] U.S. Const. art. IV, § 3, cl. 2 ("The Congress shall have Power to dispose of and make all needful Rules and Regulations respecting the Territory or other Property belonging to the United States.").

these lands such as the Wild Free-Roaming Horses and Burros Act of 1971. This Act protects and manages these animals on public lands. The U.S. Supreme Court upheld the Act as applied to federal public lands, but the Court did not decide whether the Act would apply to private lands under the Property Clause.[111] Congress assigned primary responsibility for wildlife management to the states and does not require federal permits to hunt and fish on public lands unless the federal government, in consultation with the applicable state fish and game department, designates certain federal lands as prohibiting hunting or fishing.[112] Nevertheless, in several areas Congress has asserted its power to protect and manage wildlife on federal, state, and private lands, most notably with the enactment of the ESA, which applies to all U.S. wildlife.

The U.S. Bureau of Land Management (BLM) "manages" the wild horses roaming on rangelands. Pursuant to the Wild Free-Roaming Horse and Burro Act of 1971, the BLM tracks their numbers (approximately 49,000 in 2016), corrals thousands of wild horses each year, and takes them to "temporary holding pens, where they're fattened up with rich grains and then sold for adoption. . . . Environmental groups say the bureau collects too many horses from the wild each year. This year the bureau hopes to round up 13,000 horses and over the next five years the plan is to reduce populations from about 49,000 to 27,000." Amanda Onion, *Why Are They Killing the Wild Horses*, ABC NEWS (Jan. 31, 2016), http://abcnews.go.com/US/story?id=94255&page=1.

Wildlife Management: While Congress intended that states have primary responsibility for wildlife management, states' wildlife management rights are subject to treaty claims by Native American tribes in the Pacific Northwest[113] and other areas of the country for tribal hunting and fishing rights.[114] Indian Nations manage wildlife on their own reservations so long as there are no off-reservation effects subjecting them to state control.[115] Federal government wildlife regulations may also come into conflict with tribal rights when tribal members kill wildlife protected under federal laws such as the Bald Eagle Protection Act, the Migratory Bird Treaty Act, or the Endangered Species Act (ESA).[116] Because Indian Nations have the sovereign right to regulate reservation wildlife, the Lacey Act protects against tribal and non-tribal persons who "export, sell, receive, acquire, or

[111] *See* Kleppe v. New Mexico, 426 U.S. 529 (1976) (discussing the constitutionality of the Wild Free-Roaming Horses and Burros Act of 1971, 16 U.S.C. §§1331-1340).
[112] *See* Defenders of Wildlife v. Andrus, 627 F.2d 1238 (D.C. Cir. 1980).
[113] Puyallup Tribe, Inc. v. Dept. of Game of Wash., 433 U.S. 165 (1977).
[114] Minnesota v. Mille Lacs Band of Chippewa Indians, 526 U.S. 172 (1999).
[115] New Mexico v. Mescalero Apache Tribe, 462 U.S. 324 (1983).
[116] United States v. Dion, 476 U.S. 734 (1986).

purchase any fish or wildlife . . . taken or possessed . . . in violation of any Indian tribal law."[117]

The ESA addresses concerns about the extinction of fish, wildlife, and plant species in the United States as well as concerns about the ecosystems upon which endangered and threatened species depend.[118] The ESA focuses on critical habitat for threatened or endangered species, which is "any species which is in danger of extinction throughout all or a significant portion of its range."[119] The Secretary of the Interior, Commerce, or Agriculture determines whether any species is endangered or threatened "solely on the basis of the best scientific and commercial data available," and designates critical habitat, taking into consideration the economic impact of identifying particular areas as such.[120] Agencies must then promulgate regulations to conserve, protect, recover, and monitor these identified species and habitat. In addition, all federal agencies must ensure that any action authorized, funded, or carried out by the agency does not "jeopardize the continued existence of any endangered species or threatened species or result in the destruction or adverse modification of [designated critical] habitat of such species."[121] If the agency determines that there are endangered or threatened species, or critical habitat in the area of proposed federal action, the agency must prepare a biological assessment. This assessment determines whether formal consultation with the Secretary is required because the action may adversely affect these species or habitats. A biological opinion is prepared to identify reasonable and prudent alternatives to the action and determine whether a "taking" (e.g., harming) is "incidental to the agency action" and whether alternative action will minimize or mitigate such impact.[122]

International Wildlife Law: A basic premise of international wildlife law is that sovereign nations have power over the natural resources within their borders. The Stockholm Declaration of the United Nations Conference on the Human Environment in 1972 identified this premise in Principle 21, giving sovereign nations the right to exploit their resources so long as their actions did not harm the environment of other nations. The 1992 International Convention on Biological Diversity affirmed Principle 21, but also recognized the value of wildlife in supporting biological diversity

---

[117] Lacey Act, 16 U.S.C. §3371(a)(1).
[118] Endangered Species Act, 16 U.S.C. §§1531-1544.
[119] *Id.* §1532(6).
[120] *Id.* §1533(b)(1)(A).
[121] *Id.* §1536(a)(2).
[122] *See* Babbitt v. Sweet Home Chapter of Cmtys. for a Greater Or., 515 U.S. 687 (1995); Ariz. Cattle Growers' Assn. v. U.S. Fish & Wildlife, 273 F.3d 1229 (9th Cir. 2001); Nat'l Assn. of Home Builders v. Babbitt, 130 F.3d 1041 (D.C. Cir. 1997); *see also Endangered Species Act: Issue Overview*, HOUSE COMM. ON NATURAL RES., http://naturalresources.house.gov/esa/ (last visited Sept. 29, 2017) (stating that more than 500 ESA-related lawsuits have been filed or opened against the federal government since 2009).

and ecosystem functioning to ensure the success of the human economy. The 1993 Convention on Biological Diversity incorporated sovereign rights to exploit resources so long as there was no transboundary harm but also obligated states to conserve biological diversity and use biological resources sustainably. These principles of sovereign exploitation, avoidance of harm to other nations, and conservation of biodiversity and ecosystem management may create conflicts requiring international agreements.

International wildlife protection through the 1973 Convention on International Trade in Endangered Species (CITES) and other conventions have generated conflicts between conservation and commercial trade in wildlife and wildlife products. The principle of sustainable use is a way to manage wildlife by taking into account the needs of local people in developing countries and properly valuing wildlife such that we can protect species while still allowing sustainable trade. Wildlife is a renewable resource so long as we use it sustainably and we properly account for its value. The African elephant and the ivory market illustrates how the market will not work to preserve the survival of the species since ivory poachers do not have to account for the value of lost elephants for tourism or existence value. Instead, we need regulation or liability to prevent killings.[123] The 1983 Convention on the Conservation of Migratory Species of Wild Animals ("Bonn Convention") also protects the African elephant since it crosses national boundaries.

Whales and Fish: International wildlife law began in the late 1800s with treaties among the European countries of Germany, Switzerland, France, Luxembourg, and the Netherlands to allocate fishing rights in the Rhine River. International agreements focusing on conservation instead of allocation to prevent a "tragedy of the commons" on open seas arose during this period to control industrial whaling, species preservation, and fur-seal fishing in the Behring Sea by Russia, the United States, Great Britain (for Canada), and Japan.[124] International regulation of whaling began with the Convention for the Regulation of Whaling in 1931, led to the International Agreement for the Regulation of Whaling in 1937, and culminated in the International Convention for the Regulation of Whaling (ICRW) in 1946 near the end of World War II. These agreements were the result of declining populations and near extinction of several whale species (such as right whales, bowhead whales, blue whales, and gray whales) and the oversupply of whale oil in the market from overharvesting. The ICRW recognized the history of over-fishing of whale stocks and established international

---

[123] *See* Freyfogle & Goble, *supra* note 107, at 713-734.
[124] Kurkpatrick Dorsey, THE DAWN OF CONSERVATION DIPLOMACY: U.S.-CANADIAN WILDLIFE PROTECTION TREATIES IN THE PROGRESSIVE ERA 105-165 (1998).

regulations to conserve and develop whale fisheries and allow for the "orderly development of the whaling industry."[125]

The ICRW enactment in 1948 established the International Whaling Commission (IWC) to control international whaling, but the Commission consistently set catch limits in excess of sustainable use. As a result, whales were overharvested and we needed to prevent extinction by taking drastic measures. In 1982, the IWC passed a moratorium on commercial whaling to stop whaling from the 1985–1986 season onward; this ban on whaling illustrated a shift of focus from sustainable commercial practices to species conservation. Following the moratorium, Iceland withdrew from the IWC and Norway and Japan challenged the ban as not supported by scientific evidence. Japan attempted to avoid the ban by arguing that its coastal villages traditionally relied on subsistence whaling and were "aboriginal" and exempt from IWC regulation. Japan has also obtained scientific permits to allow scientific investigations that some believe are a pretense for the commercial killings of whales.[126] The moratorium has impacted indigenous peoples, such as the Inuit in the Arctic, because their aboriginal tribal culture is centered on whaling and they are being forced to abandon it.[127] There are other international conventions that are potentially applicable to whales, such as CITES and the 1982 United Nations Convention on the Law of the Sea (UNCLOS).[128]

INTERNATIONAL CONVENTION FOR THE REGULATION OF WHALING AND *AUSTRALIA v. JAPAN*

Opened for signature in 1946, the Convention has approximately 89 member nations, including the United States. As structured, nations may leave the Convention at will and several have including the Netherlands, Norway, and Sweden, only to rejoin later. The objective of the Convention is to "provide for the proper conservation of whale stocks and thus make possible the orderly development of the whaling industry."[129] As mentioned above, pursuant to the Convention in 1982, the IWC established a moratorium on commercial whaling in response to a CITES report identifying many whale species as being in danger of extinction. The only permitted uses are aboriginal subsistence and scientific permits.

In response to the moratorium, Norway and Iceland objected and continued to issue their own quotas. Japan did not submit a reservation to the moratorium and instead continued to hunt under the scientific exception. In May 1994, the IWC voted to

---

[125] International Convention for the Regulation of Whaling, Nov. 19, 1956, 10 U.S.T. 952, 161 U.N.T.S. 72.
[126] Cinnamon Pinon Carlarne, *Saving the Whales in the New Millennium: International Institutions, Recent Developments and the Future of International Whaling Policies*, 24 Va. Envtl. L.J. 1, 18-20 (2005).
[127] Rupa Gupta, *Indigenous Peoples and the International Environmental Community: Accommodating Claims through a Cooperative Legal Process*, 74 N.Y.U. L. Rev. 1741 (1999).
[128] Celeste Black, *Whaling Update*, 5 Australian Animal Protection L.J. 82, 82-88 (2011).
[129] *History and Purpose*, International Whaling Commission, https://iwc.int/history-and-purpose (last visited Sept. 30, 2017).

create an almost 12 million square mile sanctuary habitat named the Southern Ocean Sanctuary, and it banned the use of factory ships.[130]

Japan granted permits to kill thousands of whales for scientific reasons based on Article VIII of the Convention. Permits were issued pursuant to the Japanese Whale Research Program under Special Permit in the Antarctic (JARPA II) in the Southern Ocean Sanctuary. Australia sued in the International Court of Justice claiming Japan ignored the moratorium and the prohibition on commercial hunting in the Southern Ocean Sanctuary and breached its obligations to preserve marine mammals and the marine environment under the CITES and the Convention on Biological Diversity.

The ICJ ruled that Japan must halt its current whaling program in the Southern Ocean, but that it may continue to hunt in the northern Pacific, as long as it conducts these hunts within the requirements of the Convention. The ICJ went on to rule that Japan's whaling program lacked scientific merit, specifically in the large-scale lethal sampling. The court reviewed 1) the purposes of Japan's whaling program, and 2) whether it involved scientific research under the reasonableness standard. While the court found that it could characterize JARPA II as scientific research, it held that the design and implementation (i.e., lethal take) of the research was unreasonable. Japan failed to provide any "evidence pointing to consideration of the feasibility of non-lethal methods." A "State party may not, in order to fund the research for which a special permit has been granted, use lethal sampling on a greater scale than is otherwise reasonable in relation to achieving the programme's stated objectives."[131] The United Nations Security Council is responsible for enforcing ICJ rulings, but it has not yet (as of 2017) enforced the 2014 ruling against Japan.[132]

The U.S. Marine Mammal Protection Act of 1972 prohibits the taking of mammals from U.S. waters or the high seas in order to ensure an optimum sustainable population.[133] The National Marine Fisheries Service (NMFS) and the U.S. Fish and Wildlife Service (FWS) enforce this Act to protect species such as whales, porpoises, dolphins, manatees, polar bears, sea otters, seals, sea lions, and walruses.[134] To avoid the incidental take of dolphins, the United States, as part of its regulatory program to protect these animals, required tuna importers to meet certain fishing standards. Mexico successfully challenged these requirements for restricting free trade under the General Agreement on Tariffs and Trade (GATT).[135]

---

[130] *Whale Sanctuaries*, INTERNATIONAL WHALING COMMISSION, https://iwc.int/sanctuaries (last visited Sept. 30, 2017).
[131] Whaling in the Antarctic (Australia v. Japan: New Zealand intervening), Judgment, I.C.J. Reports (Mar. 31, 2014), p. 226.
[132] Note, John Arnold, *Call Me Ishimaru: Independent Enforcement of International Agreements*, 44 B.C. ENVTL. AFF. L. REV. 331 (2017).
[133] Marine Mammal Protection Act, 16 U.S.C. §§ 1361-1407 (1972).
[134] *See, e.g.*, United States v. Hayashi, 22 F.3d 859 (9th Cir. 1993).
[135] *Dispute Panel Report on Mexican Complaint Concerning United States Restrictions on Imports of Tuna*, 30 I.L.M.J. 1594 (1991), http://www.worldtradelaw.net/reports/gattpanels/tuna dolphinI.pdf; *see also General Agreement on Tariffs and Trade: Dispute Settlement Panel Report on United States Restrictions on Imports of Tuna*, 33 I.L.M. 839 (1994), http://heinonline.org/HOL/ LandingPage?handle = hein.journals/intlm33&div = 110&id = &page = .

Similar import restrictions based on environmental concerns with shrimp trawling that harms sea turtles were also successfully challenged by India, Malaysia, Pakistan, and Thailand.[136] The North American Free Trade Agreement (NAFTA) of 1993 incorporates environmental protection and sustainable development into its goals, but side agreements such as the North American Agreement on Environmental Cooperation have been the most effective approach for discussing and settling environmental issues.[137]

International Fishing: Commercial fishing in the oceans constitutes a major use of natural resources throughout the world, but as with any common resource, these resources will be subject to a tragedy of the commons unless regulated nationally, internationally, or collaboratively.[138] Coastal nations claim sovereignty over territorial seas 200 miles from their coastlines under UNCLOS, which established exclusive economic zones (EEZ),[139] and the United States regulates its territory under the Magnuson-Stevens Fishery Conservation and Management Act (FCMA) of 1976 by asserting a 197-mile EEZ.[140] Within the United States, states may regulate fishing within three miles out from their coasts, but their regulations are subject to constitutional limitations such as the Commerce Clause and the Equal Protection Clause.[141] International agreements, such as UNCLOS, control international fishing, however, enforcement of these agreements against non-signatories has been difficult, and the agreements have not been successful in conserving the fisheries.[142] When UNCLOS established the 200-mile EEZs, countries financed bigger fishing fleets and exacerbated overfishing problems, even though UNCLOS imposed environmental responsibility on nations to ensure resource conservation.[143]

U.S. Fishing Regulations: The FCMA regulatory regime over fisheries establishes the EEZ and claims sovereign and exclusive fishery management over all of the fish in this zone, as well as exclusive authority over anadromous species that spawn in U.S. waters and all Continental Shelf fish resources.[144] The United States also pledges to cooperate with other nations to ensure conservation and promote optimal yield of fish that are highly migratory.[145] Congress enacted the FCMA as the primary domestic

---

[136] Appellate Body Report, *United States–Import Prohibition of Certain Shrimp and Shrimp Products,* WT/DS58/AB/R (*adopted* Nov. 6, 1998), *reprinted in* 38 I.L.M. 121 (1999); *see also* Freyfogle & Goble, *supra* note 106, at 648-674 (Wetlands, Trade and Wildlife: Sea Turtles and Shrimp, Dolphins and Tuna).
[137] Freyfogle & Goble, *supra* note 107, at 759-761.
[138] Freyfogle & Goble, *id.* at 924.
[139] United Nations Convention on the Law of the Sea, art. 57, Oct. 12, 1982, U.N.T.S. 1833-1835.
[140] Freyfogle & Goble, *supra* note 107, at 926.
[141] *Id.* at 925.
[142] *Id.*
[143] *Id.*
[144] *Id.* at 926.
[145] *Id.* at 927.

regulation over fish stocks based more on fishing concerns than on environmental interests.[146] The Sustainable Fisheries Act amended the FCMA in 1996 to require greater consideration of ecological factors in assessing catch levels and protecting habitats.[147] The Amendment created the Ecosystem Principles Advisory Panel to advise Congress on how best to manage fisheries in light of ecological concerns. The Panel also has authority to restrict fishing equipment, control time and area closures, and establish harvest limits.

A. Resilience and Sustainability of Fish Stocks

The fishing industry has not sustainably managed commercially important fish stocks. Although we have designed regulatory frameworks to sustain fish stocks, politics, lack of enforcement, weak and unreliable scientific data, and the poor articulation of legal standards have resulted in more than 20% of the world's freshwater fish species becoming extinct, threatened, or endangered in the last few decades.[148] *Overfishing* is the most significant problem. As illustrated in the Atlantic cod example in Chapter 1, a boat's overcapacity in terms of storage space and the enhanced technology used to find fish are often responsible for overfishing. In addition, once one species is overfished, fishers often move to another species — as was the case when the Atlantic cod was exhausted.[149]

Bycatch is another major problem. Bycatch results when the fishing process traps other aquatic life and that product dies or is thrown away by the fishing boat that is not trading in that product. Shrimp fishing in the Gulf of Mexico, for example, frequently results in four times more bycatch than the amount of target shrimp.[150]

Habitat loss is another major threat to fish. Land-based marine pollution is the greatest cause of habitat loss. For example, the agricultural runoff from states along the Mississippi River is the primary pollution source that has created up to 7,000 square miles of dead zone in the Gulf of Mexico.[151] The pollution that destroys habitat also pollutes the fish

---

[146] *See generally*, 16 U.S.C. §1801. "[T]he purposes of the Congress in this chapter [are] . . . to conserve and manage the fishery resources found off the coasts of the United States [and] to promote domestic commercial and recreational fishing under sound conservation and management principles. . . ." §1801(b)(1), (3).

[147] *Sustainable Fisheries Act of 1996*, NOAA, http://www.nmfs.noaa.gov/sfa/laws_policies/msa/sfa.html (last visited Sept 30, 2017).

[148] Freshwater Threats, NAT'L GEOGRAPHIC, http://www.nationalgeographic.com/environment/habitats/freshwater-threats/ (last visited Sept. 30, 2017).

[149] George A. Rose, COD: THE ECOLOGICAL HISTORY OF THE NORTH ATLANTIC FISHERIES 388 (2007).

[150] *What Is Bycatch?*, CONSORTIUM FOR WILDLIFE BYCATCH REDUCTION, http://www.bycatch.org/about-bycatch (last visited Sept. 30, 2017).

[151] *2015 Gulf of Mexico dead zone "above average,"* NOAA (Aug. 4, 2015), http://www.noaanews.noaa.gov/stories2015/080415-gulf-of-mexico-dead-zone-above-average.html ("above average" 2015 dead zone was 6,474 square miles).

themselves, resulting in fish consumption advisory warnings for problems such as mercury poisoning.

We will need better management of fisheries based on carrying capacity and surplus production to enhance the resilience and sustainability of aquatic life systems. The "maximum sustainable yield" is the greatest annual catch that ensures a sustainable population.[152] Sadly, there is often not enough or inadequate research to determine this annual number with any degree of accuracy and it is difficult to assess the stock that exists in the ocean at any point in time. Nevertheless, we make informed guesses as to the annual catch number and governments issue quotas to control the total allowable catch.[153] The United States issues individual transferable quotas to

---

[152] Freyfogle & Goble, *supra* note 107, at 930.
[153] *Id.* at 931.

large and small fisheries, while Greenland, Iceland, and New Zealand use community development quotas to give nonprofit groups a portion of the total allowable catch that will benefit just their community. However, because of the inherent tension between protecting both economic concerns and the environment, governments may have difficulty enforcing quotas and establishing sustainable quotas. Catch restrictions may not be followed by fisheries because of the pressure to bring back a big catch, and fishers may be encouraged to race to catch their quota before open fishing time is closed, resulting in unsafe "derby fishing."[154]

Other methods of resolving these sustainability challenges include: vessel buyback schemes to reduce the capacity of the fishing boats; environmentally protected areas where no one is allowed to fish; and consumer choice of environmentally responsible products from sustainable fisheries that comply with certification standards of an organization such as the Marine Stewardship Council to receive an eco-friendly label.

 In *Putting Resilience Theory into Practice: The Example of Fisheries Management*, 31 WTR Nat. Resources & Env't 3 (2017), Robin Kundis Craig highlights the ways in which "maximum sustainable yield" is not compatible with the concept of resilience:

Like other natural resources laws, marine fisheries laws assume the general predictability of fisheries resources. . . . This assumption is embodied in both international and U.S. law in the goal of "maximum sustainable yield" (MSY).

Under the third United Nations Convention on the Law of the Sea (UNCLOS III, which the non-party United States generally accepts as customary international law), coastal nations must enact conservation measures for marine resources "designed to maintain or restore populations of harvested species at levels which can produce the maximum sustainable yield, as qualified by relevant environmental and economic factors." UNCLOS III, art. 61(3). . . . Similarly, under the United States' Magnuson-Stevens Fishery Conservation and Management Act, management measures in federal fishery management plans "shall prevent overfishing while achieving, on a continuing basis, the optimum yield from each fishery for the United States fishing industry." 16 U.S.C. §1851(a)(1).

"Optimum" yield, in turn, "is prescribed on the basis of the maximum sustainable yield from the fishery, as reduced by any relevant social, economic, or ecological factor; . . ." 16 U.S.C. §1802(33)(B). In contrast, "overfishing" occurs when "a rate or level of fishing mortality[] jeopardizes the capacity of a fishery to produce the maximum sustainable yield on a continuing basis." 16 U.S.C. §1802(34). Thus, both international and U.S. law promote—even demand—the "full" exploitation of fisheries resources. . . .

[S]etting MSY as the goal presents a number of problems for healthy marine ecosystems in the Anthropocene. First, for both scientific and political reasons, achieving MSY without crossing into overfishing is, as a practical matter, very difficult. . . .

---

[154] *See* Clare Leschin-Hoar, *Study: Program to Protect Fish Is Saving Fishermen's Lives, Too*, NPR (Feb. 16, 2016), http://www.npr.org/sections/thesalt/2016/02/16/466612148/study-program-to-protect-fish-is-saving-fishermens-lives-too.

Second, MSY-based fisheries management makes it exceedingly difficult for managers to consider system dynamics in a constantly changing world. While optimum yield calculations under the Magnuson-Stevens Act can clearly take account of ecosystem dynamics, the MSY calculations on which they are based focus on specific stocks, 50 C.F.R. §600.310(e)(1)(i)(A), perpetuating a data gap and translation problem between the MSY and optimum yield calculations. . . . In ecological resilience terms, therefore, commercial fishing has already reduced both the total biodiversity and the functional diversity of global marine ecosystems.

In addition, fishing to MSY by definition reduces the overall populations of the target species from their natural maximums and assumes that fish are "surplus" if they are not needed for replacement breeding. H. Rep. No. 94-445 (1975), reprinted in 1976 U.S.C.C.A.N. 593, 615. . . . In terms of ecological resilience, therefore, the pursuit of MSY reduces targeted species' resilience to other kinds of shocks and disturbances in the system by reducing both response diversity (the lack of prolific breeders) and the species' simple numeric chances of survival.

For all of the above reasons, MSY-based fishing also disturbs the panarchical interactions of nested marine ecosystems in ways that are, at best, poorly understood. However, historical studies strongly suggest that marine fishing has been undermining both the engineering and ecological resilience of marine ecosystems, making ecological thresholds easier to cross. For example, extirpation of sea otters along the U.S. Pacific coast led to the transformation of many kelp forest ecosystems because the loss of sea otters allowed sea urchins to multiply unchecked, decimating the kelp on which they feed. . . .

Finally, calculating MSY assumes constant environmental conditions. . . . However, if marine environments are constantly changing, there is no scientifically valid way to calculate MSY because there is no way to know how the targeted population will respond on a long-term basis. . . . Indeed, environmental conditions in the ocean have been changing for a long time, exacerbated now by climate change. . . . Land-based pollution and habitat destruction have profoundly altered coastal ecosystems around the world. Moreover, because many coastal ecosystems serve as nurseries for species that then migrate to deeper waters, the impacts of coastal alteration ripple into deeper marine ecosystems. Toxic and plastic pollution affect every marine ecosystem on the planet, even the Southern Ocean around Antarctica. Climate change is warming the ocean, altering marine currents and causing species to migrate poleward, both of which are creating new configurations of species and altering ecosystem function. Changing marine currents can also create or exacerbate hypoxic or "dead" zones—areas of low oxygen traditionally resulting from nutrient pollution. Arctic Ocean sea ice is melting. Finally, as the ocean absorbs carbon dioxide from the atmosphere, the pH of the ocean is dropping, interfering with organisms' abilities to form shells and other life functions.

We currently have very little idea what all of these changes to marine ecosystems mean for particular species except that many of those species are, in fact, responding to these changes.

Question and Note

1. As set forth in Chapter 2, given the drastic reductions and eliminations of species since the Industrial Revolution, are the current laws sufficient to support a sustainable social-ecological system around wildlife and fish? Which systems' resilience thrives under the existing legal regime and which are made more vulnerable?

2. Scholars have raised a number of challenges concerning the 1973 Convention on International Trade in Endangered Species (CITES), including:

- CITES focuses on trade at the species level and does not address habitat loss or ecosystems approach to conservation;
- It regulates in the manner of a "negative list" such that trade in all species is permitted and unregulated unless the species in question appears on the Appendices and a showing is made to justify the listing in the Appendices;
- It seeks to prevent unsustainable use rather than promote sustainable use;
- It does not explicitly address market demand;
- It does not list some of the most important and vulnerable species, such as several fisheries;
- It allows nations to opt-out of specific listings;
- It is difficult to amend; and
- Some nations are not complying with it.[155]

VI. STRATEGY TO FACILITATE IMPLEMENTATION #6: ADAPTIVE GOVERNANCE

Enhancing ecosystem resilience and sustainability requires that systems, such as the social-ecological systems surrounding fish, adapt to changing circumstances as those changes arise. As new technologies reveal more information concerning complex social-ecological systems and the changes they are experiencing, policies will need to adapt. Adaptive Governance (AG) is an approach to policy that incorporates flexibility to accommodate change. AG provides a process that gives decision makers the opportunity to modify policies and programs and make adjustments to respond to new information. AG moves away from one-time, static decision making and embodies a process in which decisions are constantly monitored, evaluated, and altered based on the incoming information.

Once we make a decision based on the best information available, AG provides a process that facilitates the altering of that decision as information improves and shows internal and external system changes. In this way, AG is a flexible method of developing a policy that can help reduce vulnerabilities and alter unsustainable conditions. In incorporating a process for change, AG recognizes uncertainty and social-ecological system complexities and provides opportunities to learn from system changes and apply new knowledge.

---

[155] *See, e.g.,* David Favre, *Debate within the CITES Community: What Direction for the Future?,* 33 Nat. Resources J. 875 (1993); William C. Burns, *CITES and the Regulation of International Trade in Endangered Species of Flora: A Critical Appraisal,* 8 Dick. J. Int'l L. 203 (1990).

A. General Description of Adaptive Governance

Adaptive Governance fills a critical gap in policy making by instituting a process focused on the constant flow of information and on providing an outlet to incorporate that information into decision making. In doing so, AG represents a dramatic shift from the current use of static policy approaches. Traditional policy approaches are based on past information, are fixed, and do not contain a method for re-evaluation. Focusing on natural resources, Professor J.B. Ruhl describes the current predominant policy approach as:

> [N]atural resource management agencies are locked in an administrative law system that . . . shows no sign of being flexible. . . . The system's fixation on pre-decisional environmental assessment, cost-benefit analysis, records of decisions, and judicial review litigation has only pushed the system toward a "front-end" focus on reliability and efficiency.[156]

The traditional method involves the "front end" gathering of information to establish a foundation and then fixing a policy based on that foundation. There is little if any, continual evaluation and monitoring to determine if the policy is functioning according to plan and whether there are unintended consequences. "Fixed rules are likely to fail because they place too much confidence in the current state of knowledge, whereas systems that guard against the low probability, high consequence possibilities and allow for change may be suboptimal in the short run but prove wiser in the long run. This is a principal lesson of adaptive management research."[157]

In many ways, Adaptive Governance is a *learning process* through experience. With AG, policy makers observe new data—including what is actually working and how the system reacts—to adjust policies to respond to the data. For example, new information concerning climate change impacts on oceans (discussed in more depth in Chapter 10) is regularly coming to light. As that information becomes available, policies that are not subject to an AG process risk becoming obsolete or counterproductive, as they do not respond to the new conditions. Policies that integrate an AG process require constant revision and reworking to adapt to the new conditions. In this regard, AG is helpful to achieve underlying goals, such as improving system resilience or sustainability, because it allows for policy changes that are no longer consistent with the underlying goals.

---

[156] J.B. Ruhl, *General Design Principles for Resilience and Adaptive Capacity in Legal Systems: Applications to Climate Change Adaptation Law*, 89 N.C. L. Rev. 1373, 1392-1393 (2011).
[157] Elinor Ostrom, Thomas Dietz & Paul C. Stern, *The Struggle to Govern the Commons*, Sci. 302(5652), 1907-1912 (2003).

In the piece below, scientist Carl Folke and others set forth core aspects necessary to implement AG successfully. Using ecosystems (Ecosystem Services Management is discussed in Chapter 3, Section VI) as the relevant context, Folke et al. highlight how AG is well-suited to help policy makers address uncertainty and to monitor, evaluate, learn, and experiment.

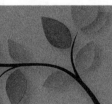

Carl Folke et al., *Adaptive Governance of Social-Ecological Systems*

30 ANNU. REV. ENVIRON. RESOUR. 441, 443 (2005)

Adaptive management is often put forward as a more realistic and promising approach to deal with ecosystem complexity than management for optimal use and control of resources. . . .

Because the self-organizing properties of complex ecosystems and associated management systems seem to cause uncertainty to grow over time, understanding should be continuously updated and adjusted, and each management action viewed as an opportunity to further learn how to adapt to changing circumstances. This is the foundation for active adaptive management wherein policies become hypotheses, and management actions become the experiments to test those hypotheses. . . .

Adaptive governance focuses on experimentation and learning, and it brings together research on institutions and organizations for collaboration, collective action, and conflict resolution in relation to natural resource and ecosystem management. . . . The notion of adaptation implies capacity to respond to change and even transform social-ecological systems into improved states.

The review highlights the following four interacting aspects of importance in adaptive governance of complex social-ecological systems:

- Build knowledge and understanding of resource and ecosystem dynamics; detecting and responding to environmental feedback in a fashion that contributes to resilience require ecological knowledge and understanding of ecosystem processes and functions. . . .
- Feed ecological knowledge into adaptive management practices; successful management is characterized by continuous testing, monitoring, and reevaluation to enhance adaptive responses, acknowledging the inherent uncertainty in complex systems.
- Support flexible institutions and multilevel governance systems. . . . The sharing of management power and responsibility may involve multiple and often polycentric institutional and organizational linkages among user groups or communities, government agencies, and

nongovernmental organizations. . . . Adaptive comanagement relies on the collaboration of a diverse set of stakeholders, operating at different levels through social networks.

● Deal with external perturbations, uncertainty and surprise; it is not sufficient for a well-functioning multilevel governance system to be in tune with the dynamics of the ecosystems under management. It also needs to develop capacity for dealing with changes in climate, disease outbreaks, hurricanes, global market demands, subsidies, and governmental policies. The challenge for the social-ecological system is to accept uncertainty, be prepared for change and surprise, and enhance the adaptive capacity to deal with disturbance.

B. Specific Description of AG's Relevance to R&S

As Carl Folke et al. note above, Adaptive Governance is about reacting to system changes, which can help avoid system vulnerabilities and catastrophic, unsustainable results. AG helps us understand whether and how changes are affecting a system, such that it is trending toward an increase or decrease in sustainability or resilience. It provides a process to give opportunities to alter policies when those policies make a system more vulnerable and unsustainable.

AG accounts for conditions relevant to social-ecological systems that are constantly changing. When we work with complex systems, unintended consequences or new conditions may arise no matter how thoroughly we plan. In addition, technology can change, providing new information on how systems are functioning. AG helps recognize the potential for these changes and their importance in affecting a system's resilience and sustainability.

> *Because ecosystems, their outputs, and adaptive cycles are complex and difficult to predict, AG can help enhance resilience by providing . . . officials with a constant flow of relevant information on how these systems are changing and a process to adapt. AG represents a [process] to help navigate the complexities embedded in social-ecological systems. "[T]he emphasis in resilience thinking is on understanding the dynamics and complexities of the [social-ecological systems], not on determining and then maintaining a fixed system state. The emphasis is building adaptive capacity rather than maintaining stationarity." "Scholars of resilience call for AG to deal with uncertainty in the face of unexpected disturbance."*[158]

---

[158]Jonathan Rosenbloom, *Fifty Shades of Gray Infrastructure: Land Use & the Failure to Create Resilient Cities*, 91 WASH. L. REV. __ (2018) (citations omitted).

AG may also help policy makers avoid decisions that result in social-ecological system failures, risking future generations' opportunities. For example, when we found that substances such as chlorofluorocarbons deplete the ozone layer, the international community adopted and altered which ozone-depleting substances it would phase out. As we discover new substances that damage the ozone layer, we add them to the list of controlled substances to phase out.

For purposes of AG, "governance" is not equivalent to public "government." Rather, it applies equally to all forms of public and private institutional arrangements. Governance may occur "through laws, regulations, discursive debates, negotiation, mediation, conflict resolution, elections, public consultations, and protests, amongst other decision-making processes."[159] Thus, AG can be useful to many people and entities across governing bodies and disciplines.

You recall from Chapter 1 that the Adaptive Cycle relevant to resilience consists of two loops (a fore and back loop). These loops help indicate the system's susceptibility to regime change and permanently alter the system. At each stage of the Adaptive Cycle, we can access information, including early information as to a system's vulnerabilities. For example, during the fore loop phases, we can access information as to which resources and inputs build resilience and which changes lead to vulnerabilities. During the back loop phases, we can assess information showing the potential for sudden change and system reorganization. All of this data is useful for helping policy makers adapt to system changes and alter policies as needed.

C. Illustration of Adaptive Governance's Application to Resilience and Sustainability

In the following piece, the authors evaluate the Adaptive Governance system used for fisheries off the coast of Kenya. The authors base their analysis on three core inquiries that help form an Adaptive Governance process: 1) the availability of information to understand environmental change, 2) the use of this information to inform decision making, and 3) the decisions that result in resilient systems.

---

[159] *Id.*

Louisa S. Evans, Katrina Brown & Edward H. Allison, *Factors Influencing Adaptive Marine Governance in a Developing Country Context: a Case Study of Southern Kenya*

ECOLOGY AND SOCIETY 16(2): 21 (2011)

Small-scale fisheries and the coastal social-ecological systems in which they are embedded are complex systems. They are difficult to govern because they are dynamic and unpredictable. . . . Adaptive management is unique as a framework for managing the uncertainty, nonlinearity, and emergent properties inherent in complex systems. . . .

Adaptive governance is society's capacity to understand and respond to environmental (and social) feedback, in the context of change and uncertainty, to sustain and enhance resilience of desirable system configurations. . . .

A variety of government agencies and others manage the Kenyan coast, using a range of approaches and tools, often with overlapping and evolving mandates. . . .

The Mombasa Marine Park and Reserve and Diani–Chale Marine Reserve are adjacent marine protected areas (MPAs). . . .

The State Level

We now turn to processes of state decision making to query the potential for adaptive management. . . . We look first at state-based understanding of complex system change, then at the integration of knowledge and its use in decision making, and finally at processes of reform.

Understanding Environmental Change: the Role of State Knowledge

There are three government agencies that collect data for the purposes of marine management in Kenya: the Kenya Fisheries Department (KFD), the Kenya Wildlife Service (KWS), and the Kenya Marine and Fisheries Research Institute (KMFRI). . . . The KFD deploys scouts along the Kenyan coast to collect data on inshore fish catch (total weight), with individual fish scouts covering relatively large areas in some cases. These data are used to monitor inshore coastal fisheries production and are reported on annually. . . . [F]ish scouts . . . work closely with one of the research organizations collecting other catch metrics. These data are also reported on annually in joint meetings with the KFD and fishers, and published internationally in scientific papers. . . .

The KWS . . . undertakes standardized, taxonomically broad monitoring of fish abundance, benthic cover, and invertebrate counts (urchin and crown of thorns), across all its MPAs on an annual or biannual basis, in partnership

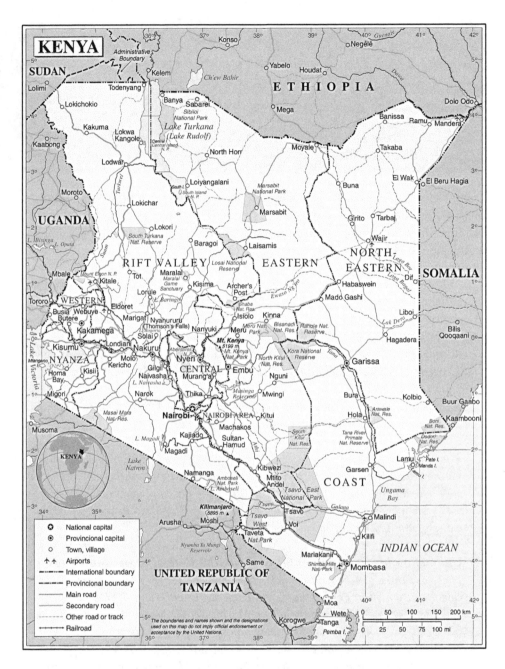

with a research organization. . . . These data are presented in yearly reports disseminated to Nairobi headquarters and communicated to the Assistant Director of the Coast. Park rangers also record boats in dive sites, occurrences of illegal entry into the park, and mooring damage, but this information is rarely aggregated and reported. . . . According to a park warden, information on the number of tourists in the park or number of fishers in the reserve, which could be gleaned by assessing park tickets or fisher licenses, are not analyzed and reported on by either. . . .

The KMFRI undertakes in-depth (species-level) fish-catch monitoring and wa-ter-quality monitoring alongside targeted research programs on different issues, including seagrass habitats and ornamental fisheries, among others. According to a KMFRI scientist, analysis of catch monitoring data is not conducted rou-tinely, but the data are available. . . .

[F]rom a complex-systems perspective, many metrics are not captured by these programs as currently designed. For instance, species-level catch data are either not collected or are not regularly analyzed, and ecological monitoring in MPAs is at the broad taxonomic level. Therefore, biodiversity and functional change may be missed. The MPA monitoring program does not assess the impact of sanctioned uses of the park, and does not compare data from within and out-side the protected areas, so it does not assess different disturbance regimes. . . .

Using Knowledge to Inform Decisions
. . . . Our data suggest several "lost opportunities" with regard to knowledge integration. . . .

Different types of collaborative fora have been created by the government agen-cies involved in coastal management in Kenya. . . . These collaborative fora ap-pear to perform different functions as environmental feedback mechanisms. For instance, fora such as policy review are essentially a debate over interests related to a preformulated document rather than opportunities for ecological knowledge to inform governance processes. By contrast, issue-based task forces, such as task forces on urchin degradation of seagrass, ornamental fisheries, or ring-net fishing, prioritize demand-driven research for decision making and so are more likely to function as effective, ongoing mechanisms of environmental feedback into government decision making. However, these fora have different criteria for participation. Local resource users, including fishers, were included in policy development with the Department of Fisheries and Tourism, but have not been included in planning phases of integrated coastal area management or in the is-sue-based task forces. The reasons for this are not clear, as there is extensive ref-erence to participation and indigenous knowledge in new policy documents. . . .

[I]n general, evidence suggests that few government actions are underpinned by an in-depth understanding of the complexities of the marine environment. . . .

Adapting Management Institutions and Practice
To what extent are new state policy, legislation, and action informed by the ecological knowledge available in the coastal zone? . . .

An example of effective management response at the state level is the amended fisheries legislation designating beach seine gears, and more recently spearguns, as illegal. However, there is evidence to suggest that, on the whole, this knowl-edge does not inform government decision making on an ongoing basis. . . .

Barriers to adaptive governance also exist at the level of action. In some cases, the issue is not a lack of understanding but, rather, a lack of regulation and enforcement capability. For instance, hoteliers continue to build seawalls on protected beach land to mitigate beach erosion when these structures are known to exacerbate the issue. In other cases, the issue is indeed one of lack of information or knowledge or, perhaps more, the lack of effective use of available knowledge. For example, . . . [new] technologies are expected to facilitate offshore, deep sea fishing, and the resting of inshore areas. However, fishers have not been provided with training in deep-sea fishing, or use of such nets with modern vessels. . . .

There is little knowledge of the status of offshore stocks, only ad hoc monitoring of the impact of these new technologies on inshore stocks through price/catch records of fishers, and no analysis of the implications of this development agenda for the vulnerability of fishers. Observations of the use of these gears suggest that actually they may reduce the resilience of inshore lagoons by exploiting source stocks more efficiently, and/or increase the vulnerability of fishers who may collectively fail to catch enough and who are required to cover costs of petrol and maintenance in the context of uncertainty and variable catch. . . .

Discussion

We argue here that adaptive marine governance, in a contemporary developing country setting, is not likely to be a smooth process of learning, knowledge-sharing, and responding. . . . At the state level, governance processes are evolving, with some processes becoming more inclusive. However, the institutions pertaining to participation, science, and local "indigenous" knowledge outlined in new conservation, fisheries, and environmental policy and/or legislation do not, in practice, ensure adequate representation of all stakeholders in opportunities for knowledge exchange and decision making. As such, new national policy relevant to coastal management continues to reflect a greater concern for inshore fisheries and terrestrial conservation, and state action does not appear to be rooted in an in-depth understanding of complex system interactions and change. . . .

[W]e argue that it is not necessarily knowledge per se, as a static and given, that is important for adaptive management, but the more dynamic processes of learning and knowledge exchange as the means by which environmental feedback continues to be captured and fed into institutional and behavioral change. . . .

[R]esilience perspectives are forward looking and emphasize uncertainty. . . . [K]nowledge sharing is central to systems understanding and ongoing learning in a context of uncertainty. . . .

Finally, the study . . . emphasizes that in many instances, considerable awareness and knowledge exists, and that substantial barriers to improved governance are found at the phase of institutional reform and collective action at the local and state levels. . . . At the level of the state, decision making remains highly centralized in Kenya. Institutional and policy reform occur, but are not necessarily tailored to needs at the coastal scale. In contrast, effective adaptive governance is expected to require flexible, responsive, and multiscale governance.

SUSTAINABILITY, ADAPTIVE GOVERNANCE, AND BIOLOGICAL DIVERSITY

In 1993, the Convention on Biological Diversity went into effect. The Convention focuses on conserving biological diversity, sustaining the use of biodiversity, and fairly and equitably sharing benefits arising from genetic resources. At the seventh biennial meeting of the nations (known as the Conference of the Parties (COP)), the parties embraced an AG approach for biodiversity, stating:

> Adaptive management should be practiced, based on:
>
>> Science and traditional and local knowledge;
>>
>> Iterative, timely and transparent feedback derived from monitoring the use, environmental, socio-economic impacts, and the status of the resource being used; and
>>
>> Adjusting management based on timely feedback from the monitoring procedures.

Rationale: Biological systems and the economic and social factors that can affect the sustainability of use of biological diversity are highly variable. It is not possible to have knowledge of all aspects of such systems before a use of biological diversity begins. Therefore, it is necessary for the management to monitor the effects of that use and allow adjustment of the use as appropriate, including modification, and if necessary, the suspension of unsustainable practices. In this context, it is preferable to use all sources of information about a resource when deciding how it can be used. In many societies, traditional and local knowledge has led to much use of biological diversity being sustainable over long time-periods without detriment to the environment or the resource. Incorporation of such knowledge into modern use systems can do much to avoid the inappropriate use and enhance sustainable use of components of biodiversity.

> **Operational guidelines**
>
> Ensure that for particular uses adaptive management schemes are in place;
>
> Require adaptive management plans to incorporate systems to generate sustainable revenue, where the benefits go to indigenous and local communities and local stakeholders to support successful implementation;
>
> Provide extension assistance in setting up and maintaining monitoring and feedback systems;
>
> Include clear descriptions of their adaptive management system, which includes means to assess uncertainties;
>
> Respond quickly to unsustainable practices;
>
> Design monitoring system on a temporal scale sufficient to ensure that information about the status of the resource and ecosystem is available to inform management decisions to ensure that the resource is conserved;
>
> When using traditional and local knowledge, ensure that approval of the holder of that knowledge has been obtained.

Convention on Biological Diversity, Conference of the Parties 7, Decision VII/12 Sustainable Use (Article 10) (Apr. 13, 2004).

Questions and Notes

1. In the third paragraph quoted on page 490, Carl Folke mentions collective action challenges (CACs) (discussed in more detail in Chapter 3, Section II.E). How would you characterize the relationship between CACs and AG? What is it about AG that can help resolve some CACs?

2. AG works in tandem with Systems Thinking (ST), described in Chapter 6, Section II. ST provides helpful information concerning system changes. AG is a process to learn from those changes and translate them into policy alternatives.

3. In Chapter 1, we discussed the example of the Atlantic cod. What do you think of this AG-based analysis of the Atlantic cod:

   In 2002, a moratorium on all fishing for northern cod was declared by the Canadian government after a collapse of this valuable fishery. An earlier near-collapse had led Canada to declare a 200-mile zone of exclusive fisheries jurisdiction in 1977. Considerable optimism existed during the 1980s that the stocks, as estimated by fishery scientists, were rebuilding. Consequently, generous total catch limits were established for northern cod and other ground fish, the number of licensed fishers was allowed to increase considerably, and substantial government subsidies were allocated for new vessels.

   Some have reported a variety of information-related problems including: (i) treating all northern cod as a single stock instead of recognizing distinct populations with different characteristics, (ii) ignoring the variability of year classes of northern cod, (iii) focusing on offshore-fishery landing data rather than inshore data to "tune" the stock assessment, and (iv) ignoring inshore fishers who were catching ever-smaller fish and doubted the validity of stock assessments.

   What went wrong? . . . This experience illustrates the need to collect and model both local and aggregated information about resource conditions and to use it in making policy at the appropriate scales.

   Thomas Dietz et al., *The Struggle to Govern the Commons*, 302 SCIENCE 1907, 1908 (2003).

4. AG is partially about learning from the past. Similar to many of the other Strategies for Implementation, AG does not recommend a course of action to enhance system resilience or sustainability. However, it does help identify conditions and policies that are vulnerable and/or unsustainable. Policymakers, however, must still make the actual decision, weighing additional factors not included in AG, including political will and resources. As you read the following quote consider the

possibility that politics, undue influence, or inertia will defeat change relevant to improving sustainability even when utilizing many of the strategies described in this book:

> *[I]t is easy to see various reasons why the simple, attractive idea of treating management as experimentation has been so difficult to put into practice. Objections to large-scale experiments range from faith in our ability to purchase answers through process research and modeling, to concerns about ecological side effects and risks of experimental policies. These objections provide a rich set of excuses to delay decisive action by those who can profit from, or find protection in, such delays. . . . [T]he public will come to realize that business as usual is no longer a viable option for sustaining and restoring riparian ecosystem values.*[160]

5. In Chapter 6, Section IV, we described Baselines and Metrics as a useful tool to help assess and understand R&S. Describe how Baselines and Metrics are relevant to AG.

VII. PRESERVATION AND RECREATION

Open land and water have nonconsumptive uses such as preservation and recreation. The United States has historically managed federal public lands based on the multiple-use doctrine, which considers consumptive uses as discussed above, as well as nonconsumptive uses. While recreation and preservation are sometimes in harmony, there are conflicts when preservationists seek to reduce the human footprint on nature, but recreationists enjoy using motorized equipment such as speedboats, snowmobiles, and all-terrain vehicles (ATVs).

Preservation: Preservation of land and water resources is important for sustaining existing natural resources for consumptive uses and for supporting the habitats needed for such uses as well as for sustaining nonconsumptive uses. In the United States, this concept of "sustainability" dates back to 1916 when the Organic Act established the National Park Service (NPS) as a bureau of the Department of the Interior. The stated purpose of this federal legislation was "to conserve the scenery and the natural and historic objects and the wild life therein and to provide for the enjoyment of the same in such manner and by such means as will leave them unimpaired for the enjoyment of future generations."[161] In addition to manag-

---

[160] Carl Walters, *Challenges in Adaptive Management of Riparian and Coastal Ecosystems*, CONSERV. ECOL. 1(2):1 (1997), http://www.ecologyandsociety.org/vol1/iss2/art1/vol1-iss2-1.pdf.
[161] National Park Service Organic Act of 1916, 16 U.S.C. §1 (repealed 2014).

ing 397 areas or "units," constituting over 84 million acres, the NPS also helps manage sites protected by the National Register of Historic Places, National Historic Landmarks, National Heritage Areas, National Wild and Scenic Rivers, and National Trails. The units managed include historical parks or sites, national parks, battlefields or military parks, preserves, recreation areas, seashores, lakeshores, reserves, and monuments.[162]

In addition to the Organic Act, which established the NPS, preservation efforts are guided by executive orders, federal regulation, and other legislation such as: the Antiquities Act of 1906,[163] as superseded by the Archaeological Resources Protection Act (ARPA) of 1979;[164] the Historic Sites Act (HSA) of 1935;[165] the Wetlands Loan Act of 1961;[166] the Land and Water Conservation Fund Act of 1963;[167] the National Wilderness Preservation Act of 1964;[168] the National Historic Preservation Act (NHPA) of 1966;[169] the Wild and Scenic Rivers Act of 1968 (WSRA);[170] the Coastal Zone Management Act (CZMA);[171] the Coastal Barrier Resources Act;[172] the Estuarine Areas Act of 1968;[173] the Clean Water Act §404;[174] the Eastern Wilderness Act of 1975;[175] the Boundary Waters Canoe Area Wilderness Act of 1978;[176] the Alaska National Interest Lands Conservation Act of 1980;[177] and the California Desert Protection Act of 1994.[178] People have interpreted differently what constitutes preservation. Generally, it means limited or non-use of land, and some believe it to mean no human use whatsoever. While some consider nonmotorized recreational use (such as hikers, skiers, canoeists, etc.) to be compatible with preservation, motorized recreational use (such as motorboats, ATVs, and jet skis) is typically inconsistent with preservation interests in ecological, scenic, and aesthetic goals.[179]

---

[162] *Id.*

[163] 16 U.S.C. §§431-433 (1906) (repealed 2014) (providing for preservation of land containing historically or scientifically significant objects and prohibiting injury to or extraction of objects of antiquity without government permission).

[164] 16 U.S.C. §§470aa-470mm (preserving archaeological resources for current and future uses).

[165] 16 U.S.C. §§461-467 (1935) (repealed 2014).

[166] 16 U.S.C. §§715k-3-715k-5 (providing federal loans and funding to prevent loss of wetlands and waterfowl habitat).

[167] 16 U.S.C. §§460l-460l-11 (repealed 2014) (providing federal funding for federal and state habitat land acquisition within the National Park System, the National Forest System, and the National Wildlife Refuge System).

[168] 16 U.S.C. §§1131 *et seq.* (1964).

[169] 16 U.S.C. §§470 *et seq.* (1980, as amend.); *see* Act of Dec. 12, 1980, Pub. L. No. 96-515, 94 Stat. 2987.

[170] 16 U.S.C. §§1271-1287 (protecting rivers throughout the nation by designation and classification).

[171] 16 U.S.C. §§1451-1464 (1972).

[172] 16 U.S.C. §3501 (1999).

[173] 16 U.S.C. §§1224-1226 (1956).

[174] 33 U.S.C. §1344 (protecting wetlands and tidelands from dredging and filling based on the definition of navigable waters).

[175] Pub. L. No. 93-622, 88 Stat. 2096 (1975).

[176] Pub. L. No. 95-495, 92 Stat 1649 (1978).

[177] 16 U.S.C. §§3101-3233 (1980).

[178] 16 U.S.C. §§410aaa-83 (1994).

[179] LAITOS HORNBOOK, *supra* note 1, at §7.02.

Conservation: We can also accomplish private land preservation and conservation by using conservation easements and covenants.[180] A conservation servitude is a private agreement to refrain from private property land uses, now and in the future, that are detrimental to the property's ecological or open space values.[181] A conservation servitude arises when a landowner donates or sells his or her property rights, such as the right to develop the land, to a private organization or a public agency. The private or public entity, which holds the benefit of the landowner's promise, may enforce the landowner's promise not to exercise the land use rights donated or sold.[182] This promise as to how the land is used will bind the landowner making the promise, but subsequent owners of the private land as well. Conservation easements protect more than 2.6 million acres of land in the United States, and their use is expanding internationally in Canada, Latin America, and Australia.[183]

Native American Rights: Regulation of federal land and resources can sometimes overlap with the sovereign interests of Native American tribes. The significance of "place" is particularly important to tribes as their oral traditions give special meaning and value to lands within existing Indian reservations as well as those located off-reservation that may be sacred for ceremonial or burial uses.[184] These cultural and spiritual resources may be protected by federal legislation such as the National Environmental Policy Act (NEPA) or the National Historic Preservation Act (NHPA), which require an environmental impact statement before taking federal action impacting areas of significant cultural, spiritual, or historical significance.[185] Congress amended the NHPA in 1992 to allow Indian tribes official responsibility for preserving these historic areas located on tribal land. Federal agencies are also required to consult with Native American tribes when they take significant action that impacts religious and cultural lands, even though these areas may not be located on tribal lands.[186] Indian tribes were unsuccessful in arguing to the U.S. Supreme Court in *Lyng v. Northwest Indian Cemetery Protective Association*[187] that logging and building roads in a National Forest violated their First Amendment rights

---

[180] *See, e.g.*, Madden v. Nature Conservancy, 823 F. Supp. 815 (D. Mont. 1992).

[181] *Private Lands Conservation: Conservation Easements*, NATURE CONSERVANCY, http://www.nature.org/about-us/private-lands-conservation/conservation-easements/index.htm (last visited Oct. 1, 2017).

[182] *Conservation Easements: Conserving Land, Water, and a Way of Life*, NATURE CONSERVANCY (Dec. 2003), http://www.nature.org/about-us/private-lands-conservation/conservation-easements/conserving-a-way-of-life.pdf.

[183] *See id.*

[184] *See* Dean B. Suagee, *Historical Storytelling and the Growth of Tribal Historic Preservation Programs*, 17 NAT. RESOURCES & ENV'T 86 (2002).

[185] *See* Pit River Tribe v. U.S. Forest Serv. (*Pit River I*), 469 F.3d 768 (9th Cir. 2006); Pit River Tribe v. U.S. Forest Serv. (*Pit River II*), 615 F.3d 1069 (9th Cir. 2010).

[186] *Tribal Historic Preservation Officers*, ADVISORY COUNCIL ON HISTORIC PRESERVATION, http://www.achp.gov/thpo.html (last visited Oct. 1, 2017).

[187] Lyng v. Nw. Indian Cemetery Protective Assn., 485 U.S. 439 (1988).

of free exercise, even though these actions "could have devastating effects on traditional Indian religious practices."[188] However, Congress later designated the sacred lands at issue in this case as protected federal wilderness, which precluded the commercial activities of timber harvesting.[189]

Tribal lands and public lands of significant cultural, spiritual, and historical significance may complicate the already existing conflict between preservation and recreation. In *Bear Lodge Multiple Use Association v. Babbitt*,[190] recreational climbing at Devils Tower National Monument was affecting wildlife, habitat, and the integrity and physical appearance of the rock, which was sacred to some Native American tribes. In response, the National Park Service issued a voluntary climbing ban, which courts upheld against a challenge that the ban violated the Establishment Clause of the First Amendment by advancing Native American worship. An Executive Order issued in 1996 during the litigation directed federal agencies to accommodate ceremonial uses of Native American sacred sites.[191]

The Native American Graves Protection and Repatriation Act (NAGPRA), which requires that cultural items found on federal lands be returned to the appropriate Native American tribes, also protects Native American sacred items.[192] The conflict between tribal practices and conservation, recreation, and tourism erupted into protests, violence, and litigation in Minnesota when the Chippewa tribe asserted its rights to hunt, fish, and gather on state lands, particularly the lands adjacent to Lake Mille Lacs.[193] The U.S. Supreme Court in *Minnesota v. Mille Lacs Band of Chippewa Indians*[194] upheld the Chippewa tribal rights based on the tribe's 1837 treaty with the U.S. government, but recognized that these "treaty-based usufructuary rights do not guarantee the Indians 'absolute freedom' from state regulation."[195] Indeed, the Court

Devil's Tower

---

[188] *Id.* at 451.

[189] Natchez Trace Parkway, 16 U.S.C. §460 (1938).

[190] Bear Lodge Multiple Use Assn. v. Babbitt, 2 F. Supp. 2d 1448 (D. Wyo. 1998), *aff'd*, 175 F.3d 814 (10th Cir. 1999).

[191] Exec. Order No. 13007, 61 Fed. Reg. 26,771 (May 24, 1996).

[192] 25 U.S.C. §§3001-3013 (1990).

[193] Klein et al., *supra* note 10, at 618; *see also* Minnesota v. Mille Lacs Band of Chippewa Indians, 526 U.S. 172 (1999).

[194] 526 U.S. 172 (1999).

[195] *Id.* at 204.

emphasized that the state has the "authority to impose reasonable and necessary nondiscriminatory regulations on Indian hunting, fishing, and gathering rights in the interest of conservation."[196]

Wilderness Preservation: Wilderness is defined by the Wilderness Act, in part, as "an area where the Earth and its community of life are untrammeled by man, where man himself is a visitor who does not remain."[197] Under this Act, the Secretary of the Interior is directed to identify roadless areas of acreage over 5,000 acres as suitable or not for inclusion in the National Wilderness Preservation System (NWPS).[198] The Secretary of Agriculture must also recommend areas within the National Forest System that are appropriate for designation. The United States has designated over 106 million acres as wilderness since the Wilderness Act's enactment in 1964. More than 57 million of these acres are in Alaska, where motorized vehicles, structures, and other limited uses are not allowed because of the distinctive characteristics of this particular wilderness region. The benefits derived from this designation include clean air, clean water, habitat preservation for plant and animals, and primitive recreation.[199] The federal agencies responsible for managing these wilderness areas are the Bureau of Land Management (BLM), the Fish and Wildlife Service (FWS), the Forest Service, and the National Park Service (NPS).[200]

According to the BLM, the uses that are allowed in the wilderness include "protection of air and watersheds; maintenance of soil and water quality, ecological stability, plant and animal gene pools, protection of archaeological and historical sites, habitat for wildlife; and livestock grazing."[201] Additional uses include limited outdoor recreation, such as horseback riding, camping, fishing, hunting, hiking, and the use of existing rights to water, mineral claims, and rights of way.[202] These designated areas generally do not permit bicycles and motor vehicles, except in special circumstances such as emergencies, area management, or the exercise of preexisting rights. Designated areas also prohibit the construction of new roads.

Conflicting Values of Preservation and Recreation: The conflict between preservation and recreation is particularly problematic in wilderness areas as we intend to maintain these lands in their natural condition

---

[196] *Id.* at 205 (reaffirming Puyallup Tribe v. Dep't of Game of Wash., 391 U.S. 392, 398 (1968)).

[197] 16 U.S.C. §1131(c) (1964).

[198] Richard J. Fink, *The National Wildlife Refuges: Theory, Practice, and Prospect*, 18 Harv. Envtl. L. Rev. 1 (1994).

[199] *Frequently Asked Questions*, U.S. Dep't Interior: Bureau Land Mgmt., https://web.archive.org/web/20161008044421/http://www.blm.gov:80/wo/st/en/prog/blm_special_areas/NLCS/wilderness2/Wilderness_FAQ.html (last visited Oct. 1, 2017).

[200] *Id.*

[201] *Id.*

[202] *Id.*

with limited human impact.[203] Motorized vehicles are prohibited and courts have upheld the statutory declaration that the possession and operation of such vehicles within a designated wilderness area is unlawful. Litigation over these conflicts has: increased permission for hunting, unless it poses a danger to safety or wilderness purposes; restricted sailboats and houseboats operated on private waters next to a wilderness; prohibited motor vehicles such as snowmobiles, unless the emergency they were responding to arose before entry into the wilderness; banned commercial fishing; and allowed for commercial towboats.[204]

The National Park Service (NPS) provides for land management of U.S. National Parks, as well as national monuments, national wild rivers, national preserves, and national recreation areas, just to name a few. The Antiquities Act provides that the President may declare lands and objects of historic or scientific interest that are located on federal lands to be national monuments.[205] U.S. presidents have used this authority to preserve wildlife habitat and other lands of historic or scientific interest. For example: President Roosevelt created the 220,000-acre Jackson Hole National Monument in Wyoming (now part of Grand Teton National Park); President Truman preserved 40 acres of land surrounding the Devil's Hole cavern in Nevada by establishing a monument based on the area's historic and scientific significance; and President Clinton designated the Grand Staircase-Escalante National Monument in Utah.[206] In 2016, "President Obama designated Bears Ears National Monument, an area of scenic rock formations and sites sacred to Native American tribes. . . . On Dec. 4, [2017] President Trump traveled to Utah to sign proclamations downsizing Bears Ears National Monument by 85 percent and Grand Staircase-Escalante National Monument by nearly 50 percent." Environmental organizations and Native American tribes filed lawsuits challenging this action and many environmental and natural resources law scholars consider this attempt to downsize these national monuments illegal and likely to be judicially overturned.[207]

The U.S. Congress has also acted to preserve land by creating national parks for the benefit and enjoyment of the people. While some individuals and businesses may view the national parks as exploitable for natural resources, the federal government has designed the park system to treat these lands as more than just physical resources or commodities.[208] The fundamental purpose of these parks is "to conserve the scenery and the natural and

---

[203] LAITOS HORNBOOK, *supra* note 1, at 240.

[204] *Id.* at 244-245 (discussing various cases, including Alaska Wildlife Alliance v. Jensen, 108 F.3d 1065 (9th Cir. 1997); *see also* Wilderness Soc'y v. U.S. Fish & Wildlife Serv., 353 F.3d 1051 (9th Cir. 2003) (en banc), *amended on reh'g en banc in part*, 360 F.3d 1374 (9th Cir. 2004).

[205] American Antiquities Act of 1906 16 U.S.C. §431-433 (1906) (repealed 2014).

[206] *See also* Utah Assn. of Counties v. Bush, 316 F. Supp. 2d 1172 (D. Utah 2004); Christine A. Klein, *Preserving Monumental Landscapes Under the Antiquities Act*, 87 CORNELL L. REV. 1333 (2002).

[207] Nicholas Bryner, Eric Biber, Mark Squillace & Sean B. Hecht, *President Trump's National Monument Rollback Is Illegal and Likely to Be Reversed in Court*, THE CONVERSATION (Dec. 4, 2017) https://theconversation.com/president-trumps-national-monument-rollback-is-illegal-and-likely-to-be-reversed-in-court-88376.

[208] Holly Doremus, *Nature, Knowledge and Profit: The Yellowstone Bioprospecting Controversy and the Core Purposes of America's National Parks*, 26 ECOLOGY L.Q. 401 (1999).

historic objects and the wild life therein and to provide for the enjoyment of the same in such manner and by such means as will leave them unimpaired for the enjoyment of future generations."[209] The same section of the statute states that the NPS is directed "to promote and regulate the use" of the parks. This dual purpose encourages recreation and tourism, while at the same time holds the NPS responsible for the sustainable preservation of these resources.

The NPS has reconciled the conflict between recreation and preservation by interpreting the Organic Act to prefer resource conservation above recreation.[210] "There can be no doubt, as NPS and the courts have concluded, that the overriding aim of the Organic Act, as well as the purpose of NPS' oversight and management of the park system, is to conserve the natural wonders of our nation's parks for future generations."[211] The NPS is responsible for making sure that the balance between recreation and conservation does not impair park resources or values to meet one of our sustainability metrics of preserving these resources for the enjoyment of future generations. This conflict between recreation and preservation exists in our designated wilderness areas, but there we are guided by the goal of preservation with very limited human impact. In the national parks, as will be discussed below, the conflict between recreation and preservation is more difficult to manage because the NPS is responsible for both of these goals.[212]

Local Governments and Preservation and Conservation: Because local governments in the United States typically have control over land uses, preservation and conservation often happen through the exercise of local zoning powers. We discuss local zoning codes and relevant preservation and conservation zones in Chapter 5.

International Preservation: Globally, international conventions and less commonly treaties deal with nature preservation. The Convention on Nature Protection and Wildlife Preservation in the Western Hemisphere of 1942 directly protects wildlife and emphasizes habitat protection by establishing national reserves, wilderness reserves, national parks, and nature monuments.[213] The Convention on Wetlands of International Importance especially as Waterfowl Habitat 1971, also known as the Ramsar Convention, recognized the importance of conserving wetlands, not only for waterfowl protection, but also for other valuable functions such as biodiversity, hydrological control of floods and droughts, and the economic interests in commercial fish and shellfish harvests.[214] Protection

---

[209] National Park Service Organic Act of 1916, 16 U.S.C. §1 (repealed 2014).
[210] Bluewater Network v. Salazar, 721 F. Supp. 2d 7, 19-21 (D.D.C. 2010).
[211] *Id.* at 21.
[212] S. Utah Wilderness Alliance v. Dabney, 222 F.3d 819 (10th Cir. 2000).
[213] Convention on Nature Protection and Wildlife Preservation in the Western Hemisphere, Oct. 12, 1940, 56 Stat. 1354, U.S.T.S. 981.
[214] Convention on Wetlands of International Importance especially as Waterfowl Habitat, Feb. 2, 1971, T.I.A.S. No. 11,084 [hereinafter "Ramsar Convention"].

of wetlands depends on a country's designation of wetlands within its territory that are eligible for listing "on account of their international significance in terms of ecology, botany, zoology, limnology, or hydrology."[215]

Recreation: Recreational uses may conflict with water resources, wildlife, forests, habitat, wetlands, land use, and preservation values. However, recreational uses of natural resources can be valuable for purposes of education and appreciation of these resources. Managing recreational uses may occur at the local, state, national, and international level. While international management of recreation appears to be mostly voluntary,[216] individual nations have a significant interest in managing these resources, not only for their citizens but also in many cases to support a vibrant tourism industry. The United Nations has established an agency, the World Tourism Organization (UNWTO), which is responsible for "the promotion of responsible, sustainable and universally accessible tourism."[217] The UNWTO states that "[a]s the leading international organization in the field of tourism, [it] promotes tourism as a driver of economic growth, inclusive development and environmental sustainability and offers leadership and support to the sector in advancing knowledge and tourism policies worldwide."[218]

U.S. Public Recreation: Public recreational lands in the United States generally include national forests, national recreation areas, and national parks and monuments.[219] As noted above in the discussion of wilderness, recreation and preservation are frequently in conflict. The public trust doctrine, in its broadest interpretation, requires that the government hold public lands, waters, and natural resources in trust for the benefit of the people. Therefore, the conflict between recreation and preservation must be resolved in a way that ultimately benefits the people so that recreational uses do not diminish the value of the public's resources.[220] The government's obligation under the public trust doctrine is a continuing one, at least in some states such as California and Idaho.[221] The Idaho Supreme Court, in a case challenging the grant of a ten-year lease of lakeshore line for a yacht club, determined that the public agency could grant such a lease, but that it would be subject to continuing review to ensure that the public's use was not impaired.[222] Therefore, even though a public agency may grant rights for the recreational use of public trust resources, it has a continuing obligation to review such grants to determine whether recreational use interferes with other public values.

---

[215] *Id.* at Art. 2(1)-(2).
[216] *See generally* INT'L FED'N PARK & RECREATION ADMIN. (IFPRA), http://www.ifpra.org/ (last visited Oct. 1, 2017); WORLD URBAN PARKS, http://www.worldurbanparks.org (last visited Oct. 1, 2017).
[217] *Who We Are*, WORLD TOURISM ORG. UNWTO, http://www2.unwto.org/en/content/who-we-are-0 (last visited Oct. 1, 2017).
[218] *See id.*
[219] LAITOS HORNBOOK, *supra* note 1, at 246.
[220] Kootenai Envtl. Alliance, Inc. v. Panhandle Yacht Club, 671 P.2d 1085 (Idaho 1983).
[221] *See id.*
[222] *See id.*

Recreation is a permitted and even a preferred use on public lands, but it is the use of motorized vehicles that is typically at the root of disputes between recreation and preservation. While the balance between recreation and preservation generally leans in favor of nonmotorized recreation over preservation, when motorized recreation is involved, preservation usually is the favored outcome.[223] Motorized recreation and nonmotorized recreation can also come into conflict in situations where the higher intensity use interferes with the peaceful enjoyment of nature by others. The Department of the Interior has the authority to limit motorized use on recreation lands, and courts have upheld limits on motorized watercraft in favor of kayakers and rafters and restrictions on off-highway vehicles (OHV) in a national forest where other visitors may be adversely affected.[224]

The federal Boundary Waters Canoe Area Wilderness Act barred motorized vehicles from a network of lakes in Minnesota, even though this ban also impacted state and privately owned land.[225] However, the Bureau of Land Management allowed off-road vehicles for recreational use on federal lands that were classified as wilderness study areas, without violating the FLPMA or NEPA.[226] Snowmobiles present problems because of their impact on wildlife and habitat[227] and personal watercraft (jet skis) may adversely impact water quality, soundscapes, air quality, wildlife, habitat, and visitor safety.[228] Even the use of nonmotorized vehicles such as bicycles may be restricted if they adversely impact national parks and environmental preservation goals.[229]

Environmental Impact of Recreation: Commercial recreation and tourism can have devastating effects on natural resources if not properly managed. In the United States, the NPS manages commercial concession activity such as food, lodging, equipment rental, and guided trips.[230] For example, the NPS has limited cruise line ship entries into

Johns Hopkins Glacier

[223] LAITOS HORNBOOK, *supra* note 1, at 241.
[224] *Id.* at 245-46 (discussing Hells Canyon Alliance v. USFS, 227 F.3d 1170 (9th Cir. 2000); Ohio Valley Trail Riders Assn. v. Worthington 111 F. Supp. 2d 878 (E.D. Kent. 2000)).
[225] Minnesota v. Block, 660 F.2d 1240 (8th Cir. 1981).
[226] Norton v. S. Utah Wilderness Alliance, 542 U.S. 55 (2004).
[227] Mausolf v. Babbitt, 125 F.3d 661 (8th Cir. 1997).
[228] Bluewater Network v. Salazar, 721 F. Supp. 2d 7, 19 (D.D.C. 2010).
[229] Bicycle Trails Council of Marin v. Babbitt, 82 F.3d 1445 (9th Cir. 1996).
[230] LAITOS HORNBOOK, *supra* note 1, at 249-251.

Glacier Bay National Park[231] and air tours of the Grand Canyon to protect against adverse environmental impacts caused by these activities.[232] The Forest Service manages private recreational facilities in the national forest areas that are not wilderness to prevent overcrowding and control usage. Permits are required for commercial ski areas and other concessionaires such as guiding and outfitting services.[233] Increased tourism in developing countries has been especially problematic as these nations attempt to foster economic development by encouraging tourist activities, such as golf courses, which consume excessive water where water is scarce.[234] Globally, nations struggle to balance tourism against ecological and cultural values to ensure the sustainability of their natural resources.

Question and Note

1. As stated above, the purpose of the legislation creating the National Park Service is "to conserve the scenery and the natural and historic objects and the wildlife therein and to provide for the enjoyment of the same in such manner and by such means as will leave them unimpaired for the enjoyment of future generations." What do you think about this provision as it relates to the resilience and sustainability of ecosystems within national parks? Why do you think it has been unsuccessful in achieving resilient or sustainable ecosystems associated with wildlife species survival?

---

[231] Nat'l Parks & Conservation Assn. v. Babbitt, 241 F.3d 722 (9th Cir. 2001).
[232] Grand Canyon Air Tour Coal. v. FAA, 154 F.3d 455 (D.C. Cir. 1998).
[233] LAITOS HORNBOOK, *supra* note 1, at 252-255.
[234] *UNESCO Water E-Newsletter No. 155: Water and Tourism*, UNITED NATIONS EDUCATIONAL SCI. & CULTURAL ORG. (Sept. 15, 2006), https://web.archive.org/web/20160912153532/http://www.unesco.org/water/news/newsletter/155.shtml.

Pollution

8

I. INTRODUCTION

Human activities to obtain basic needs and produce products and services can generate waste and result in externalities, which may adversely affect the resilience and sustainability of critical social-ecological systems. Natural events, such as volcanic eruptions, earthquakes, and hurricanes, may also affect system resilience and sustainability. To varying degrees, public and private sector entities have responded to these disruptions in both short-term and long-term approaches.

As discussed in Chapter 3, Section II.E (Collective Action Challenges), Garrett Hardin, in his influential article *The Tragedy of the Commons*, explained the tragedy of a pasture open to everyone. In the analogy, each herdsman seeks to maximize his gain by adding one more animal to his herd because he receives the short-term positive utility of selling an additional animal; however, all the herdsmen share the long-term negative utility of overgrazing the pasture. Thus, each herdsman is incentivized to increase his herd without limit until the pasture is overgrazed and the common resource destroyed.[1] Hardin described pollution as a reverse tragedy of the commons because "it is not a question of taking something out of the commons, but of putting something in — sewage, or chemical, radioactive, and heat wastes into water; noxious and dangerous fumes into the air."[2]

This chapter describes some of the major regulatory steps taken in the United States to address increasing externalities stemming from human behavior during and after the Industrial Revolution as well as the exponential growth in human population. Sustainability is relevant during at least two different stages. First, sustainability is helpful to understand how

---

[1] Garrett Hardin, *The Tragedy of the Commons*, 162 SCIENCE 3859, 1243-1248 (1968), https://www.sciencemag.org/content/162/3859/1243.full.
[2] *Id.* at 1245.

U.S. law, policy, and science respond in the short term to managing existing pollution from human activity. Second, sustainability can help raise questions concerning whether continuing to have the current amount of externalities is possible or desirable or whether we need to reduce externalities so that relevant systems are not overwhelmed.

Similarly, assessing resilience to continued short-term pollution may help determine whether greater efforts and sacrifices are necessary to reduce what may be an unsustainable degree of externalities. This may include examining whether both our response systems and our control over pollution levels are sufficiently flexible to adapt to increasing challenges. We use the 2010 British Petroleum (BP) oil spill in the Gulf of Mexico to illustrate how the United States addresses short-term responses to human externalities and how these responses are affecting the sustainability and resilience of critical systems and how we need to remediate the externalities in our changing world.

II. ADDRESSING POLLUTION: CASE STUDY, THE BP OIL SPILL—A TRAGIC EXAMPLE

On April 20, 2010, the Deepwater Horizon, a mobile BP oil-drilling unit located off the shore of Louisiana in the Gulf of Mexico, exploded killing 11 rig workers and injuring more than a dozen. Just under five million barrels of oil (42 gallons of crude oil to a barrel) gushed into the surrounding sea until workers successfully capped the well hole, approximately three months later. This was the largest oil spill disaster in U.S. history and resulted from a deep-water well blowout. Gas pressures from an oil well drilled on the sea floor were not sufficiently controlled and resulted in the destruction of the equipment designed to contain and manage the extraction of oil from below the Earth's crust.[3]

Pollution from this oil spill affected ocean waters, the sea floor, aquatic plants and wildlife, waterfowl, public health, beaches, wetlands, the Gulf seafood industry, and tourism along the Gulf Coast. U.S. law had a framework in place to address these impacts, but legal remedies for recovering monetary damages and enforcing criminal liability cannot bring about a reversal of ecological damage and restoration of environmental, economic, or societal well-being in this immensely impacted area. Assessing the resilience and sustainability of key systems affected by the oil spill can help lead to actions that reduce and prevent externalities and prepare us to respond to unforeseen events.

---

[3] The Ocean Portal Team, *Gulf Oil Spill*, OCEAN PORTAL, http://ocean.si.edu/gulf-oil-spill (last visited Nov. 30, 2017).

III. ADDRESSING POLLUTION: U.S. ENVIRONMENTAL LAW AND POLLUTION

In the United States prior to the 1960s and 1970s, litigants used common law tort actions, such as nuisance, negligence, and strict liability for ultra-hazardous activity to respond to pollution.[4] Some states, such as California and New York, led the way to more extensive federal regulation by introducing state and local legislation to control pollution.[5] Common law actions still supplement regulation, particularly in the developing area of "toxic tort" law and air pollution, including climate change,[6] but federal, state, and local governments have regulated extensively since the early 1970s to address environmental degradation from human activity. Although various federal and state pollution statutes existed prior to 1970, the era of modern federal environmental regulation began with the National Environmental Policy Act of 1970 (NEPA). Ironically, one of the catalysts for passing extensive state and federal environmental legislation was another blowout and oil spill that occurred in 1969 in the Santa Barbara Channel off California's coast.[7] We begin our exploration of pollution controls, resilience, and sustainability with the National Environmental Policy Act and environmental impact statements and waste disposal.

A. Environmental Impact Statements

1. THE NATIONAL ENVIRONMENTAL POLICY ACT

The U.S. Congress enacted the National Environmental Policy Act (NEPA) to set national environmental policy "to create and maintain conditions under which man and nature can exist in productive harmony, and fulfill the social, economic, and other requirements of present and future generations of Americans."[8] This stated purpose for NEPA illustrates that the sustainability goal of intergenerational equity—providing for future

---

[4] *See, e.g.,* William B. Johnson, *Common-law Strict Liability in Tort of Prior Landowner or Lessee to Subsequent Owner for Contamination of Land with Hazardous Waste Resulting from Prior Owner's or Lessee's Abnormally Dangerous or Ultrahazardous Activity,* 13 A.L.R.5th 600 (1993); *see also* Massachusetts v. EPA, 549 U.S. 497 (2007); Am. Elec. Power Co., Inc. v. Connecticut, 564 U.S. 410 (2011).

[5] *See, e.g.,* W. Christopher Brestel Jr., *The California Motor Vehicle Pollution Control Law,* 50 CAL. L. REV. 121 (1962), http://scholarship.law.berkeley.edu/californialawreview/vol50/iss1/7; *see also* Deirdre Carmody, *City's Air Cleaner Than in 1960's But Pollution Level Is Unknown,* N.Y. TIMES (May 26, 1981), http://www.nytimes.com/1981/05/26/nyregion/city-s-air-cleaner-than-in-1960-s-but-pollution-level-is-unknown.html.

[6] *See, e.g.,* Merrick v. Diageo, No. 14-6198, 2015 WL 6646818 (6th Cir. Nov. 2, 2015); Bell v. Cheswick Generating Station, 734 F.3d 188, 190-191 (3d Cir. 2013).

[7] PEW ENVIRONMENT GROUP, SANTA BARBARA OIL SPILL—JANUARY 28, 1969, (May 2010), https://web.archive.org/web/20130910034540/http://www.pewenvironment.org/uploadedFiles/PEG/Publications/Fact_Sheet/PEG_SantaBarbaraSpill_May2010.pdf.

[8] National Environmental Policy Act of 1969 (NEPA) §101, 42 U.S.C. §4321 (1970).

generations — has been part of modern environmental law in the United States since its beginnings. When government agencies make decisions that may have an environmental impact, NEPA requires that the decision makers have adequate information about environmental effects and alternatives before they take "major federal action significantly affecting the quality of the human environment."[9]

NEPA is not a substantive statute in that it does not require agencies to take particular pollution control actions, which has led many to criticize its effectiveness as an environmental statute. However, by requiring federal agencies to prepare a detailed environmental impact statement (EIS) before taking significant and adverse action, we hope that the EIS will guide decision makers to achieve sustainability and "productive harmony" between nature and man.

If the government agency determines that an EIS is required, litigants may challenge the detailed report and will need to address the content, scope, and level of judicial review. The report should include the environmental impacts of the proposed action as well as alternatives governed by a "rule of reason," meaning that remote or speculative alternatives need not be considered.[10] Agencies must consider reasonable alternatives to mitigate the action's adverse environmental impacts, but they need not adopt such mitigating measures so long as they have considered the measures and discussed them in the report. When scientific uncertainty exists as to the impacts of a proposed action, the agency must disclose that it is lacking adequate information. However, it is no longer necessary to produce a "worst case analysis" to identify the environmental impact of the worst possible outcome. If there are significant changes to the proposed action, or significant new information arises, the agency may need to prepare a supplemental EIS. Agencies must also be sure to address the larger project and avoid segmenting the actions into smaller, but related, pieces that independently would not require an EIS, but would cumulatively present a significant impact on the environment. Agencies address this segmentation problem by "tiering" the EIS preparation through a "programmatic EIS" which describes the overall project but relies on smaller components that consider local effects.[11]

Finally, if there are challenges to the NEPA process, federal courts will review the agency action to determine if it is procedurally adequate and rationally considered, but not whether it is substantively responsive to the environmental impacts presented. The U.S. Supreme Court explained in *Robertson v. Methow Valley Citizens Council* that NEPA only prohibits "uninformed — rather than unwise — agency decisions."[12] The scope of review is

---

[9] NEPA §102(2)(C) (1970).
[10] Vermont Yankee Nuclear Power Corp. v. NRDC, 435 U.S. 519, 551-552 (1978).
[11] *See* Kleppe v. Sierra Club, 427 U.S. 390, 397 (1976).
[12] 490 U.S. 332, 351, 375-377 (1989).

to assess agency compliance with the procedural obligations of NEPA and make sure the EIS content is responsive to NEPA requirements. Federal courts use the standard of review under the Administrative Procedure Act (APA), which validates agency action so long as it is not arbitrary or capricious.[13]

2. STATE ENVIRONMENTAL PROTECTION ACTS

In addition to federal NEPA requirements to assess significant environmental impacts, most states have similar statutes, often called "little NEPAs" or "SEPAs," to inform state and local decision makers of the environmental effects of government actions. Some states require the review of private actions in addition to state and local actions.[14] Some SEPAs go beyond the procedural functions of NEPA by requiring substantive action in the face of significant environmental impacts.[15] NEPA and state statutes operate independently, depending upon whether the government action occurs at the state or federal level. For example, the federal government generally has jurisdiction over offshore oil leasing; however, the Coastal Zone Management Act allows states with shorelines potentially impacted by these leases to review them for consistency with the states' approved coastal management plans.[16]

3. CASE STUDY OF RESILIENCE AND SUSTAINABILITY

Returning to our BP oil spill example, the U.S. Interior Department's Minerals Management Service (MMS) was the federal agency responsible for approving the oil lease to drill and operate the Deep Horizon. Approving offshore oil drilling in the Gulf of Mexico at a depth of 5,000 feet appears to qualify as a "major federal action significantly affecting the quality of the human environment," which would require the preparation of an EIS. In fact, the MMS had reviewed three previous detailed environmental reports for the area, but determined that the likelihood of a major oil spill was remote. Each report minimized the impact of an oil spill and concluded that any such spill would not reach land and would quickly dissipate. Therefore, the MMS allowed a "categorical exemption"

[13] *See* Marsh v. Or. Natural Res. Council, 490 U.S. 360 (1989).
[14] *See, e.g., The State Environmental Policy Act*, Dep't of Ecology: St. of Wash., http://www.ecy.wa.gov/programs/sea/sepa/e-review.html (last visited Nov. 30, 2017).
[15] *See CEQA: The California Environmental Quality Act*, Cal. Nat. Resources Agency, http://resources.ca.gov/ceqa/ (last visited Nov. 30, 2017).
[16] Linda Krop, *Defending State's Rights Under the Coastal Zone Management Act, State of California v. Norton*, Sustainable Dev. Law & Pol'y J. (Fall 2007), http://digitalcommons.wcl.american.edu/cgi/viewcontent.cgi?article=1160&context=sdlp.

for oil leases in this area, and BP was not required to prepare an EIS for the Deepwater Horizon.[17]

Originally, environmental reports prepared under NEPA were required to include a "worst case analysis" if information about potential impacts was uncertain. However, agency action in 1986 eliminated this requirement and required instead consideration of only reasonably foreseeable impacts.[18] Do you think the BP oil spill was a "worst case" scenario that agencies did not need to consider or was it a "reasonably foreseeable" event?[19]

The agency determines whether to prepare an EIS by conducting an initial environmental assessment (EA). The EA describes the proposed action, briefly discusses alternatives to such action, and assesses if it is a major federal action requiring an EIS. If the proposed action does not meet the threshold for an EIS, the agency will issue a "Finding of No Significant Impact" (FONSI) and explain why an EIS is not necessary. However, some agency actions are exempt from the EIS process altogether and do not require even the minimum EA investigation. For example, most of the actions of the Environmental Protection Agency (EPA) are exempt, but Congress may also adopt specific statutory exclusions called "categorical exemptions."

Categorical exemptions are intended to bypass EIS review when certain types of actions do not "individually or cumulatively have a significant effect on the human environment."[20] The Council on Environmental Quality (CEQ)—established by NEPA to advise the President regarding environment issues—is responsible for reviewing these exemptions. Following the BP oil spill, on November 23, 2010, the CEQ issued NEPA guidance on the best practices for use of these exclusions "as a way to reduce unnecessary paperwork and delay" if there are "no extraordinary circumstances that might cause significant environmental effects."[21]

The MMS categorically exempted the Deepwater Horizon lease from NEPA requirements, and just 11 days before the blowout, BP was lobbying with regulators to expand these exemptions for Gulf drilling operations.[22] However, within three months after the spill, the Secretary of the Interior reorganized MMS and renamed it the Bureau

---

[17] *See* Sandra Zellmer, Joel A. Mintz & Robert Glicksman, *Throwing Precaution to the Wind: NEPA and the Deepwater Horizon Blowout*, GEO. WASH. J. OF ENERGY & ENVTL. L., 62, 62 (Summer 2011), http://digitalcommons.unl.edu/cgi/viewcontent.cgi?article = 1112&context = lawfacpub.

[18] Robertson v. Methow Valley Citizens Council, 490 U.S. 332, 356 (1989).

[19] For further discussion, see Oliver Houck, *Worst Case and the Deepwater Horizon Blowout: There Ought to Be a Law*, 24 TUL. ENVTL. L.J. 1, 14 (2010), and Victor B. Flatt, *The "Worst Case" May Be the Best: Rethinking NEPA Law to Avoid Future Environmental Disasters*, 6 ENVT'L & ENERGY L. & POL'Y J. 181 (2011).

[20] 40 C.F.R. §1508.18 (2017).

[21] *See National Environmental Policy Act Update: New White House Guidance Recommends Procedures for Mitigating Adverse Environmental Impacts and Stresses the Importance of Public Involvement in Agency Decision-making*, SALSA LABS (2011), https://web.archive.org/web/20150320121405/https://soe.salsalabs.com/o/1/images/NEPA%20Mitigation%20and%20Monitoring%20Release.pdf.

[22] Juliet Eilperin, *U.S. Exempted BP's Gulf of Mexico Drilling from Environmental Impact Study*, WASH. POST (May 5, 2010), http://www.washingtonpost.com/wp-dyn/content/article/2010/05/04/AR2010050404118.html.

of Ocean Energy Management (BOEM). Congress authorized BOEM to carry out DOI reforms for drilling on the Outer Continental Shelf (OCS).[23] These reforms bolstered inspections of all Gulf of Mexico deep-water oil and gas drilling operations and required operators to include blowout scenarios within their Exploration Plans.[24] These reforms, among others, are expected to "improve BOEM's NEPA practices and procedures and ensure robust environmental reviews for future oil and gas exploration and development activities."[25]

Questions and Notes

1. Exemptions from NEPA raise a variety of issues relevant to resilience and sustainability. One of those issues pertains to information gathering. If a particular action is exempt from an EA or EIS, the opportunity for information is lost. For example, how might categorical exemptions, similar to the one granted to the Deepwater Horizon, positively or negatively impact the resilience of social-ecological systems associated with the Gulf? How might those exemptions affect the sustainability of coastal communities?

2. NEPA is particularly relevant to R&S because an EIS can expose system vulnerabilities and/or unsustainable conditions. As mentioned above, the MMS determined that an EIS was not required because the likelihood of a major oil spill was sufficiently remote. The MMS based part of its determination on the belief that any oil from a spill would not reach land and would quickly dissipate.

   a. How might the MMS (now the BOEM) analysis be different if it adopted a Precautionary Principle approach, described in Chapter 3, Section IV.C, to evaluate deep-water permitting?

   b. How might future requests for permitting be different if BOEM adopted an Adaptive Governance approach, described in Chapter 7, Section VI?

   c. Would either the Precautionary Principle or Adaptive Governance help us understand the resilience or sustainability of social-ecological systems in the Gulf?

---

[23] Executive Office of the President of the United States, Report Regarding the Minerals Management Service's National Environmental Policy Act Policies, Practices, and Procedures as They Relate to Outer Continental Shelf Oil and Gas Exploration and Development (Aug. 16, 2010), https://web.archive.org/web/20151003120215/https://www.whitehouse.gov/sites/default/files/microsites/ceq/20100816-ceq-mms-ocs-nepa.pdf.
[24] Id. at n.3.
[25] Id. at 3.

B. Waste Disposal and Cleanup

Congress enacted two primary legislative acts to address waste disposal and the cleanup of contaminated sites: the Resource Conservation and Recovery Act (RCRA), and the Comprehensive Environmental Response, Compensation and Liability Act (CERCLA). RCRA deals with solid and hazardous waste disposal through a regulatory structure designed to establish a "cradle-to-grave" system (Subtitle C) for tracking hazardous waste from generation to disposal, as well as through a more limited system (Subtitle D) for requiring nonhazardous waste to be disposed of in sanitary landfills.[26] RCRA also regulates storing materials in underground storage tanks (USTs) and the generation, transport, sale, and recycling of used oil. CERCLA provides the government authority to force the cleanup of hazardous waste sites and allocate liability for cleanup costs.[27]

1. RESOURCE CONSERVATION AND RECOVERY ACT

The Resource Conservation and Recovery Act (RCRA) manages the generation, transportation, and disposal of hazardous waste through the use of a manifest procedure that requires documentation for the shipment of waste from its origin to its final destination at an authorized "treatment, storage, and disposal facility" (TSDF). Generators and transporters of hazardous waste do not need a permit but they must participate in the manifest documentation system. A TSDF requires a permit in order to receive hazardous waste. Regulations require that the facility use liners and monitor groundwater and air emissions from incinerators in order to meet minimum technology standards. The permit also requires that the disposal facility provide planning and financing for facility closure once it ceases operation. Further, disposal facilities cannot dispose of hazardous wastes in landfills or by underground well injection absent a "no migration" variance. This variance requires that there is "no migration" of hazardous constituents from the land disposal, or that the waste is pretreated to a level at which the waste no longer exhibits hazardous characteristics — which can only be achieved by using the "best demonstrated available technology" (BDAT) to minimize environmental threats. Amendments to RCRA in 1986 enabled the EPA to address the environmental problems resulting from underground tanks storing petroleum and other hazardous substances.[28]

Subtitle C of RCRA regulates hazardous waste and defines it as "solid waste" that meets the criteria required to be hazardous. Solid waste can be solid, liquid, or a contained gas, and discarded as abandoned, recycled,

---

[26] See generally Resource Conservation and Recovery Act (RCRA) §82, 42 U.S.C. §6901: Solid Waste Disposal (2002).
[27] See generally, Daniel A. Farber & Ann E. Carlson, ENVIRONMENTAL LAW Chapter 8 (9th ed. 2013).
[28] Id.

or "inherently waste like." Domestic sewage and National Pollutant Discharge Elimination System permits for point source discharges may be solid wastes, but RCRA excludes them from regulation because they are subject to Clean Water Act regulation instead.

There are two primary types of hazardous wastes under RCRA — "listed wastes" and "characteristic wastes." The EPA lists (and de-lists) listed wastes through agency rulemaking. The characteristic wastes demonstrate one or more of the following characteristics: ignitability, corrosivity, reactivity, or toxicity. If a listed waste is mixed with a nonhazardous solid waste, it is still considered hazardous waste. However, if a characteristic waste is mixed with a nonhazardous solid waste, and the resulting material no longer exhibits a hazardous characteristic, then it will no longer be considered hazardous waste for purposes of RCRA. Wastes "derived from" a listed hazardous waste are hazardous, and any material containing a listed hazardous waste is treated as hazardous waste under the "contained-in" definition.[29]

RCRA regulates nonhazardous solid waste under Subtitle D. This waste is deposited into sanitary landfills, which must meet specific criteria for receiving nonhazardous waste, or into Municipal Solid Waste Landfills (MSWLFs). MSWLFs must meet stringent criteria similar to those required for hazardous waste treatment, storage, and disposal. MSWLF regulation is more stringent because Subtitle C exempts household waste from regulation, even though it may contain large amounts of hazardous waste. RCRA prohibits open dumping of nonhazardous waste and requires it to be disposed of in a sanitary landfill.[30]

Additional regulations under RCRA prohibit the exporting of hazardous waste outside of the country unless the exporter notifies the receiving country's government and it does not object. International treaties, such as the Basel Convention, also deal with exporting hazardous waste. The U.S. government may compel companies to clean up solid or hazardous waste if there is an "imminent and substantial endangerment," and citizens may bring civil actions against anyone who causes or contributes to such an endangerment. However, while RCRA has some authority to order cleanup of hazardous waste in addition to managing the waste life cycle, the legislative purview for cleanup falls under CERCLA.[31]

---

[29] *Id.*
[30] *Id.*
[31] *Id.*

2. THE COMPREHENSIVE ENVIRONMENTAL RESPONSE, COMPENSATION AND LIABILITY ACT

The Comprehensive Environmental Response, Compensation and Liability Act (CERCLA) is the principal federal statute enacted to contend with the cleanup of hazardous materials. It allows the government to compel persons identified as "potentially responsible parties" (PRPs) to clean up hazardous substances or share the cost of such cleanup activities. The law authorized a tax on the chemical and petroleum industries to create and maintain a funding source for cleaning up abandoned, hazardous sites, thus CERCLA is also known as "Superfund." The provision for collecting these special taxes expired in 1995, leaving replenishment of the fund to actions against those private parties who contributed in some way to the hazardous condition requiring remedy and funding through appropriations from general revenues.[32]

The EPA, in conjunction with the states, identifies hazardous sites that pose a serious risk to human health and the environment and lists these sites on the National Priorities List (NPL) for cleanup. For example, the human health and environmental threats from the mining and mineral processing sites on the NPL include asbestos exposure, lead poisoning, and the contamination of drinking water and waterways supporting fish. The EPA designated the Gold King Mine as a Superfund site and included it on the NPL in 2016, a year after "a team of EPA contractors released 3 million gallons of toxic mine waste into the Animas River, turning it yellow for days and kicking off an expensive and ongoing clean-up and quality monitoring effort."[33] This spill is discussed in more detail in Chapter 3 under the heading, "The Animas River and the Gold King Mine Contamination."

The EPA has put into place cleanup remedies using both private and Superfund resources for 68% of the total 1,685 sites listed since 1983. The EPA considers 36% of the listed NPL sites sufficiently protected for redevelopment or reuse.[34] The Government Accountability Office (GAO) reported that in a 15-year period from 1999 through 2013 the majority of Superfund cleanup money was spent in seven states. Over $2.0 billion was spent in New Jersey alone, which was more than 25% of cleanup funds.[35] In addition to providing for the cleanup of hazardous sites, CERCLA establishes prohibitions and requirements concerning closed and hazardous waste sites, provides for liability of those responsible for releases of

---

[32] *Id.*

[33] Devin Henry, *EPA Names Gold King Mine a Superfund Site*, THE HILL (Sept. 7, 2016, 4:25 PM), http://thehill.com/policy/energy-environment/294865-epa-names-gold-king-mine-a-superfund-site.

[34] Enesta Jones, *EPA Adds Nine Hazardous Waste Sites to Superfund's National Priorities List/Agency Also Proposes to Add an Additional Nine Sites*, U.S. ENVTL. PROTECTION AGENCY NEWSROOM (May 5, 2013), http://yosemite.epa.gov/opa/admpress.nsf/bd4379a92ceceeac8525735900400c27/dad880110407074185257b720054f6cc!OpenDocument.

[35] SUPERFUND: TRENDS IN FEDERAL FUNDING AND CLEAN UP OF EPA'S NONFEDERAL NATIONAL PRIORITIES LIST SITES, GAO (Sept. 2015), https://www.gao.gov/assets/680/672735.pdf.

hazardous waste, and authorizes the revision of the National Contingency Plan (NCP) to provide guidelines and procedures needed to respond to releases or threatened releases of pollutants.[36]

CERCLA assigns strict liability to potentially responsible parties (PRPs) and it is joint and several. CERCLA historically precluded defenses based on the divisibility of harm among the various PRPs contributing to the release. However, the U.S. Supreme Court in *Burlington Northern & Santa Fe Railway v. United States* agreed to allow a PRP to establish divisibility of the harm if they could prove that there is a rational basis for apportionment among the PRPs.[37]

There are four categories of PRPs:

1. prior owners and operators of the contaminated property at the time of disposal (which can even include underground containers that are leaking without the prior owner or operator's knowledge);
2. current owners and operators of the facility, even if the disposal occurred previously;
3. generators of the waste who arranged for its disposal or treatment; and
4. transporters of the hazardous waste, if they were substantially involved in selecting the disposal site.

Even though these various parties may have been operating in conformance with disposal laws and regulations in effect at the time, lack of negligence is not a defense to PRP liability.[38]

There are very limited defenses available to PRPs for escaping liability for hazardous waste cleanup. First, if petroleum or natural gas pollution causes the hazardous condition, it is exempt from coverage under CERCLA because other federal statutes address this pollution. Another major defense allows a current or prior landowner to avoid liability if they can show that they were an innocent purchaser. Under this exception, a landowner must show that at the time of purchase they made "all appropriate inquiries" into the condition of the property, most likely requiring a thorough environmental assessment, depending upon the property's history. There are also limited exceptions for hazardous releases caused by third parties, an act of war, or an act of God, and an exception for de minimis contributors. Finally, there is a potential exception for lenders holding or foreclosing a security interest in contaminated property, so long as they

---

[36] *CERCLA Limitation and Local Government Acquisitions and Other Activities*, EPA (Mar. 2011), https://www.epa.gov/sites/production/files/documents/local-gov-liab-acq-fs-rev.pdf; *see also Superfund: National Priorities List (NPL)*, EPA, https://www.epa.gov/superfund/superfund-national-priorities-list-npl (last updated Sept. 21, 2017).
[37] Burlington N. & Santa Fe Ry. Co. v. United States, 556 U.S. 599 (2009).
[38] See Farber & Carlson, *supra* note 27, at Chapter 8.

intend to divest themselves of ownership and do not exercise decision making or management and control over the site.[39]

In addition to prioritizing the cleanup of hazardous releases and determining who will be responsible for the cleanup, the EPA must determine the appropriate short-term and long-term remedies needed to respond to these releases (and threatened releases) and clear the site for redevelopment. Brownfields are contaminated urban sites that may not be appropriate for redevelopment as residential or high human contact uses, but may be sufficiently clean to support activities such as industrial or other commercial activities. Instead of leaving these industrial areas vacant because investors are wary of purchasing property with CERCLA liability, local, state, and federal funding have promoted appropriate infill redevelopment of urban areas and avoided the sprawl from suburban "greenfields" investment.

3. CASE STUDY OF RESILIENCE AND SUSTAINABILITY

The BP oil spill generated thousands of tons of oily waste. In response, workers laid booms in the ocean for oil containment and capture, conducted skimming operations, and cleaned the shoreline by soaking up the mess. While workers were able to extract usable oil from this collected waste, some considered the remaining material to be hazardous and deposited it in landfills in the Gulf area. The oil-soaked trash was not subject to RCRA regulation because a 1988 amendment categorically exempted oil exploration and production waste because of its alleged benign characteristics.[40] Although citizens in the Gulf region were concerned that potentially hazardous oil disposed of in local landfills would leach into the groundwater, EPA tests concluded that oily waste samples were not characteristically hazardous.[41]

Cleanup operations directed a larger percentage of the oil spill waste to landfills in minority or low-income communities, triggering environmental justice concerns.[42] The EPA defines environmental justice as "the fair treatment and meaningful involvement of all people regardless of race, color, national origin, or income with respect to the development,

---

[39] *Id.*

[40] 40 C.F.R. §261.4(b)(5) (2016) states that "drilling fluids, produced waters, and other wastes associated with the exploration, development, or production of crude oil, natural gas or geothermal energy" are solid wastes that are *not* hazardous wastes.

[41] Elana Schor, *How Has BP's Oily Waste Escaped 'Hazardous' Label?*, N.Y. Times (July 20, 2010), http://www.nytimes.com/gwire/2010/07/20/20greenwire-how-has-bps-oily-waste-escaped-hazardous-label-54942.html; *see also Questions and Answers About the BP Oil Spill in the Gulf Coast*, EPA (Feb. 14, 2013), https://web.archive.org/web/20150727155042/http://www.epa.gov/BPSpill/qanda.html.

[42] Krissah Thompson, *Waste from BP Oil Spill Cleanup Has Gulf Residents Near Landfills Concerned*, Wash. Post (Aug. 16, 2014), http://www.washingtonpost.com/wp-dyn/content/article/2010/08/15/AR2010081503185_2.html?sid=ST2010081503271.

implementation, and enforcement of environmental laws, regulations, and policies."[43] The citizens in the predominantly white and affluent community of Harrison County, Mississippi, were able to pressure BP not to deposit the oil spill waste in their nearby landfill.[44] Dr. Robert Bullard, credited with being the founder of the environmental justice movement, complained that this deal resulted in unfairly burdening local communities of color.[45] The EPA countered by explaining that "the agency approved a plan to deposit the waste in landfills close to the spill and took the racial makeup of the communities surrounding the landfills into account, along with the history of complaints about odor and other issues."[46] However, the EPA also voiced their disappointment in BP's plan not to deposit the waste from the oil spill in Harrison County.[47]

Questions and Notes

1. The EPA has spent at least $10 billion to address Superfund sites. How would the resilience and sustainability of systems associated with lands contaminated with hazardous waste be affected if that money could instead be allocated to preventative measures instead of cleanup? Can you think of a way to use funds related to pollution that would enhance ecosystems associated with land in a preventative way?

2. Unlike NEPA, RCRA and CERCLA incorporate substantive standards to address externalities. Would substantive or nonsubstantive regulations tend to increase the resilience of land-based systems? What about the wildlife on or connected to these lands? Does your answer depend on which systems? If so, which systems' resilience would be strengthened and which would be weakened?

3. As mentioned above, the oil-soaked trash was not subject to RCRA. Were the regulations governing cleanup adequate to ensure the sustainable, intergenerational equity of the coastal communities? If so, which communities? Did it depend on the community's economic status and race?

---

[43] *Environmental Justice*, U.S. EPA, https://web.archive.org/web/20150830064239/http://www.epa.gov/compliance/ej/ (last visited Nov. 30, 2017).
[44] *See* Thompson, *supra* note 42, at 2.
[45] *Id.*
[46] *Id.*
[47] *Id.*

IV. STRATEGY TO FACILITATE IMPLEMENTATION #7: LIFE CYCLE SUSTAINABILITY ASSESSMENT

Pollution and waste are often by-products. They are part of a process (typically one of the outcomes) that involves manufacturing something. However, when assessing externalities and the true costs of manufacturing a product, the costs of pollution and waste are often not calculated. Critical to R&S is the inclusion and consideration of waste disposal and all other phases of a product's life. As mentioned above, RCRA statutorily exempted the oil-soaked trash stemming from the BP oil spill. By doing so, it is difficult to ascertain the full effects of oil exploration and the products that stem from that exploration, and whether oil exploration as part of a social-ecological system is resilient. Important to decisions relevant to R&S is an understanding of the complete impacts a given policy may have.

Life Cycle Sustainability Assessment (LCSA) is a method to help identify, assess, and quantitatively analyze diverse environmental, social, and economic impacts to systems. LCSA draws from many different disciplines to obtain a broad swath of information pertaining to the potential and actual consequences of alternative decisions. Similar to Risk Analysis, described below in Section VI, LCSA helps unearth information relevant to impacts over time. That information will encourage decisions that reduce risk and result in more resilient and sustainable systems, if so desired.

A. General Description of LCSA

LCSA is a relatively new concept that derived from and expanded on Life Cycle Analysis (LCA) — also referred to as "life cycle approach," "life cycle assessment," and "life cycle management." Originally designed in the 1960s and 1970s, LCA attempts to capture some of the environmental impacts, including natural resource demands and pollution, stemming from all of the primary *stages* of a product's life — known as "cradle to cradle" or "cradle to grave." Possible stages that may be included in an LCA of a product or process are:

- researching and developing the product;
- originating, extracting, and transporting raw materials for the product;
- processing the raw materials;
- manufacturing the product;
- packaging, distributing, and transporting the product;
- purchasing, using, and maintaining the product during its normal life; and
- disposing (including recycling or reusing) the product.

At each stage, LCA helps obtain information pertaining to the environmental impacts occurring during that stage. Review of the environmental impacts may involve a number of *steps* for each stage, including:

1. The *definition and scope* are determined for the stage, including information needs, data specificity, collection methods, and data presentation.
2. A *life cycle inventory* (a quantification of system inputs and outputs, including energy flows, material flows, environmental pollution, and others) is completed through process diagrams, data collection, and evaluation of the data.
3. A *life cycle impact assessment* is established in which the data obtained from the life cycle inventory is categorized and weighted properly.
4. An *interpretation of the data* (#2 above) based on the assessment (#3 above) is completed, showing significant data, data evaluation and interpretation, conclusions, and recommendations.[48]

Although there are many variations of these *stages* and *steps*, the overall objective among the variations is focused on environmental externalities at all phases of products, processes, policies, or activities to help make decisions that are more informed. The information obtained through LCA helps connect diverse impacts to various stages of development. By doing so, it helps identify opportunities for improvement by illustrating weaknesses or high-impact areas. In addition, LCA helps policy makers more completely understand the relevant systems and potential impacts on those systems.

Performing an LCA can be difficult, as accessing the requisite system information may be complex and require advanced technology and resources (financial and human). In addition, determining which stage and step are necessary to analyze can raise critical (and often, political) questions. To help with this task, numerous LCA databases that standardize the review of specific products, processes, or activities are available. For example, Ecoinvent, an LCA database sponsored by Swiss Center for Life Cycle Inventories, provides impact analysis for building products, detergents, chemicals, wood, and many other products. Similarly, a commonly used framework for performing LCA is *ISO [International Organization for Standardization] 14040:2006, Environmental management — Life cycle assessment — Principles and framework*.[49] Choosing a standardized database may also depend on available resources.

---

[48] Aida Sefic Williams, *Life Cycle Analysis: A Step by Step Approach*, ISTC Reports, at 1 (Dec. 2009).
[49] For more information on LCA, see generally *Design for the Environment Life-Cycle Assessments*, U.S. EPA, https://www.epa.gov/saferchoice/design-environment-life-cycle-assessments (last visited Nov. 30, 2017); *See also* Williams, *supra* note 48, at 1.

ISO 14040:2006, ENVIRONMENTAL MANAGEMENT—LIFE CYCLE ASSESSMENT—PRINCIPLES AND FRAMEWORK

Founded in 1947, the International Organization for Standardization (ISO) is an independent, nongovernmental international organization that sets international standards. It is comprised of 162 representatives from around the world. Only one representative can be from each country and that representative must be from a standards organization in their respective country.

ISO 14040:2006 describes the principles and framework for life cycle assessment (LCA) including: definition of the goal and scope of the LCA, the life cycle inventory analysis (LCI) phase, the life cycle impact assessment (LCIA) phase, the life cycle interpretation phase, reporting and critical review of the LCA, limitations of the LCA, the relationship between the LCA phases, and conditions for use of value choices and optional elements.

ISO 14040:2006 covers life cycle assessment (LCA) studies and life cycle inventory (LCI) studies. It does not describe the LCA technique in detail, nor does it specify methodologies for the individual phases of the LCA.

The intended application of LCA or LCI results is considered during definition of the goal and scope, but the application itself is outside the scope of this International Standard.

International Organization for Standardization, *ISO 14040:2006 Preview Environmental Management — Life Cycle Assessment — Principles and Framework* (last visited Sept. 18, 2017).

B. Specific Description of LCSA's Relevance to R&S

LCSA is similar to LCA but broadens the scope of the analysis by exploring economic impacts ("life cycle costing") and social impacts ("social life cycle assessment"). The additional data accessed through LCSA provides a more complete picture of whether a system is approaching a threshold, which in turn informs the system's resilience, and whether that system is accomplishing its environmental, economic, and social goals. The following excerpt from the United Nations Environment Programme describes LCSA in more detail and explains how it expands on LCA.

Towards a Life Cycle Sustainability Assessment

UNITED NATIONS ENVIRONMENT PROGRAMME (2011), HTTP://WEDOCS.UNEP.ORG/BITSTREAM/HANDLE/20.500.11822/8001/UNEP_LIFECYCLEINIT_DEC_FINAL.PDF?SEQUENCE=3&ISALLOWED=Y (LAST VISITED DEC. 5, 2017)

An (Environmental) life cycle assessment (LCA) looks at potential impacts to the environment as a result of the extraction of resources, transportation, production, use, recycling and discarding of products; life cycle costing (LCC) is used to assess the cost implications of this life cycle; and social life cycle assessment (S-LCA) examines the social consequences. . . .

[I]n order to get the "whole picture," it is vital to extend current life cycle thinking to encompass all three pillars of sustainability: (i) environmental, (ii) economic and (iii) social. This means carrying out an assessment based on environmental, economic and social issues — by conducting an overarching life cycle sustainability assessment (LCSA). . . .

Increasingly, in addition to tackling economic questions when developing policies and strategies, governments and enterprises must consider impacts on the environment and society. There is now growing concern with addressing the *three pillars of sustainability*: (i) environment, (ii) economic, and (iii) social.

The crucial question is: *How do we guarantee more sustainable practices into the future?* Applying *life cycle thinking* . . . to the pillars of sustainability offers a way of incorporating sustainable development in decision-making processes. . . . [It] means taking account of the environmental, social and economic impacts of a product over its entire life cycle. . . .

Potential and future decision-makers, stakeholders, enterprises, and consumers can benefit from LCSA in the following ways:

- LCSA enables practitioners to organize complex environmental, economic and social information and data in a structured form.
- LCSA helps in clarifying the trade-offs between the three sustainability pillars, life cycle stages and impacts, products and generations by providing a more comprehensive picture of the positive and negative impacts along the product life cycle.
- LCSA will show enterprises how to become more responsible for their business by taking into account the full spectrum of impacts associated with their products and services.
- LCSA promotes awareness in value chain actors on sustainability issues.
- LCSA supports enterprises and value chain actors in identifying weaknesses and enabling further improvements of a product life cycle. For instance, it supports decision-makers in enterprises in finding more sustainable means of production and in designing more sustainable products. . . .
- LCSA helps decision-makers choose sustainable technologies and products.
- LCSA can support consumers in determining which products are not only cost-efficient, eco-efficient or socially responsible, but also more sustainable.
- LCSA stimulates innovation in enterprises and value chain actors. . . .

Walter Klöpffer put this idea [of LCSA] into a conceptual formula. . . . :

$$LCSA = (environmental)\ LCA + LCC + S\text{-}LCA$$

. . . . By identifying the various stages that a product experiences, we can more accurately understand the environmental and social impacts. . . . These are often impacts that may otherwise under existing methods and functioning be intentionally or unintentionally ignored.

C. Illustration of LCSA's Relevance to R&S

While consumption has played a limited role in environmental law and policy relevant to disposal, more research has shown the need to focus on consumption to reach more sustainable levels and avoid mass pollution.[50] However, governments, consumer product markets, and individual consumers must be involved to change unsustainable consumption patterns.[51] In the excerpt below, the authors employ LCSA to help determine which waste disposal alternative is best for Nonthaburi, Thailand, a local government of about 260,000 people outside of Bangkok. The authors describe the LCSA process and the methods they used to make decisions resulting in more sustainable conditions.

S.N.M. Menikpura, Shabbir H Gheewala, & Sébastien Bonnet, *Framework for Life Cycle Sustainability Assessment of Municipal Solid Waste Management Systems with an Application to a Case Study in Thailand*

30 WASTE MGMT. RES. 7, 708-719 (2012)

Similar to other Asian countries, open dumping and non engineered landfilling [discharging untreated waste into an uncontrolled open dump] are the two predominant waste disposal methods in Thailand. . . .

At present, the average amount of municipal solid waste (MSW) generation in [the City of Nonthaburi, Thailand] is 370 tonnes per day [one tonne is equal to almost 2,205 pounds]. Nonthaburi Municipality is making an effort to maximize recycling and minimize waste generation. As a result, 24% waste recycling was achieved in 2010. . . . The remaining 76% of generated waste is disposed of in a sanitary landfill without a

---

[50]John C. Dernbach, *Pollution Control and Sustainable Industry*, 12 NAT. RESOURCES & ENV'T 101 (1997) (discussing among other issues the need to reduce consumption of renewable and non-renewable resources in both the private and the industrial sector and suggesting that taxes and subsidies could be used to effect change).
[51]Douglas A. Kysar & Michael P. Vandenbergh, *Introduction: Climate Change and Consumption*, 38 ENVTL. L. REP. NEWS & ANALYSIS 10825 (2008).

gas recovery system. Therefore, the existing landfill is a cause of serious environmental degradation, economic losses and social burdens. In order to minimize such burdens, a potential integrated system was considered for Nonthaburi Municipality [an integrated solid waste system is one that considers waste prevention, recycling, composting, combustion, and landfilling]. In order to assess sustainability, an attempt was made to broaden the application of a traditional environmental life cycle assessment (LCA) to a more comprehensive three-dimensional sustainability assessment. . . .

Assessment of environmental sustainability

. . . [E]ven though . . . damage to human health is caused by environmental emissions, this indicator can be considered as a social indicator too. . . . Hence, only "damage to ecosystem" and "damage to abiotic resources" are selected as the major composite indicators for environmental sustainability assessment. . . .

Assessment of economic sustainability

. . . Sustainability of any MSW [municipal solid waste] management method depends on the total cost of the facility and the willingness of people to pay for a waste management service. Therefore, a detailed financial analysis via life cycle costing (LCC) has been identified as an appropriate economic method. . . .

Assessment of social sustainability

. . . There is a wide range of social impacts, both positive and negative, associated with MSW management. For instance, poor MSW management practices may lead to a serious threat to human health, including shortened length of life, as a result of environmental pollution and other negative impacts. Also, at times, there is a lack of benefits to the community resulting in public opposition, as well as a lack of stakeholder participation, coordination and commitment to waste management. In contrast, properly designed waste management systems improve the overall social environment and aesthetic conditions. The major social impact of initiating such a system is the possibility of uplifting community well-being. Improving the efficiencies of waste management systems and reducing the environmental emissions would directly help mitigate public health hazards, consequently reducing expenditure by health services. In addition, an appropriate waste management system may provide a significant number of direct and indirect employment opportunities, as well as generating additional income to households from selling recyclables, home composting, etc. Thus, damage to human health and income-based community well-being are suitable indicators to quantify the critical social impacts from waste management. . . .

[The LCSA framework adopted by the authors] includes the major phases of the life cycle, such as collection and transportation of MSW, segregation of biodegradable and combustibles fractions at the sorting facility, and treatment using different technologies. It should be noted that recycling is a different process chain as recyclables are separated at the household level. . . .

[P]olicy-makers or local authorities can develop a simple spreadsheet model by following the step-by-step procedure explained in this article to quantify the ultimate damages/effects from waste management systems. Once the damages/effects from different waste management options are quantified, the results can be compared and the most sustainable waste management system can be selected for a particular municipality.

For instance, the analysis results of the case study in Nonthaburi revealed that efficiency of the materials and energy recovery potential from different technologies are the key driving forces for the level of sustainability. . . . According to the policy targets, if Nonthaburi Municipality initiates an integrated system with a 30% recycling rate (instead of the current rate of 24%) the MSW management system would have the potential of further improving all the sustainability aspects by more than 20%. . . .

To assess the three dimensional sustainability, a comprehensive methodology was presented and the most relevant composite indicators were proposed. . . .

The proposed indicators were used to test the effectiveness of the integrated system via quantitative assessment of the sustainability attributes. Out of all the technologies assessed, recycling was found to be the most promising technology with regard to its potential for driving the entire system towards improved sustainability. AD [anaerobic digestion] and incineration were found to contribute to environmental and social sustainability. However, those technologies were found to be not economically sustainable owing to their high investment and operational costs. The enhancement of efficiencies of those technologies is therefore required to enable improving overall sustainability. Based on the proposed assessment framework detailed in this article, the research findings obtained from the case study evaluated in this work for Thailand could considerably help in strengthening law enforcement and support policy initiatives for moving towards more sustainable MSW management plans via an integrated approach.

In 2015, researchers at Yale University estimated that the average person in the United States disposes of 1,871 pounds of trash per year in landfills.[52] At the time the researchers published their findings, the U.S. Environmental Protection Agency estimated the average to be approximately half of this number. The researchers' findings are particularly troubling for climate change. When trash decomposes in landfills, it emits methane—a significant contributor to climate change since a methane molecule can trap as much as 25 times the amount of heat as a carbon dioxide molecule and can stay in the atmosphere for approximately 12 years. Almost 18% of all U.S. methane emissions originate in landfills.

Questions and Notes

1. Note how Menikpura et al. begin by choosing key metrics to inform the LSCA. They then select the stages of review (for example, trash collection), followed by the inputs and outputs affecting the system at the various stages:

   a. *Environmental: Inputs*
      i. Land consumption
      ii. Fossil fuel and mineral consumption
   b. *Environmental: Outputs*
      i. Environmental emissions (such as carbon dioxide and methane)
   c. *Social: Inputs*
      i. Labor force
      ii. Community participation
   d. *Social: Outputs*
      i. Uplifting the living standards of the community
   e. *Economic: Inputs*
      i. Costs involved in waste management
   f. *Economic: Outputs*
      i. Income generations

   Finally, the authors compared policy options to make a recommendation based on the overall sustainability of the proposals by weighing the environmental, economic, and social metrics. This process of selecting metrics, stages, and means to quantify each metric represents a typical LCSA process.

---

[52] Jon T. Powell, Timothy G. Townsend & Julie B. Zimmerman, *Estimates of Solid Waste Disposal Rates and Reduction Targets for Landfill Gas Emissions*, Nature Climate Change (Sept. 21, 2015), http://www.nature.com/nclimate/journal/vaop/ncurrent/full/nclimate2804.html.

2. Many statutes and associated regulations focus on one phase of a product's life. For example, RCRA and CERCLA primarily focus on the disposal phase of a product. Should statutes like RCRA and CERCLA consider all phases of a product's life? What would be the objective of a statute similar to RCRA that considered all phases?

3. If you were asked to work on an LCSA of grass fed versus non-grass fed beef, what inputs and outputs would you recommend? For example, would you explore: water pollution/runoff from the grass pasture versus the corn and related food croplands for an environmental output; health implications of consuming grass versus non-grass fed beef for a social input; and costs involved with grass versus non-grass fed for an economic input?

4. As illustrated in the excerpt above, LCSA has a high level of interconnectedness with other Strategies for Implementation, including Baselines and Metrics (discussed in Chapter 6, Section IV) and Risk Analysis (discussed below). What metrics would you use to measure the inputs and outputs you identified in question 3 above? For example, for water pollution/runoff in adjacent waterways, we might measure nutrient levels (such as nitrate and phosphate levels), the prevalence of microorganisms (such as Salmonella, E. coli, and Cryptosporidium), and veterinary pharmaceuticals (such as Sulfamethazine).

5. Drafted at the Earth Summit in 1992, *Agenda 21* is a nonbinding 700-page report covering a broad array of environmental, social, and economic issues. In covering toxic chemicals, the report calls for the use of LCA, stating:

   > In a wider context, risk reduction involves broad-based approaches to reducing the risks of toxic chemicals, taking into account the entire life cycle of the chemicals. . . . The objective of the programme area is to eliminate unacceptable or unreasonable risks . . . by employing a broad-based approach involving a wide range of risk reduction options and by taking precautionary measures derived from a broad-based life-cycle analysis. . . .

   > Governments, through the cooperation of relevant international organizations and industry, where appropriate, should . . . [u]ndertake concerted activities to reduce risks for toxic chemicals, taking into account the entire life cycle of the chemicals. . . .[53]

6. An integral part of Collective Action Challenges (CAC), described in Chapter 3, Section II.E, are externalities. These are negative impacts one actor has on another actor when the first uses a common resource.

---

[53] United Nations Conference on Environment and Development, Agenda 21, Ch. 19, at §§19.44-19.50 (1992).

In the context of pollution that typically means using a clean resource, such as air, land, or water, and polluting that resource. The actor polluting the source receives the economic benefit of avoiding costs associated with proper disposal or reducing disposal. Given this, how would you describe the connection between LCSA and CACs? Where does LCSA fit in and could it help avoid CACs?

V. ADDRESSING POLLUTION: U.S. ENVIRONMENTAL LAW AND POLLUTION

Continuing our discussion of U.S. environmental law from Section III, below we introduce statutes relevant to pollution and clean air, clean water, oceans, and toxins. For each area of the law, we explore its relevance to resilience and sustainability.

A. Clean Air

Even though it is purported to be the most complex environmental statute yet enacted, the Clean Air Act (CAA) of 1970—along with its major amendments, particularly those of 1990—is one of the most effective pollution controls in modern times. The CAA establishes National Ambient Air Quality Standards by identifying major air pollutants and using human health and environmental data to set nationwide goals for controlling air pollution. We achieve these goals through both a command-and-control approach, illustrated by the technology standards demanded of industrial polluters to limit emissions, and economic incentive regulation enacted through the 1990 amendments, which employ a cap-and-trade system to reduce acid rain created by power plant sulfur emissions. CAA legislation regulates both stationary sources of pollutant emissions, such as factories and power plants, and mobile sources, such as vehicles.[54]

1. NATIONAL AMBIENT AIR QUALITY STANDARDS

There are two types of National Ambient Air Quality Standards (NAAQS): primary standards, which establish the concentrations of pollutants required "to protect the public health," and secondary standards, which establish the concentrations required "to protect the public welfare," by

---

[54] Clean Air Act (CAA) §111(a)(3) (2016), 42 U.S.C. §7411(a)(3) (2016): Standards of Performance for New Stationary Sources (2006) (defines stationary source as any "building, structure, facility, or installation which emits or may emit any air pollutant").

considering the effect of pollutants on property and the environment. The EPA must establish and monitor ambient air concentrations for six "criteria pollutants." These nationwide pollutants include sulfur dioxide, particulate matter, carbon monoxide, ozone, nitrogen dioxide, and lead. When establishing these standards, the EPA cannot account for economic or technological concerns and must solely consider the most recent scientific information about the public health and environmental effects of the ambient levels established. Initially, most anticipated that we would attain the NAAQS in 1977, but instead, there were many areas in the United States that were not in attainment by the statutory deadline. Therefore, the 1977 CAA amendments included statutory strategies to foster state cooperation and address these nonattainment areas. The NAAQS require periodic review for necessary revision; however, changes to these standards are infrequent and are often challenged by industry and/or environmental advocacy groups.[55]

2. ACID RAIN

Two of the criteria pollutants—sulfur dioxide and nitrous oxide—present a special difficulty when they mix with water in the atmosphere to form precipitation called "acid rain," which can cause serious harm to human health, natural resources, and personal property.[56] Coal-burning power plants are notorious emitters of these pollutants. In 1990, Congress amended the CAA to adopt a new approach to controlling acid rain through economic-incentive regulation.

Title IV of the CAA requires ongoing reduction of sulfur dioxide emissions and establishes a program of marketable sulfur allowances. Initially, power plants specifically listed in the statute received sulfur allowances and could sell these allowances if they found it cheaper to reduce emissions. Title IV allows polluters to trade emissions, but it also allows environmental groups and individuals to purchase these allowances to "retire" them and reduce emissions by reducing allowances in the marketplace. Over time, as defined by the statute, the EPA will reduce the number of sulfur allowances allocated to facilities. Participation in the sulfur allowance programs and other regulatory controls target nitrous oxide emissions for reduction. The acid rain program requires a permit and a compliance plan under Title IV.[57]

---

[55] *See, e.g.*, Mississippi v. EPA, 744 F.3d 1334 (D.C. Cir. 2013).
[56] *See Effects of Acid Rain*, U.S. EPA, https://www.epa.gov/acidrain/effects-acid-rain (last updated June 1, 2017); *see also* University of Vermont, *Damage from Acid Rain Pollution Is Far Worse Than Previously Believed*, SCIENCEDAILY (July 18 2002), http://www.sciencedaily.com/releases/2002/07/020718075630.htm; Megan Nortrup, *Acid Rain's Slow Dissolve*, U.S. NAT'L PARK SERV. (May 22, 2012), http://www.nps.gov/nama/blogs/Acid-Rains-Slow-Dissolve.htm.
[57] Farber & Carlson, *supra* note 27, at Chapter 6.

3. NATIONAL EMISSION STANDARDS FOR HAZARDOUS AIR POLLUTANTS

The EPA must limit hazardous air pollutants by determining which air pollutants are hazardous under CAA Section 112 and promulgating emission standards. The initial statute required that the standards ensure "an ample margin of safety to protect the public health," and the EPA had difficulty discerning how carcinogenic air emissions could possibly meet this standard. In *NRDC v. EPA*, the D.C. Circuit attempted to guide the EPA in deciding that the term "safe" does not mean "risk-free."[58] The court held that the EPA had authority to determine what emission levels are "acceptable" risks to public health so long as it did not consider costs when deciding what was "safe."[59] The EPA could later use costs and technological feasibility to determine what constitutes an "ample margin" of safety.[60]

The EPA continued to struggle with the concept of what constitutes an "acceptable risk" until Congress amended Section 112 in 1990. Congress directed the EPA to establish technology-based standards that use maximum achievable control technology (MACT) and develop programs to control hazardous air pollutant emissions from various sources. The EPA has identified 189 hazardous pollutants, as compared to the initial list of seven hazardous pollutants (asbestos, benzene, beryllium, coke oven emissions, inorganic arsenic, mercury, radionuclides, and vinyl chloride). The EPA applies National Emission Standards for Hazardous Air Pollutants (NESHAPs) to both existing and new major sources and to "area sources," which are stationary sources of HAPs that are not major sources or mobile sources.[61]

4. STATE IMPLEMENTATION PLAN

Every state must prepare a State Implementation Plan (SIP) showing how it will impose and enforce restrictions on pollutant emissions in order to attain the federally mandated NAAQS by required statutory deadlines. For each criteria pollutant, the state must determine whether the "air quality control regions" within its boundaries are either in attainment or in nonattainment areas for specific pollutants. An air quality control region may be in attainment for one or more pollutants, but in nonattainment for other criteria pollutants. The state establishes a plan based on what it will take to achieve the NAAQS given existing air pollution sources and proposed emission limitations. Emission sources include both stationary and mobile sources.[62]

---

[58] NRDC v. EPA, 824 F.2d 1146 (D.C. Cir. 1987).
[59] *Id.* at 1166.
[60] *See id.* at 1165.
[61] Farber & Carlson, *supra* note 27, at Chapter 6.
[62] *Id.*

Once these restrictions are established based on modeling, estimating, and predicting air quality, the state is responsible for monitoring air quality to determine whether it has attained the NAAQS. The EPA must approve the SIP and may sanction a state for noncompliance by withdrawing federal highway funding, restricting the state's ability to allow new or modified emission sources in nonattainment areas, and even substituting a Federal Implementation Plan (FIP) for an inadequate SIP. Since air pollutants do not heed state boundaries, state SIPs must also control in-state sources that interfere with another state's ability to adhere to the NAAQS.[63]

5. CAA REGULATION OF MOBILE SOURCES

The 1970 Clean Air Act provisions established the basic structure of pollution control over vehicles. Federal emission limitations on these mobile sources are determined based on technology requirements designed to force vehicle manufacturers to improve currently existing technology to meet higher standards of emission controls. In order to prevent manufacturers from having to meet a variety of standards established by different states, the CAA preempts state standards except for those states adopting the more restrictive California standards, allowed because of California's unique air quality challenges.

In addition to imposing limits on vehicle emissions, the EPA regulates fuel ingredients. Gasoline is now lead-free and regulations in some parts of the United States require the reformulation of oxygenated fuels to reduce ozone-forming emissions and carbon monoxide. The 1990 CAA amendments encourage using alternative fuels such as ethanol, natural gas, and clean fuel vehicles to reduce pollution, particularly in nonattainment areas such as California. Regulating mobile sources is an important part of the CAA, but the extent of regulation is limited. While command-and-control regulation of manufacturers and refiners can address fuel efficiency and vehicle technology, the government cannot dictate the individual actions of drivers in a free society such as the United States. Instead, we need the market pricing of vehicles and fuel, as well as carpool lane incentives, to encourage people to use mass transit and ride sharing. City planning and land use controls are also helpful to discourage urban sprawl, promote bicycle use, and increase the walkability of cities.[64]

---

[63] CAA §110(a)(2)(D), 42 U.S.C. §7410(a)(2)(D): State implementation plans for national primary and secondary ambient air quality standards.
[64] *See* Farber & Carlson, *supra* note 27, at Chapter 6.

6. CAA REGULATION OF STATIONARY SOURCES

Command-and-control regulation based on emission limitations and tech-nology requirements works well on stationary sources. However, the CAA has also effectively established economic incentives to encourage emitters to reduce pollution through cap-and-trade and through offsets. Many of the CAA provisions address requirements for new or modified stationary sources only, and some have criticized this approach as discouraging exist-ing facilities from modernizing in order to avoid restriction. Instead, the state implementation plans are mostly responsible for controlling exist-ing stationary sources. As addressed above, officials divide states into air quality control regions and classify each region as either nonattainment or attainment for particular pollutants. States are then free to develop restric-tions on existing stationary source emissions and implement the federally mandated regulations of new and modified sources.[65]

In Southern California, the California Air Resources Board (CARB) reg-ulates mobile resources, while the South Coast Air Quality Management District (SCAQMD) uses emission and operation rules to regulate station-ary sources, such as petroleum facilities. For example, a SCAQMD rule adopted in 2013 requires petroleum refineries equipped with delayed coking units to reduce emissions from the atmospheric venting of coke drums. These rules are complex and the SCAQMD attempts to help small business owners comply by offering compliance classes and compliance inspections without penalty. [66]

7. NEW SOURCE PERFORMANCE STANDARDS

All new or modified sources, whether the source is located in an attain-ment area or a nonattainment area, must meet New Source Performance Standards (NSPS) restrictions for the target pollutant. Existing station-ary sources are not subject to NSPS restrictions unless they modify their equipment or production processes. NSPS restrictions are determined on a national basis within categories of industrial sources and restrict emis-sions according to technology standards that are based on the "best system of emission reduction" that can be demonstrated to the EPA, considering cost and achievability.[67] These technology-based standards constitute com-mand-and-control regulation, but the definition of a stationary source as any "building, structure, facility, or installation, which emits or may emit

---

[65] *Id.*
[66] *Rule 1114: Petroleum Refinery Cooking Operations*, South Coast Air Quality Mgmt. Dist. (SCAQMD) (May 3, 2013), http://www.aqmd.gov/docs/default-source/rule-book/reg-xi/rule-1114.pdf.
[67] CAA §111, 42 U.S.C. §7411 (2012).

any air pollutant,"[68] facilitates an economic-efficiency approach using the "bubble" rule.

The "bubble" rule allows an individual stationary source to claim that changes within a facility, including both new and modified sources, are not subject to NSPS restrictions so long as the overall emissions for the industrial facility do not exceed existing emissions. Using an imaginary bubble to contain all emissions from a "stationary source" — which may actually comprise multiple sources — the "bubble" rule allows an industrial facility to make cost-efficient decisions to reduce emissions from one part of its plant to offset increased emissions from another part of its operation and still avoid meeting the NSPS technology standards. The net result will be that emissions from the stationary source will be at least the same, if not less, than previous emissions, and the industrial facility may benefit economically from the change in operation. In addition to subjecting all new and modified stationary sources to NSPS limitations, the CAA restricts these sources depending upon whether the source is located in an attainment area or nonattainment area for the specific pollutants emitted.[69]

8. ATTAINMENT AREA CONTROLS

The CAA regulations govern new or modified stationary sources in attainment areas to ensure that an air quality control region currently in attainment for one or more pollutants does not deteriorate when new sources enter the area or when modifications to an existing source increase existing emissions or emit a new pollutant. Therefore, in addition to satisfying NSPS, a major new or modified emitting source must also satisfy the requirements of the "Prevention of Significant Deterioration" (PSD) program adopted in the 1977 CAA amendments.[70] The stationary source must obtain preconstruction review and approval and use the "best available control technology" (BACT) as determined individually for the particular facility seeking approval. Although this is not an industry-wide or nationally set standard like the NSPS, the BACT must be at least as strict as the NSPS. Sources subject to this program must meet the definition of a "major emitting facility," having the potential to emit 100 tons per year or more of any air pollutant. If it does not meet the definition of a "major emitting facility," it must be a stationary source with the potential to emit more than 250 tons per year.[71]

PSD areas are those regions classified as either attainment or unclassifiable relative to the NAAQS, and the goal is to allow some economic

---

[68] CAA §111(a)(3), 42 U.S.C. §7411(a)(3) (2012).
[69] *See* Farber & Carlson, *supra* note 27, at Chapter 6.
[70] CAA §101(b)(1), 42 U.S.C. §7401(b)(1) (2012).
[71] *See* Farber & Carlson, *supra* note 27, at Chapter 6.

growth in the area without endangering the air quality. There are three classes of PSD areas: Class I, which includes places such as national parks; Class II, which includes all other areas designated as attainment; and Class III, which is a designation by the state to reclassify Class I or Class II areas to allow greater emissions under certain circumstances.[72] The amount by which emissions may increase in a particular PSD area is limited based upon these classes. Similar to the "bubble" rule, used to determine whether a new or modified source within a larger facility is subject to NSPS review, the EPA uses the "bubble" concept in determining whether an entire facility, not just the individual sources, will be subject to PSD review.[73]

9. NONATTAINMENT AREA CONTROLS

When an air-quality management region does not meet the NAAQS for one or more criteria pollutants, it is a nonattainment area for the pollutant(s) at issue and it creates a dilemma as to whether new sources will be able to enter into the area. Restricting such entry affects the short-term economic vitality for nonattainment areas across the country, so the EPA and Congress developed an approach that would allow some growth while still addressing the need for emission reduction.[74]

Section 172, 42 U.S.C. §7502, requires states to include certain requirements for nonattainment areas in their SIP. First, nonattainment areas must comply with primary NAAQS "as expeditiously as practicable" within the set deadlines, but states may obtain extensions from the EPA. Second, states must make "reasonable further progress" (RFP) to achieve compliance by making "annual incremental reductions" in emissions. Third, existing stationary sources must meet the state SIP technology-based standards including "reasonably available control technology" (RACT) and "reasonably available control measures" (RACM). Fourth, areas that are nonattainment for ozone are subject to additional CAA restrictions depending upon their placement in one of five area classifications based on the severity of the ozone pollution (extreme, severe, serious, moderate, and marginal). Each classification is subject to varying requirements that include showing "reasonable further progress" by meeting a set percentage reduction, defining more stringently what constitutes a major source, requiring greater offsets to reduce overall emissions of ozone in the area, and restricting emissions from mobile sources, since vehicle emissions contribute heavily to ozone formation.[75]

---

[72] CAA §162, 42 U.S.C. §7472: Initial Classifications.
[73] *See* Farber & Carlson, *supra* note 27, at Chapter 6.
[74] *Id.*
[75] *Id.*

The major regulatory feature impacting nonattainment areas is the requirement that new or modified major stationary sources obtain a permit under Section 173, 42 U.S.C. §7503, in order to begin operation in a nonattainment area. However, the EPA applies the bubble rule, as discussed above, to NSPS requirements in nonattainment areas so that existing sources wishing to modify will not need a permit if overall emissions from the facility do not increase.[76]

To address the concern that increased emissions from new and modified stationary sources in a nonattainment area will further erode the state's ability to meet the NAAQS, the permitting process requires these sources to obtain "offsets" for new emissions and meet stringent technology-based control levels. Offsets are emission reductions achieved in the nonattainment area through purchased reductions from other existing stationary sources or from government efforts to achieve emission reductions while allowing for desired economic growth.[77] Sources subject to the offset permitting process will also be required to meet several other requirements including the "lowest achievable emission rate" (LAER), which is one of the strictest technology standards that must be at least as stringent as the applicable NSPS.[78]

The "offset" program, the "bubble" rule, sulfur allowance trading, and PSD permitting all directly or indirectly employ economic market incentives to reduce emissions. Existing sources that are able to reduce emissions cost-effectively may sell or trade these reductions to existing sources, which are unable to reduce emissions as required, or to new or modified sources with increased emissions. While economic incentives are effective in reducing pollution below the level we can achieve with command-and-control regulation, some people object that sources are able to buy a "right to pollute." Additionally, there are limitations on the effectiveness of these market-trading schemes. Since the traders must sell the same pollutant within the same air quality region, trading requires a functioning commodity market. The initial allocation of emission rights also requires fairness. Finally, emission rights might lose value as future government regulation may reduce emission levels and create market uncertainty.[79]

---

[76] *Id.*

[77] *See* Citizens Against Refinery's Effects, Inc. v. EPA, 643 F.2d 183 (4th Cir. 1981) (affirming EPA's approval of Virginia's SIP, which requires the state highway department to use less of a particular type of asphalt and thereby decrease hydrocarbon pollution in an amount sufficient to offset increased pollution from a proposed refinery).

[78] *See* Farber & Carlson, *supra* note 27, at Chapter 6.

[79] *Id.*

10. TITLE V AND STATE PERMITS

The states must develop and implement the permitting program instituted by the 1990 CAA amendments. Legislation requires the EPA to adopt the regulations guiding the state permitting process. Permits are required for stationary sources, such as those participating in sulfur trading, those emitting above a certain threshold of hazardous air pollutants, new and existing sources subject to NSPS, major sources in nonattainment areas, sources required to have a PSD permit, and other sources as identified in the statute.[80] The state permitting process, under the EPA's direction, takes into account the other types of federal permits, such as the PSD permit and the permit required under Section 173 governing nonattainment areas.[81]

TITLES I AND V: UTILITY AIR REGULATORY GROUP V. EPA, 134 S. CT. 2427 (2014)

Following the *Massachusetts v. EPA* case, the U.S. Environmental Protection Agency announced that stationary sources would be subject to the Title I, "Prevention of Significant Deterioration" (PSD) program, and Title V because they emit greenhouse gases (GHGs), and GHGs are air pollutants that endanger human health.

Pursuant to Title I (PSD), EPA is charged with formulating national ambient air quality standards (NAAQS) for air pollutants, §§7408-7409. At the time of this case, EPA had issued NAAQS for six pollutants: sulfur dioxide, particulate matter, nitrogen dioxide, carbon monoxide, ozone, and lead, 40 CFR pt. 50 (2013). States are primarily responsible for implementing the NAAQS by developing "state implementation plans," 42 U.S.C. §7410. States must designate every area within their borders as "attainment," "nonattainment," or "unclassifiable" with respect to each NAAQS, 42 U.S.C. §7407(d). Stationary sources in areas designated attainment or unclassifiable are subject to the Act's provisions relating to PSD, §§7470-7492. It is unlawful to construct or modify a "major emitting facility" in "any area to which [the PSD program] applies" without first obtaining a permit, §§7475(a)(1), 7479(2)(C).

To qualify for a permit, the facility must not cause or contribute to the violation of any applicable air-quality standard, 42 U.S.C. §7475(a)(3), and it must comply with emissions limitations that reflect the "best available control technology" (or BACT) for "each pollutant subject to regulation under" the Act, 42 U.S.C. §7475(a)(4).

Title V also makes it unlawful to operate any "major source," wherever located, without a comprehensive operating permit, 42 U.S.C. §7661a(a). Unlike the PSD program, Title V generally does not impose any substantive pollution-control requirements. Title V facilitates compliance and enforcement by consolidating all of a facility's obligations under the Act into a single document. The permit must include all "emissions limitations

---

[80] CAA §502, 42 U.S.C. §7661 (2012): Permit Programs.
[81] *See* Farber & Carlson, *supra* note 27, at Chapter 6.

and standards" that apply to the source, as well as associated inspection, monitoring, and reporting requirements, 42 U.S.C. §7661c(a)-(c).

Upon the Utility Regulatory Air Group's challenge to the EPA's determination, the Supreme Court ruled that the EPA reasonably interpreted the Clean Air Act to require major sources under Title V (requiring permits based on their emission of conventional pollutants) to comply with BACT for GHGs.

11. CASE STUDY OF RESILIENCE AND SUSTAINABILITY

While air pollution was not one of the major problems resulting from the BP oil spill, the National Oceanic and Atmospheric Administration (NOAA) monitored air quality over the area where oil was spilling and measured a variety of pollutants, including ozone and particulate matter. The EPA and Occupational Safety and Health Administration (OSHA) were also monitoring air quality in various areas to determine possible health risks to shoreline residents and cleanup workers. Measurements and predictions were consistent among these three agencies based on the regional air quality model used to project the dispersion of pollutants.[82] NOAA determined that "[t]he levels of ozone were similar to what occurs in large urban areas. During the oil spill, it was like having a large city's worth of pollution appear out in the middle of the Gulf of Mexico." [83]

NOAA's research revealed that about one of every 13 barrels of oil that reached the ocean surface became airborne particulates from either the controlled surface burning of the oil or from evaporation. NOAA researchers determined that "the total mass of organic particles formed from evaporating surface oil was about ten times bigger than the mass of soot from all the controlled burns."[84] These particles have human health effects since they are small enough for human lungs to inhale and they can damage both lung and heart functions, as well as affect climate. NOAA's study showed that while the lighter compounds from the oil evaporated quickly, the heavier compounds took longer and formed the majority of the airborne particles. This discovery will be very helpful to future research about air quality in general since vehicles and other combustion sources emit the same compounds released from an oil spill.[85]

---

[82] *NOAA Releases Data Report on Air Quality Measurements Near the Deepwater Horizon/BP Oil Spill Area*, NAT'L OCEANIC AND ATMOSPHERIC ADMIN. (NOAA) (July 21, 2010), http://www.noaanews.noaa.gov/stories2010/20100721_p3_oilspill.html.

[83] *Air Pollution Levels from Deepwater Horizon Spill Similar to Large Urban Area*, NOAA (Dec. 19, 2011), http://www.noaanews.noaa.gov/stories2011/20111219_dwhairquality.html.

[84] *Id.*

[85] *Insights from Oil Spill Air Pollution Study Have Applications Beyond Gulf*, NOAA (March 10, 2011), http://www.noaanews.noaa.gov/stories2011/20110310_airpollution_oilspill.html.

Questions and Notes

1. As mentioned above, NAAQS are rarely reviewed. How would an Adaptive Governance approach, discussed in Chapter 7, Section VI, to NAAQS work? In addition, would that improve the sustainability of air quality?

2. Air pollution raises a particular collective action challenge. Can you describe the challenge?

3. Is it possible to have a resilient or sustainable social-ecological system (any system) that pollutes the air? If so, how?

4. Do the "bubble rule" and cap-and-trade programs promote the sustainability of the atmosphere and the resilience of social-ecological systems associated with clean air? Does it depend on which systems we are analyzing?

5. Please read this excerpt from Albert C. Lin, *Myths of Environmental Law*, 2015 UTAH L. REV. 45 (2015):

   Pollution Credit Trading Programs

   Pollution credit trading programs rest on an assumption similar to that underlying wetlands mitigation: pollution emissions are fungible. Although this assumption may be less problematic than in the wetlands context, these programs nevertheless are subject to controversy.

   In the last two decades, cap-and-trade programs have become an increasingly popular mechanism for regulating air pollution. The key selling point behind cap-and-trade schemes is the promise to yield pollution reductions more cost effectively than conventional command-and-control regulation. Cap-and-trade programs require sources of pollution to possess pollution allowances in a quantity equivalent to the amount of pollution they emit. A program caps the total quantity of allowances, and program administrators distribute allowances to pollution sources either for free or via auction. A source may then purchase or sell allowances, and its decisions will depend on a comparison of allowance prices with the source's cost of reducing emissions directly.

   Cap-and-trade programs frequently allow pollution sources to satisfy program requirements by using offsets in lieu of allowances. Offsets are typically generated when sources outside the cap-and-trade program reduce their pollution. Once these reductions are verified, the sources receive offset credits that may be used or sold like allowances.

   Emission trading programs pose substantial challenges for enforcement: program effectiveness hinges on accurate emissions data, which is often difficult if not impossible to come by. To make matters worse, the financial gains made possible by allowance trading create incentives for fraud. These challenges expand when pollution sources are allowed to use offsets to satisfy program requirements. The inclusion of offsets complicates the already demanding tasks of monitoring and verification because offsets originate from sources whose emissions tend to be especially difficult and costly to measure. Sources of offsets may include, for example, small-scale polluters not subject to emissions monitoring, as well as forestry, ranching, and other land-use activities whose emissions are not readily quantified. They also may include sources located outside the jurisdiction of the agency that oversees the emissions trading program. Unfortunately, offset programs can even undermine pollution reduction goals by "encourag[ing] project hosts to gain credit when net emissions happen to be declining (whether or not they are actually declining due to some additional effort) but leav[ing] the source unregulated when net emissions are rising."

Notwithstanding these concerns, cap-and-trade programs addressing greenhouse gas (GHG) emissions have been adopted internationally (under the Kyoto Protocol), regionally (within the European Union), nationally (e.g., by Norway), and subnationally (e.g., by California in its implementation of AB 32). The stated appeal of these schemes is their ability to generate cost-effective emissions reductions. The extent to which these programs have actually reduced carbon emissions is open to debate, however. Indeed, their continued use despite accompanying doubts suggests that their appeal derives from appearing to tackle the problem while avoiding more onerous, systemic changes that might be necessary.

The Kyoto Protocol presents perhaps the most prominent example of the difficulties faced by carbon trading schemes. Under the Kyoto Protocol, industrialized nations — but not developing countries — committed to reduce their GHG emissions during a five-year commitment period (2008-2012) by approximately five percent from 1990 emission levels. On paper, the agreement pushed nations primarily to reduce emissions themselves by requiring that any emissions trading be "supplemental to domestic actions." However, the Protocol contained several "flexibility mechanisms" designed to ease compliance, including the Clean Development Mechanism (CDM) and emissions trading. These mechanisms have proven critical to fulfilling industrialized nations' commitments.

The offset system created by the CDM has had especially troubling effects. The CDM was intended to foster **sustainable** development in developing countries while reducing industrialized countries' compliance costs. Under the CDM, industrialized nations may obtain carbon credits ("certified emission reductions") for funding activities in developing countries that reduce GHG emissions. These credits essentially substitute carbon-reducing projects in developing countries for commitments to reduce existing emissions in industrialized nations. Ensuring that CDM projects actually produce a net reduction in emissions is essential to the integrity of the system, especially as the Kyoto Protocol placed no limit on the number of carbon credits that may be generated through the CDM.

* * *

Indeed, implementation of the CDM has increased net GHG emissions in some instances. Most notoriously, the easy availability of carbon credits prompted manufacturers of coolant gases (which happen to be powerful GHGs) to dramatically increase coolant production for the sole purpose of destroying waste gases (which are even more powerful GHGs), thereby generating carbon credits. These operations are responsible for nearly half of all credits awarded under the CDM, and efforts to rein them in have been stymied by concerns that manufacturers will release the waste gases directly into the atmosphere if they are not paid to destroy them.

Another flexibility mechanism of the Kyoto Protocol, emissions trading, has likewise undermined emissions reduction efforts. In particular, the shrinking of the economies in the former Soviet Republics and Eastern Europe left these nations with numerous excess allowances to sell, sometimes referred to as "hot air" allowances. Although some countries have shunned the use of these hot air allowances to meet their Kyoto obligations, other nations have relied on them to avoid drastic cuts of their own. Indeed, so many of these allowances were left over after the original Kyoto commitment period that they became the subject of contentious negotiations. Although the developed countries collectively met their pledged Kyoto reductions, their emissions were not much lower than they would have been in the absence of Kyoto, thanks to emissions trading and the global economic downturn.

Carbon trading programs ultimately rest on two key assumptions: that emissions are fungible and that calculated emissions reductions represent actual emissions reductions. The first assumption — that emissions are fungible — is relatively unproblematic. In contrast to wetlands, whose value and function depend on their location and unique characteristics, the effects of carbon emissions are independent of their locale. However, the second assumption — that calculated emissions reductions represent actual emissions reductions — is tenuous, particularly when it comes to offsets. Additionality is essential to ensuring that actual net reductions in pollution occur, yet has proven almost impossible to ensure. Moreover, hot air allowances and other accounting maneuvers call into question the sincerity of the international community in addressing climate change.

Generally speaking, pollution trading systems and other market-based mechanisms tap into fundamental beliefs regarding private property rights, utilitarianism, and virtues of the free market. These beliefs do not constitute myths themselves so much as a system of values — values that are contested not only within environmental policy circles but also in society more broadly. But just as classical myths reflected and reinforced societal values in ancient societies, the mythology of pollution trading systems likewise bolsters market-oriented values today.

B. Clean Water

The goal of the Clean Water Act (CWA), also called the Federal Water Pollution Control Act (FWPCA), is to clean and maintain waters of the United States. The approach to address water pollution differs somewhat from the approach to control air pollution under the CAA. While the CAA primarily seeks to achieve health-based ambient air quality standards, the CWA controls discharges of pollutants from point sources using a permitting system, a pretreatment program for wastes discharged into sewers, and technology standards.[86] Nonpoint source pollution, such as agricultural runoff, has not to-date been directly regulated under the CWA and has been more difficult to control. Agricultural nonpoint source pollution is the primary source of water quality impacts on rivers and streams and is a major contributor to adverse impacts on wetlands, estuaries, and groundwater.[87]

All ambient air in the United States is subject to CAA regulation, however, the CWA jurisdiction only extends to "navigable waters," which are "waters of the U.S., including territorial seas."[88] When the CWA attempts to regulate isolated, nonnavigable water bodies and wetlands, it is subject to challenge. In *Rapanos v. United States*,[89] the U.S. Supreme Court did not have a majority view as to the definition of wetlands for purposes of CWA authority, but Justice Kennedy's concurrence explained that there must be a "significant nexus" between the wetland and navigable waters.[90]

The EPA and Army Corps of Engineers attempted to provide more clarity on the CWA's jurisdiction by issuing the Clean Water Rule (aka WOTUS) in June 2015, essentially adopting Justice Kennedy's concurrence.[91] Some states challenged this new rule, but as it worked its way through litigation, President Donald Trump issued an Executive Order in February 2017 ordering the EPA and the Army Corps of Engineers to review WOTUS. The Order directed that as the EPA and Army determined whether to rescind or revise the rule, they "shall consider interpreting the term 'navigable waters,' as defined in 33 U.S.C. 1362(7), in a manner consistent with the opinion of Justice Antonin Scalia in Rapanos v. United States"[92] Justice Scalia's opinion asked lower courts to determine

---

[86] *See* Farber & Carlson, *supra* note 27, at Chapter 7.
[87] *Polluted Runoff: Nonpoint Source Pollution: Agriculture*, EPA, https://www.epa.gov/nps/nonpoint-source-agriculture (last updated Aug. 18, 2017).
[88] Federal Water Pollution Control Act (Clean Water Act) §502, 33 U.S.C. §1362 (2012).
[89] 547 U.S. 715 (2006).
[90] *See also* Solid Waste Agency of N. Cook County v. U.S. Army Corps of Eng'rs, 531 U.S. 159 (2001) (SWANCC) (finding Army Corps of Engineers has no authority under Section 404 of the CWA over a pond that is not connected to navigable waters).
[91] Clean Water Rule: Definition of "Waters of the United States," 33 C.F.R. Part 328 (2015). *See also, What the Clean Water Rule Does*, EPA (May 18, 2016), https://www.epa.gov/wotus-rule/proposed-rule-definition-waters-united-states-addition-applicability-date-2015-clean.
[92] *Presidential Executive Order on Restoring the Rule of Law, Federalism, and Economic Growth by Reviewing the "Waters of the United States" Rule*, THE WHITE HOUSE (Feb. 28, 2017), https://www.whitehouse.gov/the-press-office/2017/02/28/presidential-executive-order-restoring-rule-law-federalism-and-economic.

"whether the ditches or drains near each wetland are 'waters' in the ordinary sense of containing a relatively permanent flow."[93] In August 2017, the agencies proposed to rescind the 2015 rule and replace it "with the regulations that were in effect immediately preceding the 2015 rule."[94] The definition of wetlands is important for the functioning of the "dredge and fill" program established by Section 404, which makes the Army Corps of Engineers responsible for issuing a separate permit to allow construction that involves the dredging or filling of wetlands.[95]

1. POINT SOURCE REGULATION

A point source is "any discernible, confined and discrete conveyance."[96] Point sources may be manmade, such as a pipe or ditch, or natural, such as a channel or gully. Point sources such as factories directly discharging into a river must obtain a permit under the National Pollutant Discharge Elimination System (NPDES) Permit Program. If instead of directly discharging into a water source, the factory indirectly discharges into the sewer system, the effluent will be subject to a "pretreatment" program before it enters the municipal sewer.[97]

2. NPDES PERMIT FOR DIRECT DISCHARGES

Section 301 of the CWA prohibits "the discharge of any pollutant by any person" from a "point source" into "navigable waters" unless the point source obtains an NPDES permit. As discussed above, "navigable waters" is defined broadly as "waters of the U.S." and may include intermittent water bodies, tributaries, and wetlands, so long as there is a nexus to a navigable waterway.[98] The term "pollutant" is defined broadly to include most tangible materials and even intangible elements such as heat, so long as the pollutant is added to the water and causes a net increase in pollutants.[99]

The NPDES permit sets limits on the amount of pollutants a permitted source may discharge. The EPA has the authority to issue permits, but may delegate this authority to the states, while maintaining veto power over state permits and the right to revoke state authority. Federal

---

[93] Rapanos v. United States, 547 U.S. 715, 757 (2006).
[94] *Extension of Comment Period for the Definition of "Waters of the United States"—Recodification of Pre-existing Rules*, EPA, https://www.epa.gov/wotus-rule/extension-comment-period-definition-waters-united-states-recodification-pre-existing (last updated Sept. 27, 2017).
[95] *See* Farber & Carlson, *supra* note 27, at Chapter 7.
[96] CWA §1342, 33 U.S.C. §1342 (2012).
[97] *See* Farber & Carlson, *supra* note 27, at Chapter 7.
[98] Note the discussion above regarding the Executive Order of February 2017, which may result in narrowing this definition.
[99] CWA §1311, 33 U.S.C. §1311(a) (2012).

technology-based effluent limitations and state water-quality standards govern discharge limitations, which can be more stringent than federal standards in order to address the water quality of designated state water bodies under the Total Maximum Daily Load (TMDL) program.[100] The best pollution control equipment the particular category of the industrial facility can use to reduce pollution serves as the basis for the federal technology-based effluent limitations. A **new** facility will be required to use pollution control technology based on New Source Performance Standards (NSPS), also known as Best Available Demonstrated Technology (BADT), and **existing** facilities will be subject to Best Practicable Technology (BPT), Best Available Technology (BAT), or Best Conventional Technology (BCT).[101] A source may seek a variance from the applicable national standards if it can show that it is "fundamentally different" from a typical facility of its type.[102]

The NPDES effluent discharge limitations incorporate the state water-quality standards and Section 301(b) requires the inclusion of water quality standards in the permit when the technology-based standards do not sufficiently protect state water-quality expectations.[103] In addition, Section 302 authorizes the EPA (or delegated state) to incorporate limitations to preserve local water quality.[104] The permit may impose conditions to prevent "unreasonable degradation" of the ocean environment, if the source discharges into the ocean,[105] and to control stringently the discharge of toxic pollutants.[106] Point sources may require individual permits or may be included in a "general" permit that applies to multiple facilities that are similar in nature. Once the point source obtains an NPDES permit, it is deemed to be in compliance with the other CWA requirements and is shielded from prosecution so long as it complies with the permit requirements.[107]

3. PRETREATMENT PROGRAM FOR INDIRECT DISCHARGES

Nondomestic wastewater sources that are discharging into the municipal sewer system, rather than directly into a waterway, will be subject to pretreatment requirements for pollutants that the Publicly Owned Treatment Works (POTWs) cannot adequately treat. These dischargers will need to pretreat any industrial waste that will interfere with the biological

---

[100] *See* Homestake Mining Co. v. EPA, 477 F. Supp. 1279, 1287-1289 (D.S.D. 1979).
[101] *See* Farber & Carlson, *supra* note 27, at Chapter 7.
[102] CWA §1311, 33 U.S.C. §1311 (2012).
[103] 33 U.S.C. §1311(b)(1)(C) (2012).
[104] *Id.* §1312 (2012).
[105] *Id.* §1343 (2012).
[106] *Id.* §1312 (2012).
[107] *See* Farber & Carlson, *supra* note 27, at Chapter 7.

treatment systems employed by the POTW.[108] Pretreatment standards are technology-based standards, such as BPT, BAT, BCT, or NSPS, nationally developed based on categories of industrial sources. POTWs must obtain an NPDES permit as a point source discharger and are subject to the less stringent technology-based standard known as "secondary treatment."[109] Sometimes the sewage sludge that remains after this secondary treatment is used as fertilizer, unless it contains toxic materials from industrial waste, which will likely violate the NPDES permit.

4. NONPOINT SOURCE REGULATION

Urban, agricultural, and resource-extraction activities typically release nonpoint source pollution. Addressing this type of water pollution continues to be the most difficult challenge under the CWA regulations because we cannot track the releases to individual sources and cannot control them through permitting and technology and emission limitations. Therefore, we must take an area-wide approach to controlling the water quality levels of the receiving water bodies. Local land use planning is necessary to identify the impacted waters and attempt to control the nonpoint source pollution entering these waters.[110] We provide an illustration of the challenges raised by nonpoint sources in Chapter 3.

5. STATE WATER QUALITY STANDARDS

As discussed briefly above, water quality standards, both state and federal, play a role in establishing effluent limitations for a point source NPDES permit. These standards are even more critical in controlling nonpoint source pollution by focusing on the quality of the water body since permitting cannot control the area-wide source. To establish water quality standards, the states must specify the "designated use," such as "public drinking water supply" or "hydroelectric power," for each state water body. However, the EPA has determined that under Section 303 of the CWA, the state must set the state water-quality goals at a level sufficient to protect aquatic life and support recreation—the "fishable/swimmable" goal[111]—unless the state can show that such a goal is not attainable because of natural conditions or adverse social and economic impacts.[112]

Once the state has determined the designated use for the water body, it must set water standards related to this use by establishing the "criteria"

---

[108] 33 U.S.C §1317(b) (2012).
[109] 33 U.S.C §1311(b)(1)(B) (2012).
[110] *See* Farber & Carlson, *supra* note 27, at Chapter 7.
[111] 33 U.S.C. §1313(c) (2012).
[112] 33 U.S.C. §1251(a) (2012).

needed to preserve the designated use. Criteria establish the maximum allowable pollutant concentration in a water body to retain its designated use. States must include antidegradation provisions in their standards to prevent a deterioration of water quality below the existing designated use or a higher quality "fishable/swimmable" level if attained.[113]

6. AREA-WIDE PLANNING AND WATERSHEDS

States must identify those water bodies that are "impaired" because the effluent limitations established in the NPDES permits for point sources releasing into the water body are not sufficient to achieve the water quality standard for such waters. The CWA requires states to list impaired water bodies and establish the total amount of pollutants that any source — point or nonpoint — can discharge into these waters.[114] The states must calculate the "total maximum daily loads" (TMDLs) of each pollutant for listed water bodies and control releases into these waters through NPDES permits or land use controls over nonpoint sources.[115] States must also take special action on waters that are not meeting water quality standards for toxic pollutants, also called "toxic hot spots."[116]

Watersheds are the natural area-wide landscapes that serve as a valuable tool for water quality protection and runoff/flood management. A watershed is "that area of land, a bounded hydrologic system, within which all living things are inextricably linked by their common water course and where, as humans settled, simple logic demanded that they become part of a community."[117] Urban, agricultural, and mining runoff affects watersheds and is not subject to the NPDES permitting process. Chemical and biological waste spills also contribute to the runoff pollution of both surface and ground water.[118]

Stormwater from rain and melting snow increases the quantity and velocity of these runoff pollutants. The amount of impervious cover within the watershed, such as asphalt, cement, and roofs, exacerbates the runoff problem by preventing the natural landscape from absorbing the increased water flow.[119] Sustainable approaches to dealing with this problem include low impact development (LID) and green infrastructure to control the sources of runoff by restoring natural watershed functions

---

[113] See Farber & Carlson, *supra* note 27, at Chapter 7.

[114] 33 U.S.C. §1313(d) (2012).

[115] See Pronsolino v. Nastri, 291 F.3d 1123, 1125 (9th Cir. 2002) (holding that states may be required to prepare TMDLs even if water quality is only impacted by nonpoint source pollution).

[116] 33 U.S.C. §1314(l) (2012).

[117] *What Is a Watershed?*, Univ. of Wis. Green Bay, https://www.uwgb.edu/watershed/fox-river/overview.asp, (last visited Dec. 1, 2017) (quoting scientist geographer John Wesley Powell).

[118] Carole Browner & Dan Glickman, Clean Water Action Plan: Restoring and Protecting America's Waters (U.S. EPA, U.S. Dep't of Agriculture, EPA 840-R-98-001, 1998).

[119] See Decker v. Nw. Envtl. Def. Ctr., 133 S. Ct. 1326, (2013) (upholding EPA's view that stormwater runoff from logging roads does not require NPDES permits).

through landscape planning, site design, and using technology that captures and recycles the stormwater.[120]

The NPDES Stormwater Program[121] requires permits for three types of nonpoint sources: municipal separate stormwater systems,[122] construction sites, and discharges associated with industrial activity.[123] Unfortunately, far too many municipalities still operate with old infrastructure that combines in one piping system the sewer system with stormwater, called a Combined Sewer Overflow (CSO). In times of significant rain or snowmelt, the system may be overwhelmed, and instead of sending the sewage into a wastewater treatment plant, it may combine with the stormwater and directly discharge untreated human and industrial waste into natural waterways.[124] Even cities with separate stormwater systems[125] will often experience overflows that bypass treatment and adversely impact local waters, although these systems require an NPDES permit and are subject to TMDL restrictions.[126]

Achieving sustainable water quality management will likely require watershed programs that encourage local solutions to water issues and recognize the water cycle relationship between front-end water supply and consumption and back-end effluent discharge.[127]

7. OIL POLLUTION ACT OF 1990

The Oil Pollution Act of 1990 (OPA) was the culmination of several congressional acts originating in legislation enacted to provide a national response to oil spill disasters following a major oil spill off the coast of England in 1967.[128] An oil tanker, Torrey Canyon, ran aground in a storm and spilled 31 million gallons of crude oil into English and French waters — "the worst environmental disaster in history at that time."[129] As a result, the United

---

[120] *Stormwater Management*, EPA, https://web.archive.org/web/20150617082927/http://www.epa. gov/oaintrnt/stormwater/index.htm, (last visited Dec. 1, 2017).

[121] *Id.*

[122] Los Angeles Cty. Flood Control Dist. v. Natural Res. Def. Council, Inc., 133 S. Ct. 710, (2013) (holding that flood control district's discharge of stormwater is not a "discharge of a pollutant" requiring an NPDES permit). *See also* Paula Estornell & Peder Hansen, *Understanding Impaired Waters and Total Maximum Daily Load (TMDL) Requirements for Municipal Stormwater Programs*, EPA (Jan. 2008), https://www3.epa.gov/npdes/pubs/region3_factsheet_tmdl.pdf.

[123] *See* Decker v. Nw. Envtl. Def. Ctr., 133 S. Ct. 1326 (2013).

[124] *Combined Sewer Overflows Frequently Asked Questions*, EPA, https://web.archive.org/web/ 20130308132108/http://cfpub1.epa.gov/npdes/faqs.cfm?program_id=5 (last updated Jan. 24, 2013).

[125] *Stormwater: Frequently Asked Questions*, EPA, https://web.archive.org/web/20130308131229/ http://cfpub1.epa.gov/npdes/faqs.cfm?program_id=6 (last updated Jan. 24, 2013).

[126] Bettina Boxall, *New Storm Water Runoff Rules Could Cost Cities Billions*, L.A. TIMES (Nov. 9, 2012), http://articles.latimes.com/2012/nov/09/local/la-me-storm-water-20121109.

[127] *See* Ryan P. Murphy, *Did We Miss the Boat? The Clean Water Act and Sustainability*, 47 U. RICH. L. REV. 1267, 1298-1300 (2013).

[128] Frederick J. Kenney, Jr. & Melissa A. Hamann, *The Flow of Authority to Stop the Flow of Oil: Clean Water Act Section 311(c): Removal Authority and the BP/Deepwater Horizon Oil Spill*, 36 TUL. MAR. L.J. 349, 351 (2012).

[129] *Id.* at 353.

States, as well as other nations, recognized the importance of developing plans to deal with such emergencies and responding quickly to the release of oil and other hazardous substances.[130]

The Clean Water Act (CWA) of 1972 required that the National Oil and Hazardous Substances Pollution Contingency Plan (NCP) incorporate response provisions for oil and hazardous substance releases. Section 311 of the CWA also established the framework for the response and liability for these releases and authorized the federal government to respond if the polluter did not.[131] In addition to the grant of federal authority under the CWA to address oil spill response and cleanup, there were three other federal acts governing oil spill response.[132]

After the catastrophic 1989 Exxon Valdez oil spill in Alaskan waters, the U.S. Congress enacted OPA to replace the various federal acts regulating oil spill response with a broad structure incorporating private, local, state, and federal responsibilities.[133] OPA amended Section 311 of the CWA to give the President greater authority to respond to and monitor oil-spill release cleanup efforts.[134] OPA also provides that "responsible parties" who discharge oil into navigable waters and the adjacent coast will be strictly liable for damages such as removal costs, natural resource damage, property damage, and economic losses.[135] OPA allows the government to use the Oil Spill Liability Trust Fund, established in 1986, when the liability of a "responsible party" has reached a regulatory cap.[136] Further, "implementation of the Oil Pollution Act of 1990, which . . . authorizes the assessment and recovery of natural resources damages, provides a basis for ecosystem valuation and restoration."[137]

8. CASE STUDY OF RESILIENCE AND SUSTAINABILITY

The BP oil spill polluted Gulf waters, harming the natural ecological systems in the surrounding areas.[138] The long-term failure of environmental regulations resulted in this "sudden and devastating" environmental disaster.[139] We cover disasters in Chapter 9 as distinct from environmental regulation over pollution. However, all too often a regulatory failure

---

[130] *Id.* at 354-355.

[131] *Id.* at 357.

[132] *Id.* at 358 (citing the Trans-Alaska Pipeline Authorization Act (1973), the Deepwater Port Act of 1974, and the Outer Continental Shelf Lands Act Amendments of 1978).

[133] *Id.* at 361-362.

[134] *Id.* at 362.

[135] Michael Dore, Law of Toxic Torts §3:14.20 (2013) (discussing liability under OPA for offshore drilling activities).

[136] *Id.*

[137] Keith H. Hirokawa, *Disasters and Ecosystem Services Deprivation: From Cuyahoga to the Deepwater Horizon,* 74 Albany L. Rev. 543, 559 (2011).

[138] *See* Daniel Farber, *Navigating the Intersection of Environmental Law and Disaster Law,* 2011 B.Y.U. L. Rev. 1783, 1785 (2011).

[139] *Id.* at 1794.

in environmental law that does not properly control environmental risks may create environmental disasters.[140] This was certainly the case with the BP oil spill, which resulted from mistakes made by the private firms involved in the deep-water drilling as well as the lack of regulatory oversight to minimize the risks involved.[141] Disasters that result from such regulatory failures then act as catalysts for changes in environmental law.[142]

The BP oil spill tested the OPA federal response provisions to a major oil spill or hazardous substance release. While statutory and regulatory shortcomings were uncovered during the massive operation to respond to this disaster,[143] the overall structure of the President's authority to delegate the coordinated response and execution of removal actions was adequate to address the need for "maximizing on-scene initiative," as demonstrated by the U.S. Coast Guard.[144] Multidistrict litigation by thousands of claimants seeking to recover under OPA for economic loss, property damages, personal injury and death, and punitive damages[145] settled in 2012.[146] However, the final resolution of all of the individual claims may take years, and the defendants continue to challenge the handling of these claims in federal court.[147]

In addition to the water pollution resulting from the oil spilled into the ocean from the well blowout, the use of dispersants in response to the spill may also have adversely affected wildlife in the Gulf of Mexico. As discussed above, the CWA requires a permit for the discharge of pollutants into navigable waters. However, in the face of an oil spill, responders may use dispersants under EPA regulations so long as the National Oil and Hazardous Substances Pollution Contingency Plan (NCP) lists the dispersant[148] and it is at least 45% effective in oil spill response activities.[149]

The EPA and the U.S. Coast Guard authorized BP to use the dispersant of its choice, Corexit, which was listed on the NCP Product Schedule with an effectiveness rate of 50% for surface application.[150] Some criticized the use of Corexit because, although it is less toxic than oil, it does contain

---

[140] *Id.* at 1794.

[141] *Id.* at 1798 (citing Deep Water: The Gulf Oil Disaster and the Future of Offshore Drilling, Report to the President, Nat'l Commission on the BP Deepwater Horizon Oil Spill and Offshore Drilling 89-122 (2011)).

[142] *See* Hirokawa, *supra* note 137, at 546-548.

[143] *See* Kenney & Hamann, *supra* note 128, at 394-395 (listing "lessons learned" from the Deepwater Horizon disaster).

[144] *Id.* at 395.

[145] *See In re* Oil Spill by the Oil Rig Deepwater Horizon in the Gulf of Mexico, 808 F. Supp. 2d 943 (E.D. La. 2011), *aff'd sub nom. In re* Deepwater Horizon, 745 F.3d 157 (5th Cir. 2014).

[146] *MDL-2179 Oil Spill by the Oil Rig "Deepwater Horizon,"* E.D. La., http://www.laed.uscourts.gov/OilSpill/OilSpill.htm (last visited Dec. 1, 2017).

[147] Margaret Cronin Fisk, Brian Swint & Laurel Calkins, *BP's Oil Spill Deal Sours as Claims Add Billions to Cost,* BLOOMBERG (June 5, 2013), http://www.bloomberg.com/news/2013-06-04/bp-s-oil-spill-settlement-sours-as-claims-add-billions.html.

[148] 40 C.F.R. §300 (2002).

[149] Catherine Kilduff & Jaclyn Lopez, *Dispersants: The Lesser of Two Evils or a Cure Worse Than the Disease?,* 16 OCEAN & COASTAL L.J. 375, 377-378.

[150] *Id.* at 378, 383-384.

a petroleum solvent, which increased the amount of hydrocarbon in the water and caused the oil to more easily enter the body of animals.[151] The government reduced the number of dispersants BP was allowed to use and eventually prohibited the use altogether.[152] Subsequent research indicates that the use of dispersants may have adversely impacted deep-water ecosystems and marine wildlife.[153]

Further investigation needs to determine to what degree we should use dispersants in the future to respond to oil spills of this magnitude.[154] However, more importantly, the long-term ecosystem impacts of the oil spill itself, along with the cleanup response, must be analyzed to determine how to provide ecological, economic, and cultural sustainability in the Gulf of Mexico (and other regions) when we assess the risk of continuing to permit deep-water oil drilling.[155]

Questions and Notes

1. In Chapter 3, Section VI, we introduced Ecosystem Services Management (ESM) in which the services ecosystems provide are properly assessed and valued. What would a clean water statute focused on cleanup and remediation consist of if it incorporated ESM? Would that help strengthen the resilience and sustainability of water-based systems? What Baselines and Metrics (discussed in Chapter 6, Section IV) might be helpful if directed at agricultural runoff?

2. How could the CWA's failure to regulate nonpoint agricultural runoff pollution affect the resilience of clean, freshwater-based systems? What about the sustainability of the fishing industry?

3. How might limiting WOTUS in the way proposed by President Trump's 2017 Executive Order impact clean, freshwater-based systems?

4. In *Disasters and Ecosystem Services Deprivation: From Cuyahoga to the Deepwater Horizon*, 74 ALBANY L. REV. 543, 552-560 (2011), Keith Hirokawa draws the connection between ecosystem services management and disasters:

   > When we value ecosystem resources in reference to the costs and benefits of changes in ecosystem circumstances, we acquire a fuller and deeper understanding of the reasons for repairing ecosystem damage and avoiding

---

[151] *Id.* at 385-386.
[152] *Id.* at 388.
[153] *Id.*
[154] *Id.* at 394.
[155] *See* Hirokawa, *supra* note 137, at 553–554.

future disasters. Indeed, it is typically the case that—the value of ecosystem services becomes apparent only after such services are diminished or lost, which occurs once the natural processes supporting the production of these services have been sufficiently degraded. Here, then, is where the ecosystem services approach can be cast as an opportunistic feature of environmental disaster: the information that we gather about ecosystem processes and services is especially helpful for valuing lost ecosystem services, and when focusing on ecosystem changes, the damage that environmental disasters cause to human wellbeing can be subjected to a useful accounting. . . .

The problem apparent in the response to the Deepwater Horizon spill has been a general lack of understanding of the potential costs of ecosystem services deprivation. . . . The Gulf of Mexico houses a diverse network of interconnected and immensely productive ecosystems that have proven essential to the Gulf's ecological, economic, and cultural sustainability. The Gulf boasts thousands of miles of coastal features and habitats, spanning the shores of five U.S. states (Alabama, Florida, Louisiana, Mississippi, and Texas) and six Mexican states. The Gulf's shoreline includes bays and bayous, beaches, marshes, forested wetlands, and mangroves that provide a wide range of ecosystem services to the region and to the world. The waters of the Gulf offer a variety of vulnerable habitat systems throughout the water column, including the floating Sargussum mat habitats, bottom habitats in geological features and coral reefs, and even the open waters, where oil may encounter planktonic eggs and larvae. The region enjoys billions in economic revenue from the Gulf's aesthetic value, productive fisheries, and recreational opportunities, all of which provide jobs and safety. Regional residents are protected through the natural infrastructure of the Gulf coast, including climate-absorbing coastal wetlands. . . .

To understand the intricacies of the project, the range of ecosystem services might be separated into the four categories proposed in the Millennium Ecosystem Assessment. . . . The Gulf's provisioning services affect the entire nation's seafood markets and the region's economy. In 2008, commercial fishermen in the Gulf of Mexico supported a commercial fishing harvest of 1.27 billion pounds of finfish and shellfish at a value of $659 million in landings revenue. . . .

The Gulf's regulating services relate to the safety and security of a region that is already vulnerable to natural changes. Oceans are essential for nutrient and waste cycling and gas regulation, including carbon dioxide absorption and atmospheric composition. A recent report estimates that coastal wetlands benefit the United States with $23.2 billion in annual storm protection services. . . .

As a cultural resource, the Gulf provides history, recreation, and employment for millions of residents and visitors to the region: Estuaries and coastal seas have been focal points of human settlement and marine resource use throughout history. The National Marine Fisheries Service *estimated that the Gulf region enjoyed approximately $12.5 billion in fishing trip and equipment expenditures in 2008, with an annual average of 22 million fishing trips made by 3.1 million anglers. During this time, the commercial harvest supported $8.8 billion in seafood industry sales in Florida, Louisiana, and Texas. . . .*

Uncertainty about the Gulf's supporting services is also commanding attention during the response. Exposure to discharged oil can disrupt habitat functions, or otherwise cause displacement, due to avoidance of contaminated areas or loss of phytoplankton and other food sources. . . .

Given even this brief introduction to the ecosystem services at risk, it should seem clear that successful restoration of the Gulf ecology and economy will require an immense information-gathering exercise. . . . Employing an ecosystem services approach will direct the restoration process, as well as subsequent regulatory developments, towards the importance of functional ecosystems in the creation of economic value. . . .

It is important to recognize that environmental disasters offer constructive opportunities to identify systemic defects and past practices that threaten human well-being by depriving us of essential ecosystem services. Hence, although the practice of disaster-driven regulation casts a long shadow over our foresight, it is worth noting that environmental disasters can also compel a more searching inquiry into the ecological consequences of a given activity. What we get from environmental disasters materializes in the context of knowledge about ecosystems, and a drive toward more certainty in our environmental management decisions.

C. Oceans and Coastal Management

Oceans and coastal zones are particularly susceptible to serious sustainability challenges. First, coastal zones are experiencing and will experience the direct effects of climate change impact on sea levels and ocean acidification. In addition, coastal zones are subject to adverse impacts such as nonpoint source pollution from urban and agricultural runoff, aquaculture, recreation and tourism, the siting of energy facilities, marine debris, marine habitat destruction, biofouling, overfishing, the depletion of marine resources, and changes to thermohaline circulation (deep-ocean currents influenced by the water's temperature and salinity).[156]

Ocean acidification, caused by increased carbon dioxide emissions absorbed by the ocean, greatly threatens aquatic species, livelihoods,

---

[156] *See* Josh Eagle, Coastal Law, Chapter 1 (2011).

tourism, and sea-faring cultures.[157] Recent problems with ocean chemistry in the Pacific Northwest waters of the United States have threatened commercial species of shellfish and marine life and introduced increasing numbers of nuisance species, such as jellyfish.[158] Scientists have been exploring solutions to acidification, including recycled shells and selective breeding of acidity-resistant shellfish, but ultimately we must reduce carbon dioxide emissions using the same recommendations for controlling climate change, discussed in Chapter 10.

With increased transportation, ocean species are struggling with biofouling, which occurs when aquatic species such as plants, algae, and shellfish accumulate on a surface that is in contact with the ocean, such as a dock or a ship's hull. Exposure to this accumulation, particularly of non-native species transported by boat, can cause adverse environmental impacts by their introduction into the area such as reducing biodiversity and endangering existing aquatic species.[159]

In the United States, the Department of Commerce is responsible for Ocean and Coastal Management programs under the direction of the National Oceanic and Atmospheric Administration (NOAA).[160] NOAA's Office of Ocean and Coastal Resource Management (OCRM) administers six major programs including the Coastal Management Program, the Coral Reef Conservation Program, the National Estuarine Research Reserve System, the Coastal and Estuarine Land Conservation Program, the National Marine Protected Areas, and the Coastal Nonpoint Pollution Control Program. In addition, OCRM is responsible for licensing Ocean Thermal Energy Conversion projects that harness ocean power to generate electricity.[161] Federal legislation and presidential executive orders authorize the work of OCRM in performing its responsibilities.[162]

---

[157] See Study Outlines Threat of Ocean Acidification to Coastal Communities in U.S., OR. STATE UNIV. (Feb. 23, 2015), http://oregonstate.edu/ua/ncs/archives/2015/feb/study-outlines-threat-ocean-acidification-coastal-communities-us.

[158] Id.

[159] Kathleen D. Oppenheimer & Todd K. BenDor, A Comprehensive Solution to the Biofouling Problem for the Endangered Florida Manatee and Other Species, 42 ENVTL. L. 415 (2012).

[160] U.S. DEPARTMENT OF COMMERCE: OCEAN & COASTAL RESOURCE MANAGEMENT, https://coast.noaa.gov/, (last visited Dec. 1, 2017).

[161] Id.

[162] Id. "The work OCRM performs is authorized by the Coastal Zone Management Act, the Marine Protected Areas Presidential Executive Order, the Coral Reef Conservation Act. The Coastal and Estuarine Land Conservation is codified under 16 USC §1456d."

PLASTICS AND OCEANS

A recent six-year study estimates that more than five trillion pieces of plastic are floating in the world's oceans, weighing over 250,000 tons.[163] This does not account for all ocean plastic, as the study notably does not include sunken and degraded plastics.[164] One recent study estimates that eight million tons of plastic have entered into the oceans per year and that the rate is increasing.[165] Eight million tons of plastic is enough to line the world's coastlines with five garbage bags per linear foot.[166] Ocean plastic comes from a variety of sources, including ineffective or improper waste management, intentional or accidental dumping and littering on shorelines or at sea, or through stormwater runoff.[167] The researchers found plastic in every ocean zone and identified regions where it accumulates.[168]

These pieces of plastic affect the environment in subtle and remarkable ways, including environmental, social, and economic impacts.[169] Photodegradation and other environmental forces gradually break down the plastic into smaller and smaller pieces.[170] Although some plastics degrade to the molecular level, most common types of plastic turn into microplastics, particles smaller than 5mm.[171] Marine life ingests pieces of plastic and sometimes becomes entangled in it.[172] Wind and ocean currents circulate plastics between ecosystems,[173] and the traveling plastic facilitates the migration of species to non-native habitats.[174] Invasive species can then outcompete native species, which can lead to loss of biodiversity and other significant environmental changes.[175] Marine litter can also affect human activities by reducing beach tourism or by causing human injuries, such as when swimmers become entangled in monofilament.[176] In 2011, David Osbourne of UNEP summarized this concern: "Marine debris is a wicked problem, one that is difficult to define, multi-causal, socially complex with no clear solution."[177]

Despite the lack of a clear solution, one company has developed a program that seeks to make an impact. Method®, a manufacturer of household cleaning products, has formed partnerships with other organizations to harvest plastic debris from

---

[163] Marcus Eriksen et al., *Plastic Pollution in the World's Oceans: More than 5 Trillion Plastic Pieces Weighing over 250,000 Tons Afloat at Sea*, PLOS ONE (Dec. 10, 2014), http://journals.plos.org/plosone/article?id = 10.1371/journal.pone.0111913.

[164] *Id.*

[165] Laura Parker, *Eight Million Tons of Plastic Dumped in Ocean Every Year*, NAT'L GEOGRAPHIC (Feb. 13, 2015), http://news.nationalgeographic.com/news/2015/02/150212-ocean-debris-plastic-garbage-patches-science/.

[166] *Id.*

[167] *Marine Debris Program: Plastics*, NAT'L OCEANIC AND ATMOSPHERIC ADMIN. (Aug. 11, 2016), http://marinedebris.noaa.gov/info/plastic.html, (last visited Dec. 1, 2017).

[168] Eriksen et al., *supra* note 163.

[169] Tavis Potts & Emily Hastings, *Marine Litter Issues, Impacts and Actions*, MARINE SCOTLAND (May 2011), http://www.gov.scot/Resource/0040/00402421.pdf.

[170] Eriksen et al., *supra* note 163.

[171] *What We Know About: Plastic Marine Debris*, NAT'L OCEANIC AND ATMOSPHERIC ADMIN. (Sept. 20, 2011), https://marinedebris.noaa.gov/sites/default/files/publications-files/Gen_Plastic_9-20-11%281%29.pdf.

[172] Potts & Hastings, *supra* note 169, at 17.

[173] *See* Eriksen et al., *supra* note 163.

[174] Potts & Hastings, *supra* note 169, at 19.

[175] *Id.*

[176] *Id.* at 20-21.

[177] Stephen Leahy, *Fight Against Marine Garbage Runs into Plastics Lobby*, INTER PRESS SERV. (Mar. 28, 2011), http://www.ipsnews.net/2011/03/fight-against-marine-garbage-runs-into-plastics-lobby/.

beaches and turn it into their recycled bottles, diverting the material back into the stream of commerce.[178] So far, volunteers in the Method program have cleaned up over a ton of plastics from the beaches of Hawaiʻi. Envision Plastic, a recycling company, processes the material, incorporating the salvaged ocean plastics with other recycled plastics into the bottle for one of their product lines.

While the decision makers at Method acknowledge the scope of their operation and the relatively small impact on the global problem of marine plastic debris, they have still chosen to operate their ocean plastic program. It may not be realistic for them to expect volunteer beachcombers to continue to provide a reliable source of plastics for years to come, and paying employees to collect packaging materials by hand would probably be too expensive to maintain. Why do you think Method would operate such a program? The company says, "we can raise awareness about the issue and use our business to demonstrate smart ways of using and reusing the plastics that are already on the planet."[179] Who derives benefits from the program? What are those benefits? Consider benefits that relate to each of the pillars of sustainability and resilience of the ocean.

The success of NOAA programs depends on the cooperation of local, state, and federal governments as well as the private industry's commitment to sustainability. Historically, coastal states and the federal government struggled over which entity had jurisdiction over marine resources offshore. Eventually, the Submerged Lands Act of 1952 established state jurisdiction over coastal waters three nautical miles from shore.[180] At the same time, the Outer Continental Shelf Lands Act established federal jurisdiction over waters beyond three nautical miles.[181] However, coastal states continued to have concerns over the impact of offshore oil operations permitted by the federal government, and inevitably the destructive oil spill six miles off the coast of Santa Barbara, California in 1969 led to the enactment of the Coastal Zone Management Act of 1972 (CZMA).[182]

[178] METHOD, http://methodhome.com/beyond-the-bottle/ocean-plastic/ (last visited Dec. 1, 2017).
[179] *Id.*
[180] Submerged Lands Act, 43 U.S.C. §§1301-1315 (1952).
[181] Outer Continental Shelf Lands Act, 43 U.S.C. §§1331-1356 (1952).
[182] Coastal Zone Management Act, 16 U.S.C. §§1451 *et. seq.*

The CZMA provides for cooperation between the state and federal agencies to ensure that offshore activities permitted by the federal government do not interfere with the state's protection of its coastline. The CZMA encourages but does not require coastal states to develop plans to protect, restore, manage, and preserve coastal resources.[183] The federal government provides assistance to encourage participation, and in 1990, it reauthorized the CZMA and identified nonpoint source pollution as a major factor in coastal degradation.[184] The CZMA, as interpreted by the Ninth Circuit in *California v. Norton* in 2002, gives the state a right to review a federally permitted project that may impact the coastal zone to ensure that the activity is consistent with the state's coastal plan.[185] NOAA's Office of Ocean and Coastal Resource Management (OCRM) "interprets the CZMA and oversees the application of federal consistency; provides management and legal assistance to coastal states, federal agencies, tribes and others; and mediates CZMA related disputes."[186] This concept of cooperative federalism allows state and local authorities to work with federal agencies to protect and preserve state interests.[187]

An example of a state coastal zone management plan is the 2013 Hawaii Ocean Resources Management Plan, which considers Native Hawaiian cultural solutions when establishing goals and priorities for protecting and conserving ocean and coastal resources.[188] The five-year plan contemplates consultation with the public and Hawaiian groups to "incorporate native practices for sustaining plants, animals, and land together in an inclusive manner."[189] The state plans to coordinate with the federal government and even other countries, such as Japan, in order to achieve continued sustainability by managing biological and species resources across different ecosystems.[190]

The Marine Protection, Research, and Sanctuaries Act (MPRSA), also called the Ocean Dumping Act, protects ocean and coastal area integrity. MPRSA prohibits transporting materials to be dumped in the ocean which will "unreasonably degrade or endanger" human health or the marine

---

[183] Krop, *supra* note 16.

[184] 16 U.S.C. §1455(b).

[185] *See* California v. Norton, 311 F.3d 1162, 1173 (2002).

[186] *Federal Consistency*, Nat'l Oceanic and Atmospheric Admin., https://coast.noaa.gov/czm/consistency/, (last visited Dec. 1, 2017).

[187] Sam Kalen, Ryan M. Seidemann, James G. Wilkins & Megan K. Terrell, *Lingering Relevance of the Coastal Zone Management Act to Energy Development in Our Nation's Coastal Waters?*, 24 Tul. Envtl. L.J. 73, 83-84 (2010).

[188] *See generally Hawai'i Ocean Resources Management Plan*, Hawaii St. Off. of Plan. (July 2013), http://files.hawaii.gov/dbedt/op/czm/ormp/ormp_update_reports/final_ormp_2013.pdf.

[189] B.J. Reyes, *New Ocean Management Plan Considers Native Hawaiian "Cultural solutions,"* Star Advertiser (July 26, 2013), http://www.staradvertiser.com/hawaii-news/new-ocean-management-plan-considers-native-hawaiian-cultural-solutions/.

[190] *Id.*

environment.[191] The EPA is responsible for developing ocean dumping criteria meeting this standard and evaluates applications before issuing a permit.[192] While the EPA's criteria and approval governs the management of dredging materials, the U.S. Army Corps of Engineers is responsible for issuing the appropriate permits for such materials.[193]

Case Study: The federal government regulates energy development in the Outer Continental Shelf (OCS), but states have input into this development through state coastal management plans. As discussed above, one of the major goals of the CZMA is to ensure consistency of federal actions with state policies addressing the adverse impacts of such activity on state shorelines.[194] Prior to the BP oil spill in 2010, Louisiana governor Kathleen Blanco sued the federal Minerals Management Services (MMS) agency to protest the lack of MMS oversight for OCS oil drilling leases and sales.[195] Louisiana, motivated by the massive damages inflicted by Hurricanes Katrina and Rita, disagreed with the MMS determination that oil leases and sales did not adversely affect coastal resources, did not require environmental analysis, and were consistent with the CZMA.[196]

The court in *Blanco v. Burton*[197] determined that the MMS was lax in its environmental impact analysis, even after the devastating 2005 hurricanes.[198] However, the MMS did little to change its lax approach to enforcing safety and environmental standards by the oil and gas industry, leading some to speculate that we could have avoided at least some of the problems that led to the Deepwater Horizon disaster had MMS paid attention to the judge's decision.[199] As mentioned earlier in this chapter discussing NEPA, the Secretary of the Interior disbanded and reorganized MMS to address the programmatic shortcomings in managing OCS development. Ultimately, states may need more authority under the CZMA to question federal consistency determinations and assess the viability of environmental assessment and review of offshore activities.[200]

---

[191] 16 U.S.C. §§1431 *et seq.*; 33 U.S.C. §§1401 *et seq.* (1988). *See also Summary of the Marine Protection, Research, and Sanctuaries Act*, U.S. EPA, http://www2.epa.gov/laws-regulations/summary-marine-protection-research-and-sanctuaries-act, (last updated Feb. 7, 2017).
[192] *Id.*
[193] *EPA History: Marine Protection, Research and Sanctuaries Act (Ocean Dumping Act)*, U.S. EPA, https://www.epa.gov/aboutepa/epa-history-marine-protection-research-and-sanctuaries-act-ocean-dumping-act (last updated Oct. 25, 2017).
[194] *See* Kalen et al., *supra* note 187, at 77.
[195] Blanco v. Burton, No. Civ. A. 06-3813, 2006 WL 2366046 (E.D. La. Aug. 14, 2006).
[196] Kalen et al., *supra* note 187, at 95-96.
[197] Blanco v. Burton, No. Civ. A. 06-3813, 2006 WL 2366046 (E.D. La. Aug. 14, 2006).
[198] Kalen et al., *supra* note 187, at 97.
[199] *Id.* at 97-98.
[200] *Id.* at 106-112.

Questions

1. For years, the ocean's resilience has been tested and strained. At what point should law and policy be more aggressive in ensuring a strong and resilient ocean and the ecosystems associated with it?

2. If the ocean's resilience to a variety of pollution-based disturbances crosses a threshold due to increased pollution, is there any way to achieve a sustainable future for the next generations?

D. Toxins

Controlling toxins, including pesticides, chemical products, and toxic waste, is a daunting challenge for the modern world. The regulation of toxins in the United States increased in the 1970s, as did the adoption of other major environmental regulations. This increased toxin regulation was spurred by public awareness of the potential adverse impacts of insecticides and pesticides revealed in Rachel Carson's influential book, *Silent Spring*, published in 1962. Discussed briefly below, several federal statutes address toxic substances including the Federal Insecticide, Fungicide and Rodenticide Act (FIFRA), the Toxic Substances Control Act (TSCA), the Food, Drug, and Cosmetic Act (FDCA), and portions of the Clean Air Act (CAA) and Clean Water Act (CWA). Other statutory provisions, not discussed here, address exposure to toxic substances and include the Occupational Safety & Health Act (OSHA),[201] the Safe Drinking Water Act (SDWA),[202] the Consumer Product Safety Act (CPSA),[203] the Federal Hazardous Substances Act (FHSA),[204] the Emergency Planning and Community Right-to-Know Act of 1986 (EPCRA),[205] and state legislation such as California's Proposition 65.[206]

---

[201] Toxic Substances Control Act (TSCA) §§6(b)(5), 3(8), 29 U.S.C. §§652(8) & 655(b)(5) (regulating workplace exposure to toxic substances). *See also* Indus. Union Dep't, AFL-CIO v. Am. Petroleum Inst., 448 U.S. §607 (1980) (Benzene Case).

[202] 42 U.S.C.A. §300(g) (requiring EPA to set maximum contaminant level goals (MCLG), which are generally set at zero for known carcinogens, to reduce toxins in drinking water).

[203] 42 U.S.C.A. §§2051-2084.

[204] 15 U.S.C.A. §§1261 *et seq.*

[205] 42 U.S.C.A. §§11004-11049 (EPA requires reporting of toxic releases for listed hazardous substances and prepares a national toxic release inventory (TRI) for public information).

[206] CAL. HEALTH & SAFETY CODE §§25249.5-25192 (requiring public disclosure of toxic releases and toxic substances contained in consumer products).

1. FEDERAL REGULATION OF TOXINS

a. Toxic Substances Control Act

The Toxic Substances Control Act (TSCA) is the federal statute designed to require chemical manufacturers to test the safety of their products and allow the EPA to control or halt such chemical use or production if it determines that there is a "reasonable basis to conclude" that the product "presents or will present an unreasonable risk of injury to health or the environment."[207] The basic structure of TSCA requires manufacturers to submit a premanufacture notification (PMN) to the EPA before producing a new chemical substance or putting an existing chemical to a signifi-cant new use.[208] The notification may require the manufacturer to submit chemical testing information, and the EPA may prohibit the manufacture or use of the product pending additional testing data. However, TSCA does not require that manufacturers extensively test the safety of all new chemicals and does not order specific tests. Thus, many of the chemicals regulated by TSCA have not had extensive testing.[209]

The EPA may also require testing of new and existing substances if it finds that the production, distribution, processing, use, or disposal of the product presents an unreasonable risk.[210] This additional information gathered pursuant to testing rules issued by the EPA, may persuade the EPA to limit the use, labeling, marketing, or disposal of these chemical substances by adopting restrictions "to the extent necessary to protect ade-quately against such risk using the least burdensome requirements."[211] A major goal of the legislation is to increase the information about chemicals and the effects of human and environmental exposure to these toxic sub-stances throughout a chemical's life cycle.

b. Federal Insecticide, Fungicide, and Rodenticide Act

The Federal Insecticide, Fungicide, and Rodenticide Act (FIFRA) is a fed-eral statute that controls the production, distribution, and use of pesti-cides. Unlike TSCA, which does not require extensive testing of chemical products, FIFRA requires manufacturers to perform toxicology tests before producing and selling agricultural chemicals that could potentially cause harm to consumers, farm workers, and those living in farming communi-ties. State, local, and tribal entities may also regulate pesticides, as FIFRA does not preempt additional restrictions.[212]

---

[207] TSCA §6(a), 15 U.S.C.A. §2605(a) (2016).
[208] 15 U.S.C.A. §2604 (2016).
[209] James Salzman & Barton Thompson, Jr., ENVIRONMENTAL LAW & POLICY 180 (3d ed. 2010).
[210] Federal Insecticide, Fungicide, and Rodenticide Act (FIFRA) §4(a), 15 U.S.C. §2604(a)(1) (2016).
[211] 15 U.S.C. §2605(a) (2016).
[212] See Farber & Carlson, *supra* note 27, at Chapter 9.

Producers of agricultural chemicals must conduct tests to determine the cancer-causing (carcinogenic) risks of these chemicals before manufacturing and selling these products. The EPA must approve registration of the product to ensure, among other things, the manufacturer has properly labeled the product and that the product "will not generally cause unreasonable adverse effects on the environment." "Unreasonable adverse effects" include "any unreasonable risk to man or the environment taking into account economic, social and environmental costs and benefits of the use of any pesticide."[213] Once the EPA registers the product, it does not need retesting, even though scientific knowledge has improved. However, a 1988 amendment to FIFRA addressed concerns about early testing and approval of many of these chemicals by requiring retesting and reregistration. By 2008, this reregistration process was completed. After registration, the EPA may cancel or suspend the pesticide use, pending cancellation, if the EPA determines that the use presents an "imminent hazard."[214]

c. Food, Drug, and Cosmetic Act

In addition to testing requirements under FIFRA, the EPA must set tolerance levels under the Food, Drug, and Cosmetic Act (FDCA) for pesticide residue on raw agricultural products. FDCA also requires extensive testing of chemicals added to food or cosmetics. Under the "Delaney Clause," named after a Congressman from New York, additives to food, animal drugs in meat and poultry, and color additives are prohibited as unsafe if they have been "found . . . to induce cancer in man or animal."[215] However, even with extensive testing of the carcinogenic risks of these chemicals, there is still much uncertainty due to the difficulty of determining risk from epidemiological studies, where humans are exposed to carcinogenic substances, but cancer symptoms may not appear for decades. Other difficulties include establishing causation when people are exposed to other health risks besides the tested chemical, translating animal exposure to human exposure when relying on animal bioassays for testing, and determining the actual level of exposure that consumers, workers, and rural communities experience.

d. CAA and CWA

Both the CAA and the CWA have special provisions to address toxic substances in the air and water. As mentioned earlier, the CAA sets national standards for a small number of hazardous air pollutants. The EPA sets these National Emission Standards for Hazardous Air Pollutants (NESHAPs) as technology-based standards according to "maximum achievable control technology" (MACT) because of the difficulty in determining under

---

[213] 7 U.S.C. §§136a(c)(5), 136(bb).
[214] *See* Farber & Carlson, *supra* note 27, at Chapter 9.
[215] 21 U.S.C. §348(c)(3)(A); 7 U.S.C. §136(d) (1996).

a health-based standard what constitutes "an ample margin of safety to protect the public health."[216] However, the EPA may impose additional limitations on carcinogenic hazardous air pollutant (HAP) emissions, if after applying MACT limitations it cannot sufficiently reduce a residual risk of "lifetime excess cancer risk."

The CWA specifically calls for designating toxic pollutants, which are then subject to EPA effluent limitations set at Best Available Technology (BAT) standards, as well as possible EPA water-quality-based toxic effluent standards and state water-quality control standards. Variances to these toxic pollutant standards are not allowed unless an individual point source can show that its operation is "fundamentally different" from other sources of its type that were analyzed to set the original effluent guidelines.[217] The point source seeking the variance must show that the factors used to set the guidelines are "fundamentally different factors" (FDF) from its own operation such that an FDF variance is justified. For example, if the production processes of one plant are fundamentally different from the other plants in its category that were used to set the national effluent standards, then such a variance might be allowed. However, the individual point source requesting an FDF variance cannot assert economic affordability as a factor distinguishing it from other industrial plants in its category.[218]

States are required to identify toxic "hot spots" under CWA Section 304(l) and list water body segments that are not meeting the toxic pollutant water-quality standards, as well as identify point sources that are causing segments of the water body to be out of compliance.[219] States must then prepare "individual control strategies" (ICS) to enable these segments to meet water quality standards by controlling the NPDES permits of point sources identified as offending dischargers. While the CAA does not have a special toxic "hot spots" provision, several states have established programs to identify and control air quality regions suffering from toxic emissions. California, for example, enacted the Air Toxics "Hot Spots" Information and Assessment Act in 1987 to collect emissions data, identify polluting facilities, notify residents of significant risks, and reduce significant risks to acceptable levels.[220]

e. Nanotechnology Impacts

Nanotechnology is defined as "the understanding and control of matter at dimensions between approximately 1 and 100 nanometers, where unique

---

[216] 42 U.S.C. §7412 (1999).
[217] Chem. Mfrs. Assn. v. NRDC, 470 U.S. 116, 131-133 (1985) (holding that toxic pollutant limitations are subject to an FDF variance).
[218] Id.
[219] 33 U.S.C. §1314 (2000).
[220] AB 2588 Air Toxics "Hot Spots" Program, CALIFORNIA ENVIRONMENTAL PROTECTION AGENCY: AIR RESOURCES BOARD (Apr. 25, 2016), http://www.arb.ca.gov/ab2588/ab2588.htm (last visited Dec. 1, 2017).

phenomena enable novel applications."[221] In order to understand the size of a nanometer, the thickness of a sheet of paper is approximately 100,000 nanometers, and one nanometer is one million times smaller than the length of an ant.[222]

Nanotechnology has many uses including consumer products, biomedical technology, electronics, and pesticides. At the nanoscale, gases, liquids, and solids may exhibit properties that are different from their bulk form properties. Nanomaterials may show enhanced abilities as to strength, magnetic properties, heat or electricity conduction, light reflection, or color changes. However, using nanotechnology has potential health and environmental risks from nanoparticles and engineered nanomaterials (ENMs), but there is incomplete understanding and little direct regulation of these risks. Nanoparticles and ENMs can easily penetrate cell membranes once they have entered the human body and can disrupt ecosystems in the environment.[223]

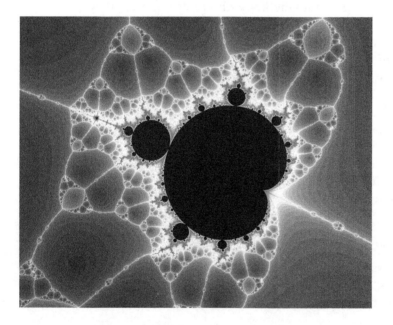

The EPA is taking action under TSCA and FIFRA to identify and regulate ENMs as chemical substances and pesticides that contain nanoscale materials. OSHA standards do not yet include nanomaterials, but employers are required to keep workplaces clear of "recognized hazards," which may include nanomaterials if they are shown to present a known hazard.[224] International organizations, including the European Union, are also moving toward regulating nanomaterials in consumer products and the environment.[225]

---

[221] Nat'l Sci. and Tech. Council, National Nanotechnology Initiative (NNI) Strategic Plan 1 (Feb. 2014), http://www.nano.gov/sites/default/files/pub_resource/2014_nni_strategic_plan.pdf.

[222] *Nanotechnology 101*, Nat'l Nanotechnology Initiative, http://www.nano.gov/nanotech-101#content (last visited Dec. 1, 2017); *see also* Jean M. Eggen, *Nanotechnology and the Environment: What's Next?*, 26 Natural Resources & Environment no. 3 (Winter 2012).

[223] Eggen, *supra* note 222.

[224] *Id.*

[225] Dr. Basila Kattouf, *The Impact of Nanotechnology on Industry Sectors—A Review*, NanoFine Technologies (May 23, 2016), http://www.nanofine-technologies.com/#!The-impact-of-nanotechnology-on-industry-sectors-a-review/c64n/5742b1000cf2aa150f1fb837.

f. Electronic Waste

Consumer electronics such as computers, music devices, and cell phones may present health and environmental hazards during the manufacturing, use, disposal, and recycling of these products. Most electronic waste (e-waste)[226] in the United States is dumped into landfills, but it is also exported to developing countries such as China and Africa for recycling and dumping. EPA is concerned about these exports, partly because the safety and environmental hazards associated with recycling and discarding consumer electronics may not be properly managed and also because the United States is passing up the opportunity to retain valuable resources through domestic recycling.[227] In 2011, the United States Interagency Task Force on Electronics Stewardship released a report, the National Strategy for Electronics Stewardship, which recommended several actions to enhance electronic device design and improve the way we manage discarded electronics.[228]

Only about 20% of people in the United States properly dispose of electronic waste.[229] The other 80% throw it in the trash, which ends up in landfills, where mercury, lead, and other toxins may leak from this e-waste to contaminate soil and groundwater.[230] Exporters may ship the recycled electronics overseas because dismantling devices to recover valuable resources may be too time-consuming and costly in the United States. Instead, the receiving country, such as China, pulls the electronics apart and burns them with minimal management of the risks to human health and the environment.[231]

---

[226] *National Strategy for Electronics Stewardship*, INTERAGENCY TASK FORCE ON ELECTRONICS STEWARDSHIP (July 20, 2011), https://www.epa.gov/sites/production/files/2015-09/documents/national_strategy_for_electronic_stewardship_0.pdf. Note that the Interagency Task Force on Electronics Stewardship "considers 'e-waste' a subset of 'used electronics'" and encourages return of these products to the supply chain through various routes such as reusing, restoring, or recycling in order to reduce waste. *Id.* at 5.

[227] *E-Waste* U.S. EPA, https://www.epa.gov/international-cooperation/international-priorities#ewaste (last updated Oct. 26, 2017).

[228] INTERAGENCY TASK FORCE ON ELECTRONICS STEWARDSHIP, *supra* note 226.

[229] Bryan Walsh, *E-Waste Not: How — and Why — We Should Make Sure Our Old Cell Phones, TVs and PCs Get Dismantled Properly*, TIME MAGAZINE (Jan. 8, 2009), http://content.time.com/time/magazine/article/0,9171,1870485,00.html.

[230] *Id.*

[231] *Id.*

As discussed briefly in the previous RCRA section, U.S. regulation prohibits exporting hazardous waste outside the country unless the exporter notifies the government of the country receiving the wastes and it does not object. However, the United States has signed, but not ratified, the Basel Convention, which is an international treaty regulating the export of hazardous waste to developing countries.[232] U.S. environmentalists advocate prohibiting the export of this waste and push electronics manufacturers to take greater responsibility for managing their products throughout the life cycle.[233] The European Union already requires these manufacturers to ensure responsible recycling and disposal and encourages "green design" by limiting the use of toxic substances in products.[234]

Note

1. In Chapter 3, Section IV.C we described the Precautionary Principle (PP). We noted one common definition as *"when there is uncertainty as to the risks associated with a policy, that risk should be removed through alternative policies prior to exposing humans and the environment to such risk."* As stated above, the Toxic Substances Control Act allows the EPA to halt or regulate chemical use when there is a "reasonable basis to conclude" that the product "presents or will present an unreasonable risk of injury to health or the environment." Because there is a difficulty with identifying the risk involved and the appropriate level of risk posed by the substance to human health and the environment, the PP plays an important role in regulating toxins in a sustainable manner.

2. LITIGATION

Civil and Criminal Liability for Environmental Harm: If the government provides incentives for compliance and improvement and forces behavior changes through command-and-control regulation and common law principles, these mechanisms may achieve environmental responsibility. Providing incentives through economic tools has an advantage over command-and-control regulation and common law principles because it does not require compliance monitoring, causation evidence, and enforcement actions and penalties. However, when incentives do not sufficiently encourage compliance with regulation or adherence to common law rules

[232] *Id.*

[233] *Id.*

[234] Chris Carroll, *High-Tech Trash: Will Your Discarded TV End Up in a Ditch in Ghana?*, Nat'l Geographic (Jan. 2008), http://ngm.nationalgeographic.com/2008/01/high-tech-trash/carroll-text.

of liability and responsibility, we must impose private civil penalties or governmental civil or criminal penalties. Below we briefly discuss civil tort law principles for toxic torts, trespass, and nuisance, before we address governmental action to discourage noncompliance with regulatory requirements.

Civil Liability through Tort Law: Tort law requires intentional, negligent, or wrongful action that causes harm to another person. In order to establish liability, the plaintiff must prove that 1) the defendant had a legal duty to act in a particular manner, 2) the defendant breached the duty by failing to act in such a manner, and 3) the plaintiff suffered injury directly caused by the breach. Tort law, through either common law or statute, allows the judicial system to allocate civil liability and provide remedies for personal injuries caused by the release of toxins into the environment.[235]

Toxic torts are a subset of tortious conduct that directly causes personal injury based on the exposure to toxic chemicals. Toxic torts occur through workplace exposure; environmental exposure through contamination of land, water, or structures; ingestion of pharmaceutical products; or exposure to toxic consumer products, such as pesticides.

Exposure to toxins does not necessarily result in immediate, recognizable, personal injuries. Sometimes it takes many years for toxic exposure to manifest itself through diseases such as cancer, asbestosis, mesothelioma, and leukemia. **Signature diseases** are those diseases, such as asbestosis and mesothelioma, that are directly traceable to a specific toxin exposure, in this case, asbestos. However, diseases such as cancer, leukemia, lung disease, or aplastic anemia may be caused by factors other than exposure to toxins. This uncertainty as to causation creates a significant obstacle to toxic tort cases. First, the plaintiff must prove general causation by showing that exposure to a particular toxin, through ingestion, inhalation, or contact, *can cause* the illness complained of and that plaintiff was exposed to a dosage level sufficient to cause the illness. Second, the plaintiff must show specific causation by demonstrating that the exposure *did cause* the illness.

The plaintiff cannot establish specific causation just by proving exposure to a toxin and must instead present expert testimony by physicians, toxicologists, epidemiologists, and other specialists to prove that the exposure was the cause of the illness.[236] The U.S. Supreme Court held in *Daubert v. Merrell Dow Pharmaceuticals* that such expert testimony must meet some threshold of scientific validity and that trial courts must demand significant evidentiary showings that the testimony is relevant and reliable, as required under Rule 702 of the Federal Rules of Evidence governing admissibility.[237] When there are multiple sources of exposure,

---

[235] *See* Farber & Carlson, *supra* note 27, at Chapter 2.
[236] *Id.*
[237] Daubert v. Merrell Dow Pharms., 509 U.S. 579, 597 (1993).

the plaintiff must also show that the defendant was the source of the exposure that specifically caused the illness.

Toxic tort litigation is a relatively new area of practice, taking form in the 1970s as people were exposed to industrial synthetic chemicals produced after World War II.[238] The litigation process has created toxic torts as new causes of action, new remedies, or a combination of both. There may be a long latency period between the time of exposure to the toxin and the manifestation of an injury caused by the exposure. This delay between breach and injury creates legal complications in determining what remedies are appropriate when tortious exposure to a toxin has occurred, but the injury is not yet discernible and may not be for years. Statutes of limitation govern when a litigant must file a lawsuit after the date of tortious conduct. However, in toxic tort cases such statutes should follow the discovery rule so that the statutory time does not begin to run until an injury has manifested through the diagnosis of a disease or other injury.[239]

Tortious exposure to a carcinogenic toxin is particularly problematic because it is not certain that the exposure will cause cancer and the latency period until the physical injury appears may be long and emotionally distressing to the person exposed. However, the traditional tort of emotional distress requires that plaintiffs show physical injury or physical manifestation of the distress, and this will be difficult, if not impossible for the toxic tort plaintiff to demonstrate. Through toxic tort litigation in various U.S. states, new theories have developed to handle this problem of recovering damages without being able to show a physical injury. Courts treat these theories as causes of action or remedies for a toxic tort injury and include emotional distress based upon cancerphobia (the fear of developing cancer), medical monitoring to identify diseases that may occur in the future, and an immediate injury based on an increased risk of cancer.[240]

Trespass and Nuisance: Property-based torts of trespass and nuisance were some of the first approaches courts used to deal with modern-day pollution. While these common law legal theories no longer provide the basis for regulatory control over pollution, they remain viable legal actions to address harms not otherwise addressed by government regulation. Trespass requires a physical entry onto the property of another without permission, and nuisance law allows property owners to prevent others from substantially and unreasonably interfering with the use and enjoyment of their land.

---

[238] Robert F. Blomquist, *An Introduction to American Toxic Tort Law: Three Overarching Metaphors and Three Sources of Law*, 26 VAL. U. L. REV. 795 (1992); David E. Bernstein, *Getting to Causation in Toxic Tort Cases*, 74 BROOK. L. REV. 51 (2007).

[239] Bernstein, *supra* note 238.

[240] James T. O'Reilly, TOXIC TORTS PRACTICE GUIDE (1992).

The case of *Gill v. LDI*[241] illustrates nicely the intersection of federal regulatory law and state-law tort claims of trespass and nuisance. In this case, plaintiff landowners brought claims against their neighbors, LDI, which established a quarry operation that discharged silt, debris, and rocks into the plaintiffs' pond and a nearby river. The court determined that LDI violated the Clean Water Act, which justified a civil action by the plaintiffs.[242] Based on Washington State's four-part test for trespass, the court found:

1. LDI's discharge of silt was a physical invasion of plaintiffs' property;
2. LDI intentionally carried on the rock quarry operation;
3. LDI must have realized that the quarry, which was on top of the springs that supplied plaintiffs' pond with water, was the likely cause of the silt discharges into the pond; and
4. the actual entry onto plaintiffs' land by the tangible silt was presumed to be damaging to the plaintiffs' property interest, since only intangible and indirect trespass requires substantial damage.[243]

The *Gill* court also determined that LDI's quarry operation constituted a nuisance per se because it violated CWA permit regulations and exceeded the state and county noise limits. Plaintiffs were not required to show that the quarry operation unreasonably interfered with their use and enjoyment of the property because the activity was unlawful.[244]

Government Enforcement of Regulation—Civil and Criminal: Many of the federal and state pollution statutes provide for government civil and criminal enforcement as well as private enforcement in the form of **citizen suits** between private parties. Government enforcement mechanisms include:

- **compliance orders** to require a violator to come into compliance with statutory requirements;
- **administrative penalties** requiring the violator to pay more in penalties than they can save from their noncompliance;
- **civil penalties** obtained through judicial action such as injunctive relief or financial fines; and
- **criminal prosecution** resulting in fines or incarceration based on willful or knowing violations.[245]

---

[241] Gill v. LDI, 19 F. Supp. 2d 1188 (W.D. Wash. 1998).

[242] *Id.* at 1197.

[243] *Id.* at 1197-1198 (describing four-part test for "intangible and indirect trespass of microscopic airborne particles deposited on their property" as "(1) an invasion affecting an interest in the exclusive possession of plaintiffs' property, (2) an intentional doing of the act which results in the invasion, (3) reasonable foreseeability that the act done could result in an invasion of plaintiffs' possessory interest, and (4) substantial damage to the *res*").

[244] *Id.* at 1198-1199.

[245] *See* Jeffrey M. Gaba, BLACK LETTER OUTLINE ON ENVIRONMENTAL LAW, Chapter 9 (2008).

Private enforcement through a **citizen suit** requires appropriate notice to the defendant and government authorities. If government authorities are already diligently prosecuting an action against violators, either civilly or criminally, the government will generally preclude a citizen suit.[246] Plaintiffs may not bring citizen suits against polluters for past violations of a statute, but only for intermittent or ongoing violations.[247] In *Friends of Milwaukee's Rivers v. Milwaukee Metropolitan*,[248] a citizen group concerned about ongoing discharges from sanitary sewers into Lake Michigan and Milwaukee rivers brought a citizen suit under the Clean Water Act against the State of Wisconsin (State) and the Milwaukee Metropolitan Sewerage District (MMSD) for failure to take action to eliminate these discharges.[249] The Seventh Circuit Court of Appeals determined that the State's judicial enforcement actions, which began in 1976 and did not result in any legally binding agreement to remedy the Clean Water Act (CWA) violations, did not constitute a diligent prosecution.[250] In addition, "the State did not timely 'commence' and diligently prosecute an administrative enforcement action," so the citizen suit for civil penalties was not barred by any non-judicial action.[251]

Criminal prosecutions require some type of "guilty knowledge" to provide the mens rea needed to use criminal penalties to enforce pollution control. The court in *United States v. Sinskey*[252] determined that the defendant receiving punishment for exceeding the NPDES permit for ammonia nitrate discharges did not need to have knowledge that his acts violated the CWA or permit. Liability required only that the ammonia nitrate discharges, resulting from increasing the hogs slaughtered and processed at the plant, exceeded the one part per million NPDES limit.[253] The government is not required to prove that the violator knew that his actions violated the law.[254] The knowledge required for prosecution may not be actual knowledge of the illegal action but it can include deliberate ignorance of the illegality of pollution disposal. In *United States v. Wilson*,[255] the defendant hired his cousin to haul away barrels filled with a known

---

[246] *See, e.g.*, 33 U.S.C. §1365(b)(1)(B) (citizen suit barred "if the Administrator or State has commenced and is diligently prosecuting a civil or criminal action in a court of the United States, or a State to require compliance with the standard, limitation, or order").

[247] *See* Gwaltney v. Chesapeake Bay Found., Inc., 484 U.S. 49, 64 (1987) (interpreting Clean Water Act to bar citizen suits for wholly past violations).

[248] Friends of Milwaukee's Rivers & Lake Michigan Fed'n v. Milwaukee Metro. Sewerage Dist., 382 F.3d 743 (7th Cir. 2004).

[249] *Id.* at 748.

[250] *Id.* at 752-754.

[251] *Id.* at 757.

[252] United States v. Sinskey, 119 F.3d 712 (8th Cir. 1997).

[253] *Id.* at 714-716.

[254] *Id.* at 716 (citing United States v. Int'l Minerals & Chem. Corp., 402 U.S. 558, 562-563, (1971), which held that a criminal conviction under a statute prohibiting the knowing violation of regulations governing the interstate shipment of hazardous materials required that the person being punished "knowingly committed the specific acts or omissions contemplated by the regulations at issue," not knowledge of the relevant law).

[255] United States v. Wilson, 151 F. App'x 295 (5th Cir. 2005).

pollutant. When the defendant asked his cousin where he would be disposing of the barrels, before his cousin could answer the defendant stated, "I don't want to know."[256]

TRAGEDY IN FLINT, MICHIGAN—A FAILURE TO ENFORCE

In their essay, "After Flint: Environmental Justice as Equal Protection," Professors David A. Dana and Deborah Tuerkheimer argue that Michigan's failure to enforce the regulations governing lead in water sources should be considered unequal protection and that "a firm historical basis exists for conceiving of equal protection as a guarantee of protection against the underenforcement of protective laws." The professors begin their essay with a concise background of the tragedy that occurred in Flint.[257]

The story of Flint is one of gross government failure—a failure impacting a population comprised of 57% of African-Americans and nearly 42% of citizens living below the federal poverty line. When it most mattered, officials opted not to enforce the rules designed to keep these residents safe from toxic hazards. Most striking in this regard was the failure to treat the contaminated Flint River water, which then flowed through and corroded lead pipes. As summarized by a report issued by the Governor's Water Task Force in March 2016:

> With the City of Flint under emergency management, the Flint Water Department rushed unprepared into full-time operation of the Flint Water Treatment Plant, drawing water from a highly corrosive source without the use of corrosion control. Though MDEQ [Michigan Department of Environmental Quality] was delegated primacy (authority to enforce federal law), the United States Environmental Protection Agency (EPA) delayed enforcement of the Safe Drinking Water Act (SDWA) and Lead and Copper Rule (LCR), thereby prolonging the calamity. Neither the Governor nor the Governor's office took steps to reverse poor decisions by MDEQ and state-appointed emergency managers until October 2015, in spite of mounting problems and suggestions to do so by senior staff members in the Governor's office, in part because of continued reassurances from MDEQ that the water was safe.

The Task Force report makes clear that, from the time it began drawing water from the highly corrosive Flint River, MDEQ officials were under a legal obligation to implement corrosion control measures. Neglecting to do so caused "chronic toxic exposure of an entire population"—most troublingly, Flint's children. A host of further missteps, like violating federal mandates to appropriately sample water quality, compounded the harm created by the initial decision not to treat the river water.

MDEQ appears to bear primary responsibility for the disaster. But across the board, governmental workers at the state Department of Health and Human Services, the Governor's office, the county health department, and the EPA, among others, all fell short of their responsibilities to the citizens of Flint. The clear picture that emerges is one of systemic disregard for the city's residents—again, residents who are disproportionately poor and

---

[256] *Id.* at 297.
[257] David A. Dana & Deborah Tuerkheimer, *After Flint: Environmental Justice as Equal Protection*, 111 Nw. U. L. Rev. 879 (2017).

predominantly African-American. This disregard led officials charged with enforcing the law to ignore it.

The government failure in Flint is, in some sense, exceptional: Flint's finances are far worse than most localities; and, ostensibly because of that, the governance of the city had been assumed by the state as a receiver. However, while the lack of local control in Flint and the brazen indifference to community well-being may be unusual, the perils faced by the people of Flint are not. Scores of poor, often minority, communities across the United States bear extreme risks from lead and other hazards—risks that should not be tolerated in a civilized nation.

3. CASE STUDY OF RESILIENCE AND SUSTAINABILITY

The BP oil spill litigation involved multiple common law and regulatory claims. These claims included personal injury claims for wrongful death, injuries from the explosion, fire, exposure to oil and chemicals used to disperse the oil, damages to property and natural resources along with economic loss from the spill, contract breach, and statutory violations of the Oil Pollution Act of 1990, the Clean Water Act (CWA), and other federal and state regulations.[258] The federal claims were consolidated into two Multidistrict Litigations (MDLs) labeled *In re BP p.l.c. Securities Litigation* (MDL-2185) and *In re Oil Spill by the Oil Rig "Deepwater Horizon" in the Gulf of Mexico, on April 20, 2010* (MDL-2179).[259] Complex jurisdictional conflicts among state law, federal maritime law, and federal statutes, as well as preemption challenges, required judicial resolution before the courts could address the underlying substantive claims.[260]

In 2012, BP agreed to a class settlement estimated at $8 billion to compensate a multitude of claimants for personal, economic, and environmental injuries.[261] Challenges to the administration and interpretation of this settlement resulted in an order by the U.S. Court of Appeals for the Fifth Circuit in October 2013 requiring the district judge to reconsider the settlement terms.[262] Without such reconsideration, some were estimating that the actual settlement might cost $16 billion, more than twice the original BP estimate.[263] BP also contributed $20 billion to the Deepwater

---

[258] Carl J. Barbier & Benjamin S. Allums, *Selected Issues Encountered in MDL No. 2179, In re: Oil Spill by the Oil Rig "Deepwater Horizon" in the Gulf of Mexico*, 61 THE ADVOC. (STATE BAR OF TEXAS) 47 (2012).

[259] *Id.* at 47.

[260] *Id.* at 48-49.

[261] *Questions of Ethics Arise as BP Class Action Claims Process Gets Second Look*, LEGAL MONITOR WORLDWIDE (JORDAN) via THOMPSON REUTERS NEWSROOM, 2013 WLNR 28467400 (Nov. 12, 2013).

[262] *Id.*

[263] Trefis Team, *BP's Settlement Could Top $16 Billion Amid Failed Attempts to Limit Its Liabilities*, TREFIS TEAM, 2013 WLNR 22467520 (Sept. 9, 2013).

Horizon Oil Spill Trust fund "to pay individual and business claims, penalties resulting from litigation judgments and settlement of litigations, state and local response costs and claims, as well as natural resource damages and related costs."[264]

As a result of the Deepwater Horizon spill and its impact on the region, Congress passed the Resources and Ecosystems Sustainability, Tourist Opportunities, and Revived Economies of the Gulf Coast States Act of 2012 (RESTORE Act). This Act established a trust fund to receive deposits of a large percentage of any CWA regulatory penalties collected from parties determined to be responsible and liable for the spill. The fund will assist restoring the coastline and creating jobs in the five Gulf Coast states affected—Alabama, Florida, Louisiana, Mississippi, and Texas.[265]

In addition to the numerous civil claims filed in response to the oil spill, **criminal charges** were filed against two BP supervisors for manslaughter based on their alleged negligence in conducting safety tests and their disregard of high-pressure readings before the explosion that killed 11 workers.[266] In 2015, the manslaughter charges were dropped against both supervisors.[267] A former BP engineer was accused of obstructing the oil spill investigation by allegedly deleting text and voice mail messages about the amount of oil spilling from the blowout.[268] A former Halliburton cementing technology director was also charged with destroying evidence because he allegedly instructed employees to delete data about the cement work performed on the blown-out well during a review of the BP spill.[269]

Criminal charges, civil suits, regulatory penalties, and common law claims may all be necessary to obtain the appropriate remedies of restitution, restoration costs, economic and personal injury damages, punitive damages, and traditional notions of justice for the impacts caused by the oil spill. The environment and those people who have been adversely impacted by negligence, intentional wrongdoing, and the general risks associated with deep-water drilling should be fairly compensated for losses incurred.

---

[264] *Id.*

[265] Gerald J. Pels & Julia C. Rinne, *The Restore Act: Legislation That Works for the Gulf Coast*, 27-SPG NAT. RESOURCES & ENV'T 40 (2013).

[266] *Delay Granted in BP Oil Spill Manslaughter Trial*, THE TIMES (SHREVEPORT, LA), 2013 WLNR 22981743 (Sept. 14, 2013).

[267] Janet McConnaughey & Michael Kunzelman, *Manslaughter Charges Dropped Against 2 BP Supervisors over 11 Rig Worker Deaths*, ASSOCIATED PRESS via U.S. NEWS (Dec. 2, 2015), http://www.usnews.com/news/us/articles/2015/12/02/bp-supervisor-pleads-guilty-to-misdemeanor-in-2010-oil-spill.

[268] Rick Jervis & Kevin Johnson, *3 BP Executives Indicted over Gulf Oil Spill*, USA TODAY (Nov. 15, 2012), https://www.usatoday.com/story/money/business/2012/11/15/bp-near-settlement-with-us-over-gulf-spill/1706209/.

[269] *Oil Exec Charged with Destroying Spill Evidence*, VICTORIA TIMES COLONIST (CANADA), 2013 WLNR 23535085 (Sept. 20, 2013).

Questions

1. What do you think about citizen-initiated lawsuits, such as those based on nuisance? Are they a good way to regulate the environment? What are their advantages? Disadvantages?

2. Can citizen suits lead to more sustainable conditions? Do they help with the equity portion of the triple bottom line? If so, how?

VI. STRATEGY TO FACILITATE IMPLEMENTATION #8: RISK ANALYSIS

Helpful to assessing and understanding resilience and sustainability is risk analysis. Assessing risks facing social-ecological systems can help illuminate system vulnerabilities. Scientists, policy makers, regulatory analysts and agencies, economists, and scholars have struggled with how to deal with scientific uncertainty and the assessment of risk. For example, there are different approaches to risk regulation of occupational and environmental exposure to toxins and carcinogens. Regulation may be risk-based by determining whether significant risks exist and how to reduce these risks to the maximum extent feasible.

When environmental regulations require controlling toxins at a level that protects human health and the environment, the challenge for regulators is to determine what constitutes a "safe" level of exposure. Unfortunately, any level of exposure to many toxins will pose a risk such that a "safe" level does not exist. The U.S. Supreme Court in *Industrial Union Department, AFL-CIO v. American Petroleum Institute* (also known as the *"Benzene Decision"*)[270] distinguished between regulating to a level that is "risk-free" and regulating to a level that is "safe," even though some risk is involved. Recognizing the importance of chemical use in industrial workplaces, the Court in the *Benzene Decision* required the Occupational Safety and Health Administration (OSHA) to regulate the exposure level only to the degree it constitutes a "significant risk" in the workplace.[271] Safety does not mean risk-free, and regulations must be set at a level to ensure the workplace is not "unsafe," which requires a showing of "significant risk."[272]

Economic approaches to risk regulation require cost-benefit analysis to evaluate the immediate economic impacts of the regulation in relation to the benefits accrued in the future. Valuing human health and

---

[270] 448 U.S. 607, 642 (1980).
[271] *Id.* at 641.
[272] *Id.* at 642.

environmental benefits, as well as discounting these benefits into the future make benefit analysis very difficult. For example, placing a monetary value on reducing mortality risks requires valuing "life" by determining how much money someone would demand in return for being exposed to a 1 in 1,000 risk of death. Economists distinguish between the values of a statistical life versus the individual life. Discounting future benefits to account for the time value of money is also problematic for exposure to a carcinogen, which may have a long latency period before cancer develops or for determining the benefits of climate change regulation. For example, "[i]f a human life is valued at $8 million, and if an agency chooses a 10% discount rate, a life saved 100 years from now is worth only $581."[273]

Professor Lisa Heinzerling has devoted a great deal of important research and scholarship to confront the ongoing debate regarding risk assessment. In one of her articles, "The Rights of Statistical People," she explains some of the difficulties with risk assessment:

> *Modern risk assessment, which forms the basis of much health-related regulation, attempts to determine the probability of future harm to individuals exposed to particular hazards. This analysis requires many assumptions about the potency of the hazard, the magnitude of exposures, and the susceptibility of the individuals to the harm in question. Often the assumptions must be made in the absence of conclusive proof. For example, many risk assessments attempt to determine the probability of cancer in a human population exposed to a particular substance by considering the effect of that substance on an animal population, such as rats or mice. Extrapolating the results in animal studies to the human population requires an assumption about the similarity between the relevant responses of animals and humans. Risk assessments must also, to take another example, attempt to predict what level of exposure the relevant human population will experience with regard to the substance in question. Will the individuals in the population eat the substance, drink it, breathe it, or all of these and more? How often? For how many days or weeks or years? These are difficult questions to answer in advance. Risk assessors must therefore make assumptions about what the future exposures will be to estimate the risk the population faces.[274]*

We can properly manage risks only if we can identify and value them. Once we identify and value them, they can help address the complexities embedded in assessing resilience and sustainability by providing data to weigh trade-offs. In essence, we need to recognize potential problems in order to avoid them. Making decisions that intentionally address resilience and sustainability requires us to understand what

---

[273] *See* Farber & Carlson, *supra* note 27 at Chapter 2 (quoting Cass R. Sunstein, *Cost-Benefit Default Principles*, 99 MICH. L. REV. 1652, 1711 (2001)).
[274] 24 HARV. ENVTL. L. REV. 189 199-200 (2000); *see also* Frank Ackerman & Lisa Heinzerling, *Pricing the Priceless: Cost-Benefit Analysis of Environmental Protection*, 150 U. PA. L. REV. 1553 (2002).

could happen so that we can make decisions that not only avoid undesirable, vulnerable, and unsustainable outcomes, but also promote positive resilient and sustainable systems. Risk analysis (RA) provides a process to do just that. It helps identify risks associated with a particular decision so that we can evaluate the acceptable levels of risk under the specific circumstances.

A. General Description of Risk Analysis

Ascertaining the applicable risks relative to toxins or other issues involves a complex process. For starters, there is no single universally agreed-upon definition of risk. "[O]ne reason is that the concept is multidimensional and nuanced. It requires an understanding that risk to a system is inherently and fundamentally a function of the states of the system and of its environment (and of course of the initiating event)."[275]

Risk analysis (RA) identifies risk in complex systems by using a three-phase process including **risk identification, risk evaluation,** and **risk management**.

The **risk identification** phase predominantly focuses on locating the potential risks facing social-ecological systems. There are two basic types of risk identification: quantitative and qualitative. A quantitative risk assigns a numeric value to the likelihood of exposure to danger and the consequences of such exposure. In this way, quantitative risk considers the probability of an event happening and the level of damage if that event occurs. Quantitative risk is expressed as:

$$\text{Risk } (R) = \text{Probability of Exposure } (p) \times \text{Consequence } (C)$$

More recently, scholars have attempted to capture the resilience of a system by adding the system's vulnerabilities (i.e., areas in which a system is susceptible to crossing a threshold described in Chapter 1). In this regard, quantitative risk is expressed as:

$$R = p \times C \times \text{Vulnerability } (V)$$

Identifying qualitative risks involves judgments based on societal and/ or individual assumptions and perceptions relevant to one's tolerance, but not actual data. Qualitative risk incorporates subjective factors and individualized values that influence decisions pertaining to risk identification

---

[275] Yacov Y. Haimes, *On the Complex Definition of Risk: A Systems-Based Approach*, 29 RISK ANALYSIS 1647-1654 (2009).

(i.e., whether or not the specific facts amount to a risk) and risk tolerance (i.e., the severity of the risk).

Where quantitative risk is often illustrated by numerical values, the qualitative risk is shown by scale, such as high, medium, and low. For example, one might identify sharks as presenting a high risk to humans and riding a motorcycle presenting a comparably lower risk. Actual data, however, shows that one is far more likely to be injured or killed by riding a motorcycle than from a shark bite.

Once we identify the risk, the next phase in RA is **risk evaluation** in which we ascertain the acceptable level of risk. This step involves understanding the relevant stakeholders' level of tolerance to a specific risk. This phase can be difficult to administer as it may involve diverse views and varying acceptable levels of risk. Subjectivity may play a role and can assert influence over this phase of RA as individuals may view risks differently depending on their individual circumstances.

The type of risk identification plays an important role in risk evaluation. In the context of qualitative risk, perceptions and bias can influence the evaluative process. In the context of quantitative risk, we can use numerical data to influence decision making by comparing data from multiple risk scenarios.

Once we identify and evaluate the risks, the final RA step is **risk management.** In this step, stakeholders determine the best policy to move forward based on the risks identified and the acceptable level of tolerance relative to those risks.

B. Specific Description of Risk Analysis's Relevance to Resilience and Sustainability

In the context of resilience and sustainability, risk analysis helps identify and account for vulnerabilities to systems. RA provides a method to identify and then consider those vulnerabilities in the decision-making process so that we can intentionally address resilience. Similarly, RA elucidates the pros and cons of making specific decisions, and thus, can illustrate environmental and social challenges to enhance sustainable conditions.

Each step in the RA process has the ability to provide information useful to make decisions relevant to R&S. The following two pieces set forth the importance of RA in identifying and assessing R&S. The first piece focuses predominantly on resilience, highlighting threats and their relation to vulnerabilities. The second piece focuses on sustainability as incorporated into business management.

Yacov Y. Haimes, *On the Complex Definition of Risk: A Systems-Based Approach*

29 RISK ANALYSIS, NO. 12 (2009)

Vulnerability and resilience are key concepts in risk analysis.

To perform effective risk assessment and management, the analyst must understand the system and its interactions with its environment, and this understanding is requisite to modeling the behavior of the states of the system. . . .

Consider a future hurricane scenario similar to Katrina making a land-fall at New Orleans. The challenges associated with both the perception of risk and the quantification and management of the risk vector are a loss of lives, the number of people displaced, damage to infrastructures, and other varied costs. Each of these consequences is a function of the *threat* (e.g., the time of the landfall, its wind speed, and its expected water surge), the *vulnerability* of the community (e.g., those in the area below sea level, the states of the levee system, the canals, etc.), the *resilience* of the levee system (the reliability of the water pumps, preparedness, first responders, etc.), and the *time* of the hurricane. All these factors and many others must be included in any modeling efforts to assess and quantify the likely consequences associated with this scenario. Similarly, the risk management process must also address each element of the risk vector individually and the entire set as a whole.

The implicit and explicit purpose of an investment in risk manage-ment is to render the states of the system less vulnerable and more resil-ient. Preparedness is one important way with which risk managers change the states of natural and constructed environmental systems. . . . *Since the present is deterministic and the future is not, there is an imperative need to assess the future states of the system as they might respond and evolve as a consequence of emergent forced changes.* . . .

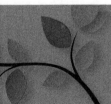

James Lam and Francis Quinn, *The Role of Sustainability in Enterprise Risk Management*

WORKIVA (2013)

[S]ustainability has worked its way up to the top tier of management prior-ities. . . . Once little more than statements of environmental stewardship . . . sustainability has become a critical strategic objective.

Major multinationals, including General Electric (GE), L'Oreal, and Unilever, realized early on that sustainability was neither a distraction nor simple public image posturing. Properly executed, sustainability policies promote faster growth and reduce risk. . . . In fact, sustainability touches every aspect of a company's ability to manage risk and grow its business. . . .

Whenever possible, companies should assess and measure risks to facilitate monitoring of progress. . . . [T]he key players should meet at least quarterly to share their concerns and discuss enterprise-wide, cross-discipline solutions. Each unit should prepare a risk control self-assessment (RCSA), setting out the probability and severity of key risks, what risk controls exist, and how effective they are [risk identification]. Risk managers use RCSAs to develop risk mitigation strategies appropriate for the company as a whole. By adding new pieces, sustainability simply completes the risk management puzzle — it does not require separate or special treatment. . . .

[A] company cannot manage a risk until it has determined how much of that risk it is willing to bear [risk evaluation]. It needs to make business decisions within the context of a risk appetite statement, prepared by risk professionals but reviewed and approved by the board. The statement spells out quantitative limits applicable across the entire company. . . .

Once risk appetite is defined, risk managers can prioritize the risks they need to mitigate and how best to achieve the desired result [risk management]. . . .

In the sustainability context, risk transfer demands an intense focus on the supply chain, including indirect sources. For example, a consumer products company is at risk not only for the ingredients it purchases but also the supply chain behind those ingredients. If child labor is used to gather saffron for a chemical company that makes a yellow pigment sold to a branded food manufacturer, the media would pounce on the consumer products company. . . .

Risk and sustainability data are complex and distributed throughout an organization. To report effectively on a regular basis, companies must invest in technology that aids in the collection, analysis, and management of risk, financial performance, and sustainability data.

Questions and Notes

1. As a general matter, Risk Analysis is not normative. RA does not necessitate the normative assumption that we want to reduce toxins and strengthen system resilience or sustainability. While RA may not be normative, it may involve value judgments. A common issue involved

with RA is determining which risks we should identify, evaluate, and manage. Who the audience is and what we are trying to accomplish can often narrow the possible risks and outcomes involved with RA. For example, as stated in Section III above, an initial environmental assessment (EA) conducted by the government agency is used to determine whether the action is a major federal action requiring an EIS. If the proposed action does not meet the threshold for an EIS, the agency will issue a "Finding of No Significant Impact" (FONSI) and explain why no EIS is needed. In many ways, the EA is a form of Risk Analysis. The outcome very much depends on what the agency uses to evaluate during its analysis.

2. Can you identify an activity or policy by a public or private entity that presents risks? Which system or systems are threatened by those risks? Are the risks to the environment? Economy? Society? How likely are those risks to come true? What could happen if the risk does come to fruition?

3. In Chapter 6, we noted that the natural gas pipeline grid is made of more than 305,000 miles and more than 161,000 miles of liquid pipelines. What issues relevant to resilience and sustainability do you see with this? How could a Risk Analysis help?

4. In Section III above, we note that NEPA no longer requires a "worst case analysis" about potential impacts and that it only requires the applicant to show reasonably foreseeable impacts. Do you think the BP oil spill was a worst-case scenario that did not need consideration or was it a "reasonably foreseeable" event? What might a Risk Analysis of the BP oil spill illuminate?

5. RA can be particularly helpful in evaluating R&S in the context of toxins. It can help arrive at the appropriate level of chemical present in the selected environment, how much exposure a person or the environment has to this contamination, and the toxicity of the chemical.[276] In regard to the three steps above, we need to identify the substances and regulate them if they pose a risk. Second, we need to evaluate the exposure level to determine the acceptable level of risk. Third, we must manage or regulate the substance based on the risks and our level of tolerance to those risks.[277]

6. What are the trade-offs involved with the *Benzene Decision*, distinguishing between "risk free" and "safe"?

---

[276] *Risk Assessment*, U.S. EPA, http://epa.gov/riskassessment/basicinformation.htm#arisk (last updated Oct. 12, 2017).
[277] Guidelines for Carcinogen Risk Assessment, 70 Fed. Reg. 17765-17817 (2005).

7. Based on the three-step process for Risk Analysis, how would you identify, evaluate, and manage risk relative to the typical household garbage disposal? Where does it come from? What should happen with it? Where does it go? How does it get there?

VII. GLOBAL ENVIRONMENTAL REGULATION

The concepts of risk analysis, economics, sustainable development, the precautionary principle (described in more detail in Chapter 3, Section IV.C), and the Polluter Pays Principle (described in more detail below) are the dominant environmental guidelines espoused by the international community.[278] The Rio Declaration on Environment and Development, Principle 15, was adopted by the United Nations Conference on Environment and Development on June 14, 1992, and encapsulates risk, economics, and precaution in stating: "In order to protect the environment, the precautionary approach shall be widely applied by States according to their capabilities. Where there are threats of serious or irreversible damage, lack of full scientific certainty shall not be used as a reason for postponing cost-effective measures to prevent environmental degradation."[279] The Polluter Pays Principle was adopted in Principle 16, which states: "National authorities should endeavor to promote the internalization of environmental costs and the use of economic instruments, taking into account the approach that the polluter should, in principle, bear the cost of pollution, with due regard to the public interest and without distorting international trade and investment."[280]

Pollution crosses international boundaries using transitory mediums such as water, the wind, creatures, and air. Managing pollution requires agreement and cooperation among nations. For example, the European Union (EU) is an organization that has some control over member states to protect and restore surface waters and groundwater, in order to promote sustainable water use, protect aquatic ecosystems, and reduce pollution.[281] Air pollution is particularly difficult to address as many of the issues are global in scale, including transboundary pollution, ozone depletion, and climate change.[282] International human rights law may protect the populations most vulnerable to climate change — such as the Inuit in

---

[278] Stephen McCaffrey & Rachael Salcido, GLOBAL ISSUES IN ENVTL. L., 4-13 (2008).
[279] REPORT OF THE UNITED NATIONS CONFERENCE ON ENV'T & DEV., UNITED NATIONS (Sept. 28, 1992), http://www.un.org/documents/ga/conf151/aconf15126-4.htm.
[280] *Id.*
[281] *See* McCaffrey & Salcido, *supra* note 278, at 107-109 (discussing the EU Water Framework Directive, adopted in 2000).
[282] *Id.* at 113-115.

the Arctic—from those nations, such as the United States, which have failed to regulate greenhouse gas emissions.[283]

China is the leading polluter and emitter of total greenhouse gases per year in the world, but it has struggled to maintain its rapid economic growth and has asserted its right to unlimited emissions in the future.[284] Simultaneously, China has taken a number of actions on climate, including announcing a national cap-and-trade program. China must commit to enforcing its own environmental regulations to protect its people and international economic leaders, such as the United States, must cooperate with China and other large polluters to reduce the harmful air pollutants that affect us all.[285]

The U.S. commitment to international agreements to reduce greenhouse gas emissions has been politically controversial. While the United States became a party to the 2015 Paris Agreement to address climate change via an Executive Order and has generally complied with its terms, as of 2016 the Senate had not ratified the agreement. In June 2017, President Trump announced that the United States would withdraw from the Paris climate accord and noted, "I was elected to represent the citizens of Pittsburgh, not Paris."[286]

The United States has attempted to address international pollution in the CAA by requiring states to modify their State Implementation Plans to control sources that are causing or contributing to air pollution problems in another country.[287] Title VI of the CAA, added in the 1990 amendments, implements the U.S. responsibilities under the Montreal Protocols to address ozone depletion. Executive Order 12114, signed by President Carter in 1979, provides that "responsible officials of Federal agencies be informed of environmental considerations and take those considerations into account when making decisions on major Federal Actions which could have environmental impacts anywhere beyond the borders of the U.S., including Antarctica."[288] This Executive Order requires an assessment similar to that required by NEPA for federal actions that have significant environmental effects, but it "does not preempt the application of NEPA extraterritorially."[289]

---

[283] *See, e.g.*, Inuit Petition to the Inter-American Commission on Human Rights to Oppose Climate Change Caused by the United States of America, Inuit Circumpolar Council Canada (Dec. 7, 2005), http://www.inuitcircumpolar.com/inuit-petition-inter-american-commission-on-human-rights-to-oppose-climate-change-caused-by-the-united-states-of-america.html.

[284] John Copeland Nagle, *How Much Should China Pollute?*, 12 Vt. J. Envtl. L. 591 (2011).

[285] *Id.* at 612, 629.

[286] Michael D. Shear, *Trump Will Withdraw U.S. from Paris Climate Agreement*, N.Y. Times (Jun. 1, 2017), https://www.nytimes.com/2017/06/01/climate/trump-paris-climate-agreement.html?_r=0.

[287] CAA §115, 42 U.S.C. §7415.

[288] *See generally* Executive Order 12114: Environmental Effects Abroad, Bureau of Oceans Energy Mgmt., http://www.boem.gov/Environmental-Stewardship/Environmental-Assessment/12114/index.aspx.

[289] Daniel R. Mandelker, NEPA Law and Litigation §5:19 (2d ed. 2013).

A. Polluter Pays Principle

Can we continue to develop and pollute at current rates and, if not, how do we alter course? In the context of R&S, one method to avoid depletion of resources and potentially address collective action challenges is the Polluter Pays Principle. The Polluter Pays Principle is a policy approach that helps more accurately account for the costs associated with consuming resources by internalizing the costs associated with externalities. We often see the Polluter Pays Principle in the international context to address pollution issues. The following excerpt discusses this method and how it can address CAC.

Jonathan Remy Nash, *Too Much Market? Conflict between Tradable Pollution Allowances and the "Polluter Pays" Principle*

24 HARV. ENVTL. L. REV. 465 (2000)

The core of the polluter pays principle argues that neither the government nor society-at-large should subsidize pollution and polluters and that polluters should internalize the costs of pollution abatement. The internalization of costs leads to two corollary goals: waste reduction and the development of more efficient and effective pollution abatement technologies. Finally, the principle has a pedagogical effect of encouraging individual responsibility for pollution and in general. . . .

In 1992, the UN Conference on Environment and Development included the principle in its Rio Declaration on Environment and Development ("Rio Declaration"). . . . Principle 16 of the Rio Declaration provides:

> *National authorities should endeavor to promote the internalization of environmental costs and the use of economic instruments, taking into account the approach that the polluter should, in principle, bear the cost of pollution, with due regard to the public interest and without distorting international trade and investment.*

The precise contours and breadth of the polluter pays principle remain unclear. . . . [T]he "'weak' form" of the polluter pays principle . . . can be seen to require only that the government should not subsidize polluters or pollution costs. It calls for polluters to internalize the costs of reducing their pollution emissions to the level established by the government. . . .

[The] "strong approach" calls for polluters to internalize at least pollution abatement costs. . . . If, for example, a single factory discharges waste into a river and affects a farmer downstream, equitable internalization calls for the proper apportionment of the costs of abatement and of residual pollution between the factory and the farmer — with the polluter bearing those costs. . . .

By requiring polluters to internalize abatement costs, the principle creates incentives for polluters to reduce their waste output and to develop new technologies that allow them either to reduce their waste production or to reduce the harmful effects of the waste they do produce. . . .

Cap-and-trade (CAT) systems represent an example of how the Polluter Pays Principle can address collective action challenges (CAC). Climate change is the "ultimate" CAC in which actors across the globe use the atmospheric resource. CAT attempts to internalize the costs associated with emitting greenhouse gas emissions (GHG), such as carbon dioxide and methane, which contribute to climate change. A CAT system places a cap for the maximum allowed GHG emissions. Each emitter of a regulated GHG must pay to comply with the cap by cutting their emissions (thus, internalizing the cost of improvements), or purchasing excess allowances from other emitters (thus, internalizing the cost of emitting, but not reducing emissions). We discuss CATs in more depth in Chapter 10, Section III.B.1.

With any policy involving the internalization of costs, it is important to acknowledge the possibility of leakage (discussed in more depth in Chapter 10, Section III.B.1). Leakage occurs when some actors use a resource but are able to avoid internalizing the costs associated with that usage. Leakage typically results in an unequal system in which some actors absorb the costs of their actions, while other actors continue to push those costs onto others. For example, leakage occurring in a CAT system may involve some GHG emitters avoiding the internalization of costs by operating outside of the CAT's jurisdictional boundaries, but those same emitters are permitted to sell their goods in the CAT's jurisdiction. This would create an unfair advantage, where those avoiding the costs can sell goods at lower rates, achieve similar profits, and defeat the CAT's objectives. Leakage must be considered in any Polluter Pays Policy.

Questions and Note

1. One of the biggest issues with the Polluter Pays Principle is that it is difficult to determine the appropriate cost that is externalized and that should be internalized. Environmental degradation is so widely dispersed over space and time it is often hard to discern who should be

responsible for what and who is harmed. Can you think of a natural-resource-based example where there may be many polluters and it may be difficult to assign a precise cost to one or a group of actors? What should we do in this instance?

B. Public Health

Critical to the resilience and sustainability of many social-ecological systems is the public health implications involved with pollution. Under the auspices of the United Nations, the World Health Organization (WHO) is the health authority and "is responsible for providing leadership on global health matters, shaping the health research agenda, setting norms and standards, articulating evidence-based policy options, providing technical support to countries and monitoring and assessing health trends."[290] WHO has found that "[e]ach year, 13 million deaths are due to preventable environmental causes" and that 23% of global disease can be attributed to environmental issues such as climate change, air pollution, water, sanitation and hygiene, and other risks.[291] WHO asserts that proper environmental management could avoid these preventable illnesses.[292]

In the 2000 U.N. Millennium Declaration,[293] the Committee on Economic, Social and Cultural Rights affirmed the link between health and the environment when it adopted General Comment No. 14:

> *The Committee interprets the right to health, as defined in article 12.1, as an inclusive right extending not only to timely and appropriate health care but also to the underlying determinants of health, such as access to safe and potable water and adequate sanitation, an adequate supply of safe food, nutrition and housing, healthy occupational and environmental conditions, and access to health-related education and information, including on sexual and reproductive health. A further important aspect is the participation of the population in all health-related decision-making at the community, national and international levels.*[294]

---

[290] *About WHO*, WORLD HEALTH ORGANIZATION (WHO), http://www.who.int/about/en/ (last visited Dec. 1, 2017).

[291] A. Prüss-Üstün & C. Corvalán, *Preventing Disease Through Healthy Environments—Towards an Estimate of the Environmental Burden of Disease*, WHO (2006), http://www.who.int/quantifying_ehimpacts/publications/preventingdisease.pdf.

[292] *Global Health Observatory Data Repository: Public Health and Environment*, WHO, http://apps.who.int/gho/data/node.main.122?lang=en (last visited Dec. 1, 2017).

[293] United Nations Millennium Declaration, U.N. GAOR, 55th Sess., 2d mtg., U.N. Doc. A/res/55/2 (2000), http://www.un.org/millennium/declaration/ares552e.htm.

[294] Sumudu Atapattu, *The Public Health Impact of Global Environmental Problems and the Role of International Law*, 30 AM. J. L. & MED. 283, 286 (2004) (quoting Committee on Economic Social and Cultural Rights General Comment 14, ¶ 11, U.N. ESCOR, 22d Sess., U.N. Doc. E.C.12/2000/4 (2000)).

In August 2002, the U.N. Commission on Human Rights appointed a Special Rapporteur to study the right to health. In his 2003 report, the Rapporteur noted, "the right to health is an inclusive right, extending not only to healthcare but also to the underlying determinants of health such as access to safe and potable water and adequate sanitation, healthy environmental conditions and access to health-related education and information."[295] The report emphasized "the importance of a healthy environment (both workplace and natural) for people to enjoy their right to health. In other words, a healthy environment is a sine qua non for the right to health to be meaningful."[296]

Questions

1. In this chapter and Chapter 3, Section IV.C, we described Ecosystem Services Management, Risk Analysis, and the Precautionary Principle. Can you see how public health is relevant to all of these? What about their impact on resilience and sustainability?

2. In the context of public health, how can risk assessment help understand the resilience of urban areas and communities?

3. How can the Precautionary Principle as applied in the context of public health help improve the sustainability of urban areas and communities?

C. Population

Returning to Garrett Hardin's *The Tragedy of the Commons*, we are confronted with the concept that population problems may be tied to the societal commitment to the welfare state, such that families adding children beyond their capacity of adequate care do not experience the full negative utility of the impact of overpopulation.[297] Hardin explains that "[i]f each human family were dependent only on its own resources; if the children of improvident parents starved to death; if thus, overbreeding brought its own 'punishment' to the germ line — then there would be no public interest in controlling the breeding of families."[298]

---

[295] *Id.* at 286-287 (citing Paul Hunt, *The Right of Everyone to the Enjoyment of the Highest Attainable Standard of Physical and Mental* Health, U.N. Economic and Social Council, 59th Sess., Agenda Item 10, at 8, U.N. Doc. E/CN.4/2003/58 (2003)).
[296] *Id.* at 287.
[297] Hardin, *supra* note 1, at 1246.
[298] *Id.*

In a society where many resources are treated as common, the government may limit the number of children in order to avoid a tragedy created by overpopulation. China's program of limiting each family to one child demonstrates how a government may attempt to regulate the tragedy that it cannot otherwise avoid. While this policy has been softened to allow a second child if one of the parents was an only child, Chinese citizens are subject to mandatory abortions, severe fines, and public censure for violating these family planning regulations.[299] Given the lower status of females in many parts of the world, such population limitations have had a perverse effect on gender percentages, as sex-selection in utero or infanticide limits the number of female children, particularly in China and India.[300]

The world population now exceeds seven billion people and the United Nations projects it to increase to 9.3 billion by 2050 if the average birth rate declined from 2.5 children to 2.1, or 11 billion by 2050 if the birth rate remains the same.[301] While these birthrates may seem relatively low, high birth rates in the past along with decreased child mortality have created a momentum that will continue to increase the population into the next century.[302] Without government regulation, fertility rates in many poor countries remain high because of family and cultural traditions, religious beliefs, lack of birth control options, and the subordinate status of women.[303] These developing countries will be the least prepared to handle a rapid population rise because of political instability, chronic hunger, and the degradation and destruction of environmental and natural resources.[304]

Urban growth and the loss of good farmland through erosion, chemical contamination, and drought will strain the food supply and a growth in population will require an increase in the food supply.[305] The effects of climate change will likely displace large numbers of people and increase the conflicts over land, food, and shelter. Population control in the poorest countries, hardest hit by the inability to support sharp increases in the birthrate, will require renewed emphasis on access to contraception. However, religious, traditional, and political pressures against preventing births through government aid or regulation will hamper these efforts unless the world recognizes that the issue of population control is

---

[299] Ma Jian, *China's Brutal One-Child Policy*, N.Y. Times (May 21, 2013), http://www.nytimes.com/2013/05/22/opinion/chinas-brutal-one-child-policy.html?_r=0; Ben Child, *Zhang Yimou Could Be Fined for Breaching China's One-Child Policy*, The Guardian (Dec. 30, 2013), http://www.theguardian.com/film/2013/dec/30/zhang-yimou-fine-one-child-policy-china; Denver Nicks, *China Eases One-Child Policy and Ends System of Re-Education Through Labor in Historic Change*, Time (Dec. 28, 2013), http://world.time.com/2013/12/28/china-eases-one-child-policy/.

[300] Jian, *supra* note 299; *see also Female Infanticide*, BBC Ethics Guide, http://www.bbc.co.uk/ethics/abortion/medical/infanticide_1.shtml (last visited Dec. 1, 2017).

[301] Kenneth R. Weiss, *Fertility Rates Fall, but Global Population Explosion Goes On*, L.A. Times (July 22, 2012), http://www.latimes.com/news/nationworld/world/population/la-fg-population-matters1-20120722-html,0,7213271.htmlstory#axzz2p1NWMtSy.

[302] *Id.*

[303] *Id.*

[304] *Id.*

[305] *Id.*

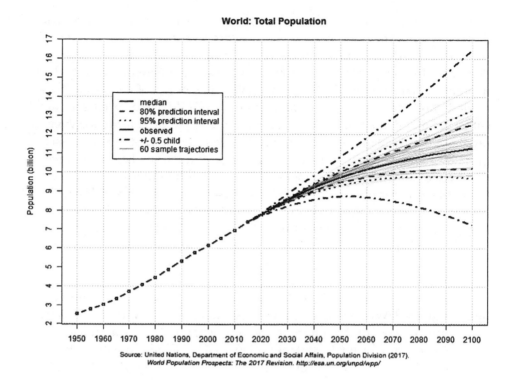

Source: United Nations, Department of Economic and Social Affairs, Population Division (2017).
World Population Prospects: The 2017 Revision. http://esa.un.org/unpd/wpp/

a significant environmental challenge, and individual men and women act to limit their families in order to break the cycle of poverty.[306]

Questions and Note

1. Hardin's statement above is consistent with the themes we discussed in Chapter 2, concerning the intersection of population, consumption, and R&S. How would you characterize the connection among these concepts relative to resilience? How about sustainability? Can you articulate how and where sustainability and resilience might diverge on the issue of population depending on the system at issue?

2. How would you address issues of population relative to sustainability?

3. What, if any, is the obligation of wealthy countries to help feed countries with malnourished populations? Is such a system sustainable? Resilient?

---

[306] *Id.*

Disasters

9

I. INTRODUCTION

Disaster law and policy received greater attention in 2005 when Hurricane Katrina hit the Louisiana/Mississippi coast in the Gulf of Mexico as a Category 5 hurricane, killing over 1,800 people, leaving millions homeless, and causing economic losses in excess of $125 billion.[1] This was the "costliest disaster in American history" and while it "is often described as a natural event," anthropogenic climate change, poor engineering and construction of the levee system by the federal government contributed to the devastation.[2]

Natural disasters are generally the focus of disaster law and are the result of natural geological or meteorological forces such as hurricanes, wildfires, and earthquakes.[3] While most people think of these natural disasters as "acts of god," there is typically a human element, an "act of man," that contributes to the magnitude of the event and its aftermath. Professor Dan Farber, the author of *Disaster Law and Policy*, defines disasters "in terms of the governmental and legal responses they demand" and explains that disasters require risk management through "mitigation, emergency response, compensation, and rebuilding."[4] Hurricane Katrina was a meteorological event of enormous proportions, but decades of land use patterns, the levee system failure, and lack of timely and effective government response were "acts of man" that exacerbated the effects.[5]

---

[1] Karl Tate, *Hurricane Katrina History and Nu (Infographic)*, LIVESCIENCE (Aug. 24, 2010), http://www.livescience.com/11235-hurricane-katrina-history-numbers.html.
[2] Dan Farber, DISASTER LAW AND POLICY 2 (2d ed. 2009).
[3] *Id.* at 3.
[4] *Id.* at 3.
[5] *Id.* at 2-3.

Hurricane Harvey, Texas National Guard

In 2017, Hurricane Harvey made landfall on the Texas coast as a Category 4 hurricane and then stalled over south Texas, dropping between 45 and 52 inches of record-breaking rainfall.[6] This natural disaster brought catastrophic flooding to hundreds of thousands of homes across Texas and resulted in 82 storm-related deaths and billions of dollars in damages.[7] However, as with Katrina, "societal decisions that place people in the path of harm are Acts of Man."[8] Climate change has increased storm strength due to the rise in air and water temperature, and poor land use planning (discussed in Chapter 5) also "contributed to the increased flooding and devastation from Harvey."[9]

"John Jacob, director of the Texas Coastal Watershed Program and a professor at Texas A&M, said he was particularly incensed to hear about a nursing home in Dickinson, southeast of Houston, where residents in wheelchairs were sitting in waist-deep water. They were rescued after photos of them went viral on social media. 'That should never have been built,' Jacob said of the nursing home that sits across the street from the floodplain boundary. 'We're putting people in harm's way.'"[10]

Shortly after Hurricane Harvey made landfall in south Texas, Hurricane Irma struck the Florida Keys as a Category 4 hurricane in September

---

[6] *Historic Hurricane Harvey's Recap*, WEATHER (Sept. 2, 2017), https://weather.com/storms/hurricane/news/tropical-storm-harvey-forecast-texas-louisiana-arkansas.

[7] Eva Ruth Moravec, *Texas Officials: Hurricane Harvey Death Toll at 82, "Mass Casualties Have Absolutely Not Happened*," WASH. POST (Sept. 14, 2017) https://www.washingtonpost.com/national/texas-officials-hurricane-harvey-death-toll-at-82-mass-casualties-have-absolutely-not-happened/2017/09/14/bff3ffea-9975-11e7-87fc-c3f7ee4035c9_story.html?utm_term = .eaecf2a51955.

[8] Andrew Buncombe, *Hurricane Harvey Was a Natural Disaster, but a Man-Made Catastrophe that Will Hurt the Poor the Most*, THE INDEPENDENT (Sept. 3, 2017), http://www.independent.co.uk/news/world/americas/harvey-texas-houston-impact-poor-natural-disaster-man-made-catastrophe-environmental-justice-a7926261.html.

[9] *Id.*

[10] Shawn Boburg & Beth Reinhard, *Houston's Wild West Growth*, WASH. POST (Aug. 29, 2017), https://www.washingtonpost.com/graphics/2017/investigations/harvey-urban-planning/?utm_term = .23a9172e4053.

2017 after decimating the Caribbean Island of Barbuda, which suffered damages to 95% of its structures and required all 1,800 residents to evacuate leaving the island uninhabited for the first time in 300 years.[11] The Caribbean Islands, including Antiqua, Anguilla, St. Bart's, St. Martin and St. Maarten, Cuba, Puerto Rico, and the U.S. and British Virgin Islands also suffered greatly. Irma was responsi-

Hurricane Irma

ble for the death of 82 people in the Caribbean and the Southeastern United States, and more than five days after the storm passed over, two million homes and businesses remained without power.[12] Financial analysts estimated that storm damages could range from $64 to $92 billion.[13] According to meteorologist Phil Klotzbach at Colorado State, Irma broke many records including "generat[ing] enough accumulated cyclone energy — the total wind energy generated over a storm's lifetime — to meet the National Oceanic and Atmospheric Administration's definition of an average full Atlantic hurricane season. By itself, it was more powerful than 18 of the 51 full hurricane seasons since 1966, according to Klotzbach's calculations."[14]

Hurricane Maria followed in Irma's path a little more than one week later, hitting the Virgin Islands and making landfall in Puerto Rico on September 20, 2017.[15] The Puerto Rico Department of Public Safety certified that 64 deaths were caused by Hurricane Maria as of December 29, 2017. However, according to estimates by the New York Times, CNN, and others, the actual death toll likely exceeds 1,000.[16] Some project that it will take four to six months to restore electricity to the U.S. territory's

---

[11] T.J. Raphael, *For the First Time in 300 Years, There's Not a Single Living Person on the Island of Barbuda*, USA TODAY (Sept. 14, 2017), https://www.usatoday.com/story/news/world/2017/09/14/barbuda-hurricane-irama-devastation/665950001/.

[12] Zachary Fagenson, *About 1.5 million, Mostly in Florida, Without Power in Irma's Wake*, REUTERS (Sept. 15, 2017), https://www.reuters.com/article/us-storm-irma/nearly-2-million-mostly-in-florida-without-power-in-irmas-wake-idUSKCN1BQ1C6.

[13] Alex Johnson, *Hurricane Irma Winds Down, Leaving a Trail of Destruction and Broken Records*, NBC NEWS (Sept. 12, 2017), https://www.nbcnews.com/storyline/hurricane-irma/hurricane-irma-winds-down-leaving-fearful-legacy-behind-n800536.

[14] *Id.*

[15] Doreen McCallister, *Puerto Rico Energy Infrastructure Is "Completely Down" Governor Says*, NPR (Sept. 20, 2017), http://www.npr.org/sections/thetwo-way/2017/09/20/552284324/hurricane-maria-makes-landfall-in-puerto-rico.

[16] Alexis R. Santos-Lozada, *Why More than 1,000 Deaths Are Missing from Puerto Rico's Official Death Toll*, PBS NEW HOUR SCIENCE (Jan 4, 2018), https://www.pbs.org/newshour/science/heres-why-more-than-1000-deaths-are-missing-from-puerto-ricos-official-death-toll.

Puerto Rico after Hurricane Maria

3.4 million people.[17] Because Puerto Rico is an island, it has been more difficult for first responders to reach those in need. In addition, Puerto Rico's infrastructure was already in poor condition suffering frequent power outages, the island's electric utility company is $9 billion in debt and already defaulted on interest payments, and there is an insufficient workforce in Puerto Rico to perform the repairs.[18]

Some have criticized the government response to the Puerto Rican disaster, as not enough FEMA resources have reached the island after the storm struck. CNN compared the FEMA response for Hurricanes Maria, Harvey, and Irma as follows:

> **Hurricane Harvey**: *For Hurricane Harvey, FEMA had supplies and personnel positioned in Texas before the storm made landfall on August 25. Within days, the number of FEMA employees, other federal agencies, and the National Guard deployed topped 31,000, FEMA said. In addition, FEMA supplied 3 million meals and 3 million liters of water to Texas to be distributed to survivors.*

> **Hurricane Irma**: *Even more federal personnel responded to Hurricane Irma when it made landfall in Florida on September 10. More than 40,000 federal personnel, including 2,650 FEMA staff, were in place by September 14. In addition, FEMA had transferred 6.6 million meals and 4.7 million liters of water to states in the Southeast after Irma as of the 14th.*

> **Hurricane Maria**: *By comparison, Puerto Rico and the Virgin Islands have seen much fewer personnel since Hurricane Maria hit, according to FEMA. In a tweet on Monday, FEMA said that more than 10,000 federal staff were on the ground in Puerto Rico and the Virgin Islands assisting search and rescue and recovery efforts.*[19]

---

[17] Brian Resnick & Eliza Barclay, *What Every American Needs to Know About Puerto Rico's Hurricane Disaster*, Vox, https://www.vox.com/science-and-health/2017/9/26/16365994/hurricane-maria-2017-puerto-rico-san-juan-humanitarian-disaster-electricty-fuel-flights-facts (last updated Oct. 16, 2017).
[18] *Id.*
[19] Nicole Chavez & Holly Yan, *Puerto Ricans Still Waiting for Aid a Week After Maria's Devastation*, CNN (Sept. 27, 2017), http://www.cnn.com/2017/09/27/us/puerto-rico-hurricane-maria/index.html.

This chapter focuses on disaster response and not prevention. How is it possible to deal with such monster storms? Certainly, improving disaster planning, incorporating adaptive governance, managing risk, and increasing emergency response will be critical as we anticipate future disasters. We must do better at coping with the aftermath of restoring power and transportation corridors to supply food and water to survivors. Such efforts are key to preventing additional deaths and injuries such as the eight deaths that occurred in a Florida nursing home when the storm knocked out the transformer supporting the air conditioning system leaving "the center's elderly and frail residents vulnerable to the heat and humidity."[20]

While losing one life is too many, it appears that the United States has greatly improved its response to hurricane and flooding disasters as evidenced by the stark differences in the number of fatalities from Katrina and the fatalities from Harvey and Irma. Katrina caused "some $160 billion in damage, compared to $70 billion for Hurricane Sandy in 2012."[21]

Even records like these can't capture the full, shocking impact of Katrina, though. More than a storm, it was a punctuating event in modern American history, setting off a kind of social and political reckoning.

Tales of abandoned citizens and failing hospitals laid bare a shocking lack of preparedness stretching from the New Orleans City government to the DC headquarters of the Federal Emergency Management Agency. The ensuing public outrage damaged President Bush's reputation and led to wide-ranging reforms at FEMA.

Also, because the storm hit poor, black communities so much harder than nearby white neighborhoods, it exposed a dimension of American inequality that had gone long overlooked. Even when it came to natural disasters, the risk seemed tilted against the most vulnerable.

Whether Harvey will have the same far-reaching impact on the American psyche depends a lot on how the aftermath is handled, which we can't yet know. But there are a lot of ways for things to go wrong.

Much of the damage in Houston is likely to be flood-related—which isn't always true of hurricanes, where wind is sometimes the greater punisher. And the trouble with flood-damage is that it isn't generally covered by insurance. Homeowners need a separate policy for that.

---

[20] Bill Chappell, *Florida Nursing Home Case: Many Questions, and Few Answers, After 8 Patients Die*, NPR (Sept. 14, 2017), http://www.npr.org/sections/thetwo-way/2017/09/14/550996932/8-die-at-florida-nursing-home-after-irma-leaving-a-host-of-questions.

[21] Evan Horowitz, *How Bad Is Harvey, Compared to Katrina*, Boston Globe (Aug. 28, 2017), https://www.bostonglobe.com/metro/2017/08/28/how-bad-harvey-compared-katrina/lehGM6Hd5BMVhdLypOKVuN/story.html.

In and around Houston, very few people have flood insurance; only about one-sixth of all homeowners. Which means that many people are in for a big surprise when they call to file a claim to fix their buckled floors or moldy walls, only to find it isn't covered by their standard homeowners' policy.

In this regard, the situation in Houston could actually be worse than Katrina. By one estimate, about half of Katrina losses were insured, compared to a quarter of expected losses from Harvey.

. . .

In the end, comparing Harvey with Katrina may come to seem overblown. Katrina was not just a big storm. In many ways it was the biggest: the most damaging and deadly hurricane in the US since the New Deal was actually new.

But many of Katrina's post-flood struggles are likely to repeat themselves in Houston: the effort to keep people from abandoning the city, the need to ensure that the poor don't face a disproportionate burden.

And then there's this question, which seems especially acute in Houston: what happens to the people with waterlogged homes and no flood insurance?[22]

The Deepwater Horizon disaster, discussed in Chapter 8, was regarded as "one of the worst human-caused environmental disasters in American history" and has required significant investigation into, and understanding of, the complex ecosystems impacted by the oil spill.[23] Because of its enormous impact on the environment through pollution, the BP oil spill served as the case study to explore various national and international laws governing pollution. In this chapter on disaster law, we will use the Fukushima earthquake and resulting tsunami as the case study to explore a natural disaster created by a geological event and the subsequent human disaster from locating a nuclear power plant in the path of the resulting tsunami.

A. Case Study: *The Fukushima Earthquake and Tsunami*

An earthquake and tsunami struck off the coast of Japan in March 2011, damaging a nuclear plant in Fukushima and causing core damage to three of the six reactors.[24] This disaster is estimated to be "the costliest natural disaster on record" with estimated economic losses of $210 billion, as compared with the $125 billion in economic losses from Hurricane Katrina.[25] The confirmed death toll from the Fukushima disaster is well

---

[22] *Id.*
[23] Keith H. Hirokawa, *Disasters and Ecosystem Services Deprivation: From Cuyahoga to the Deep-Water Horizon*, 74 ALB. L. REV. 543, 544-545 (2010-2011).
[24] Massachusetts v. U.S. Nuclear Regulatory Commn., 708 F.3d 63, 70 (1st Cir. 2013).
[25] *See* Daniel Farber, *Navigating the Intersection of Environmental Law and Disaster Law*, 2011 BYU L. REV. 1783, 1795 (2011).

over 15,000 people and the damage estimates are as high as $300 billion.[26] As of September 2013, CNN reported: "Japan's only operating nuclear reactor is shut down for maintenance. All 50 of the country's reactors are now offline. The government has not said when or if any of them will come back on."[27]

Shortly following this nuclear disaster, the U.S. Nuclear Regulatory Commission (NRC) appointed a task force to study the U.S. regulations and processes in place in the event of such a disaster in the United States.[28] The task force concluded that "NRC's 'current regulatory approach, and more importantly, the resultant plant capabilities' demonstrate 'that a sequence of events like the Fukushima accident is unlikely to occur in the United States and some appropriate mitigation measures have been implemented, reducing the likelihood of core damage and radiological releases.'"[29] While this conclusion supported the NRC's refusal to order a supplemental Environmental Impact Statement (EIS) for a nuclear power plant license and Environmental Assessment (EA) for a reactor design certification,[30] the United States and the rest of the world can learn much about disaster risk management from this devastating catastrophe.

Professor Farber suggests that the rise of legal scholarship in disaster law and policy since Hurricane Katrina has helped disaster decision making and highlighted the "role the legal system plays in disaster prevention, response, and recovery."[31] The events surrounding the Fukushima meltdown can help us learn about "the network of legal rules and institutions that deals with disaster risks" and can be put in the context of the disaster cycle, which provides a unifying approach to disaster law.[32]

---

[26] *2011 Japan Earthquake—Tsunami Fast Facts*, CNN, http://www.cnn.com/2013/07/17/world/asia/japan-earthquake---tsunami-fast-facts/ (last updated Mar. 5, 2017).

[27] *Id.*

[28] Blue Ridge Envtl. Def. League v. U.S. Nuclear Regulatory Commn., 716 F.3d 183, 189 (D.C. Cir. 2013).

[29] *Id.*

[30] *Id.* at 187.

[31] Daniel A. Farber, *Introduction: Legal Scholarship, the Disaster Cycle, and the Fukushima Accident*, 23 DUKE ENVTL. L. & POL'Y F. 1, 1-2 (2012).

[32] *Id.* at 2.

II. NATURAL DISASTERS

Earthquakes, volcanoes, hurricanes, tornadoes, typhoons, floods, forest fires, and extreme weather conditions, such as heat, drought, snow, and ice, are natural disasters that can impact humans and the environment by impairing air quality, contaminating and damaging water supplies, and polluting waterways and land by debris deposit.[33] Scientists categorize these disasters more generally as either geophysical or climate-related.[34] Data obtained from the EM-DAT International Disaster Database, Center for Research on the Epidemiology of Disasters, University of Louvain[35] show that the number of geophysical disasters since 1950 has remained relatively stable, but the number of climate-related disasters since 1950 has increased dramatically.[36]

Human preparation and response to natural disasters can also harm the environment by releasing chemicals and toxins and prematurely rebuilding areas without taking into consideration the resilient building required to face future disasters.[37] Some say that "[t]here are no truly 'natural' disasters" because the severity of the impact is based on the nature of the community it strikes.[38] Women and children suffer more than a tenfold risk of dying during a disaster than men, and the poorest and most vulnerable populations are at the greatest risk from floods, rising sea levels, droughts, earthquakes, storms, and coping with recovery.[39] As more people settle near the ocean and refuse to move away from dangerous coastlines, the human and financial costs incurred from natural disasters will surge.[40] Local land use planning, discussed in more detail in Chapter 5, becomes increasingly important as both affluent communities and developing countries determine which areas are most dangerous and whether to invest in infrastructure for these at-risk locations.[41]

Hurricanes, Cyclones, and Typhoons: Hurricanes, cyclones, and typhoons are the same weather occurrence but have different names based on the

---

[33] *Natural Disasters*, MOTHER NATURE NETWORK, http://www.mnn.com/eco-glossary/natural-disasters (last visited Dec. 2, 2016).

[34] Jennifer Leaning, M.D. & Debarati Guha-Sapir, Ph.D, *Natural Disasters, Armed Conflict, and Public Health*, 369 N. ENGL J. MED. 1836 (2013), *available at* http://www.nejm.org/doi/full/10.1056/NEJMra1109877.

[35] EM-DAT: The International Disaster Database, CTR. FOR RES. ON THE EPIDEMIOLOGY OF DISASTERS — CRED, www.emdat.be/ (last visited Dec. 2, 2017).

[36] Leaning & Guha-Sapir, *supra* note 34, at fig. 1.

[37] Christopher Joyce, *How and Where Should We Rebuild After Natural Disasters?*, NPR (Nov. 18, 2013), http://www.npr.org/2013/11/18/245949244/how-and-where-should-we-rebuild-after-natural-disasters.

[38] Anthony Spalton & Lisa Guppy, *Disaster Risk Reduction and Rio+20*, NAT'L GEOGRAPHIC NEWSWATCH (June 21, 2012), http://newswatch.nationalgeographic.com/2012/06/21/disaster-risk-reduction-and-rio20/.

[39] *Id.*

[40] Joyce, *supra* note 37.

[41] *Id.*

location of the storms, which must involve wind speeds of at least 74 miles per hour or 119 kilometers per hour. Hurricanes occur in the Atlantic and northern Pacific, typhoons occur in the northwestern Pacific, and cyclones occur in the southeastern, southwestern, and northern Indian Ocean, along with the southwestern Pacific.[42] The strongest storms can constitute severe natural disasters because even though weather forecasters can predict storm days in advance and track them with satellites, they still have difficulty predicting their path after formation.[43] While scientific consensus that there is a link between climate change and hurricanes continues to grow, "[t]he number of Category 4 and 5 hurricanes worldwide nearly doubled from the early 1970s to the early 2000s [and] both the duration of tropical cyclones and their strongest wind speeds have increased by about 50 percent over the past 50 years."[44] Scientists predict that an increase in overall global temperatures may increase the risk of drought and the intensity of hurricanes, cyclones, and typhoons.[45]

Earthquakes: Earthquakes, also called temblors, can be extremely destructive, and while they occur throughout the world, 80% of the activity takes place in the Pacific Ocean rim's "Ring of Fire." This is an area of high volcanic activity, where tectonic plates meet and are in constant

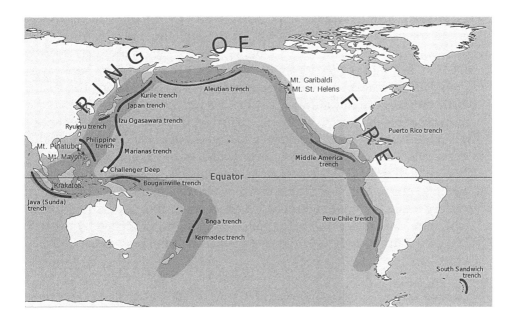

[42] Ker Than, *Typhoon, Hurricane, Cyclone: What's the Difference?*, Nat'l Geographic (Oct. 15, 2013), http://news.nationalgeographic.com/news/2013/10/131023-typhoon-hurricane-cyclone-primer-natural-disaster/.
[43] *Id.*
[44] *Id.*
[45] *The Impact of Climate Change on Natural Disasters*, Earth Observatory, http://earthobservatory.nasa.gov/Features/RisingCost/rising_cost5.php (last visited Dec. 2, 2017).

Tsunami that Struck Southeast Asia

tension with each other. When the stress built up from colliding plates in these fault zones is suddenly released, or when the plates are pushed and pulled in areas outside the fault zones, seismic waves of vibrations are sent hundreds of miles through rock and impact the Earth's surface. Seismologists rank the magnitude of an earthquake on a scale of 1 to 10 based on the duration and intensity of the seismic waves.[46] In addition to an earthquake causing mass destruction in a populated region, it can also trigger a devastating tsunami, such as the one that occurred in southeastern Asia in 2004, killing over 230,000 people.[47]

In 1700, a 9.0 earthquake occurred on the west coast of the North American continent in Northern California along the Cascadia subduction zone. This violent quake caused some sections of the Pacific Coast to drop up to five feet and generate tsunami waves causing damage as far away as Japan. The Cascadia subduction zone extends 700 miles along the Pacific Northwest coast from California to Canada, and scientists predict that this zone is capable of causing another 9.0 earthquake. The tsunami generated by such a quake would result in widespread destruction of the Pacific Coast, including an estimated 10,000 deaths and $70 billion in damage.[48] The installation of deep-sea tsunami detectors may help provide earlier warnings about the size of incoming waves by increasing the current warning time of about 5 minutes to 30 minutes, giving populations on the coast more time to seek higher ground. Illustrations produced by the U.S. Geological Survey and the University of Washington Press were published

---

[46] *Latest Earthquakes — and How Earthquakes Work*, Nat'l Geographic, http://environment.nationalgeographic.com/environment/natural-disasters/earthquake-profile/ (last visited Dec. 2, 2017).

[47] *Asia Marks 10 Years Since Indian Ocean Tsunami Killed 230,000*, Chi. Trib. (Dec. 26, 2014), http://www.chicagotribune.com/news/nationworld/chi-indian-ocean-tsunami-anniversary-20141226-story.html.

[48] Rong-Gong Lin II & Rosanna Xia, *A Potent Threat of Major Earthquake off California's Northern Coast*, L.A. Times (Mar. 12, 2014), http://www.latimes.com/local/la-me-triple-junction-quakes-20140312,0,2124861.story#axzz2vrwtyKxN; Graphic by Matt Moody, Rong-Gong Lin II, *Infographic: Lurking Quake Danger on California's North Coast*, L.A. Times (Mar. 12, 2014), http://www.latimes.com/nation/shareitnow/la-me-cascadia-graphic-20140312-g-dto,0,1034857.htmlstory#axzz2vrwtyKxN.

by the Los Angeles Times and show the potential devastation of such an earthquake and tsunami.[49]

Beyond the immediate death, injury, economic loss, and environmental destruction that result from an earthquake or a tsunami, long-term health difficulties, including the spread of communicable diseases, mental health problems such as post-traumatic stress disorder and depression, and the disruption of health services infrastructure, will likely follow. Natural disasters can also lead to increases in poverty if healthcare infrastructure, schools, and roads are not resilient to the challenges presented in rebuilding and recovery activities.[50] Developing countries, such as the Philippines (discussed below), must improve emergency response, building code enforcement, and risk-reduction laws at both the local and the national levels. The Philippines, located on the "Ring of Fire," is "one of the world's most naturally deadly countries" and suffers from seismic activity, flash floods, and typhoons.[51] Its geography and poverty make this country particularly vulnerable to large-scale human and economic loss from disasters, but the susceptibility of the very poorest is exacerbated by denuding hillsides and building towns in low-lying areas.[52] Conversely, developed countries with modern economies, such as Japan, are likely to recover from disasters without any long-term effects on their economic growth. Economists have found that healthy economies often experience an increase in economic growth rate following either a geological or a climate disaster. The rebuilding process redistributes resources and upgrades infrastructure and technology.[53]

Law and policy responses to the potential for earthquake and tsunami destruction include:

- zoning and building code regulations directing building away from active faults;[54]
- the availability of private insurance policies (and, at times, the unavailability of insurance policies — encouraging people to move out of those uninsured areas);
- tsunami warning systems; and
- local land use and building decisions creating vertical evacuation centers, such as artificial hills, in areas where there is no natural high ground to escape a tsunami.[55]

---

[49] *Id.*

[50] R. Jai Krishna, *Natural Disasters Keep People Poor*, Wall St. J. (Oct. 21, 2013), http://blogs.wsj.com/searealtime/2013/10/21/qa-could-natural-disasters-and-climate-change.

[51] *Id.*

[52] *Id.*

[53] James Surowiecki, *Creative Destruction?*, The New Yorker (Mar. 28, 2011), http://www.newyorker.com/talk/financial/2011/03/28/110328ta_talk_surowiecki?printable.

[54] *See, e.g.*, Alquist-Priolo Earthquake Fault Zoning Act, Cal. Pub. Res. Code §§2621-2630 (regulating building projects with an Earthquake Fault Zone).

[55] Lin II & Xia, *supra* note 48.

In light of discoveries made in Hawai`i of a sinkhole on Kauai, the Pacific Tsunami Warning Center is exploring the need to revise existing evacuation plans. The sinkhole shows evidence of a massive tsunami strike between 1540 and 1660, most likely from an earthquake that occurred in the Aleutian Islands.

The 1964 earthquake in Alaska with a magnitude of 9.2 is the largest recorded earthquake to occur in the United States and the second largest in the world, surpassed only by the 9.5 earthquake in Chile in 1960. Less than two hours after the Alaskan quake, tsunami waves hit the Hawaiian Islands, causing mild damage but no deaths. Crescent City, California, was not as fortunate because most of the seismic energy struck the West Coast, killing 11 people and causing major damage. Hawai`i has improved its tsunami warning system in the years since but is reviewing existing evacuation plans in anticipation of the possibility that an earthquake in the Aleutian Islands—instead of in the Prince William Sound as occurred in 1964—would cause much greater inundation.[56]

Volcanic Eruptions: In addition to contributing to seismic activity, actual eruptions can have a severe impact on human life and the environment. Most volcanos are located at the juncture of tectonic plates, and 90% of them are in the Pacific Ocean's "Ring of Fire." Volcanos are caused when the force of the tectonic plates or another movement in the Earth's interior push molten rock and gases to the surface through vents in the Earth's crust. These vents may grow larger over time and form cones from the deposit of lava flows and expulsion of rocks from the vent. There are approximately 1,900 active volcanos in the world that scientists expect to erupt again, as well as dormant volcanos that could become active at any time. [57]

The local danger to people living near volcanos, such as death, injury, or displacement, will depend on whether the build-up of energy from the Earth's interior is released slowly or violently. Lava flows, spewing rocks and debris, and the volcanic gas and ash released from an eruption can cause devastating human, economic, and environmental damage at the local level. The explosion of Mount St. Helens in Washington State in 1980 not only killed 57 people but also drastically changed the forest ecosystem in the area.[58] Plant and wildlife in the region suffered from the layer of ash, the existence of which also increased the likelihood of mudslides during rainstorms. Hydrochloric acid (HCl) and hydrofluoric acid (HF) gases released during the eruption dissolve in water and fall as acid rain.

---

[56] Karl Kim, *2004 Tsunami Offered Lessons We Must Not Forget*, STAR ADVERTISER, (Jan. 14, 2015), http://www.staradvertiser.com/editorial/2004-tsunami-offered-lessons-we-must-not-forget/.

[57] *Latest Earthquakes—and How Earthquakes Work*, NAT'L GEOGRAPHIC, *supra* note 46.

[58] Ker Than, *Mount St. Helens Pictures: Before and After the Blast*, NAT'L GEOGRAPHIC (May 20, 2010), http://news.nationalgeographic.com/news/mount-st-helens-30th-anniversary-before-after-science-environment-pictures/.

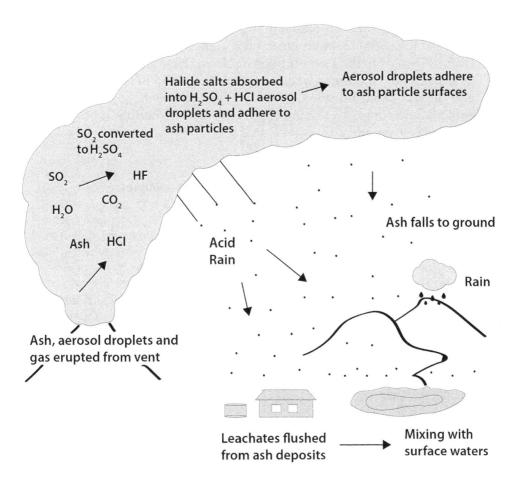

Halide salts absorbed into H_2SO_4 + HCl aerosol droplets and adhere to ash particles

Aerosol droplets adhere to ash particle surfaces

SO_2 converted to H_2SO_4

SO_2 → HF

H_2O CO_2

Ash   HCl

Ash falls to ground

Acid Rain

Rain

Ash, aerosol droplets and gas erupted from vent

Leachates flushed from ash deposits → Mixing with surface waters

Sulfur dioxide (SO_2) is converted to sulphuric acid (H_2SO_4) aerosols, which adhere to the surface of ash particles, and leachates from the fallen ash are absorbed into the underlying soil or washed away by water, changing the chemical balance and quality of both soil and water resources.[59] These aerosols can affect short-term changes in the climate by reflecting the sun's energy. For example, global temperatures temporarily dropped following massive eruptions at Agung (Bali, Indonesia), El Chichon (Chiapas, Mexico), and Pinatubo (Botolan, Philippines).[60]

Volcanic eruptions also cause widespread damage to the environment when they release gases and ash into the air. Volcanic ash consists of small particles of jagged rock and glass, and, unlike the ash from burning wood, leaves, or paper, does not dissolve in water. It also conducts electricity and is extremely abrasive.[61] The ash plume from Iceland's

---

[59] *Volcanic Ash Impacts & Mitigation*, Volcanic Ashfall Impacts Working Grp., http://volcanoes.usgs.gov/ash/properties.html (last updated Sept. 12, 2017).
[60] Karen Harpp, *How Do Volcanoes Affect World Climate?*, Sci. Am. (Apr. 15, 2002), https://www.scientificamerican.com/article/how-do-volcanoes-affect-w/.
[61] *Id.*

Eyjafjallajökull volcanic eruption in 2010 severely disrupted air travel as it spread to continental Europe and threatened to clog airplane engines in flight.[62] Dust from the 1991 eruption of Mount Pinatubo in the Philippines, after 500 years of dormancy, blew around the world in less than a month, and the ash cloud reflected 2% of the sunlight reaching the Earth. This sunlight reflection lowered the temperature of the Earth's atmosphere by one degree Fahrenheit for several years.[63]

Extreme volcanic activity may impact the sustainability of human populations if a particular population is isolated and located near the activity. For example, one controversial study has hypothesized that extreme volcanic activity 40,000 years ago in the area surrounding the Caucasus Mountains that separate Europe and Asia virtually wiped out the Neanderthals. One of the blasts in a series of eruptions, the Campanian Ignimbrite, is believed to be the most violent European eruption in the last 200,000 years. Studying soil sediments, scientists speculated that ash layers caused plant loss and led to a decline in the large plant-eating mammals hunted by the Neanderthals. The study postulates that *Homo sapiens* survived extinction because even though they had populations in Europe, these eruptions did not affect their larger populations in areas such as Africa and Asia. In contrast, the Neanderthals lived in small population groups, mostly in Europe, and were not able to reestablish their populations after the extreme volcanic events.[64]

Floods: Deforestation, wetland modification, and urbanization are land uses that contribute significantly to the increase in river and coastal flooding disasters. Dredging and filling wetlands, increasing the amount of impervious land cover through paving, and destroying or reducing nature's infrastructure of vegetation and trees have decreased the Earth's capacity to absorb excess water. What were previously considered "acts of god" have now been exacerbated by "acts of man" in disrupting nature's capability to deal with flooding in low-lying areas, coastal regions, and rivers, especially those that are downstream from dams. [65]

Hurricane Katrina serves as a sobering example of how human acts in building levees to protect the low-lying area of New Orleans prevented

---

[62] Brian Handwerk, *Electric Ash Found in Iceland Plume Miles from Volcano*, Nat'l Geographic (May 29, 2010), http://news.nationalgeographic.com/news/2010/05/100527-science-environment-iceland-volcano-ash-electric-flights/.

[63] Chris Newhall, James W. Hendley II & Peter H. Stauffer, *The Cataclysmic 1991 Eruption of Mount Pinatubo, Philippines*, U.S. Geological Survey, http://pubs.usgs.gov/fs/1997/fs113-97/ (last updated Feb. 28, 2005).

[64] Ker Than, *Volcanoes Killed Off Neanderthals, Study Suggests*, Nat'l Geographic News (Sept. 22, 2010), http://news.nationalgeographic.com/news/2010/01/100922-volcanoes-eruptions-neanderthals-science-volcanic-humans/.

[65] Matt Rosenberg, *Floods and Flooding*, ThoughtCo. (June 19, 2015), http://geography.about.com/od/physicalgeography/a/floods.htm (last updated Mar. 6, 2017).

natural wetlands from serving as a buffer against hurricanes. Just 2.7 square miles of wetlands will help reduce storm surges by one foot according to researchers. Some may ask whether human engineering or our natural landscape protects us better against natural disasters. The Netherlands, famous for its engineering of dikes to protect this low-lying country, reconsidered its flood control approach after experiencing heavy flooding and evacuations in 1993 and 1995 and then witnessing from afar the Katrina disaster in 2005. Rather than building higher dikes, the Netherlands has begun to address sustainability and disaster preparedness by retreating its populations and restoring the natural floodplains of its rivers.[66]

Thailand offers yet another example of how flooding disasters have increased in magnitude because of human activity. Losses of life have declined because of early warning systems and better education about evacuation, but economic costs of such disasters have increased. In 2011 and 2013, heavy monsoons inundated reservoirs in northern Thailand and caused flooding in the central plain, now occupied by industry, but formerly used for rice cultivation. Farther south, the City of Bangkok (once called the "Venice of Asia") had to face the political decision as to which neighborhoods would be flooded in order to save others. Dikes protecting the industrial region were overwhelmed, and Bangkok continues to increase its population and economic activity in this flood-prone area.[67]

Forest Fires: Wildfires have the capacity to injure people, domestic animals, and wildlife, as well as to cause property and ecological damage. However, they can also provide ecological benefits by increasing ecosystem health and functioning. Some ecosystems depend on the cycles of fire to maintain diverse animal and plant habitats and reduce brush to prevent a devastating fire.[68] Wildfire managers must balance these harms and benefits in real-time firefighting situations in order to decide where to deploy resources and whether to contain a fire or allow it to naturally burn.[69] An increase in the proximity of urban populations to wildlands has put more communities at risk of damage from prescribed burns, designed to reduce the risk of a wildfire, or from unplanned burns from natural causes, such as a lightning strike, or from human negligence or arson.[70]

In the United States, five federal land agencies, in conjunction with state and local agencies, manage wildland fires. These federal agencies

---

[66] Andrew Curry, *Sustainable Earth: Disasters*, Nat'l Geographic News, http://environment.nationalgeographic.com/environment/sustainable-earth/disasters/ (last visited Dec. 2, 2017); *Counting the Cost of Calamities*, The Economist (Jan. 14, 2012), http://www.economist.com/node/21542755/print.

[67] *Counting the Cost of Calamities*, The Economist, *supra* note 66.

[68] *About Wildland Fire*, Nat'l Park Serv., http://www.nps.gov/fire/wildland-fire/about.cfm#sthash.QeGLWSAp.dpuf (last visited Dec. 2, 2017).

[69] Robert E. Keane & Eva Karau, *Evaluating the Ecological Benefits of Wildfire by Integrating Fire and Ecosystem Simulation Models*, 221 Ecological Modelling 1162 (2010), *available at* http://www.fs.fed.us/rm/pubs_other/rmrs_2010_keane_r003.pdf.

[70] Farber, *supra* note 2, at 41.

include the National Park Service, the Bureau of Land Management, U.S. Fish and Wildlife Service, the Bureau of Indian Affairs, and the U.S. Forest Service.[71] A recent federal study found that the vast majority of federal wildfire suppression activities protected private property in the areas located within the wildland-urban interface (WUI).[72] While the federal agencies are responsible for protecting public natural resources, they are compelled to give private-property protection the highest priority in their fire suppression activities within the WUI.

The Federal Wildland Fire Management Policy defines the federal role in the WUI as assisting tribal, state, and local government entities in their primary role of structural fire protection. The Policy also requires the federal agencies to make protecting natural resources in equal priority to protecting private property. Despite this allocation of responsibility for structural protection and the balancing of these priorities, the federal government has continued to bear the financial responsibility for WUI protection.

The sustainability of WUI populations will require that more efforts be made at the state, local, and individual level to change landowner behavior in these interface areas. Landowners move into WUI areas without recognizing the wildfire risks and with the assumption that firefighting services will be available when needed or that insurance policies or federal disaster relief will cover property damage. Local and state governments will need to mandate zoning and building regulations and enforce them in order to reduce fire suppression costs. Local land use regulations may assess impact fees against development activity in high-risk areas to pay for the costs of fire suppression. Appropriate planning of subdivisions in these areas could help protect homes from wildfire by avoiding firefighting equipment hazards, such as narrow winding roads on steep sites, large lot sizes, and limited access to an adequate water supply.[73]

Extreme Weather: Droughts, Rain, Snow, Ice. Extreme weather events have increased throughout the world with what was a once-in-a-millennium event now happening more frequently. Torrential rains in Rio de Janeiro, Nashville, Pakistan, and Thailand have caused deadly flooding and mudslides. Severe droughts in California, Texas, Australia, Russia, and East Africa have caused massive economic and population disruptions. While these extreme weather events may be driven by natural climate cycles, such as an El Niño that pushes rain storms over the United States and Peru and causes drought and fire in Australia, scientists suspect that the warming of the Earth and the resulting increase in atmospheric moisture have contributed to these excessive, record-breaking weather events. Scientists are

---

[71] *About Wildland Fire*, Nat'l Park Serv., *supra* note 68.
[72] Farber, *supra* note 2, at 41.
[73] *Id.* at 42-47.

less certain about whether climate change affects individual storms, with some predicting that climate change will increase hurricane and typhoon strength by between 2 and 11%. However, as the Earth's temperatures change, there will be a greater potential that heat waves, wildfires, intense rainfall, and other extreme weather events will no longer be rare.[74]

Questions

1. What criteria would you draft into laws addressing disasters (for example, floods) to ensure a more resilient coastal community and a more sustainable life along the coasts?

2. Should disaster laws focus on prevention or response?

3. Should insurance companies issue policies within WUI areas? What would be the effects of not offering insurance? Should state and local governments allocate funds to projects in fire prone areas? Does doing so strengthen or weaken the community's resilience or sustainability to flooding disasters?

III. DISASTER PREPAREDNESS, PREVENTION, AND RESPONSE

The Disaster Cycle: The legal system is an important part of managing disaster risks and the **disaster cycle** provides a helpful structure for incorporating legal rules and institutions in the strategic processes of "mitigation, emergency response, insurance/liability compensation, [and] rebuilding."[75] The stages of this closed cycle involve interactions and strategies that consider the connections among different phases of the cycle. For example, the anticipated emergency response level will influence risk mitigation strategies and emergency responder planning will vary depending upon whether the planners assume that risk mitigation will be successful. Insurance availability will reduce the incentive to invest in preventing a disaster through mitigation and protecting property during emergency response. Finally, the rebuilding stage connects back to the beginning of the cycle by taking into consideration the need to mitigate future disaster risks. Disaster law, by operating within a framework of disaster risk management provides a systematic and effective approach to addressing the

---

[74] Peter Miller, *Weather Gone Wild*, Nat'l Geographic (Sept. 2012), https://www.nationalgeographic.com/magazine/2012/09/extreme-weather-global-climate-change-effects/.
[75] Farber, *supra* note 31, at 3.

The Cycle of Disaster Law. Daniel A. Farber, *Introduction: Legal Scholarship, the Disaster Cycle, and the Fukushima Accident*, 23 Duke Envtl. L. & Pol'y F. 1, (2012).

disorder encountered when disaster strikes.[76]

The Fukushima Disaster: Professor Farber examined the 2011 Fukushima disaster through the lens of the disaster cycle and described serious issues that occurred at each stage of the cycle. First, risk mitigation measures failed because government and industry did not consider the risk of a tsunami of the magnitude exhibited, which was "beyond imagination," even though there were warnings that such a tsunami could occur and a historical record of an enormous tsunami in 869. Regulatory failure was also to blame, as inadequate nuclear plant design and the failure to follow international best practices and standards contributed to risk management failures. The second stage of the cycle, emergency response, was also problematic. The extreme nature of the disaster, which involved a 9.0 magnitude earthquake and a 45-foot-high tsunami that breached the 18-foot-high seawall, created a catastrophic emergency and resulted in a disorganized and highly confused emergency response. Efforts to shield the public from information that might cause panic only served to engender public distrust and hamper response efforts. In addition, the emergency response did not take into consideration vulnerable populations, such as the elderly and chronically ill evacuees, who experienced a higher risk of evacuation death.[77]

Following the disaster, recovery and rebuilding efforts required post-disaster compensation to the victims based on the initial premise that Tokyo Electric Power Co. (TEPCO), the owner and operator of the nuclear power plant, was strictly liable for the harm. The government set up a Dispute Reconciliation Committee for Nuclear Damage (DRC) to expedite the settlement of claims, but it is unknown whether TEPCO will have sufficient assets to pay these claims. Finally, the reconstruction phase will necessarily involve decontamination of radioactive land and rebuilding that takes into account risk mitigation measures for future disasters.[78]

United States Preparedness and Response: Governmental responses to disasters experienced in the United States require the cooperation of

---

[76] *Id.* at 3-6.
[77] *Id.* at 5-15.
[78] *Id.* at 16-20.

federal, state, and local authorities. This federalism approach presents challenges to disaster response efforts that require quick and coordinated action under catastrophic conditions. The division of responsibility among these government entities may create paralysis in efforts to respond because of confusion and uncertainty over which entity is controlling response efforts. This confusion may also hamper accountability for response failures. The Federal Emergency Management Agency (FEMA) administers federal assistance during emergencies and major disasters pursuant to the authority of the Stafford Disaster Relief and Emergency Assistance Act (Stafford Act).[79] In most cases, the Governor of an affected state will request the President to declare that an emergency exists, and the President has authority to declare such an emergency and provide federal emergency assistance to the state, local government, and/or private individuals. In some circumstances, FEMA may declare a "major disaster" and provide federal assistance, even without a request from the state.[80]

Hurricane Katrina's aftermath and FEMA's poor response led to statutory changes that allowed federal disaster assistance to states and localities in the form of Public Assistance Grants and Community Disaster Loans. This financial support funded hazard mitigation assistance pre-disaster and during recovery and provided individual assistance for food, medical care, housing, transportation, legal services, unemployment benefits, counseling services, and debris removal. Statutory amendments also give the federal government the authority to direct precautionary evacuations, assist individuals in rescuing and caring for pets, and provide a clearinghouse for information to locate children and reunite families.[81]

Congress also enacted the **Post-Katrina Emergency Management Reform Act** of 2006 (Post-Katrina Act)[82] to address some of the organizational weaknesses following the creation of the Department of Homeland Security (DHS) by the Homeland Security Act of 2002.[83] The Homeland Security Act was intended to strengthen terrorism prevention and response after the 9/11 attack, but the reorganization subsumed FEMA into a federal structure focused on terrorism. The Post-Katrina Act transferred authority for emergency preparedness back to FEMA and affirmed that FEMA's primary mission was

> to reduce the loss of life and property and protect the Nation from all hazards, including natural disasters, acts of terrorism, and other man-made disasters, by leading and supporting the Nation in a risk-based, comprehensive

---

[79] 42 U.S.C. §§5121-5208 (2012).
[80] Farber, *supra* note 2, at 83-94.
[81] *Id.* at 94-103.
[82] Pub. L. No. 109-295.
[83] 6 U.S.C. §§101-557 (2016).

emergency management system of preparedness, protection, response, recovery, and mitigation.[84]

However, some people question whether Congress should reestablish FEMA as an agency independent of the DHS.[85]

Federal statutory schemes addressing emergency regulations are complex and multi-layered with several federal agencies providing various emergency support functions.[86] Legislation that supplements the Stafford Act and authorizes the federal government to act in specific types of emergencies or disasters includes:

- the Defense Against Weapons of Mass Destruction Act,[87] which provides aid to state and local agencies responding to terrorist incidents;
- the Public Health Service Act,[88] responding to public health disasters caused by a disease or disorder, or "significant outbreaks of infectious diseases or bioterrorist attacks"; and
- the Volunteer Protection Act[89] and the Public Health Security and Bioterrorism Preparedness and Response Act of 2002,[90] which protect volunteer healthcare professionals during emergencies.

Additionally, federal military personnel and troops provide disaster relief, subject to the general constraints of the Posse Comitatus Act, which prohibits the direct military enforcement of civilian law.[91]

State and Local Emergency Response: State and local entities are the "first responders" to any emergency and are the government units primarily responsible. A local government may possess "home rule" authority to operate independent of state authority, or the state may have delegated police power authority to local entities through the state constitution or by statute. Therefore, there may be some question as to whether the state or the local municipality has the authority to issue evacuation orders in anticipation of an impending disaster. While communities affected by emergency conditions will rely initially on state and local government response, federal involvement and monies may be required. Interstate cooperation based on the Emergency Management Assistance Compact (EMAC)[92] may supplement federal assistance. EMAC provides for mutual assistance between states to manage an emergency disaster. This interstate compact provided

---

[84] 6 U.S.C. §313(b)(1)(2007).

[85] Farber, *supra* note 2, at 131-135.

[86] See *id.* at 135-160 for a detailed explanation of these regulations and agencies.

[87] 50 U.S.C. §§2301-2368 (2012).

[88] 42 U.S.C. §§201-300hh-11.

[89] 42 U.S.C. §§14501-14505.

[90] Pub. L. No. 107-188.

[91] Farber, *supra* note 2, at 103-129.

[92] Pub. L. No. 104-321 (1996).

successful assistance to the states impacted by Hurricane Katrina and serves as a form of insurance against disaster risks that any one state must face.[93]

United States Response to Fukushima Disaster: In addition to providing international assistance (discussed below), the U.S. military, in partnership with the Japanese Self-Defense Forces (SDF), provided 19 naval vessels, 18,000 personnel, and 140 aircraft for disaster relief. Because of the radiation danger, U.S. troops could not operate within 80 km from the Fukushima nuclear power plant under U.S. Nuclear Regulatory Commission (NRC) criteria and instead were deployed to the Iwate and Miyagi communities. U.S. relief response was rapid, due in part to the fact that the Marine Corps force deployed is stationed on a U.S. military base in Okinawa. However, critics in Okinawa claimed that a three-day response is not rapid and that linking disaster response to the continued use of a military base in Okinawa was using the earthquake for political gain. Indeed, in addition to the main task of providing effective disaster response, the United States and Japan viewed this response, called Operation Tomodachi, as an important exercise in increasing military cooperation between the two countries. Neighboring Asian countries were not as enthused about this partnership because of concerns about the strengthening of this military alliance.[94]

The U.S. nuclear energy industry also worked to learn as much as it could about the Japanese experience with the nuclear accident that followed the earthquake and tsunami in March 2011. The U.S. nuclear energy industry immediately inspected all plants to make sure they could withstand a similar catastrophic event. It adopted a strategy to address the major difficulties experienced by Japan, in particular, the loss of power to maintain necessary cooling, and to enhance the safety of reactors in the United States. The industry moved backup equipment to multiple locations within the United States and established plans to move this equipment to impacted plants as required in case of disaster.[95]

International Preparedness and Response: The International Federation of Red Cross and Red Crescent Societies (IFRC), founded in 1911, have directed efforts to address disaster preparedness and response by focusing on legal issues that can help or hinder disaster risk management.[96] The Disaster Law Programme, originally created in 2001 and renamed in 2012, examines the role that law plays in regard to

---

[93] Farber, *supra* note 2, at 161-179.

[94] Asaho Mizushima, *The Japan-US "Military" Response to the Earthquake, and the Strengthening of the Military Alliance as a Result*, Fukushima on the Globe, http://fukushimaontheglobe.com/the-earthquake-and-the-nuclear-accident/whats-happened/the-japan-us-military-response (last visited Dec. 6, 2017).

[95] *Fukushima Response*, Nuclear Energy Inst., http://www.nei.org/Issues-Policy/Safety-Security/Fukushima-Response (last visited Dec. 2, 2017).

[96] *About the Disaster Law Programme*, Intn'l Fed'n of Red Cross & Red Crescent Societies, http://www.ifrc.org/en/what-we-do/disaster-law/about-idrl/ (last visited Dec. 2, 2017).

international disaster preparedness and relief.[97] Key legal issues identified by IFRC include:

1. strengthening laws to support disaster risk reduction, especially at the community level;
2. assessing barriers to providing emergency and transitional shelter created by property laws and regulation;
3. providing guidelines to help nations facilitate and oversee international assistance; and
4. supporting and protecting volunteers as they respond to the disaster and operate in difficult and complex circumstances.[98]

In the United States, the American Red Cross is the most important nongovernmental organization involved in disaster response and operates as a "federal instrumentality" based on the Congressional charter. While it is not a federal agency and receives its financial support from the public instead of the federal government, the federal government delegates disaster relief responsibilities to the Red Cross to provide emergency relief and services, such as food, shelter, and emergency first aid, to communities in need.[99]

Private Entities, Nongovernmental and Nonprofit Organizations, and Religious Organizations Response: Private entities and nongovernmental actors are essential to the task of restoring infrastructure and services to areas affected by disaster. However, some have criticized them for unintentionally contributing to human rights violations because of poor coordination and the lack of formal rules in what has been called "the world's largest unregulated industry."[100] Because private entities in the United States own much of the critical infrastructure, such as telecommunications and utilities, and key resources, such as water, ice, food, energy, transportation, and shelter, the government must work with private, for-profit companies that engage in disaster relief response.

In the aftermath of Katrina, there was confusion as to whether private entities could legally receive federal assistance under the Stafford Act to respond to emergency infrastructure needs. The Stafford Act provides federal assistance to state and local governments for disaster response but

---

[97] *Background on the Programme*, INTN'L FED'N OF RED CROSS & RED CRESCENT SOCIETIES, http://www.ifrc.org/en/what-we-do/disaster-law/about-idrl/background-on-the-programme/ (last visited Dec. 2, 2017).

[98] *Key Disaster Law Issues*, INTN'L FED'N OF RED CROSS & RED CRESCENT SOCIETIES, http://www.ifrc.org/en/what-we-do/disaster-law/about-disaster-law/ (last visited Dec. 2, 2017).

[99] Farber, *supra* note 2, at 182-183.

[100] David Fisher, *International Disaster Relief: A Growing Regulatory Dilemma*, 101 AM. SOC'Y INT'L L. PROC. 114, 114 (2007) (quoting *World Disasters Report 2005: Focus on Information in Disasters*, INTN'L FED'N OF RED CROSS & RED CRESCENT SOCIETIES 93 (2005)); *see also* Sarah E. Jordan, *The Aftershock of Haiti's Earthquake: Response Efforts in the Wake of Natural Disasters Perpetuate the Violation of Internally Displaced Persons' Human Rights*, 42 CAL. W. INT'L L.J. 221, 225 (2011).

does not expressly grant authority to the federal government to provide assistance to private, for-profit entities. Congress amended the Stafford Act to preclude federal agencies from denying an "essential service provider" access to a disaster site, but the Act does not expressly allow federal assistance to either essential service providers or other private companies that contribute to emergency relief efforts.[101] For-profit and nonprofit sectors may be able to provide additional disaster response capacity by utilizing Stafford Act sections that integrate these organizations with federal government response and recovery actions. Through better disaster management and coordination, public, nongovernmental, and private sectors organizations should be able to partner and harness individual citizen generosity to respond to survivor needs.[102]

Private entities have been very effective at providing important assistance following a disaster. After Hurricane Katrina, private companies, such as Wal-Mart and Home Depot, voluntarily provided relief supplies to the public almost immediately, while it took the government several days or even weeks to respond. A private hospital in New Orleans was also better prepared than the government-owned hospital across the street to evacuate patients and provide emergency supplies. Finally, privately owned utilities were able to reestablish services to their customers within two to three weeks, even though they experienced severe damage to and destruction of their generating, transmitting, and distributing infrastructure.[103]

"Hurricane Irma knocked out power to about half of Florida's customers. The president of Florida Power and Light (FPL) says it's the worst outage it has dealt with."[104] Residents in Florida, especially the elderly, expressed frustration with the power utilities' inability to restore power more than a week after Hurricane Irma hit.[105] Customers criticized FPL's slow response to the outage and one Miami resident complained, "'What really set me off was when I heard from a cousin in Cuba who had power restored in two days. . . . FPL promoted their plans for recovery, but it's been worse than a third-world

---

[101] Farber, *supra* note 2, at 179-182.
[102] M. Jude Egan & Gabor H. Tischler, *Using National Voluntary Organizations in a Disaster: A Direct Provision of Resources Approach*, 36 ADMIN. & REG. L. NEWS 12, 14 (2011).
[103] Farber, *supra* note 2, at 179-182.
[104] Angela Fritz, *Most of Florida Lost Power in Hurricane Irma. Here's What it Looks Like from Space.*, WASH. POST (Sept. 12, 2017), https://www.washingtonpost.com/news/capital-weather-gang/wp/2017/09/12/most-of-florida-lost-power-in-hurricane-irma-heres-what-it-looks-like-from-space/?utm_term=.c915866b2c76.
[105] Anne Geggis & Aric Chokey, *Desperation Spreads Among Seniors Week After Hurricane Irma*, SUN SENTINEL (Sept. 17, 2017), http://www.sun-sentinel.com/news/weather/hurricane/fl-sb-outage-elderly-20170917-story.html.

country.'"[106] The U.S. Territory of Puerto Rico, which was struck by Hurricanes Irma and Maria, had only 9% of the power restored to customers on the island more than two weeks after Maria landed. Puerto Rican Gov. Ricardo Rossello stated "the government hopes to have the power back on for a quarter of the island within a month, and for the entire territory of 3.4 million people by March [2018]."[107]

Private citizens provide effective and immediate response to disasters as survivors work to aid their families and neighbors. Because an organized response to disaster by either government or private groups will not be instantaneous, individuals are encouraged to develop personal emergency plans and stock emergency supplies.[108] At least half of the individuals in any given community are not prepared with emergency kits, food, water, personal evacuation plans, and knowledge of community evacuation plans. The public's failure to recognize the community risk and the public's unrealistic expectation that organized emergency responders will be available within the first 72 hours after a disaster contribute to this lack of preparedness.[109]

Nongovernmental (NGOs) and nonprofit organizations are comprised of individuals who have decided to work together to attain particular goals that tend to be charitable and humanitarian in nature. NGOs are voluntary citizen groups that may operate on a local, national, or international level and are generally dedicated to a common cause, such as the environment or human rights. NGOs and nonprofit organizations have been increasingly helpful in providing services to disaster-stricken areas in light of the rise in the number of global natural disasters. However, this voluntary assistance is not without complication. With the growth of the NGO sector in recent years, more donor nations are channeling their disaster assistance through these organizations, and more entities are getting involved in assisting areas in need. While the increase in assistance is encouraging, there are regulatory problems.[110]

The complexity of an international response to disaster presents a challenge to local, national, and global regulatory frameworks and requires a comprehensive international structure to manage these operations. The

---

[106] *Frustration Mounts for Floridians Still Lacking Power After Irma*, Fox News (Sept. 16, 2017), http://www.foxnews.com/us/2017/09/16/frustration-mounts-for-floridians-still-lacking-power-after-irma.html.

[107] Linda A. Johnson, *FDA: Drug Shortages Possible Due to Puerto Rico Power Outage*, ABC News (Oct. 6, 2017), http://abcnews.go.com/Health/wireStory/fda-drug-shortages-due-puerto-rico-power-outage-50334592.

[108] Farber, *supra* note 2, at 183-185.

[109] *Id.* at 185.

[110] David Fisher, *International Disaster Relief: A Growing Regulatory Dilemma*, 101 Am. Soc'y Int'l L. Proc. 114, 115-116 (2007).

major problems faced by NGOs and nonprofits engaged in disaster-response efforts include:

- barriers to entry, such as problems with customs, duties, or tariffs on relief supplies and with visas for relief personnel;
- legal facilities for operation, such as registration requirements to legally recognize foreign organizations under national law; and
- the quality and accountability of NGOs and the sovereign government to affected individuals, donors, and to each other.

Most voluntary responses are well-intentioned, but in some cases, the aid can be harmful to disaster victims when goods that are inappropriate or unneeded block and delay distribution channels for critical supplies, and when international assistance replaces local capacity and increases dependency. With international initiatives to address these regulatory problems, the "efficiency, effectiveness, and quality of response" to disasters can hopefully be improved through a "comprehensive international framework for disaster response."[111]

Religious Organizations: Religious institutions and charitable organizations supported by religious groups can play a role in disaster response at the local, as well as national and international levels. Many religious institutions make their home within local communities and they are thus in a position to offer immediate relief and aid to members of their institutions and to surrounding neighbors. A report about the role played by congregations, interfaith organizations, and faith associations during disasters found that 60% of Americans rely on religious leaders during crises.[112]

Religion can be a powerful ingredient in the relationships needed within a local community to respond effectively to disaster. Following the 2005 Kashmir earthquake in Pakistan, local Islamic NGOs and volunteers from faith communities came to the aid of victims. Thailand temples, unaffected by the 2004 Indian Ocean tsunami, served as a shelter for survivors, and monks cared for the physical and spiritual needs of the survivors as well as the ceremonial requirements for the dead.[113] Two-thirds of the agencies involved in the aftermath of the 2001 terror attacks in New York and Hurricane Katrina in New Orleans were faith-based organizations.[114] In August 2017, after Hurricane Harvey struck and while Hurricane Irma moved across the Caribbean Islands and Florida, dozens

---

[111] Elyse Mosquini, *Are Lawyers Unsung Disaster Heroes?: The Importance of Well-Prepared Domestic Legal and Regulatory Frameworks for Effective Disaster Response*, 25 EMORY INT'L L. REV. 1217 (2011).
[112] Ruxandra Guidi, *New Report Highlights Importance of Religious Groups' Involvement in Disaster Response and Recovery*, 89.3 KPPC (Nov. 1, 2012), http://www.scpr.org/news/2012/11/01/34802/new-report-highlights-importance-religious-groups-/#comments.
[113] Andreana Reale, *Acts of God(s): the Role of Religion in Disaster Risk Reduction*, HPN (Sept. 2010), https://odihpn.org/magazine/acts-of-gods-the-role-of-religion-in-disaster-risk-reduction/.
[114] Guidi, *supra* note 112.

of religious groups worked with the Voluntary Organizations Active in Disaster to help flood victims in the Houston area clean out and sanitize their homes to save them from mold and destruction. The LDS Church, Texas Baptist Men, the United Methodist Committee on Relief, Catholic Charities, and other religious and nonprofit groups volunteered to work in crews to tear out wet walls and insulation and spray the remaining structure with mold retardant.[115]

Following Hurricane Katrina, a Mississippi Church of Christ congregation of 90 families experienced the homelessness of 27 of the families, including their pastor, Al Sturgeon. The congregants cooked, slept, and shared basic needs at the church. They also offered food, water, and prayers to all. Pastor Sturgeon, on the board of the Jackson County Habitat for Humanity, worked with Latan Griffin, from the Harrison County Habitat affiliate, to merge the two affiliates and address the problems of the 95,000 people living in FEMA trailers 20 months after Katrina. Before the merger, the affiliates built five houses each year, but after they combined forces, they built 120 homes in one year.

Religious institutions additionally serve the function of collecting and funneling individual charitable donations into larger religiously affiliated nonprofit organizations, which operate on a national or international scale. Examples of just a few of the many religious organizations that may be involved in disaster relief include the Salvation Army, Samaritan's Purse, Catholic Charities, Catholic Relief Service, World Vision, the Jewish Federations of North America, the American Jewish World Service, Islamic Relief Worldwide, and the Islamic Circle of North America Relief USA.

Religious beliefs can impact disaster preparedness and response as some religions, especially in the Western world, tend to view humanity's relationship to nature as adversarial. Some religions and indigenous peoples tend to view nature as closely linked with humanity, such that they see natural disasters as the consequence of human abuse of the Earth. For instance, viewing water as a source of life, rather than as a source of dangerous floods, can affect a community's approach to disaster mitigation and response—people build their houses on stilts instead of building levees to keep back the waters. Religious views can also inhibit disaster mitigation and preparation, as leaders may see natural disasters as divine retribution and punishment from God. Nevertheless, the cultural connection that religious institutions or faith-based NGOs may share with

---

[115] Tad Walch, *While Irma Raged 11,000 Mormon Volunteers Worked to Save Texas Homes*, DESERT NEWS (Sept. 11, 2017), https://www.deseretnews.com/article/865688556/While-Irma-raged-11000-Mormon-volunteers-worked-to-save-Texas-homes.html.

local communities can be enormously valuable in disaster areas, where locals are suspicious of assistance offered by agencies of a different faith and country.

International, National, and Nongovernmental Response to the Fukushima Disaster: As discussed above, both Japanese and U.S. military forces responded to the crisis. The cooperation between these two nations strengthened their military alliance and the Japanese Self-Defense Forces (SDF) had the largest organized force to provide vehicles, aircraft, and ships to perform rescues immediately following the earthquake and tsunami.[116] France, Korea, and the Ukraine also provided technical assistance and nuclear specialists to assist in the aftermath. Outside of the national military action, the Japanese government regulatory agencies and the nuclear operator of the Fukushima Daiichi plant, Tokyo Electric Power Co. (TEPCO), were the major players in the disaster response. Nonprofit organizations, religious groups, and individual citizens have also been involved in the ongoing process to recover from what some consider a "profoundly man-made disaster."[117]

The Japanese government agencies and TEPCO were heavily criticized for their lack of earthquake-safety planning and poor communication following the tsunami. While TEPCO argued that the tsunami was "beyond imagination," investigative reports found that it was likely that the 9.0 earthquake, which was foreseeable, caused the major damage to the Fukushima Daiichi plant, leading to the series of meltdowns.[118] The Japanese parliamentary report accused regulators and TEPCO of ignoring safety risks and failing to strengthen the facility against a foreseeable massive earthquake while hampering emergency response after the disaster through slow and faulty communication.[119] In

---

[116] Mizushima, *supra* note 94.

[117] Japan issued a Parliamentary Report on the disaster, which is discussed at: Chico Harlan, *Report Blasts Japan's Preparation for, Response to Fukushima Disaster*, Wash. Post (July 5, 2012), http://www.washingtonpost.com/world/new-report-blasts-japans-preparation-for-response-to-fukushima-disaster/2012/07/05/gJQAN1OEPW_story.html.

[118] *Id.*

[119] *Id.*

addition to the report of the Japanese Parliament (Diet), the government launched three other investigations to determine the causes of the accident, analyze the disaster response, and recommend future policies. The Japanese Cabinet, TEPCO, and a private-sector group established investigative commissions and issued separate reports in a process "characterized by a lack of confidence by each entity in the findings expected from counterparts."[120]

An in-depth analysis of the four commission reports concluded that "[w]hile the four reports identify similar key problems, they place different emphasis on each issue and offer diverging perspectives, interpretations, and degrees of criticism."[121] To address the issue of poor safety planning that precipitated the earthquake, Japan has established the Nuclear Regulation Authority (NRA), which, unlike its predecessor regulator, is not part of the same organization that promotes nuclear energy. The NRA is responsible for all aspects of nuclear power regulation and issued new stricter safety standards that will require utilities to implement costly improvements. In response to the second major issue of crisis management and disaster prevention, Japan established the Nuclear Emergency Preparedness Commission, chaired by the Prime Minister, to encourage regulators and the government to work together to make joint decisions before and during a disaster. This Commission will serve as a clearinghouse of public information and crisis management, designed to prevent the confusion and chaos that occurred in the chain of command when responding to the Fukushima disaster response.[122]

The NRA continues to investigate whether the earthquake caused the damage to the cooling system at the Fukushima plant, because the four investigations, which completed final reports in 2012, were not able to conduct onsite inspections due to the high radiation levels. While three of the commissions concluded that the earthquake did not cause the critical damage at the nuclear power plant, the fourth commission reported that the earthquake possibly damaged the reactors. If seismic activity did cause the breakdown of these systems, the industry should establish new seismic safety standards. Unfortunately, this investigation may take years because of the volatility and radioactivity of the plant site.[123] Some of the buildings contain deadly levels of radiation so workers cannot enter, and TEPCO does not expect to start working in these areas for several years. Four hundred tons of radioactive water is being pumped out of the reactor basement and ground each day and stored at the plant, while another three hundred tons per day escapes. Even under the best circumstances,

---

[120] Kerstin Lukner & Alexandra Sakaki, *Lessons from Fukushima: An Assessment of the Investigations of the Nuclear Disaster*, Asia-Pacific J., Vol. 11 Issue 19, No. 2 (May 13, 2013).
[121] *Id.*
[122] *Id.*
[123] *Id.*

the Fukushima nuclear plant will continue to pose lethal threats for several decades.[124]

Nonprofit and nongovernmental organizations also responded to the Fukushima tragedy by sending funds, supplies, and volunteers. Japan has several disaster-relief laws including the Disaster Relief Act of 1947. These laws generally delegate authority to local governments for disaster relief, but in the Fukushima aftermath, the local governments were ill equipped to respond effectively. Nonprofit organizations (NPOs) must register for legal status under the NPO Act of 1999 and are accountable to the state for their ongoing operations. The Japan National Council of Social Welfare coordinates the work of these NPOs and volunteer centers.[125]

Direct Relief and the Japanese American Citizens League (JACL) contributed more than $5 million to support projects in the Fukushima Prefecture and surrounding prefectures. The Japan NGO Center for International Cooperation (JANIC) operates an NGO Collaboration Space in Fukushima to deal with more than 300,000 homeless and tens of thousands who have evacuated the area for fear of radiation or for loss of jobs. The NGO, Living Dreams, supports children's homes in the area, but again, the threat of radiation exposure requires that the children tie dosimeters around their necks with yarn so that parents and teachers can check the child's cumulative exposure. The Japanese International Volunteer Center (JVC) provides temporary housing for those who lost homes in the tsunami or had to evacuate their homes because of the radiation danger.[126]

Children's health issues from radiation exposure include an increase in the incidence of thyroid cancer. It is important to detect this at the early stage because it can be treated successfully if found early enough. The local government in Fukushima was offering to test children, but the government did not allow parents to be with their children during the test nor see the test results. This lack of transparency angered parents and thyroid specialists and as a result, a nonprofit organization, Tarachine, began offering thyroid cancer screening to children for free and to adults for a minimum fee. It is difficult to prove that there is a relationship between radiation exposure and cancer because the cause of cancer is still unknown. However, it is likely that the higher thyroid cancer rate found in the children of Fukushima is directly connected to the nuclear disaster.[127]

Nonprofit organizations in countries outside of Japan have also viewed the Fukushima disaster as a chance to encourage their governments

---

[124] Victor Kotsev, *TEPCO Risks All at Fukushima*, Asia Times (Nov. 18, 2013), http://www.atimes.com/atimes/Japan/JAP-02-181113.html.

[125] Minako Sakai, Edwin Jurriëns, Jian Zhang & Alec Thornton, Agency in Asia Pacific Disaster Relief: Agency and Resilience 53-55 (2014).

[126] Jenny Hutain, *From the Field: Fukushima, Japan*, DirectRelief (Mar. 11, 2014), http://www.directrelief.org/2014/03/from-the-field-fukushima-japan/.

[127] Yumiko Sato, *Thyroid Specialists Helping Children of Fukushima, One Child at a Time*, Discover Japan (Mar. 2, 2014), http://discoverjapannow.wordpress.com/2014/03/02/thyroid-specialists-helping-children-of-fukushima-one-child-at-a-time/.

to reexamine the threat from nuclear power plants. For example, the Natural Resources Defense Council (NRDC) has pressed U.S. policy makers and the public to examine the causes of the Fukushima meltdown and take measures to prevent such disasters in the future at other nuclear facilities. NRDC is seeking review of the safety issues at the 104 nuclear plants in the United States to address the regulatory controls over the siting, licensing, and operation of these existing facilities, as well as any new plants. NRDC encourages the phase-out of outdated nuclear technology, the responsible management of spent nuclear fuel disposal, and the planning necessary to address emergency preparedness for existing and future nuclear facilities in the United States[128]

Religious organizations from inside and outside Japan were active in answering the needs of Fukushima disaster victims and survivors. Prior to the late 1970s, the activities of religious organizations in Japan were limited. An increase in these activities led religious NGOs to begin forming networks in the 1990s to coordinate their activities and share their knowledge. While religious groups, such as the Buddhist Network and the Religious Network on Humanitarian Support, provided social relief efforts in a wide variety of situations, including following the Kobe earthquake of 1995, the Japanese public did not generally acknowledge these efforts.[129]

After the Tohoku earthquake hit in 2011, resulting in the Fukushima disaster, more than 100 religious organizations networked through a new website, Faith-Based Network for Earthquake Relief in Japan, to provide information about the damage to religious facilities, response and relief activities, calls for financial donations, and counseling, prayers, and memorial ceremonies. Similar to the churches in New Orleans that housed and provided for people after Katrina, religious facilities in Japan that were relatively undamaged and still safe opened their temple and mosque doors to evacuees. The Japan Islamic Trust provided meals to some of those affected. Involving religious groups in disaster relief can help encourage compassion and a better understanding of Japan's diverse religious terrain, which includes Buddhism, Shintoism, Islam, Christianity, as well as new religious movements.[130]

Public Health: Public health under normal circumstances is dependent upon a healthy environment, but communities seeking to recover from natural disasters must overcome the **long-term health problems, both physical and mental**, that result from these disasters. While these

---

[128] Christopher Paine, Nuclear Program Director, *Memorandum: The Fukushima Nuclear Accident and Its Implications for Nuclear Power in the U.S. and Globally*, NRDC (June 17, 2011), https://www.nrdc.org/resources/fukushima-nuclear-accident-and-its-implications-nuclear-power-us-and-globally.
[129] Sakai et al., *supra* note 125.
[130] *Id.*; *see also* Barbara Ambros, *My Take: Japanese New Religions' Big Role in Disaster Response*, CNN Belief Blog (Mar. 22, 2011), http://religion.blogs.cnn.com/2011/03/22/my-take-japanese-new-religions-big-role-in-disaster-response/.

communities must deal with the immediate emergency phase of rescue and recovery activities, such as acute trauma care, clean water, food, shelter, and health services, the redevelopment phase must address the long-term residual impacts. These long-term health challenges "include mental and psychological issues, vaccinating and eliminating the outbreak of communicable diseases like cholera, malaria, and measles and reinstating the infrastructure of the health services system."[131]

Mental health problems, such as post-traumatic stress disorder, depression, and anxiety, may not be evident in the emergency phase of a disaster, but they become more visible over time. A majority of people suffer grief and shock right after the disaster, but signs of continuing mental health problems may arise when people are not able to resume the normalcy of their life by returning to their homes, jobs, and schools. Thus, to avoid the onset of depression and anxiety, health professionals counsel those who have suffered from a natural disaster to return to their daily activities and routines as soon as possible.[132] In addition, the culture of the community impacted by a disaster can provide a protective system to help individual members and the community as a whole mitigate the trauma and stress they experience.[133]

Communicable diseases also pose long-term health challenges to disaster-struck communities. These diseases transfer easily from person to person or animal to person, and problems with hygiene following an emergency, particularly in emergency settlement camps, contribute greatly to these diseases. Vaccinations and hand-washing can help prevent lethal outbreaks, but crowded conditions, population displacement, and a general lack of cleanliness can result in an increase in controlled diseases and even the introduction of new diseases. For example, after the 2010 earthquake in Haiti, the population experienced a cholera epidemic, even though cholera had not been present in Haiti for more than 100 years. It was determined that foreign aid workers had brought the disease with them to the island.[134]

Disasters adversely affect the health service infrastructure by causing physical damage to hospitals, rehabilitation facilities, medical equipment, and medicines. If the health service infrastructure is already poor, as it was in Haiti before the 2010 earthquake, recovery and redevelopment of these services will remain inadequate. Even in communities with sufficient health services in advance of the disaster, the exodus of people from the disaster area will further impact the ability of communities to restore the health service infrastructure. Aid organizations must commit

---

[131] Katherine Beard, *Long-term Health Problems After Natural Disasters Strike*, U.S. News (Jan. 6, 2014), http://www.usnews.com/news/articles/2014/01/06/long-term-health-problems-after-natural-disasters-strike.

[132] *Id.*

[133] Farber, *supra* note 2, at 227.

[134] Beard, *supra* note 131.

to continuing assistance to support communities damaged by disaster, as these communities confront long-term public health issues after the initial emergency response.[135]

Public health issues resulting from the earthquake, tsunami, and Fukushima power plant disaster included the immediate impact of the floodwaters and loss of life and the longer-term concern about the release of radioactive material from the power plant. Initial impacts included downed power lines, damaged gas lines that could result in both fire and explosion, loss of communication hampering rescue and relief efforts, limited and contaminated food and water supplies by radioactive fallout and bacteria in floodwaters, and biohazards from human remains.[136]

Japan's government and TEPCO officials initially addressed the radioactivity concerns. In a 12-mile radius surrounding the damaged nuclear plant, they dispensed potassium iodide tablets to help prevent radioactive materials from being absorbed into the thyroid gland. In addition, the government monitored radiation levels in the air, ocean, and water and food supplies within a 50-mile radius.

Some expect that the long-term effects of the disaster will be as psychological as physical in nature even though continued monitoring has shown that the radiation levels are below the governmental limits in almost 95% of the samples, because as with previous events such as Chernobyl, people remain fearful of radiation and its long-term effects.[137] Nevertheless, others claim that even with the immediate distribution of potassium iodide, pre-cancerous thyroid abnormalities are affecting at least 48% of the children in the Fukushima prefecture, and thyroid cancer rates in local children are more than 40 times what experts consider normal.[138] The World Health Organization (WHO) released a health risk assessment in 2013 and concluded that for Japan "the lifetime risk for some cancers may be somewhat elevated above baseline rates in certain age and sex groups that were in the areas most affected," but "that no discernible increase in health risks from the Fukushima event is expected outside Japan."[139] WHO did observe that the psychological impact of the disaster and the stresses of evacuation could have a harmful impact on the health of those who were affected by Fukushima.[140]

[135] *Id.*
[136] K.Y. Williams, David Milen, Traci Foster, Matthew Lloyd Collins & Mark Gordon, *Public Health Concerns in the Aftermath of the Japanese Earthquake, Tsunami and the Fukushima Reactor Breach,* PA TIMES (Mar./Apr. 2011), http://patimes.org/public-health-concerns-in-the-aftermath-of-the-japanese-earthquake-tsunami-and-the-fukushima-reactor-breach/.
[137] *Fukushima Response, supra* note 95.
[138] Harvey Wasserman, *Fukishima's Children Are Dying,* GLOBAL RESEARCH (June 14, 2014), http://www.globalresearch.ca/fukushimas-children-are-dying/5387242.
[139] *Health Risk Assessment from the Nuclear Accident After the 2011 Great East Japan Earthquake and Tsunami Based on a Preliminary Dose Estimation,* WORLD HEALTH ORG. (2013) 4, http://apps.who.int/iris/bitstream/10665/78373/1/WHO_HSE_PHE_2013.1_eng.pdf?ua=1.
[140] *Id.; see also* Hiroko Tabuchi, *W.H.O. Sees Low Health Risks from Fukushima Accident,* N.Y. TIMES (Feb. 28, 2013), http://www.nytimes.com/2013/03/01/world/asia/who-sees-low-health-risks-from-fukushima-accident.html?pagewanted=all&_r=0.

In the United States, the federal Food and Drug Administration (FDA) has continued after the accident to monitor the radiation levels in food products imported from Japan as well as seafood caught off the U.S. coast. The government of Japan has restricted the sale or export of some products and U.S. authorities do not allow these products to enter the United States. Authorities in the United States monitor and test other products that Japan's government does not restrict as stringently, although less than 4% of U.S. food imports come from Japan.[141] The California Department of Public Health (CDPH) has worked closely with state and federal agencies to ensure that California residents are not in danger from the Fukushima plant emergency. CDPH monitored and sampled the coastline and concluded, "there are no health and safety concerns to California residents."[142] The World Health Organization emphasizes the importance of continued food and environment monitoring to refine risk estimates, as required, based upon new data from further studies.

Concerns still linger, whether based on science or psychologically generated, about continued exposure to radiation in Japan. Three years after the disaster, a group founded in Tokyo in 1987, Physicians Against Nuclear War in Japan, protested the government's pressuring of displaced people to return to contaminated areas. The group demanded that the government provide better monitoring, information, and healthcare for those living in contaminated areas or those whom the disaster displaced.[143]

Human Rights and Environmental Justice: Disasters have unequal impacts on various parts of society, even though they appear not to discriminate in how they strike. As demonstrated vividly by Hurricane Katrina and the 2010 earthquake in Haiti, disasters disproportionately harm lower-income groups because of preexisting social and economic vulnerability. Disasters also unequally harm individuals based on gender, race, and age. Income may affect the ability of people to evacuate, and the elderly have more health problems that expose them to special risks from heat waves, hurricanes, and evacuations.[144]

Environmental justice concerns directly link to disaster inequality issues based on the unequal exposure to risk. Disasters may strike rich and poor alike so that the exposure to risk for these populations is equal. However, the vulnerability and the lack of access to resources experienced

---

[141] *FDA Response to the Fukushima Dai-ichi Nuclear Power Facility Incident*, U.S. FDA, http://www.fda.gov/newsevents/publichealthfocus/ucm247403.htm (last updated July 7, 2015).

[142] Katsumi Hirose, *2011 Fukushima Dai-ichi Nuclear Power Plant Accident: Summary of Regional Radioactive Deposition Monitoring Results*, J. ENVTL. RADIOACTIVITY (Sept. 2012), http://www.sciencedirect.com/science/article/pii/S0265931X1100213X.

[143] *Japanese Physicians Demand Better Post-Fukushima Monitoring and Public Health Measures*, INT'L PHYSICIANS FOR THE PREVENTION OF NUCLEAR WAR (Apr. 24, 2015), http://peaceandhealthblog.com/2014/04/24/japanese-physicians-demand-better-post-fukushima-monitoring-and-public-health-measures/.

[144] Farber, *supra* note 25, at 1807-1810.

by lower-income and racial minority neighborhoods creates unequal harm, even though the risk may be the same. The inequality experienced by vulnerable populations is not exclusively race-based, and so the concept of environmental justice is more complex and not necessarily caused by societal oppression. Disasters reveal these inequities and can give insight into those who are exposed to risk, their vulnerability, and how well they are able to recover.[145]

International human rights treaties and agreements, including the U.N. Guiding Principles on Internal Displacement and the Sphere Project's Humanitarian Charter and Minimum Standards in Disaster Response, protect disaster victims and direct relief efforts to provide for basic human rights, such as food, shelter, medical care, and protection against human traffickers who target the most vulnerable. However, there are populations with existing vulnerabilities because of poverty or discrimination based on race, religion, class, or gender and, as mentioned above, disasters intensify these vulnerabilities. The international guidelines recognize that national authorities have the primary duty to protect their people, but some of these countries may not have the resources, the will, or the competence to assist properly their internally displaced populations.[146] The tension between respecting a nation's sovereignty and protecting human rights is a dilemma faced by the international community in responding to disaster victims when the nation is either unable or unwilling to provide relief.[147]

Both developing and developed countries provide examples of failures in response to disasters. The 2010 earthquake in Haiti struck a vulnerable population, and when the government was unable to provide response and relief, international humanitarian aid flowed into the country. Unfortunately, some believe that agencies distributed aid inefficiently and ineffectively because international agencies made decisions about what victims needed without receiving input from the communities impacted.[148] In the United States, all levels of government and relief agencies were unprepared to respond adequately to victims of Hurricane Katrina in 2005. Vulnerable populations based on poverty and race were disproportionately impacted, and some have argued that this inequality is "part of a pattern of environmental disasters in which low-income communities and communities of color are overlooked in the preparations before such disasters occur and receive less rapid assistance afterwards."[149]

---

[145] *Id.* at 1811.
[146] Farber, *supra* note 2, at 210-211.
[147] Tyra Ruth Saechao, *Natural Disasters and the Responsibility to Protect: From Chaos to Clarity*, 32 Brook. J. Int'l L. 663, 671-672 (2007).
[148] Meena Jagannath, Nicole Phillips & Jeena Shah, *A Rights-Based Approach to Lawyering: Legal Empowerment as an Alternative to Legal Aid in Post-Disaster Haiti*, 10 Nw. U. J. Int'l Hum. Rts. 7 (2011) (advocating a victim-centered approach to human rights lawyering).
[149] Farber, *supra* note 2, at 224 (quoting Center for Progressive Reform, *An Unnatural Disaster: The Aftermath of Hurricane Katrina* 35-36 (2005)).

Environmental and climate injustice is again an issue in the aftermath of Hurricane Maria that hit Puerto Rico in September, 2017. While the story continues to unfold at the time of this writing, some point to Puerto Rico's plight as an example of climate injustice. Puerto Rico's outdated and now destroyed electric grid will need to be rebuilt entirely. Many predict a large percentage of the island's population will leave and not return, an acceleration of the population drain that has been sapping the island for years. And storms like Maria are expected to get even more damaging and more costly as climate change raises sea levels and warms oceans.

"Puerto Rico today is a living, breathing, suffering symbol of climate injustice," said Elizabeth Yeampierre, executive director of UPROSE and steering committee co-chair of Climate Justice Alliance, in a press release. "The devastation left in the wake of Hurricane Maria is the culmination of centuries of colonialism, extraction, and repression. As Puerto Rico rebuilds, it must revolutionize the society's decaying systems of survival by confronting the dominant political and financial institutions that have profited from this decay."[150]

Human rights issues following the **Fukushima disaster** mostly center on concerns about the accuracy and transparency of government information regarding the radiation levels in the air, food, and water. Some have accused Japan's government of violating human rights by encouraging displaced populations to return to the Fukushima prefecture before they had assessed properly the radiation levels and determined them to be "safe."[151] Human rights activists are calling for more testing of these levels and better information regarding the health risks from both short-term and long-term exposure. The United Nations Scientific Committee on the Effects of Atomic Radiation prepared a report, which concluded that for the public, "no discernible increased incidence of radiation-related health effects are expected."[152] However, a U.N. special rapporteur on the right to health, Anand Grover, disagreed with this conclusion about the lack of health effects on those exposed to radiation.[153] The U.N. Human Rights Council supported the special rapporteur and issued a report in June 2013, urging

---

[150] Dana Drugmand, *How Will Puerto Rico, Devastated and Drowning in Debt, Pay to Rebuild?*, CLIMATE LIABILITY NEWS (Oct. 23, 2017), https://www.climateliabilitynews.org/2017/10/23/puerto-rico-hurricane-maria-climate-damages/.

[151] Ekaterina Blinova, *Radiation Killing Fukushima Children, Japan's Gov't Violating Human Rights — Former Mayor*, VOICE OF RUSS. (Apr. 21, 2014), http://voiceofrussia.com/news/2014_04_21/Radiation-killing-Fukushima-children-Japan-s-gov-t-violating-human-rights-former-mayor-9277/.

[152] *Sources, Effects, & Risks of Ionizing Radiation* (UNSCEAR 2013 Report), UNITED NATIONS SCIENTIFIC COMM. ON THE EFFECTS OF ATOMIC RADIATION 10 (2013), http://www.unscear.org/docs/publications/2013/UNSCEAR_2013_GA-Report.pdf. The 2013 Report's conclusion of "no discernible" health effects was criticized as "inconsistent with the international scientific consensus that there is no threshold below which radiation poses no harm." *Fukishima 2015 White Paper*, UNITED NATIONS SCIENTIFIC COMM. ON THE EFFECTS OF ATOMIC RADIATION 31, http://www.unscear.org/docs/publications/2015/UNSCEAR_WP_2015.pdf.

[153] *Human Rights Experts Rap U.N. Report on Fukushima Radiation*, JAPAN TIMES (Oct 25, 2013), http://www.japantimes.co.jp/news/2013/10/25/national/human-rights-experts-rap-u-n-report-on-fukushima-radiation/.

the government to adopt measures to implement the Victims Protection Law and "provide funding for relocation, housing, employment, education and other essential support needed by those who chose to evacuate, stay or return to any area where radiation exceeds 1mSv/year. These measures should include relief packages reflecting the cost of rebuilding lives."[154] The Fukushima disaster has shown again that officials must do more to include public health and human rights needs in disaster risk reduction and response efforts.

National Security: Governments recognize that natural disasters can be some of the greatest threats to national security by damaging lives and property more than any other circumstance. The United States emphasized this connection when it reorganized its federal agencies after the failed response to Hurricane Katrina. The Post-Katrina Emergency Management Reform Act of 2006 expanded the mission of the Federal Emergency Management Agency (FEMA) to include homeland security as a responsibility and promote emergency management teams involving federal, state, local, tribal, private sector, nonprofit, faith-based groups, and the public. FEMA is now part of the Department of Homeland Security (DHS) and is responsible for coordinating "the federal government's role in preparing for, preventing, mitigating the effects of, responding to, and recovering from all domestic disasters, whether natural or man-made, including acts of terror."[155] The White House National Security Strategy also links disaster management to national security and specifically states:

> At home, the United States is pursuing a strategy capable of meeting the full range of threats and hazards to our communities. These threats and hazards include Terrorism, natural disasters, large-scale cyber-attacks, and pandemics. As we do everything within our power to prevent these dangers, we also recognize that we will not be able to deter or prevent every single threat. That is why we must also enhance our resilience—the ability to adapt to changing conditions and prepare for, withstand, and rapidly recover from disruption.[156]

The government of Indonesia has also recognized the connection between disasters and national security and has made disaster reduction a national priority. Natural disasters of all kinds have been the greatest threats to Indonesia's national security and the well-being of its citizens. Because Indonesia is geographically located in one of the most volatile

---

[154] Nancy Foust, *UN Human Rights Report on Fukishima Finds Considerable Problems*, THE FUKUSHIMA PROJECT (June 10, 2013), http://www.fukuleaks.org/web/?p=10465.

[155] *About the Agency*, U.S. DEP'T OF HOMELAND SECURITY, http://www.fema.gov/about-agency (last updated May 16, 2017); *Disasters Overview*, U.S. DEP'T OF HOMELAND SECURITY (MAY 17, 2017), http://www.dhs.gov/disasters-overview.

[156] *Disaster Response, Resilience & National Security*, NAT'L SECURITY NETWORK, http://nsnetwork.org/disaster-response-resilience-and-national-security/ (quoting *National Security Strategy*, THE WHITE HOUSE, (May 2010)).

seismic and tectonic regions in the world, this nation is under the real and recurrent threat of a natural disaster, and must work to be resilient to these disasters. Indonesia must rely on local governments to be the first responders, but the central government can supply additional assistance.[157]

Natural disasters can be a threat to peace as they cause economic, social, and political impacts that could lead to conflict over food, water, energy, medicine, and other key resources. We expect these events to increase in the future, and as we expand the population in urban and coastal areas, which are the most vulnerable to impacts from a major disaster, we should expect a rise in tensions and anxieties that could lead to social disruption and political conflict.[158] Resilient infrastructure and first responder systems are critical to preparing for, withstanding, and recovering from natural disasters and other major hazards. Individuals, communities, and governments at all levels must be prepared to respond, adapt to changing conditions, and recover with speed and competence.

National security in Japan relies heavily on **resource security** since Japan has very few natural resources in energy. The nuclear disaster in Fukushima forced Japan into a position where it is not capable of generating more than a small fraction of its domestic energy needs because of the public outcry against nuclear plants. Instead, it must obtain resource supplies from sources other than nuclear energy. Immediately following the disaster, Japan replaced nuclear power with oil and natural gas. However, this is not a viable long-term resource strategy as it is expensive, generates environmental concerns, and the earthquake weakened this strategy when it destroyed several coal-fired electric plants. Japan has the infrastructure necessary to import liquefied natural gas from the United States, and it is strengthening the U.S.-Japan alliance in order to secure these imports.

Japan has linked its national security concerns with its reliance on nondomestic energy resource supplies. It is currently the third largest oil importing country in the world, behind the United States and China, and the second largest coal importing country behind China. Some view the alliance with the United States as a national strategy to avoid relying on China or Russia to obtain energy resources. As Japan struggles with local opposition to the ramifications of this alliance, such as the building of a new airbase on Okinawa, the Japanese may eventually soften their stance against the future use of nuclear energy. With political and governmental assurances of increased safety measures, such as earthquake retrofitting,

---

[157] *Disasters are "Greatest Threats to our National Security"*, United Nations Office for Disaster Risk Reduction (Oct. 29, 2012), http://www.unisdr.org/archive/29378.
[158] Fredrick S. Tipson, *Natural Disasters as Threats to Peace*, U.S. Institute of Peace (Feb. 2013), http://www.usip.org/sites/default/files/resources/Natural%20Disasters%20as%20Threats%20to%20Peace%20SR324.pdf.

Japan may return to using nuclear energy to supply one-third or more of its energy needs.[159]

Insurance and Compensation: Victim compensation in disaster law uses a patchwork of government assistance, private insurance, and tort claim litigation. In the United States, FEMA provides loans and grants to disaster victims, and private insurance policies are also available but are generally limited in coverage for disaster damages. For example, many insurance policies cover wind damage but not flood damage, and earthquake insurance, if available, is generally expensive with a high deductible before granting compensation. In addition, a major disaster may overwhelm insurance companies and their ability to process claims. Tort law is available when government or private entities are partially responsible for the impact from a natural disaster.[160]

Government assistance in providing victim compensation can take at least five forms, including expediting private compensation payouts; providing insurance when private entities do not; compensating victims when the government should have prevented or mitigated the disaster; providing compensation in lieu of tort claims; and assisting victims when communities are overwhelmed based on altruism and national unity.[161] In the United States, the federal government created a National Flood Insurance Program (NFIP) in 1968 to fill the void left by the private insurers. This program is a combination of insurance, land use management, and public disclosure that requires communities to adopt and enforce floodplain management regulations in order for individuals in that community to obtain flood insurance. In addition, the NFIP maps flood hazard areas to provide information for flood-plain management and new construction. This program is not actuarially sound because the premiums collected are not sufficient to support long-term flood damage compensation. Instead, FEMA has borrowed money from the U.S. Treasury to help pay out on flood insurance claims from multiple hurricane losses, including Hurricane Katrina.[162]

The government intends that federal aid programs supplement, but not replace, insurance and other financial means to deal with catastrophe. Many in the affected areas of Hurricane Harvey did not have flood insurance, and FEMA only deals with short-term aid for medical help and temporary housing. Long-term recovery assistance may require renters and homeowners to apply for Small Business Administration (SBA) loans,

---

[159] Francisco A. Laguna & Jennie Linder Cunningham, *Japan's Resource Security: Three Years after Fukushima*, TRANSLEGAL (Mar. 21, 2014), http://translegalllc.wordpress.com/2014/03/21/japans-resource-security-three-years-after-fukushima/.

[160] Farber, *supra* note 2, at 291; Farber, *supra* note 25, at 1811-1812.

[161] Stephen D. Sugarman, *Roles of Government in Compensating Disaster Victims*, 6 ISSUES IN LEGAL SCHOLARSHIP no. 3 (Jan. 2007), *available at* http://www.degruyter.com/view/j/ils.2007.6.issue-3/ils.2007.6.3.1093/ils.2007.6.3.1093.xml.

[162] Farber, *supra* note 2, at 311-313.

which are available to them for property losses and real estate repairs.[163] Even flood victims who have insurance through the NFIP program, discussed above, will likely experience difficulty in collecting promised assistance as the government has insufficiently funded this federal insurance program. Victims of Hurricane Sandy, which ravaged New York and New Jersey coastal communities in 2012, are struggling to pay back SBA disaster loans on top of their mortgages and five years later they are still trying to collect the assistance they were promised.[164]

Insurance may be available to help with the financial impacts of a disaster. Private insurance that may be useful to compensate disaster victims includes life insurance, health insurance, disability insurance, accidental death and dismemberment insurance, business interruption insurance, and several types of property insurance. There are certain types of disaster damages, including nuclear radiation, floods, and sometimes earthquakes, that may not be insurable or that an insurance policy may exclude. Insurers may find that catastrophic events are too unpredictable and that there is not enough time to collect sufficient premiums to prevent the risk of insurer insolvency if the disaster occurs too early and is more severe than anticipated. Even if insurance is available, individuals may not take advantage of the opportunity to insure for several different reasons. Some people think the insurance is too expensive, some do not appreciate the risk they face or believe it won't happen to them, some decide to take the chance and save money by not buying insurance, and finally, some believe that in the case of a major disaster the government will come to the rescue.[165]

The government may provide tort law compensation for disaster damages by establishing no-fault compensation plans such as the September 11 Victim Compensation Fund. The government may also be liable for personal injury and fatality negligence claims for its failure to properly build, inspect, and maintain disaster-prevention structures. Sovereign immunity may protect the government from liability, but such immunity depends on how courts interpret state or federal statutes authorizing such claims.[166]

Compensating the victims of the Fukushima disaster has been a continuing controversy as some complain that they are not receiving sufficient

---

[163] Stacy Cowley, *Harvey Victims Face Hurdles, and Maybe Bills, in Getting Aid*, N.Y. Times (Aug. 30, 2017), https://www.nytimes.com/2017/08/30/business/harvey-aid-sba-disaster-loans.html.

[164] *Id.*

[165] Sugarman, *supra* note 161, at 6-8; *see also Counting the Cost of Calamities*, The Economist, *supra* note 66 (discussing the perverse incentive against buying insurance because the federal government will step in with aid once it declares a disaster).

[166] Farber, *supra* note 2, 292-311 (discussing Paterno v. State of California, 113 Cal. App. 4th 998 (2003) (finding State liable for foreseeable failure of levee), and *In re* Katrina Canal Breaches Consol. Litig., 417 F. Supp. 2d 684 (E.D. La. 2007) (plaintiffs brought suit under the Federal Tort Claim Act alleging that Army Corps of Engineers did not exercise due care during the construction of the Mississippi River Gulf Outlet)).

compensation and that the reparation is inadequate for the injuries experienced. Heavy support from the government after the accident essentially nationalized TEPCO, which is responsible for paying compensation to the victims. In addition, the Japanese government set up a mediation center to assist in resolving claims against TEPCO. Few lawsuits have been filed in comparison to the many legal claims brought following the BP oil spill for several reasons. Japan's 1967 Act on Compensation for Nuclear Damage provides that only the nuclear plant operator, in this case, TEPCO, will be liable for victim compensation.[167] Manufacturers of the nuclear reactors, such as Toshiba, Hitachi, and General Electric, as well as TEPCO individual employees, are shielded from liability under these circumstances. In addition, victims and lawyers in Japan contend that there is a national "distaste for confrontation" and that the judicial system does not allow class actions or punitive damages.[168]

Victims have received compensation for property damage, evacuation and relocation due to radiation levels, mental anguish, business damages, and wrongful death, among other claims. Most people expect that it will take from three to five years following the disaster to resolve all of the compensation claims.[169] Nevertheless, some assert that TEPCO and the government are evading responsibility by requiring unreasonable documentation to substantiate claims and paying out "temporary compensation" that must be repaid when claims are finally settled.[170]

Those who have studied previous responses to disasters in Japan are not surprised by the **lack of government involvement** in Fukushima. The general norm in Japan appears to be: "compensate if the law requires, but not otherwise; compensate symbolically, but not enough to truly cover losses; compensate uniformly, but not tailored to individual loss."[171] The compensation process is complicated, ad hoc, political, and lacks transparency and accountability leading many to believe that the needs of TEPCO and the government outweigh the victims' needs. It appears as though TEPCO and the government are not fully addressing the needs of victims.[172]

In January 2014, **TEPCO announced a plan** to address the continuing cleanup, which will take decades, compensate victims, and strengthen its financial position so that it can return to private capital markets rather

---

[167] Act on Compensation for Nuclear Damage (Act No. 147 of 1961, as amended Apr. 2009), *available at* http://japan311disaster.com/wp-content/uploads/2013/05/Japan-Nuclear-Damage-Compensation-Act.pdf.
[168] Chico Harlan, *Japan's Nuclear Victims Seek Compensation, but not a Day in Court*, WASH. POST (June 25, 2012), http://www.washingtonpost.com/world/japans-nuclear-victims-seek-compensation-but-not-a-day-in-court/2012/06/25/gJQAe8GO1V_story.html.
[169] *Id.*
[170] Mark Willacy, *Residents Paying Back Fukushima Compensation*, ABC (Feb. 18, 2013), http://www.abc.net.au/news/2013-02-19/companies-not-paying-compensation-at-fukushima/4528150.
[171] Eric Feldman, *Fukushima: Catastrophe, Compensation, and Justice in Japan*, 62 DEPAUL L. REV. 335, 355 (2013).
[172] *Id.*

than rely on Japan's taxpayers. TEPCO will also focus on decommissioning and decontaminating the Fukushima nuclear facility.[173] However, victims of radiation exposure from the disaster remain **fearful of the long-term health effects**, such as thyroid and breast cancer, which may not appear for several years. Some citizens have refused to rely on government testing for radioactive iodine deposited in thyroid glands and have instead received the help of some local physicians who offer more frequent testing. Cancer cases are almost four times higher than the world average for all age groups, but the government can neither confirm nor deny whether the radiation exposure will result in an increased chance of cancer and so it continues to pay damages for the psychological injury.[174]

IV. CONCLUSION

Infrastructure and community resilience in the face of disaster is key to coping with both the natural and man-made disasters we will confront in the future. Connecting the concepts of resilience and disaster planning is critical to coastal communities developing strategies to deal with anticipated weather-related disasters such as superstorm Sandy, which had a devastating impact on New York City and surrounding communities in 2012. For coastal cities, there are two principal strategies to strengthen community resilience—protection of the coastline, buildings, and infrastructure and accommodating sea level rise through zoning and siting in a managed retreat from coastline development.[175]

> As a concept, resilience is highly developed in the psychological and ecological sciences, though the concept has also become more salient in the fields of international aid, disaster planning, management, and governance, including planning that specifically addresses climate change. A recent Rockefeller Foundation-funded literature review of resilience across disciplines has identified three principal frameworks in which resilience is discussed: engineering resilience, which, in its concern with the capacity to withstand external disturbances and to return rapidly to a normal state, accords with "colloquial" and "intuitive" conceptions of resilience; systems resilience, which refers to the ability of a system to maintain its functions in the face of a disturbance; and complex adaptive systems resilience, which includes the capacity to devise new ways of working, or reorganizing, when a disturbance occurs.

---

[173] *Fukushima Daiichi NPS Prompt Report 2014*, TEPCO (Jan 21, 2014), http://www.tepco.co.jp/en/press/corp-com/release/2014/1233729_5892.html.

[174] Martin Fritz, *Fukushima's Radiation Victims*, Deutsche Welle (Mar. 11, 2014), http://www.dw.de/fukushimas-radiation-victims/a-17488269. *But see* James Conca, *There's a Big Downside to Unprecedented Payoffs for Fukushima Refugees*, Forbes (Nov. 4, 2013), https://www.forbes.com/sites/jamesconca/2013/11/04/the-fukushima-refugee-business/2/.

[175] Andrea McArdle, *Storm Surges, Disaster Planning, and Vulnerable Populations at the Urban Periphery: Imagining a Resilient New York after Superstorm Sandy*, 50 Idaho L. Rev. 19, 20 (2014).

In psychology, evolving definitions have shifted emphasis from a more static, outcome-focused conception to an understanding of resilience as a dynamic process involving "positive adaptation in the context of significant adversity," a process that accords with a systems framework. Psychological analyses of resilience appear in the literature of child development and family relations. However, psychological resilience also applies in discussions of responses to trauma and disaster, and thus overlaps in some respects with disaster planning literature.

Discussions of resilience in ecological systems increasingly conjoin the ecological with the social, recognizing the impact of human activity on natural ecosystems. One inclusive definition of resilience encompasses the "ability of a social or ecological system to absorb disturbances while retaining the same basic structure and ways of functioning, the capacity for self-organisation [sic], and the capacity to adapt to stress and change."

Another application of resilience emphasizes the interaction between the social and the ecological systems, particularly the human capacity to turn to nature and realize an "ecological identity" as a mechanism of recovery after an extreme circumstance:

> *The ways in which we as humans reorganize, learn, recover and demonstrate resilience through remembering and operationalizing the value of our relationships with elements of our shared ecologies in the direst of circumstances such as disaster and war hold clues to how we might increase human resilience to new surprises, while contributing sources of social-ecological resilience to ecosystems.*

In the international aid context, resilience refers to the capacity of a nation, community, or household unit to resist and recover from a disaster. The United Nations International Strategy for Disaster Reduction defines resilience as the "ability of a system, community or society exposed to hazards to resist, absorb, accommodate to and recover from the effects of a hazard in a timely and efficient manner."

In the specific context of climate change, resilience has been defined as:

> *The capacity of an individual, community, or institution to dynamically and effectively respond to shifting climate impact circumstances while continuing to function at an acceptable level. Simply put, it is the ability to survive and recover from the effects of climate change. It includes the ability to understand potential impacts and to take appropriate action before, during, and after a particular consequence to minimize negative effects and maintain the ability to respond to changing conditions.*

Climate change resilience encompasses adaptation and recovery strategies and presumes "systems [that] build redundancies of resources, multiple response paths, and safety nets."

In a similar vein, a preliminary report of the New York State 2100 Commission, recommending steps to protect the state's infrastructure from weather-related disasters, defines resilience as:

> *The ability of a system to withstand shocks and stresses while still maintaining its essential functions. Therefore systems that are more vulnerable — i.e., those that are brittle, at stretched capacity, or with very low diversity — are more at risk of catastrophic consequences when the next shock event happens. Resilient systems are also better able to repair and recover afterwards.*

Taken together, there are several features that are common to most resilient systems, including having spare or latent capacity (redundancy); ensuring flexibility and responsiveness; managing for safe failure (building resistance to domino effects); and having the capacity to recover quickly and evolve over time — to thrive, not just survive major disruptions.[176]

Question

1. Besides resiliency planning for sea-level rise and weather-related disasters, what other types of disasters does your community experience and are there plans in place to deal with this potential disruption? For a dramatic example of how a lack of community planning can lead to even greater tragedy following a natural disaster, please read "The School Beneath the Wave: The Unimaginable Tragedy of Japan's Tsunami" by Richard Lloyd Parry.[177]

---

[176] *Id.* at 30-33.
[177] Richard Lloyd Parry, *The School Beneath the Wave: The Unimaginable Tragedy of Japan's Tsunami*, THE GUARDIAN (Aug. 24, 2017), https://www.theguardian.com/world/2017/aug/24/the-school-beneath-the-wave-the-unimaginable-tragedy-of-japans-tsunami?CMP=share_btn_link.

Climate Change

10

Throughout this book, we stressed the challenges raised when identifying and assessing the R&S of complex social-ecological systems and when finding ways to integrate those assessments into law and policy. Some of those challenges stem from system changes that can have unknown and cascading impacts across many systems and disciplines. Thus, while we divided this book into substantive chapters, such as food and water, many of the issues raised in each chapter cut across disciplines, implicating issues raised in other chapters. This is particularly true with climate change.

Climate change raises complex issues associated with many social-ecological systems discussed throughout this book. We begin our exploration of climate change by setting a foundation in the first section. This section defines "climate change," and then sets forth some of the relevant science, including the greenhouse gas effect, greenhouse gases generally, and greenhouse gas sinks. Establishing this foundation is necessary to understand how climate change may impact system resilience and sustainability. It is also necessary to design effective solutions that address the straining of these systems. After we review the science, we turn to three major approaches to address climate change — mitigation, adaptation, and geoengineering.

In Section II, we provide an overview of the global climate impacts and take a closer look at how climate change can affect the resilience and sustainability of social-ecological systems. To illustrate these impacts, we focus on changes to the "Ocean" (by which we mean the World Ocean, as opposed to individual "oceans") and how those changes affect the R&S of systems related to the Ocean. Finally, in Section III, we rely on many of the Strategies for Implementation described throughout this book to explore how assessing R&S can help provide information to mitigate and adapt to climate change.

I. SETTING THE FOUNDATION: CLIMATE BASICS, GREENHOUSE GASES, SOURCES, AND SINKS

Climate change law is fascinating. It challenges us to create new, innovative, and adaptable solutions. Before we can create solutions though, we need to understand some climate change basics. The following two subsections cover basic climate change information beginning with greenhouse gases, sources of GHGs, and sinks in subsection A and ending with three general frameworks to address climate change in subsection B.

A. Greenhouse Gases, Sources, and Sinks

Climate is the average weather at a specific place and time of year over a long period (typically 30 years). For example, measuring the average weather in August each year in Iowa from 1916–1946 would provide us with a picture of Iowa's climate. Part of that weather may include the average temperature, which is 71.7 degrees Fahrenheit in August in Iowa.[1] While we expect the weather to change from day to day, we expect the climate (average weather) to remain relatively constant.

When the long-term average weather changes, it is called climate change. One way to measure the amount of such change is by comparing two different climate points, perhaps the climate of Florida, between 1916–1946 and 1986–2016. Of course, such change can occur through natural events, such as volcanic eruptions, but what we are more concerned with are the human-made, or anthropogenic, actions that propel the changes.

To maintain a constant temperature and steady climate, the Earth must absorb and radiate a consistent level of heat. The Earth is warmed by absorbing the sun's solar energy. If, however, the Earth radiated the same total amount of heat it received from the sun's energy (in other words, failed to capture any heat), the global temperatures would be well below freezing. In order to maintain an average global temperature around 57–59 degrees Fahrenheit,[2] the Earth must trap some of that heat.

The atmosphere is what traps the sun's solar energy and warms the Earth. The atmosphere is made of hundreds of different molecules, such as water vapor, which both reflect and trap the sun's energy. About one third of the sun's solar radiation is reflected out of the inner atmosphere by clouds, the atmosphere itself, and the Earth's surface (for example, ice from

---

[1] *See Climatology Rankings*, NAT'L OCEANIC AND ATMOSPHERIC ADMIN., http://www.ncdc.noaa.gov/temp-and-precip/climatological-rankings/index.php (last visited Dec. 5, 2017) (using the search tool to find the relevant data per year and calculating the average accordingly).

[2] *State of the Climate: Global Analysis for April 2016*, NAT'L OCEANIC AND ATMOSPHERIC ADMIN., http://www.ncdc.noaa.gov/sotc/global/201604 (last visited Dec. 5, 2017).

the polar ice caps).[3] The remaining two thirds of the solar radiation is converted to heat and warms the Earth's surface.[4] Some of the heat radiates upward from the Earth's surface and is trapped by gases in the atmosphere. These gases are called greenhouse gases (GHGs). Most of the atmosphere (oxygen and nitrogen, for example) allows the heat to pass through.[5]

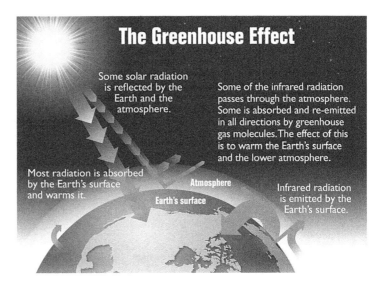

GHGs do not. They trap some of the heat and then re-radiate some of it back to the Earth's surface. Most of the GHGs that are trapping heat are caught in a portion of the atmosphere called the troposphere, ranging from approximately 7 to 16 kilometers above the Earth's surface. The more GHGs there are in the troposphere, the more heat gets trapped and re-radiated to Earth. The radiation of heat back and forth between the surface and the atmosphere creates the greenhouse gas effect.

Increases in the amount and changes in the type of GHGs in the atmosphere cause the average Earth temperature to increase by trapping and re-radiating more heat. GHG emissions from anthropogenic sources such as oil refineries have predominately caused the recent increases and changes.[6] Figure 10-1 below, from a report drafted by the Intergovernmental Panel on Climate Change (IPCC) (see the text box for more information on the IPCC), indicates the major anthropogenic emissions in 2010, separated by various types of GHGs (for example, carbon dioxide (CO_2)). According to this chart, carbon dioxide accounts for approximately 76% of anthropogenic emissions (65% from direct emissions and 11% from forestry and other land uses), while the other GHGs make up the remaining 24%, notably methane at approximately 16%, and nitrous oxide at approximately

[3] *IPCC Fourth Assessment Report: Climate Change 2007: Working Group I: The Physical Science Basis: FAQ 1.3: What Is the Greenhouse Effect?*, INTERGOVERNMENTAL PANEL ON CLIMATE CHANGE, https://www.ipcc.ch/publications_and_data/ar4/wg1/en/faq-1-3.html (last visited Dec. 5, 2017).
[4] *Id.*
[5] *Id.*
[6] Core Writing Team, R.K. Pachauri & L.A. Meyer, *Climate Change 2014: Synthesis Report*, INTERGOVERNMENTAL PANEL ON CLIMATE CHANGE 40 (2015), http://ar5-syr.ipcc.ch/ipcc/ipcc/resources/pdf/IPCC_SynthesisReport.pdf [hereinafter *2014 IPCC Synthesis Report*].

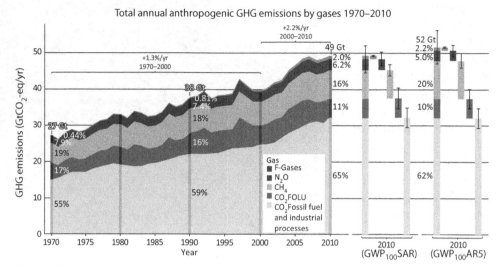

Figure 10-1

6.2%.[7] The chart also illustrates an increase in total emissions of almost 40% between 1970 and 2010.[8]

![IPCC logo] **INTERGOVERNMENTAL PANEL ON CLIMATE CHANGE (IPCC)**

The IPCC is a scientific, intergovernmental body operating under the auspices of the United Nations. Established in 1988 at the request of the World Meteorological Organization (WMO) and the United Nations Environment Programme (UNEP) and endorsed by the United Nations General Assembly in December 1988, its membership is open to all members of the WMO and UNEP.

The IPCC produces reports that support the Framework Convention on Climate Change (UNFCCC) (discussed further in Section III below). The reports collect and summarize the current knowledge on climate change, covering "the scientific, technical and socio-economic information relevant to understanding the scientific basis of risk of human-induced climate change, its potential impacts and options for adaptation and mitigation."[9]

The IPCC's *Fifth Assessment Report* resulted in three in-depth reports and a summary report issued throughout 2013 and into 2014. Working Group I issued the first report, which assesses scientific aspects of the climate system and climate change. Working Group II issued the second report, which assesses vulnerabilities related to social-economic and natural systems. Working Group II's report also explores the consequences of continuing on certain paths and various adaptation options. Working

---

[7] *Id.* at 5.
[8] *Id.*
[9] *History*, INTERGOVERNMENTAL PANEL ON CLIMATE CHANGE, https://www.ipcc.ch/organization/organization_history.shtml (last visited Dec. 5, 2017).

Group III issued the third report, which covers options for limiting GHG emissions and otherwise mitigating climate change. Authors from each working group collaborated to issue the final summary of all of the reports.[10]

Not all GHGs are equal. The U.S. Environmental Protection Agency (EPA) notes that we need to know the following factors to calculate the potential a GHG has to affect the climate:

1. How much of the gas is emitted.
2. How long the gas will stay in the atmosphere before leaving or breaking down.
3. How efficient the gas is at trapping heat.[11]

Once we obtain this information, we can get a better sense of the overall impacts to the climate and to the resilience and sustainability of many systems. Below is a table setting forth some of the most prominent GHGs and their "global warming potential" or GWP. GWP reflects the differences in gases based on factors 2 and 3 above. GWP provides for a standardized way to compare GHGs. We measure GWP relative to CO_2 over a specified timeframe. Thus, we always indicate CO_2 as a "1."

The specific GHGs compared in this table are carbon dioxide, hydro-fluorocarbon (or floroform), methane, perfluorinated chemicals, nitrous oxide, sulfur hexafluoride, trichlorofluoromethane, and black carbon. The second row of the table lists the time each gas remains in the atmosphere and traps heat. It ranges from less than one year to 10,000 years. The last two rows set forth the GWP over 20 years and 100 years. For example, the GWP of methane is 25 over 100 years, which means one unit of methane released into the atmosphere will have a warming impact 25 times greater than the same unit of CO_2 over 100 years.[12]

Substance	CO_2	HFC-23	CH_4	PFCs	N_2O	SF_6	CFC-11	Black Carbon
Atmospheric Life	5–200	270	12	10,000	114	3,200	45	<1
GWP over 20 years	1	12,000	72	5,230	289	16,300	6,730	2,200
GWP over 100 years	1	14,800	25	7,390	298	22,800	4,750	680[13]

---

[10] *Id.*

[11] *Overview of Greenhouse Gases*, U.S. EPA, https://www.epa.gov/ghgemissions/overview-green-house-gases (last updated Apr. 14, 2017).

[12] Importantly, GWP does not calculate the secondary greenhouse gas effects when a compound breaks down. For example, methane can break down into CO_2, which can continue to trap heat. Gavin Schmidt, *Methane: A Scientific Journey from Obscurity to Climate Super-Stardom*, LA RECHERCHE (Sept. 2004), https://www.giss.nasa.gov/research/features/200409_methane/ (last visited Nov. 8, 2017).

[13] Chris Wold, David Hunter & Melissa Powers, CLIMATE CHANGE AND THE LAW 8 (2d ed. 2013).

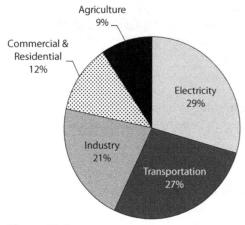

Figure 10-2
U.S. GHG emissions

GWP calculates each gas's efficiency in trapping heat and considers it in relation to the time it is in the atmosphere resulting in its potency compared to other gases. For example, we might consider nitrous oxide (N_2O) more potent than methane (CH_4), because it has a higher GWP over 20 years and an even higher GWP over 100 years.[14] While helpful, this information does not provide us with the entire story, as we do not know how much of each gas was emitted.

In order to address the emission of GHGs in a way that addresses or reverses impacts to critical systems' resilience and sustainability, we also need to know: 1) where the gases are coming from, 2) what anthropogenic sources and behaviors are associated with which GHGs, and 3) how much of each GHG is removed from the cycle.

The EPA notes that 81% of U.S. GHGs in 2014 were carbon dioxide, 11% were methane, and 6% were nitrous oxide.[15] Figure 10-2 indicates the primary sources of GHG emissions in the United States.[16]

The EPA explains which GHGs relate to which anthropogenic sources in the United States:

- **Carbon dioxide (CO_2)**: Carbon dioxide enters the atmosphere through burning fossil fuels (coal, natural gas, and oil), solid waste, trees, and wood products, and certain chemical reactions (e.g., manufacture of cement). Carbon dioxide is removed from the atmosphere (or "sequestered") when plants absorb it as part of the biological carbon cycle.
- **Methane (CH_4)**: Methane is emitted during the production and transport of coal, natural gas, and oil. Methane emissions also result from livestock and other agricultural practices and by the decay of organic waste in municipal solid waste landfills.
- **Nitrous oxide (N_2O)**: Nitrous oxide is emitted during agricultural and industrial activities, as well as during combustion of fossil fuels and solid waste.
- **Fluorinated gases**: Hydrofluorocarbons, perfluorocarbons, sulfur hexafluoride, and nitrogen trifluoride are synthetic, powerful greenhouse gases that are emitted from a variety of industrial processes.

---

[14] *Id.*
[15] *Overview of Greenhouse Gases, supra* note 11.
[16] *Id.*

Fluorinated gases are sometimes used as substitutes for stratospheric ozone-depleting substances (e.g., chlorofluorocarbons, hydrochlorofluorocarbons, and halons). These gases are typically emitted in smaller quantities, but because they are potent greenhouse gases, they are sometimes referred to as High Global Warming Potential gases ("High GWP gases").[17]

There are several ways to absorb GHGs before they enter the atmosphere. The largest absorption of GHG emissions comes from carbon sinks. The vast majority of carbon sinks are found in nature. Many natural resources feed in and out of natural cycles that are relevant to climate change, such as the water and carbon cycle. Many of these natural resources participate in moderating the climate by absorbing carbon dioxide and other GHGs. A carbon sink is anything in the carbon cycle that absorbs more carbon than it releases. For example, as plants grow, they absorb carbon dioxide from the air, and through photosynthesis they use solar energy to convert carbon dioxide into carbon, which is stored in the plant. By storing the residual carbon, plants are carbon sinks. Additional carbon sinks include forests, soils, regenerative agriculture, wetlands, savannah grasslands, and the ocean.

Many of these sinks play a dual role. They serve as a carbon sink in the carbon cycle, but they also can be a major source of carbon emissions when they decompose or are used in a way that releases the stored carbon. For example, deforestation, something discussed in more detail in Chapter 2 and in the notes below, not only releases carbon into the atmosphere, but also eliminates a carbon sink. Similarly, agricultural practices, which can be a carbon sink, also emit GHGs during planting and harvesting activities by releasing those gases from soil and vegetation.

To illustrate the dual role sinks play consider: 1) over the past 150 years, a large percentage of carbon dioxide was absorbed into sinks; and 2) over the past 40 years, between 20-40% of GHG emissions originated from releasing the GHGs stored in these sinks.[18] As shown in Figure 10-3 below, concentrations in the atmosphere of 280 parts of carbon per million (ppm) in 1750 increased to 393 ppm by 2012 and 400 ppm by 2015.[19] While forests and agriculture practices were responsible for absorbing 68 ppm and the ocean for absorbing 76 ppm, coal was responsible for emitting 86 ppm, oil 64 ppm, and land use practices (such as clearing forest and wetlands) 76 ppm, resulting in a net growth of 84 ppm that can be attributed to the destruction of carbon sinks.[20]

---

[17] *Id.*

[18] *See 2014 IPCC Synthesis Report, supra* note 6, at 45.

[19] *Global Carbon Emissions and Sinks Since 1750*, SHRINK THAT FOOTPRINT, http://shrinkthatfootprint.com/carbon-emissions-and-sinks (last visited Dec. 5, 2017).

[20] *Id.*

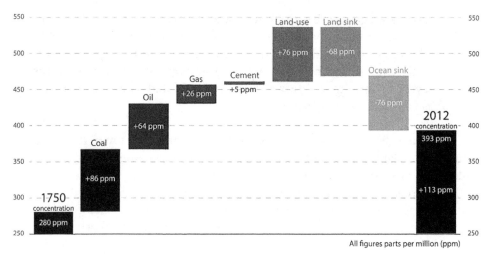

Figure 10-3

Questions and Notes

1. In general, forests have been in great decline, although at varying rates at different times and places. Most of the forests in the United States were cut down by the beginning of the twentieth century, emitting an enormous amount of GHGs. While deforestation has slowed in the United States — mostly due to availability and cost — deforestation in other countries continues to be a major source of GHG emissions. Emissions from land use and forestry, for example, amount to significant percentages of GHGs in several countries including:

   1. Bolivia — 69.6% of total national emissions
   2. Brazil — 64.4% of total national emissions
   3. Cameroon — 65.6% of total national emissions
   4. Democratic Republic of Congo — 65.4% of total national emissions.[21]

2. Assume there is a fictitious new bill to help reduce statewide greenhouse gas emissions by reforestation. The reforestation effort is part of the state's goals to reduce its climate impact. Over the past 70 years, the state has lost 60% of its forested area to development (35%) and agriculture (65%). The new bill states:

   (a) Any person seeking approval from any city in the State to remove a tree shall:

---

[21] Chris Wold et al., *supra* note 13, at 419.

(1) Submit a statement explaining why the proposed tree removal is necessary; and

(2) Submit an inventory of all trees to be removed. Such inventory shall contain the individual diameters and species of each tree.

(b) Any person subject to this section shall reforest trees equivalent to the economic value of the trees removed. Such value shall be based on the National Tree Benefit Calculator (NTBC). The NTBC can be found at: http://treebenefits.com/calculator/.

(1) For example, a 10-inch Oregon Ash tree has a value of $100 a year in total benefits. Because a 2-inch Higan Cherry tree has an annual value of $5, the person removing the tree would need to plant 20 Higan Cherry trees in the State if s/he chooses to reforest with 2-inch Higan Cherry trees.

(c) Trees reforested pursuant to this section must be planted on conservation land anywhere in the State.

What would be your top three to five priorities as to why you support or do not support the measure and/or how you would amend the law if you represented: 1) an association of developers, 2) an association of farmers, 3) an association of local governments, and 4) an environmental advocacy group? In answering this question, be clear on your client's objectives. Discuss the following in your answer: Are they a carbon source? Carbon sink? Do they have a personal stake? Who are the key stakeholders affected by climate change and affected by the proposed law? Where are the competing interests? Who are the winners and losers? What are the equity issues at stake?

B. Three Approaches to Addressing Climate Change

Responses to climate change take three general approaches: 1) mitigation, 2) adaptation, and 3) geoengineering. These three approaches provide general policy and law approaches to climate change. Some actions can meet more than one of these approaches, as we will discuss below.

1. MITIGATION

Mitigation is the reduction of GHG emissions to limit the extent of climate change. James Hansen et al.'s article describing the "carbon budget" illustrates the importance of mitigation.[22] In the article, the authors

---

[22] James Hansen et al., *Assessing "Dangerous Climate Change": Required Reduction of Carbon Emissions to Protect Young People, Future Generations, and Nature*, PLOS One (Dec. 3, 2013), http://journals.plos.org/plosone/article?id = 10.1371/journal.pone.0081648.

recognized that the previously accepted target of limiting human-made global climate warming to 2 degrees Celsius (3.6 °F) above preindustrial levels is too high.[23] The authors believe we need to strive for a target of 1 degree Celsius (1.8 °F), if not lower, instead.[24] This is possible, they state, if cumulative industrial-era fossil fuel emissions are limited to 500 gigatonnes carbon (GtC, see adjacent box), and 100 GtC is drawn down or "restored" into the biosphere (i.e., sinks).[25] This kind of total output would lower the make up of the atmospheric GHGs from over 400 parts per million (ppm) to 350 ppm by 2100.[26] In order to do this, the authors state that we need to reduce emissions or mitigate output by 6% per year.[27]

CLIMATE CHANGE IN DEGREES

In 2012, the World Bank issued a report drafted by the Potsdam Institute for Climate Impact Research and Climate Analytics. In the report, the authors described the impact of a 4 degree Celsius temperature increase by 2100 as a world where there are "unprecedented heat waves, severe drought, and major floods in many regions, with serious impacts on ecosystems and associated services." The report continued by stating:

[G]iven that uncertainty remains about the full nature and scale of impacts, there is also no certainty that adaptation to a 4°C world is possible. A 4°C world is likely to be one in which communities, cities and countries would experience severe disruptions, damage, and dislocation, with many of these risks spread unequally. It is likely that the poor will suffer most and the global community could become more fractured, and unequal than today.

Report No. 1, *Turn Down the Heat: Why a 4°C Warmer World Must Be Avoided*, (November 2012). The World Bank and Potsdam Institute for Climate Impact Research and Climate Analytics issued Report No. 3, *Turn Down the Heat: Confronting the New Climate Normal*, in November 2014.

MEASURING CARBON DIOXIDE

There are several ways to measure carbon dioxide. Gigatonnes of carbon (GtC) is one common way to measure the amount of CO_2 *emitted* into the atmosphere; and parts per million is one common way to measure the amount of CO_2 *stored* in the atmosphere. Because CO_2 can

---

[23] *Id.* The 2-degree limit is what is used in most international documents; *see, e.g.*, United Nations Framework Convention on Climate Change, May 9, 1992, S. Treaty Doc No. 102-38, 1771 U.N.T.S. 107, although as we will see, the most recent agreement in Paris sets 2 degrees as the limit with the intent to strive for 1.5 degrees. *Paris Agreement, Decision 1/CP.21* (Dec. 11, 2015) http://unfccc.int/resource/docs/2015/cop21/eng/10a01.pdf.

[24] James Hansen et al., *supra* note 22.

[25] *Id.*

[26] *Id.*

[27] *Id.*

change form as it cycles into the atmosphere, GtC is helpful for measuring emitted gases. For example, 6 units of stored CO_2 may be counted as part of a compound like $C_6H_{12}O_6$ (glucose) because the compound contains six carbons.

There are many forms of mitigation and law and policy can support many of them. For example, the IPCC divides mitigation approaches into three core categories:

1. Reducing energy use (end user)
2. Decarbonizing energy supply (producer)
3. Enhancing carbon sinks.[28]

The IPCC's summary report lists additional factors to consider when mitigating climate change. These factors include approaching mitigation as an integrated approach and designing mitigation strategies in systemic, cross-sectoral, and interdisciplinary ways. The IPCC then provides several examples of more specific mitigation steps. In Figure 10-4, the IPCC provides an example based on improving the efficiency of buildings. The IPCC divides its integrated approach into six columns. The first three set forth the projected emission reductions stemming from the mitigation strategy, the percentage of low-carbon fuel resulting from adoption of the strategy, and the final total energy demand from the strategy.

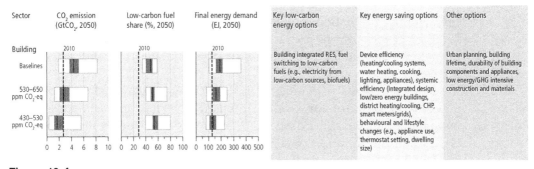

Figure 10-4

In the fourth column, IPCC describes the low-carbon energy options relevant to reducing emissions from buildings. For example, the IPCC

---

[28] *2014 IPCC Synthesis Report, supra* note 6, at 98-102; *see also* S. Pacala & R. Socolow, *Stabilization Wedges: Solving the Climate Problem for the Next 50 Years with Current Technologies*, SCIENCE 968-972 (Aug. 13, 2004) (Stephen Pacala and Robert Socolow, through something they call "wedges," provide a number of options that can help mitigate climate change).

suggests ensuring the buildings meet the International Energy Conservation Code (referenced as "RES") and that buildings switch to getting their electricity from low-carbon fuels.[29] The fifth column refers to energy savings on the end-user side. For example, the IPCC suggests device efficiencies (like heating and AC), system efficiencies, and lifestyle or behavioral changes.[30] In the final column, the IPCC suggests other mitigation options relevant to buildings including urban planning, durability of buildings and appliances, and low energy construction and materials.[31]

The IPCC report provides a glimpse of the various mitigation options available for each sector. Other commonly discussed mitigation options include cap-and-trade and the carbon tax. Many of the mitigation strategies implicate the R&S of systems that rely on the climate and/or the emission of GHGs — something we discuss in more detail in Sections II and III.

2. ADAPTATION

Adaption is the preparation for and response to climate impacts. Adaptation, unlike mitigation, does not focus on reducing GHG emissions. Rather, adaptation focuses on addressing the impacts of climate change and the ramifications of those impacts, such as property loss from sea-level rise or flooding. The IPCC defines adaptation as:

> *The process of adjustment to actual or expected climate and its effects. In human systems, adaptation seeks to moderate or avoid harm or exploit beneficial opportunities. In some natural systems, human intervention may facilitate adjustment to expected climate and its effects.*[32]

Importantly, adaptation includes all of the efforts undertaken at multiple levels of governance to prepare for climate change, whether the intent is to maximize advantages or minimize disadvantages associated with climate change.

In recent years, a number of scholars have stated that adaptation is a necessary step to address climate change because impacts are already happening and we can expect them to intensify.[33] Due to the amount of GHGs and the duration of some of them in the atmosphere where they can trap heat for decades, climate impacts will continue to unfold in *uncertain* ways. In other words, even if we were able to reduce GHGs to pre-industrial levels (i.e., mitigate), the GHGs already emitted will continue to trap heat and alter the climate.

---

[29] *2014 IPCC Synthesis Report, supra* note 6, at 101.
[30] *Id.*
[31] *Id.*
[32] *Id.* at 76.
[33] *Id.*

In terms of law and policy, adaptation and mitigation need not work exclusive of each other and can often work in tandem. For example, wetlands can be both an effective adaptation and mitigation option.[34] Wetlands simultaneously serve as a sink, absorbing more carbon dioxide than they emit, and add resilience by absorbing rising waters thus reducing flood risks. When considering adaptation strategies, the following factors may help weigh the various options:

- Political realities
- Economic resources
- Available technologies
- Accessible information
- Human capacities
- Natural resource assets
- Infrastructure assets
- Institutional (legal) support
- Needs of the region
- Possible consequences
- Priorities
- Cost
- Ease of implementation
- Biggest impact

How, and if, we adapt to climate change will impact the resilience and sustainability of communities across the country.

3. GEOENGINEERING

A third general approach to climate change is geoengineering. Geoengineering is the use of technology to reverse climate change *or* its impacts. A less used approach to-date than mitigation or adaption, the U.S. National Academy of Sciences defines geoengineering as: "[O]ptions that would involve large-scale engineering of our environment in order to combat or counteract the effects of changes in atmospheric chemistry."[35] Similar to adaptation, geoengineering does not focus on altering human behaviors to reduce anthropogenic emissions. Rather, if it attempts to reduce emissions, it does so in a way that does not alter our actual output of emissions, but rather engineers a solution to reduce GHG emissions from reaching the atmosphere or the sun's radiated energy from hitting Earth.

---

[34] *Wetlands*, THINK GLOBAL GREEN, http://www.thinkglobalgreen.org/wetlands.html (last visited Oct. 8, 2017).
[35] National Academy of Sciences et al., PANEL ON POLICY IMPLICATIONS OF GREENHOUSE WARMING COMMITTEE ON SCIENCE, ENGINEERING, AND PUBLIC POLICY, POLICY IMPLICATIONS OF GREENHOUSE WARMING 433 (1992).

The arguments that we need geoengineering to address climate change include:

1. There are too many long-lasting GHGs in the atmosphere already (this is a similar argument as to why we need adaptation).
2. We have, thus far, been unable and/or unwilling to reduce our GHGs and limit behaviors to safe levels.
3. Geoengineering allows us to adopt a "business as usual" stance while limiting the GHG impact on the climate.[36]

Geoengineering is often categorized into two basic, but different, approaches — solar radiation management and carbon dioxide removal. The two approaches function very differently because they address GHGs and carbon emissions at different stages. Solar radiation management (SRM) — also known as albedo modification — seeks to increase reflectivity, thus reducing the amount of solar energy reaching the Earth. SRM increases reflectivity either on the Earth's surface or in the atmosphere. The theory is if too much of the sun's solar energy is reaching the Earth, we just need to block it out.

Examples of SRM include:

- Releasing sulfur dioxide into the atmosphere. Sulfur dioxide converts to an aerosol when it joins with water vapor in the stratosphere. Aerosols create tiny reflective surfaces — basically millions of tiny mirrors — that block the sun's solar energy from reaching the Earth.[37]
- Installing a giant mirror or mirrors in the atmosphere. This would work similar to aerosols, but instead of millions of tiny mirrors, this would include enormous ones.[38]
- Increasing cloud cover by something called cloud seeding. Because clouds reflect light this would attempt to replicate natural cloud reflectors. Clouds are part of the water cycle involving evaporation, condensation, and precipitation. This strategy would involve increasing evaporation to get more cloud coverage.[39]

In addition to SRM, carbon dioxide removal (CDR) is a form of geoengineering. CDR involves physically removing carbon from the environment so that it does not enter the atmosphere and trap heat. Most CDR strategies differ from SRM in that they seek to stop emissions before they reach the atmosphere, while SRM allows GHGs to reach the atmosphere.

---

[36] Leon Clarke et al., *Assessing Transformation Pathways, in* Climate Change 2014: Mitigation of Climate Change. Contribution of Working Group III to the Fifth Assessment Report of the Intergovernmental Panel on Climate Change, Ch. 6, Sec. 6.9 (2014), https://www.ipcc.ch/pdf/assessment-report/ar5/wg3/ipcc_wg3_ar5_chapter6.pdf (last visited Oct. 8, 2017).

[37] National Academy of Sciences et al., *supra* note 35, at 449.

[38] *Id.* at 448.

[39] *Id.* at 455.

Some examples of CDR include:

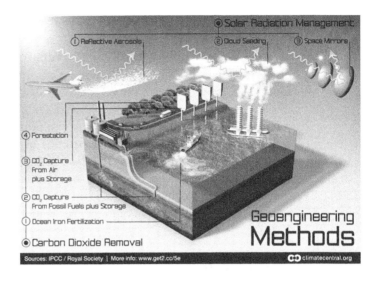

- Increasing micronutrients (for example, iron) in the ocean. Increasing micronutrients may spur growth of phytoplankton, which absorbs carbon dioxide, increasing the oceans' capacity to serve as a carbon sink. Other marine life then consumes the phytoplankton. They ultimately decay and release CO_2 either back into the atmosphere or sequester it by sinking and decomposing into the ocean floor.[40]
- Sequestering carbon in the ground. Similar to the micronutrient strategy, carbon capture and storage is another example of sequestering carbon. Here, we modify smokestacks with built-in "scrubbers," which trap the waste carbon dioxide gas and turn it into a highly compressed liquid that could be stored in the ground.[41]
- Adding massive pipes in the ocean. This method is similar to the micronutrients solution because it is an attempt to spur ocean growth to consume carbon dioxide. Massive pipes in the ocean would circulate cold water from the deeper ocean with warm water at the top to spur algae growth and absorb more carbon dioxide.[42]

Not surprisingly, geoengineering raises many concerns relevant to R&S. First, it is unclear what consequences may stem from SRM and CDR. For example, how will an increase in sulfur dioxide in the atmosphere affect the ozone layer? Second, geoengineering is often a short-term fix. We have to repeat the fix or we will experience quick, and potentially catastrophic, bumps in temperature increases. For example, aerosols remain in the atmosphere for a relatively short time. If we discontinue pumping sulfur dioxide into the atmosphere, it may dissipate very quickly and a sudden increase of solar energy may hit the Earth's surface, raising temperatures rapidly. Third, many geoengineering strategies do not address

[40] Clarke et al., *supra* note 36, at 485.
[41] National Research Council et al., COMMITTEE ON GEOENGINEERING CLIMATE, CLIMATE INTERVENTION: CARBON DIOXIDE REMOVAL AND RELIABLE SEQUESTRATION (2015).
[42] Richard Black, *Lovelock Urges Ocean Climate Fix*, BBC NEWS, http://news.bbc.co.uk/2/hi/science/nature/7014503.stm (last updated Sept. 26, 2007).

non-atmospheric GHG challenges. For example, SRM approaches do little to help with the amount of carbon dioxide absorbed in the ocean, leading to ocean acidification. Finally, and potentially most importantly, geoengineering does not address the cause of climate change — human behaviors — and provides little incentive to control GHG emissions.

To date, there are few, if any, legal doctrines directly addressing geoengineering. This raises critical concerns, including how the law should address geoengineering. What should the process be for drafting a law to integrate geoengineering? Who should decide whether geoengineering should go forward? What assurances should be required to make sure unintended consequences do not occur? And how do we incorporate the assessment of R&S into considerations of geoengineering? Which systems should we assess?

Questions and Notes

1. Below are two articles from the U.N. Framework Convention on Climate Change. These articles are relevant to the context of geoengineering. Article 2 provides:

   The ultimate objective of this Convention . . . is to achieve, in accordance with the relevant provisions of the Convention, stabilization of greenhouse gas concentrations in the atmosphere at a level that would prevent dangerous anthropogenic interference with the climate system.[43]

   Article 4 states:

   (b) Formulate, implement, publish and regularly update national and, where appropriate, regional programmes containing measures to mitigate climate change by addressing anthropogenic emissions by sources and removals by sinks of . . . greenhouse gases . . . and measures to facilitate adequate adaptation to climate change.[44]

   What are the arguments that these articles justify geoengineering or at least the exploration of geoengineering? Do you agree? Are they broad enough to encompass geoengineering?

2. Describe the differences between mitigation, adaptation, and geoengineering to someone who is unfamiliar with them. What are their key differences? How are they similar?

3. Which do you prefer as a general approach to climate change: mitigation, adaptation, or geoengineering? Does it have to be one or the other?

---

[43] United Nations Framework Convention on Climate Change, *supra* note 23.
[44] *Id.*

II. CLIMATE CHANGE IMPACTS

The effects of climate change are vast and have deep implications for the R&S of many social-ecological systems. In this section, we expand on the effects first mentioned in Chapter 2. We then focus on one area—the Ocean—to provide a more in-depth example of how climate change can alter the R&S of several systems.

REVIEW OF THE SCIENTIFIC SCHOLARSHIP ON CLIMATE CHANGE

While there has been much debate over how much human behavior affects the climate, it is well established that human actions impact global warming. In 2013, John Cook et. al published a review of almost 12,000 abstracts on climate change or global warming, from the years 1991–2011, and made the following findings:

- 66.4% of the papers expressed no position on anthropogenic global warming (AGW)
- 32.6% endorsed AGW
- .7% rejected it
- .3% were uncertain

Cook et al. concluded that when scientific scholarship addresses AGW, 97.1% supported the position that humans are causing global warming.

John Cook et al., *Quantifying the Consensus on Anthropogenic Global Warming in the Scientific Literature*, 8 ENVIRON. RES. LETT. (Jan. 18, 2013), http://iopscience.iop.org/article/10.1088/1748-9326/8/2/024024/pdf.

A. Summary of Climate Change Effects

In its summary, the IPCC makes the following over-arching conclusion:

Human influence on the climate system is clear, and recent anthropogenic emissions of greenhouse gases are the highest in history. Recent climate changes have had widespread impacts on human and natural systems.[45]

The IPCC's statement contains at least two critical parts: 1) humans are affecting the climate, and 2) by doing so, humans are having "widespread impact[s]" on socio-ecological systems.[46] Those systems cut across disciplines, including those discussed earlier in this book such as water and

---

[45] *2014 IPCC Synthesis Report, supra* note 6, at 40.
[46] *Id.*

pollution. In this way, climate change represents one of the most, if not the most, pressing issues impacting the R&S of social-ecological systems.

We are already experiencing a broad array of climate change effects that impact many systems, as illustrated by the following information:

- Temperature increases (slow and rapid changes)
  - The last 30 years have likely been the warmest in the last 800–1,400 years.[47]
- Precipitation increases and decreases (slow and rapid changes)
  - July 2016 was both extremely wet and extremely dry in the United States When compared to the last 122 years Kentucky faced its second wettest July, Illinois its third, and Minnesota its fourth.[48] At the same time, 21.1% of the United States experienced drought conditions and the drought in the western states entered its third decade.[49]
- Water flow increases and decreases, simultaneously increasing the risk of flooding and droughts
  - An increase in the intensity of rainfall leads to increased instances of flooding, particularly in areas where the ground is unable to absorb the rain due to either oversaturation or extreme under-saturation where the sheer volume and rate of rainfall means more water is shed than absorbed.[50]
- Land soil condition change
  - The permafrost is thinning which causes the soil to release previously sequestered carbon. Additionally, melting permafrost negatively impacts "drainage, ground water, river runoffs, ecological systems (such as plants and ponds) . . . and infrastructure (such as houses, roads, airports, pipelines, and other facilities based on permafrost)."[51]
- Biodiversity migration and extinctions (both flora and fauna)
  - Ecological systems are intimately intertwined and any effect of climate change on one inherently affects the others. For example, climate change has caused phonological changes that result in the mismatch of pollinators and plants, which can lead to extinction of both flora and fauna. It is estimated that 6,300 species could disappear following the extinction of a single member of an interrelated system.[52]

---

[47] *Id.*

[48] *State of the Climate: Drought for July 2016*, NAT'L OCEANIC & ATMOSPHERIC ADMIN., http://www. ncdc.noaa.gov/sotc/drought/201607 (last visited Dec. 5, 2017).

[49] *Id.*

[50] NASA, *The Water Cycle and Climate Change*, EARTH OBSERVATORY, http://earthobservatory.nasa. gov/Features/Water/page3.php (last visited Dec. 5, 2017).

[51] PMEL Arctic Change, *Land—Permafrost*, NAT'L OCEANIC AND ATMOSPHERIC ADMIN., http://www. pmel.noaa.gov/arctic-zone/detect/land-permafrost.shtml (last visited Dec. 5, 2017).

[52] Céline Bellard et al., *Impacts of Climate Change on the Future of Biodiversity*, 15(4) ECOLOGY LETTERS 365-377 (2012), https://www.ncbi.nlm.nih.gov/pmc/articles/PMC3880584/.

- Fires and risk of fire increases
  - 2017 has seen the second lowest number of forest fires but the sixth highest number of acres burned.[53] The wildfires have become harder to contain once they erupt resulting in more acres lost per fire.
- Invasive species incident increases
  - The increase in severe weather due to global warming has the potential to bring devastating numbers of invasive pathogens (Asian soybean rust) and insects (soybean aphid) from Asia to the U.S. in globetrotting storms. Such cross-continent contamination can lead to severe destruction of crops.[54]
- Sea level rise
  - From 1901–2010 sea level rose by .19 meters (about 8 inches) and continues to rise from both ice melt and thermal expansion.[55]
- Sea ice loss
  - Two major ice sheets (Greenland and Antarctic) have been losing mass at more rapid rates in the last ten years.[56]

Exploring the effects of climate change can be depressing and even, at times, give one a sense of hopelessness. For another perspective on the current climate conditions, see this clip from *The Newsroom*, https://www.youtube.com/watch?v=XM0uZ9mfOUI.

The clip was fact-checked by *Mother Jones* in the following article: http://www.motherjones.com/blue-marble/2014/11/climate-desk-fact-checks-aaron-sorkins-climate-science-newsroom.

Simply listing the impacts of global warming can be overwhelming and divorced from reality. It is important to see the connections between climate change impacts, such as those listed above, and the R&S of many social-ecological systems. For example, we can expect climate change to affect the R&S of the food and agriculture systems discussed in Chapter 4. Climate change will alter, shift, and reduce worldwide food production as changes in global temperature and rainfall patterns, along with any unforeseen changes, affect agricultural systems.[57] Regional effects will vary and may even increase the resilience and sustainability of some regionalized crops or economies, but it is predicted that climate change will negatively impact global food security

---

[53] *Wildfires—July 2016*, NAT'L OCEANIC & ATMOSPHERIC ADMIN., https://www.ncdc.noaa.gov/sotc/fire/201607 (last visited Dec. 5, 2016).

[54] *See generally* Lewis H. Ziska et al., *Invasive Species and Climate Change: An Agronomic Perspective*, CLIMATE CHANGE, vol. 105, 13 (Aug. 19, 2010), https://www.ars.usda.gov/ARSUserFiles/33472/24.%20 Ziska%20et%20al%202010%20-%20Climatic%20Change%20-%20Invasive%20species%20 and%20climate%20change%20-%20an%20agronomic%20perspective.pdf.

[55] *2014 IPCC Synthesis Report, supra* note 6, at 42. Water is typically at its smallest volume or greatest density at about 4 degrees Celsius or 39 degrees Fahrenheit. When it is hotter or colder it expands. Because there is an enormous quantity of water on Earth, a little warming can cause a significant amount of sea rise through thermal expansion.

[56] *Id.* at 74.

[57] *State of the Climate: Drought for July 2016, supra* note 48.

as a whole as food production decreases, food prices increase, and nutritional values decline.[58] This is particularly true for vulnerable communities. Communities that are poorer and/or underdeveloped will experience a widening of the inequality gap based on race, ethnicity, and income. "Meaningful and equitable access to land and water for affordable food production is essential to ensuring climate resiliency for environmental justice communities."[59]

"Eco-agriculture" is a sustainable alternative to industrialized agricultural practices by those concerned about the predicted impacts of climate change on worldwide production. Eco-agriculture "seeks to promote agricultural sustainability through the use of farming practices that employ the concept of the farm as a healthy, sustainable living system, not an industrial production facility."[60] The three goals of eco-agriculture are: 1) to conserve and enhance biodiversity and ecosystem services; 2) to produce sustainably agricultural products and services; and 3) to encourage viable jobs for local people.[61] For example, industrialized agriculture uses vast amounts of pesticides and other chemicals, massive machinery, and relatively few employees. Eco-agriculture on the other hand uses pesticide alternatives such as ladybugs, oxen instead of tractors, and employs a relatively large portion of the surrounding community. Eco-agriculture illustrates the interdisciplinary nature of climate change impacts, as it addresses agriculture, employment, and climate change. At the same time, eco-agriculture works toward eliminating the inequality gap — a critical aspect of sustainability that climate change threatens to widen.

This brief description of climate change, food systems, and eco-agriculture illustrates the importance of assessing sustainability in fostering a more complete understanding of climate change and its impacts. Sustainability provides a framework in which to assess the direct and indirect impacts of climate change in a more systematic way. In addition, a sustainability-based approach can help craft innovative solutions to address these complex multi-discipline issues. Below, we take this a step further and explore the broad implications climate change has on another area — the Ocean.

---

[58] Mary Jane Angelo & Joanna Reilly-Brown, *Whole-System Agricultural Certification: Using Lessons Learned from LEED to Build a Resilient Agricultural System to Adapt to Climate Change*, 85 U. COLO. L. REV. 689, 693-698 (2014).

[59] Liza Guerra Garcia, *"Free the Land": A Call for Local Governments to Address Climate-Induced Food Insecurity in Environmental Justice Communities*, 41 WM. MITCHELL L. REV. 572, 573 (2015).

[60] Angelo & Reilly-Brown, *supra* note 58, at 693-698.

[61] *Id.* at 723-724.

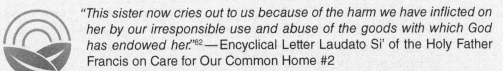

"This sister now cries out to us because of the harm we have inflicted on her by our irresponsible use and abuse of the goods with which God has endowed her."[62] —Encyclical Letter Laudato Si' of the Holy Father Francis on Care for Our Common Home #2

In May 2015 the Vatican published Pope Francis' Laudato Si. In the Laudato, the Pope highlights various ethical issues raised by the challenges of climate change. First, the Pope writes "Saint Francis of Assisi reminds us that our common home is like a sister with whom we share our life, and a beautiful mother who opens her arms to embrace us."[63] This idea that humans are a part of Earth, ecology, and nature (as opposed to supreme or dominant over it) is repeated throughout the Laudato: "If we no longer speak the language of fraternity and beauty in our relationship with the world, our attitude will be that of masters, consumers, ruthless exploiters."[64] Second, the Pope asks, "What kind of world do we want to leave to those who come after us, to children who are now growing up?"[65] Here, the Pope raises an ethical component of sustainability, namely, intergenerational equity. Third, the Pope raises intragenerational equity, stating "In the present condition of global society, where injustices abound . . . the principle of the common good immediately becomes a summons to solidarity with the poorest of our brothers and sisters."[66] This point raises the ethical challenge involved with having a disproportionate impact stemming from climate change on the poor. The Pope concludes by noting, "Living our vocation to be protectors of God's handiwork is essential to a life of virtue; it is not an optional or a secondary aspect of our Christian experience."[67]

B. Climate Change, R&S, and Ocean Acidification

Above we set forth some of the impacts stemming from climate change. In this subsection, we take a closer look at how climate change and its impacts can affect a number of systems' resilience and sustainability. To illustrate the relationship between climate change, resilience, and sustainability, we discuss climate in relation to the Ocean. The questions and connections we explore in this subsection concerning climate change, resilience, sustainability, and the Ocean can apply in similar ways to other social-ecological systems, discussed throughout this book.

1. THE OCEAN SYSTEM

The Ocean has a substantial effect on the climate, and vice versa. "The fact that 71% of the [E]arth's surface is ocean determines a significant part

---

[62] Pope Francis, *Encyclical Letter Laudato Si' of the Holy Father Francis on Care for Our Common Home*, para. 2.
[63] *Id.* at para. 1.
[64] *Id.* at para. 11.
[65] *Id.* at para. 160.
[66] *Id.* at para. 158.
[67] *Id.* at para. 217.

of its climate and ecology."[68] With an average depth of almost 12,100 feet, the Ocean is an enormous body of water that is critical to many essential cycles, including the carbon and water cycles.[69] It heavily influences the weather and climate, including precipitation, which is nearly entirely dependent on Ocean evaporation.

> *The hydrologic cycle is dependent on the vast amounts of water evaporated by solar energy from the oceans and deposited as rain on the land. Without this reservoir of open water, the earth would quickly become a desert. The oceans also provide a sink for nutrients eroded from the land. The seas regulate the global climate by serving as an enormous thermal mass for heat storage and as a reservoir for CO_2. From a purely physical point of view, the presence of the oceans can be seen as essential for a climate on earth suitable for human life.*[70]

While there is one World Ocean (which we refer to as the "Ocean") in that it is inter-connected through slow-moving currents, called Thermohaline Circulation, the Ocean is often divided into four or five popular oceans: Pacific, Atlantic, Indian, and Arctic, and sometimes Southern.

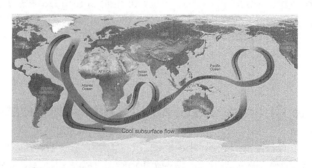

Thermohaline Circulation: The lines represent deep-water cold currents and warmer-water shallower currents.

Approximately 4.3 billion people live within 60 kilometers of the Ocean's coast.[71] As the sea level rises, these individuals' homes, cultures, environments, and economies are threatened. The Ocean is also home to hundreds of thousands of species.[72] These species include those permanently living in the Ocean, such as fish, cetacean (ex. whales), cephalopods (ex. squids), crustaceans (ex. lobsters), and others partially living in the

---

[68] Robert Costanza, *The Ecological, Economic, and Social Importance of the Oceans*, 31 ECOLOGICAL ECONOMICS 199, 200 (1999).

[69] *How Deep Is the Ocean?*, NAT'L OCEANIC AND ATMOSPHERIC ADMIN., http://oceanservice.noaa.gov/facts/oceandepth.html (last updated Oct. 10, 2017).

[70] Costanza, *supra* note 68, at 200.

[71] U.N. Atlas of the Oceans, *Coasts and Coral Reefs*, UNITED NATIONS EDUC., SCI., & CULTURAL ORG., http://www.oceansatlas.org/subtopic/en/c/304/ (last visited Dec. 5, 2017).

[72] *See Interesting Ocean Facts*, SAVE THE SEA, http://savethesea.org/STS%20ocean_facts.htm (number 35) (last visited Dec. 5, 2017).

Ocean, such as penguins and seagulls.[73] Approximately 3 billion people rely on the Ocean for sustenance.[74] Loss of these species as a food source would place immense pressure on other food systems.

In addition to serving as a means of sustenance, Ocean species and habitats provide a wealth of jobs. Approximately 43.5 million fishers in the world rely on the Ocean and its species for employment.[75] Ocean-based tourism provides a significant number of jobs as well, approximately 235 million, representing almost 9.2% of global GDP.[76]

2. IMPACTS ON THE OCEAN

Climate change is rapidly increasing the temperature of the Ocean. "Most of the heat from human-induced warming since the 1970s — a staggering 93% — has been absorbed by the ocean, which acts as a buffer against climate change, but this comes at a price."[77] As Figure 10-5 indicates, this means that only about 7% of the heat stemming from anthropogenic climate change is stored in other locations. The Ocean's absorption of heat results in temperature increases from the Ocean surface to approximately 2000 meters deep.[78] The IPCC concluded that:

> It is virtually certain that the upper ocean (0 to 700 m) warmed from 1971 to 2010. This result is supported by three independent and consistent methods of observation . . . the warming rate is 0.11 [0.09 to 0.13]°C per decade in the upper 75m, decreasing to about 0.015°C per decade by 700m. . . . Deeper in the ocean, it is likely that the waters from 700 to 2000 m have warmed on average between 1957 and 2009. . . . Sparse sampling is the largest source of uncertainty below 2000m depth.[79]

---

[73] See Ocean Animal Encyclopedia, OCEANA, http://oceana.org/marine-life (last visited Dec. 5, 2017).

[74] Stéphanie Ijff &, Marie-Pauline van Voorst tot Voorst, An Ocean Full of Opportunities, NETH. STUDY CTR. FOR TECH. TRENDS, at 8 (2016), https://stt.nl/stt/wp-content/uploads/2016/06/An-ocean-full-of-possibilities-web.pdf (last visited Dec. 5, 2017).

[75] Resumed Review Conference on the Agreement Relating to the Conservation and Management of Straddling Fish Stocks and Highly Migratory Fish Stocks, U.N. DEP'T OF PUB. INFO. (May 2010), DPI/2556 D, http://www.un.org/depts/los/convention_agreements/reviewconf/FishStocks_EN_A. pdf.

[76] Livelihoods: Jobs and Wages, OCEAN HEALTH INDEX, http://www.oceanhealthindex.org/methodology/components/marine-jobs (last visited Dec. 5, 2017).

[77] Latest Ocean Warming Review Reveals Extent of Impacts on Nature and Humans, INT'L UNION FOR CONSERVATION OF NATURE (Sept. 5, 2016), https://www.iucn.org/news/latest-ocean-warming-review-reveals-extent-impacts-nature-and-humans.

[78] Monika Rhein et at., Observations: Ocean, in CLIMATE CHANGE 2013: THE PHYSICAL SCIENCE BASIS. CONTRIBUTION OF WORKING GROUP I TO THE FIFTH ASSESSMENT REPORT OF THE INTERGOVERNMENTAL PANEL ON CLIMATE CHANGE, at 263 (2013), http://www.ipcc.ch/pdf/assessment-report/ar5/wg1/WG1AR5_Chapter03_FINAL.pdf.

[79] Id.

Where is global warming going?

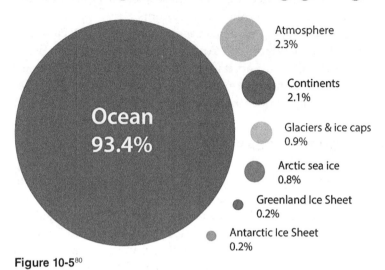

Ocean
93.4%

Atmosphere
2.3%

Continents
2.1%

Glaciers & ice caps
0.9%

Arctic sea ice
0.8%

Greenland Ice Sheet
0.2%

Antarctic Ice Sheet
0.2%

Figure 10-5[80]

Increases in Ocean temperature exacerbate sea level rise through thermal expansion. Because water is at its densest (smallest) at about 39.2 degrees Fahrenheit, heating water that is already warmer than 39.2 degrees, such as most of the Ocean (the World Ocean average surface temperature is about 62 degrees), results in an expansion of the Ocean's volume.[81] As the volume expands, the sea level rises, exacerbating increased levels from sea ice melt.[82]

Sea level rise under warming is inevitable. Thermal expansion would continue for many centuries after GHG concentrations have stabilised, for any of the stabilisation levels assessed, causing an eventual sea level rise much larger than projected for the 21st century. . . . The long time scales of thermal expansion and ice sheet response to warming imply that stabilisation of GHG concentrations at or above present levels would not stabilise sea level for many centuries.[83]

Temperature increases and sea level rise are only two of the challenges facing the Ocean. Another severe consequence of increased carbon

---

[80] *See also* NOAA Paleoclimatology, *What Are Positive Feedbacks?*, Nat'l Oceanic and Atmospheric Admin., http://www.ncdc.noaa.gov/paleo/abrupt/story2.html (last updated Aug. 20, 2008).
[81] *2014 IPCC Synthesis Report, supra* note 6, at 42.
[82] *Causes of Sea Level Rise: What the Science Tells Us*, Union of Concerned Scientists (Apr. 2013), http://www.ucsusa.org/sites/default/files/legacy/assets/documents/global_warming/Causes-of-Sea-Level-Rise.pdf.
[83] Intergovernmental Panel on Climate Change (IPCC), *Fourth Assessment Report: Synthesis Report, Summary for Policymakers* (2007), at 20, http://www.ipcc.ch/publications_and_data/publications_ipcc_fourth_assessment_report_synthesis_report.htm.

dioxide (CO_2) emissions is ocean acidification. Because nature is typically striving to achieve some form of equilibrium, there is a constant give and take of carbon between the Ocean's surface and the atmosphere. This results in the Ocean serving as a vital sink that absorbs approximately 25% of CO_2 emissions.[84] The more CO_2 emitted into the atmosphere, the more CO_2 is absorbed into the Ocean.

> *[W]here water and air come into contact there's an exchange. Gases from the atmosphere get absorbed by the ocean and gases dissolved in the ocean are released into the atmosphere. When the two are in equilibrium, roughly the same quantities are being dissolved as are being released. Change the atmosphere's composition, as we have done, and the exchange becomes lopsided: more carbon dioxide enters the water than comes back out. In this way, humans are constantly adding CO_2 to the seas.*[85]

CLIMATE CHANGE AND INTERGENERATIONAL EQUITY

"Ocean warming is one of this generation's greatest hidden challenges—and one for which we are completely unprepared," says International Union for Conservation of Nature Director General Inger Andersen. "The only way to preserve the rich diversity of marine life, and to safeguard the protection and resources the ocean provides us with, is to cut greenhouse gas emissions rapidly and substantially." *Latest Ocean Warming Review Reveals Extent of Impacts on Nature and Humans*, INT'L UNION FOR CONSERVATION OF NATURE (Sept. 5, 2016), https://www.iucn.org/news/secretariat/201609/latest-ocean-warming-review-reveals-extent-impacts-nature-and-humans.

As set forth in Figure 10-6, when CO_2 joins with water it commonly causes a chemical reaction resulting in bicarbonate ions (H_2CO_3).[86] Once this happens, the hydrogen ions that partially make up bicarbonate ions are easily broken off. These hydrogen ions elevate the acidity of the water, reducing pH and leading to "ocean acidification."[87]

---

[84] PMEL Carbon Program, *Ocean Acidification*, NAT'L OCEANIC AND ATMOSPHERIC ADMIN., http://www.pmel.noaa.gov/co2/story/Ocean+Acidification (last visited Dec. 6, 2017).
[85] Elizabeth Kolbert, THE SIXTH EXTINCTION (2014).
[86] PMEL Carbon Program, *supra* note 84.
[87] *Id.*

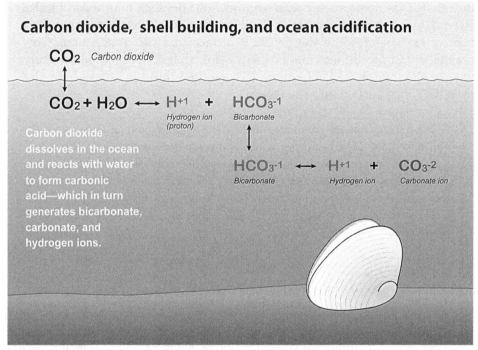

Carbon dioxide, shell building, and ocean acidification

CO_2 *Carbon dioxide*

$CO_2 + H_2O \longleftrightarrow H^{+1} + HCO_3^{-1}$
Hydrogen ion (proton)   *Bicarbonate*

Carbon dioxide dissolves in the ocean and reacts with water to form carbonic acid—which in turn generates bicarbonate, carbonate, and hydrogen ions.

$HCO_3^{-1} \longleftrightarrow H^{+1} + CO_3^{-2}$
Bicarbonate   *Hydrogen ion*   *Carbonate ion*

Figure 10-6[88]

All pH levels are logarithmic, which means, the difference between 7 and 6 in Figure 10-7 is ten times the hydrogen ion concentration.[89] The additional carbon dioxide emitted since the Industrial Revolution has resulted in a drop in pH levels from 8.2 to 8.1. The Ocean is "now thirty percent more acidic than [it was] in 1800."[90]

The top half of Figure 10-8 below shows the carbon dioxide parts per million as measured in the atmosphere over Mauna Loa, Hawai'i.[91] The bottom half of the image indicates the pH levels of the Ocean measured during the same timeframe. As the CO_2 emissions increase, pH levels show a corresponding decrease.[92]

[88] *See also* John Cook, *Where Is Global Warming Going?*, SKEPTICAL SCI. (Apr. 20, 2010), http://www.skepticalscience.com/Where-is-global-warming-going.html.

[89] PMEL Carbon Program, *A Primer on pH*, NAT'L OCEANIC AND ATMOSPHERIC ADMIN., http://pmel.noaa.gov/co2/story/A+primer+on+pH (last visited Dec. 6, 2017).

[90] Kolbert, *supra* note 85.

[91] Mauna Loa is one of the volcanoes that form Hawaii Island. On the island is located NOAA's Mauna Loa Observatory, where NOAA measures GHG concentrations.

[92] U.S. GLOBAL CHANGE RESEARCH PROGRAM, 2014 NATIONAL CLIMATE ASSESSMENT, *Overview and Report Findings* 10, http://nca2014.globalchange.gov/downloads.

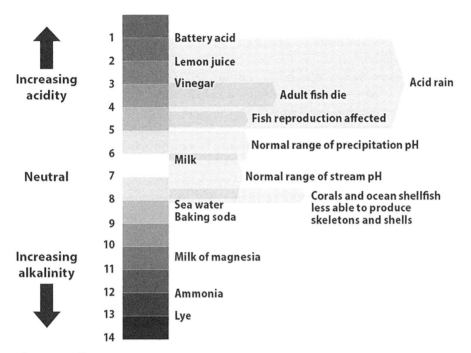

Figure 10-7[93]

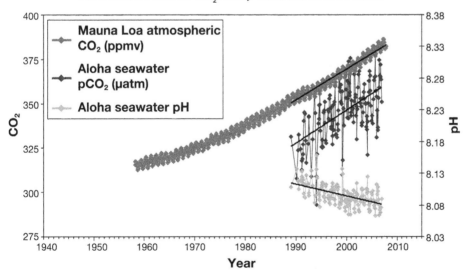

Figure 10-8[94]

---

[93] *Id.*

[94] PMEL Carbon Program, *A Primer on pH, supra* note 89.

3. OCEAN ACIDIFICATION AND ASSESSING R&S IN THE ERA OF CLIMATE CHANGE

While scientists continue to research the effects of decreasing pH levels (increasing acidity), thus far the decreased levels have had drastic impacts on the resilience and sustainability of many social-ecological systems. Rising Ocean acidity wears away at habitats and shells for several species at the bottom of the oceanic food web.[95] Researchers have witnessed numerous aquatic species' shells developing "deep lesions" from the acidic water.[96] These lesions threaten the species' ability to reproduce and survive.[97] The sustainability and resilience of systems relying on these aquatic species are greatly stressed. Can you think of any Ocean-based systems that might experience an increase in their resilience due to ocean acidification?

Further, Ocean acidification damages coral reefs, which are disappearing at rapid rates. As mentioned in Chapter 2, coral reefs "are among the most biologically diverse and economically valuable ecosystems on earth."[98] They "are a source of food for millions; protect coastlines from storms and erosion; provide habitat, spawning and nursery grounds for economically important fish species; provide jobs and income to local economies from fishing, recreation, and tourism; are a source of new medicines."[99]

Some researchers have estimated that coral reefs will not last through this century, taking an untold amount of species with them and making them "the first major ecosystem in the modern era to become ecologically extinct."[100] "Thousands — perhaps millions — of species have evolved to rely on coral reefs, either directly for protection or food, or indirectly, to prey on those species that come seeking protection or food."[101] As these critical habits are lost, so too will be the many species that rely on them.

Loss of vital habitats and species at the bottom of the food web is having, and will continue to have, trophic cascading effects up the food chain, impacting the sustainability and resilience of numerous systems.[102] One change in an ecological system initiates other changes, which can continue to cascade through the system and perhaps even into other systems. For example, Figure 10-9 below shows cascading impacts stemming from the warming of the ocean surface. As it warms a number of new challenges arise: fish shift; Hypoxia may increase (dead zones); coral reefs die, leading to further cascading on biodiversity; sea ice melts, further cascading, and so on.[103]

---

[95] Nova — Lethal Seas (PBS 2015), https://www.youtube.com/watch?v=vhR7KlaBa2A.
[96] Kolbert, *supra* note 85.
[97] Nova — Lethal Seas, *supra* note 95.
[98] *The Value of Corals*, Coral Reef Systems, Scripps Inst. of Oceanography and San Diego St. Univ., http://coralreefsystems.org/content/value-corals (content borrowed from coralreef.noaa.gov that has since been moved or deleted) (last visited Dec. 5, 2017).
[99] *Id.*
[100] Kolbert, *supra* note 85.
[101] *Id.*
[102] We discuss tropic cascading in more detail in "Case Study: *Catching Water in a Net, the Population Collapse of the Atlantic Cod*," Chapter 1, Section II.B.2.a.i.
[103] *2014 IPCC Synthesis Report*, *supra* note 6, at 52.

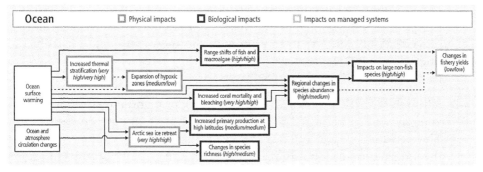

Figure 10-9[104]

In addition to ecological systems, the resilience of social systems relying on the Ocean will be stressed. Systems built around jobs, economies, cultures, aesthetic beauty and others will be strained and may become vulnerable as the Ocean struggles. For example, "[i]n South-East Asia, harvests from marine fisheries are expected to fall by between 10% and 30% by 2050 relative to 1970-2000, as the distributions of fish species shift, under a high 'business as usual' greenhouse gas emission scenario, the report states."[105]

Ocean acidification represents one of the many impacts stemming from climate change. For each system that climate change alters, there are many known and unknown impacts. These impacts can have broad effects on many systems. In the next and final section, we explore how we might use law and policy to respond to climate change and enhance system R&S.

Questions and Notes

1. Climate change is increasing temperatures and precipitation levels such that some areas are experiencing increased risk of wildfires. What cascading impacts might stem from an increase in number and size of wildfires? What systems might be affected? How would we test the R&S of these systems? Are there some systems that may become more resilient in the wake of a wildfire?

2. Coal is the largest energy source in the world for the production of electricity through combustion. It is not a clean source of energy because of the adverse environmental impacts from the extraction and burning of coal, which is one of the leading contributors to smog, acid rain, toxic air quality, and global climate change.[106] Thousands of individuals

---

[104] U.S. GLOBAL CHANGE RESEARCH PROGRAM, *supra* note 92, at 10.

[105] INT'L UNION FOR CONSERVATION OF NATURE, *supra* note 77.

[106] *Environmental Impacts of Coal Power: Air Pollution*, UNION OF CONCERNED SCIENTISTS, http://www.ucsusa.org/clean-energy/coal-and-other-fossil-fuels/coal-air-pollution#.WduuRGhSyUk (last visited Dec. 6, 2017); *Environmental Impacts of Coal*, CTR. FOR MEDIA AND DEMOCRACY, http://www.sourcewatch.org/index.php/Environmental_impacts_of_coal (last visited Dec. 6, 2017).

depend upon the production of coal as employment. What would justify phasing out coal, such that these individuals would become unemployed? What can we do to eliminate the inequality gap left from the unemployment? In terms of sustainability, what trade-offs would be involved with phasing out coal?

3. Ultimately, reducing unsustainable production and consumption of oil and gas will be required to address humanity's impact on the Ocean. The private sector, United States, European Union, China, India, and the international community must continue to cut carbon emissions by recycling, conserving, reducing, and substituting cleaner forms of energy to meet economic demands, achieve energy stability, and create a more resilient and sustainable energy sector.[107]

III. ASSESSING SYSTEM RESILIENCE AND SUSTAINABILITY AND RESPONSES TO CLIMATE CHANGE

Throughout this book, we explore resilience and sustainability as both concepts and frameworks to help understand complex social-ecological systems and the challenges they face. We began by defining and dissecting R&S in the context of systems in Chapter 1. We then explored the many challenges facing those systems in Chapter 2. We concluded Chapter 2 with an excerpt from *The Collapse of Western Civilization: A View from the Future*, in which the authors describe a world where social-ecological systems are deteriorated or destroyed following a failure to address the challenges and alter behaviors and policies. In Chapters 3 through 9, we explored R&S's relevance to systems in seven critical areas. While doing so, we described eight "Strategies for Implementation" that can help operationalize R&S.

We now come full-circle. Relying on many of the Strategies for Implementation, this final section explores proposals to mitigate and adapt to climate change and enhance the R&S of several systems. These proposals in turn affect many of the social-ecological systems explored in Chapters 3 through 9. In subsection III.A, we describe the contemporary use of R&S in the context of law and climate change. The examples in this subsection stem predominantly from international negotiations and provide an overview of how we incorporate R&S assessment in legal and policy documents to address climate change. In subsection III.B, we explore specific proposals to address climate change that reflect the eight Strategies for Implementation. Although typically we do not structure law and policy by isolating the Strategies in a manner similar to that set forth

---

[107] Zhong Xiang Zhang, *Assessing China's Energy Conservation and Carbon Intensity: How Will the Future Differ from the Past?*, Fudan U. (May 24, 2010), *available at* http://papers.ssrn.com/sol3/papers.cfm?abstract_id=1604867.

below, we chose these proposals to illustrate the individual Strategies' relevance to system R&S threatened by climate change.

A. R&S and Climate Change

Many international, national, and subnational documents recognize the benefits and importance of building a climate strategy in consideration of system resilience and/or sustainability. Generally, the international community has employed sustainability and sustainable development to facilitate the reduction of GHGs to help mitigate climate change. The international community has assessed resilience in the context of adaptation to help communities prepare for the effects of climate change.[108] However, this is not always the case. Some agreements, such as the Paris Agreement (discussed below), turn to "sustainable development" in both mitigation and adaptation contexts:

> *Article 8: "(1) Parties recognize the importance of averting . . . loss . . . including extreme weather events and slow onset events, and the role of sustainable development in reducing the risk of loss and damage."*
>
> *Article 4(1): "Parties aim to . . . undertake rapid reductions . . . so as to achieve a balance between anthropogenic emissions by sources and removals by sinks of greenhouse gases in the second half of this century, on the basis of equity, and in the context of sustainable development and efforts to eradicate poverty. . . ."*

The legal regime governing climate action at the international level illustrates how we have drafted policies to integrate R&S in the climate change context. Governance of climate change at the international level begins with the *United Nations Framework Convention on Climate Change* (UNFCCC). Opened for signature in 1992 and entering into force in 1994, the UNFCCC is the umbrella treaty under which all subsequent agreements on climate change have fallen. The over-arching objective, as set forth in Article 2 of the UNFCCC, is a mitigation-based goal to "stabilize greenhouse gas concentrations in the atmosphere at a level that would prevent dangerous anthropogenic interference with the climate system."[109] Pursuant to the UNFCCC, developed countries and Annex I parties are to formulate policies to mitigate climate change and implement those policies.

The UNFCCC set general commitments such as reducing global GHGs to 1990 levels.[110] It also set in place financing and technological assistance.

---

[108] The opposite is also true, however, sustainability and sustainable development have been used, albeit less frequently, to facilitate adaptation responses, and assessing resilience has been employed even less frequently to support mitigation efforts. *But see* United Nations Framework Convention on Climate Change, *supra* note 23, at Art. 7(1) ("Parties hereby establish the global goal on adaptation of enhancing adaptive capacity, strengthening resilience and reducing vulnerability to climate change, with a view to contributing to sustainable development and ensuring an adequate adaptation response in the context of the temperature goal.").

[109] *Id.* at Art. 2.

[110] *Id.* at Art. 4(2).

In accomplishing the goals, the UNFCCC set forth several approaches relevant to sustainability. Because we needed a holistic approach to climate change to induce participation and cooperation among nations, sustainability (intergenerational equity and the triple bottom line) provided a useful framework. Social and economic factors needed to be included in the discussion of the environment. We find these considerations for sustainability throughout the UNFCCC including:

- *Preamble*:
  - "Determined to protect the climate system *for present and future generations*"
  - "Recognizing that States should enact effective environmental legislation, that environmental standards, management objectives and priorities should reflect the *environmental and developmental* context to which they apply"
  - "Recognizing that steps required to understand and address climate change will be *environmentally, socially and economically* most effective if they are based on relevant scientific, technical and economic considerations and continually re-evaluated in the light of new findings in these areas"
- *Article 3(1)*: "The Parties should protect the climate system for the benefit of *present and future generations of humankind*, on the basis of equity and in accordance with their common but differentiated responsibilities and respective capabilities."
- *Article 3(2)*: "The specific needs and special circumstances of developing country Parties, especially *those that are particularly vulnerable to the adverse effects of climate change*, and of those Parties, especially developing country Parties, that would have to bear a disproportionate or abnormal burden under the Convention, should be given full consideration."
- *Article 3(3)*: "The Parties should take precautionary measures to anticipate, prevent or minimize the causes of climate change and mitigate its adverse effects. *Where there are threats of serious or irreversible damage, lack of full scientific certainty should not be used as a reason for postponing such measures, taking into account that policies and measures to deal with climate change should be cost-effective so as to ensure global benefits at the lowest possible cost.*"
- *Article 3(4)*: "The Parties have a right to, and should, promote *sustainable development*."
- *Article 4(1)(d)*: "Promote *sustainable management* . . . of sinks and reservoirs of all greenhouse gases"
- *Article 4(1)(f)*: "Take climate change considerations into account, to the extent feasible, in their relevant *social, economic and environmental policies and actions.*"

- *Article 7(2)(e)*: "Assess . . . the implementation of the Convention by the Parties . . . in particular *environmental, economic and social effects* as well as their cumulative impacts."[111]

Thus, in achieving its mitigation goals under Article 2, the UNFCCC adopts a sustainability approach relying on intergenerational equity and the triple bottom line.

After the UNFCCC established a framework, the parties began to meet as a Conference of the Parties (COP) to operationalize the UNFCCC. Accordingly, on December 11, 1997, the parties agreed on the language for the 1997 Kyoto Protocol. Entered into force on February 16, 2005, the Protocol sets emission reduction targets for six GHGs: carbon dioxide, methane, nitrous oxide, hydrofluorocarbons, perfluorocarbons, and sulfur hexafluoride.

CLIMATE CHANGE AND INTERGENERATIONAL EQUITY II

Carbon dioxide and nitrous oxide, two of the most common GHGs, remain in the atmosphere for approximately 5–200 and 114 years, respectively (others, such as sulfur hexafluoride (SF_6), can stay in the atmosphere for thousands of years). Because GHGs are emitted by current generations, but have the potential to impact future generations, climate change has raised significant intergenerational equity issues.

In November 2015, a King County Superior Court Judge in Washington State issued an opinion finding that children and future generations have a state constitutional right to have the climate protected. In a ruling echoing intergenerational equity, the court held that children's "survival depends upon the will of their elders to act now, decisively and unequivocally, to stem the tide of global warming . . . before doing so becomes first too costly and then too late." The court went on to rule that the "scientific evidence is clear that the current rates of reduction mandated by Washington law . . . cannot ensure the survival of an environment in which [youth] can grow to adulthood safely." Accordingly, the court ruled that Washington has a duty to "preserve, protect, and enhance the air quality for the current and future generations." *Foster v. Wash. Dep't of Ecology*, No. 14-2-25295-1 SEA (Wash. Sup. Ct. Nov. 19, 2015); *see also Foster v. Wash. Dep't of Ecology*, No. 14-2-25295-1 SEA (Wash. Sup. Ct. Apr. 29, 2016) (ordering state agency to promulgate emission reduction rules by the end of 2016).

After the court issued its decision, one of the children petitioners noted the importance the decision placed on intergenerational equity: "This ruling means that [the State of Washington] . . . has to protect us, the kids of Washington, and not just us, but future generations too, like my children and those to come." James Conca, *Future Lives Matter — Seattle Judge Rules for Children on Climate Change*, Forbes (Nov. 24, 2015), https://www.forbes.com/sites/jamesconca/2015/11/24/future-lives-matter-judge-rules-for-children-on-climate-change/#4e1730a8773d.

---

[111] United Nations Framework Convention on Climate Change, *supra* note 23.

Pursuant to the Protocol's first commitment period (2008–2012), Annex I parties were required to reduce their overall emissions of GHGs by at least 5% below 1990 levels.[112] During the first commitment period, 37 industrialized countries and the European Community committed to reduce GHG emissions. In doing so, Annex I parties were assigned specific goals.

To help accomplish its goals, the Protocol, similar to the UNFCCC, relies on sustainability. Article 2 states that each country shall meet its reduction limits by promoting sustainable development. It goes on to provide a number of sustainable mitigation strategies including enhancing energy efficiency in relevant national economy sectors, sustainably managing forests, promoting sustainable agriculture practices, limiting methane emissions, and better managing waste. Article 2 continues by stating: "The Parties . . . shall strive to implement policies and measures . . . in such a way as to minimize adverse effects, including the adverse effects of climate change, effects on international trade, and social, environmental and economic impacts on other Parties."[113]

The Protocol also provides for the Clean Development Mechanism, which helps countries achieve "sustainable development."[114] Another Conference of the Parties meets every year and oversees the Clean Development Mechanism. Further, this Conference of the Parties (COP) is obligated to "[a]ssess . . . the overall effects of the measures taken pursuant to th[e] Protocol, in particular environmental, economic and social effects,"[115] thus, further integrating sustainability into the regulation of climate change.

In Doha, Qatar, on December 8, 2012, the Doha Amendment to the Kyoto Protocol was adopted. The amendment included new commitments for Annex I parties to the Kyoto Protocol. They agreed to take on additional commitments in a second period from 2013–2020. Parties agreed to reduce GHG emissions by at least 18% below 1990 levels in the eight-year period from 2013 to 2020.[116]

The previous year, at the 2011 COP in Durban, South Africa, the parties agreed to establish a new treaty to limit carbon emissions. They also recognized that maintaining global average temperature below 2 degrees Celsius may be too high to curb climate change and that 1.5 degrees above pre-industrial levels may be more appropriate.[117]

---

[112] Kyoto Protocol to the United Nations Framework Convention on Climate Change, Dec. 10, 1997, U.N. Doc FCCC/CP/1997/7/Add.1, 37 I.L.M. 22 (1998) (3(1)).

[113] *Id.* at 2(3). A similar provision is set forth in Article 3(14).

[114] *Id.* at 12(2).

[115] *Id.* at 13(4)(a).

[116] Kyoto Protocol to the United Nations Framework Convention on Climate Change, Dec. 10, 1997, U.N. Doc FCCC/CP/1997/7/Add.1, 37 I.L.M. 22 (1998) (Amended by Doha Amendment (Dec. 8, 2012), http://unfccc.int/files/kyoto_protocol/application/pdf/kp_doha_amendment_english.pdf.

[117] Report of the Conference of the Parties to the Kyoto Protocol, Dec. 11, 2011, U.N. Doc. FCCC/CP/2011/9/Add.1, (Distr.: General Mar. 15, 2012), http://unfccc.int/resource/docs/2011/cop17/eng/09a01.pdf#page = 2.

CANCUN ADAPTATION FRAMEWORK AND RESILIENCE

In 2010, the COP placed a heavy focus on adaptation. In doing so, it produced the "Cancun Adaptation Framework," in which resilience began to play a more important role:

14. Invites all Parties to enhance action on adaptation under the Cancun Adaptation Framework, taking into account their common but differentiated responsibilities and respective capabilities, and specific national and regional development priorities, objectives and circumstances, by undertaking, inter alia, the following . . . (d) Building resilience of socio-economic and ecological systems, including through economic diversification and sustainable management of natural resources.

Report of the Conference of the Parties to the Kyoto Protocol, Dec. 10, 2010, U.N. Doc. FCCC/CP/2010/7/Add.1, (Distr.: General Mar. 15, 2011), http://unfccc.int/resource/docs/2010/cop16/eng/07a01.pdf. Note how the report uses resilience and the connection between building a resilient social-ecological system and sustainable management of natural resources.

The Durban Platform made a few additional contributions that the ultimate agreement in Paris in 2015 incorporated. Most prominently, reductions would be nationally determined, rather than established by the international community. The distinction between Annex 1 (developed countries) and non-Annex 1 (developing countries) disappeared — it became "applicable to all."[118]

Leading up to the 2015 COP in Paris, countries submitted their Intended Nationally Determined Contribution (INDC) pledges in which they described how they would achieve GHG reductions. In addition, many countries included their adaptation plans in their INDCs.[119] As submitted, the INDCs represent only around one-half of the reductions necessary by 2030 to keep global temperatures below the 2 degrees Celsius mark.[120] In INDCs, countries set forth a baseline, reduction, and target date/goal. For example, the United States set a goal of 26–28% below 2005 levels by 2025.[121] In addition, countries describe the relevant gases, sinks, and sources that are or will be regulated and a strategy for moving forward.

---

[118] *Id.*

[119] For submitted INDCs, see United States' *Intended Nationally Determined Contribution*, UNFCC, http://www4.unfccc.int/submissions/indc/Submission%20Pages/submissions.aspx (last visited Dec. 6, 2017).

[120] *IEA Says INDCs Will Slow Energy Emissions Growth Dramatically: Estimates National Climate Plans Set Path for 2.7 Celsius Rise*, UN CLIMATE CHANGE NEWSROOM, http://newsroom.unfccc.int/unfccc-newsroom/iea-says-pledges-for-cop21-slow-energy-emissions-growth-dramatically/ (last visited Dec. 6, 2017).

[121] *See United States' Intended Nationally Determined Contribution, supra* note 119.

On December 12, 2015, at COP21 the parties "adopted" the Paris Agreement.[122] The Agreement went into effect on November 4, 2016, when at least 55 parties to the UNFCCC representing at least 55% of total global greenhouse gases ratified the Agreement.[123]

Some of the key principles of the Paris Agreement include a desire to "hold the increase" in global average temperature to well below 2 degrees Celsius and "to pursue efforts to limit" temperature increases to 1.5 degrees Celsius above pre-industrial levels.[124] The Agreement requires the parties to achieve "rapid reductions" in GHG emissions "so as to achieve" net zero GHG emissions ("a balance between anthropogenic emission by sources and removals by sink[s]") between 2051 and 2100. Each country makes a voluntary pledge. Starting in 2020, each country is to "prepare, communicate and maintain successive nationally determined contributions that it intends to achieve" every five years. New pledges must get successively stronger in reductions.

Like the Protocol, the Agreement partially relies on sustainability. This time, however, it also integrates resilience. Below are several provisions where the Agreement taps into resilience and sustainability:

- *Article 2(1)*: "This Agreement . . . aims to strengthen the global response to the threat of climate change, in the context of *sustainable development* and efforts to eradicate poverty, including by . . . (b) Increasing the ability *to adapt to the adverse impacts of climate change and foster climate resilience*. . . ."
- *Article 4(1)*: "Parties aim to . . . undertake rapid reductions . . . so as to achieve a balance between anthropogenic emissions by sources and removals by sinks of greenhouse gases in the second half of this century, *on the basis of equity, and in the context of sustainable development* and efforts to eradicate poverty. . . ."
- *Article 6(2)*: "Parties shall, where engaging on a voluntary basis in cooperative approaches that involve the use of internationally transferred mitigation outcomes towards nationally determined contributions, promote *sustainable development* and ensure environmental integrity and transparency. . . ."
- *Article 7:*
  - "(1) *Parties hereby establish the global goal on adaptation of enhancing adaptive capacity, strengthening resilience and reducing vulnerability*

---

[122] The legal character of the Paris Agreement is different from the Kyoto Protocol. The "natural" form would have been to draft a Protocol like Kyoto, as provided for in Art.17 of the UNFCCC. The parties, however, chose to draft neither an amendment nor a protocol. The Paris Agreement is a separate, but dependent treaty under international law. It is dependent on the UNFCCC because only parties to the UNFCCC may ratify it and because it cannot stand alone as many clauses refer to the respective procedures and bodies of the UNFCCC.

[123] *Paris Agreement—Status of Ratification*, United Nations Framework Convention on Climate Change, http://unfccc.int/paris_agreement/items/9485.php (last visited Dec. 6, 2017).

[124] *Paris Agreement, supra* note 23.

to climate change, with a view to contributing to sustainable develop-ment and ensuring an adequate adaptation response in the con-text of the temperature goal. . . ."

○ "(9) Each Party shall . . . engage in adaptation planning processes and the implementation of actions, including. . . . (e) *Building the resilience of socioeconomic and ecological systems,* including through economic diversification and *sustainable management of natural resources.*"

● *Article 8:*

○ "(1) Parties recognize the importance of averting . . . loss . . . including extreme weather events and slow onset events, and the role of *sustainable development* in reducing the risk of loss and damage."

○ "(4) Accordingly, areas of cooperation and facilitation to enhance understanding, action and support may include. . . . (h) *Resilience of communities, livelihoods and ecosystems.*"[125]

The Paris Agreement marked a heightened attention to adaptation. It was also the first agreement under the UNFCCC that included a focus on resilience. These provisions begin to illustrate some of the many ways we can draft resilience and sustainability into law and policy to address climate change.

Subnational governments have also stressed the importance of R&S in the context of climate change. Washington, Oregon, New York, and other states have plans specifically devoted to resilience and resilience planning.[126] These plans include many adaptation measures, such as:

Improve the resilience of forested watershed communities to fire by increasing the diversity of forest species used in reforestation. . ., Improve the capacity of local health offices to respond to climate-related health risks. . ., [and] Protecting critical areas of watersheds should allow for resilience to change.[127]

Resilience planning in these states crosses disciplines and requires integration between agencies and areas of the environment. Finding the right agencies and persons to plan and implement R&S strategies can be difficult given the cross-reaching nature of these policies.

The Alliance of Small Island States (AOSIS) within the UNFCCC has spearheaded international responses to water quality and quantity issues due to climate change because these island states are directly vulnerable to the impacts of sea level rise,

---

[125] *Id.*

[126] *See* Judith Curry, *Forget Sustainability—It's About Resilience,* Climate Etc. (May 29, 2013), https://judithcurry.com/2013/05/29/forget-sustainability-its-about-resilience/.

[127] Jeffery A. Weber, Regional Framework for Climate Adaptation: Clatsop and Tillamook Counties (Feb 10, 2015), https://www.oregon.gov/LCD/OCMP/docs/Publications/Regional_Framework_Adapt_Clat_Till.pdf.

ocean acidification, and extreme heat.[128] It has been estimated that up to 25 million of these islanders may become refugees due to these impacts and that questions as to the status of a submerged nation under international law and the status of its citizens will need to be addressed.[129] While the UNFCCC has not led the efforts to reduce GHG emissions to combat climate change, it may be the appropriate forum for establishing a framework to mobilize financial and technical resources to assist those nations most likely to suffer from these severe impacts as they adapt to these threats.[130]

Questions and Notes

1. Which concepts of sustainability can you identify in the three bullet points listed under the UNFCCC's Preamble? Do you see those concepts repeated in other provisions of the UNFCCC? Why would a single document utilize more than one definition for sustainability? If they convey different meanings, what are those meanings in the context of the UNFCCC?

2. Article 4(1)(d) of the UNFCCC mentions "sustainable management . . . of sinks and reservoirs." How would you describe the definition of sustainable management? How would you operationalize that definition?

3. The Paris Agreement sets forth goals of both resilience *and* sustainability. The Agreement typically states them as independent concepts in separate provisions. Article 7, however, lists them both. How does Article 7 of the Paris Agreement, set forth in this chapter, envision the overlap between resilience and sustainability?

4. How would you characterize the difference in the use of "sustainable development" under the Paris Agreement Article 4(1) and Article 8(1)?

5. The United States has a particularly high rate of energy consumption as evidenced by its per capita GHG emissions of 19.78 metric tons in 2006, as compared to the 2006 global per capita average of 4.48 metric tons.[131] This level of consumption plays a critical role in addressing resilience, sustainability, and, in particular, climate change.[132] Reducing consumption and changing to alternative energy sources will help

---

[128] Maxine Burkett, *Rehabilitation: A Proposal for a Climate Compensation Mechanism for Small Island States*, 13 SANTA CLARA J. INT'L L. 81, 82-83 (2015).

[129] Shaina Stahl, *Unprotected Ground: The Plight of Vanishing Island Nations*, 23 N.Y. INT'L L. REV. 1, 3-4 (2010).

[130] David Freestone, *Can the UN Climate Regime Respond to the Challenges of Sea Level Rise?*, 35 U. HAW. L. REV. 671, 684 (2013).

[131] *See* Alice Kaswan, *Climate Change, Consumption, and Cities*, 36 FORDHAM URB. L.J. 253, 256 & nn.5-6 (2009).

[132] *Id.* at 312.

reduce GHG emissions.[133] However, as discussed in Chapter 6, one of the biggest barriers to using renewable power is the ability to bring this power from remote generation sites to consumers. Investments in the electricity grid infrastructure throughout the world will encourage using renewable energy sources and help make energy delivery more efficient, economic, secure, and reliable.[134] Some have suggested prohibiting individuals from living in certain areas or prohibiting the provision of electricity to these remote areas. Do you think this is a good idea? Explain why or why not? Consider whether this is any different than providing other city utilities like sewer, water, and gas, which cities do not generally provide to rural properties.

6. Scientist Stephen Hawking warns that President Donald Trump's decision in June 2017 to withdraw the United States from the Paris Agreement could "cause avoidable environmental damage to the planet for generations to come."[135] What is the impact of Trump's decision and how are states responding? For guidance, see Science Friday, *The US Will Be the Only Country Not in the Paris Agreement. Now What?*, (Nov. 10, 2017), https://www.sciencefriday.com/segments/the-u-s-will-be-the-only-country-not-in-the-paris-agreement-now-what/.

B. Strategies to Facilitate Implementation in the Climate Change Context

In this final subsection, we bring together climate change and the Strategies for Implementation studied throughout this book. Our goal is to illustrate how we can use an assessment of R&S in both the private and public sectors to help further action on climate change. How those actions overlap with other substantive areas is important to understand. We are not trying to cover all actions addressing or all systems impacted by climate change, as they are many and constantly changing. Instead of simply listing actions, we set forth examples that we base on some of the eight Strategies for Implementation to illustrate their usefulness in incorporating R&S into climate change mitigation and adaption law and policies.

---

[133] *See generally* Alice Kaswan, *Greening the Grid and Climate Justice*, 39 Envtl. L. 1143 (2009).

[134] *See, e.g., Officials Dedicate Sunrise Powerlink*, ABC News (July 26, 2012), http://abclocal.go.com/kgo/story?section=news/state&id=8750590; *see also* Timothy P. Duane, *Greening the Grid: Implementing Climate Change Policy Through Energy Efficiency, Renewable Portfolio Standards, and Strategic Transmission System Investments*, 34 Vt. L. Rev. 711 (2010).

[135] Loulla-Mae Eleftheriou-Smith, *Stephen Hawking Says Donald Trump Could Turn Earth into Venus-Like Planet with 250C and Sulphuric Acid Rain*, Independent, http://www.independent.co.uk/news/science/stephen-hawking-donald-trump-paris-climate-change-agreement-earth-brink-global-warming-us-fossil-a7820336.html (last visited Oct. 9, 2017).

1. MITIGATION: CARBON PRICING, COLLECTIVE ACTION CHALLENGES, POLLUTER PAYS PRINCIPLE, AND ECOSYSTEM SERVICES MANAGEMENT

Some have described climate change as the "ultimate" collective action problem.[136] Climate change is part of a particularly complex collective action challenge because climate change:

1. Is global in nature. Almost every citizen participates in the collective challenge by emitting GHGs or destroying sinks that contribute to climate change. Every citizen also suffers the consequences of others' GHG emissions.
2. Implicates several additional resource challenges. For example, those involving carbon sinks like wetlands and forests.
3. Raises a temporal collective challenge. Many of the GHGs will re-radiate heat for centuries, impacting future generations (intergenerational equity).
4. Affects the current generation unequally. Some of the smaller GHG emitting countries, as measured by both volume and per capita, are some of the most affected by climate change (intragenerational equity).
5. Involves every national and subnational jurisdictional boundary. Politics complicates planning and developing solutions.

Carbon pricing is a mitigation strategy that attempts to alter behaviors by requiring actors to internalize the costs associated with emitting GHGs. It is similar to a Polluter-Pays-Principle-approach, discussed in Chapter 8. Carbon pricing assigns a monetary value to the emission of CO_2 or other GHGs. It essentially requires emitters to pay for the GHGs they emit. Policymakers have adopted a number of approaches that incorporate carbon pricing, including instituting both a carbon tax and a cap-and-trade (CAT) program.

---

[136] Benjamin Ewing & Douglas A. Kysar, *Prods and Pleas: Limited Government in an Era of Unlimited Harm*, 121 YALE L.J. 350, 369 (2011).

Figure 10-10[137]

A CAT system places a cap on the maximum allowable GHG emissions.[138] Each emitter of a regulated GHG must pay to comply with the cap by: 1) cutting their emissions (thus, internalizing the cost of improvements), or 2) purchasing excess allowances from other emitters (thus, internalizing the cost of emitting, but not reducing emissions). To illustrate how CAT can address collective action challenges raised by climate change, we explore the largest international cap-and-trade regime — the EU Emission Trading System (ETS). Launched in 2005, the ETS has 28 EU member states plus Iceland, Norway, and Liechtenstein. Within these countries 11,000 power plants, manufacturing plants, and energy producing stations must comply with the ETS's provisions to limit CO_2, nitrous oxide, and perfluorocarbon emissions. In 2008, the installations regulated by the ETS were collectively responsible for close to half of the EU's anthropogenic emissions of CO_2 and 40% of its total greenhouse gas emissions. The EU

---

[137] Tom Randall, *Paris UN Climate Conference 2015: Here's the Climate Deal the World Really Wants*, The Sydney Morning Herald (Dec. 11, 2015), http://www.smh.com.au/business/paris-un-climateconference-2015-heres-the-climate-deal-the-world-really-wants-20151210-glkxqf.html (last visited Oct. 9, 2017).

[138] Cap-and-trade programs are utilized to address other collective action challenges as well. EPA, Clearing the Air: The Facts About Capping and Trading Emissions, EPA-430F-02-009 (May 2007), https://www.epa.gov/sites/production/files/2016-03/documents/clearingtheair.pdf. "The oldest and arguably most successful emissions trading system in place is for sulfur dioxide under the acid rain program of the 1990 Clean Air Act Amendments, which has reduced SO_2 emissions at a fraction of anticipated costs and engendered health benefits exceeding program costs by more than 40 to 1." Benjamin Goldstein, *Learning from Europe: Designing Cap-and-Trade Programs that Work*, Ctr. for American Progress (June 1, 2007), https://www.americanprogress.org/issues/green/news/2007/06/01/3173/learning-from-europe-designing-cap-and-trade-programs-that-work/.

estimates that installations covered by the ETS will have 21% lower emissions by 2020 and 43% by 2030.[139]

The ETS cap establishes a limit on the total emissions from the participating installations. Starting in the third phase, which began in 2013, the cap is reduced regularly (1.74% per year, and 2.2% per year beginning 2021, which will be the fourth phase).[140] Once the overall cap is set, each country receives emission allowances based on its percentage of emissions in 2005 with an additional allowance of 10% allocated to the least wealthy EU member states. Each country then grants the allocations for free or auctions them off. Free allowances will be phased out by 2027.

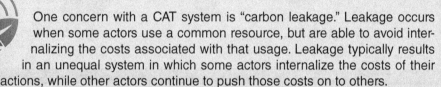

LEAKAGE

One concern with a CAT system is "carbon leakage." Leakage occurs when some actors use a common resource, but are able to avoid internalizing the costs associated with that usage. Leakage typically results in an unequal system in which some actors internalize the costs of their actions, while other actors continue to push those costs on to others.

With any policy involving the internalization of costs, it is important to acknowledge the possibility of leakage. If power plants, manufacturing plants, and energy producing stations in countries outside of the CAT area, such as the participating members of the EU ETS, are able to sell their products and services inside the CAT area, those plants and stations could provide the same product or service at lower costs without the CAT regulations. These plants and stations outside of the CAT area thus receive a competitive advantage, which constitutes leakage.

Once allowances are allocated, a participating installation may either surrender the allowance — one allowance for every tonne of CO_2 equivalent — or trade it in the market place. Participating installations must monitor and report their emissions. If its emissions exceed its allowances, the installation must either purchase additional allowances or pay a €100 per CO_2 equivalent tonne fee.[141]

The first trading period (called the "Learning by Doing" phase) lasted three years, from January 2005 to December 2007. During this period, there was an excess of allocations, such that the market price for an allocation in 2007 was €0. The second trading period, which ran from January 2008 until December 2012, coincided with the first commitment period of the Kyoto Protocol and similarly produced surplus allocations. The third trading period

---

[139] EUROPEAN COMMISSION, CARBON MARKET REPORT 2015, BRUSSELS, 18.11.2015 COM (2015) 576 FINAL, 1-3, https://ec.europa.eu/clima/sites/clima/files/strategies/progress/docs/com_2015_576_annex_1_cover_en.pdf.
[140] *Id.* at 31.
[141] *Id.* at 29.

began in January 2013 and will span until December 2020, coinciding with the second commitment period of the Kyoto Protocol.[142] A report issued on August 26, 2016, stated that the 27 EU member states shared €4.88 billion in allowances revenue in 2015, which was almost 50% more than 2014 and surpassed the previous record-year, 2013, by over a billion euros.

CAT seeks to reduce GHGs and address collective action challenges by requiring actors to internalize the cost of using the resource. By capping the total GHG emissions and by placing a monetary value on GHG emissions, the ETS limits the ability of the actors to use the atmosphere commons (the cap) and incentivizes the actors to reduce their use of the commons (the trade).

CAT systems adopt an ecosystem services management approach by placing a value on the atmosphere. To do this effectively we must base either the fee or a floor market-trading price on an ecosystem services valuation relative to emitting carbon. Some CAT systems incorporate a floor price, however, that price is rarely based on an ecosystem services valuation that accounts for the actual cost of emitting GHGs.

CARBON TAX

A carbon tax can be applied to many sources and GHGs. The tax can apply to end users (for example, British Columbia's (BC) carbon tax, discussed in more detail below, requires end users to pay at gas pumps about 7-8 cents per liter) or source users (extractors of the fossil fuels by taxing power plants or fossil fuel extractors).

Although called the "carbon" tax, this taxing scheme could regulate any GHG. For example, N_2O, nitrous oxide, does not contain carbon, but could be taxed as one of the most common and damaging GHGs. It could be taxed by converting it to a CO_2 equivalent and assigning it a comparative value.

BC was the first North American jurisdiction to implement a stand-alone carbon tax. It is revenue-neutral, meaning tax revenue is redistributed to reduce personal income taxes and corporate taxes by approximately the same amount gained in revenue. To make it more desirable to voters, the tax has a social component, which includes a low-income tax credit. In 2014, BC collected $1.2 billion in revenue from the tax "and a little more was returned" to the taxpayers under the program. The carbon tax revenue is redistributed to reduce personal income taxes and corporate taxes by approximately the same amount gained in revenue. BC has the lowest income tax rate in Canada for individuals earning up to $122,000 and the general corporate income tax rate is among the lowest in North America. However, similar to many solutions to collective action challenges, BC struggles with leakage. Up to one-quarter of BC's electricity may originate from sources outside BC, whose carbon emissions are not subject to the tax. The competition created by the leakage can negatively impact national businesses when consumers buy from sources outside BC.

---

[142] *Climate Action: Phase 1 and 2 (2005-2012)*, European Commission, http://ec.europa.eu/clima/policies/ets/pre2013/index_en.htm (last visited Dec. 6, 2017).

CAT and carbon tax have many similarities and may work in conjunction with each other. Both attempt to address collective action challenges by correcting the market's failure to account for external consequences stemming from GHG emissions. Both also rely on the free market to regulate efficiently, as opposed to command-and-control regulation. In addition, both can generate revenue. The revenue can offset economic impacts or further mitigation and adaptation efforts.

Some have advocated for one strategy over the other citing a host of reasons. Those advocating for CAT state the carbon tax does not actually require a reduction in emissions, while the cap portion of CAT guarantees meeting the GHG reduction objectives. Those in favor of the carbon tax cite its lower administrative cost. Additionally, the carbon tax is less susceptible to market manipulation and avoids price volatility because the cost of carbon on the open market can fluctuate with the economy (as the demand for economic growth goes up, the cost of emissions will likely also rise).

Questions and Notes

1. Pricing can influence decisions, which can alter systems' R&S. Should the public sector be involved with manipulating pricing? For example, should government assign a price for the emission of carbon based on ecosystem services in an attempt to alter decisions by private actors? How can the public sector regulate in a way that more accurately reflects the true costs of one's actions? For example, burning fossil fuels has a cost on the environment and climate. If there is a way to quantify that cost, should the entities burning the fossil fuels pay the tax or should those consuming the fuels pay the tax? By requiring tax payments, how could we alter behaviors around fossil fuels? Can we help create a more resilient or sustainable climate system? In doing so, are we making trade-offs? What systems might we make more vulnerable?

2. What do you think about trusting regulation of the climate to the market? Or turning carbon into a commodity?

3. How does CAT motivate installations and plants to reduce their emissions? How does it compel them to reduce emissions?

4. The fee per tonne of CO_2 (or CO_2 equivalent) provides an incentive to comply with CAT, unless what happens? Think of situations in which the fee is not a compelling incentive.

5. The price of carbon on the ETS has been a challenge, fluctuating from $0-20 per unit. What is the connection between the number of allocations and the price per carbon? How does the number of allocations impact GHG emissions?

6. Assume you have the choice of representing the European Union; a large "developing country," such as China or India; a small coastal developing country that climate change will seriously affect, such as Maldives; an industrialized country, such as the United States or Canada; or a large developing country that climate change will likely impact, such as Bangladesh. How would you respond to a proposal to institute a global carbon tax that imposes a direct fee on GHG emissions from private sector businesses based on the amount of GHGs emitted per business? Businesses may emit as much GHGs as they would like, however, the more they emit, the more they will pay. Take into account the most recent scientific information as set forth by the IPCC and be sure to consider commitments or percentage reductions in emissions, corresponding time tables, types of commitments (by sector? by country?), differentiated burdens by country (scientific and economic advancement), cost sharing, enforcement, and implementation.

2. SYSTEMS THINKING AND CLIMATE CHANGE

In Chapter 6, we described Systems Thinking (ST) as a critical strategy to help understand and assess R&S. ST plays a variety of roles in addressing climate change. One of those roles concerns *feedbacks* and *feedback loops.* Recall from Chapter 1, a system is comprised of distinct parts that work together to make-up a more complex entity. An open system is a system that receives information from and informs its environment. A feedback loop consists of both the inputs, in which the environment informs the system, and the outputs, in which the system informs the environment. A feedback is when a system's output loops back to become an input.[143]

There are two types of feeds back — negative and positive. A negative feedback consists of an input that feeds back into the system in a way that tends to limit the system's outputs. In this way, the system is resisting change. The system is acting to reduce, control, or reverse the stimulus or environmental change. Negative feedbacks create a more stable system

---

[143] *What Are Positive Feedbacks?, supra* note 80; Mary Jane Porter, *2.1 Systems Analysis in Environmental Science: Systems Analysis,* UNIT 1 THE EARTH SYSTEM AND ITS COMPONENTS, http://www.soas.ac.uk/cedep-demos/000_P500_ESM_K3736-Demo/unit1/page_14.htm (last visited Dec. 6, 2017).

that tends toward equilibrium.[144] Think of equilibrium as zero excess stimuli to be looped back into the system resulting in a stable cycle. A positive feedback tends to amplify a system's output, which produces a positive cycle of uncontrolled growth, pushing the system toward thresholds.[145] Instead of moving toward zero excess stimuli, the system puts out an increasing amount of stimuli looping back into the system and feeding an ever-growing cycle. A positive system is an unstable one that is constantly changing.

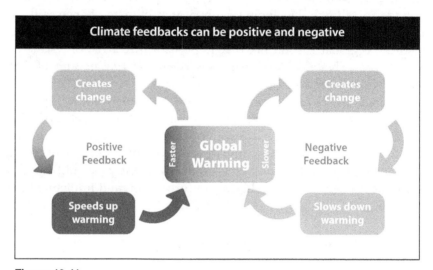

Figure 10-11

As part of climate change, scientists have been identifying and tracking a number of potential tipping points that produce positive feedback loops. These are points where changes in the climate system begin to snowball, leading to irreversible damage and a permanent positive loop. As shown on the left side of Figure 10-11, a positive feedback loop involves changes that stem from global warming, create additional temperature increases, intensify global warming, and produce additional changes and associated temperature increases. These positive feedback loops exacerbate global warming and its associated impacts. For example, in the case of water vapor, global warming increases the movement of water vapor into the atmosphere through evaporation (caused by increased temperatures) and potential changes in vegetation. Because water vapor is a GHG, increases in water vapor will speed up warming, increasing global warming and continuing the positive feedback loop.

---

[144] *What Are Positive Feedbacks?*, *supra* note 80; Porter, *supra* note 143.
[145] *What Are Positive Feedbacks?*, *supra* note 80; Porter, *supra* note 143.

CLIMATE CHANGE AND FEEDBACKS

[C]ontinued climate change impacts are inevitable because carbon dioxide persists in the atmosphere for a few centuries, plus 25 percent . . . lasts essentially forever. . . . [E]ven if the world immediately implements comprehensive efforts to significantly reduce emissions of carbon dioxide and other greenhouse gases, there will be a substantial time lag between implementation of those efforts and either actual stabilization of greenhouse gas concentrations in the atmosphere or cessation of climate change impacts. . . . As a result, climate change impacts will vary from location to location, necessitating different specific adaption strategies in different places.

Robin Kundis Craig, *"Stationarity Is Dead"— Long Live Transformation: Five Principles for Climate Change Adaption Law,* 34 HARV. ENVTL. L. REV. 9, 23-25 (2010).

Climate change affects all sectors of social-ecological systems (SESs). Climate change impacts on SESs can set in motion feedback loops (positive and negative) and non-linear changes, none of which are entirely (or even mostly) predictable. For example, as ice melts in the Arctic Ocean, and as permafrost melts in the Arctic tundra, the exposed surface changes from white to dark. Consequentially, that surface absorbs more heat, rather than reflecting it and creates a positive feedback loop that accelerates regional warming. This consequence leads scientists to predict an ice-free summer Arctic Ocean in the near future and the conversion of the Arctic tundra to the Arctic shrub land.

The right side of the image in Figure 10-11 illustrates negative feedback loops in the climate change context. A negative feedback would involve outputs that create environment changes, resulting in inputs that decrease or offset more global warming. Scientists have identified fewer negative feedback loops relative to climate change and the climate system. A potential negative feedback may occur through changes in plant growth stemming from increases in CO_2 (the change). Increases in CO_2 can be considered part of a negative feedback loop because it can spur vegetation growth (the feedback), which can remove carbon dioxide from the atmosphere, thus, partially reducing the greenhouse gas effect. The more plants grown, the more CO_2 removed from the atmosphere.

Climate change, similar to many aspects of social-ecological systems, has both known and unknown feedback loops. Examples include those associated with the thermohaline circulation (changes in the Ocean flow), jet stream, cloud cover, migration of invasive species, land carbon cycles, and methane hydrates (methane stored in frozen water). For example, some permafrost (soil that remains at or below freezing for more than two years) locks in CO_2 and methane. As the permafrost melts, it releases

---

[146] Ben Booth, *Climate Feedbacks*, MET OFF. (June 16, 2016), https://www.metoffice.gov.uk/climate-guide/science/science-behind-climate-change/feedbacks.

methane and other GHGs, which make it hotter, melting more permafrost and releasing more GHGs. Similarly, as sea ice melts, it reflects less solar energy to the atmosphere. The darker Ocean absorbs more energy and converts it to heat, making it hotter, which melts more sea ice. In the context of R&S, it is important to recognize these feedbacks and their ability to both support and inhibit the R&S of the climate system and other related systems.

3. ADAPTATION: BASELINES AND METRICS, ADAPTIVE GOVERNANCE, AND HUMAN HEALTH

As discussed in Chapter 6, Baselines and Metrics (B&M) are standards chosen and results monitored by a decision-making body. They help address the complexities embedded in assessing R&S by providing data that we can assess and then act upon. B&M "require[] ongoing dialogue among scientists, decision makers, and those affected by decisions. . . . This interaction, properly structured, can enhance our understanding of biophysical and social systems, help interested and affected parties develop trust in uncertain science, and help direct analysis towards the key issues for shaping decisions."[147]

B&M are useful to R&S because they help identify social-ecological system harms and unintended consequences and whether those systems are trending toward resilience or sustainability. That information can indicate the need for new strategies or policies to adapt to changing circumstances. From a resilience perspective, choosing baselines and tracking metrics help expose vulnerabilities within a system. A threshold—the point at which a system irreversibly changes—provides an essential baseline from which we can measure resilience. Depending on the scenario, one may want to avoid crossing a threshold baseline and, thus, may devise a strategy to track the relevant metric and use that data to determine when to adapt. Knowing when a system reaches that tipping point is critical to determining how and when to adapt. Crossing a threshold baseline could create a positive feedback and cascading impacts. B&M help to avoid such system change and provide policy makers with information to help us draft law and policy to support resilient systems.

Similarly, in the context of sustainability, the absence of B&M makes it difficult to draft policies and determine whether those policies achieve some measure of success. Incorporating B&M help sustainability efforts by identifying unknown harms and unintended consequences, thus influencing the choice of one discipline or strategy at the expense of another. They also serve as the foundation for a system of Adaptive Governance (AG).

---

[147]Thomas Dietz, Elinor Ostrom & Paul C. Stern, *The Struggle to Govern the Commons*, 302 Sci. 1907, 1912 (2003).

For example, at the beginning of the book in Chapter 1 (Section II.B.2.b.i), we introduced the City of Los Angeles' pLAn.[148] The pLAn adopted an aggressive monitoring system comprised of B&M. The pLAn also incorporated targets and action steps to achieve those targets. In doing so, the pLAn integrates B&M, AG, and Ecosystem Services Management. The pLAn identifies 14 key principles, including carbon and climate leadership, energy-efficient buildings, and urban ecosystems.[149] For each principle, the pLAn measures a mixture of complex and diverse aspects of social-ecological systems (36 in total). For each metric, the city set a baseline goal for what it hopes to achieve for that metric by 2017, 2025, and 2035 and a strategy to achieve its goal.[150]

The city's vision for "carbon & climate leadership," for example, is to be "a proactive leader on climate issues" and to "strengthen LA's economy by dramatically reducing GHG emissions and rallying other cities to follow our lead."[151] Part of achieving that goal is to "reduce GHG emissions below 1990 baseline by 45% in 2025, 60% in 2035, and 80% in 2050."[152]

In its *Sustainable City pLAn, 2nd Annual Report (2016–2017)*, the city marked the following five metrics and their corresponding progress (indicated in the sub-bullet):

- Establish a pathway to derive 50% of L.A. Department of Water and Power's (LADWP) electricity from renewable sources by 2030
  - LADWP's 2015 Integrated Resource Plan (IRP) sets a path toward 50% renewable energy. The updated 2016 IRP scenario will beat the state mandate, hitting 55% renewable energy by 2030 and at least 65% by 2036.
- Develop a comprehensive climate action and adaptation plan, including an annual standardized greenhouse gas (GHG) inventory
  - Expanding on the 2015 Climate Action Report, the Mayor's Office is developing pathways to meet 80% GHG reduction by 2050. L.A. was among the first cities to publish its GHG inventory (2013) in the C40/Compact of Mayors Global Protocol for Community Scale Greenhouse Gas Emissions Inventories (GPC) format, and will release 2014-15 inventories this year. The Resilient L.A. Strategy, set to launch in 2017, includes climate adaptation strategies and recommendations. . . .

---

[148] The City of Los Angeles, *pLAn: Transforming Los Angeles*, at 8, https://d3n8a8pro7vhmx.cloudfront.net/mayorofla/pages/17002/attachments/original/1428470093/pLAn.pdf?1428470093 (last visited Dec. 6, 2017).

[149] As the Mayor notes: "To ensure our bright future, we must protect what makes our city great: our incredible natural environment, our diverse economy, and the people that make our city thrive." *Id.* at 6.

[150] On its website, http://plan.lamayor.org/, the city provides up-to-date data that helps inform whether the city is meeting its designated goals.

[151] *pLAn, supra* note 148, at 35.

[152] *Id.*

● Accelerate the decarbonization of the electricity grid, including ceasing delivery of power from Navajo Generating Station
  ○ With the July 2016 sale of LADWP's 21% share in Navajo Generating Station, Intermountain Power Plant remains the last coal-fired plant in the city's portfolio, now slated to close two years early, in 2025. LADWP has already reduced GHG emissions by 40% below 1990 levels, 13 years ahead of schedule[153]

Other baselines and targets associated with climate change include:

● reducing wait-time for residential solar PV interconnection;
● installing at least one megawatt of solar on L.A. Convention Center roof;
● increasing installed capacity of local solar photovoltaic (PV) power to 400 MW with authority for an additional 200 MW;
● avoiding cumulative 1250 gigawatt-hours (GWh) of energy use through 2014- 2017 thanks to efficiency programs;
● retrofitting 12,500 homes with residential Property Assessed Clean Energy (PACE) financing;
● reducing daily vehicle miles traveled (VMT) per capita by at least 5% by 2025;
● increasing the percentage of all trips made by walking, biking or transit to at least 35% by 2025; and
● improving preparedness and resiliency so the city can quickly "Return to Normal" after a disaster.

UNITED STATES ACTION ON CLIMATE ADAPTATION

On November 1, 2013, President Barack Obama signed an Executive Order stating:

The Federal Government must build on recent progress and pursue new strategies to improve the Nation's preparedness and resilience. In doing so, agencies should promote: . . . risk-informed decisionmaking and the tools to facilitate it . . . [as well as] adaptive learning, in which experiences serve as opportunities to inform and adjust future actions.

Section 3 of the President's Executive Order required several agencies to:

[C]omplete an inventory and assessment of proposed and completed changes to their land- and water-related policies, programs, and regulations necessary to make the Nation's watersheds, natural resources, and ecosystems, and the communities and economies that depend on them, more resilient in the face of a changing climate.

Section 4 states:

---

[153] City of Los Angeles, *Sustainable City pLAn, 2nd Annual Report (2016–2017)*, http://plan.lamayor.org/wp-content/uploads/2017/03/sustainability_pLAn_year_two.pdf (last visited Aug. 18, 2017).

Providing Information, Data, and Tools for Climate Change Preparedness and Resilience. (a) In support of Federal, regional, State, local, tribal, private-sector and nonprofit-sector efforts to prepare for the impacts of climate change, . . . [eleven federal agencies] and any other agencies as recommended . . . shall . . . work together to develop and provide authoritative, easily accessible, usable, and timely data, information, and decision-support tools on climate preparedness and resilience.

The sections set forth above rely on many of the Strategies for Implementation described in prior chapters to accomplish resiliency-based goals. Can you identify which Strategies are embedded in the sections above?

President Obama, *Executive Order — Preparing the United States for the Impacts of Climate Change* (Nov. 1, 2013), https://www.whitehouse.gov/the-press-office/2013/11/01/ executive-order-preparing-united-states-impacts-climate-change. On March 28, 2017, President Trump withdrew this Executive Order. President Trump, Executive Order, Sec. 3(a)(i), *Presidential Executive Order on Promoting Energy Independence and Economic Growth*, https://www.whitehouse.gov/the-press-office/2017/03/28/ presidential-executive-order-promoting-energy-independence-and-economi-1.

Adaptive Governance (AG) and Baseline and Metrics (B&M) often represent the foundation of numerous climate change policies. B&M provide information pertaining to the direction the climate system is trending, while AG helps avert collapse of the system by establishing a process by which we can alter policies contributing to climate change. This is particularly true with complex, interdisciplinary issues, such as energy and climate change. For example, a single action, such as burning inexpensive coal, could simultaneously enhance economic prosperity (trending toward short-term sustainable economic conditions), while exacerbating climate changing conditions (trending toward unsustainable environmental and social conditions). B&M can help identify key data points in these scenarios, which we can evaluate to assess *trade-offs* and assess performance relative to R&S.

The Centers for Disease Control and Prevention (CDC), a federal administrative agency under the Department of Health and Human Services, has documented numerous impacts on human health stemming from climate change. As can be seen in Figure 10-12, many of those impacts are also related to subjects previously covered in this book, including water, food, pollution, and energy.

In response to the impact of climate change on human health, the CDC drafted the Building Resilience Against Climate Effects (BRACE) framework to help state and local officials and health departments prepare for uncertainty and changing circumstances from climate change. As set forth in the excerpt below, BRACE relies on baselines, metrics, and adaptive governance to help promote resilience and adapt to climate change.

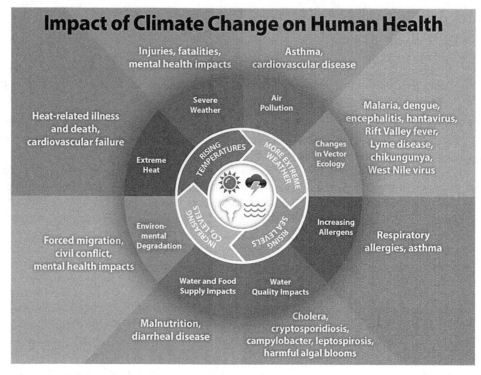

Figure 10-12[154]

Gino D. Marinucci et al., *Building Resilience Against Climate Effects — A Novel Framework to Facilitate Climate Readiness in Public Health Agencies*

INT. J. ENVIRON. RES. PUBLIC HEALTH 2014, 11(6), 6433-6458; DOI:10.3390/ IJERPH110606433

Climate change is likely to have broad public health impacts, from the direct impacts of weather extremes to shifting geographies of infectious diseases and the potential for destabilization of critical societal support systems such as food, energy and transportation. . . .

The public health community has identified several potential constraints and barriers to public health adaptation to climate change . . . includ[ing] uncertainty about future socioeconomic and climatic conditions. . . .

To build climate change adaptation capacity in the public health community, CDC has devised a comprehensive framework for developing local

---

[154] *Climate Effects on Health*, CLIMATE AND HEALTH, CDC, http://www.cdc.gov/climateandhealth/ effects/default.htm (last updated Oct. 9, 2017).

climate change adaptation plans. . . . [BRACE] is an iterative approach to adaptively manage the health effects of climate change. The adaptive management approach has shown promise in other sectors, such as the water and natural resources management sectors. . . . Moreover, BRACE is designed to clarify and assess the most concerning public health risks in a given region, acknowledging the place specificity of many emerging climate change health threats. . . .

Adaptive management explicitly acknowledges that complex systems are incompletely understood, that management interventions can affect system behavior in unexpected ways, and that management strategies need to be regularly updated as system managers and stakeholders learn through interactions with the system and each other. Systems well suited to an adaptive management approach are typically incompletely understood and sometimes exhibit unexpected attributes in response to management efforts; ecosystems are an oft-cited example. Adaptive management principles posit that the key to managing these complex, non-linear systems is a learning-based strategy that uses models and emphasizes the need to periodically gather information about their behavior, particularly in response to management actions and shifting stressors over time. . . .

BRACE incorporates adaptive management principles in its recognition that the public health impacts of climate change are complex and that the many systems involved are incompletely understood. . . .

There are five sequential steps in BRACE [set forth in Figure 10-13]. . . .

BRACE . . . enables the incorporation of learning into future decisions. . . .

We describe the steps of BRACE that can be implemented by public health agencies of various sizes and locations and the key considerations for agencies embarking on becoming climate-ready.

The first step of BRACE [forecasting climate impacts and assessing vulnerabilities] involves two inter-related tasks: (1) working with weather, climate variability, and change data sources to identify climate sensitive health outcomes; and (2) identifying vulnerable populations. More specifically, the first

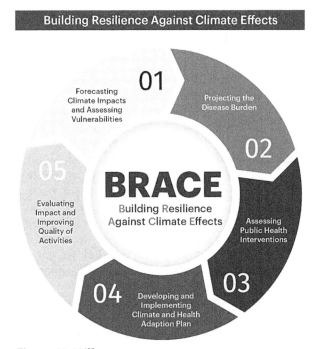

Figure 10-13[155]

---

[155] *CDC's Building Resilience Against Climate Effects (BRACE) Framework*, Climate & Health, CDC, http://www.cdc.gov/climateandhealth/brace.htm (last updated Oct. 2, 2015).

task focuses on finding data sources, relating weather to health outcomes and identifying the range of health outcomes that may be affected by climate change and variability within the jurisdiction. . . . By the conclusion of this task a public health agency will have the information to prepare a climate and health profile report (CHPR) that compiles the list of health outcomes of concern for a jurisdiction and details the climate-health exposure pathways. . . . Then after familiarizing itself with the range of likely climate changes and public health impacts, a public health agency will characterize vulnerability within a jurisdiction. . . . There are several methods used to conduct a vulnerability assessment. Vulnerability assessments can take on both qualitative and quantitative components. . . .

At the conclusion of Step 1, a public health agency has developed a profile of how the climate is changing, the likely effects on health, and the populations and systems most vulnerable to these changes. In Step 2, the agency examines shifting disease burdens more closely. Step 2 can be done qualitatively to yield a general impression of how climate change may affect the risk for certain outcomes, at least capturing general climatic trends and environmental exposures, population vulnerability, and expected human health impacts. However, a quantitative effort, the results of which can be used in comparative health assessments and cost-benefit analyses, is likely to be of greater use to a range of stakeholders if the relevant exposure pathways are adequately understood and if there is sufficient data to drive projections. . . .

RISK ANALYSIS AND CLIMATE CHANGE

As described in Chapter 8, Risk Analysis (RA) helps identify and evaluate risks. It helps us understand the threats facing systems and changes in systems. It also provides policy makers with information to avoid catastrophic loss. RA often results in a document that puts the B&M into a context policy makers can understand and use. Knowing the probability that an event will occur, and the damage that may result if the event occurs, helps policy makers adopt decisions that can avoid crossing system thresholds and enhance systems' R&S.

Climate change poses many known and unknown risks. Each stage of the RA process contains questions and variables that are subject to change. We need to account for these questions and variables to make accurate policy. For example, climate change can alter habitats making them suitable for invasive species. RA can help explain how these migrations may affect social-ecological systems and how we can alter policies to better adapt. Importantly, an RA that exposes the potential damage invasive species might have on the R&S of a system only informs policymakers. RA does not require that policymakers take action.

While RA may not be normative in nature, it may involve value judgments. RA requires a determination of which risks to identify, evaluate, and manage. For example, an evaluation of invasive species may be limited to its effects on commercial activities and exclude social, environmental, or ecosystem services impacts. This exclusion will produce different results than a more inclusive RA. Selecting an RA that incorporates the relevant data to inform policy is vital. An under-inclusive RA may result in policy changes that have unintended consequences or fail to adapt as needed.

Climate change health impact projections can be data intensive. However, many uncertainties arise, and efforts to increase the precision of projected outcomes may result in unstable estimates due to small sample sizes and other potential biases. In general, the longer the time horizon used in the projection, the greater the uncertainty in the estimates. . . .

The focus of Step 3 of BRACE is identifying the most suitable interventions to adapt to the climate change related health threats identified as of greatest concern in Steps 1 and 2. For various clinical and public health interventions, the evidence-based public health (EBPH) approach provides practitioners an opportunity to assess the efficacy of alternative interventions. . . . The general EBPH approach entails the following steps: (i) assessment of the problem; (ii) a systematic review of the public health literature to identify relevant interventions; and (iii) assessment of the efficacy of interventions. In the case of climate change, the problem assessment step includes both assessment of the shifting exposures resulting from climate change and the likely health impacts. Step 3 of BRACE is focused, in particular, on the latter parts of the EBPH process, in which intervention efficacy is examined closely. . . . Undertaking Step 3 of BRACE employs several elements of adaptive management. This step studies and considers a range of management choices . . . and in its most collaborative form enables extensive opportunities for stakeholder participation and learning. . . .

The focus of Step 4 of BRACE is synthesizing information generated in the prior steps into a focused climate and health adaptation plan. BRACE emphasizes the need for a unified adaptation plan for the public health sector to foster collaboration across disciplines and interest groups and to align efforts to a common objective of protecting and promoting health. . . . [S]takeholder engagement, communication, iterative learning, and adaptive management are key principles of both "successful" adaptation frameworks and BRACE, and are reflected in BRACE guidance for climate and health adaptation plans. . . . The process of developing and implementing a climate and health adaptation plan crosses all of the elements of adaptive management. In particular, a plan is a means for defining the management objectives . . . of the strategy, the prioritized interventions and adaptations . . . measures for monitoring and evaluating progress . . . quality improvement processes . . . and the role of stakeholders. . . .

Step 5: Evaluating Impact and Improving Quality of Activities

Implementing BRACE is an iterative process. Climate change considerations are relatively new for the public health community, therefore, gathering information on the processes used to address the health effects of climate change and the potential outcomes and impacts of those processes are critical. It is important to note that, while evaluation is positioned in Step 5 to better accommodate discussion and communication, in reality, monitoring and evaluation of processes, outcomes and key indicators are central considerations throughout the entire process. The value of explicitly making processes iterative is that management decisions can be revisited with new information, not only general knowledge about the threats being managed, but also information gleaned from experience since the process began. This ability to continually improve interventions is a fundamental adaptive management tenet.

At any point in the implementation of BRACE, process evaluation measures can help to validate methods employed and to reveal flaws in the plan. In addition to assessing the execution of key methods, process metrics can help to determine if the most appropriate stakeholders have been engaged and if the stakeholders' engagement added critical input. . . . Evaluating impact is influenced by the quality of assessment performed in Steps 1 and 2 of BRACE. Rigorously evaluating public health intervention requires baseline climate and health relationships (Step 1). Similarly, adaptations can be evaluated against counterfactuals (Step 2) that estimate climate change attributable disease burden in the absence of adaptation. . . .

While each agency will have different evaluation resources, the agency should be able to answer some basic questions after its evaluation activities:

- Does the public health agency have a reasonable estimate of the health impacts of climate change in its jurisdiction?
- Has the process allowed the public health agency to prioritize health impacts of greatest concern and the most suitable interventions?
- Has the public health agency prepared an adaptation plan for the public health sector within the jurisdiction?
- Are climate change considerations accommodated in public health planning and implementation activities?
- Are public health considerations accommodated in climate change planning and implementation activities?
- Are indicators in place that will evaluate the interventions implemented as a result of utilizing BRACE?
- How can the process be improved in the next iteration?
- What are the agency's top learning priorities in the next iteration of BRACE?

Climate change is an evolving concern. For public health agencies, climate change presents a number of adaptation challenges, not least of which is the incompletely understood nature of the impacts and the ecological systems in which these impacts will unfold. Managing the public health risks associated with climate change requires an iterative framework consistent with the principles of adaptive management. BRACE incorporates the features of adaptive management into a stepwise process tailored for public health agencies.

CASE STUDY ON BRACE: ARIZONA v. MINNESOTA

The growing weather extremes due to climate change have negatively impacted both Arizona and Minnesota. In Arizona, extreme heat waves have become the number one weather-related cause of death. Every degree of temperature increase creates a 6% increase in mortality risk.

Hot and dry is a breeding ground for wildfires and, when rain does come, flash flooding. Minnesota is the third fastest warming state in the nation. Additionally, it faces increased humidity and rainfall. It too faces a drastic increase in heat-related mortality risk and flooding. The difference between these states is their BRACE approach to the problem.

Arizona gathered data from both weather reporting and public health agencies. It also evaluated education and outreach across sectors. It gathered all relevant agencies, federal, state, and local, across weather and public health sectors, to share data and establish a plan. The resulting program connected all four weather-reporting stations with healthcare facilities, schools, and the public. When extreme weather is located, agencies send out an alert via email and social media. The alert includes advice on health and safety concerns during the heat wave. Additionally, they developed "heat safety toolkits" for children and older adults. These toolkits include educational components. This BRACE approach improved the state's response to the extreme weather incidents in summer 2013 (wildfires) and Sept. 2014 (flooding).

Minnesota also created toolkits, but it released them to public safety and healthcare agencies. The toolkits contained relevant data on heat wave responses statewide and how to partner with other agencies across sectors. Minnesota has also mapped out which communities are vulnerable and where the nearest resources are for those communities. It has developed and expanded training for public health professionals. The next step for Minnesota is to take its statewide vulnerability reports and education to the local level.

While both Arizona and Minnesota used the BRACE approach to develop toolkits and responses to the extreme weather caused by climate change, their programs are quite different. Arizona targeted citizens and Minnesota designed educational and cooperative programs for its agencies. Consider the ways in which different entities can use the same BRACE approach to create strategies specific to their unique needs and challenges to address climate change. ADAPTATION IN ACTION: GRANTEE SUCCESS STORIES FROM CDC'S CLIMATE AND HEALTH PROGRAM, AM. PUB. HEALTH ASS'N (Mar. 2015), http://www.cdc.gov/climateandhealth/pubs/adaptation-in-action.pdf.

Questions and Notes

1. What role can adaptive governance play in climate change? And how can it be used to help address climate change and enhance community resilience to climate change?

2. The above excerpt describing BRACE focuses mostly on climate adaptation and building resilience. How can we use adaptive governance to address climate mitigation and incorporate sustainability?

3. What is the connection between Baselines and Metrics and adaptive governance?

4. "Climate science does contain uncertainties, of course. The biggest is the degree to which global warming sets off feedback loops, such as a melting of sea ice that will darken the surface and absorb more heat, melting more ice, and so forth. It is not clear exactly how much the feedbacks will intensify the warming; some of them could even partially offset it. This uncertainty means that computer forecasts can give only a range of future climate possibilities, not absolute predictions."[156] This quote raises many issues, including those relevant to the relationship between systems thinking and adaptive governance. How would you describe the connection between systems thinking and adaptive governance?

5. What parallels do you see between BRACE and NOAA Fisheries Climate Science Strategy described below?

> From warming oceans and rising seas, to droughts and ocean acidification, these impacts are expected to increase with continued changes in the planet's climate system. . . . The NOAA Fisheries Climate Science Strategy (Strategy) is part of a proactive approach to increase the production, delivery, and use of climate-related information in fulfilling NOAA Fisheries mandates. The Strategy identifies seven objectives which will provide decision-makers with the information they need to reduce impacts and increase resilience in a changing climate. The Strategy is designed to be customized and implemented through Regional Action Plans that focus on building regional capacity, partners, products and services to address the seven objectives.[157]

---

[156] Justin Gillis, *Short Answers to Hard Questions About Climate Change*, N.Y. TIMES, http://www. nytimes.com/interactive/2015/11/28/science/what-is-climate-change.html?_r = 1 (last updated Jul. 6, 2017).

[157] *NOAA Fisheries Climate Science Strategy*, NOAA, https://www.st.nmfs.noaa.gov/ecosystems/ climate/national-climate-strategy (last visited Jan. 28, 2018).

Index